1991

Politics and Policy
in States and Communities

Politics and Policy in States and Communities

THIRD EDITION

John J. Harrigan
Hamline University

Scott, Foresman/Little, Brown College Division
Scott, Foresman and Company
Glenview, Illinois
Boston
London

Library of Congress Cataloging-in-Publication Data

Harrigan, John J.
   Politics and policy in states and communities.

   Includes bibliographies index.
   1. State governments.   2. Municipal government—United
States.   3. Local government—United States.   I. Title.
JK2443.H37   1987   320.973   87-24322
ISBN 0-673-39725-4

   2   3   4   5   6   7   8   9   10 — RRC — 93   92   91   90   89   88

Printed in the United States of America

Produced by R. David Newcomer Associates

Acknowledgments:
Page 37: Quotation from John J. Harrigan, *Political Change in the Metropolis,* 3rd ed.,
pp. 230–231. Copyright © 1985 by John J. Harrigan. Reprinted by permission of Little, Brown
and Company.
Page 197: Excerpt from Rochelle L. Stanfield, "Economic Development Aid—Shell Game or
Key to Urban Rejuvenation?" *National Journal,* March 21, 1981. Copyright 1981 by *National
Journal* Inc. All Rights Reserved. Reprinted by permission.
Page 464: Quotation from Ann Gorsuch Burford in *Congressional Quarterly Weekly Report,*
November 27, 1982, p. 2917. Reprinted by permission.
Page 468: List from James L. Regens, "State Policy Response to the Energy Issue: An Analysis
of Innovation," *Social Science Quarterly* 61, No. 1 (June 1980):44–55. Reprinted by permission
of the University of Texas Press.
Page 490: Quotation from Susan B. Hansen, "State Perspectives on Economic Development:
Priorities and Outcomes," a paper presented at the Midwest Political Science Association
convention, Chicago, IL; April 10–12, 1986. Used by permission of the author.

Preface

Since the original publication of *Politics and Policy in States and Communities* in 1980, the media as well as scholarly publications have focused more and more attention on three general topics of American domestic politics. These topics are:

- the unprecedented rejuvenation of state and local governments over the past quarter century, with special attention to the consequences of this rejuvenation in the 1980s.
- the unprecedented developmental role that state and community governments play today in the political economy.
- the never-ending ideological conflict over the public issues that dominate state and community politics.

These three themes played important roles in the earlier editions of *Politics and Policy in States and Communities,* and their importance has been highlighted in this third edition as well. Examples of the three themes abound.

Item: A quarter century ago, as we shall see, state government was decried as "dullsville" and local government as a "lost world." so complete has been the rejuvenation of state and local government in the past two decades that these complaints no longer ring true. Today some of the most exciting political leaders around the nation are emerging from state politics (e.g., New York's Democratic governor Mario Cuomo, and Republican senators Richard Lugar and Pete Wilson who came to the Senate from the mayor's office in Indianapolis and San Diego respectively).

Item: States and municipalities have gone into the economic development business in a big way in recent years. They seek to stimulate business activity to create more jobs, attract new industries, and keep existing ones. This has sparked an intense interstate and inter-regional competition for corporate investment dollars. When General Motors decided to build a factory to manufacture a new automobile to be called the Saturn, over half the states offered packages to GM in their competition to get the site of the new Saturn plant.

Item: Barely a quarter century ago, a prominent scholar published a book lamenting the end of ideology. Today ideology is alive and well in state and community politics. Too alive, in some people's judgment. On virtually every major domestic issue area (education, social welfare, crime, infrastructure, regulation) political leaders divide themselves into a variety of ideological positions on the left–right spectrum which we shall examine shortly. Overriding all of this through most of the 1980s has been the turn toward political conservatism and the dominance of national politics by President Reagan. These trends have had profound consequences for the conduct of state and community politics.

Conceptual Themes

Rejuvenation of state and local government, the role of those governments in state political economies, and the influence of political ideology in state and community politics are the unifying themes of this book. Rejuvenation of state and local government is particularly the dominant theme for Chapters 2 through 12 which deal with the institutions and processes of state and local politics. Political ideology is most relevant in the material for Chapters 12 through 16 which deal with the major policy areas confronting state and local governments (crime, education, social welfare, infrastructure, and regulation). The object of examining the ideological aspect of these issue areas is twofold: (1) to help the reader better understand his or her own value orientations toward these issues and (2) to provide conceptual tools that the reader can use to make evaluations of these issues as they arise in the readers' own communities. Finally, the theme of political economy is relevant in several chapters of the book but nowhere more directly than in Chapter 17, which is a new chapter added to discuss the role that state and local governments play in promoting economic development.

New Features of the Third Edition

- A new chapter (17) on economic development policy. So important has economic development politics become in the 1980s, that I decided a special chapter should be devoted specifically to it. Especially useful to the readers in this chapter is a set of analytical questions the reader can use to assess proposed economic development projects in his or her own state.

- A unique appendix on career prospects in state and community government and politics. This appendix gives students a guide to numerous career possibilities in state and local politics. This is especially helpful given today's demand that the college curriculum be relevant to the work place.
- End-of-chapter glossaries. Important terms are now defined in glossaries at the end of each chapter where they can easily be found by the reader.
- Up-to-date coverage of recent developments in state and community politics.

Teaching Features of this Book

This book contains numerous pedagogical features that aid the instructor in teaching the course and aid the student in learning the material.

- "You Decide" exercises. These are boxed case studies that ask the reader to respond to lively issues that range from deciding welfare eligibility in a complicated case to anticipating how the Supreme Court would rule in affirmative action cases.
- Chapter previews and summaries. Chapter previews have been inserted in this edition to give the reader a brief outline of the major issues in each chapter. The end-of-chapter summaries seek to wrap up the most important points.
- Highlight boxes in each chapter. These are short, boxed case studies that seek to illustrate important points made in the body of the text.
- A comprehensive *Instructor's Manual*. This manual provides: (1) chapter outlines, (2) twenty-five to thirty multiple choice questions for each chapter, (3) suggested classroom exercises to promote discussion of key issues and topics, (4) proposed research projects designed to have the student investigate how well the chapter's assertions apply to his or her state or community, (5) a film guide, and (6) study guides that can be given to the student. The two-page study guide for each chapter can be duplicated and distributed to the class as an aid for mastering the material of the course. Each contains (a) learning objectives for the chapter, (b) identification terms that the student should understand, and (c) mastery questions for which the student should be able to outline answers.
- Detailed footnotes that the reader can use as a guide to basic literature on research topics.

Acknowledgments

For me it is exciting to write and teach about state and local politics, because it is a topic that is directly involved in people's daily lives and one that has changed dynamically over the past decade. If some of that excitement rubs off on some of the student users of this text, I have many people to thank. First, are the many users of the earlier additions of the book. They will see retained the approaches they responded to positively in the earlier editions and will note substantial additions in this edition to accommodate changing events and perspectives. Additionally and more directly, I am greatly indebted to the following reviewers who read part or all of the manuscript and gave me their invaluable comments: Barbara Burt, Texas A&M University, William Dowd, Manchester Community College, James Lester, Colorado State University, and Tom Oberlink, Kalamazoo Valley Community College. John Covell and his talented colleagues once again shepherded me through the difficult task of turning many disparate ideas into a coherent book. But most of all my appreciation is to Sandy for her support.

John J. Harrigan
St. Paul, Minnesota

Contents

Politics and Policy
in States and Communities

Chapter 1
Introduction to State and Community Politics

Chapter Preview

Chapter 1 introduces the central concerns of state and community government today and outlines the plan of this book. In this chapter we will discuss in turn:

1. How state and local government responsibilities have increased in recent decades.
2. How state and local governments have reformed and rejuvenated themselves to handle their new responsibilities.
3. What conflicts arise in states and communities as those governments seek to carry out their responsibilities.
4. How state and local governments have become increasingly concerned with political economy and the politics of economic development.

Introduction

State and local governments affect our lives much more directly than does the national government in Washington. Most of the governmental services we receive are delivered by state or local units, not by Washington. That includes most of the federal government's domestic services, such as public housing and Aid for Families with Dependent Children. Many people feel they can influence what goes on in their city hall or state capitol much more than they can influence what goes on in Washington. For most of us, Washington seems very far away, with most of its money being spent elsewhere, in somebody else's neighborhood, somebody else's state, or somebody else's country. State and local governments spend their money locally, and their projects are literally carried out before our eyes, sometimes in our own neighborhoods.

Not only do state and community governments have a more direct impact on our lives than does the government in Washington, but their role in domestic policy is steadily growing. This growth is illustrated in Figure 1–1, which shows that growth of state and local government employment and expenses since midcentury has outstripped the growth of both the federal government and the gross national product (or GNP, the most common measure of the nation's economic output).

Washington, by contrast, has been slowly restricting its domestic role in recent years. Since Ronald Reagan's election as president in 1980, the federal government has shifted dozens of domestic programs to the states, has sharply curtailed its spending for social services, and has softened its regulatory punch in such important areas as the environment, civil rights, and occupational health and safety. And as Washington has reduced its domestic role in the 1980s, state and local governments have been forced to pick up the slack and to make difficult political choices themselves. Which public services should be maintained? At what levels? Who should receive them? Who should pay their cost? And how should the great burden of regulating the environment, the economy, health, and safety be divided among the three levels of government (national, state, and local)?

Rejuvenation of State and Local Government

If these great tasks had been handed to the states twenty years ago, in the 1960s, the states probably would not have been up to the task. In those years, scholars and journalists usually viewed state and community governments as incompetent at best. State governments were described as "sick,"[1] and state legislatures were caricatured as "horse-and-buggy" institutions.[2] States for the most part shirked their responsibilities for dealing with urban problems.[3] And as states ignored their growing urban problems in the 1950s and 1960s, the federal government picked up much of the slack with a vast expansion of social services and domestic programs. Journalists and social scientists increasingly turned their attention to Washington or to the central city, largely ignoring state government as "Dullsville."[4]

Today, these charges no longer ring true. State and community governments have profoundly rejuvenated themselves in recent years. With few exceptions, the legislatures have become more professional and competent. Governors have enjoyed a broad expansion of their political powers. State and local court systems are modernizing. Bureaucracies have come more fully under civil service systems and attract a much higher caliber of employee than before. And state ability to cope with domestic problems has been enhanced

Figure 1-1. Growth of the Public Sector

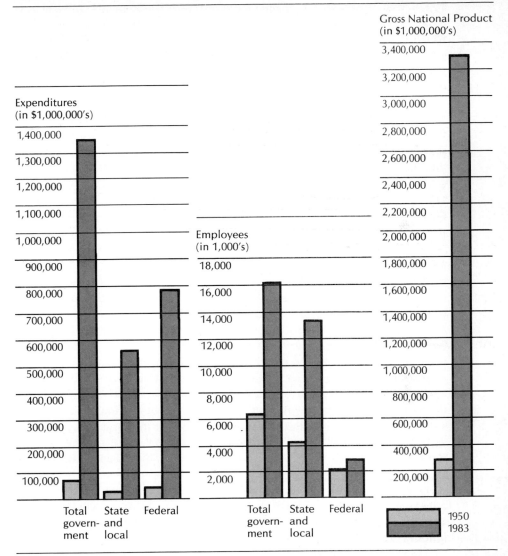

Source: Bureau of the Census, *Statistical Abstract of the United States: 1986* (Washington, D.C.: U.S. Government Printing Office, 1985), pp. 262, 294, 432.

by more effective revenue collection systems.[5] According to the Advisory Commission on Intergovernmental Relations, this transformation of state government capability in such a short period of time "has no parallel in American history."[6]

State and Community Political Economies

One of the most dramatic symbols of state and community rejuvenation has been their growing role in stimulating economic development. Indeed, as states and communities have been obliged to provide more public services, they have come under great pressure to find the revenues to pay for those services. One of the best ways for a community to increase its revenues is, of course, to increase the amount of its economic activity. As the number of local jobs increases and new buildings are constructed, more tax revenues are generated. For these reasons, state and local governments have become increasingly active in the **political economy** (the interaction between state economic conditions and public economic policy).

For a variety of reasons, some communities are better than others at promoting economic development. Some also are more favorably located. For instance, Houston, Texas, located near bountiful oil fields and the Gulf of Mexico, seemed destined to become a great metropolis no matter what governments did. In fact, however, governments did a great deal to help Houston's growth. They dredged the Houston Ship Channel, built the Astrodome, put pressure on Congress to provide favorable tax treatment for oil exploration, and got the National Aeronautics and Space Administration (NASA) to locate a huge space center just outside the city. Although Houston's economy suffered when oil prices dropped in the mid-1980s, its status as a great metropolis has remained secure. In contrast to Houston, some other communities labor under such extreme disadvantages geographically and economically that it is equally hard to see how they could prosper no matter what their governments did. Exhausted iron-mining towns of northern Minnesota and copper-mining towns in Montana, for example, subsist on products that face stiff, low-priced foreign competition, and it is difficult to imagine how governments can stave off the impending decline of those areas.

Most communities, however, are neither as well situated as Houston nor as poorly situated as northern Minnesota mining towns; thus, political leaders in most communities find themselves under pressure to use the political process to foster economic growth. Later chapters will examine various aspects of the political economy and the impact of political institutions on state and local economies.

Conflict in State and Community Politics

As states and communities go about providing domestic services and promoting economic development, they necessarily find themselves in the middle of intense political conflict over what the proper role of the state should be and how that role should be carried out. Such conflicts tend to involve some of the most fundamental issues of American politics: ideology, the distribution of government benefits, and the role that individual citizens play in the public economy.

Conflict over Ideology

The sharpest ideological conflicts over public services probably are those that arise over the question of whether public services should be redistributive. **Redistributive policies** serve people at the lower end of the income scale but are financed by revenue collected disproportionately from people at the higher end of the income scale.*

Not everybody agrees that public services should be redistributive, and there are ways to ensure that they are not redistributive. The first is to minimize the role of government and let it provide the least amount of services. A second is to limit government to providing the services that disproportionately benefit the middle and upper classes—higher education, public freeways and highways, redevelopment of big-city central-business districts, and support for the arts. A third is to finance public services through regressive taxes rather than through progressive taxes. (A *regressive tax* is one that takes a bigger percentage of poor people's income than it takes from high-income people. A *progressive tax* is one in which the percentage of income taken in taxes goes up as people's income goes up and goes down as people's income goes down.) Generally, income taxes are believed to be more progressive than sales taxes or property taxes. Progressive and regressive taxes are discussed more fully in Chapter 4.

People on the left or liberal end of the **ideological spectrum** generally support the expanding of government services for low-income people and paying for these services out of a progressive tax system. This system redistributes income from the rich to the poor. In contrast, people on the right or conservative end of the ideological spectrum support minimal government services and regressive tax systems. This leads to distributive policies; that is,

*Redistribution can also work in the opposite direction—taking from the poor and giving to the well-off. As the term is used in this book, however, redistribution means taking from the well-off and giving it to the not-so-well-off.

Figure 1–2. The Ideological Spectrum: 1985

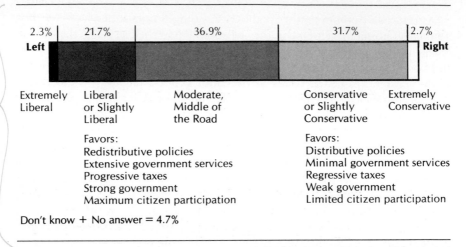

2.3%	21.7%	36.9%	31.7%	2.7%
Left				**Right**

Extremely Liberal	Liberal or Slightly Liberal	Moderate, Middle of the Road	Conservative or Slightly Conservative	Extremely Conservative

Favors:
Redistributive policies
Extensive government services
Progressive taxes
Strong government
Maximum citizen participation

Favors:
Distributive policies
Minimal government services
Regressive taxes
Weak government
Limited citizen participation

Don't know + No answer = 4.7%

Source: James Allan Davis: *General Social Surveys, 1972-85.* [machine-readable data file]. Principal Investigator, James A. Davis; Senior Study Director, Tom W. Smith. NORC ed. (Chicago: National Opinion Research Center, producer, 1985; Storrs, Conn.: Roper Public Opinion Research Center, University of Connecticut, distributor).

people receive back about as much in government services as they pay in taxes. Ideological differences are illustrated in Figure 1–2, which shows that the overwhelming majority of people are middle of the road or lean just slightly away from the center.

Conflict over Group Benefits

Although it is very difficult to link these ideological positions with specific groups in the society, redistributive policies usually draw their greatest support from interest groups representing people low on the socioeconomic scale. These include labor unions (which may want more jobs), welfare rights organizations (which may want higher welfare benefits), minority groups (which may want higher expenditures on health and educational services), and the elderly (who may want better transportation facilities, other services for senior citizens, and property tax relief).

Opposition to redistributive policies usually comes from interest groups representing people who expect to see their taxes rise as a result of higher expenditures—chambers of commerce (which may fear potential tax increases) and ad hoc taxpayers associations (which may resent potential tax increases, welfare expenditures, or higher salaries for public employees).

Most groups and individual citizens lack a consistent ideological position. This fact was dramatized after California residents voted to reduce their property taxes by 60 percent in 1978. Television reporters asked citizens for their views on the service cutbacks that followed the voting on the proposition. Many parents interviewed expressed resentment that public school services were being cut. But the same people admitted that they had voted for the proposition to cut property taxes. They apparently wanted to have the best of both worlds. They wanted to retain a high level of school services for their children, but they wanted somebody else's taxes to pay for those services. This same phenomenon is seen among interest groups. Groups traditionally support programs that benefit their members, and they tend to resist taxes that hurt their members. Bankers, for example, supported urban redevelopment and the construction of the World Trade Center in New York City. After the New York City fiscal crisis of 1975–76, however, the same bankers urged a cutback in the city's social services that went to nonbankers.

Chapters 12–15 of this book will illustrate how different ideological perspectives lead to different value judgments about the policies enacted by state and local governments. The different effects that these policies have on different groups of people will be further explored to show that some groups benefit disproportionately from specific policies.

Government and Personal Values

In the process of observing the conflicts inherent in state and community politics, most people inevitably find that their personal values are challenged. When the state takes a major initiative (reforming the tax structure, for example), you might discover that your own value system is violated by the initiative or that it is promoted. When an important issue is put before the state legislature or the city council, you may find yourself agreeing with people on one side of the issue and disagreeing with people on the other side.

This book will repeatedly attempt to help you clarify the ideological assumptions and values that underlie major issues. Does a particular idea stem from the conservative side of the ideological spectrum or the liberal side? It is consistent with or opposed to the reformist tradition in state and community politics? Which groups stand to benefit or bear the burden of paying for the benefits? And most of all, how do these issues relate to your own value system? One device to help you explore your own values on some of these issues is the "You Decide" exercises that appear in most chapters. In the nearby "You Decide" exercise, for example, you are asked to weigh the value of efficiency in the delivery of public services against a number of other values that are widespread in our society.

What Role for the Citizen?

As governments have gotten bigger, the role of the individual citizen has gotten smaller. The problems of public services increasingly have been addressed by professional bureaucracies rather than citizen-dominated legislatures, and the citizen has suffered a declining influence. The citizen has become a passive consumer of public services rather than an active participant in shaping the public policies for the services that he or she receives.

You Decide
Is Efficiency the Answer to the Problem of Governance?

As state and local governments find their budgets squeezed by strong demands for services and reduced financial resources to provide those services, critics have begun to demand that governments become more efficient and increase their productivity. Efficiency, in this sense, refers to providing more public services without increasing their cost.

This drive for greater efficiency draws support from a mounting body of evidence that considerable waste exists in state and local governments around the nation. A comparison of city-run water-meter readers in Chicago with privately run meter-readers in Indianapolis found that Chicago's meter-reading costs were over four times as high as those of Indianapolis. An enterprising *New York Times* reporter spent a day following a garbage collection crew in that city to find that the crew actually collected garbage only two-and-a-half hours out of its six-and-a-half-hour workday. Similar wasteful abuses most likely exist in many communities. We thus see that a glaring need exists for greater efficiency and productivity in the delivery of public services.

But is efficiency always the highest value to be sought in delivering public services?

And does efficiency always mean greater effectiveness? Public school systems, for example, could probably handle more pupils for fewer dollars by increasing pupil–teacher ratios fifty percent. But this increased efficiency might actually decrease teaching effectiveness and learning. Or judges might devise routines to process more civil and criminal cases each day, but such speed might result in hastily considered outcomes: guilty persons might be let off and innocent persons punished; or inequitable decisions might be made in divorce and child custody suits. Local welfare departments, for another example, might lower their costs for disturbed children in treatment centers by reducing the amount of time each child is permitted to spend in such centers. In one sense, this would increase the department's efficiency by increasing the number of children being treated per dollar. But sending disturbed children back to their home environments before they are ready might well exacerbate their problems, and thus possibly increase future assaults and vandalism.

In short, the way that state and local governments provide services reflects such societal values as efficiency, effectiveness, justice, equity, and public order.

It is perhaps expected that individuals would perform a very small role in national affairs. There is only one president and 535 congressmen to serve over 240 million people, and the chances of any one citizen being elected to federal office are very slim. At the state and local levels, however, there are 7,000 state legislators and hundreds of thousands of other elective offices. Thus, virtually anyone who is seriously interested in government can get elected to *some* office if he or she does the right things and persists long enough. With a little luck and a lot of persistence, the average citizen *can* affect what his or her governments do. Nearly all college students could, if they seriously pursued that goal for a number of years, become important figures in the politics of some state or community.

We all have opinions about such matters. What is your opinion? This exercise lets you decide that for yourself. On each of the issues discussed here, indicate the value (efficiency, effectiveness, justice, equity, or public order) that you consider most important, least important, and of moderate importance.

	Most important value	Value of moderate importance	Least important value
Water-meter reading	___	___	___
Garbage collection	___	___	___
Pupil–teacher ratios	___	___	___
Criminal cases (*e.g.*, robbery)	___	___	___
Civil cases (*e.g.*, divorce)	___	___	___
Length of treatment for disturbed children	___	___	___

Are there any patterns to your answers and those of your classmates? Does this exercise give you any insight into your own feelings about these issues? On the basis of these reflections, how would you respond to someone arguing for efficiency as the highest value in the delivery of governmental services? Agree totally? Agree partially? Disagree totally?

Sources: For meter-reading data: E. S. Savas, "Municipal Monopolies versus Competition," *Improving the Quality of Urban Management,* vol. 8, Urban Affairs Annual Reviews, ed. Willis D. Hawley and David Rogers (Beverly Hills, Calif.: SAGE Publications, 1974), p. 483. On garbage collection: *New York Times,* August 8, 1980, p. B-4.

If state and local political systems are sufficiently open that the average citizen can realistically aspire to elective office and the average college graduate can realistically aspire to a position of considerable influence, then in what sense can it be said that the average citizen has been reduced to a passive consumer of public services rather than an active participant in policymaking? What role does the average citizen really play in state and local governance? Are these governments really as close to the people as they are said to be in the American political mythology?

The Plan of This Book

State and local governments, then, are highly relevant to our lives. They directly affect how well or how poorly we live. Some of the time they give benefits to us, and other times they tax us to pay for services that we never receive. Whether these benefits, taxes, and services are redistributive deeply touches our own personal values about the role of government and about the kind of society we want to live in. Finally, whether we can influence what these governments do is a direct challenge to our belief in democracy.

In order to discuss these important aspects of state and local government in as orderly a way as possible, the first group of chapters examines the constraints or limitations within which state and local governments operate. Chapter 2 studies the constitutional and cultural constraints. Chapter 3 analyzes how federalism has evolved into an elaborate intergovernmental system. State and local governments are no longer autonomous. Each governmental unit is limited by actions of the federal government and by actions of other governments at the state and local levels. Chapter 4 examines the financial constraints on state and local governments. State and local governments can provide only as many services as they can pay for. And deciding which of their citizens will pay for what services is a bitter political question.

The next four chapters study the political processes. Chapter 5 looks at public opinion and interest groups, Chapter 6 at political parties and elections, Chapter 7 at forms of local government, and Chapter 8 at the dynamics of community politics.

The next four chapters discuss the state-level policymaking institutions—the legislatures (Chapter 9), the executives (Chapter 10), the administrative apparatus (Chapter 11), and the courts (Chapter 12). A primary concern of these chapters is to show the impact of the reformist movement on the organization and policies of these institutions as well as the nature of political conflicts that surround these institutions.

The final group of chapters examines several policy areas—poverty and welfare (Chapter 13); education (Chapter 14); the infrastructure policies regarding housing, community development, and transportation (Chapter 15); the regulatory policies toward the environment, energy, and the economy (Chapter 16); and the politics of economic development (Chapter 17).

Summary

1. Recent years have seen a dramatic reform and rejuvenation of state and local governments in the United States.

2. One of the major additions to state and local government responsibilities during the recent period of rejuvenation has been responsibility for state and local political economies.

3. As state and local governments carry out their responsibilities they become focal points for important political conflicts, especially conflicts over political ideology and group benefits.

4. Because of budget squeezes and administrative reform movements, state and local governments are increasingly assessed by the value of efficiency in their delivery of public services. The "You Decide" exercise in this chapter presents a situation in which efficiency as a value is compared to other values in the assessment of government's effectiveness.

5. As state and local governments become increasingly central to our lives, it also becomes increasingly important to have an effective system of citizen participation in order to keep government accountable to the people.

Key Terms

Ideological spectrum The traditional left–right spectrum in which liberal (or left-leaning) ideological positions are on the left side of the spectrum and conservative (or right-leaning) ideological positions are on the right side.
Political economy The interaction between public policy and economic growth.
Redistributive policies Policies that provide extensive public services for people on the low end of the income scale and finance those services with revenues collected from people on the high end of the income scale.

References

1. Charles Press and Charles Adrian, "Why Our State Governments Are Sick," *Antioch Review* 24, no. 2 (1964): 154–165.

2. James Nathan Miller, "Our Horse-and-Buggy State Legislatures," *Reader's Digest* (May 1965): 49–54.

3. Roscoe C. Martin, *The Cities and the Federal System* (New York: Atherton Press, 1965), pp. 45–47.

4. Coleman Ransone, "Scholarly Revolt in Dullsville: New Approaches to the Study of State Government," *Public Administration Review* 26, no. 4, (December 1966): 343–352.

5. See David C. Nice, "Revitalizing the States: A Look at the Record," *National Civic Review* 72, no. 7 (July–August 1983): 371–376.

6. Advisory Commission on Intergovernmental Relations, *In Brief: State and Local Roles in the Federal System* (Washington, D.C.: Advisory Commission on Intergovernmental Relations, 1981), p. 3. Also see the most comprehensive review of state government rejuvenation, Advisory Commission on Intergovernmental Relations, *The Question of State Government Capability: An Authoritative Catalogue of State Action to Modernize State Governments in Recent Decades,* Report A–98 (Washington, D.C.: Advisory Commission on Intergovernmental Relations, 1986).

Chapter 2
The Constitutional and Cultural Environment of State and Local Governments

Chapter Preview

Chapter 2 outlines the constitutional and cultural environments within which state and local politics take place. In this chapter we will discuss in turn:

1. The constitutional framework for state and community politics.
2. The criticisms of state constitutions and the politics of constitutional reform.
3. The impact that political cultural values have on the conduct of state and community politics.

Introduction

State and local governments exert a powerful influence on our lives. However, they cannot do everything they might wish. They are hemmed in by a number of constraints, two of the most important being constitutions and political culture. State constitutions outline the powers of government and restrict the actions that governments may take. The cultural beliefs and values of the citizens impose a vague boundary on the kinds of things governments are expected to do.

This chapter examines the constitutional and cultural environments that surround state and local governments. First we will look at state constitutions, problems with those constitutions, the model state constitution, and the constitutional reform movement. Then we will examine the importance of political culture to state and local politics.

13

State Constitutions

A constitution establishes the structure of government and prescribes the fundamental rules of the game of politics. Constitutions may be unwritten (as in the case of Great Britain) or written (as in all fifty American states). Because the state constitution outlines government structures and the basic rules of the political game, it is the **fundamental law** of a state and takes precedence over the **statutory laws,** that is, the laws passed by the legislature. If the statutory laws contradict the constitution, judges may declare them unconstitutional and not enforce them in the courts.

This feature of constitutional government is called **judicial review.** In the United States (but not in very many other countries), judges have authority to review the constitutionality of laws and other acts of governments. Because of judicial review, the wording of constitutions is important. A well-written constitution provides an effective and efficiently structured framework of government, protects the civil liberties of its citizens, and promotes stable governance. In contrast, a poorly written constitution shields special interest groups from state regulation, gives tax breaks that are difficult to rectify, and contains confusing and contradictory details that ensure a maximum amount of court litigation to determine the meaning of these unclear provisions.

Problems with State Constitutions

State constitutions have generally been viewed much more negatively than the federal constitution. The federal constitution is concise and well written, and it focuses on prescribing the fundamental law. In contrast, as illustrated in Table 2–1, state constitutions are often long, poorly written, and full of petty details that many observers feel should be left to statutory law. The state constitutions have been criticized as archaic documents reflecting the biases of 100 years ago. For example, Mississippi's constitution provides a religious test for public officeholders and also regulates dueling.[1] In addition, reformers say that many state constitutions place too many restrictions on state legislatures, create fragmented executive branches and inefficient court systems, and hamper the operations of local governments.[2]

Too Long and Too Detailed

Although the United States Constitution has only about 8,700 words, the average state constitution has 26,000. Alabama's, with about 172,000 words, is the longest. Such excessive length makes the document very difficult to understand. Reformers advocate shorter constitutions that deal only with the

Table 2-1. Differences Between the Federal and State Constitutions

	Federal	The average state constitution
Length	About 8,700 words	About 26,000 words
Frequency of amendments	Seldom. Only 16 amendments since 1800.	Frequent. The average state passes at least one amendment every two years.
Focus	Broad focus on setting fundamental law, with emphasis on the structure of government, the powers of government, and citizens' rights.	Narrow focus on details that might be better left to ordinary statutory law.
Legal theory	The federal government possesses only those powers specified in the Constitution.	The state governments possess any powers that are not specifically prohibited.
Supremacy	The Constitution is the supreme law of the land.	State constitutions are subordinate to the federal Constitution and to federal law.

fundamental structures of government. The New England constitutions and most of the constitutions that have been rewritten since 1960 have been substantially shortened (they average only about 16,000 words) and expound only the basic state laws.

Length itself is probably not so serious a problem as excessive detail, which is usually included to protect particular interests, for example, tax breaks for mining companies or public utilities. Lewis Froman found that the states with the strongest interest groups tend to be the states with the longest constitutions.[3]

Legislative Restrictions

Many constitutions put such rigid restrictions on the state legislatures that those bodies find it difficult to establish state policies. The most significant restrictions are the ones on finance and taxation powers of the legislatures. Most constitutions limit the amount of debt that the state may incur. Nebraska, for example, puts a $100,000 debt limit on most government construction projects. To build something larger than that (except for highways or university facilities) requires a constitutional amendment.[4] All constitutions restrict the classification of property taxes. They typically exempt some property (such as church-owned property) from taxation and place other property in special categories that the legislatures cannot change.

Not only do most constitutions limit the state's debt and restrict the legislature's ability to raise taxes, they also earmark certain revenues (those raised from specific taxes) to be spent only in specific **dedicated funds** (funds set aside for specific activities). One of the most important **earmarked revenues** is the state gasoline tax, most of which goes directly into a highway users' fund. This fund can be spent only for highway maintenance or construction. The revenues from fishing and hunting licenses are often earmarked for conservation and natural resources.

The problem with earmarked revenues and dedicated funds is that they restrict the legislature's ability to control the services delivered by the departments that receive the earmarked funds. Too many dedicated funds prevent the legislature from controlling the overall state budget. Although there has been a general decline in reliance on earmarking over the past few decades, the average legislature still lacks control over about a fifth of its budget because of earmarked funds.[5] In some states as much as 65 percent of the budget is earmarked.

Fragmented Executive Branches

Most state constitutions provide numerous independent administrative agencies and departments that are not directly accountable to the governor or to the legislature. The typical state constitution also provides for several independently elected state officials. Consequently, the executive power is fragmented into many different offices, making it harder for the governor to provide strong leadership. Political reformers prefer that the state executive branch be modeled after the business corporation. In the corporation, all ad-

Highlight
Reducing Legal Jargon: The Case of California

In the 1970s, several states substantially reduced the size and improved the clarity of their constitutions simply by rewriting the cumbersome nineteenth-century prose. Article I, Section I, of California's constitution was shortened in 1974 as follows:

Before

The privilege of the writ of habeus corpus shall not be suspended unless when, in cases of rebellion or invasions, the public safety may require its suspension.

After

Habeus corpus may not be suspended unless required by public safety in cases of rebellion or invasion.

Source: Helene K. Nemschoff, "Language, Constitutions and Laws," *Public Affairs Report,* 21, no. 3 (June 1980): 3 (Berkeley: Institute of Governmental Studies, University of California).

ministrative units are ultimately accountable to a chief executive, who in turn answers to a policymaking board of directors. By analogy the governmental reformers view the governor as the corporate chief executive and the legislature as the policymaking board of directors. Reformers want state executive power to be integrated and accountable to a limited number of policymakers.

④ Inefficient Court Systems

The typical court system is not integrated. Rather, it is composed of dozens of courts that are independent of each other. No one body ensures the enforcement of high judicial standards. The procedures by which cases are given to one court rather than another are unclear and confusing. In civil cases when one person sues another, conflict or confusion over which court has jurisdiction can delay the case. In criminal cases when a person is tried for breaking the law, the fragmented court systems are not tied into the correctional system; law enforcement, adjudication, and corrections are not integrated. This compounds the already difficult task of creating a corrections system that actually corrects the antisocial behavior of criminals.

⑤ Hamstrung Local Governments

Most constitutions restrict how much debt local governments can incur, and this often limits their ability to provide public services efficiently. Many state constitutions prescribe the type of governments for localities, making it impossible for residents to choose the type of government they want. In sum, local governments are legally creatures of the state and possess only those powers that the state constitutions and legislatures permit them to have. Reformers advocate giving local governments more financial flexibility, giving local officials enough authority to meet their responsibilities, and giving local residents a form of home rule that would allow them to choose the type of local government they want.

The Model State Constitution

A number of reformers have called for the systematic overhauling of the worst state constitutions. These constitutional reformers come from various places—the National Municipal League, the Council of State Governments, public administration specialists, and citizen groups such as the League of Women Voters. The ideal sought by these reformers is a constitution similar to the **model state constitution** drafted by the National Municipal League.[6] The model constitution is short and deals in fundamental principles

Figure 2–1. The Model State Constitution

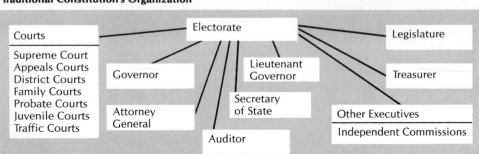

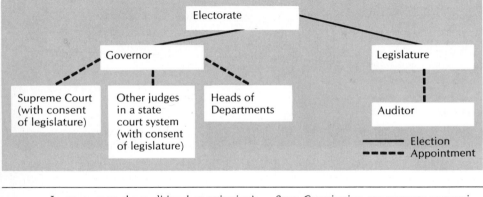

In contrast to the traditional constitution's large number of elected offices and the fragmentation of authority, the Model State Constitution concentrates responsibility in the governor and legislature.

Source: Adapted from *Model State Constitution,* 6th ed. (New York: National Municipal League, 1963).

of government instead of specific legislative details. It provides a bill of rights to protect the civil liberties of its citizens. Rather than a large number of elected executive offices, it permits only the governor and lieutenant governor to be elected, with the other state officials being appointed by the governor. The legislature is granted considerable authority and flexibility as the chief policymaking and taxing body in the state. In short, as Figure 2–1 shows, the model state constitution is the exact opposite of the typical state constitution, which is subject to the five criticisms just outlined.

The Politics of Constitutional Reform

In later chapters we will see that constitutional reform has not always improved governments as much as expected. For now it is sufficient simply to understand the reformist critique of state constitutions: unreformed constitutions create an inefficient, anachronistic governmental structure that is unable to respond effectively to the needs of the late twentieth century. Reformers urge that the constitutions be changed. Practical politicians attempt to get around the more cumbersome constitutional restrictions in several ways.

Circumvention and Interpretation

Many restrictive constitutional provisions are simply circumvented. *(over looked)* For example, although some state constitutions require that a proposed law be read aloud three times in the legislature before it can be approved, this rigid requirement is regularly circumvented by having the presiding officer read only the title of each bill. Critics say such circumvention encourages disrespect for the constitution and the law without changing outmoded constitutional provisions.

The most common way of adjusting rigid constitutional language to the needs of the times is by filing lawsuits that require the courts to interpret the constitution. Judicial interpretation does not change the wording of the constitution, but it changes the way in which the constitution is applied. Kentucky's constitution, for example, limits state salaries to $7,200 per year. This may have been a reasonable sum in 1890 when it was added to the constitution, but it is quite unreasonable today. Kentucky courts got around this limit, however, by a so-called "rubber dollar" ruling that permitted the dollar limit to be adjusted for inflation.[7]

Amendment

Amending a constitution is a two-step process requiring, first, initiation and then ratification. The most common procedure for initiation is for both houses of the legislature to pass the amendment by a simple majority (although some states require a three-fifths or a two-thirds majority). Fourteen states permit citizens to put a constitutional amendment directly on the ballot if they can gather enough signatures on a petition.

Ratification usually requires a majority vote of all those people voting on the amendment. But some states make amendments difficult to pass by either requiring passage in two sessions of the legislature in order to initiate the amendment, limiting the number of amendments that may be put on the ballot in any election, or requiring more than a simple majority vote for initiation or ratification.

Constitutional Conventions

Constitutions can also be completely rewritten by **constitutional conventions.** Unlike the federal constitution, which has never been rewritten, the fifty state constitutions have been rewritten ninety-six times since independence in 1776. Louisiana and Georgia with eleven lead in number of constitutional rewritings.

As shown in Table 2–2, three-fourths of the rewritings of the constitutions have occurred in three relatively short periods, periods of great national turbulence. From 1776 to 1799 ten constitutions were revised. During the years immediately preceding and following the Civil War, fifty-two constitutional revisions occurred. Many of these were in the southern states, which rewrote their constitutions following the collapse of the Confederacy, and once again

You Decide
Constitutional Circumvention

The Minnesota Constitution stipulates that "No law shall embrace more than one subject, which shall be embraced in its title." The title of one law passed by the Minnesota legislature in 1982 embraced the following:

Collection of taxes
Distribution of campaign funds
Interest rate limits on municipal bonds
Provisions to withhold income tax refunds from child support debtors
Requiring registration of rental housing in Minneapolis
Provisions for residential energy credits
Sale of unstamped cigarettes to members of Indian tribes
Lease and sale of equipment by local governments
Eligibility for property tax refunds
Restrictions on tax increment financing
Issuance of bonds to promote tourism
Allowing one county a levy for fire protection purposes
Allowing another county to exceed its levy limitation
Providing for lease of hydroelectric power

In your view, is the inclusion of all these topics in one law consistent with the constitutional provision that a law embrace no more than one subject? Or is this a circumvention of the constitutional provision quoted above? If you were a state Supreme Court justice being asked to determine whether the topics listed here did violate the state constitutional provision, how would you decide?

To see how the Minnesota Supreme Court ruled, see the Highlight on p. 21.

Source: Minnesota Laws, 1982, ch. 523, An Act Relating to the Financing of Government in this State.

Table 2-2. Incidence of Constitutional Revision

Time period	Number of constitutional rewritings
1980s	2
1960s–1970s	10
1940s–1950s	3
1920s–1930s	1
1900s–1910s	4
1880s–1890s	7
1860s–1870s	39
1840s–1850s	13
1820s–1830s	6
1800s–1810s	1
1780s–1790s	9
1770s	1
	96

Source: Calculated from *The Book of the States: 1986-87* (Lexington, Ky.: Council of State Governments, 1986), p. 14.

at the end of the Reconstruction period. Finally, during the 1960s and 1970s, ten states completely rewrote their constitutions.

The process of rewriting a constitution requires several steps, which in turn take several years to carry out. First, a constitutional convention must be called. In some states the legislature can call the convention whenever it wants. In most states, however, the legislature must vote to have a referendum on the question of whether a convention should be held. If the legislature approved the referendum in 1989, for example, the second step would be putting the question of a constitutional convention on the general election ballot for voter approval in 1990. The third step would be for the legislature in its 1991 session to provide for holding the convention and electing the delegates. The fourth step would be the elections and convention. These would take place in 1991 and 1992. The fifth and most crucial step would be ratification by the voters at the 1992 general election. If approved, the new constitution would take effect in 1993. Thus, the very shortest period for completely rewriting the constitution would be four years. Because of the time and difficulty it takes to establish a constitutional convention, some

Highlight
Constitutional Circumvention: Ruling

In 1986, the Minnesota Supreme Court struck down as unconstitutional a law, similar to the one on p. 20, that embraced many different subjects.

states require that a call for a convention be periodically put on the ballot. New York, for example, requires that this question be put before the voters every twenty years.

When constitutional conventions are held these days, they usually are non-partisan. The delegates usually are elected on ballots that do not identify their party affiliation, and once the convention starts, the delegates normally do not divide themselves into Republican and Democratic factions. Instead of perceiving themselves as representatives of political parties, most constitutional convention delegates today view themselves as "idealistic statesmen" concerned about the good of the state as a whole.[8]

Conventions today also are often limited to making proposals on only specified constitutional provisions. Although an unlimited convention can do a more thorough job of overhauling the constitution, the more radically the constitution is revised, the less likely it is to be approved by the voters.[9] Because of this, constitutional reformers tend to prefer more limited reforms that have a better chance of being adopted. Slightly more than half of the constitutional conventions since 1960 have been limited in scope.

One of the most successful unlimited constitutional conventions in recent years was Hawaii's, held in 1978. It put curbs on state expenditures, provided for open meetings of the state legislature, created an intermediate appellate court, added a privacy provision to the state Bill of Rights, and replaced all male gender words with words having no reference to gender. The delegates were heavily lobbied by interest groups seeking to beat back amendments that might threaten their position in the status quo. Public employee groups, for example, defeated attempts to eliminate public employee collective bargaining.

One of the most noteworthy features of Hawaii's new constitution is the way in which its provisions were approved by the voters. One hundred and sixteen changes were incorporated into thirty-four proposals, so that the voters could vote separately on each proposal. Submitted to the voters in 1980, all thirty-four proposals passed.[10]

The ease of getting Hawaii's new constitution adopted by the voters, however, was extraordinary. In recent years, North Dakota, Arkansas, Maryland, New Mexico, and New York have all held extensive constitutional conventions only to have the proposed constitution rejected by the voters. These unsuccessful experiments suggest that the dynamic period of rewriting state constitutions, which began in the mid-1960s, has peaked.[11]

Constitutional Revision Commissions

If reform through constitutional conventions has indeed peaked, then constitutional revision commissions might play a greater role in constitutional reform. A **constitutional revision commission** may serve as either a preparatory commission or a study commission. The study commission meets, studies the constitutional problems, and proposes a number of changes to the legislature. Utah has found such commissions to be so useful that in 1977 it created a permanent Constitutional Revision Commission to propose changes on a regular basis. In contrast to the study commission, which reports to the legislature, the constitutional preparatory commission actually conducts the background work for a constitutional convention. Since the convention meets for a very limited period of time, it needs as much prior preparation as possible. New Hampshire created a constitutional study commission in 1983 that held public hearings in different locations throughout the state to consider proposals for change. With this groundwork layed, a limited constitutional convention was held the following year. It put ten proposed changes before the voters, six of which were accepted.[12]

Although constitutional study commissions have become very useful and popular, they are not without their drawbacks. One drawback lies in the fact that many state constitutions prohibit amendments dealing with more than one specific subject. Thus, for example, it becomes constitutionally impossible to use a simple amendment to reorganize the entire executive branch. One proposal to remedy this has been the **gateway amendment,** which changes the constitution so that subsequent amendments can cover more than one subject and can pass with a smaller majority.

Political Culture

In addition to being limited by their constitutions, state and local governments are also affected by their citizens' attitudes, beliefs, and expectations about what governments should do, who should participate, and what rules should govern the political game. These attitudes, beliefs, and expectations are called the **political culture.**[13] Some political cultures may place very strict limits on what a state or local government can do, whereas other political cultures may allow their governments considerable freedom.

Daniel Elazar has described three state political cultures—the individualistic, the moralistic, and the traditionalistic.[14] These three cultures differ sharply in the way they view the purpose of government and the role of the average citizen.

The **individualistic political culture** believes government exists primarily to distribute favors to government supporters and to regulate the economic marketplace so that everyone can freely pursue his or her own self-interest. It also believes politics exists primarily to help politicians make a living and get ahead. The individualistic culture favors large bureaucracies, because they offer opportunity for providing services for voters and patronage jobs for political party workers. But it does not expect the average citizen to participate much beyond voting for candidates selected by professional politicians.

The **moralistic political culture,** in contrast, believes government exists to achieve moral goals that are in the public interest. It gives governments a broader role, permitting them to initiate new programs even if there is no public pressure for them, as long as the programs can be justified as being in the public interest. The moralistic culture places a high value on citizen participation and expects public officials to follow higher standards of ethical conduct than the individualistic culture expects. The moralistic culture also favors large bureaucracies, because they are believed to enhance political neutrality in the provision of services. Unlike the individualistic culture, however, the moralistic culture rejects a patronage system of employment (government jobs given to political supporters) and favors a merit system, in which people are hired and promoted on the basis of their qualifications and job performance.

The **traditionalistic political culture** believes government exists to preserve the social order. It permits governments to initiate new programs only if they serve the interests of the governing elites. It limits political participation to the few appropriate elites. Political parties are less important than family or social ties. And bureaucracy is viewed negatively as a force for depersonalizing government. The traditionalistic culture rejects the merit system of employment.

Elazar traces these three political cultures in historical development. The moralistic culture is traced to the colonial New England Puritans and the Scandinavian and German Protestants. As these peoples migrated across the northern states to the west, they imposed their cultural values on those regions. The individualistic culture is traced to nineteenth-century European immigration, especially of Catholics, and to the rise of the business centers in the mid-Atlantic states of New Jersey, New York, Pennsylvania, and Delaware. The traditionalistic culture is traced to the plantation economy of the South.

Combinations of these cultures predominate in the states where the westward migration of population caused these peoples to move, as shown in the map of Figure 2–2. Thus the moralistic culture is most strongly rooted along the northern tier of states following a stream of New England migrants in that direction. The individualistic culture is most strongly rooted in the mid-Atlantic and the lower Great Lakes states of Illinois, Indiana, Ohio, and Pennsylvania; and the traditionalistic culture is most strongly embedded in the South.

While Elazar cautions us not to identify particular states as completely dominated by a single political culture, different combinations of cultures

Figure 2–2. Distribution of Political Culture in the United States

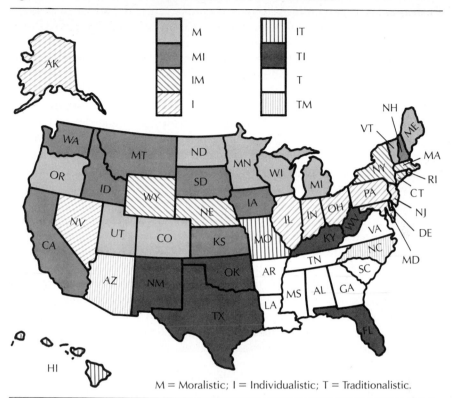

M = Moralistic; I = Individualistic; T = Traditionalistic.

Source: From *American Federalism: A View from the States,* 2nd ed. by Daniel Elazar, p. 117. Copyright © 1972 by Harper & Row, Publishers, Inc. Reprinted by permission of the publishers.

lead some states to develop peculiar political styles. This can be seen most clearly in the Midwest. In the moralistic states of Michigan, Wisconsin, and Minnesota, an **issue-oriented politics** developed, while in the individualistic states of Illinois, Indiana, and Ohio, a **jobs-oriented politics** developed.[15] In issue-oriented states, the Democratic party is strongly allied with organized labor, and it promotes liberal policies such as civil rights, public welfare, strong worker-protection legislation, and progressive taxes. The Republican party draws its greatest strength from rural areas, the suburbs, and the business community, and it is ideologically opposed to the Democrats on most of these issues.

In contrast to these three issue-oriented states, Ohio, Indiana, and Illinois developed a jobs-oriented politics consistent with their dominant individualistic cultures. Rather than fighting over issues, Republicans and Democrats in these states fight mostly over who will get to distribute the benefits of government to their supporters. All three states have extensive patronage employment in which government workers get jobs because they supported the winning political party. When government changes hands, large numbers of public employees are replaced by new employees who belong to the party that is coming to power. Graft and political corruption are much more extensive in Illinois, Indiana, and Ohio than they are in Michigan, Wisconsin, or Minnesota. Politics is viewed as much dirtier. These states have not provided the progressive reform movement leadership provided by their three northern neighbors. And whereas political machines have pretty much withered away in the moralistic, issue-oriented states, machine politics is still alive where politics is individualistic and jobs-oriented, especially in Chicago.

Impact of Political Culture

What impact does political culture have on the politics and policies of the different states? Research into this question has produced several conclusions. First, citizen participation in politics is highest in the moralistic cultures and lowest in the traditionalistic cultures.[16] This is due in great measure to the fact the moralistic states facilitate participation by having more lenient requirements for voter registration and voting in elections than do the traditionalistic states, and the institutions of government are more open to citizen input than they are in the traditionalistic states.[17]

Second, numerous studies have found that political culture influences the kind of policies adopted by states. Moralistic states tend to pursue more redistributive policies than do the traditionalistic states, but this may be because the moralistic states are also more affluent.[18] In a number of other policy areas, political culture was found to have an independent influence. States with the moralistic culture are much more likely than states with the traditionalistic culture to have lenient divorce legislation,[19] to engage in a broader scope of governmental activity, to spend more money on welfare and economic development policies, to rely on local governments for administering state programs, and to pursue innovative government actions.[20] For instance, the moralistic states are more likely than the others to adopt uniform state laws and to engage in cooperative ventures with other states.[21]

A third important impact of political culture on state politics is that the moralistic states do indeed have higher ethical standards of public conduct than other states.[22] Public officials in moralistic states are convicted for corrupt behavior much less frequently than are public officials in the individualistic and traditionalistic states.[23]

Finally, although Elazar's theory of political culture has been a powerful concept for understanding the variations in politics and policy from one state to another, it is not clear *how* or by what mechanism the political cultures have this impact.[24] Nor is it clear that states will continue in the future to fit as neatly into Elazar's three categories as they have in the past. Since Elazar formulated this theory two decades ago, population migrations have been leading to a dynamic mixing of cultures that will possibly create new types and combinations of cultures. There has been a heavy migration of people from the individualistic and moralistic regions to the South and Southwest, leading to a very turbulent mixing of cultural values in those regions. The South in particular appears to be becoming much less traditionalistic. And the Southwest is, in a sense, becoming the new melting pot of the nation. It has absorbed substantial in-migration of peoples from all three political cultures. It is absorbing millions of Latin American immigrants who are leaving their imprint on the political culture. And the substantial number of Asian immigrants has influenced local culture, especially on the West Coast.

Summary

1. Constitutions are the fundamental laws of a state and take precedence over the statutory laws.

2. The state constitutions have been heavily criticized for five weaknesses: They are too long and too detailed. They place too many restrictions on state legislatures. They create ineffective, fragmented executive branches. They create outmoded, ineffective court systems. They hamstring local governments.

3. The National Municipal League has drafted a model state constitution that it encourages the states to adopt.

4. Many detailed constitutional provisions are evaded through circumvention or judicial interpretation.

5. The two major strategies for overhauling state constitutions are constitutional conventions and constitutional revision commissions. Although a fifth of the states have rewritten their constitutions since 1965, the majority of constitutional conventions are not successful in getting their new constitutions adopted by the voters. Limited conventions have been more successful at getting their constitutions adopted than have unlimited conventions.

6. Political cultures constrain what state and local governments are permitted to do. Daniel Elazar has identified three political cultures—the individualistic, the moralistic, and the traditionalistic.

7. Political culture has had a much greater impact on political participation than it has on public policy results.

Key Terms

Constitutional convention A convention that drafts a new constitution and proposes it to voters for ratification.

Constitutional revision commission A commission appointed by the legislature to study the constitution and make recommendations for change. The revision commission may be either a study commission (which presents its results to the legislature) or a preparatory commission (which presents its results to the constitutional convention).

Dedicated fund A portion of a budget set aside for a specific purpose.

Earmarked revenues Revenues raised from specific sources (such as gasoline taxes) that can only be spent for related purposes (such as transportation).

Fundamental law The law of a constitution.

Gateway amendment A constitutional amendment that makes it easier to pass future constitutional amendments.

Individualistic political culture A viewpoint that believes government exists to distribute favors and believes politics should be dominated by professional politicians.

Issue-oriented politics A politics characterized by a liberal–conservative split between political parties as they compete over the direction of public policy.

Jobs-oriented politics A politics characterized by competition over the power to control a patronage apparatus and to distribute benefits to political followers.

Judicial review The power of courts to determine the constitutionality of acts of other government actors.

Model state constitution A proposal for constitutions advanced by the National Municipal League that would concentrate authority in the governor and legislature and would reduce the number of elected executives.

Moralistic political culture A viewpoint that believes government should seek to achieve moral goals in the public interest. Places a high value on citizen participation.

Political culture People's attitudes, beliefs, and expectations about what governments should do, who should participate, and what rules should govern the political game.

Statutory law A law enacted by a legislature.

Traditionalistic political culture A viewpoint that believes government's purpose is to preserve the existing social order.

References

1. *Wall Street Journal*, August 19, 1986, p. 50.

2. This agenda for reform appears in a number of critiques. The one relied on most heavily here is: Committee for Economic Development, *Modernizing State Government* (New York: Committee for Economic Development, 1968). A more recent summary of

the constitutional reform agenda can be found in Advisory Commission on Intergovernmental Relations, *The Question of State Government Capability*, Report A-98 (Washington, D.C.: U.S. Government Printing Office, 1985), pp. 35–44.

3. Lewis A. Froman, Jr., "Some Effects of Interest Group Strength in State Politics," *The American Political Science Review* 60, no. 4 (December 1966): 956.

4. A. B. Winter, "The State Constitution," in *Nebraska Government and Politics,* Robert D. Miewald, ed. (Lincoln: University of Nebraska Press, 1984), p. 15.

5. Steven D. Gold, "The Pros and Cons of Earmarking," *State Legislatures* 13, no. 6 (July 1987): 30.

6. National Municipal League, *Model State Constitution,* 6th ed. (New York: National Municipal League, 1963).

7. Carl Chelf, "The Kentucky Constitution," in *Kentucky Government and Politics,* Joel Goldstein, ed. (Bloomington, Ind.: Tichenor Publishing, 1984), p. 29.

8. Wayne R. Swanson, Sean A. Kelleher, and Arthur English, "Socialization of Constitution Makers: Political Experience, Role Conflict, and Attitude Change," *Journal of Politics* 34 (February 1972): 183–198.

9. Albert L. Sturm, *Trends in State Constitution Making 1966-1972* (Lexington, Ky.: Council of State Governments, 1973). Of fourteen constitutional conventions from 1966 to 1975 described in *The Book of the States,* five were limited to specific subject matters, and all five were successful in getting all or most of their suggested provisions adopted by the voters (Louisiana, Rhode Island, Tennessee, New Jersey, Pennsylvania). Of the nine states with unlimited constitutional conventions, the new constitutions were adopted by only three states (Montana, Illinois, and Hawaii). See *The Book of the States: 1974-75* (Lexington, Ky.: Council of State Governments, 1974). Also see the editions for 1972–73, 1970–71, and 1968–69.

10. Norman Meller and Richard H. Kosaki, "Hawaii's Constitutional Convention—1978," *National Civic Review* 69, no. 5 (May 1980): 248–257.

11. See Albert L. Sturm, "State Constitutional Conventions During the 1970s," *State Government* 52, no. 1 (Winter 1979): 24–30; and Albert L. Sturm and Janice C. May, "State Constitutions and Constitutional Revision: 1980–81 and the Past 50 Years," *Book of the States: 1982-83* (Lexington, Ky.: Council of State Governments, 1982), pp. 115–125.

12. Albert L. Sturm, "State Constitutional Developments During 1984," *National Civic Review* 74, no. 1 (January 1985): 27, 37.

13. Lucian Pye defines political culture as the "set of attitudes, beliefs, and sentiments that give order and meaning to the political process." See his "Political Culture," *International Encyclopedia of the Social Sciences,* ed. David L. Sills, vol. 12 (New York: Macmillan, 1968), p. 218.

14. Daniel J. Elazar, *American Federalism: A View From the States,* 2d ed. (New York: Thomas Y. Crowell, 1972), Ch. 4, especially pp. 100–101.

15. John Fenton, *Midwest Politics* (New York: Holt, Rinehart & Winston, 1966).

16. Ira Sharkansky, "The Utility of Elazar's Political Culture: A Research Note," *Polity,* (Fall 1969): pp. 66–83. This pattern of participation rates was also found in another study that was generally unsupportive of Elazar's theory on the geographic dispersion of the cultures. See Timothy D. Schiltz and R. Lee Rainey, "The Geographic Distribution of Elazar's Political Subcultures Among the Mass Population: A Research Note," *Western*

Political Quarterly 31, no. 3 (September 1978): 410–415. In support of Elazar's theory, see Robert L. Savage, "Looking for Political Subcultures: A Critique of the Rummage-Sale Approach," *Western Political Quarterly* 34, no. 2 (June 1981): 331–336.

17. Eric B. Herzik, "The Legal-Formal Structuring of State Politics: A Cultural Explanation," *Western Political Quarterly* 38, no. 3 (September 1985): 413–423.

18. Sharkansky, "The Utility of Elazar's Political Culture."

19. Gillian Dean, "The Study of Political Feedback Using Non-Recursive Causal Models: The Case of State Divorce Policies," *Policy Studies Journal* 8, no. 6 (Summer 1980): 920–927.

20. Charles A. Johnson, "Political Culture in American States: Elazar's Formulation Examined," *American Journal of Political Science* 20, no. 3 (August 1976): 491–509.

21. David C. Nice, "Cooperation and Conformity Among the States," *Polity* 16, no. 3 (Spring 1984): 494–505.

22. John G. Peters and Susan Welch, "Politics, Corruption, and Political Culture: A View From the State Legislature," *American Politics Quarterly* 6, no. 3 (July 1978): 345–356.

23. See *Ibid.*, and David C. Nice, "Political Corruption in the American States," *American Politics Quarterly* 11, no. 4 (October 1983): 507–517.

24. David Lowery and Lee J. Sigelman, "Political Culture and State Public Policy: The Missing Link," *Western Political Quarterly* 35, no. 3 (September 1982): 376–384.

Chapter 3
The Intergovernmental Framework for State and Community Politics

Chapter Preview

In the previous chapter we saw how constitutions and political culture limit what state and community governments can do. In this chapter we examine the limiting impact of federalism, or intergovernmental relations, as it is increasingly being called. We shall discuss in turn:

1. The federal division of powers between the national and state governments.
2. The constitutional evolution of federalism.
3. The New Federalism.
4. Other intergovernmental politics.
5. Intersectional rivalries.
6. Intergovernmental relations and state–community political economies.

Let us begin with a look at the importance of federalism in American history.

Introduction

Conflicts between states, regions, and the national government have been the source of some of the bitterest political battles in American history. The results of these battles continue to have a profound influence on our lives.

Example: In 1832 John C. Calhoun got a South Carolina convention to proclaim the Nullification Ordinances. Calhoun argued that the United States Constitution was a compact between the state governments rather than a charter from the people. This **compact theory** proposed that any state could nullify a congressional law. At issue was a high tariff being considered by

31

Congress. Although the tariff would protect the industries of the Northeast from imported competition, it would hurt the South's ability to export cotton and agricultural products to Europe. In reaction to the Nullification Ordinances, congressmen from the Northeast compromised, and the South won a moderate tariff that would not damage its export economy.

Example: From 1861 to 1865, in order to keep eleven southern states in the Union, the nation fought its bloodiest war, a war that claimed half a million lives. As a result, the southern slave economy was destroyed, the economic dominance of the North was established, and the South's status as an underdeveloped region was determined for at least the next two generations.

In the 1980s we no longer fight wars or issue nullification ordinances to protect states' rights. Yet the competition and conflict between governments is just as vital to the well-being of citizens today as it was a hundred years ago.

Example: In recent years, the conflict between regions has begun to take new forms. One form of interregional conflict is North–South, or frostbelt–sunbelt, as the regions are sometimes called. The cities of the Northeast and Midwest are declining in population and industry, while many cities of the South and Southwest are growing. These regions compete for new industry, for federal aid, and for other federal expenditures. Another form of interregional conflict is East–West. Most of the nation's domestic supplies of energy are found in the West, while the East is energy-poor. The stakes in these interregional conflicts involve billions of dollars and affect the life-styles of millions of people.[1]

Example: A visible symbol that state and local governments are giving more and more importance to their relations with the federal government is the Hall of the States in Washington, D.C. This building houses the Washington offices of several state lobbying organizations, such as the National Governors Association, the National Conference of State Legislatures, and the Council of State Community Affairs Agencies. Located right next to the Capitol, these offices give the governors, state legislators, and other state and local officials convenient access to those federal officials who write regulations and design federal aid programs that have such an important impact on state and local governments.[2]

As these examples illustrate, intergovernmental relations historically have been, and today continue to be, important facets of American political life. This chapter examines the changing dynamics of intergovernmental relations by exploring (1) the evolution from federalism to intergovernmental relations, (2) the New Federalism, (3) other intergovernmental politics, (4) a case study of intergovernmental politics—the East–West conflict and the Sagebrush Rebellion, and (5) the impact of intergovernmental relations on state and local political economies.

The Division of Powers Between National and State Governments

Federalism divides authority between a national government and state governments. It is distinguished from unitary government and confederacy. A *unitary government* concentrates all authority at the national level; subnational units exist only if the national government creates them. England, for example, is a unitary government. A *confederacy* reverses this relationship: The national government is created by the states and has only as much authority as the states give it. From 1781 to 1789, the United States lived under a confederacy, the Articles of Confederation.

In a federal government, one of the most critical issues is the formal division of powers between the national and the state governments. The United States Constitution delegates certain powers to the national government and reserves all other powers to the states or to the people.

The Federal Government

The federal government possesses only those powers delegated to it by the Constitution. Included among those **delegated powers** (or **enumerated powers**) are the powers to coin money, to regulate foreign and interstate commerce, to establish a post office, to declare war, and to provide for the defense and general welfare of the United States.

According to strict constructionists of the Constitution, Congress can exercise only those powers that are specifically enumerated. However, this limitation is partially undone by the clause that grants Congress the power to make all laws "necessary and proper for carrying into execution" the enumerated powers. Loose constructionists argue that this **necessary-and-proper clause** gives the federal government implied powers to act even if such actions have not been specifically enumerated.

Strict and loose constructionists clashed in the very first presidential administration. Secretary of the Treasury Alexander Hamilton (a loose constructionist) wanted Congress to establish a national bank, arguing that such a bank would promote the general welfare of the nation. Secretary of State Thomas Jefferson (a strict constructionist) objected to the proposal, since the Constitution did not specifically give Congress the authority to charter banks. Hamilton prevailed, and the bank was established for a period to end in 1808.

In 1811 a second national bank was chartered. The state of Maryland charged that Congress had no authority to issue such a charter and placed a tax on the bank's operations, hoping to drive it out of the state. The United States Supreme Court held that the necessary-and-proper clause did indeed authorize Congress to charter the bank, and Maryland's tax on it violated the **national-supremacy clause.** As a result of this court case, *McCulloch* v. *Maryland* (1819), the powers of the federal government were expanded, and it became impossible for the states to tax the federal government.[3]

A third constitutional clause that facilitated the expansion of the federal government's power is the **commerce clause.** In a very early interpretation, the Supreme Court ruled that the authority to regulate interstate commerce belongs exclusively to Congress.[4]

In addition to enumerating the powers of the federal government, the Constitution also places significant limits on it. Article I, Section 9, lists a series of prohibitions on Congress; the Bill of Rights (the first ten amendments) places other limitations; and the fact that the states possess the **reserve powers** (all those powers *not* assigned to the federal government) also limits the federal government.

You Decide
Should Cities Conduct Their Own Foreign Relations?

Fewer federal powers are more firmly entrenched than the U.S. government's exclusive authority to conduct foreign relations. But foreign relations can cause headaches for communities in which foreign diplomats reside. For example, such diplomats are immune from prosecution for violation of local traffic ordinances and are exempt from paying taxes for the local services they receive.

The city of Glen Cove, Long Island, New York, became incensed in 1982 over the suspected installation of electronic eavesdropping equipment in a local mansion that was owned and used by the Soviet Union mission to the United Nations. Pointing out that diplomatic occupancy of the mansion deprived Glen Cove of $100,000 in property taxes each year, the city council voted to ban Soviet diplomats from using city beaches, tennis courts, and other recreational spots until the Soviet Union or the State Department (or somebody) paid the taxes.

Three years later, in another local conflict over foreign policy, the Los Angeles City Council directed city workers to stop helping federal authorities locate and deport "political refugees." At issue was the Council's desire to give sanctuary to illegal immigrants from places such as Haiti, Guatemala, and El Salvador who faced execution if sent back. From the federal viewpoint, such sanctuary movements not only interfered with U.S. foreign policy, but they compounded the already difficult task of keeping track of illegal aliens. By the end of 1985 at least six other cities had adopted their own sanctuary measures.

You decide! Do Glen Cove and Los Angeles have a constitutional right to take the actions they did? Do they have a moral right?

For more on these cases, see the Highlight on p. 35.

The State Governments

Whereas the federal government has only those powers delegated to it, the Tenth Amendment of the Constitution reserves all other powers "to the states respectively, or to the people." In practice the states and their local governments have primary responsibilities over most domestic matters. They administer the election process; conduct most court trials; operate the public school systems; and provide most of our public services, such as streets, sewers, water supply, public recreational facilities, and public health facilities. Although the states enjoy primary responsibility in these policy areas, the federal courts have often relied on three constitutional clauses to restrict the states' authority. These are the commerce clause, the equal-protection clause, and the due-process clause.

The commerce clause gives the federal government the exclusive authority to regulate interstate commerce. The **equal-protection clause** of the Fourteenth Amendment says that no state may deny any person the "equal protection of the laws." And the Fifth and Fourteenth Amendments' **due-process clause** says that no person shall be deprived of "life, liberty, or property without due process of law." Relying on one or more of these clauses, the federal courts over the past forty years have struck down most state segregation laws, have imposed minimum standards of criminal justice on the states, have struck down state prohibitions on abortions, and have sometimes limited the regulatory capacity of the states.[5]

Since the mid-twentieth century, Supreme Court interpretation of these clauses has generally tended to restrict state authority and expand the authority of the federal government. In the 1980s, however, the pattern has become

Highlight
Local Foreign Relations

Glen Cove: Two years after Glen Cove, N.Y., banned resident Soviet diplomats from using the city's recreational facilities, and following a suit by the U.S. government, a federal court order, and a change in mayors, Glen Cove withdrew its ban on the Soviet diplomats.

Sanctuary Movement: The sanctuary-movement ordinances are mainly symbolic gestures that have not yet faced a test of law. But in 1986, eight church workers were convicted in federal court of felony charges that they had smuggled illegal aliens into the United States.

Sources: New York Times, July 29, 1982, p. 8; August 26, 1983, p. 1; April 18, 1984, p. 12; November 29, 1985, p. 12; May 6, 1986, p. 9.

less clear. In support of federal supremacy, the Supreme Court in 1985 forced local governments to adhere to the federal minimum wage standards.[6] Cities complained that this ruling drove up their annual overtime pay costs by $1.75 billion.[7] Counter to the trend of federal supremacy, however, state and local governments have also won some important federalism cases before the Supreme Court.[8] And with the establishment of the State and Local Legal Center to help them better prepare their federal cases, states and communities seem likely to enjoy improved success when federalism cases come before the Supreme Court in the future.[9]

The Evolution of Federalism

Federalism today is very different from federalism in 1787, when the Constitution was written. Federalism has evolved through different stages,[10] which has led us from a dual-federalism concept of state–national relations to cooperative federalism.

Dual Federalism: Pre-1937

Before 1937, **dual federalism** was the prevailing view of the relations between the state and national governments. Each level of government was viewed as having its own separate source of authority and areas of responsibility.[11] The states were not supposed to interfere in foreign affairs, for example, and the federal government was not supposed to intervene in areas of state responsibility.

The entire history of dual federalism was marked by intense conflicts for dominance between the federal government and the states. The Civil War (1861–1865) established the ultimate dominance of the national government by determining that states could not secede from the union. After the Civil War, the main conflicts centered on federal government attempts to regulate business and stimulate the economy. National dominance in this sphere was affirmed by the Supreme Court in 1937,[12] when it legitimized the federal government's right to regulate major aspects of the national economy.

Cooperative Federalism: 1933–1961

The dual federalism concept concentrates on formal divisions of authority. In the actual operation of governments, however, the division of powers is not so tidy as it seems in the Constitution. The very achievement of federal dominance by the 1930s brought basic changes in the federal system. The federal government began working directly with local governments, thus introducing a three-level relationship. By the end of the 1930s, the three levels had become deeply intertwined. How these three levels of government interact can be seen in the operation of the child-protection program, a program in which federal grants are given to local governments to combat child abuse and child neglect by parents and other adults. The key official in fighting child abuse is the child-protection worker.

> Usually employed and paid by the local county welfare department, the child protection worker is financed partly from county funds, partly from state funds, and partly from federal welfare grants. Although a county employee, the child protection worker functions as an official of many different governments, acting as a federal officer when getting a client to apply for federally funded food stamps or AFDC, and as a state officer when investigating a complaint about a violation of state laws prohibiting abuse of children. When bringing a client to a mental health center in a county hospital, the worker functions as a county officer; because the center is funded by a federal program, however, the worker also functions as a federal officer. When the worker investigates a complaint that a city family lets its infant crawl on a floor strewn with the feces of family pets, he or she is acting as a city officer, concerned both with the ordinance on health and the ordinance on the number of pets permitted in a home. When the worker follows up on court orders that abusing parents continue with family counseling, he or she is serving as an officer of the court. When the worker visits a man in jail, who has sexually abused his daughter, to see whether he is taking part in the counseling program there, he or she is serving in part as a state corrections officer. The child protection worker may also act as a negotiator with several other local governments and private agencies; for example, he or she may negotiate with local school districts to get clients into special programs, or with neighboring counties to purchase services for clients that the worker's own county does not provide, or with private agencies, foster homes, halfway houses, or church groups to get their resources applied to clients.[13]

In short, this county-hired social worker acts partly as an agent of the federal government, partly as an agent of the state, and partly as an agent of the county.

The example of the child-protection worker shows that the levels of government are no longer separate, like the layers of a layer cake. Rather, as Morton Grodzins has said, the functions of government overlap so much among all three levels of government that they have the appearance of a "rainbow or marble cake, characterized by an inseparable mingling of differently colored ingredients, the colors appearing in vertical and diagonal strains and unexpected whirls. As colors are mixed in the marble cake, so functions are mixed in the American federal system."[14] This feature of federalism is labeled **cooperative federalism,**[15] because the federal government is seeking to cooperate with state and local governments to provide financial support for their traditional services. It is also sometimes called **marble cake federalism,** in contrast to **layer cake federalism,** or dual federalism.

Creative Federalism: 1961-1969

During the administrations of Presidents Kennedy and Johnson (1961–1969), intergovernmental politics moved into a third phase. The national government increasingly relied on the grant-in-aid system (see below) to impose the federal government's priorities on the states. The number of federal grant programs increased dramatically from about one hundred at the start of the decade to about five hundred at the decade's end—from about $7 billion to about $24 billion. President Johnson labeled his administration the Great Society. He persuaded Congress to pass a variety of imaginative programs with catchy names such as the War on Poverty, Model Cities, Headstart, legal services for the poor, and compensatory education.

This phase of intergovernmental relations was called *Creative Federalism* because the policy initiatives were often created at the national level and then imposed on the states. As such, it also entailed a massive shift of power over domestic policies from the state–local levels to the federal level. With its superior ability to raise revenues and the willingness of federal courts to impose desegregation, affirmative action, and other guidelines throughout the nation, the federal government by 1969 had in fact become supreme over the states. In reaction to this, Republican Presidents Nixon (1969–1974) and Reagan (1981–1989) pushed for a *New Federalism* that would reverse the flow of power to Washington. Before discussing New Federalism, however, we need to examine the main device by which Creative Federalism had brought Washington to dominance—the grant-in-aid.

The Grant-in-Aid System

The major device for implementing cooperative and creative federalism is the grant-in-aid. A **grant-in-aid** is a federal payment to a state or local government for some activity, such as running a child-protection program. As shown in Table 3–1, there are three types of federal grants to state and local governments—categorical grants, block grants, and general revenue sharing.

Categorical Grants

A **categorical grant** is a federal payment to a state or local government to carry out a specific activity. The Interstate Highway Program, for example, provides federal funds to states to build the interstate highway system. Federal funds under this categorical grant cannot be used for any other purpose. The

Table 3–1. Types of Federal Aid

Type of aid	Billions of dollars (fiscal year 1987)	Percent of total
Categorical grants (e.g., Interstate Highway Program)	$ 94.1	85.6%
Block grants (e.g., Education Block Grant)	13.4	12.2
General revenue sharing	0.1	0
Other general assistance	2.3	2.2
	$109.9	100

Source: United States Office of Management and Budget, *Special Analyses of the Budget of the United States Government: FY 1988* (Washington, D.C.: United States Government Printing Office, 1987), p. H–2.

grants usually are accompanied by extensive federal guidelines stipulating in great detail how the programs should be implemented. Grants-in-aid also contain a matching provision requiring the recipient governments to match a certain percentage of the federal grant. In the interstate highway program, a state has to contribute only $10 for every $90 contributed by the federal government.

Categorical grants are either project grants, formula grants, or open-ended reimbursements. In a **project grant** (e.g., the Urban Development Action Grant, which funds community construction projects), a state or local agency makes a grant application to some federal agency, which has considerable discretion in deciding who gets the money. In a **formula grant** (e.g., the Interstate Highway Program, which funds freeway construction), the federal aid is distributed automatically to state or local governments according to a formula drawn up by Congress. In an **open-ended reimbursement** program (e.g., unemployment compensation, which gives cash grants to workers who have lost their jobs), states and communities are reimbursed for whatever expenses they incur implementing the federal share of the program. These programs are open-ended because their costs vary greatly with the economy, rising in times of recession but dropping in periods of economic boom. Three-fourths of all federal aid is now dispensed by formulas or open-ended reimbursements.[16]

Block Grants

In contrast to the categorical grant, which can only be used for a very specific purpose, a **block grant** is one that can be used for a wider variety of purposes and has far fewer federal guidelines on how programs are to be implemented. Most block grants have been formed through the consolidation of several specific categorical grants. For example, in 1981 Congress consolidated thirty-eight specific educational categorical grants into one education block grant that increased state flexibility and responsibility for administering federal education dollars.

Because of this greater flexibility, state and local elected officials generally prefer block grants over categorical grants.[17] Congress, on the other hand, is concerned that federal aid be used to meet priorities set at the national rather than the local level. For this reason, Congress tends to favor categorical grants over block grants. There are currently eleven block grant programs, nine of them established during the Reagan administration.[18]

General Revenue Sharing

General revenue sharing was a program that turned federal funds over to local governments to use as they see fit. Started in 1972, the program originally funded both state and local governments. But in 1980 all state grants were dropped from the program, and local governments began to get about $4.6 billion annually, with very few strings attached. Each community's share was determined by a complex formula based primarily on population but adjusted to give more money to poor, urban states with high levels of taxation. The program was ended in 1986 because of the need to reduce the federal budget deficit.

Criticisms of Cooperative Federalism

Cooperative federalism, and the grant-in-aid system described here, is neither simple nor unbiased, and those two facts make it the target of continual political criticism. More than 400 categorical grant programs have evolved in a piecemeal fashion over the last generation to form a confusing, uncoordinated approach to hundreds of the nation's problems, ranging from highway construction to child protection. Not only is the system exceedingly confusing, it is rife with biases. Northern, industrial states complain that too many funds go to the South and Southwest. Southerners, of course, charge the opposite. Some critics complain that the categorical grants go not to cities with the greatest need for financial aid, but to cities most adept at "grantsmanship" (writing grant proposals).

Political questions also arise over the proportion of federal aid that should take the form of categorical grants, block grants, and general revenue sharing. As indicated above, Congress prefers to use categorical grants because they permit greater Congressional influence in determining how the federal monies are spent. Private interest groups also tend to prefer categorical grants, and they pressure Congress to use such grants whenever possible. State and local elected officials prefer block grants and general revenue sharing, because those two forms of aid give state and local officials greater discretion in implementing federal domestic programs.

The most important political question in all of these conflicts over federal aid is: To what extent should federal aid be used as an instrument of national dominance over the states? In theory, the $110 billion in aid gives the federal government substantial leverage to dominate state budgetmaking and set program priorities for the states. In some policy areas this in fact happens. For example, the salaries of child-protection workers are funded heavily by federal grants, as are many of the programs these social workers use to carry out their child-protection responsibilities. If these federal programs were eliminated, some states would lack the financial resources or the political willpower to take them over. In this sense, federal aid is used to get the states to spend more money on the child-abuse problem than they would spend without the federal prodding.

The New Federalism

Each presidential administration reacted differently to those complaints about cooperative federalism. During the Eisenhower years (1953–1961), grants-in-aid came under attack by conservatives as undermining state autonomy. President Eisenhower formed a national committee to find grant-in-aid programs that could be turned over to the states, but after two years' work, not a single program had been shifted to the states.

The Kennedy–Johnson years (1961–1969) saw a dramatic increase in the number of grant programs, from 100 to about 500. These were the Great Society years, in which categorical grants were used to entice the states to participate in a number of federally initiated social welfare programs: Model Cities, Medicaid, Food Stamps, legal services for the poor, compensatory education, and the War on Poverty, among others.

During the 1970s, the number of categorical grant programs ceased growing as the Nixon administration (1969–1974) sponsored general revenue sharing and the first extensive block grants. Although the number of grant programs stayed stable in the 1970s, the money involved grew rapidly to $94 billion in 1981, supplying about a fourth of all state and local government revenue.

In the early 1980s the Reagan administration proposed a **New Federalism,** the keynote of which was "devolution," or spinning off the federal government's responsibilities to state and local governments and to the private sector. Devolution has four components: the budget, regulation, the private sector, and courts.

Budgetary Devolution

Reagan's goal of spinning off substantial federal budgetary responsibilities to state and local governments was to be accomplished through three major devices: (1) the consolidation of seventy-seven categorical grants into nine new block grants, which would be administered by the states with minimal federal strings attached; and (2) severe budget cutbacks in social service programs in an effort to shift more of the burden for these services onto the states; and (3) the *Great Swap,* which tried to sort out which programs could best be handled by the states and which could best be handled by the national government. Under the Great Swap, Reagan proposed that the federal government assume all responsibility for Medicaid, a very expensive and rapidly growing program of health care for the indigent, the elderly, and people on welfare. In exchange, the states would take over responsibility for Food Stamps, Aid to Families with Dependent Children (AFDC), and forty-three other categorical programs.

The important point about these complicated proposals is that they were the most significant attempts to date to reverse federal dominance of the federal-fiscal partnership that has existed since the 1930s. The original intent of the Reagan administration was to cut the total amount of federal grants almost in half. And the federal government would lose much of its ability to set budget priorities for the states.

While Reagan scored stunning successes on his block grants and social services cutback proposals, Congress rejected his Great Swap proposal. As satirized in the cartoon, local officials were not overwhelmingly pleased at taking on these new responsibilities from the federal government. Many of them viewed poverty and welfare as national problems, and for years they had urged the federal government to assume full financial responsibility for the major welfare programs. Reagan's Great Swap proposal to devolve Food Stamps and AFDC onto the states directly contradicted this goal. Against opposition from the states, Reagan succeeded in cutting federal grants-in-aid back to $86 billion in 1982. Despite this reduction, federal aids continued to grow and by 1987 reached $110 billion.

Regulatory Devolution

A second aspect of Reagan's New Federalism might be called regulatory devolution. Between 1965 and 1980, there was a virtual explosion of federal laws, administrative agency rules, and court orders that put the sharpest regulation in American history on several aspects of the economy, ranging from environmental protection to antidiscrimination and occupational health and safety. Because these new regulations added to the cost of doing business, American business leaders bitterly resented many of them. Thus the Carter

Isn't it wonderful, Orville? And after we thought he'd be whisked off to Washington forever?

The Reagan administration's New Federalism sought to turn more governmental responsibility over to state and local governments. As this cartoon suggests, however, not all local and state officials were pleased with the prospect.

Source: C. P. Houston, *The Houston Chronicle,* 1981.

administration took some early steps toward deregulation by phasing out federal controls over the price of petroleum and natural gas and deregulating the airline industry. President Reagan made further reductions of federal regulatory activities and sought legislation that would shift major regulatory responsibilities to the states, especially in environmental protection. Under Reagan, the Environmental Protection Agency cut back sharply the number of regulations it issued. Thus, as discussed in Chapter 16, Reagan threw his support behind attempts to rewrite the Clean Air Act in ways that would put greater responsibility on the states for reducing air pollution.

Devolution to the Private Sector

When the Reagan administration cut funds for social programs in the early 1980s, it called on the private sector to take up the slack. In cutting social expenditures, for example, Reagan argued that some federally funded programs providing food and shelter for the destitute could be replaced by volunteers from churches and nonprofit organizations. The heart of his proposals for tackling urban problems was to create so-called urban enterprise zones. These would be city neighborhoods in which taxes and regulatory restrictions (such as occupational safety and minimum wages) would be relaxed for companies that moved facilities into those neighborhoods and created jobs there. This reliance on the private sector to accomplish public goals did not, of course, initiate with Reagan. But he pushed for this objective more strongly than any other recent president.

Curbing Federal Courts

Finally, the early 1980s saw concerted efforts to pressure the federal courts into a strict constructionist posture in dealing with highly volatile issues such as abortion, desegregation, and voting rights, in which the federal courts have ordered states to comply with federal laws and with the Supreme Court's interpretation of the Constitution. Pressure on the courts came in the form of bills introduced by conservative members of Congress to reduce the Supreme Court's authority to hear cases on school busing and abortion, as well as proposals for Constitutional amendments that would reverse Supreme Court rulings on those subjects. To date, none of these proposals have passed.

Assessing the New Federalism

Did Reagan's New Federalism achieve his goal of returning more power and authority to the states? On the surface it may seem the goal was not achieved, since the president lost most of the major battles involved and eventually seemed to lose interest in the issue itself. But in some respects he may well have won the war. He capped the growth rate of most domestic social programs, reduced the number of federal grant-in-aid programs, got nine new block grants passed, and provoked an ongoing debate over the sorting out of federal from state and local responsibilities. Furthermore, as federal grants were cut back, states and communities were forced to set their own priorities on what social services they would fund. Although a definitive study of the state response to New Federalism has yet to be conducted, one highly respected study that monitored the implementation of the block grants in fourteen states concluded that those states effectively made up for federal cutbacks in social programs and that they used the block grants to increase their own influence over cities and the federal bureaucracies.[19]

These considerations remind us that the New Federalism is not a neutral program. It contains biases of its own. It is not simply a conflict between the states and the federal government. It is primarily a conflict between those who want political power to lie with state governments and those wanting it in the federal government, because they believe they will receive greater benefits in these respective situations. At the risk of oversimplification, the groups that perceive that they will benefit more through state rather than federal regulation include business groups, conservative groups, and development-oriented groups. Those that perceive they will benefit more through federal regulation include consumerists, environmentalists, racial minorities, organized labor, and groups representing low-income people. As we will see in later chapters, consumerists, environmentalists, and labor leaders often seek regulations (such as stringent occupational safety rules) that put a state adopting them at a disadvantage when competing for industrial growth and economic development. A state with stringent occupational safety rules may be less attractive for industrial expansion than a state with lenient rules. But this disadvantage would disappear if the rules were applied evenly across all states by the federal government. For this reason, consumerists, environmentalists, and labor unions would prefer that this type of regulation be federally directed.

Other Intergovernmental Politics

Federalism refers to the relationship between the national and the state governments. In addition, there are so many other ways in which governments interact with each other that scholars use the term **intergovernmental relations** (IGR) to refer to this phenomenon. Two of these patterns of interaction deserve notice. They are the role of local governments in the IGR system and the patterns of politics among states.

Local Governments in the IGR System

The evolution of cooperative federalism has had the long-term effect of eroding local autonomy. In federal and local relations this has taken the form of weakening the general-purpose local governments. In state and local relations, a long-term centralization process has eroded much local autonomy.

Federal and Local Relations

Until the 1930s the federal government had little direct involvement with local governments. To cope with the Great Depression, however, the federal government gave grants-in-aid directly to cities. This practice expanded during the 1960s. Between 1960 and 1970 the percentage of federal aid going to urban areas, for example, increased from 55 percent to 70 percent.[20] During the 1970s, city governments became very dependent on federal funds to ward off economic recessions and on federal employment funds to hire public service workers.

While federal aid has had many positive effects, it has also weakened the general-purpose local governments, strengthened the functionally organized bureaucracies, and contributed to the decline of the cities. Federal aid was organized on a program basis and quite often was channeled through single-purpose governments that used the federal funds and federal regulations to insulate themselves from the local government political leaders.[21] Federal aid also has contributed to the population declines and the relative impoverishment of the central cities. Federal mortgage subsidies under the Federal Housing Administration and Veterans Administration plans reinforced the movement from central cities to suburbs. Federally supported freeway systems facilitated access to suburban shopping centers and made it unnecessary to go downtown to shop. Urban renewal programs tore down many white ethnic neighborhoods, thus depriving the central cities of a stabilizing social structure.[22]

During the Johnson administration, many Great Society programs sought to bypass traditional city governments by sending federal aid directly to the local level or, as in the case of the community action and model cities programs, directly to subcity neighborhood units. In contrast, the Nixon and Reagan administrations sought to channel such urban aid through the state governments rather than directly to the cities and neighborhoods.[23]

State and Local Relations

If communities rely heavily on federal money, they rely even more strongly on the states for their legal authority. City governments are creatures of the state, and the legal principle known as **Dillon's Rule** holds that city governments' powers must be interpreted very narrowly. Because of Dillon's Rule, cities are usually permitted to exercise only those authorities granted to them by their state constitutions or their state legislatures. Boulder, Colorado, relearned this lesson the hard way in 1982 when the Supreme Court struck down that city's attempt to regulate cable television.[24]

Probably the most visible impact states have on local governments is financial. State governments provide general and categorical aids to local governments. They determine how much debt local governments can have, and they limit how much local governments may increase their property taxes from year to year.

Although local autonomy has generally eroded in the twentieth century, it must not be concluded that local politics are irrelevant. Local communities remain as the key political bases of state legislators, congresspersons, and, in some instances, statewide officials. Local leaders are able to call on their elected officials or congresspersons to exert influence on the administration of national policies. In many ways state officials have taken on the new role of advocate for local governments in the quest for greater federal aids.[25] And nearly half the states have established intergovernmental advisory commissions to promote smoother cooperation between the states and their local governments.[26]

Interstate Politics

Some interstate relationships are required by the United States Constitution. The Supreme Court has jurisdiction over legal conflicts between states. The full-faith-and-credit clause requires each state to recognize the official acts of other states. Thus, people divorced in one state do not find their divorce nullified when they cross into another state. The privileges-and-immunities clause prohibits a state from discriminating against nonresidents.

In addition to these clauses, the Constitution also contains a rendition clause that requires governors to return fugitives from justice to the state from which they fled. If a governor refuses to return a fugitive, however, the Supreme Court is unlikely to intervene. Florida, for example, once refused to return to Missouri a man who had stolen a chimpanzee from the St. Louis Zoo but had left behind in the chimp's cage enough money to pay for the animal. Missouri could hardly complain about Florida's reluctance to cooperate in this case, however, because Missouri itself annually refuses about a half-dozen rendition requests from other states.[27]

The most popular mechanism for resolving interstate problems is probably the interstate compact.[28] This is an agreement made by two or more states and ratified by Congress. Interstate compacts are commonly used to settle problems in corrections, education, transportation, or natural-resources management.[29] The most famous interstate compact is the one that created the Port Authority of New York and New Jersey in 1921 to regulate and develop transportation facilities. This Authority quickly developed bridges, tunnels, commuter railroads, bus terminals, airports, and, more recently, the World Trade Center.

Rising Regionalism

One significant interstate development in recent years has been the resurgence of sectional rivalries. The best-known regional rivalries are the sunbelt–frostbelt and the East–West ones. At the heart of these conflicts, as shown in Figure 3–1, has been the long-term demographic and economic decline of the Midwestern and Northeastern **frostbelt** states in comparison with the more rapidly growing **sunbelt** and Western states. The problem is especially acute

Figure 3–1. Sunbelt and Frostbelt Prosperity: 1970–1984

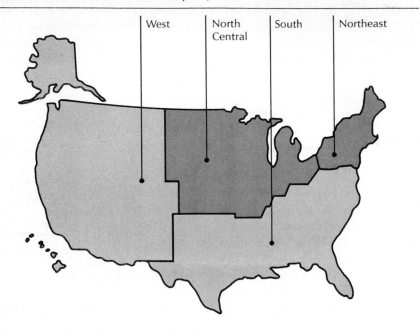

Regions above the national average in growth

Regions below the national average in growth

	Population growth		Growth in nonagricultural employment	
Region	1970–1984	1980–1984	1970–1984	1980–1984
Northeast	1.2%	1.2%	14.9%	4.5%
North Central	4.4	0.3	16.5	− 1.5
South	28.3	6.9	54.5	7.5
West	34.2	8.1	58.4	6.6
United States	16.2	4.3	33.6	4.4

Sources: Calculated from the Bureau of the Census, *Statistical Abstract of the United States: 1986* (Washington, D.C.: U.S. Government Printing Office, 1986), pp. 9, 411; *Statistical Abstract: 1971,* p. 218.

in the Midwestern (North Central) region, which, in the first half of the 1980s, actually lost more jobs than it gained.

Northerners argue that their economic problems are compounded by the way in which federal expenditures are spread around the country. The residents of each state pay income taxes to the federal government. The federal government then spends money in the states so each state's economy may receive back from federal expenditures either more or less money than its residents send to the federal government in taxes. In order to determine which states actually make out best from this arrangement, the Advisory Commission on Intergovernmental Relations calculated an expenditure-to-tax ratio that shows how much each state received in federal expenditures from 1982 to 1984 for each tax dollar the state's residents sent to the federal government during those years. For example, Texas residents received only 78¢ for each dollar they paid in federal taxes, while their neighbors in New Mexico reaped $1.80 for each dollar they paid in federal taxes.

Table 3–2 shows that three-fourths of the sunbelt states received more in federal expenditures than they paid in federal income taxes. Less than half of the remaining states received more in federal expenditures than they paid in taxes. The most disadvantaged region was the Northeast–Midwest manufacturing belt stretching from the Hudson River in New York to the Mississippi River. Not a single state within that stretch received as much in federal expenditures as it paid in federal taxes. This fact led frostbelt leaders to charge that they were not getting a fair deal from fiscal federalism.

As the states have pursued economic growth and more federal expenditures, they have found it useful to band together in multistate regional associations. The New England Governors' Conference, for example, has become an important force in promoting development in that region.[30] The Northeast Coalition of Governors and the Northeast-Midwest Coalition of Congressional Members were formed in part to get a greater share of federal funds spent in their regions. In 1977, in response to these frostbelt initiatives, Southerners reacted by forming their own lobbying organization, the Southern Growth Policies Board.[31] Southerners respond to Northern complaints about the distribution of federal grants by pointing out that their rapid growth in recent decades has not come without costs. They have had to make substantial investments in such public construction projects as roads and schools to handle the rapidly expanding population. Nor have all southern states benefited from the sunbelt boom. Some states, such as Mississippi and Kentucky, still have the highest poverty levels in the nation. And the migration of laid-off northern industrial workers to places such as Houston during the 1980–1982 recessions put a heavy burden on unemployment compensation, welfare, and other social services of some sunbelt states.[32]

Table 3–2. Expenditure-to-Tax Ratios: 1982–1984

Frostbelt states		Sunbelt states		Rest of the nation	
Illinois	$ .70	New Mexico	$1.80	Hawaii	$1.38
New Jersey	.70	Mississippi	1.61	Utah	1.27
Michigan	.78	Virginia	1.52	Idaho	1.13
Iowa	.80	Alabama	1.29	Washington	1.09
Wisconsin	.82	Arkansas	1.27	Montana	1.07
Delaware	.83	South Carolina	1.25	Alaska	1.01
Indiana	.83	Tennessee	1.20	Nevada	.92
Minnesota	.85	Arizona	1.14	Colorado	.91
Ohio	.85	Kentucky	1.10	Oregon	.89
New York	.92	California	1.09	Wyoming	.75
Nebraska	.95	Florida	1.09		
Pennsylvania	.96	Georgia	1.09		
New Hampshire	.98	West Virginia	1.07		
Connecticut	1.02	North Carolina	.95		
Kansas	1.02	Louisiana	.90		
Rhode Island	1.05	Oklahoma	.88		
North Dakota	1.06	Texas	.78		
Massachusetts	1.10				
Vermont	1.10				
South Dakota	1.24				
Maryland	1.27				
Maine	1.30				
Missouri	1.43				

Source: Advisory Commission on Intergovernmental Relations, *Intergovernmental Perspective* 11, nos. 2/3 (Spring/Summer 1985): 19.
   *Note: Figures represent the amount of federal dollars state economies received for each dollar state residents paid in federal taxes.

East–West Conflict and the Sagebrush Rebellion

Western concerns attracted national attention in July 1979, when the Nevada Legislature passed a resolution demanding that 49 million acres of federal land in Nevada be turned over to the state. Termed the **Sagebrush Rebellion,** the idea quickly spread and similar legislation was introduced in other western states where the federal government was a big land owner.[33] Three issues prompted this Sagebrush Rebellion, and they are likely to be important in western politics for some time. These are land, energy, and water.

Land Issues

Land is an issue because the federal government owns over half of the land in five western states and over a third of the land in ten states. Until 1976, the federal government leased its land mostly for traditional uses such as mining, logging, and grazing livestock. This arrangement changed with the federal Land Policy and Management Act of 1976, which sought to protect the environmental quality of these federally owned lands. Ten-year leases were replaced by one-year leases, and the tenants were required to file environmental impact statements indicating how their use of the land would affect the overall environment. When the Bureau of Land Management sought to carry out those provisions, it sparked a strong reaction from some of the traditional users who sought to get the federal government "off our backs."

The land issue in the West is only partly a conflict between the western states and the federal government. It is also a conflict between the New West and the Old West. Old West interests seek to use the land primarily for ranching, farming, and mining, which are called "dominant" traditional uses. New West interests want to use the land for industrial development, urbanization, intensified energy exploration, and recreation, which are called "multiple uses." Under its 1976 mandate, the Bureau of Land Management is managing the land for "multiple uses" rather than for "dominant" traditional uses, a situation that angers Old West interests. Bureau of Land Management officials also resist turning the federal land over to the states for fear that the states will not protect the environmental quality of the land as it is used for more industrial and urban purposes. Many of these complaints were put to rest by the Reagan administration that clamped down on the regulatory efforts of the Bureau of Land Management[34] and slowly began increasing the sale of federal lands.[35]

Energy Issues

Energy issues are also prominent in the Sagebrush Rebellion. Most of the nation's energy-producing areas are found in the West. Only twelve states produce as much energy as they consume each year, and all but two of those are west of the Mississippi River.[36]

The disproportionate concentration of energy resources in a few states creates a serious issue for intergovernmental politics. When the acute energy shortages of the 1970s produced an **energy crisis,** oil, coal, and natural gas companies responded by dramatically expanding their energy explorations. Each coal-mining site or energy-processing plant brought in new people who needed houses, schools, and public services while they worked in the energy production enterprises. To pay for these services, some energy-producing states drastically increased their **severance taxes** (the tax on resources extracted from the ground). Louisiana, for example, sharply increased its tax on natural gas that was piped out of state, and Montana increased its coal tax to 30 percent of the value of coal that was mined. Energy-consuming states bitterly complained that these increases were a blatant attempt by energy-producing states to gouge the rest of the country by exporting their tax burdens. In 1981 the Supreme Court voided the Louisiana tax on natural gas because it exempted Louisianans,[37] but the Court let stand the Montana tax because it fell on Montanans as well as non-Montanans.[38]

By the mid-1980s, the energy shortage was replaced by an energy glut, and the wellhead price of oil fell by 50 percent. This development eased greatly the financial problems of energy-consuming states, but it wreaked financial havoc on much of the West. Some of the energy boomtowns created a decade earlier now faced the prospect of becoming ghost towns still burdened with the task of paying for the school buildings, water systems, and other public facilities they built to accommodate their then-growing populations. Some of them no longer have the population and tax base required to raise the needed revenues.[39] States, such as Texas and Oklahoma that relied heavily on energy taxes to expand their public facilities in the 1970s, suddenly in the mid-1980s found their tax base shrinking as the price of oil dropped.

Water Issues

Although the West is energy-rich, it is water-poor. It is the driest region of the country, and water politics have often been bitter. The West traditionally has sought to meet its water needs through federally sponsored projects that dammed up rivers and moved large volumes of water huge distances through long aqueducts to growing urban populations. Some urban locations became overdeveloped in relation to their water supply. Such cities have attempted to increase their water supply by sinking wells deeper and deeper into the underground aquifers, with the result of increasingly lowering the groundwater levels. Houston's underground aquifers have been so dramatically reduced that the city has sunk four feet since 1900, and scientists warn that the downtown area could sink by another fourteen feet in the next forty years if remedial steps are not taken.[40]

Because of urbanization, industrialization, and the desire to exploit natural resources, many competing interests want access to scarce western water rights. One proposal for allocating water resources is to let the marketplace determine the allocation by selling water as most other commodities are sold. But there appears to be little support for this proposal.[41] A survey of legislators and the public in four western states found no support for re-allocating

The water problems inherent in development of the sunbelt are graphically
portrayed here by the frostbelt cartoonist
Jerry Fearing.

Source: Jerry Fearing, *St. Paul Pioneer Press,* January 18, 1981.

existing water supplies among competing users.[42] Rather, they wanted to increase the water supply. In 1980 Arizona passed legislation that sought simul-
taneously to increase water supplies and to decrease consumption through
conservation.[43] Crucial to this plan is the Central Arizona Project, a huge
system of aqueducts to pipe water hundreds of miles away into Arizona at a
cost to federal taxpayers of $180 million per year.

Several questions arise for interregional water politics. From how far can
water actually be transported to the West? From the Mississippi River? From
the Great Lakes? Even if such feats were technologically possible, would they
make sense as public policy? Will nonwestern states be willing to pay the
costs for projects that will benefit mainly the West? The only answer we can
give with much certainty is that the political fight over western water is likely
to intensify over the next decade.

The Scope of Intergovernmental Conflict in the West

One of the most important aspects of these political conflicts has been their expansion from the state level to the federal level. State governments have been unable to resolve the competition for use of land and water, so some of the interests have turned to the federal government. As these interests looked to Washington for help, the Bureau of Land Management played a stronger role as mediator of multiple versus dominant land uses. But it was just this role that helped precipitate the Sagebrush Rebellion. And under the Reagan administration the Bureau of Land Management became less aggressive than it had been in earlier years.

Intergovernmental Impact on State and Local Political Economies

It is apparent from our review here that federalism and intergovernmental relations have important consequences for the ability of state and local governments to deliver public services and facilitate economic growth in their private sectors. Two of these consequences are very important: (1) the forces for interregional conflict, and (2) the strengths and weaknesses of the intergovernmental system in dealing with regional and state diversity.

Cooperation versus Conflict

Underlying much of what occurs in intergovernmental politics is the fact that the states and regions differ widely in their economic resources and assets. The West has an abundance of energy resources, but it is the nation's driest region and lacks the water to develop its resources. The Northeast and Midwest regions have the world's most extensive network of factories and productive capacity, but they have been hit hard in recent years by foreign competition. The South has benefited immensely from population and economic growth in recent years, but it is still the poorest region; indeed, during the 1980–1982 recessions the in-migration of displaced northern industrial workers put a burden on the unemployment compensation systems and social services of such metropolises as Houston and Dallas.

Not only are there disparities in assets among regions, there are also dramatic disparities within regions. The sunbelt includes impoverished rural Mississippi as well as dynamic growth centers in Texas and Florida. The northeastern–midwestern frostbelt not only includes Detroit, whose unemployment rates exceeded 20 percent during the early 1980s, but it also includes one of the nation's highest concentrations of dynamic high-technology industry in the Boston suburbs near Harvard University and the Massachusetts Institute of Technology.

These disparities in economic assets create forces both for cooperation and conflict among the states. Interstate cooperation has been enhanced by the emergence of regionally based economies. States are still the dominant political units for dealing with local economies, but states have been forced to band together to cope with economies that overlap state boundaries. The Great Lakes, for example, are an economic asset to eight different states, and there are many questions on managing water rights, navigation rights, and other matters that force the Great Lakes states into cooperation. Similar overarching economic interests exist in other regions also. Hence the devices of cooperation discussed earlier are used more and more frequently; they include interstate compacts, regional commissions, and regional lobbying groups such as the Southern Growth Policies Board and the Northeast-Midwest Coalition.

Working against interstate cooperation, however, are other forces leading the states into conflict with each other. The widespread desire for economic growth sometimes leads states into destructive bidding wars to offer unreasonable concessions to companies to expand in their states. These bidding wars involve extensive tax concessions, the promise of low tax rates, minimal regulation of the environment, health, and safety, promises to keep down costly welfare services, and the promise to enact right-to-work laws that make it difficult for unions to organize employees.

Free market competition is, of course, one of the basic values of the American culture, and it has the benefits of promoting greater efficiency and a wider variety of products. But an unbridled competition between cities and states to attract industry also has seriously unhealthy consequences. Because economic resources and assets are not evenly divided across the country, most places will make out poorly while a few places will prosper handsomely. In the early 1980s, for example, increasing numbers of cities entered the competition to entice service industries and high-technology industries in computers, software, biomedical engineering, and genetics. A critical resource needed for this strategy to succeed, however, is a major research university such as Harvard or MIT outside of Boston or the University of California and Stanford near that state's famous Silicon Valley, which had an early start in making silicon chips for computers. Cities without major research universities to provide personnel and other attractions to high-technology companies could well invest large sums of money into the competition and get very little payoff.[44]

Unbridled bidding wars for industry might also drastically weaken the ability of states to carry out their constitutional responsibilities to raise revenues for public services and to regulate the public health, safety, and environment. A state or city that gives away too many tax concessions to attract new industries may find itself financially strapped for police, fire, education, welfare, and other services. Or neighboring states may find themselves being played off against each other by a major industry threatening to relocate out of state. For years, for example, Oregon found itself in a weak position for forcing paper mills to clean up the pollution they dumped into the Columbia River, because the companies threatened to move their operations into neighboring states.[45] Federal action was needed to enforce environmental regulation.

Unbridled competition for industry, finally, might well lead to a self-defeating imbalance in economic growth, whereby people from the faltering regions will migrate to the growth regions in search of jobs. During the first two-thirds of the twentieth century, for example, there was a massive migration of poor southern blacks into northern cities in the search of jobs and less discrimination. During the 1930s, Oklahoma farmers, impoverished by the Great Depression, migrated to California. During the recessions of the early 1980s, unemployed industrial workers migrated to prosperous places like Houston and Dallas in search of jobs. In all three instances, the job markets were overloaded by migrants and the large number who failed to find work put pressure on local welfare and social service agencies. Then when the oil boom faded in the mid-1980s, New England reported influxes of Texans seeking to capitalize on New England's resurgence.[46]

Summary

1. The Constitution divides authority between the national and state governments. The national government possesses those powers delegated to it by the Constitution. All other powers not otherwise forbidden are reserved to the states or to the people. (not local gov't)

2. Although the federal government is restricted to exercising only delegated powers, some constitutional provisions have permitted the Supreme Court to make a loose constructionist interpretation of those delegated powers. The most significant constitutional clauses are the necessary-and-proper clause, the national supremacy clause, and the commerce clause.

3. Although the states are given the reserved powers, a number of constitutional provisions put limits on the states' exercise of those powers. The most significant constitutional clauses are the commerce clause, the equal-protection clause, and the due-process clause.

4. Federalism evolved from dual federalism to cooperative federalism and creative federalism. The major mechanism for cooperative federalism has been the system of grants-in-aid, including categorical grants, block grants, and general revenue sharing.

5. President Reagan sought a New Federalism in the 1980s that would devolve federal responsibilities to the states and the private sector for many social services and for much governmental regulation. He succeeded in obtaining nine new block grants but to date has not achieved his Great Swap proposal.

6. In addition to state and national relations, there are also several other forms of intergovernmental relations: local and national, local and state, local and local, and state and state. Over the long term, the changes in intergovernmental relations have caused local autonomy to decline. The major instrument of state-to-state relations is the interstate compact.

7. Two patterns of interregional conflicts are sunbelt–frostbelt and East–West.

8. State and community political economies are greatly affected by contemporary intergovernmental relations. Fiscal federalism redistributes income from the richer states to the poorer states. The competition for economic growth often pits regions, states, and communities against each other.

Key Terms

Block grant A grant that can be used for a much wider variety of purposes than a categorical grant. Usually created by consolidating several categorical grants into a single block grant.

Categorical grant A grant-in-aid given for a specific purpose. Also called a *categorical aid.*

Commerce clause The provision in Article II, Section 8, of the Constitution that grants Congress the authority to control interstate and international commerce.

Compact theory The theory of John C. Calhoun that the United States Constitution was a compact between the state governments rather than a charter from the people.

Cooperative federalism The theory of federalism in which federal and state levels of government cooperate in differing programs in areas previously considered reserved to the states. The opposite of *dual federalism.*

Delegated powers See *enumerated powers.*

Dillon's Rule The principle that city government powers must be interpreted very narrowly.

Dual federalism The concept of federalism in which the state and national levels of government have separate areas of authority. Popular until the 1930s. Distinct from *cooperative federalism.*

Due-process clause The provision of the Fifth and Fourteenth Amendments that protects a person from deprivation of life, liberty, or property without due process of law.

Energy crisis A situation in the 1970s when petroleum and natural gas sources were scarce, and prices for them increased precipitously.

Enumerated powers The powers specifically granted to Congress by the Constitution. Also called *delegated powers.*

Equal-protection clause The provision of the Constitution's Fourteenth Amendment that forbids any state to deny any person in its jurisdiction the equal protection of the laws.

Federalism A formal division of authority between a national government and state governments.

Formula grant A grant-in-aid in which the funds are dispensed automatically according to a formula specified by Congress.

Frostbelt The Northeast and Midwest.

General revenue sharing A program in which the federal government turned funds over to local governments to use as they saw fit with very few federal guidelines on how the money is to be spent.

Grant-in-aid A federal payment to a state or local government to carry out some activity or run some program.

Intergovernmental relations A term used for contemporary federalism in which many different layers of government interact with each other in a complex system.

Layer cake federalism See *dual federalism.*

Marble cake federalism See *cooperative federalism.*

National-supremacy clause The provision in Article VI of the Constitution that makes the Constitution and all legislation passed under its authority the supreme law of the land.

Necessary-and-proper clause The clause in Article I, Section 8, of the Constitution, that gives Congress power to pass all laws necessary and proper for carrying into execution the enumerated powers.

New Federalism Attempts by the Nixon and Reagan administrations to turn federal responsibilities over to the states, usually through general revenue sharing and block grants. The Reagan administration added the concept of "devolution" and sharp cutbacks in federal aid to states and communities.

Open-ended reimbursement A grant-in-aid in which the federal government automatically reimburses state or local governments for the federal share of whatever program funds are spent. Applies only to entitlement programs, such as unemployment compensation, in which the funds spent will vary greatly with economic conditions.

Project grant A grant-in-aid in which the recipient government has to make an application to the granting agency and the granting agency has considerable discretion in deciding which applicants will receive the grant.

Reserve powers The powers reserved to the states or to the people of the United States by the Tenth Amendment to the Constitution.

Sagebrush Rebellion The rebellion of many states in the West against federal ownership and management of significant amounts of western land.

Severance tax A tax levied on natural resources extracted from the earth.

Sunbelt The South and Southwest.

References

1. On frostbelt–sunbelt conflicts, see Jacqueline Mazza and Bill Hogan, *The State of the Region 1981: Economic Trends in the Northeast and Midwest* (Washington, D.C.: The Northeast-Midwest Institute, 1981). On East–West conflicts, see *National Journal*, November 11, 1979, p. 1928, and March 22, 1980, p. 469.

2. Denise Akey, ed., *National Organizations of the U.S.*, vol. 1, *Encyclopedia of Associations* (Detroit: Gale Research Co., 1981).

3. *McCulloch* v. *Maryland*, 4 L. Ed. 579 (1819).

4. *Gibbons* v. *Ogden*, 6 L. Ed. 23 (1824).

5. Federal court rulings are not wholly consistent on the issue of state regulatory powers where interstate commerce is concerned. On the one hand, federal courts prohibited states from imposing safety standards on nuclear power plants in excess of the standards imposed by the Nuclear Regulatory Commission. See *Northern States Power Company, Inc.* v. *The State of Minnesota*, 447 F. 2d 1143 (1971). On the other hand, federal courts allowed California to set higher automobile emission-control standards than those set by the federal Environmental Protection Agency.

6. *Garcia* v. *San Antonio Metropolitan Transit Authority* 105 S.Ct. 1005 (1985). Specifically, this ruling required the San Antonio Transit Authority and other public bus companies to increase the overtime pay for its drivers. Because bus use is not spread evenly throughout the day, bus drivers often work split shifts during the daily rush hours, with long breaks in between.

7. *Intergovernmental Perspective* 11, no. 2/3 (Spring/Summer 1985): 23. Actually, in response to this problem Congress amended the Fair Labor Standards Act to let state and local governments use compensatory time off in lieu of overtime pay for its workers. *State Government News* 29, no. 1 (June 1986): 6.

8. The most important state victory so far in the 1980s is probably *Container Corporation of America* v. *Franchise Tax Board* (June 2, 1983), in which the Supreme Court upheld a controversial California method of taxing corporations.

9. See David B. Walker and Cynthia Cates Colella, "Federalism 1983: Mixed Results from Washington," *Intergovernmental Perspective* 10, no. 1 (Winter 1984): 30–31. Also see Rochelle L. Stanfield, "All the Way to the Supreme Court: States Make Federalism a Federal Case," *National Journal*, 16, no. 2 (January 14, 1984): 71–74, in which the author argues that states lost so many federalism cases prior to 1980 because they so often opposed progress in areas such as civil rights and criminal justice. In the 1980s the states are much more in the mainstream of political currents than they were two decades ago and hence can be expected to enjoy more federalism victories.

10. See Deil S. Wright, "Intergovernmental Relations: An Analytical Overview," *Annals of the American Academy of Political and Social Science* 416 (November 1974): 5.

11. See Daniel J. Elazar, *The American Partnership* (Chicago: University of Chicago Press, 1962), p. 20.

12. *National Labor Relations Board* v. *Jones and Laughlin Steel Corp.*, 300 U.S. 1 (1937).

13. John J. Harrigan, *Political Change in the Metropolis*, 2d ed. (Boston: Little, Brown and Co., 1981), p. 207.

14. Morton Grodzins, "The Federal System," *Goals for Americans: The Report of the President's Commission on National Goals* (Englewood Cliffs, N.J.: Prentice-Hall, 1960), pp. 365–366. In this article, Grodzins provided the example of the sanitarian on which the example of the child-protection worker is modeled.

15. Elazar, *The American Partnership*, p. 20.

16. George E. Hale and Marion Lief Palley, *The Politics of Federal Grants* (Washington, D.C.: Congressional Quarterly Press, 1981), pp. 76–77.

17. For the position of the National Governors' Association supporting the consolidation of categorical grants into block grants, see "Governors' Bulletin," no. 80–20 (Washington, D.C.: National Governors' Association, May 16, 1980).

18. For an excellent history of the origins and development of block grants, see Timothy J. Conlan, "The Politics of Federal Block Grants from Nixon to Reagan," *Political Science Quarterly* 99, no. 2 (Summer 1984): 247–270.

19. Richard P. Nathan and Fred C. Doolittle, "The Untold Story of Reagan's 'New Federalism'," *Public Interest* no. 77 (Fall 1984): 96–105.

20. Wright, "Intergovernmental Relations: An Analytic Overview," p. 15.

21. The Advisory Commission on Intergovernmental Relations has traced the rise of special districts to grants-in-aid. It found twenty-four programs as of 1972, "which had resulted in the formation of 1,800 regional or substate districts which handle special programs in a narrow functional manner. It further identified 4,005 such districts as having been funded or designated by the federal government." Quote from Philip J. Rutledge, "Federal-Local Relations and the Mission of the City," *Annals of the American Academy of Political and Social Science* 416 (November 1974): 80–81.

22. See Richard Krickus, *White Ethnic Neighborhoods—Ripe for the Bulldozer?* (New York: American Jewish Committee, Middle America Pamphlet Series, 1970).

23. For a positive assessment of these efforts, see David B. Walker, "The State-Local Connection: Perennial, Paramount, Resurgent," *National Civic Review* 73, no. 2 (February 1984): 53–63.

24. *Community Communications Company, Inc.* v. *City of Boulder* 102 S.Ct. 835 (1982).

25. David Bresnick, "New Roles for State Officials in the Age of Fiscal Federalism," *State Government* 53, no. 2 (Spring 1980): 81–83.

26. Dan B. Mackey, "Spotlight on the South Carolina ACIR," *Intergovernmental Perspective* 11, no. 2/3 (Spring/Summer 1985): 7.

27. Richard J. Hardy and Michael P. McConachie, "Missouri in the Federal System," *Missouri Government and Politics*, Hardy and Dohm, eds. (Columbia, Mo.: University of Missouri Press, 1985), p. 10.

28. Brevard Crihfield and H. Clyde Reeves, "Intergovernmental Relations: A View from the States," *Annals of the American Academy of Political and Social Science* 416 (November 1974): 99–107.

29. Harvey C. Mansfield, "Intergovernmental Relations," *The 50 States and Their Local Governments,* ed. James W. Fesler (New York: Knopf, 1967), p. 176.

30. Thad L. Beyle, "New Directions in Interstate Relations," *Annals of the American Academy of Political and Social Science* 416 (November 1974): 108–119.

31. See *New York Times,* February 8–11, 1976; November 14, 1976, p. 1; and December 18, 1977, p. 21.

32. See *New York Times,* June 14, 1982, p. 13.

33. See *National Journal,* November 11, 1979, p. 1928.

34. See *New York Times,* February 14, 1983, p. 1, and June 18, 1982, p. 11. State complaints were not totally put to rest, however. Alaskans, in particular, got upset in the 1980s when the amount of National Park land was expanded in that state; see *New York Times,* August 4, 1986, p. 1.

35. Frank J. Popper, "The Timely End of the Sagebrush Rebellion," *The Public Interest* no. 76 (Summer 1984): 61–73.

36. They are Kentucky and West Virginia. *National Journal,* March 22, 1980, p. 469.

37. *Maryland* v. *Louisiana,* 451 U.S. 725 (1981).

38. *Commonwealth Edison* v. *Montana,* 453 U.S. 609 (1981).

39. See, for example, *New York Times,* September 30, 1985, p. 8.

40. See *New York Times,* September 26, 1982, p. 19.

41. See *New York Times,* May 12, 1986, p. 9.

42. John C. Pierce, "Conflict and Consensus in Water Politics," *The Western Political Quarterly* 32, no. 3 (September 1979): 307–317.

43. Michael F. McNulty and Gary C. Woodward, "Arizona Water Issues: Contrasting Economic and Legal Perspectives," *Arizona Review* 32, no. 2 (Fall 1984): 1–13.

44. See Aaron S. Gurwitz, "The New Faith in High Tech," *Wall Street Journal,* October 27, 1982.

45. Council on Environmental Quality, *Environmental Quality Annual Report: 1973* (Washington, D.C.: U.S. Government Printing Office, 1973), pp. 43–71.

46. See *Wall Street Journal,* December 18, 1984, p. 35.

Chapter 4
Financial Constraints on State and Local Government

Chapter Preview

Chapter 4 examines the financial constraints on state and local governments. There is a reciprocal relationship between state fiscal policies and state economic conditions. The overall economic trend in a region sharply affects how expansive or restrictive a state or community government can be. And at the same time, state and community fiscal policies also affect how vibrant their economy is. We shall examine these relationships in this chapter by asking:

1. For what purposes do state and local governments spend your money?
2. How do state and community governments raise their revenues?
3. What major conflicts and issues concern states and communities in the late 1980s?
4. What is the importance of the political economy in state and community finances?

Let us begin this excursion into state and community finances with a look at one of the most symbolically important events of the last two decades—Proposition 13 in California.

Introduction

One of the most important events in recent American politics took place on June 6, 1978. California voters that day struck terror into the hearts of most California state and local officials and a good many other public officials around the country by overwhelmingly passing an initiative* called **Proposition 13.** This vote cut local government property tax revenues by

*The *initiative* is a device in some states that enables voters to pass laws directly without having to go through the state legislature.

over $6 billion and gave property owners a 57-percent tax relief. Immediately after the proposition passed, tax or expenditure limitation movements gathered steam in virtually every state, ushering in an era of financial tightfistedness. More than any other event, the passage of Proposition 13 separates the period of governmental expansion (1960s and 1970s) from the contemporary period of general governmental retrenchment (1978 to the present).[1]

Government officials could not have been surprised by the success of Proposition 13, however. Resentment against high taxes and government spending had been building throughout the 1970s. When voters were given the chance to vote on bond issues or school budgets, they often defeated them.[2] A speculative real estate boom in the 1970s drove up California home prices dramatically, and most real estate taxes went up even faster. In contrast to the property tax squeeze on homeowners, the California State treasury in 1978 had a surplus of over $3 billion, although the state legislators disagreed on how to use it to provide property tax relief.

At that point, retired businessmen Howard Jarvis and Paul Gann took matters into their own hands. With very little effort or expense, they quickly gathered 1.2 million signatures on a petition to place on the June 1978 ballot a constitutional amendment initiative that:

1. Reduced the maximum property tax rate to 1 percent of the 1975–1976 assessed value of the property.
2. Limited future assessment increases to 2 percent per year, except when the ownership changes, at which point the property can be reassessed at current market value.
3. Barred the state legislature from raising any state taxes to make up for those cuts unless the new taxes pass by a two-thirds majority vote.

Despite denials by prominent state officials before the vote that the state would help finance local communities, the legislature passed a bill after the vote that did precisely that. In 1978 the state distributed $5 billion in grants and loans to cities, school districts, and other local governments.[3]

From the average taxpayer's viewpoint, Proposition 13 was an unmitigated success. He or she received a substantial property tax reduction. The spirit that led to Proposition 13 also helped index the state income tax so that it would not rise faster than the inflation rate and also helped put a limit on state government expenditures. Furthermore, distribution of the state's huge surplus to local governments helped prevent the immediate decimation of local public services that had been resoundingly predicted by critics of Proposition 13. California voters appeared to have gotten exactly what their critics said was impossible—tax reduction without public service reductions, or to use the critics' imagery, something for nothing, a free lunch.[4]

Seldom can you get something for nothing in the long run, however, and when California's big budget surpluses disappeared in the early 1980s, the costs of Proposition 13 became apparent. Governmentally, the main cost was a sharp reduction in most public services, especially for welfare services and road maintenance (although some services, such as police and fire protection barely suffered at all).[5] These reductions became increasingly severe in the late 1980s when the state bumped up against a constitutional expenditure limit imposed during the height of the tax reduction movement. Politically, the increased reliance on state funding led to a shift in power from local officials to the state capitol in Sacramento.[6] And socially, the tax reduction benefits were not distributed evenly across the population. Older, upper-middle-income people who had bought their homes before 1975 got substantial benefits, while renters and young people who bought their homes after 1978 received much less. In fact, the biggest winners were not homeowners at all, but corporations. A lower-middle-income homeowner saved a few hundred dollars, but Standard Oil Corporation, for example, saved an estimated $13.1 million. The ten largest utilities and railroads saved $400 million.[7]

Since these corporations do not buy and sell their property as often as individuals do, they would not have to worry about being reassessed every time they bought. The long-term effect of Proposition 13 was clear (but apparently irrelevant to most voters). It would shift the property tax burden from corporations to homeowners. Praised by conservatives, it was condemned by liberals.[8]

Although it may have disturbed liberals, the victory of Proposition 13 in California bolstered fiscal conservatives to push for other **tax or expenditure limitation movements (TEL)** around the nation. Other states with statewide initiative provisions, such as Iowa, Michigan, and Oregon, soon saw similar measures put before their voters. While few of these had the dramatic results of Proposition 13, Massachusetts' 1980 Proposition 2½ had a large impact. By limiting a community's property tax revenue to 2.5 percent of the full value of taxable property, it gave Massachusetts homeowners a $1.3 billion tax reduction.[9]

After the passage of Massachusetts' Proposition 2½, however, the tax-cutting movement seemed to wither, as state and local governments began to face a **budget retrenchment** challenge. Budget surpluses, which were quite common in the 1970s, began disappearing in the 1980s, as the economic recessions (of 1980–1982) and cutbacks in federal grants-in-aid began to make themselves felt. Instead of being able to vote themselves tax cuts, citizens in most states saw their taxes begin to rise to cover revenue shortfalls. By the late 1980s, most states had increased their taxes.

In sum, the few short years from the passage of Proposition 13 to the late 1980s changed the intellectual climate within which public services are offered and revenues are raised to pay for them. In the current era of fiscal constraint, public officials find it much more necessary than previously to ask where revenues will come from before they enact new programs or expand existing ones. To understand the dynamics of this new climate, this chapter addresses the following.

1. What services should state and local governments offer? That is, on what should these governments spend their money?
2. Where should government money come from? The property tax? Sales tax? Income tax? Entrepreneurial activities? Other sources?
3. What is meant by the variety of technical terms used in the discussion of Proposition 13 and other government finances—terms like *assessed valuation, mill rates, market value, property tax relief, circuit breaker, tax burden, tax effort,* and others?
4. How should the tax burden be distributed? For example, if a state lets most of its services be provided by local governments and paid for by local property taxes, who gets stuck with the biggest share of the taxes? The rich? The poor? Business people? The elderly? The young? Or you?

How State and Local Governments Spend Your Money

State and local governments spend a lot of money. Figure 4–1 shows that state and local government spending rose slightly faster than either federal government expenditures or the economy as a whole until the late 1970s. The major index of national economic growth is the gross national product (GNP). As Figure 4–1 shows, state and local government spending has risen almost 2,000 percent since 1950, while the GNP rose at barely half that rate (1,052 percent).

When these figures are adjusted to compensate for inflation and population growth, however, we find that state and local spending peaked in 1978.[10] Today state and local governments are spending no more per capita in constant dollars than they were almost a decade ago.

Why Costs Have Gone Up

There are several explanations for these rapid increases in state and local expenditures. First is inflation. Between 1967 and 1984, the purchasing power of the dollar declined from one dollar to thirty-two cents. Rising government expenses may anger many people, but in practical terms, just to maintain the same levels of services that existed in 1967, governments today have to spend about three times as many dollars as they spent then.

Figure 4–1. Trends in Government Spending

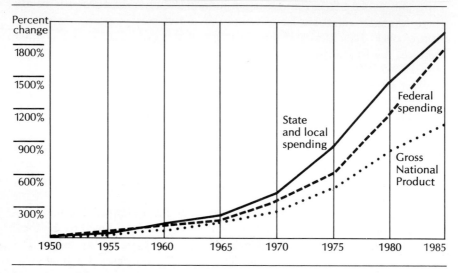

Source: Bureau of the Census, *Statistical Abstract of the United States 1986* (Washington, D.C.: U.S. Government Printing Office, 1986), pp. 262, 431.

During that period, however, citizens and interest groups were not content with simply maintaining the same level of services; this trend is a second explanation for the rise of government spending. During the entire post–World-War II period, but especially during the mid-1960s and the mid-1970s, Americans demanded more services in education, health care, transportation, law enforcement, housing, and other areas. Each increase in services meant an increase in dollars spent and employees hired. As Figure 4–2 shows, the number of state and local employees nearly tripled between 1954 and 1984, compared to a more modest increase in federal employment. Most of this rapid increase in employment occurred at the local level.

Where Your Money Goes

About 40 percent of the money spent by state and local governments goes for just two services: education and public welfare. But Figure 4–3 shows that states spend their money slightly differently than do local governments. For states, the single biggest expenditure is for aids to local governments, followed by education, public welfare, and the other purposes shown in Figure 4–3. States also spend considerable amounts of money on insurance trust fund payments for such items as public employee pension benefits, workers' compensation payments, and unemployment compensation payments. How-

Figure 4–2. Rise in State and Local Employment

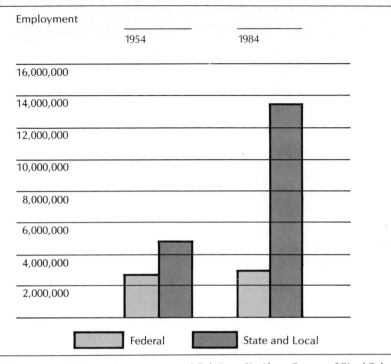

Source: Advisory Commission on Intergovernmental Relations, *Significant Features of Fiscal Federalism: 1985-86 Edition,* Report M-146 (Washington, D.C.: U.S. Government Printing Office, 1986), p. 132.

ever, since most of these trust fund expenditures are covered by employee and employer contributions to the trust funds, it must be remembered that they are not a direct drain on the tax dollar.

For local governments, the single largest expenditure is for public education, followed by utility systems and the other purposes shown in Figure 4–3. However, utility systems, like the states' trust fund expenditures, also generate off-setting revenues and thus are not a direct cost to the taxpayer.

Conflict over Expenditures

In the Proposition 13 battle described earlier, two aspects of these expenditure patterns became the subjects of bitter conflict. First, the architects of Proposition 13 complained that the expenditures were simply too high. They

Figure 4–3. Where State and Local Governments Spend Your Money

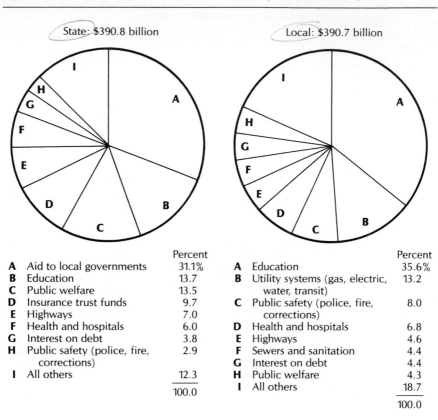

State: $390.8 billion   Local: $390.7 billion

		Percent
A	Aid to local governments	31.1%
B	Education	13.7
C	Public welfare	13.5
D	Insurance trust funds	9.7
E	Highways	7.0
F	Health and hospitals	6.0
G	Interest on debt	3.8
H	Public safety (police, fire, corrections)	2.9
I	All others	12.3
		100.0

		Percent
A	Education	35.6%
B	Utility systems (gas, electric, water, transit)	13.2
C	Public safety (police, fire, corrections)	8.0
D	Health and hospitals	6.8
E	Highways	4.6
F	Sewers and sanitation	4.4
G	Interest on debt	4.4
H	Public welfare	4.3
I	All others	18.7
		100.0

Source: Bureau of the Census, *Governmental Finances in 1984-85,* GF 84, no. 5 (Washington, D.C.: U.S. Government Printing Office, December 1986), pp. 2, 13.

Note: These are direct expenditures for fiscal year 1984–1985. Local expenditures include $121.6 billion in aid from state governments. Both the state and the local levels include $107.2 billion in aid from the federal government.

argued that state and local budgets included so much fat and waste that they could easily be cut back. The level of government spending is a key issue in the conflict between liberals and conservatives. Conservatives are much more inclined than liberals to argue for cutting government expenditures. Table 4–1 shows that in 1986 slightly less than a third of the public at large agreed with this conservative position. About half of the public agreed with the more liberal position of keeping services and taxes as they are. And only a small minority wanted to increase spending and taxes.

Table 4–1. Desired Level of Taxes and Services

| | "Considering all government services on the one hand and taxes on the other, which of the following comes closest to your view?" | | | | | |
	1975	1977	1979	1980	1982	1986
Keep taxes and services about where they are	45%	52%	46%	45%	42%	51%
Decrease services and taxes	38	31	39	38	36	31
Increase services and taxes	5	4	6	6	8	9
No opinion	12	13	9	11	14	9

Source: Advisory Commission on Intergovernmental Relations, *Changing Public Attitudes on Governments and Taxes: A Commission Survey: 1986*, Report S-15 (Washington, D.C.: Advisory Commission on Intergovernmental Relations, 1986), pp. 3, 28–29.

If the level of spending is the first key conflict between liberals and conservatives, the second is how money should be spent. After the tax or expenditure limitations were put into place, and as federal aid declined, states and communities were forced to make bitter choices among programs that had to be reduced. Initially, many officials approach this task by asking for equal cuts across all state services. If carried on long enough, however, this approach can cut so much from all areas of government that all programs begin to suffer, the essential ones as well as the nonessential ones. Eventually officials may be forced to set priorities among their programs.

You Decide
Cutting Budgets

Suppose the budgets of your state and local governments have to be curtailed. Which of these programs would you limit most severely? Put a number 6 by that program. Then rank the rest of the programs in priority from 1 (the one with the least cuts) to 5 (the one with the most cuts).

1. Public safety
   (fire, police, criminal justice) _____

2. Public schools
   (kindergarten–12th grade) _____
3. Tax-supported colleges
   and universities _____
4. Aid to the needy _____
5. Streets and highways _____
6. Parks and recreation _____

To compare your choices with those of the American public, see Table 4–2.

Table 4–2. Popular Candidates for Budget Cuts

| | "If the budgets of your state and local governments have to be curtailed, which of these parts would you limit most severely?" | | | |
| | August 1981 | | September 1981 | |
	Percent	Rank	Percent	Rank
1. Public safety (fire, police, criminal justice)	4%	1	3%	1
2. Public schools (kindergarten–12th grade)	7	2	3	1
3. Tax-supported colleges and universities	10	4	24	5
4. Public welfare programs	39	6	xx	
Aid to the needy	xx		7	3
5. Streets and highways	9	3	10	4
6. Parks and recreation	24	5	45	6
7. None of these or don't know	9		10	

Source: Advisory Commission on Intergovernmental Relations, *Changing Public Attitudes on Government and Taxes: 1981,* Report S-10 (Washington, D.C.: U.S. Government Printing Office, 1981), p. 2.
Note: xx = choice not offered.

The "You Decide" exercise on p. 69 asks you to take a shot at setting priorities among competing public purposes. And Table 4–2 shows how the public at large reacted to the same task in 1981. Note how much peoples' priorities were affected simply by changing the program labels for item number four. The people questioned in August were asked to respond to a category called "public welfare," but in the September survey that term was relabeled "aid to the needy." In contrast to "public welfare," which was the program people most wanted to cut, "aid to the needy" fared much better, ranking only a few percentage points behind the most favored programs (public safety and schools).

Where State and Local Revenue Comes From

If the first part of dealing with fiscal stress is to hold down expenditures, the second part, of course, is to increase revenues. In general, state and local governments have four sources of revenue: taxes, intergovernmental transfers, charges on services or enterprises they operate, and borrowing. Figure 4–4 shows that the revenue sources for state governments differ significantly from those for local governments. Local governments rely heavily on state and federal aid, property taxes, and charges levied on services (such as parking meters and sewer fees). State governments place little reliance on either prop-

Figure 4-4. Where State and Local Governments Get Their Revenues: 1983-1984

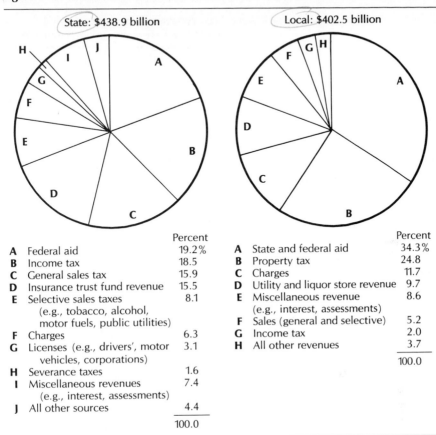

State: $438.9 billion

Local: $402.5 billion

		Percent
A	Federal aid	19.2%
B	Income tax	18.5
C	General sales tax	15.9
D	Insurance trust fund revenue	15.5
E	Selective sales taxes	8.1
	(e.g., tobacco, alcohol,	
	motor fuels, public utilities)	
F	Charges	6.3
G	Licenses (e.g., drivers', motor	3.1
	vehicles, corporations)	
H	Severance taxes	1.6
I	Miscellaneous revenues	7.4
	(e.g., interest, assessments)	
J	All other sources	4.4
		100.0

		Percent
A	State and federal aid	34.3%
B	Property tax	24.8
C	Charges	11.7
D	Utility and liquor store revenue	9.7
E	Miscellaneous revenue	8.6
	(e.g., interest, assessments)	
F	Sales (general and selective)	5.2
G	Income tax	2.0
H	All other revenues	3.7
		100.0

Source: Bureau of the Census, *Governmental Finances in 1984-85*, GF 84, no. 5 (Washington, D.C.: U.S. Government Printing Office, December 1986), pp. 2, 13.

erty taxes or service charges. They rely most heavily on aid from the federal government, income taxes, sales taxes, and insurance trust fund revenues.

Conflict over Revenue Sources

The revenue sources a government chooses strongly affect the distribution of the tax burden. **Tax burden** is the total amount of taxes paid as a percentage of a person's income. A **progressive tax** system is one that increases the tax burden for upper-income people while reducing it for lower-

Table 4–3. The Worst Tax from the Public's Viewpoint

	"What do you think is the worst tax—that is, the least fair?"					
	March 1972	May 1975	May 1978	September 1981	May 1984	May 1986
Federal income tax	19%	28%	30%	36%	36%	37%
State income tax	13	11	11	9	10	8
State sales tax	13	23	18	14	15	17
Local property tax	45	29	32	33	29	28
Do not know	11	10	10	9	10	10

Source: Advisory Commission on Intergovernmental Relations, *Changing Public Attitudes on Governments and Taxes: A Commission Survey,* Report S-15 (Washington, D.C.: U.S. Government Printing Office, 1986), pp. 1, 22–23.

income people. A **regressive tax** system increases the tax burden for lower-income people while reducing it for upper-income people. In short, progressive taxes are based on the ability to pay. Some states have very progressive tax systems, and others have very regressive ones, as will be shown at the end of this chapter.

Taxation as a Revenue Source

Few of us like to pay taxes, but we dislike some taxes more than others. Table 4–3 shows that the most unpopular taxes are the federal income tax and the local property tax. However, as the table shows, the property tax has become less unpopular since Proposition 13 started the property tax revolt in 1978, whereas the federal income tax has become even more unpopular. In contrast, state income and sales taxes are consistently viewed much more favorably.

Evaluating the Major Taxes

In order to evaluate taxes we need to go beyond public opinion about them. Table 4–4 provides six criteria for evaluating taxes—equity, yield, certainty, administrative convenience, economic effect, and appropriateness. *Equity* has various meanings,* but it will be used here to mean taxation based on the ability to pay. *Yield* means how much money a tax will raise; closely

---

*Economists distinguish between vertical equity, horizontal equity, and equity in relation to benefits received from the tax. *Vertical* equity refers to whether the tax is based on the ability to pay. *Horizontal* equity refers to levying the same tax rate on all persons within the same taxable class. For example, if identical houses on the same block have different property taxes, that violates horizontal equity. Equity *in relation to benefits received* refers to whether the value of benefits a person receives from paying a tax equals the amount of the tax paid.

Table 4–4. Criteria for Evaluating Taxes

Criterion	Property tax	Income tax	Sales tax
Equity	Most regressive, but regressivity can be reduced	Most progressive	Regressive, but regressivity can be reduced
Yield and certainty	High yield and the most certain	Yield depends on other variables; least certain	High yield; less certain than property tax; more certain than income tax
Administrative convenience	Most costly	Least costly	Less costly than property tax; possibly more costly than income tax
Economic effect	Associated with no incentives for improving property; fiscal disparities	Useful for controlling economy's growth	Incentive for saving and investing
Appropriateness	Best for local	Best for federal and state	Best for state

akin to the concept of yield is the *certainty* that the tax can be counted on to yield the same amount year after year. *Administrative convenience* refers to how difficult it is to collect the tax. *Economic effect* refers to the consequences the tax can have on the economy that surrounds the government levying it. Finally, *appropriateness* refers to the level of government that gets the best use out of the tax.

Property Tax.   A person's **property tax** is based on two factors—the assessed value of the real estate property and the mill rate, which local governments levy on property. The assessed value is determined periodically by an assessor. A mill is the thousandth part of a dollar. Thus a 1-mill levy means that for every $1,000 of assessed value, $1 will be raised in taxes. Your house, for example, may have a taxable assessed value of $100,000. If your mill rate is 20, then your property tax will be $2,000 ($100,000 × .020 = $2,000). If your home's value and the mill rate each go up by only 10 percent this year, your total taxes will go up by 22 percent ($110,000 × .022 = $2,420). This combined effect was one of the things that drove up Californians' property taxes in the 1970s and led to the Proposition 13 tax revolt.

Property taxes receive their heaviest criticism on the criteria of equity, administrative convenience, and economic effect. The property tax is not based on the ability to pay. You must pay that $2,420 next year, whether you get a big salary increase or whether you lose your job. Most states have taken four measures either to make the tax more equitable or to shift the tax burden off of certain kinds of property. The most recent of these is the **circuit breaker,** which limits how much of your income can be taken in property taxes. If the state sets a 4 percent limit, then your property taxes cannot exceed 4 percent of your income. If they do exceed that amount, the circuit breaker protects you by giving you a tax deduction or credit to reimburse you.

In addition to the circuit breaker, most states have *homestead* and *senior citizens' credits.* Your taxes will be lower for a building that you make your home than for a building in which you operate a business. Many states have adopted a special credit for senior citizens that freezes their property taxes once they stop working.

States also grant *exemptions* to certain property. Non–income-producing church property or property used for charitable purposes is often exempt from taxation. Finally, states shift the property tax burden by creating different property tax *classifications.* Farmland usually is classified in a lower bracket than land in a city.

Although the property tax has historically been considered regressive, circuit breakers, credits, and exemptions have made the property tax much more equitable than it was ten or twenty years ago. Economists and tax experts are consequently beginning to view the property tax more positively.[11]

The other criteria on which property taxes are heavily criticized are administrative convenience and economic effect. The need to hire assessors, create boards of appeal, process complaints about assessments, and make fair assessments of different kinds of property can cause the property tax to be difficult and costly to administer. Property owners may be penalized with increased assessed valuations for making needed improvements. And, as will be shown in the special case of schools, property taxes breed fiscal disparities between communities. The same $100,000 house might have taxes twice as high in one municipality as in a neighboring community.

Property taxes score high on the criteria of yield and certainty. This is because the property tax is the most certain of all the taxes. It will bring in exactly as much money as the assessors project. Nobody can escape it. Property taxes not paid this year must be paid next year, and if you go too long without paying them, the government will sell your property for the amount of back taxes that you owe. Finally, the property tax is the most appropriate at the local level.

Income Taxes.   Forty-three states levy personal income taxes, but the rates are much lower than are federal income tax rates. Compared to the top federal income tax rate of 28 percent, only eight states have rates over 10 percent, and the state with the highest rate, Iowa, charges a maximum of only 13 percent.

State income taxes score highest on the criteria of equity, administrative convenience, and economic effect. They have the greatest chance of taxing people on their ability to pay, especially in states that use a graduated income tax. In these states the rate goes from a very small percentage for low-income residents to higher percentages for people with higher incomes. The income tax is the easiest to administer, since it is collected automatically by employers. However, some administrative costs are incurred in auditing returns and in trying to discourage tax evasion. It is a very positive tool for influencing the overall economy, since tax rates can be manipulated to stimulate or retard growth rates. However, this works much more successfully at the federal level than at the state level.

On the questionable side, the yield from state income taxes depends on several factors—the rate of inflation, the rate of unemployment, the tax rates, and the amount of tax money lost because of credits, deductions, exemptions, and loopholes. The income tax is therefore the least certain of all taxes. During years of economic boom, income tax revenues often exceed estimates, giving the state treasury a surplus. When the economy has a recession, however, income tax revenues lag behind forecasts and a treasury deficit results.

The income tax works best at the federal and state levels. Many cities (New York City, for example) impose a small income tax on people who live or work there. But cities that impose an income tax risk driving residents and employers out of the city and into suburbs that levy no such tax.

In addition to the personal income tax, forty-five states charge a corporate income tax, which in many respects is even more controversial than the personal income tax. Critics complain that the corporate tax can create an unfriendly environment for business and that it is simply a personal tax in disguise, since corporations pass the tax on to their customers. Supporters of the corporate income tax argue that corporations should pay their share of the cost of government just as citizens do. The most controversial aspect of the corporate income tax today concerns the *unitary tax.* This tax irritates multinational companies, because it enables a state to figure each company's tax on a portion of the company's worldwide profits rather than just its profits within the United States. Although some states still use the unitary tax, California—which was the biggest user—effectively dropped it in 1986. And this muted much of the criticism of the unitary tax.

Sales Tax.   Forty-five states levy a general **sales tax.** This tax scores negatively only on the criterion of equity. Mississippi, for example, has a 5 percent sales tax on all retail items. This tax is traditionally considered regressive because it inherently takes a higher percentage of the incomes of poor people than it takes from rich people. Some states seek to reduce this regressivity by granting tax credits and exempting certain categories of purchases, such as food, clothing, medicines, and textbooks. Since poor people spend a greater percentage of their income on food and medicine than do the wealthy, these exemptions help shift the tax burden from the poor onto the higher-income groups in those states. Current thinking, however, argues that progressivity could be best achieved if no exemptions were granted and a circuit-breaker tax credit were given to poor people.

On all the other criteria, the sales tax scores high. It generally produces a high yield, although this yield is reduced if the states grant a lot of exemptions in order to make it less regressive. Sales tax revenues are much less certain than those from the property tax but much more certain than those from the income tax. Sales tax revenues fluctuate with changes in the national economy, but not nearly as much as revenue from income taxes. The sales tax is easy and inexpensive to administer, since it is collected by retailers, who send their tax receipts to the state tax office. In theory its economic effect is to encourage people to save and invest, since it taxes retail purchases.

Finally, sales taxes work best at the state level. Many local governments do impose local sales taxes. However, if these are too high or too inconvenient, shoppers go to neighboring communities to shop.

Other Tax Sources

In addition to the three major taxes, state and local governments rely on a number of other taxes (see Figure 4–4). Major among these other taxes are motor fuel taxes, alcohol and tobacco taxes, and severance taxes. About three-fifths of the states levy **severance taxes** on industries that extract (that is, "sever") natural resources such as timber, ore, coal, and natural gas. But few states rely on severance taxes for more than 10 percent of their tax revenue.

The beauty of severance taxes is that they *export* the tax burden to people in other states who buy the natural resources. One state's beauty, however, is another state's beast, as Louisiana discovered when other states protested bitterly in the late 1970s against a Louisiana tax on natural gas drilled in Louisiana but piped to other states. The United States Supreme Court struck this down because the tax exempted Louisianans.[12] The Court upheld Montana's 30 percent coal tax, however, because the tax had to be paid by Montanans as well as by others.[13] In these two cases the Court seemed to be saying that it would not interfere with a state's severance taxes unless that state was blatantly using such taxes to export the tax burden to other states; this is just what Louisiana did when it exempted its residents from its new gas tax.

Tax-Base Breadth

One final consideration, which has become of increasing concern in the 1980s, is the **tax-base breadth.** If too many people are exempted from the tax base (through property tax classification, income tax loopholes, sales tax exemptions, or untaxed so-called underground transactions such as getting paid in cash to paint your neighbor's house), then the tax base is narrow, which has a number of consequences. Principally, states relying on a narrow tax base tend to have a much more volatile flow of tax revenue than do states with a broader tax base, and they also need to have higher tax rates on the smaller number of people and businesses that pay the taxes. The traditional reason for narrowing the tax base has been to achieve progressivity or some other *social good* (see p. 78). But current thinking asserts that progressivity could be obtained just as easily by broadening the tax base and building in income tax credits for low-income people.

Entrepreneurial Sources of Revenue

In addition to taxes, state and local governments operate enterprises that generate almost one-fourth of their revenue. At the state level, about 15 per-

Highlight
Alaska Uses Its Oil and Gas Income

Following the discovery of huge oil and natural gas reserves in the 1970s, Alaska became the biggest user of severance taxes. By the 1980s, oil and gas revenues amounted to a billion dollars yearly and paid for over half of the state budget.

To safeguard against the day when the oil and gas stop flowing, Alaskans in 1976 approved a Permanent Fund, which now receives 10 percent of all the oil and gas royalties. By 1987, the Permanent Fund reached $7 billion, an enormous surplus for a state whose population is barely 500,000 people. So big was this surplus, in fact, that Alaska abolished its income tax, raised salaries for state officials, initiated numerous economic development projects, and began sending each resident an annual check that started

out at $400 and by 1987 had reached $675.

By the mid-1980s, however, the worldwide oil shortages of just a few years earlier had turned into an oil glut. Oil prices plummeted from over $30 per barrel to under $12 per barrel in 1986 before rebounding to the lower twenties. Alaskans were suddenly faced with scarcity rather than abundance. Although continuing the annual check to each resident, the state was forced to cancel a number of economic development projects, reduce state aids to local governments, and begin talk of reinstating the income tax.

Sources: New York Times, November 29, 1977, p. 11; June 5, 1981, p. 7; June 18, 1982, p. 11; March 17, 1983, p. 1; April 8, 1986, p. 1; February 21, 1987, p. 5; *State Legislatures* 12, no. 10 (November/December 1986): 8.

cent of all revenue is raised from insurance programs. These include workers' compensation, unemployment compensation, and public employee retirement funds. The monies contributed to these programs by workers and employers are kept in large trust funds run by the state. The interest from these funds is earmarked for the benefits of the programs. States collect another 13 percent of their revenue from state-owned liquor stores and from charges for college tuition, highway tolls, and public hospitals and health facilities.

At the local level, the major entrepreneurial sources of revenue are public utilities (bus companies, power plants, water supply companies). Local governments also earn substantial revenues from fees for sewer service, garbage collection, parking facilities, building permits, franchises, and the use of publicly owned facilities, such as golf courses, tennis courts, or swimming pools. Municipalities also have licensing powers and can tax commercial establishments such as movie theaters, bars, restaurants, sports arenas, and hotels. In the budget retrenchment of the early 1980s, many communities doubled and tripled the fees and taxes they collect in order to cover revenue shortfalls.

If local governments can raise money by charging fees and running profit-making enterprises and if state governments can run lotteries at a profit, we might ask why they do not run more and more enterprises until their profits are such that they do not need to levy taxes at all. The answer seems to be that, in a capitalist economy, governments traditionally run only certain kinds of enterprises. Economists distinguish between private goods to be distributed by private companies and public goods to be distributed by governments. One of three criteria can be used to make this distinction.[14] First, some public goods are **social goods,** which are goods (such as a city's unpolluted drinking water supply) that nobody can be excluded from and that cannot be divided up among the users so that what is used by one person is unavailable to be used by another. In contrast, a prime rib dinner at your favorite restaurant is a private good. People unwilling to pay the price are excluded, and the portion consumed by one customer is no longer available to be used by another. Thus, social goods are nonexclusive and nondivisible, in contrast to private goods, which are exclusive and divisible.

A second criterion for distinguishing public from private goods is that of merit. **Merit goods** are those (such as minimal public health care or free public education) that society judges all citizens should have, whether or not they can personally afford them.

Finally, the criterion of **externalities** can be used to distinguish between public and private goods. Private economic activities produce certain external costs that are not reflected in the purchase price of the good. The construction of a major shopping center, for instance, requires police protection, streets, and storm sewers, costs not borne by the shopping center owners or passed on to the consumers. Although the costs are external to the shopping

"When I grow up, I hope to win the lottery."

Opponents of the state-run lottery dislike   attitude satirized in this cartoon.
the state's involvement in promoting the

Source: Drawing by Mulligan; Copyright © 1984, The *New Yorker* Magazine, Inc.

center, they are nevertheless real and somebody must pay them. They are paid by the neighboring local governments.

Following these criteria, the economist argues that governments normally engage in entrepreneurial activity only when that activity involves a good that cannot be produced by private entrepreneurs. The goods that cannot be produced profitably by private entrepreneurs are the social, merit, and external goods.

Intergovernmental Aid as a Revenue Source

As shown in Figure 4–4, intergovernmental transfers are the single largest source of state and local revenues. In 1981, the federal government provided $94 billion in aid to the states and localities. With the New Federalism of President Ronald Reagan, federal aid dropped to $86 billion the next year, then rose to $110 billion by 1987. As a percent of state and local revenue, federal aid peaked in 1978 at 31.7 percent.[15] By 1982 it had dropped back to 25.7 percent, the same level that existed a decade earlier.

Federal Aid

Federal aid has a number of important financial consequences. First, it has been one of the major reasons for the rapid increase in state and local expend-

Highlight
Legalized Gambling as a Way to Reduce Direct Taxes on Citizens

With the fiscal stress of recent years, it is not surprising that states have increasingly looked to legalized gambling as a revenue source. The biggest revenue winners are pari-mutuel betting and lotteries. Nevada is the most extensive user of gambling taxes, collecting 40 percent of its revenue from them. Only four states (Hawaii, Mississippi, Missouri, and Utah) prohibit all gambling.

Lotteries have been the fastest-growing form of state-sanctioned gambling since New Hampshire started its lottery in the 1960s. Twenty-two states currently have lotteries. California's brings the state $500 million annually in revenues, but other states earn substantially less, and lottery revenues seldom exceed 2 or 3 percent of a state's budget. Many state lotteries have run into scandals and start-up problems that reduced their potential profits.

Even after start-up problems have been corrected, lotteries have been disappointing revenue earners in most states. Keeping revenues high requires an imaginative administration capable of introducing new games, offering the games frequently, and avoiding scandals. Lotteries have additionally been criticized as a regressive form of taxation.

Casino gambling exists in only two states, Nevada and New Jersey. Although other states are considering it, New Jersey's experiences may well dissuade them. Highly promoted in the mid-1970s as a sure-fire means to revitalize the decaying Atlantic City, in fact Atlantic City has gained very little from the casinos, and it has paid an enormous price in escalating property values, housing shortages, higher crime rates, and the disappearance of hundreds of retail business establishments.

In addition to lotteries and casinos, many other forms of gambling can also raise state revenue. Bingo is permitted in all but five states. It has recently become a very popular fund raiser for Indian tribes and led to legal controversy over the extent to which states can regulate gambling on Indian reservations. The next most popular form of legalized gambling is horse racing. Others are numbers games, sports betting, off-track betting, dog racing, and jai alai. If all states were to adopt all these forms of gambling, then—some people project—state gambling revenues would rise from the $1.2 billion prevailing in the late 1970s to about $9 billion yearly. To keep these projections in perspective, however, we must also recognize the possibility that expansion to all types of legalized gambling could simply increase the competition between the types for existing customers. Gambling revenues exceed 10 percent of total state revenues only in Nevada and New Hampshire.

Sources: State Government News 20, no. 9 (September 1977): 2–5; Judy Heffner, "Legalized Gambling in the States: Who Really Wins?" *State Legislatures* 7, no. 8 (September 1981): 6–16; George Sternleib and James Hughes, *Atlantic City Gamble* (Cambridge, Mass.: Harvard University Press, 1984).

itures in the past decade.[16] Second, much federal aid has been channeled into human services programs, and this has forced state and local budgets to provide more money for programs such as Medicaid, AFDC,* and other social services.

Third, since much federal aid is deliberately used to get state and local governments to carry out federal objectives, federal aid has the effect of determining how state and local governments will spend their money. This is especially true for the states' matching portion of federal categorical grants (see p. 39).[17]

State Aid to Local Governments

State aid to local governments follows the same pattern as federal aid. Some aids are **categorical aids.** Others are similar to revenue sharing in that they simply support local budgets and give local governments great discretion in spending the money. In the education sector, for example, states finance public schools primarily through categorical aids and foundation aids. The foundation aids are based on a per-pupil amount that the state contributes to each local school district. The foundation aids also frequently include highly complex equalization formulas aimed at equalizing the differences among school districts. They do this by giving more assistance to districts with poor property tax resources and high concentrations of poor families.

In contrast to the overall budget support provided by the foundation aids, educational categorical aids are aimed at a specific program objective, such as transportation, aiding children with special learning disabilities, or providing special assistance to children from low-income backgrounds.

The biggest complaint local officials have about state aid is probably over *mandating.* Many state programs are mandated (required) by state law, and most have matching-fund provisions. This forces local governments to adopt the program but does not provide all the finances for it. The local governments thus must either raise local taxes or, if that is impossible, cut other programs to pay for the state-mandated programs. Because local governments may not cut programs mandated by the federal or state government, they have mostly cut their own discretionary programs. In this way, mandating has contributed to the declining autonomy of local governments discussed in Chapter 3. For all these reasons, local officials prefer general state aid rather than categorical aids or mandated programs.

---

*Medicaid is a program that provides health care to poor people. AFDC (Aid for Families with Dependent Children) provides cash payments for the care of dependent children in low-income, single-parent families.

Borrowing as a Revenue Source

If state and local governments had to finance every operaton on a pay-as-you-go basis, it would become virtually impossible for them to function in the twentieth century. They need to borrow money to build school buildings, universities, and prisons, or install sewer systems or water purification projects. All of these large construction projects are referred to as **capital expenditures** and are financed by long-term debt. State and local governments also borrow money on a short-term basis to meet immediate payroll or other obligations when they have not yet received the taxes levied to pay for those obligations. This short-term borrowing is accomplished through **revenue-anticipation notes** or **tax-anticipation notes.**

Long-term borrowing is accomplished by selling bonds. The person who buys a $5,000 municipal bond actually lends the city $5,000. The city pledges to repay the $5,000 and to pay a fixed amount of interest.

A **general-obligation bond** puts the full faith and credit of the issuing agency behind it. The issuing government guarantees that it will use its taxing powers to pay off the bonds. These bonds become in effect a charge against the property of all homeowners in the jurisdiction. For this reason general-obligation bonds usually require approval by a voter referendum. Because these bonds are backed by the taxing power of the government, they are very safe; and because their interest is exempt from federal income taxes, they usually pay very low interest rates.

Distinct from general-obligation bonds are **revenue bonds.** These are not guaranteed by the taxing power of the issuing government. Rather, they are paid off from the revenue earned by the facility for which they were issued. Toll bridges, toll roads, convention centers, industrial parks, and municipally owned athletic stadiums are common examples of projects financed by revenue bonds. Interest on these bonds is exempt from federal income taxes. Since the bonds are slightly riskier than general-obligation bonds, they carry a slightly higher interest rate. A special type of revenue bond is the **Industrial Development Revenue Bond** (IDRB), through which a city uses its tax-exempt status to raise money for commercial development projects. IDRBs will be discussed more fully in Chapter 17, "State and Community Economic Development Policies."

Conflicts and Issues in State and Local Finance

As should be apparent from the discussion up to this point, state and local finances are highly politicized. If there is a major shift in the expenditure or revenue patterns of these governments, some people win and others lose.

Usually the shifts are bitterly contested by the losers and supported by the winners.

These conflicts are probably most apparent in three specific problems affecting state and local finance during the 1980s. These are (1) the special problem of property taxes and the public schools, (2) the regressivity or progressivity of the tax burden, and (3) attempts to reform state tax structures.

The Special Problem of Property Taxes and Public Schools

The biggest portion of most people's property tax bill supports public schools. The amount of money the local school district can raise is based directly on the assessed valuation of property within its boundaries. Assume that school districts A and B have the same number of pupils. School district A has a large shopping center, a number of commercial and manufacturing establishments, and many expensive homes. District B, in contrast, has no large shopping center or commercial or manufacturing establishments. It has only small supermarkets and gas stations, and it has few expensive homes. School district B has a much lower total assessed valuation than does district A. To provide the same level of educational services as those provided in district A, the residents in district B will have to pay a much higher property tax rate. If the district B homeowners are less affluent than the district A homeowners, which is likely since they live in cheaper houses, they may be unable to pay higher taxes. In that case, their children will get fewer educational services. This will mean a higher pupil–teacher ratio, older textbooks, fewer extracurricular activities, and fewer course offerings. The term given to this situation is **fiscal disparities.** Especially within metropolitan areas, communities have large disparities in property tax rates and in the level of public services.

Many critics of the property tax argue that the quality of a child's education should not depend on whether he or she lives in a district that has a shopping center or other expensive commercial real estate. Critics look to the states to alleviate fiscal disparities. One obvious way to do this is to shift the financing burden from the local property tax to the state income and sales taxes. By financing schools from the state level, the burden is borne throughout the state, and the fiscal disparities are evened out. In the past decade, the states have assumed increasing shares of the cost of public education.

This movement to shift the education tax burden from the local to the state level has not been easy. In its famous *Serrano* v. *Priest* decision, the California Supreme Court in 1971 ruled that financing public education through local property taxes violated both the California and the federal constitutions.[18] Despite this decision, the California legislature failed to implement it well until voters passed Proposition 13. Residents of a tax-poor school district in San Antonio, Texas, asked the federal courts to strike down the property tax as a basis for funding Texas schools. However, the United States Supreme Court, in *Rodriguez* v. *San Antonio School District,* decided that the United States Constitution did not preclude property taxes as the method for funding local schools.[19] The Supreme Court did agree that fiscal disparities in public education should be eliminated but felt that this action should come from state legislatures.

Subsequently, a number of suits have been filed in state courts. The most dramatic case occurred in New Jersey, which had neither a statewide income tax nor a sales tax. The New Jersey Supreme Court in its *Robinson* v. *Cahill* decision in 1973 ordered the legislature to find an alternative to the property tax for funding the public schools.[20] Only after the state supreme court ordered all the schools to be closed could the legislature agree upon and pass an income tax that would meet the court's requirements.

A second imaginative approach to easing fiscal disparities was taken by Minnesota in 1971. The Minnesota Fiscal Disparities Act of that year provided that after 1972 all new commercial real estate tax base created in the Minneapolis–Saint Paul metropolitan area would be shared between the local community receiving the new real estate and the rest of the metropolis. By 1987 property taxes from more than $1.5 billion of commercial real estate were being shared as a result of this act. This amounted to about 28 percent of all the commercial real estate tax base in that metropolitan area.[21]

A third approach to the fiscal disparities problem is simply to have expensive services such as education and welfare run by the state rather than by local government. The leader in this approach is Hawaii, where there are no local school districts and education is completely funded by the state.

Shifting the Tax Burden

The hottest tax controversy, not surprisingly, is over the distribution of the tax burden. How heavy will it be, and who will bear the brunt of it? As Figure 4–5 shows, about half the states have a regressive tax structure in which low-income people bear the heaviest tax burden. A proportionate tax structure that is neither progressive nor regressive would collect twice as much in taxes from a $50,000 income as from a $25,000 income. For this reason a ratio of 2.00 can be considered the dividing line between progressive and regressive taxes. The higher the ratio, the more progressive the state and local tax structure. Thus, Oklahoma City has the most progressive tax structure because it collects 2.79 times as much from the $50,000 earners as it does from the $25,000 earners. Manchester, New Hampshire, has the most regressive, because it collects only 1.22 times as much from the $50,000 earners as it does from the $25,000 earners.

Figure 4–5. Progressivity of State and Local Taxes

City and state	Ratio of total state and local taxes on a high income to the taxes on a middle income[a].
Oklahoma City, Okla.	2.79
Columbia, So. Car.	2.68
Wilmington, Del.	2.60
Minneapolis, Minn.	2.54
Little Rock, Ark.	2.40
Los Angeles, Calif.	2.38
New York, N.Y.	2.36
Charlotte, No. Car.	2.35
Atlanta, Ga.	2.33
New Orleans, La.	2.33
Portland, Maine	2.30
Jackson, Miss.	2.29
Charleston, W. Va.	2.24
Phoenix, Ariz.	2.21
Albuquerque, N. Mex.	2.21
Wichita, Kan.	2.18
Boise, Idaho	2.18
Billings, Mon.	2.11
Honolulu, Hawaii	2.10
Burlington, Ver.	2.09
U.S. median	**2.05**
Omaha, Neb.	2.05
Norfolk, Va.	2.04
Denver, Col.	2.03
Portland, Ore.	2.03
Providence, R.I.	2.01
St. Louis, Mo.	2.01
Louisville, Ky.	2.01
Baltimore, Md.	1.97
Cleveland, Ohio	1.93
Salt Lake City, Utah	1.93
Milwaukee, Wis.	1.91
Des Moines, Iowa	1.89
Fargo, No. Dak.	1.89
Birmingham, Ala.	1.87
Detroit, Mich.	1.83
Philadelphia, Pa.	1.82
Indianapolis, Ind.	1.75
Boston, Mass.	1.74
Houston, Tex.	1.65
Memphis, Tenn.	1.63
Jacksonville, Fla.	1.60
Chicago, Ill.	1.58
Newark, N.J.	1.49
Seattle, Wash.	1.42
Sioux Falls, So. Dak.	1.41
Casper, Wyo.	1.40
Las Vegas, Nev.	1.37
Bridgeport, Conn.	1.33
Anchorage, Alas.	1.23
Manchester, N.H.	1.22

Source: Advisory Commission on Intergovernmental Relations, *Significant Features of Fiscal Federalism: 1985–86,* Report M-146 (Washington, D.C.: U.S. Government Printing Office, 1986), pp. 127–128.
[a]Figures are for a couple with two dependents. "High income" here means $50,000; "middle income" means $25,000. The higher the ratio, the more progressive the state and local tax structure.

The most direct way to shift the tax burden in a progressive manner is to adopt the graduated income tax. This, however, often draws strong opposition from upper-middle-income earners, who get hit the hardest by graduated income taxes and who also tend to be the most active and influential participants in state and local political processes. Four states (Illinois, Massachusetts, Michigan, and Florida) prohibit a graduated income tax.

Even when graduated income taxes are adopted, it is difficult to keep their graduations meaningful. Through a process called **bracket creep,** inflation pushes everybody into higher tax brackets so that eventually middle-income earners pay the same rate as high-income earners. To avoid this, several states adopted **indexation** of their income taxes so the tax brackets go up to match inflation.

A less controversial way of shifting the tax burden is for the states to import large amounts of federal money. The more a state gets from federal grants, the less it needs to raise from its own citizens. Some states also seek to shift their tax burden by exporting it. Energy-rich states such as Alaska do this with severance taxes. Nevada does it with gambling taxes. And tourist-oriented states do it with high sales taxes. Hawaii is probably the most obvious example, gaining about 30 percent of its tax revenue from nonresidents.[22] But few states would be able to make a significant shift in their tax burden this way.

State Tax Reform

The past decade has witnessed extreme turmoil in state tax systems due to the tax limitation movements symbolized by Proposition 13, the deep recessions of 1980–1982, federal aid cutbacks under the Reagan administration, and interstate competition to reduce taxes in order to create a more attractive business climate. Most states responded to Proposition 13 by enacting some form of tax or expenditure limitation after 1978.[23] Next they were forced by the 1980s recessions (1980–1982) and the federal aid cutbacks to raise taxes. Then as the economy rebounded in the mid-1980s, most states reduced taxes once again. And throwing another ingredient into the pot, Congress in 1986 passed federal income tax reforms that dramatically cut rates, eliminated the federal deductability of state sales taxes, and sharply restricted the use of tax-favored economic-development tools. These measures at the federal level had a profound fiscal impact on most states and communities. And in reaction to these far-reaching changes, the states once again, in the late 1980s, were forced to make significant changes in their own tax laws.

In short, the events of the past decade have thrown most states and communities into a fiscal turmoil, which in turn has prompted half of the states to conduct tax reform studies.[24] Two major concerns seem to predominate

"We therefore feel that a person should be taxed according to his inability to do anything about it."

The reality of tax reform is probably not quite as bad as the cynical viewpoint expressed in this cartoon. But no one would doubt that some people are better able to protect themselves from the tax burden than are others.

Source: Dunagin's People by Ralph Dunagin. © 1980 Field Enterprises, Inc. Reprinted by permission of North America Syndicate, Inc.

among these studies: reducing reliance on the progressive income tax and broadening the tax base.[25] These, in fact, were the major features of the most comprehensive state tax reform so far in the 1980s, that of Wisconsin in 1985. In that year Wisconsin drastically simplified its income tax from eight brackets to four, reduced the top rate from 10 percent to 7.9 percent, broadened the tax base by eliminating several deductions and exclusions, and sharply increased the standard deduction to $7,200 for low-income people so as to avoid shifting the burden on to the poorest families.[26] It remains to be seen whether other states will follow Wisconsin's example. But Congress's 1986 tax legislation has put considerable pressure on most states to rewrite their tax structures.

State–Community Finance and the Political Economy

The ability of states and communities to finance their public services is tightly interwoven with the overall economy within which they operate. Revenue raising is easiest, obviously, when the economy is booming, most people have jobs, and tax collection is relatively simple. Holding down expenditures is easier in low-inflation periods than in periods of high inflation, because the cost of government purchases and payrolls will not escalate so rapidly. This fact of life gives states and communities a lot of incentive to do whatever they can to promote economic growth. How they go about that will be examined in Chapter 17, "State and Community Economic Development Policies." At this point we merely note a number of generalizations about the reciprocal relationship between state–community finances and the economies within which they live.

The Impact of Economic Trends

In the 1980s, national economic trends are both a plus and a minus for state fiscal systems. On the plus side has been the low inflation of the 1980s (through 1987, at least). On the minus side is the simple fact that the national economy has been growing much more slowly than it did in the previous two decades. The gross national product (GNP) grew at a real annual rate (that is, adjusted for inflation) of 4.6 percent in the 1960s and 3.5 percent during the 1970s. During the first part of the 1980s, the real annual growth rate dropped to 2.7 percent.[27] For the balance of the 1980s, expectations are for a growth rate closer to that of the 1970s than that of the 1960s.[28]

Regional Economic Dislocations

In addition to the prospects for slower economic growth, the national economy affects each region of the country differently. In the 1970s, the Northeast and Midwest were devastated by escalating energy prices and a rising tide of good-quality, cheaply priced imported manufactured goods. During the same period, the Southwest prospered from the energy boom and, not being dependent on heavy manufacturing, was only marginally affected by foreign competition in manufactured products.

In the 1980s these situations partially reversed. Energy-producing states of the Southwest, such as Texas and Oklahoma, were badly hit by the petroleum glut and the 50 percent drop in oil prices in 1986.[29] The Northeast, in the meantime, has staged a vibrant recovery.[30] The Midwest, still staggering from its industrial losses, fell into the worst agricultural depression in fifty years.

Federal Budget Cutbacks

In real dollars (that is, adjusted for inflation), federal aid to state and local governments peaked in the late 1970s and has been declining ever since. Given the severe pressures on the federal government to curb its budget deficits, there seems to be no likelihood in the immediate future of significant increases in federal aid to state and local governments.

Interstate Tax Competition

There is today an intense competition among states to maintain an attractive tax climate in order to attract high-income in-migrants and foster business expansion. Many state leaders fear their states will not attract new businesses or even keep existing businesses if their tax rates are too much higher than those of neighboring states. To measure state tax collections and to take into account the fact that rich states find it easier to raise revenues than do poor states, the Advisory Commission on Intergovernmental Relations constructed an index of tax effort, which measures each state's actual tax level in comparison to its capacity to impose taxes. The higher the index number, the higher a state's tax effort. As Table 4–5 indicates, the lowest tax efforts are found in the Southeast and Southwest, while the highest tax efforts are found in the Mideast and Great Lake regions.

In sum, the interaction between state–local fiscal policy and regional economies is quite complicated. In a growing economic period, such as the 1950s and 1960s, fiscal policies are probably less critical than they are in a period of slower growth, such as that which has prevailed since 1970. As

Table 4–5. Tax Effort

Region	Tax effort score
United States average	100
New England	99
Mideast	110
Great Lakes	104
Great Plains	99
Southeast	88
Southwest	81
Rocky Mountains	97
Far West	91
State with lowest score (Nevada)	65
State with highest score (New York)	158

Source: Carol E. Cohen, "1984 State Tax Wealth: Preview of the RTS Estimates," *Intergovernmental Perspective* 12, no. 3 (Summer 1986): 25.

Note: These index scores, based on an average score of 100 for all fifty states, show how far a state is above or below the national average. Alaska (141), District of Columbia (139), and Hawaii (99) have been excluded.

growth slows down and as major transformations occur in the national economy, the competition among states and regions becomes much more acute.

Urban Fiscal Crisis

The devastating impact that some of these trends can have on cities can be seen in the near bankruptcy crisis of New York City in the mid-1970s. Although this occurred over a decade ago, it still is relevant as a warning to other cities of what can happen if they lose control over their public finances. Responding to demands for high expenditures, New York City saw its budgets soar during the 1960s.[31] The number of city workers grew rapidly, their salaries increased much faster than salaries of workers in private enterprise, and even more importantly, their fringe benefits such as pensions increased generously. Some city employees could retire in their forties with pension benefits equal to half their final year's salary. Liberalizing pensions was an easy way for political leaders to give benefits to city employees without having to raise the revenue, for the costs would not be incurred until the future, when somebody else would be in office. The dramatic rise in welfare benefits and programs also increased city government expenditures. The City University of New York, with its 265,000 students, dropped tuition charges for undergraduates and assessed them only a flat $110 fee.

The money for all these expenditures had to come from some revenue source. The city regularly had borrowed short-term money by issuing municipal notes in order to pay off long-term obligations. By 1975 the deficit was $800 million, and the debt repayments totaled $1.6 billion per year. New York City was unable to make these payments in 1975 without borrowing more short-term money, but because the city was in danger of defaulting on its bonds, its credit rating dropped and it was unable to sell new bonds or municipal notes.

New York's plight did not spark much sympathy around the nation. Public opinion polls indicated that many people did not want the federal government to bail out New York City. At the federal level, both the Secretary of the Treasury and President Ford castigated the city for its poor money management over the years and objected to using federal funds to help.

Nevertheless, the problem was too severe to be ignored. A substantial portion of the city's bonds were owned by the State of New York, and a default by the city would threaten the safety of state bonds as well. Default on the city's bond payments would also cause sharp losses to the various pension funds, banks, and individuals that owned those bonds and counted on their interest payments for income. These possibilities diminished confidence in the municipal bond market in general, and other cities that needed to market municipal bonds during those years had to pay higher interest charges.

New York State responded to the city's crisis by creating two new institutions—the Municipal Assistance Corporation (called Big MAC) and the Emergency Financial Control Board. Big MAC was authorized to issue $3 billion of long-term bonds and to use those funds to buy up the city's short-term obligations. In this way the city would be saved from immediate default. The Big MAC bonds themselves did not become marketable, however, until the federal government guaranteed them. The federal government would not issue such guarantees until it was assured that the city's financial management was being put back in order. To straighten out the city finances, the Emergency Financial Control Board was given power to oversee the city budget. It used these powers to ensure that city costs were cut, tens of thousands of employees laid off, welfare benefits reduced, tuition reinstated at the City University, wages frozen for city workers, and severe cutbacks made in public service levels. After a number of short-term guarantees to get the city over immediate crises in 1976 and 1977, the federal government finally in 1978 extended a number of long-term loan guarantees that got the city back on a timetable for meeting its financial obligations.

New York City was not the only city to face near bankruptcy in these years. In 1979–1980 Chicago flirted with default on its debts when it discovered a cumulative deficit of $100 million that the city had to repay and $500 million that the public school system had to repay.[32] Cleveland's fiscal situation was even worse; it actually defaulted on some bond payments and at one point sold off city property to get funds to meet other bond payments.[33]

By the late 1980s, most cities had put their fiscal houses in order enough so that there were few bankruptcies being threatened. But a new set of fiscal woes had befallen cities. The service cutbacks needed to balance city budgets, the loss of General Revenue Sharing, the sharp reductions in other federal aid, and the continuing deterioration of their tax bases left many cities ill-prepared to cope with the problems of deteriorating infrastructure, the elderly, and the high rates of teenage pregnancy, drug abuse, and illiteracy that plague them today. We will return to these problems in later chapters.

Summary

1. The experience of Proposition 13 in California introduces some important questions about state and local finances. What services should state and local governments offer? On what sources of revenue should these governments rely? How should the tax burden be distributed? How can property tax relief best be implemented?

2. Between 1950 and 1978, state and local government expenditures and employment rose much faster than the gross national product or federal government expenditures. Since 1978, state and local expenditures have begun to lag behind inflation.

3. The major state government expenditures are for insurance trust benefits, public education, welfare, and highways. The major local government expenditures are for education and utility operations.

4. State governments get over half their revenues from federal aid, sales taxes, and income taxes. Local governments get about 60 percent of their revenues from state and federal aid and from property taxes.

5. Six criteria for evaluating taxes are equity, yield, certainty, administrative convenience, economic effect, and appropriateness.

6. In deciding what kinds of entrepreneurial activities are proper for governments in capitalist societies, economists have presented the criteria of social goods, merit goods, and externalities.

7. In borrowing money, governments rely on general obligation bonds and revenue bonds.

8. Key problems for state and local finance during the 1980s are the special problem of property taxes and public schools, shifting the tax burden, tax reform, and the interplay between public fiscal policy and economic development.

Key Terms

Bracket creep The phenomenon of a person's being boosted into a higher income tax bracket by inflation.

Budget retrenchment The phenomenon of governments having to raise taxes and cut back expenditures in order to balance their budgets.

Capital expenditure Expenditure for buildings and other fixed equipment.

Categorical aid A grant-in-aid for a specific purpose. Also called *categorical grant*.

Circuit breaker A device that limits the amount of income that can be taken in property taxes.

Externalities Costs that are not borne directly by the buyers or sellers of a particular product, for example, air pollution produced by automobiles but whose cleanup costs are not included in the price of cars.

Fiscal disparities The situation in which neighboring governmental jurisdictions vary widely in their ability to raise revenue. One jurisdiction may have a substantial property tax base while a neighboring one has a meager tax base.

General-obligation bond A government bond that is backed by the taxing authority of the issuing government.

Indexation The practice of adjusting income tax brackets to rise with the cost of living. Also refers to the practice of making benefit levels in certain programs adjustable for inflation.

Industrial Development Revenue Bond A revenue bond issued by a government to enable a particular company or a collection of companies to raise funds to develop a site by selling bonds with the tax and interest rate advantages of government bonds.

Merit goods Goods that society judges all citizens should have as a matter of right.

Progressive tax A tax that takes a higher percentage of the income of upper-income people than it does of lower-income people.

Property tax A tax levied on real estate.

Proposition 13 An initiative proposition in 1978 that cut California property taxes by 60 percent.

Regressive tax A tax that takes a higher percentage of the income of lower-income people than it does of upper-income people.

Revenue-anticipation note A short-term note a government uses to borrow money to make payments that will come due before a next revenue payment comes in. The note is payed off from the proceeds of the next revenue payment.

Revenue bond A public bond that is payed off from revenue earned by the facility that was built with the bond's proceeds.

Sales tax A tax levied on retail sales.

Severance tax A tax levied on natural resources extracted from the earth.

Social goods Goods whose benefits are nondivisible and nonexclusive. Their enjoyment by one person does not prevent their enjoyment by others.

Tax-anticipation note A short-term note a government uses to borrow money to make payments that will come due before a next tax payment comes in. The note is payed off from the proceeds of the next tax payment.

Tax-base breadth Refers to the broadness or narrowness of the base on which a tax is levied.

Tax burden The total amount of taxes paid as a percentage of a person's income.

Tax or expenditure limitation movement (TEL) The movement of the late 1970s and early 1980s to put legal or constitutional limits on the amount of money a government can raise or the amount of money it can spend.

References

1. From 1954–1978, expenditures for all states increased at an annual rate of 4.9 percent and local expenditures at an annual rate of 4.2 percent. Over the four-year period following the passage of Proposition 13 (1978–1982), state expenditures *declined* at an annual rate of 0.4 percent, and local expenditures *declined* at an annual rate of 2.1 percent (figures adjusted for inflation and population changes). See John Shannon and Susannah

E. Calkins, "Federal and State–Local Spending Go Their Separate Ways," Advisory Commission on Intergovernmental Relations, *Perspectives* 8, no. 4 (Winter 1983): 24.

2. See *New York Times,* November 6, 1975, p. 1.

3. Terry Christensen and Larry N. Gerston, *The California Connection: Politics in the Golden State* (Boston: Little, Brown and Co., 1984), p. 217.

4. On the "something for nothing" concept, see Jack Citrin, "Do People Want Something for Nothing? Public Opinion on Taxes and Government Spending," *National Tax Journal* 32 (supplement) (1979): 113.

5. K. Bacon, "The Los Angeles Times Survey of Local Government Responses to Proposition 13 of 1978," in *California and The American Tax Revolt,* T. Schwadron and P. Richter, eds. (Los Angeles: University of California Press, 1984).

6. See Robert Lindsey, "California Agencies Begin to Feel Tax Revolt," *New York Times,* April 21, 1986, p. 11.

7. See *Time,* June 19, 1978, p. 16.

8. See *New Republic,* June 3, 1978, p. 6.

9. Sherry Tvedt, "Enough is Enough! Proposition 2½ in Massachusetts," *National Civic Review* 70, no. 10 (November 1981): 527–533.

10. In constant dollars on a per-capita basis, local government spending appears to have peaked in 1975 and state spending in 1977. Advisory Commission on Intergovernmental Relations, *Significant Features of Fiscal Federalism, 1982–83* (Washington, D.C.: Advisory Commission on Intergovernmental Relations, 1983), p. 34.

11. See Henry J. Aaron, *Who Pays the Property Tax? A New View* (Washington, D.C.: Brookings Institution, 1975); James A. Maxwell and J. Richard Aronson, *Financing State and Local Governments,* 3rd ed. (Washington, D.C.: Brookings Institution, 1977).

12. *Maryland* v. *Louisiana,* 451 U.S. 725 (1981).

13. *Commonwealth Edison* v. *Montana,* 453 U.S. 609 (1981).

14. These arguments are taken from Richard Musgrave, *Fiscal Systems* (New Haven, Conn.: Yale University Press, 1969), Chapter 1.

15. See *Public Administration Times,* May 1, 1981.

16. Susan B. Hansen, "Extraction: The Politics of State Taxation," *Politics in the American States: A Comparative Analysis,* 4th ed., eds. Virginia Gray, Herbert Jacob, and Kenneth N. Vines (Boston: Little, Brown and Co., 1983), p. 433.

17. On the consequences of federal grants, see David C. Nice, *Federalism: The Politics of Intergovernmental Relations* (New York: St. Martin's Press, 1987), pp. 57–60.

18. *Serrano* v. *Priest,* 5 Cal. 3d 584 (1971).

19. *Rodriguez* v. *San Antonio School District,* 411 U.S. 59 (1973). By 1987, Texas's school financing policy was back in the courts. A Texas district court ruled that unequal distributions of state aid were illegal. This set the stage for Texas appellate courts to examine the issue. See *New York Times,* April 30, 1987, p. 11.

20. For background on this case, see Richard Lehne, *The Quest For Justice: The Politics of School Finance Reform* (New York: Longman, 1978).

21. *Minnesota Journal* (a publication of the Minnesota Citizens League) 4, no. 1 (November 11, 1986), p. 1.

22. Steven Gold, "State Tax Studies: The Best Ideas," *State Legislatures* 11, no. 9 (October 1985): 11.

23. It is important to note that all states did not react in the same way to the tax and expenditure limitation movement. Some states cut property taxes or income taxes, others indexed their income tax or cut expenditures, and still others combined tax and expenditure cuts. See Frank Levy, "On Understanding Proposition 13," *The Public Interest* no. 56 (Summer 1979): 66–89.

24. Gold, "State Tax Studies," p. 11.

25. See Steven Gold, "Taxing Problems Spark State Reforms," *State Legislatures* 12, no. 3 (March 1986): 14–17.

26. Steven Gold, "Income Tax Reform—Wisconsin Style," *State Legislatures* 12, no. 1 (January 1986): 8–9.

27. Bureau of the Census, *Statistical Abstract of the United States: 1986* (Washington, D.C.: U.S. Government Printing Office, 1985), p. 434.

28. See Roy Bahl, *Financing State and Local Government in the 1980s* (New York: Oxford University Press, 1984), pp. 166–167.

29. For an assessment of the impact of falling oil prices on the Texas budget, see *New York Times,* February 14, 1986, p. 8. On Oklahoma, see *New York Times,* January 4, 1983, p. 9. On oil-producing states generally, see *New York Times,* April 8, 1986, p. 1.

30. See "Northeast Sees Upturn," *National Civic Review* 74, no. 8 (September 1985): 325.

31. On New York City's fiscal crisis, see Martin Shefter, "New York City's Fiscal Crisis: The Politics of Inflation and Retrenchment," *Public Interest* no. 48 (Summer 1977): 98–127. To place the crisis in historical perspective, see Shefter's *Political Crisis/Fiscal Crisis: The Collapse and Revival of New York City* (New York: Basic Books, 1985).

32. See *New York Times,* January 30, 1980, p. 16; December 16, 1979, p. 30; Sidney Lens, "The City That Doesn't Work Anymore: Chicago in the Crunch," *Progressive* 44, no. 4 (April 1980): 34–38.

33. See *New York Times,* January 4, 1980, p. 10.

Chapter 5
Channels of Citizen Influence: Participation, Public Opinion, and Interest Groups

Chapter Preview

If democracy is to have any meaning, there must be channels through which ordinary citizens can influence government policies. This chapter examines three of these channels. We shall discuss in turn

1. The patterns of political participation and the attempts to increase participation of the poor and the racial minorities.
2. The influence of public opinion on government and public policy.
3. Interest groups—their types, tactics, and patterns of influence.

Let us begin with an incident that illustrates how important it is to one's well-being to understand how to use the channels of citizen influence.

Introduction

In 1967 and 1968 the village of Weston, Illinois, and seventy-one surrounding farms were removed to make way for a large atom smasher in the form of an enormous underground ring two miles in diameter. The needed properties were donated to the Atomic Energy Commission (currently known as the Nuclear Regulatory Commission) by the State of Illinois, which used its power of eminent domain to buy the Westonites' houses. In purchasing the homes, state officials used pressure tactics that got most of the homeowners and farmers to sell their property to the state at a price far below what they could have received had they consulted one another, hired lawyers, maintained a united front, and confronted the state as an adversary.

According to a critical study of Weston, the residents of that town unwittingly helped bring about their own financial losses and the demise of their village by not being skeptical enough about the project when it was first proposed and by trusting political leaders who either let them down or proved incapable of defending their interests.[1] The residents also faced a hostile county board of commissioners that was unsympathetic to the village because it was perceived as an undesirable working- and lower-middle-class community in the middle of one of the nation's richest counties. The atom smasher would bring in upper-middle-class professionals and scientists as residents; the Westonites could move elsewhere.

Interestingly, at the same time that Weston was being considered as the site for the atom smasher, the nearby upper-income suburb of Barrington was also being considered as the site. Barrington residents effectively communicated with their political leaders that they did not want the atom smasher near Barrington, and they immediately organized such strong local opposition to the project that the Atomic Energy Commission quickly decided against placing the atom smasher near Barrington.

The tale of Weston and Barrington lays bare one of the starkest truths of American democracy: People who know how to participate in government and who have the means to do so are able to protect their self-interest. People who do not know how to do this or who lack the means find themselves at the mercy of persons who may not understand their circumstances and who often have little sympathy for them.

The outcome of Weston and Barrington also raises some important questions about the channels of political participation. Why did the channels work so well for the residents of Barrington and so poorly for Weston? We might ask the same question more generally. How do the channels of participation work, and who benefits from them? In order to deal with this question, this chapter will first explore the patterns of political participation and then examine two channels of citizen influence—public opinion and interest groups. The following chapter, Chapter 6, will examine three other channels of citizen influence—political parties, elections, and direct democracy.

Political Participation

Political participation refers to individual or group activity that seeks to influence the selection of government officials or actions that these officials take.[2] A hierarchy of political participation is shown in Figure 5–1, which distinguishes between several types of conventional participation. Lester Milbrath has labeled political participants as gladiators and spectators. **Spec-**

Figure 5–1. The Hierarchy of Political Involvement

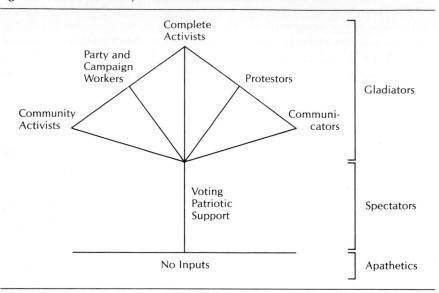

Source: Lester W. Milbrath and M. L. Goel, *Political Participation: How and Why Do People Get Involved in Politics?* 2d ed. Copyright © 1977 Houghton Mifflin Company. Used with permission.

tators, who comprise 60 to 70 percent of the population, vote regularly and display support through activities such as flying the flag or attending patriotic events. The **gladiators** participate in all spectator activities, plus they invest time and money in political activity. As Figure 5–1 suggests, they tend to specialize in a specific kind of political activity, such as community organizing, party or campaign work, protesting, or contacting—that is, communicating their views about community problems to political officials through letters or protest messages. At the top of the hierarchy of political involvement are the complete activists, who engage in several kinds of activity. And at the bottom are the people Milbrath calls **political apathetics,** who neither vote nor consciously put other demands on the political system.[3]

Who Participates?

The standard measure of political participation is the percentage of eligible voters who turn out on election day. The most pronounced pattern to voter turnout is its systematic association with either upper-status people or people with strong organizational ties. In all the social categories shown in Table 5–1, voter turnout is higher among the upper socioeconomic levels than among the lower socioeconomic levels. This difference is even more pronounced among the gladiators. The gladiator positions shown in Figure 5–1 are held overwhelmingly by people with college degrees; and research on elective officeholders consistently shows that elected officials tend to be slightly above the average socioeconomic level of their constituents.

At the bottom of Milbrath's hierarchy of participation are what he calls the *apathetics*, those people who rarely vote or engage in the other forms of conventional participation. However, a much less biased term for them would be *nonparticipants*, since many nonvoters regularly engage in a variety of activities that either support the political system or place demands on it. They work, obey laws, pay taxes, use public services, collect benefits from government programs, raise families, send their children to school, serve in the

Table 5–1. The Socioeconomic Base to Participation

	Percent of eligible voters who voted in the 1984 presidential election
Income	
Poorest third	62%
Middle third	73
Richest third	82
By education	
High school degree or less	67
Associate of arts degree or more	85
By race	
Black	67
White	72
By organizational membership*	
No memberships	52
1 or 2 memberships	73
3 or more memberships	89
By church attendance	
Infrequent	59
Frequent (at least 2–3 times per month)	56
By Democratic or Republican party attachment	
Independent, or weak attachment	60
Strong, or moderate attachment	76
All eligible voters	69

Source: James Allen Davis: *General Social Surveys, 1972–1985.* [machine-readable data file]. Principal Investigator, James A. Davis; Senior Study Director, Tom W. Smith. NORC ed. Chicago: National Opinion Research Center, producer, 1985; Storrs, Conn.: Roper Public Opinion Research Center, University of Connecticut, distributor.

*Organizational membership was calculated for the 1980 election; 1984 data were unavailable.

armed forces, support the national economy through their purchases, and do a variety of other things that are politically relevant. They are apathetic only in the sense that they do not engage in the very narrow range of conventional gladiator and spectator political activities. And there are many reasons why they abstain.

Why Do Some People Not Participate?

Table 5–1 shows that the nonparticipants tend to be heavily concentrated among poor people, those who do not belong to organizations, and those with little education. Raymond Wolfinger and Steven Rosenstone sorted out the relative association of various socioeconomic variables with nonvoting and concluded that education was the most important of these variables.[4] Thus, poor people vote less often than middle-class people not because they are poor but because they have much less education. Less-educated people are more likely than middle-class people to lack the confidence and the communications skills needed to engage in community organizing, campaign work, or lobbying. They are less knowledgeable about political issues and candidates than college-educated people are, and they are less likely to have internalized a **sense of civic duty,** the belief that they have a community obligation to vote and take part in community affairs.[5]

One form of political participation is not explained very fully by socioeconomic status, however: the contacting of local or state officials about neighborhood problems. This is especially so in neighborhoods with serious needs. In such neighborhoods, people of low socioeconomic status are just as likely to contact local officials as are people of higher status.[6]

For most forms of political activity, however, the poor and undereducated have the lowest participation rates, and this is one of the great paradoxes of American society. If poor people are most in need of governmental benefits and if political participation is a way of gaining those benefits, why then do the poor not participate more actively? Four explanations have been advanced: (1) individual psychological and skill barriers, (2) political barriers, (3) lack of organizations to mobilize them, and (4) indifference of the governing institutions to their demands.

Psychological Barriers

Psychological and skill barriers prevent poor people's participation. As indicated above, the poor often lack the self-confidence that comes with education. They do not work in the highly verbal or analytical occupations that business people, union organizers, lawyers, doctors, or other professionals do. Thus, persuasion tactics, organizing activities, and seeking cooperative solutions to common problems do not become second nature to the poor as they do to the more educated. If poor people attend a city council meeting and clash with an articulate lawyer, for instance, they are very likely to lose the argument and come away with bruised egos. Repeated experiences such as this reduce one's **sense of political efficacy, a term used by political scientists to describe a person's belief that one's participation in politics can have some impact**. Voting research has demonstrated that the lower a person's sense of political efficacy, the less likely that person is to vote.[7]

How the various psychological factors affect participation is rather complicated. Using voter turnout as a measure of participation, Arthur Hadley divided nonvoters into six different types,[8] four of which result from psychological factors. First, the largest group of nonvoters are the *positive apathetics,* about 35 percent of his sample of nonvoters. These people are contentedly involved in their jobs and family lives and perceive politics as irrelevant. Second, about 13 percent of the nonvoters are the *bypassed,* people who have such low levels of information that they do not bother to participate. A third category of nonvoters, about 6 percent, is composed of the *naysayers,* those who have philosophically rejected voting. Fourth are the *cross-pressured,* about 5 percent of the nonvoters. They choose not to vote so that they can escape the pressures of the forces pushing them to vote Democratic and the contrary pressures pushing them to vote Republican.

Legal and Political Barriers

The fifth category of nonvoter found by Hadley was the *physically disenfranchised.* Comprising about 18 percent of nonvoters, these people are knowledgeable and have a relatively high sense of civic duty. Yet either they do not meet voter registration requirements, or physical or health reasons keep them from going to the polls.

Historically there were many legal barriers to voting. In colonial times property requirements were common; but these have now been stripped away. Until the passage of the Nineteenth Amendment to the Constitution in 1920, several states denied women the right to vote. And until the ratification of the Twenty-sixth Amendment in 1971, few states permitted eighteen-year-olds to vote.

The most enduring and pervasive voting discrimination was that against racial minorities prior to the passage of the Voting Rights Act of 1965. The historical experience of the racial minorities—especially blacks before 1965—best illustrates how legal impediments have been used to deny the vote to large minority groups.

Although the Fifteenth Amendment (1870) guaranteed racial minorities the right to vote, southern states applied a number of discriminatory devices that nullified the Fifteenth Amendment in practice. The *poll tax* reduced turnout among minorities and the poor, because it had to be paid each election year and it accumulated for each year it was not paid. In a short time, one could owe a considerable amount of money just for the right to vote. The poll tax was finally prohibited by the Twenty-fourth Amendment in 1964. Many states also required voters to pass *literacy tests* before being allowed to register; but these were usually conducted in a blatantly discriminatory fashion. In some instances, blacks with graduate degrees were failed on the test. In other instances, black applicants would be given obtuse passages of the state constitution to interpret. Some states, such as Oklahoma, had a *grandfather clause,* which exempted people from the literacy test if they had a grandfather who had voted in 1866. This obviously was designed to exempt whites but not blacks from the literacy test, and it was struck down by the Supreme Court in 1915. Other states, such as Texas, had *white primaries.* Blacks were allowed to vote in the general election but not in the primary election of the Democratic Party. Because Texas was a one-party Democratic state, the Democratic primary really determined who got elected to office. The white primary was struck down by the Supreme Court in 1944.[9] When black voters became numerous enough to determine local elections, local communities often changed their boundaries or gerrymandered election districts to dilute the impact of black voters. The most flagrant case of this was Tuskegee, Alabama, which in the 1950s changed its boundaries from the shape of a square to a twenty-eight-sided polygon in order to dilute black voting in city elections. This practice was struck down by the Supreme Court in 1960.[10]

The key that enabled racial minorities to enter the electorate as full citizens was the **Voting Rights Act of 1965.** This law and its amendments of 1970, 1975, and 1982 set up provisions for eliminating the literacy test, placing federal registrars in counties with the worst records of voting discrimination, and requiring federal government approval before changes in the voting laws could take effect. (See the Highlight on p. 103). The results of this act have been dramatic. Since 1965, the number of black voters and black officeholders has increased not only in the South but throughout the country. In 1969 only 1,185 black officials had been elected throughout the United States; by 1985, this number had more than quintupled to 6,016.[11]

Ironically, as the more recent legal barriers to voting were overcome, the percent of eligible voters who actually turned out and voted decreased. This has led some critics to push for relaxing voter registration requirements and holding elections on Sundays instead of workdays. Wolfinger and Rosenstone estimate that voter turnout would increase by 9 percent if all states relaxed their voter registration laws to the level of the most lenient states.[12] It is not clear how much other reform devices would increase turnout.

Concerning the lower participation rates of the poor, especially in the gladiator activities, there are no legal barriers against poor people. However, a few moments' reflection will show that poor people face more practical barriers to such participation than do middle-class professionals. Lawyers, doctors, businesspeople, or college professors can rearrange their work schedules in order to take a few hours off to testify before a legislative committee or some government agency in the middle of the day. This is impossible for the hourly wage earner whose pay will be docked for time missed from work. The professional also has ready access to an office telephone, a secretary, copying machines, and other office assets that ease the task of preparing position papers, contacting people, and arranging meetings. The hourly wage earner has none of these assets. Finally, if a baby-sitter has to be hired to watch children while the mother and father attend an evening school board meeting or other community event, the baby-sitter costs will be much more significant to the poor family than to the middle-class family.

Lack of Mobilizing Organizations

A third factor reducing political participation among the poor is the lack of organizations to mobilize them. Among working-class people, labor unions, for example, make strenuous efforts to mobilize their members to participate.

Highlight
The Voting Rights Act

1. *A Triggering Formula*

   The provisions of the act would apply to any state, county, or municipality that had (a) used a literacy test for voter registration in 1964 and (b) experienced less than a 50 percent turnout in the 1964 presidential election. This was called the triggering formula.

2. *Voting Examiners*

   The Department of Justice was authorized to use federal voting examiners to register people in any jurisdiction identified by the triggering formula.

3. *Literacy Tests*

   The Justice Department was authorized to suspend literacy tests in any jurisdiction identified by the triggering formula.

4. *Preclearance Requirement*

   Voting laws, municipal boundaries, and election districts could not be changed in any community identified by the triggering formula unless the change was cleared in advance by the Justice Department or a three-judge district court panel in Washington, D.C. The object of this provision is to prevent dilution of the minority vote by gerrymandering election districts or by annexing substantial white subdivisions.

5. *Enforcement Machinery*

   The act gave the Attorney General considerable authority to prosecute violations and stipulated fines and imprisonment for convictions.

The importance of union-organizing activities was seen in a study comparing West Virginia counties with neighboring Virginia counties of a similar economic character. The West Virginians voted much more regularly than the Virginians. The reason for this was that unions had organized the West Virginia coal miners in the early twentieth century and those miners had developed the habit of participation. In Virginia, in contrast, politics were dominated by a political organization called the Byrd Machine, which discouraged participation because it thrived on low voter turnouts.[13]

Voters can also be mobilized by voter registration drives. A study of such drives in Houston in 1976 found not only that the voter registration drives increased turnout that year but that the drive had long-term impacts as well: A majority of the people who registered during the 1976 voter registration drive also turned out to vote in the elections four years later.[14]

System Nonresponsiveness

A final category of nonvoters in Hadley's typology (about 22 percent of his sample) is the *political impotent,* who has an extremely low sense of political efficacy. The political impotents do not think that they can influence political outcomes. Anthony Downs applies a form of cost–benefit analysis to explain this form of nonvoting.[15] With thousands of voters in a typical legislative race, for example, an individual's chance to affect the outcome is negligible. If a person thinks the material circumstances of his or her life will be the same no matter who wins, even the minimal cost of taking a few minutes to stop at the polling place may outweigh the apparently nonexistent benefits, especially if one has no sense of civic duty to nag the conscience.

Does the political impotent shun voting because he or she feels inadequate and has a low sense of efficacy, or because he or she realizes that the government will most likely remain unresponsive to his or her demands? Michael Parenti argues strongly that poor people especially are politically impotent because of governmental unresponsiveness rather than because of any sense of personal inadequacy. In his view the government does not pay attention to the demands of the poor when they do participate. As a result, participation is fruitless. When looked at this way, the withdrawal of the poor and the bottom two-thirds of the population from gladiator status is not a result of psychological misperceptions. Rather it is an accurate assessment of their self-interest. The American political process at all levels is a process of bargaining and negotiation among elites, and the commitment of elites to democratic procedures is a commitment to procedures in which mostly the elites participate.[16] Revolutionizing those procedures so that the poor can have an effective voice is frowned on by the elites.

Parenti studied three unsuccessful attempts of poor people in Newark, New Jersey, to obtain major gains for the residents of a poor, black neighborhood during the mid-1960s.[17] The Newark Community Union Project (NCUP) was organized by local black militants and radical white members of the Students for a Democratic Society. Over a three-year period, NCUP attempted to get the city government to enforce the city's building codes and to install a traffic light at a particularly dangerous intersection. When these attempts failed, NCUP tried to elect new black candidates to the city council and the state legislature. But this attempt failed, too. Throughout these efforts, the tactics employed by NCUP ranged from traditional voter registration and electioneering to protest activity, which involved rent strikes, sit-ins, and blocking traffic at the intersection where the traffic light was desired. Although NCUP held together and persisted in its efforts for three years, none of its three major projects was successful.

From this discouraging experience, Parenti concluded that the poor simply did not have the resources to make the governing elites pay attention to them and to respond to their demands. One of the crucial elements of power is the capacity to set the agenda of politics and to determine which questions will be considered by government agencies. Parenti found that Newark officials kept NCUP's demands off the decision-making agenda. The political resources of the poor to place certain demands such as building code enforcement on the agenda are infinitesimal in comparison to the resources of interest groups such as absentee slum landlords who do not want the building codes enforced.

What Are the Channels of Participation?

Much of the rest of this chapter and the next is devoted to the question of whether the participation of the poor in general is as fruitless as Parenti indicates it was in Newark. In order for participation to work, the political system must provide what political scientists call *linkages* between the individual citizen and the governing officials. These linkages can be thought of as channels through which individuals have input into the governing process. The major channels to be examined in these two chapters are: (1) public opinion, (2) interest groups, (3) political parties, (4) elections, and (5) direct democracy. For any of these channels to serve as effective means of allowing citizens to influence government policy, two conditions must prevail. The channels themselves must effectively influence government policy, and the channels must be responsive to citizen demands.

Public Opinion

Public opinion refers to peoples' views on politically relevant issues.[18] If democracy has any meaning at all, there must be some correlation between public opinion and government policy. By this criterion, how democratic are the American states?

Fifteen years ago, the preponderant research would have concluded, Not Very! Most research until that time had concluded that a state's per-capita income and its level of economic development had a bigger impact on the kind of policies it adopted than did any political factors, including public opinion.[19] Recent research, however, has found that public opinion has a much greater impact on public policy than previously thought. Researchers have found a consistency between preferences expressed in public opinion polls and public policies on about two-thirds of all public opinion preferences. They have also identified many instances (but not all) in which public opinion directly influences policy outcomes.[20] One team of researchers used *New York Times*/CBS telephone surveys from 1976–1982 to rank each state on an index of liberalism. When this index was correlated with eight different policy outcomes (such as welfare expenditures, consumer policies, legalized gambling policy, and tax progressivity), the researchers found that public opinion had a greater impact on public policy than did economic variables such as per-capita income or level of education. In short, states with the most liberal populations also have the most liberal policies, and states with the most conservative populations have the most conservative policies.[21]

How Does Public Opinion Influence Policy?

In Theory

There are basically three theoretical models that describe how public opinion can influence public policy.[22] The first is a *sharing* or *consensus* model. In this view, the legislators share the same values that their constituents hold. When the legislators cast their votes, they automatically bring the values of their constituents to bear on the policy questions before the legislature. Legislators' policy decisions reflect popular opinion not because they fear voter retaliation but because they share that opinion. The second model is the *rational activist model*,[23] which holds that people choose their legislators rationally on the basis of their issue positions. While there is some evidence to support the first model,[24] there is very little evidence in support of the rational activist model. Voters seldom know the candidates' stands on a range of issues, and legislators' votes seldom correlate perfectly with their constituents' opinions.[25] The third model is the *role-playing model*, in which the legislators play the delegate role of finding out what their constituents want before voting on critical issues.[26] Some evidence exists that local leaders can accurately predict public opinion on specific issues;[27] but there is very little evidence that this knowledge affects the decisions of these local officials.[28]

In Practice

Given these theoretical models, is there any evidence showing how, in practice, public opinion affects policy? Four important generalizations can be made. First, public opinion has its strongest impact on issues that are highly visible and emotional. This can be seen most clearly in the history of the civil rights movement. A study of the relationship between the voting of congress-persons and the attitudes of their constituents found civil rights to be the issue in which congressional voting most strongly reflected constituents' opinions.[29] An attempt to correlate public opinion in the states with policy outputs found the strongest correlations in the area of prohibiting racial discrimination in public accommodations.[30] Where public opinion was strongly against this, it was difficult to enact.

The second generalization, following from the first, concerns the **intensity problem.** When an issue is visible and emotional, public opinion is often sharply divided. Some constituents feel more intensely about the issue than do others. On gun control, for example, an individual legislator may find that two-thirds of the constituents favor stricter controls but are not excited about it. The other one-third may oppose tighter controls vociferously and may agitate for the defeat of legislators who support those controls. Since the minority feels much more intensely about its position than does the majority, the legislator will lose votes by going along with the majority public opinion. Anne Hopkins found that gun permit legislation typically was not passed until more than 70 percent of people supported it.[31]

A third generalization is that some parts of the public have more influence on public policy than do others. Legislators identify **attentive constituents** in their districts[32] who are politically aware, especially those who hold office at the local level. The legislators not only respect the opinion of these constituents but actively seek their advice. These attentive constituents have more effect on public policy than does the public at large.

Finally, even when a correlation can be found between public opinion and public policy, it is not always possible to know which caused which. Comparing 1930s survey data with later public policy changes, Robert Erikson studied public opinion on capital punishment and argued that public opinion preceded the public policy. That is, states with the strongest antideath-penalty feelings in the 1930s were the first states to abandon capital punishment in later decades.[33] However, examples can also be found where the policy shapes opinion. Scholars have noted, for example, that public opinion on foreign policy tends to change in response to the government's policies.[34]

In summary, public opinion's influence on public policy cannot be ignored. It is difficult for legislators to enact policies that violate deeply held values of a substantial majority of the population. Public values help establish the overall boundaries within which policymakers have much discretion but outside of which they cannot act decisively. On the day-to-day operations of government that are less visible and less emotional than civil rights or gun control, policymakers find themselves responding more to other channels of influence than to public opinion.

Interest Groups

A second conventional channel of citizen influence is the political **interest group,** any organization that tries to influence government decisions. Interest groups differ from political parties in several respects. They do not run candidates for office. It is true that candidates are *endorsed* by interest groups, such as labor unions, gun clubs, environmental groups, and business associations, but the candidates are *not nominated* by interest groups. They are nominated by political parties (in partisan elections), and they appear on the ballot with their party designation. Interest groups also do not organize the government once the election is over. Parties do. The legislature (except for Nebraska's) is formally divided between the Republican and Democratic parties, not a series of interest groups. Finally, whereas parties represent geographic entities, interest groups represent functional entities.

Kinds of Interest Groups

So many varied interest groups are found in the states that it is impossible to categorize them all. Four kinds can be identified that account for most of the interest group influence on state and local governments.

Economically Motivated Groups

First are the economically motivated groups, groups that have a direct economic interest in government policy. Government policies will either cost or save their members' money. Business and labor are the most obvious examples. Business corporations are especially concerned with a state's taxing and spending policies. They seek to minimize their taxes and to channel government spending into areas from which they will benefit. Trade associations are organizations of individual businesses in an industry. Thus, the state association of electrical contractors pursues the economic interests of that specific occupation. Chambers of commerce, on the other hand, include so many kinds of businesses that they often cannot speak with a single voice on a given issue.

Labor unions are also economically motivated. Their sole purpose is to improve the working conditions and economic status of their members.

Hence, they support government policies that promote unionization of workers. They also tend to promote civil rights and social welfare legislation. While unions are often opposed to management on many social issues, they often work together on issues that affect jobs. Thus, unions usually support public construction projects because these create jobs, and they oppose ban-the-can legislation that prohibits no-deposit, no-return containers, because such a ban means workers in those industries would lose jobs. When large manufacturers threaten to close down rather than install expensive pollution-control equipment, the unions at those companies frequently support the industry rather than the environmentalists.

In the 1980s, unions have come under their sharpest attack in fifty years. The decline of the manufacturing sector of the American economy has seen corresponding declines in the membership of industrial unions such as the United Auto Workers (UAW) and the United Steel Workers (USW)[35] (although *total* union membership has remained stable). Corporations during the 1980s took a hard line when negotiating contracts with unions, often refusing to bargain collectively and using union-busting consulting firms to stymie union-organizing activities.[36] Union strength during this period was further diluted by the retirement of an older generation of successful union leaders, for example, George Meaney of the AFL-CIO, and their replacement by younger leaders (such as Lane Kirkland of the AFL-CIO), who came out of the union bureaucracies rather than out of the union-organizing battles of the 1930s.[37] Unions in the 1980s were also hampered by an unsympathetic Reagan administration, which appointed anti-union people to head agencies that are very important to organized labor, such as the National Labor Relations Board and the Department of Labor.[38]

Professionally Motivated Groups

A second category is the *professionally motivated group,* whose primary purpose is to provide services to its members. The state medical association, for example, might distribute medical journals to members, or it might sponsor conferences on important medical issues. Since professionally motivated groups also often attend to the economic well-being of their members, some groups are difficult to categorize as either professionally or economically motivated. Among teachers' groups, for example, there has been recurring friction between the oldest and largest group, the National Education Association (NEA), and the newer American Federation of Teachers (AFT). The NEA has traditionally looked upon itself as a professional association that has tried to play down collective bargaining and other union-organizing activities. The AFT, however, from the very beginning regarded itself primarily as a union. It eagerly pursued collective bargaining in order to improve the wages and working conditions of teachers. As the AFT increased its membership in the big city school districts, which were the first to embrace collective bargaining, the NEA has been forced to move away from the professional association model to the union model.

Public Agency Groups

A third category of interest groups is the public agency group, an organization of public agencies. The seven most prominent are the Council of State Governments, the United States Conference of Mayors, the National Governors' Association, the National Conference of State Legislatures, the National Association of County Officials, the National League of Cities, and the International City Management Association. These groups provide opportunities for public officials to exchange ideas, to lobby collectively at the regional and national levels, and to get up-to-date information about the latest developments and concepts that affect their own public agency.

Ideological Groups

A final category is the ideological group, such as the Sierra Club, the Audubon Society, Common Cause, and similar organizations that claim to represent a public interest not represented by the economic or professionally motivated interest groups. The Sierra Club, for example, is an aggressive group devoted to conserving the environment. Unlike a labor union or a medical association, the ideological group offers its members no direct economic or professional benefits; rather, members are attracted by an ideological concern—protecting the environment, in the case of the Sierra Club. The most relevant ideological groups for college students are the Public Interest Research Groups (PIRGs), established on college campuses by Ralph Nader in the early 1970s. Many PIRGs are supported by student fees collected by the colleges and passed on directly to the local or state PIRG. The PIRG then uses the funds to hire students to research social issues, prepare position papers, and lobby for these issues before the state legislatures and other public agencies. The PIRGs usually lobby for liberal and environmental causes. In many states they have become quite effective. Other politically important ideological groups in the 1980s are women's groups, gay rights groups, and fundamentalist Christian groups.

Interest Group Political Tactics

The most common political tactics of interest groups are *public relations, electioneering,* and *lobbying.* **Public relations** probably absorbs more time than any other interest group activity. The objective normally is to create a favorable climate within which the interest group can operate. The advertising strategies of many electric power companies provide an example. Prior to the

1970s these companies advertised principally to get people to use more electricity. Since 1970, however, they have come under pressure from environmentalists to stop polluting the atmosphere with their power plants. Many companies then began public relations efforts designed to create opinion favorable to the construction of more electric power plants, including nuclear plants.

Electioneering is the tactic of trying to elect legislators who are sympathetic to your point of view. Thus, farmers' groups are partial to rural-based candidates for office, business groups lean toward conservative candidates, labor unions favor economic liberals, and teachers' associations unite behind candidates who support public employee collective bargaining and more expenditures for public schools.

Whereas business groups tend to make the most effective use of public relations tactics, labor unions and teachers' associations are probably most skilled at electioneering, especially in the Northeast and Midwest and on the West Coast, where union membership is very large. Unions endorse candidates, collect campaign contributions from their members, and donate these contributions to the endorsed candidates. Their most effective electioneering asset, however, lies in their large and active memberships. Teachers, in particular, are accustomed to persuading people and to organizing their activities. Thus, they have many skills that are useful in an election campaign. Additionally, they perceive a direct benefit to themselves from electing candidates who favor collective bargaining and greater expenditures for public schools. As a consequence, they contribute a disproportionate number of people to deliver campaign literature, make telephone calls, organize coffee parties, set up fundraising parties, and plan campaign strategies.

As a counter to union electioneering, business corporations and independent professionals such as doctors and lawyers are increasingly relying on the **political action committee (PAC)** to influence the electoral process. A PAC collects money to use as a campaign contribution in an effort to get friendly people elected to public office. Many states prohibit unions or corporations from directly contributing money to campaigns. But unions or corporations can legally set up a PAC that will collect money from potential contributors. In this way the PAC can effectively give the union or corporation political influence without violating the law.

PACs are beginning to have a major impact on the outcome of elections. Texas PACs in 1980 spent an average of $31,000 per seat for the House and Senate races in that state. Some candidates received up to 75 percent of their campaign funds from Texas PACs. PACs representing banks and savings and loan associations spent $267,000; the AFL-CIO spent $120,000. Most of the PAC money goes to incumbents.[39]

As the role of PACs in elections has grown, political reform groups such as Common Cause have sought to have states limit the amount of money a PAC may contribute to a campaign. By the mid-1980s, over 20 states had adopted some form of limit on PACs.[40] Despite this move to impose limits, few observers expect the influence of PACs to decline.

Lobbying is the tactic of trying to influence a decision of the legislature or some other governmental body. Lobbying is done directly by interest groups, by individuals, and by professional lobbyists who make a career of representing the interests of various groups before the legislature. This year it may be the electrical contractors' association that is seeking to prevent a change in the state's building codes; next year it may be the savings and loan association that is seeking to make a change in the state's building codes. Such lobbying is often defensive in nature, seeking to prevent new legislation that might undo some existing privilege or right.

At the local level the crucial feature of lobbying is the existence of informal civic interest groups such as chambers of commerce, which represent primarily business interests. Theodore Lowi argues that these groups are so pervasive and the overlap between their members and public policymaking boards is so great that public officials have virtually abdicated policymaking responsibility to private interests.[41] This may be an overstatement, but the history of state and local government is filled with examples of interest groups directing local policymaking. Local business corporations dominated Pittsburgh's air pollution policies for two decades. The highway lobbies appeared to have more influence on urban freeway locations than did big city councils. Local realtors and other business people dominated land use planning commissions.

One of the most effective ways for business to influence local policies is to form nonpartisan research or civic groups that study public issues and make policy recommendations. These include associations such as the New Detroit Committee, the Cleveland Citizens League, the Pennsylvania Economy League, and various taxpayers associations. Being nonpartisan and attracting highly respected members, their policy recommendations often acquire a legitimacy that gives them considerable influence on local officials.[42]

State and local lobbying is generally thought to be more corrupt than congressional lobbying. State legislators are suspected much more of accepting bribes and other favors in exchange for their votes.[43] One Illinois legislator, for example, charged in the mid-1960s that it was a common practice for state senators to receive direct cash payments for assuring the passage of key bills.[44] The belief that these practices are common has made some legislatures and lobbying organizations the butt of political satire such as the cartoon on p. 113.

Of course daddy loves us, why do you ask?

Source: Jerry Fearing, *St. Paul Dispatch,* April 27, 1971.

States have found it difficult to pass effective controls over lobbying, despite the fact that most states have passed lobby regulation laws. Typical is California's attempt to pass a Political Reform Act in 1974, which required lobbyists to register with the Secretary of State and make detailed reports on their income and expenditures. Despite the act's seemingly strict provisions, one California analyst commented that it "has not significantly altered lobbyist activity in Sacramento [the capital], although wining and dining has been drastically curtailed."[45]

Most lobbying is not corrupt. A study of lobbying in four states found that both lobbyists and legislators regarded bribery as the least effective tactic for influencing legislators. Entertainment also ranked low, and personal presentations to legislators was thought to be the most effective lobbying technique.[46] This is because accurate and timely information contained in good presentations is very useful to legislators. In fact, providing legislators with useful information may be the most valuable thing lobbyists do. AFL-CIO lobbyists in Oregon, for example, once got a legislative committee to delete from a civil rights bill a phrase that would have prohibited denying anyone a job because of membership or nonmembership in any organization. The quick-witted lobbyists realized that this wording would have outlawed Oregon's union shop.[47]

Effective lobbying simply involves a lot of hard work and concern for details. The activities of a state School Boards Association (SBA) during the legislative session provide a typical example of lobbying in practice. The School Boards Association represents all the local school boards in the state. It holds regular conventions at which the school board members present and approve resolutions. These resolutions constitute the association's lobbying agenda for that legislative session. The officers and professional staff members of the SBA contact legislators and get them to introduce the resolutions as bills in the legislature. The SBA sets up liaison committees composed of local school board members in each legislative district. When a senator is faced with a committee vote on some matter of importance to the School Board Association, the SBA contacts the legislative liaison committee members in that senator's district, and they call the senator to express their concerns about the issue. Moreover, the SBA compiles a weekly log of all bills in the legislature that relate to education, where they are in the legislative mill, and what the SBA's concern is about them. When a committee is wrestling with a difficult piece of legislation, such as equalizing the state's school aid formula, SBA officials spend inordinate amounts of time working with the appropriations committee members and staff.

Do Interest Groups Affect Public Policy?

How much influence interest groups have on public policy is a difficult question to answer. Although we know that interest groups draft bills that become legislation, it is not clear just how much impact they have on legislative policy output.[48] It is clear, however, that the patterns of interest group influence differ in the various states.

Patterns of Interest Group Influence

Harmon Zeigler has identified five different patterns of interest group influence in the fifty states. First, the rural, one-party states with weak legislative parties are often characterized by an *alliance of dominant groups*. In Maine, for example, state politics has traditionally been dominated by power companies, timber interests, and manufacturers. "Over three-fourths of the state is woodland and most of this land is owned by a handful of timber companies and paper manufacturers. These interests, combined with power companies and textile and shoe manufacturers, are able—insofar as their well-being is directly involved—to control Maine politics."[49] This pattern was true also of the southern one-party states.

As most of these states have become more urbanized in recent years, the traditional alliance of dominant groups has come under attack from environmentalists, conservationists, labor unions, and changing economic conditions. In Maine, for example, foreign competition has cut heavily into the economic security of the state's shoe industry. The growth of tourism and the desire for vacation homes by people living in the nearby metropolitan areas of Massachusetts and Connecticut have created more diverse economic interests to challenge the traditional dominance.

The second interest group pattern of influence is a *single dominant interest,* found mostly in rural, two-party states with moderately strong parties in the state legislatures. West Virginia, for example, has been dominated by coal mining companies largely owned by non-West Virginians. These companies have so successfully opposed the coal severance tax that, until recently, that tax brought less revenue into the state than the cigarette tax, a minor tax source.[50]

The third pattern of interest group influence is a *conflict between two dominant groups.* The prime example of this phenomenon occurs in Michigan, where politics are polarized by the conflict between the automobile manufacturers and the United Automobile Workers (UAW). The UAW typically takes a liberal position on tax issues, social legislation, and labor legislation; and it regularly backs candidates from the Democratic party. The automobile manufacturers, in contrast, regularly back the Republican candidates and take more conservative positions on tax and social issues. One observer of Michigan politics wrote, "No major issues of policy (taxation, social legislation, labor legislation, and so on) are likely to be decided in Michigan without the intervention, within their respective parties and before agencies of government, of automotive labor and automotive management."[51]

The fourth pattern of interest group influence is a *triumph of many interests,* and here Zeigler points to California. In that state, as noted earlier, the political parties are very weak. The state is highly urban and industrial, leading to a heterogeneous economy and society. The interest groups become forces in initiating proposals, influencing the election of public officials, and generally influencing public policy.

The final pattern is that of *party dominance* over the interest groups, which occurred principally in Connecticut from the 1940s to the early 1960s. Although Connecticut had a well-diversified economy and population with many interest groups, it was also characterized by two strong, competitive political parties. Party cohesion in the legislature was high, enabling party leaders to dominate interest group lobbyists in swaying the vote of individual legislators.[52] Oklahoma, in contrast, has been known for very weak legislative parties. Interest groups have had a great influence on voting patterns in that state.[53] Strong political parties protect individual legislatures from interest group coercion.

The Resources for Interest Group Influence

Not only do the states have different patterns of interest group influence, interest groups themselves also vary in their strength. Some groups have more of the resources leading to strength than others. Three of the most important resources are size of membership, quality of the leadership, and status.

Size of the membership can be a source of interest group strength. Cities and states with large labor union memberships usually have public policies that are pro-union.[54] States with large Catholic populations tend to be much more receptive to aiding parochial schools than are states with small Catholic populations. The size of groups is important because their members are a source of campaign contributions, campaign workers, and potential lobbyists during the legislative session.

Although large memberships can be an asset for group influence, they can also weaken its influence if the group's policy positions become too broad or vague. Chambers of commerce, for example, seek to represent the business community in general and thus must avoid certain specific issues that might alienate significant businesses. In contrast, a trade association such as a Savings and Loan Association League can target its efforts to issues that concern its members. Some scholars argue that the large membership groups tend to win symbolic benefits for their members, while the small membership groups tend to win tangible benefits.[55]

The leadership and cohesion of an interest group is also an important power resource. The AFL-CIO is powerful in the Northeast and Midwest not only because of its size but also because it enjoys capable leadership. Some observers argue that group leadership over the long term tends to gravitate into the hands of a small circle of staff and self-perpetuating leaders. Roberto Michels called this the **iron law of oligarchy.**[56] Groups have a tendency to become less democratic and more oligarchic over time.

Finally, the status of a group also affects its level of influence. In a Republican-dominated state, business groups are likely to have more status than labor unions and to get a better reception among legislators. In a Democratic-controlled legislature of the Northeast or Midwest, however, the reverse may often be true.

In addition to a group's resources and tactics, interest group influence is also determined by the overall political and economic environments of the states. Table 5–2 lists the states whose interest group systems are considered

Table 5–2. Comparative Interest Group Strength:
States in Which Interest Group Influence Is Considered

Strong	Moderately strong	Weak
Alabama	Arizona	Colorado
Alaska	California	Connecticut
Arkansas	Delaware	Massachusetts
Florida	Idaho	Michigan
Georgia	Illinois	Minnesota
Hawaii	Indiana	New Jersey
Iowa	Kansas	New York
Kentucky	Maine	North Dakota
Louisiana	Maryland	Rhode Island
Mississippi	Missouri	Wisconsin
Montana	Nevada	
Nebraska	Ohio	
New Hampshire	Pennsylvania	
New Mexico	South Dakota	
North Carolina	Utah	
Oklahoma	Vermont	
Oregon	Virginia	
South Carolina	Wyoming	
Tennessee		
Texas		
Washington		
West Virginia		

Source: Adapted from *State Politics, Parties and Policy* by Sarah McCally Morehouse. Copyright ©
1981 by CBS College Publishing. Reprinted by permission of Holt, Rinehart and Winston, Inc.

to have strong, moderately strong, or weak influence in state governments.
The pattern shown in the table is not a random one. With a few exceptions
(such as Texas), the states with the strongest interest group systems tend to
have less complex economic systems than do the states with weak interest
groups. That is, strong-interest-group states tend to have lower per-capita
incomes, lower population densities, lower levels of education among the
adult population, and less-industrialized economies and are more likely to
have state economies dominated by a single industry.[57] The weak-interest-
group states also tend to have stronger political parties, although that relationship is not nearly as pronounced as it was two decades ago. The weak-
interest-group states additionally tend to have stronger governors and more
professional legislatures than the strong-interest-group states. In general, one
could safely conclude that the more diversified a state's economy is, the more

affluent is its population, and the stronger its political party system and governing institutions, the less likely that state is to be dominated by a single-interest group or a single combination of groups.

Which Groups Are Most Influential?

A study of legislators in four states (Tennessee, Ohio, New Jersey, and California) found considerable agreement as to which interest groups the legislators thought were the most influential. In all four states the legislators selected business interests as the most powerful. Teacher groups were the second most powerful, and organized labor ran third. Beyond these three, the pattern varied from one state to another, and an assortment of interests were named as influential—farm interests, public agency interest groups, and others.[58] Note that the highest influence in this ranking is attributed to the economically motivated groups. Few ad hoc or ideological groups are perceived as being among the most powerful.

Conclusion: A Comparison of Public Opinion and Interest Groups

Table 5–3 summarizes the preceding discussion. Public opinion and interest groups are rated as channels of political participation by their policy impact, the ease through which a citizen can use the channel to affect public policy, and the responsiveness of the channels.

For policy impact, public opinion is a very weak channel of citizen input. Public opinion does not have a direct effect on most issues that governments face. Public opinion is most effective on visible and highly emotional issues. As discussed earlier, there is some evidence that elected public officials share a consensus of values with the majority of their constituents. By contrast, interest groups exert a very strong influence on public policy, although their influence varies from state to state.

In the ease with which an outsider can use the channel to affect public policy, public opinion is paradoxically the least effective. Outsiders can manipulate public opinion only when they have a charismatic appeal and only when the issue is visible and emotional. Most established interest groups are not accessible to manipulation by outsiders. Yet if enough outsiders feel strongly enough about a policy, they are free to organize their own interest group. In the environmental politics of the 1970s, many environmentalists formed ad hoc interest groups, which exerted influence on environmental policymaking.

Table 5-3. Public Opinion and Interest Groups as Conventional Channels of Political Participation

Channel	Policy impact	Ease through which an outsider can use this channel to change public policies	Most responsive to whom?	Least responsive to whom?
Public opinion	Very weak, except for visible and emotional issues; unreliable	Very difficult (except when a charismatic candidate manipulates an emotional issue)	Vocal minorities	Poor and unorganized people
Interest groups	Very strong, especially on the day-to-day, unemotional issues that give tangible benefits to particular groups	Difficult, but possible	Existing institutions; members of the interest groups	Poor and unorganized people

119

Finally, and most important from the point of view of representative democracy, Table 5–3 examines the responsiveness of these channels. Public opinion and interest groups as channels of political participation are most responsive to the middle- and upper-middle classes, to people who participate, to the gladiators, and to such existing institutions as unions, corporations, and professional associations. Neither of these conventional channels is particularly responsive to the demands or needs of the poor and the unorganized.

To place interest groups and public opinion in a broader comparative context, we need to examine the other channels of political influence. We will do this in the next chapter.

Summary

1. Several patterns of participation arise in conventional political activities. Participation is concentrated among a small part of the population and is disproportionately an upper-status and middle-status phenomenon. This is especially true for demanding gladiator activities. Poor people do not participate nearly as much as do affluent people. To explain these patterns of participation, scholars have focused on psychological and skill barriers among the poor, political barriers, the lack of mobilizing organizations, and the indifference of the governing institutions to the demands of the poor.

2. Three models try to explain the impact of public opinion on public policy—the sharing or consensus model, the rational activist model, and the role-playing model. Public opinion appears to have its strongest voice in issues that are visible and emotional. In deciding how much importance to attach to public opinion on a given issue, legislators have to cope with the intensity of voters' reactions. Policymakers also tend to be more responsive to their attentive constituents than they are to constituents in general. Even when public policy does correlate with public opinion, it often is not possible to know which one caused the other.

3. Interest groups are organizations that try to influence government decisions. A distinction can be drawn between economically motivated groups, professionally motivated groups, public interest groups, and ideological groups. Interest groups engage in a variety of tactics to influence government decisions—public relations, electioneering, and lobbying. There are five patterns to interest group influence—an alliance of dominant groups, a single dominant interest, a conflict between two dominant groups, a triumph of many interests, and party dominance over the interest groups.

Key Terms

Attentive constituent The constituent, often a local official, who is aware of a legislator's activity and voting behavior in the legislature.

Electioneering The interest group tactic of trying to get favorable people elected to the legislature.

Gladiator A person very active in political activities, campaigning, contributing to campaigns, and lobbying.

Intensity problem The legislators' problem in deciding whether they should support the legislative preferences of a small minority that feels very intensely about an issue or the majority that feels much less intensely about it.

Interest group Any organization of people who try to influence government decisions.

Iron law of oligarchy The tendency of groups to become less democratic over time and to fall under the dominance of a small group of leaders.

Lobbying The interest group tactic of trying to influence a decision of the legislature or some other governmental body.

Political action committee (PAC) A group that collects money from various sources and uses it to make campaign contributions and to try to influence election outcomes.

Political apathetics People who neither vote nor put other conscious demands on the political system.

Political participation Individual or group activity that seeks to influence the selection of government officials or the actions that those officials take.

Public opinion The general population's views on politically relevant issues.

Public relations The use of the media to create a favorable public opinion.

Sense of civic duty One's belief that one has a community obligation to vote and take part in community affairs.

Sense of political efficacy One's belief that one's participation in politics can have some effect.

Spectator A person whose main political activity is voting and observing politics.

Voting Rights Act of 1965 This law was very effective in striking down the legal barriers that had prevented the majority of racial minorities in the South from registering and voting.

References

1. The tale of Weston is described and analyzed in Theodore J. Lowi et al., *Poliscide* (New York: Macmillan, 1976).

2. Sidney Verba and Norman Nie, *Participation in America* (New York: Harper & Row, 1972), p. 2.

3. See Lester W. Milbrath and M. L. Goel, *Political Participation: How and Why Do People Get Involved in Politics?* 2nd ed. (Chicago: Rand McNally, 1977), pp. 19–21. Also see Robert Lane, *Political Life: Why People Get Involved in Politics* (Glencoe, Ill.: Free Press, 1959).

4. Raymond E. Wolfinger and Steven J. Rosenstone, *Who Votes?* (New Haven, Conn.: Yale University Press, 1980), pp. 23–30.

5. The importance of a sense of civic duty to voting is discussed in the work of William Riker and Peter Ordeshook, "A Theory of the Calculus of Voting," *The American Political Science Review* 62, no. 1 (March 1968): 25–42.

6. This was the major finding of Elaine B. Sharp's study of citizen-contacting in Kansas City, Missouri, in 1982–1983. See her "Citizen Demand Making in the Urban Context," *American Journal of Political Science* 28, no. 4 (November 1984): 654–670.

7. Angus Campbell et al., *The American Voter* (New York: Wiley, 1960), Ch. 4.

8. Arthur T. Hadley, *The Empty Polling Booth* (Englewood Cliffs, N.J.: Prentice-Hall, 1978), pp. 67–103.

9. *Smith* v. *Allwright,* 321 U.S. 649 (1944).

10. *Gomillion* v. *Lightfoot,* 364 U.S. 339 (1960).

11. Bureau of the Census, *Statistical Abstract of the United States: 1986* (Washington, D.C.: U.S. Government Printing Office, 1985), p. 252.

12. Wolfinger and Rosenstone, *Who Votes?,* p. 73.

13. Gerald W. Johnson, "Research Note on Political Correlates of Voter Participation: A Deviant Case Analysis," *American Political Science Review* 65, no. 3 (September 1971): 768–776. One study found that black voting increased when outside organizers and federal registrars appeared. See Lester M. Salamon and Stephen Van Evera, "Fear, Apathy, and Discrimination: A Test of Three Explanations of Political Participation," *American Political Science Review* 67, no. 4 (December 1973): 1288–1307.

14. Arnold Vedlitz, "Voter Registration Drives and Black Voting in the South," *Journal of Politics* 47, no. 2 (May 1985): 643–651.

15. Anthony Downs, *An Economic Theory of Democracy* (New York: Harper & Row, 1957), Ch. 14.

16. See Kenneth Prewitt, "Political Ambitions, Volunteerism, and Electoral Accountability," *American Political Science Review* 64, no. 1 (March 1970): 5–17; Peter Bachrach, *The Theory of Democratic Elitism* (Boston: Little, Brown & Co., 1967); Jack L. Walker, "A Critique of the Elitist Theory of Democracy," *American Political Science Review* 60, no. 2 (June 1966): 285–295; Walter Dean Burnham, "The Changing Shape of the American Political Universe," *American Political Science Review* 59, no. 1 (March 1965): 7–28; Geraint Parry, *Political Elites* (London: George Allen and Unwin, 1969).

17. Michael Parenti, "Power and Pluralism: A View From the Bottom," *Journal of Politics* 32, no. 3 (August 1970): 501–530.

18. M. Margaret Conway and Frank B. Feigert, *Political Analysis: An Introduction,* 2nd ed. (Boston: Allyn and Bacon, 1976), p. 130.

19. Thomas R. Dye was one of the most persistent and influential advocates of this view. See his *Politics, Economics, and the Public: Policy Outcomes in the American States* (Chicago: Rand McNally and Company, 1966). Dye, in this book, does not directly test public opinion as a possible independent variable; rather he uses measures such as interparty competition and voter turnout, which presumably reflect public opinion partially.

20. On the consistency between public policy and public opinion preferences, see Benjamin I. Page and Robert Y. Shapiro, "Effects of Public Opinion on Policy," *American Political Science Review* 77, no. 1 (March 1983): 175–191; and Alan D. Munroe, "Consistency Between Public Preferences and National Policy Decisions," *American Politics Quar-*

terly 7, no. 1 (January 1979): 3–20. For instances when public opinion has influenced policy outcomes, see Robert Weissberg, *Public Opinion and Popular Government* (Englewood Cliffs, N.J.: Prentice-Hall, 1976), p. 137.

21. Gerald C. Wright, Jr., Robert S. Erikson, and John P. McIver, "Public Opinion and Policy Liberalism in the American States," a paper presented at the 1986 meeting of the Midwest Political Science Association, Chicago, Ill., April 10–12, 1986; and "Measuring State Partisanship and Ideology with Survey Data," *Journal of Politics* 47, no. 2 (May 1985): 469–489.

22. Robert. S Erikson, "The Relationship Between Public Opinion and State Policy: A New Look Based on Some Forgotten Data," *American Political Science Review* 20, no. 1 (February 1976): 25–37.

23. Norman R. Lutbeg, *Public Opinion and Public Policy,* rev. ed. (Homewood, Ill.: Dorsey Press, 1974), p. 4.

24. See David R. Morgan, "Political Linkage of Public Policy: Attitudinal Congruence Between Citizens and Officials," *Western Political Quarterly* 26, no. 2 (June 1973): 209–223; and Eric Uslaner and Ronald E. Weber, "Representing People Who Have Interests," Paper delivered at the annual conference of the Midwest Political Science Association, Chicago, Ill., April 24–26, 1980. Also see Uslaner and Weber, "U.S. State Legislators' Opinions and Perceptions of Constituency Attitudes," *Legislative Studies Quarterly* 4 (November 1979): 563–585.

25. Warren E. Miller and Donald E. Stokes, "Constituency Influence in Congress," *American Political Science Review* 57, no. 1 (March 1963): 15–56.

26. Lutbeg, *Public Opinion and Public Policy,* p. 8.

27. Roberta S. Sigel and H. Paul Friesema, "Urban Community Leaders' Knowledge of Public Opinion," *Western Political Quarterly* 18, no. 1 (December 1965): 881–895.

28. See Prewitt, "Political Ambitions, Volunteerism, and Electoral Accountability," pp. 5–17.

29. Miller and Stokes, "Constituency Influence in Congress," pp. 45–56.

30. Ronald E. Weber and William R. Shaffer, "Public Opinion and American State Policy Making," *Midwest Journal of Political Science* 16, no. 4 (November 1972): 683–699.

31. Anne H. Hopkins, "Opinion Publics and Support for Public Policy in the American States," *American Journal of Political Science* 18, no. 1 (February 1974): 167–177.

32. G. R. Boynton, Samuel C. Patterson, and Ronald D. Hedlund, "The Missing Links in Legislative Politics: Attentive Constituents," *Journal of Politics* 31, no. 3 (August 1969): 700–721.

33. Erikson, "The Relationship Between Public Opinion and State Policy," pp. 25–37.

34. See Weissberg, *Public Opinion and Popular Government,* pp. 159–162.

35. Between 1965 and 1985, USW membership dropped 485,000, from 1,062,000 to 577,000, and UAW membership dropped 176,000, from 1,150,000 to 974,000. See *New York Times,* October 27, 1985, p. 4E.

36. Jack Barbash, "Trade Unionism from Roosevelt to Reagan," *The Annals of the American Academy of Political and Social Science,* no. 473 (May 1984): 21.

37. Arthur R. Schwartz and Michele M. Hoyman, "The Changing of the Guard: The New American Labor Leader," *The Annals of the American Academy of Political and Social Science,* no. 473 (May 1984): 64–75.

38. Barbash, "Trade Unionism from Roosevelt to Reagan," p. 18.

39. Wendell M. Bedichek and Neal Tannahill, *Public Policy in Texas* (Glenview, Ill.: Scott Foresman and Co., 1982), p. 141.

40. Candace Romig, "Placing Limits on PACs," *State Legislatures* 10, no. 1 (January 1984): 22.

41. See Theodore J. Lowi, *The End of Liberalism: Ideology, Policy and the Crisis of Public Authority* (New York: Norton, 1969).

42. See Edward F. Cooke, "Research: An Instrument of Power," *Political Science Quarterly* 76 (March 1961): 69–87; Ted Kolderie and Paul Gilje, "The Citizens League," *National Civic Review* 65, no. 7 (July 1976): 322–342.

43. See Lester Milbrath, *The Washington Lobbyists* (Chicago: Rand McNally, 1973), pp. 241–243.

44. Paul Simon, "The Illinois Legislature: A Study in Corruption," *Harper's Magazine,* September 1964, p. 78.

45. Michael J. Ross, *California: Its Government and Politics* (North Scituate, Mass.: Duxbury Press, 1979), p. 66.

46. L. Harmon Zeigler and Michael A. Baer, *Lobbying: Interaction and Influence in American State Legislatures* (Belmont, Calif.: Wadsworth, 1969), p. 61.

47. L. Harmon Zeigler and Harvey J. Tucker, *The Quest for Responsive Government: An Introduction to State and Local Politics* (North Scituate, Mass.: Duxbury Press, 1978), p. 117.

48. See L. Harmon Zeigler, *Interest Groups in American Society* (Englewood Cliffs, N.J.: Prentice-Hall, 1964); Zeigler, *The Politics of Small Business* (Washington, D.C.: Public Affairs Press, 1961); Lester W. Milbrath, "Lobbying as a Communications Process," *Public Opinion Quarterly* 24, no. 1 (Spring 1960): 32–53; Raymond A. Bauer, Ithiel de Sola Pool, and Lewis Dexter, *American Business and Public Policy* (New York: Atherton Press, 1963).

49. L. Harmon Zeigler and Hendrik van Dalen, "Interest Groups in State Politics," in *Politics in the American States,* 3rd ed. Herbert Jacob and Kenneth Vines (Boston: Little, Brown & Co., 1976), p. 96.

50. Neal Peirce, *The Border South States* (New York: Norton, 1975), p. 154.

51. Joseph La Palombara, *Guide to Michigan Politics* (East Lansing: Michigan State University Press, 1960), p. 104.

52. See Duane Lockard, "Legislative Politics in Connecticut," *American Political Science Review* 48, no. 1 (March 1954): 166–173. Also see the description of Connecticut politics in Joyce Gelb and Marian Lief Palley, *Tradition and Change in American Party Politics* (New York: Crowell, 1975), pp. 189–192.

53. Samuel C. Patterson, "Dimensions of Voting Behavior in a One-Party Legislature," *Public Opinion Quarterly* 26, no. 2 (Summer 1962): 185–200; and Patterson, "The Role of the Lobbyist: The Case of Oklahoma," *Journal of Politics* 25, no. 1 (February 1963): 72–95.

54. See Weber and Shaffer, "Public Opinion and American State Policy Making," pp. 683–699.

55. This argument is especially made by Thomas R. Dye and L. Harmon Zeigler in their *The Irony of Democracy: An Uncommon Introduction to American Politics,* 4th ed. (North Scituate, Mass.: Duxbury Press, 1978), pp. 209–210.

56. Roberto Michels, *Political Parties: A Sociological Study of the Oligarchical Tendencies of Modern Democracy,* trans. Eden Paul and Cedar Paul (New York: Free Press, 1962).

57. Sarah McCally Morehouse, *State Politics, Parties and Policy* (New York: Holt, Rinehart & Winston, 1981), pp. 108–113, 491–492.

58. John C. Wahlke et al., *The Legislative System: Explorations in Legislative Behavior* (New York: Wiley, 1962), p. 314.

Chapter 6
Channels of Citizen Influence: The Ballot Box, Parties, and Direct Action

Chapter Preview

This chapter explores the efficacy with which various channels of citizen input enable citizens to influence the actions of state and local governments. Examined in turn are:

1. The election process.
2. Political parties.
3. Direct democracy devices, such as initiative, referendum, and recall.
4. Direct action tactics, such as protests, demonstrations, and sit-ins.

Let us begin by discussing how election systems operate.

Introduction

The ultimate test of democracy is whether people can effectively influence their government through the electoral process. At the national level most people can expect to influence events only indirectly and in very small ways. Washington, for most people, is very far away. State capitols and city halls, however, are much closer. And it is at the state and local levels of government that democracy would seem to have the best prospects for success. How effective the electoral channels of influence are will be examined in this chapter.

The Ballot Box

In a representative democracy such as that in the United States, the election process is the central means by which people are expected to hold the government accountable.

How Election Systems Operate

Elections are regulated by the states and generally administered by local governments. In all states, you must meet minimal requirements in order to vote. You must be a United States citizen, eighteen years of age, and a resident of your state for a given period. Forty-nine states also require you to register in order to vote.

Except for the Nebraska Legislature and most judgeships, state elections use a partisan ballot on which the political party of each candidate is indicated near his or her name, so you know whether you are voting for a Democrat, a Republican, or a member of another party.

At the local level there is a much wider variety of election systems. In general, local election systems can be categorized as either *reformed* or *unreformed*. A **reformed election system** tends to have nonpartisan, at-large elections, which are held at times separate from state or national elections. In nonpartisan elections, the ballots do not list the party designation of the candidates. In at-large elections, city council members are elected from the entire city. They are distinguished from **ward elections** or **district elections,** in which the council members are elected from neighborhood areas usually called *wards* (sometimes *districts*). Reformed elections also protect against voter fraud by voter registration, voting machines, election judges from all parties and factions, and safeguards in counting the ballots. An **unreformed election system,** in contrast, tends to be partisan, ward rather than at-large, held at the same time as statewide elections, and lacks effective protection against voter fraud. Reformed election systems predominate in suburbs and in the Far West. Unreformed election systems predominate in the central cities of the East, the Midwest, and the South.

One consequence of reformed election systems is reduced voter turnout. Most of the reform devices slightly increase the difficulty of voting. Since nonvoting tends to be highest among the poor, one inevitable bias of reformed election systems is to reduce the influence of poor people in the election process.[1] These considerations are discussed more fully in Chapter 7.

Elections as Instruments of Accountability

Do elections hold governing officials accountable to the voters? Three general propositions can be made. First, elections in general do not give mandates; rather, they let the voters judge candidates on past performance.[2] Voters simply do not know enough about the issue positions of legislative or gubernatorial candidates to choose one set of policies over another. The winners will have to face reelection two or four years later, and at that time the voters make a retroactive judgment about whether they are dissatisfied enough to replace the incumbent.

Next, in local communities most evidence suggests that elections do not keep the officials accountable. Kenneth Prewitt interviewed over 400 city council members in the San Francisco area and discovered that most of them really did not worry about getting defeated at the polls if they angered their constituents.[3] A fourth of them got their council positions through appointment rather than election. During elections, voter turnout was so small that the average candidate could win by getting the vote from as little as 6 to 8 percent of the population. Once in office, 80 percent were reelected when they chose to run. The offices had low salaries, and few council members cared to run for higher office. In short, they were community volunteers doing a civic duty, not professional politicians attempting to build a career. We can call this phenomenon **volunteerism.** These voluntary public officials followed their own judgments and the judgments of trusted associates. Despite the election process, the council members were in practice unaccountable to the majority. Joseph Schlesinger has written, "No more irresponsible government is imaginable than one of high-minded men unconcerned for their political futures."[4] That is, the volunteer does not have to worry about displeasing the majority, because he or she has little to lose if ousted from office. Even when the volunteer is ousted, he or she is replaced by another volunteer, who also has no compelling reason to worry about majority opinion. At best the majority can hope to make its will felt only in fits and starts when voters occasionally rise in rebellion against occasional unpopular decisions. Usually, however, this occurs retroactively, as when a neighborhood group is upset by the cost of installing sewers or sidewalks or some other public amenity and votes out the local council members at the next election. By this time, however, the unpopular action has usually been accomplished and cannot be reversed. The problem of holding local elected officials accountable to the majority is also complicated by the fact that most local governments are severely constrained by state and federal regulations in what they can do (see Chapters 7 and 8).

A third generalization about elections as instruments of accountability is that government is probably much more accountable at the state level than at the local level. Although people do not follow state affairs any more closely than they follow local ones,[5] state elections have higher turnout rates than local elections, and this suggests that state officials represent a broader spectrum of the population than do local officials. State legislators, as one study found, more often share the public policy preferences of the majority of the population than do state agency heads or party leaders.[6] Since state government has more autonomy and freedom than local government has, it probably is easier for state officials than it is for local officials to respond to popular demands.

Elections as Channels of Citizen Input

Related to the question of elections as instruments of accountability is the question of whether citizens can use the election process as a means to get the government to enact favorable policies. This question is especially important for low-income people, who—as we saw in Chapter 5—have lower voter turnouts than do middle-income people. If more low-income people voted, could they get more favorable policies and programs from government?

Most research on this question is not very encouraging. The most systematic study was done by Thomas R. Dye, using data from the 1950s and 1960s.[7] Dye correlated each state's voter turnout rate with several policy outcomes, including education expenditures, welfare expenditures, and state tax revenue. Realizing that wealthier states can afford to spend more than poor states, he used statistical techniques to eliminate the effect of wealth on his findings. Dye found that increases in voter turnout have no effect on the amount of money spent on services for the poor, especially on education and welfare.

Nor does turnout appear to affect whether the state is controlled by Democrats (who presumably would be more favorable to low-income voters) or by Republicans. Raymond Wolfinger and Steven Rosenstone estimated that even if voter turnout were increased by as much as 10 percent, it would make only a marginal difference in the vote outcome for Democrats and Republicans. It would increase the net Democratic vote by only 0.3 percent.[8]

These studies suggest that the ballot box is not a very effective tool for giving people a voice in governmental policymaking. But these studies all deal with relatively small increases in voter turnout. When one looks instead at instances in which a distinctive category of people goes from practically no voter turnout to a relatively high turnout, one notices that the political system does indeed become more responsive to their concerns. Quantum leaps in voter turnout for distinct categories of people happened twice in this century—following the Nineteenth Amendment's enfranchisement of women in 1920 and following enfranchisement of racial minorities after the Voting Rights Act of 1965. Enfranchisement enabled them to take on gladiator roles (see Chapter 5) that previously had been reserved for white males. Also, in both cases, the emergence of increasing numbers of minorities and women into gladiator roles was followed by the emergence of public policies aimed at their concerns. In the case of women, this development included such issues as abortion, affirmative action programs, and antirape and anti–wife-abuse measures. In the case of minorities, we have seen the emergence of bilingual programs, affirmative action programs, and social welfare programs, because disproportionate numbers of minorities live in poverty and benefit from such programs.

In sum, the right to vote does not necessarily give a particular category of people a great deal of influence in public policymaking, but the absence of the right to vote virtually ensures that their influence will be minimal. How influential they can make their voice depends on several factors in addition to the right to vote—whether they are united, whether their leaders can mobilize them to vote, whether their leaders are effective, and whether the political system has the resources to meet their demands.

Financing State and Local Elections

It is very expensive to run for public office. A governor's race, even in a small state, can cost over $1 million, and a state legislative race could cost tens of thousands of dollars. Texas governor Bill Clements spent over $7 million in his 1978 election, and Tom Hayden spent $1.8 million winning a California legislative race in 1982.[9] As at the national level, an increasing source for campaign finance has been the political action committee, or PAC (see Chapter 5, pp. 111–112).

In the wake of the Watergate scandal in Washington (1972–1974), many states began enacting campaign finance legislation, and by 1980, forty-nine states had some campaign regulation provisions. The most common provisions are disclosure of contributors (forty-nine states) and limits on either campaign contributions or expenditures (twenty-six states). Seventeen states provide some public funding for campaigns, and twenty states give people tax checkoffs or tax deductions or credits for campaign contributions. To oversee campaign finance law, twenty-nine states have set up bipartisan election commissions, although most of these commissions are so understaffed that they have little practical ability to enforce the law.[10]

There are two essential ideas behind these elaborate provisions. First, the financial disclosure requirements are intended to let voters know if the candidates themselves have any potential conflicts of interest between their governmental responsibilities and either their sources of income or their campaign contributions. Some citizens, for example, might want to vote against candidates who get contributions from labor unions; others might want to do the opposite. In either case, campaign finance disclosure helps the voter make a more informed choice. Second, the public finance provisions are designed to give the average voter financial incentives to contribute, in the hopes that such contributions will offset the influence of contributions from PACs and wealthy individuals.

Political Parties

Whether or not elections are effective instruments of accountability depends on whether the voters are grouped together in political parties that offer clear alternatives in candidates and public policy proposals. Political parties are organizations that nominate candidates for public elective office, help those candidates win elections, and organize the government once the election is over. The political party is most accurately visualized, according to Frank Sorauf, as a **tripartite organization** composed of the party in its organization, the party in the electorate, and the party in government.[11]

Party Organization

Party organization refers to the structures and people that nominate the party's candidates for office and seek to get them elected. The party structure, or organization, is divided into semi-independent units at different levels of government (see Figure 6–1). The highest levels have traditionally exerted very little influence over the lower levels. The national convention's authority over the lower levels is limited to setting its own rules for seating each state's delegates. If two competing delegations both demand to be seated, the national convention must decide which delegation is legitimate.

Figure 6–1. Political Party Organization

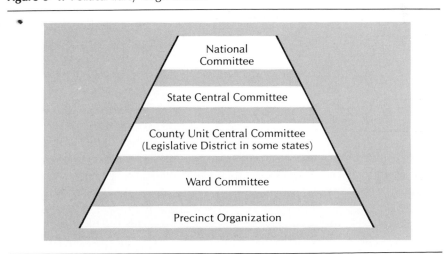

You Decide
What Would It Take to Get You to Contribute?

The integrity of the democratic process is undermined to the extent that campaign finance is left to wealthy individuals, interest groups, and political action committees. Few Americans ever contribute to political campaigns. The democratic process in most states would probably be healthier if more people contributed or if there were a broader base of contributions. As a student you may not have the spare funds now to contribute to political causes. But a few years after graduation your finances will stabilize, and you will find yourself with the discretionary income to support causes and candidates. Listed below are several steps proposed by various groups to encourage a broader range of participation in campaign finance. Assuming you had an extra hundred dollars, above and beyond your normal spending needs, what would it take to get you to contribute half of that $100 to a political campaign for a candidate or party of your choice?

	Yes	No
1. No special incentive needed. I would willingly contribute.	☐	☐

Rationale: _____

_____

| 2. A state tax credit for one-half the contribution, so that the $50 contribution would actually only cost me $25. | ☐ | ☐ |

Rationale: _____

_____

| 3. A state tax credit for one-half the contribution and an additional federal tax credit for the other half so that the $50 contribution would actually cost me zero. | ☐ | ☐ |

Rationale: _____

_____

| 4. I would not contribute $50, but I would willingly earmark $1 of my state income tax refund to a public campaign fund distributed to the candidates of my party. | ☐ | ☐ |

Rationale: _____

_____

5. I would not contribute $50 or earmark $1 of my state income tax refund for candidates of a particular party, but I would willingly earmark $1 of my state income tax refund to a public campaign fund distributed equally to all candidates of all parties.   ☐   ☐

   Rationale: _____

   _____

6. I would not make any of the above contributions, but I would support tax dollars from the general fund to being spent on public funding of campaigns, with equal amounts going to all candidates for the office. To hold down the number of frivolous candidacies, candidates would have to get a minimum percentage of the vote.   ☐   ☐

   Rationale: _____

   _____

7. None of the above tax concessions or public funding proposals appeal to me, but I would contribute if it were likely to lead to an appointment to some public advisory commission for me.   ☐   ☐

   Rationale: _____

   _____

8. I would not contribute the $50, and I would not support any of the public funding or tax incentives listed.   ☐   ☐

   Rationale: _____

   _____

Having decided what incentives, if any, would be needed to get you to contribute under these ideal conditions in which you had a spare $100, what percentage of the people in your state do you think would support each of the eight options? What percentage of your classmates? How many of the options exist in your state? What are some of the advantages and disadvantages of each option?

The leading party organization officials are the state and the county chairpersons. Despite negative stereotypes of political party leaders, state chairpersons are successful, well-educated people who often are attracted to politics because of their philosophical and ideological concerns. They administer the party organization and promote the party image.[12] If the state chairperson is the most significant party official, the county (legislative district in some states) is probably the most important level of party organization.

The precinct is the basic level of political organization. There is one precinct for each polling place. The precinct chairperson's job is to keep a list of all voters in the precinct, to identify which ones are Republicans, Democrats, or Independents, and to get the voters from his or her party to the polls on election day. The precinct chairperson is normally elected at the precinct caucus or mass meeting. In strong machine cities, he or she is appointed by the ward leader.

Within these general patterns of political party organization there is considerable variation from state to state. Malcolm E. Jewell and David M. Olson have identified three different patterns of party organization: a cohesive state party organization, a bifactional pattern of organization, and a multifactional pattern.[13] The cohesive pattern of party organization exists where a strong leader (such as former New York Republican governor Nelson Rockefeller [1955–1975]) pulls the disparate factions of the party together into a well-functioning unit. More common, however, are the bifactional and multifactional patterns. An example of a bifactional party is the Michigan Democratic Party from the 1940s to the 1960s, which was split between organized labor and middle-class liberals. Examples of multifactional parties include both the Democrats and the Republicans of California, in which the influences of volunteer groups, ideological groups, and multiple candidacies have prevented a cohesive party organization from developing. The California Republican Party, for example, is divided among the conservative California Republican Assembly, the more conservative United Republicans of California, and the moderate California Republican League.[14]

Nominating Candidates

The main task of the party organization is to nominate candidates for public office. Candidates are nominated through a combination of conventions and primary elections. The **nominating convention** is usually dominated by party activists, and it endorses candidates for the party nomination. In most states, however, the official nomination comes not from the convention but from the primary election. If no candidate gets enough votes to win endorsement at the convention or if the losing candidate at the convention thinks he or she can do better in the primary, then a **primary election** will be held to determine the nominee. Connecticut has a **challenge primary.**

The losing candidate at the convention can challenge the winner to a primary election only if the loser received at least 20 percent of the vote. Primaries may be open or closed. In the **closed primary,** only identifiable party sup-porters may vote. That is, to vote in the Republican primary, a person must present evidence that he or she is Republican. In the **open primary** anyone can vote, regardless of party affiliation. The open primary is greatly frowned upon by party leaders because it allows members of one party to cross over and vote for the weakest candidates in the other party's primary.[15] The open primary was given a boost in 1986 when the Supreme Court struck down state laws requiring a closed primary.[16] The Republican Party of Connecticut had wanted to allow Independents to vote in its primary elections but had been prevented from doing so by that state's closed primary law. Although thirty-six other states had similar laws, it is not clear yet how many state parties will follow the example of Connecticut Republicans and try to draw Independents into their primaries.

Electing the Party Nominees

The main value of the party to the nominated candidate is the party label. For all practical purposes one cannot get elected to the governorship or the state legislature (except in Nebraska) unless one has been nominated by the Republican or Democratic party.

Whether the party organization will contribute much assistance beyond the party nomination varies greatly from state to state, depending on the strength or weakness of the state party system. Historically, the parties contributed a great deal, especially where the **political machines** dominated electoral politics, as under Chicago's legendary Mayor Richard J. Daley from 1955–1976. The key to the Chicago machine was the Cook County Democratic Central Committee, which controlled nominations by endorsing a slate of organization candidates to run in the primary elections. Since thousands of city workers would lose their patronage jobs if their precincts failed to deliver enough votes for the party slate, those employees always canvassed their precincts thoroughly. With all those workers, the party slate seldom lost its primary contests. Mayor Daley, the Central Committee chairman, personally approved all persons put on the party slate and all significant patronage appointments. Nobody stayed on Chicago's payroll if Mayor Daley wanted him or her out. With his tight reign over Chicago's Democrats, Daley con-trolled the City Council plus a substantial block of votes in the state capitol and in Congress. Since Daley's death in 1976, the Chicago machine has gone through successive battles for control, which have left it fragmented.

In contrast to Mayor Daley's hold over Chicago, nobody controls the political parties in California. In that state, the parties have been deliberately weakened. Early in the twentieth century California's government was dominated by the Southern Pacific Railroad. Hiram Johnson, elected governor in 1910 as a Progressive Republican, sought to break the ties between the government, the Southern Pacific Railroad, and both political parties. While governor he pushed through a series of progressive reforms including the initiative, referendum, recall, the direct primary, the short ballot, and nonpartisanship.

California deliberately weakened the parties by establishing open primaries and putting restrictions on the party organizations. The formal party organizations were not allowed to endorse, raise money for, or campaign for candidates. As a result, the party activists formed extralegal clubs to perform these campaign functions unofficially. Some of these reforms, such as cross-filing, were later undone, but the net effects weakened the parties permanently, strengthened the role of special interest groups in endorsing and financing candidates, and put a premium on modern campaign tools such as television.[17]

Until recently, the role of the political parties in running elections was much closer to the California weak-party model than to Chicago's former strong-machine model. One of the major reasons for this is the rising importance of television, polling, and computers in the conduct of election campaigns. For a statewide race, or even a mayoral race in a big city, the most effective campaign techniques are television appearances, imaginative advertising in the media, favorable endorsements by influential interest groups, and computerized information banks for direct mailings to target groups. Old-fashioned political parties usually lack the expertise and skills needed to conduct television-oriented races of this sort, and this lack of expertise among party leaders created an opportunity for campaign management firms to provide election services to candidates on a fee basis. To a great extent these firms displaced the parties as campaign managers, since the firms provide "all of the campaign services which could be provided by a party organization: fundraising, voter communication, scheduling, campaign events and appearances, voter canvassing and polling, and election-day staffing of polling places."[18] The growth in importance of the campaign management firms has been accompanied by a corresponding weakening of the role of the party in getting party nominees elected.

In the 1980s, however, political parties have become much stronger organizationally than they were a decade earlier.[19] A majority of state party organizations now provide financial assistance to candidates, help in polling, media consultation, and campaign seminars.[20] The Republicans in general are much better organized at these activities than are the Democrats.

The Party in the Electorate and the Party in Government

The party in the electorate refers to the mass of people who identify themselves regularly as Republicans or Democrats. We can make three generalizations about the party in the electorate. First, partisan attachment differs from region to region. Two-party competition is the strongest in the Northeast, the Midwest, and the Far West. Although Democrats have traditionally dominated the South, that region is becoming increasingly competitive, with white anti–civil rights activists turning to the Republican Party and a black–white coalition emerging in the Democratic Party.[21] Republicans have an edge in the northern New England states[22] and in four western states.

Second, party attachment varies by social class, religious affiliation, and ethnic origin. Table 6–1 shows that in each socioeconomic category the upper-status people are more likely to be Republicans. Blacks, Jews, and Catholics are more likely to be Democrats. Whites and Protestants are more likely to be Republicans.

Third, over time the trend has been away from strong party identification and toward independence (Figure 6–2). In 1960 only 23 percent of the people identified themselves as political independents; by 1986 this had grown to 29

Table 6–1. The Social Basis of Partisanship (1985)

	Percent Republican	Percent Democrat	Percent Independent
Education			
College	37%	33%	30%
High school	30	36	33
Grade school	25	50	25
Income			
$50,000 and over	46	25	29
25,000–49,999	30	37	32
15,000–24,999	31	40	29
10,000–14,999	28	40	32
under $10,000	23	47	30
Race			
White	34	35	31
Black	3	73	24
Religion			
Protestant	34	39	27
Catholic	25	43	33
Jewish	22	47	31

Source: James Allen Davis, *General Social Surveys, 1972–1985.* [machine-readable data file]. Principal Investigator, James A. Davis; Senior Study Director, Tom W. Smith. Chicago: National Opinion Research Center, producer, 1985; Storrs, Conn.: Roper Public Opinion Research Center, University of Connecticut, distributor.

percent. The trend toward independence is particularly strong among the young, suggesting that Democrats and Republicans are likely to continue losing party identifiers.[23] A peculiar variation of the move to partisan independence has been the emergence of dual partisan identification in the South. Charles Hadley surveyed Louisiana state convention delegates in 1982 and 1983 and found that nearly one out of five viewed themselves as belonging to one particular party at the state level and not belonging to it at the national level.[24] Finally, Figure 6–2 also shows that the Reagan years have enabled the Republican Party to make significant inroads in the Democrat's long-standing status as majority party.

The last component of the tripartite political party is the *party in government,* which refers to the public officeholders such as governors and legislators. The division of state government into Democrat and Republican control raises two important questions: Does it make any difference in policy outcomes whether strong competition exists between the parties? Does it matter which party controls the government?

Two-Party Competition: Does It Make Any Difference?

According to American democratic theory, strong two-party competition ensures that the parties will be responsive to the needs of the majority of the voters. V. O. Key argued also that the parties' attempts to satisfy constituent

Figure 6–2. The Decline of Party Identification

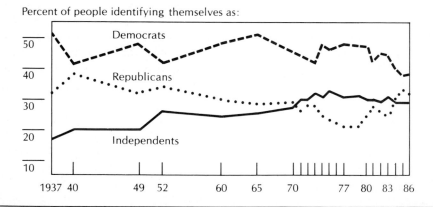

Source: The Gallup Poll: Public Opinion 1981 (Wilmington, Del.: Scholarly Resources, Inc., 1982), p. 128; *The Gallup Report,* no. 250 (July 1986), p. 21.

needs would force the states with competitive parties to give more generous benefits than the states that lacked competitive parties.[25]

Contemporary political scientists have invested enormous time and energy studying whether two-party competition leads to more generous government benefits. By comparing the level of government benefits provided by the competitive and the one-party states, two generalizations about competition and government benefits can be made. First, interparty competition is firmly based in the socioeconomic, regional, and organizational characteristics of a state. With few exceptions, two-party competition is the keenest in states that have large populations, high educational levels, substantial socioeconomic diversity, and strong political party organizations. With few exceptions the one-party states tend to lack these characteristics.[26] Second, the two-party states provide more generous welfare benefits and educational benefits than do the one-party states. Early studies, especially those of Thomas R. Dye, attributed this to the greater wealth of the competitive states, not to their greater competitiveness.[27] More recent studies, however, have used increasingly sophisticated statistical tests and discovered that competition, especially when combined with high turnouts, did have an effect on education and welfare expenditures.[28]

Democrats or Republicans: Does It Make Any Difference?

Does it matter which party controls a state? In most states, the answer to that question clearly is yes! Two important differences exist between the parties. In many states the party leaders differ sharply in ideology. A survey of Republican and Democratic delegates to the national conventions found that the party leaders differed from each other much more than did the party supporters. The Democratic voters were just slightly liberal, and the Republican voters just slightly conservative. In contrast, the Democratic leaders were very liberal, and the Republican leaders very conservative.[29] Even in a state such as Indiana, where political struggles are renowned for their lack of ideological content, researchers found sharp ideological differences between Republican leaders and Democratic leaders on issues such as support for prayer in public schools, lotteries, abortion, and nuclear power plants.[30]

Second, because Democratic leaders differ sharply from Republican leaders on issues and because Democrats draw their voting strength from different social groups than do Republicans (see Table 6–1), it is plausible to hypothesize that when Democrats control a state they will enact policies that Republicans would not enact. To some extent this hypothesis is borne out by research. Robert Erikson traced the enactment of civil rights legislation outside the South.[31] He discovered that civil rights laws were three times as likely to get passed when the Democrats controlled the legislature as when it was

There is no doubt that this initiative has forced California government to become more responsive to an important segment of its citizens who had tired of increasing taxes to pay for increasing services. But the initiative process introduces an element of political instability. Two prominent scholars of the American legislative process charged that the initiative and referendum "encroach upon legislative authority, and that occasionally they lead to legislative timidity and irresponsibility. Manifestly, they add nothing to legislative initiative or autonomy."[40]

For these reasons, direct legislation is viewed negatively by most political scientists. From his research on referenda in Toledo, Ohio, Howard Hamilton asserts that direct democracy is governance by an active minority and that "minority may be far from a mirror image of the populace."[41] There is no way to balance the intense wishes of a minority with the less intense wishes of the

Highlight
Direct Democracy in Practice

Direct democracy is a two-edged sword that can have either liberal or conservative outcomes:

Liberal Outcomes	*Conservative Outcomes*
In 1986 voters in Massachusetts, Oregon, and Rhode Island defeated measures to outlaw abortion or to prohibit state funds for abortions.	In 1986 Vermont voters rejected a state Equal Rights Amendment.
In 1982 voters in eight states passed propositions calling for a freeze in nuclear weapons possessed by the United States and the USSR.	In 1982 voters in Arizona rejected a call for a nuclear freeze.
In 1978 voters in four states refused to set tax and spending limits on their state governments.	Voters in eleven states in 1978 set tax and spending limits on their state governments.
Madison, Wisconsin, voters in 1977 recalled a judge who had made antifemale remarks during a juvenile rape case.	In 1978 voters in Miami, Saint Paul, and several other cities repealed gay rights sections of their cities' human rights ordinances.
Colorado voters in 1976 refused to repeal the state Equal Rights Amendment and the state sales tax.	Maine voters in 1977 repealed a statewide property tax distribution plan designed to equalize educational financing.

majority. The rights of minorities seem bound to suffer. Raymond Wolfinger and Fred I. Greenstein sum up the conventional wisdom on direct democracy:

> Asking voters to pass judgment on substantive policy questions strains their information and interest, leading them to decisions that may be inconsistent with their own desires. The consequence is subversion of representative government and the exercise of undue influence by groups that can afford to gather the signatures to qualify a measure for the referendum ballot and then wage a publicity campaign that will have an impact on voters.[42]

Despite these strong feelings against direct democracy, it is not likely to be dropped where it exists, and evidence suggests that it keeps political leaders in tune with the wishes of substantial portions of the population. A study of sixty years' use of the initiative in Washington State reached several positive conclusions about direct democracy. "Time and again the sponsors have been ahead of the legislature."[43] The initiative also provided some of Washington State's most exciting political battles and enhanced the citizenry's political education.

The threat of an initiative victory will often lead the legislature to adopt a compromise bill before the initiative balloting begins. In California, for exam-

. . . But for me, stuffing the ballot box is perfectly legal!

In the eyes of critics, direct democracy gives undue influence to well-organized and well-financed special interest groups, contrary to the theory that it returns influence to the average citizen.

Source: Reprinted by permission of Mike Keefe.

ple, a 1976 initiative banning nuclear power plant construction prompted the legislature to impose a temporary ban on new such construction and tighten safety restrictions on all plants.[44]

Direct Action

Direct action is not an electoral activity. Rather it is the attempt to influence public policy outcomes through the use of tactics such as citizen contacting, group protests, civil disobedience, strikes, rent strikes, sit-ins, and takeovers. These may or may not lead to violence. Some important distinctions can be made between these types of direct action. *Citizen contacting* refers to communications of demands or grievances by citizens to public officials, both elective and appointive. *Protest* occurs when a group complains about something by staging a march down a main thoroughfare, confronting a mayor in his or her office, or even passing out leaflets in a shopping center. A common protest tactic during the 1960s was for groups of blacks to gather in a mayor's office and demand more jobs for black teenagers. *Civil disobedience* occurs when someone deliberately breaks a law for the purpose of turning public opinion against that law. The most famous advocate of civil disobedience was Henry David Thoreau, who refused to pay taxes in support of the Mexican-American War and was jailed.

A *strike* occurs when a group of employees refuse to work until management agrees to collective bargaining or other demands. *Rent strike* refers to the refusal to pay rent until some grievance has been met. Tenants pay the rent to an escrow account held by an attorney until the landlord complies.

A *sit-in* is the tactic of people simply sitting in a place where they are not supposed to be until someone in charge responds to their demands. During the civil rights movement, the Student Nonviolent Coordinating Committee (SNCC) brought groups of black and white college students to lunchroom counters that were supposed to be segregated. The lunchroom business could not go on until the manager responded by serving the demonstrators or having them removed. When the demonstrators were convicted of violating the local segregation ordinances, they expanded the scope of the conflict to the federal courts, which usually declared the segregation ordinances unconstitutional.

A *takeover* is similar to a sit-in. A group simply occupies a facility and refuses to give it up. This tactic was used by some antiwar demonstrators who took over college buildings in the late 1960s. At Columbia University the demonstrators had to be removed by the New York City police.

These direct action tactics are normally used to achieve some broader goal, such as greater leverage for bargaining. This was a common objective of black protesters during the 1960s. By demonstrating in front of a city hall where they received television and newspaper attention, the black protesters made the mayors and city councils uncomfortable and forced the mayors to negotiate with the protest leaders. Without the protest pressure, black leaders often found it difficult even to get appointments with the mayor. Another common objective is to change policies. Protesters often want more minority police or firefighters hired by the city. Antiabortion advocates often demonstrate for the purpose of pressuring state legislators not to liberalize state abortion laws, and women's movement groups often demonstrate for the opposite purpose.

A Successful Example of Direct Action in Practice

The most successful use of direct action tactics came with the civil rights movement, which refers to thousands of isolated activities during the 1950s and 1960s that sought to overturn segregation laws and policies. While civil rights activities had existed for decades, they did not draw broad support from blacks and white liberals until the Montgomery bus boycott of 1955. (See Highlight on p. 146.) Encouraged by the success of Montgomery's bus boycott, black leaders organized other protest demonstrations and sit-ins that sought to desegregate other facilities, such as lunch counters, hotels, restaurants, libraries, schools, universities, rest rooms, and parks. A key strategy was expanding the scope of the conflict beyond local southern communities to the federal level, which culminated with the Civil Rights Act of 1964 and the Voting Rights Act of 1965. Perhaps the most successfully implemented feature of the 1964 act was the prohibition of racial discrimination in public accommodations, such as movies, theaters, hotels, and restaurants. The 1965 act extended the voting franchise to blacks throughout the South.

The civil rights movement did not eliminate all the inequities that blacks suffered and continue to suffer; nor did it end racial discrimination. However, it did give middle-class blacks access to the mainstream facilities and institutions in American society that previously had been closed to them. In this respect, the civil rights movement was clearly the most successful use of direct action in the history of the United States.

An Unsuccessful Example

So successful was the civil rights movement in the South that northern blacks began to apply direct action tactics to their problems. One example was the Harlem rent strikes of 1963 and 1964. While these rent strikes may seem quite dated today, they merit examination because they exemplify some inherent difficulties in protest strategies that are still relevant in the 1980s.

Many apartment buildings in Harlem were owned by absentee landlords who refused to maintain their buildings. Cockroaches and rats were common in the apartments. Ovens, plumbing, and other amenities did not work well. The apartments often did not meet the city's building codes. In an attempt to force landlords to bring their buildings up to the city's building codes, black leaders in Harlem organized a rent strike. Renters paid their rent into a fund that was to be held in escrow until the landlords made the demanded repairs.

However, few landlords made the concessions that the rent strike leaders expected. The rent strikes were hindered by severe limitations in the use of protest tactics that had not hindered the civil rights movement. Protest groups are inherently unstable and difficult to keep together. To get the attention of the mass media, rent strike leaders would overstate their strengths and accomplishments, then lose credibility with reporters when they were unable to back up the statements and claims they made. For the protests to be successful, leaders had to capture the sympathy and the financial support of third parties, particularly white liberals. This often meant the protest leaders had to moderate their position or make compromises, which lost them the support of their followers. In the Harlem rent strikes of 1963 and 1964, government officials and slum landlords used delaying tactics and waited for the indignation aroused by reporting of slum conditions to wane. When public interest declined, the rent strike coalition collapsed.[45]

Highlight
The Montgomery Bus Boycott

A critical point in the civil rights movement came late on an afternoon in 1955 when a black domestic maid, Rosa Parks, sat down in the front of a bus in Montgomery, Alabama. A Montgomery ordinance, typical of other ordinances throughout the South, specified that blacks could sit only at the back of the bus. But the back seats were full that day, so Rosa Parks would have to stand if she moved to the rear of the bus. She later stated that she had no intention of starting a bus boycott; she was simply too tired to ride home standing up. So she refused to move and was arrested.

The plight of Rosa Parks captured the imagination of Montgomery blacks who began protesting against the arrest and the rear-of-the-bus rule. They joined a well-organized boycott designed to get the bus company to change its policy. A key figure in the boycott was a young minister, Martin Luther King, Jr., who led much of the protest activity and went to jail himself for his demonstrations. Not only did the boycott get the company policy changed, the litigation following the boycott resulted in a federal court decision declaring all such bus segregation unconstitutional.

Source: Gayle v. Browder, 352 U.S. 903 (1956).

Some Criteria for Successful Direct Action

Why was direct action so successful in the civil rights movement in the South and so unsuccessful in the Harlem rent strikes only a few years later? The Harlem rent strikes and many other northern protest activities lacked several of the conditions present in the successful civil rights movement in the South. Whereas it had proved impossible in the South for authorities to ignore the lunchroom demonstrators, New York City authorities did eventually find it possible to ignore the rent strikers in Harlem. Further, whereas the southern authorities responded brutally and gained public sympathy for the demonstrators, New York housing officials responded in another way: They listened politely to the demonstrators while delaying the issue, and eventually the demonstrators got discouraged at their lack of progress.

Compounding the difficulty of the Harlem rent strikers was the lack of a clear remedy for the city's housing problem. In the South the response had been reversal of the segregation statutes. In Harlem there were no segregation statutes; the problem was more complicated. Many of Harlem's apartment buildings were old and would require considerable investment to rehabilitate them. This rehabilitation was discouraged by the city's rent controls, which prevented the landlords from raising the rents high enough to recover their investment in rehabilitation. Even in cities without rent controls, slum landlords rarely fixed their buildings, for it was frequently cheaper to abandon the buildings than to fix them.

A final difference between the southern civil rights movement and the Harlem rent strikes was the failure of the rent strikers to expand the scope of their conflict to the federal courts and to Congress. Segregation statutes violate the United States Constitution; footdragging in the implementation of building codes does not raise a constitutional issue. Without a constitutional issue, the Supreme Court is unlikely to take jurisdiction over a local conflict.

What Does Direct Action Accomplish?

Two strong proponents of the notion that direct action forces governments to respond in some way to the grievances of the protesters are Frances Fox Piven and Richard Cloward.[46] Although a specific protest action may not lead to a specific policy change, Piven and Cloward argue, the repeated use of direct action tactics during the 1930s and the 1960s definitely produced policy benefits for working-class and poor people. During the 1930s, the policy benefits for working-class people centered around organized labor. The National Labor Relations Act of 1935 forced employers to bargain collectively with unions and to refrain from certain strikebreaking tactics. The

1930s also saw the introduction of a number of other labor programs, such as unemployment compensation and workers' compensation. During the 1960s, the policy benefits for the poor were AFDC, Food Stamps, Medicaid and health care, poverty programs, and a broad increase in the number of programs targeted at poor people.

Piven and Cloward argue that when the fear of lower-class insurrection passed, the political system once again contracted. Although the 1930s saw the federal government protect union-organizing activities, the next two decades saw numerous attempts to restrict the influence of unions. The 1960s saw a broad expansion in federal programs for the poor, but the early 1970s saw the Model Cities program, the Office of Economic Opportunity, and several other innovations of the poverty program either discontinued or substantially cut back. In the view of Piven and Cloward, this historical record is evidence that governments expand benefits to lower-class people when those people use direct action to threaten rebellion, and governments restrict benefits when those people become peaceful.

Whether direct action is really as effective as Piven and Cloward believe is debatable. Arguing from historical trends is always dangerous. One could also use historical developments to argue that the most notable consequence of direct action such as the Irish draft riots, the ghetto revolts of the 1960s, or the labor disturbances of the early twentieth century was the direct, violent, and deadly repression of the participants.

In many respects the most notable beneficiaries of direct action have not been the poor, but the upwardly mobile middle class. The civil rights movement was led by the black middle class, which derived most of the benefits from civil rights legislation. Benefits gained by labor strikes primarily go to people who already have jobs, and most of those people are above the poverty class.

Perhaps the most serious shortcoming of direct action tactics is their failure to lead to the creation of permanent institutions to represent the interests of the protesters. The most successful transition from direct action tactics to institution-building occurred in organized labor. What began as movements by militant agitators during the 1880s was transformed in the 1930s into organized labor unions, which are officially recognized by the government and have the legal right to bargain collectively and to strike.

Most direct action movements, however, have not transformed themselves into permanent institutions, and this is especially true of the civil rights movement. After the Civil Rights Act of 1964 and the Voting Rights Act of 1965 were passed by Congress, most of the established civil rights organizations declined in membership and political impact.[47] The success of the civil rights movement and the growing voting power of blacks had broadened the political horizons of all black leaders. Middle-class blacks gained many new opportunities that they never had before; they could become business executives, mayors, congressmen, academics, or anything else that was open to white middle-class people. But no permanent institutions were created to represent the economic interests of lower-class blacks the way that labor unions represent the economic interests of their members.

Conclusion

One theme that has pervaded the past two chapters has been that state and local governments are more responsive to established institutions and to special interests than they are to the public interest, to the interests of isolated citizens who are unrepresented by existing institutions, or to the poorest part of the population. The conventional channels of citizen influence (public opinion, elections, political parties, and interest groups) tend to be dominated by large, economic-based institutions. These channels of citizen influence also are more capable of communicating middle-class concerns to the government than of transmitting concerns of either the poor or isolated individuals who do not speak for some specific interest.

In contrast to these conventional channels of political influence, the 1960s and 1970s saw significant use of the more unconventional tactics of direct action and independent political action. Many of the tactics of direct action and independent political action seem to depend on face-to-face contacts and the mass mobilization of people in relatively small communities, such as in a business establishment, a small town, a suburb, or a big-city neighborhood. Because these tactics seem most appropriate for community-level politics, we need to make a closer examination of such politics. Chapter 7 will examine the institutions of local government, and Chapter 8 will look into the dynamics of community politics.

Summary

1. The election process is the most fundamental institution of democracy. However, elections were found to be very limited channels for citizen input to public policy for several reasons. Elections do not give mandates. At the local level, elected officials are not greatly concerned with the opinions of the mass of the electorate, since reelection is not a worry.

2. Political parties play roles in nominating candidates to office and in organizing the government once the election is over. The parties tend to be decentralized organizations with the strongest units at the county and state

legislative district levels. Recent years have seen a decline in people's tendency to identify as strong Democrats or strong Republicans. Despite these declines, recent scholarship attributes more importance to interparty competition than was thought a decade earlier. The thrust of policymaking, as well, will depend on whether a state is controlled by the Republicans or the Democrats.

3. Direct democracy refers to the initiative, referendum, and recall. These controversial practices are most popular in the West. They can be used for either liberal or conservative causes.

4. Direct action strategies were extremely successful during the civil rights movement of the 1950s and 1960s. They have had more limited success, however, in trying to combat such complicated urban problems as slum housing. To be successful, direct action requires excellent leadership, sympathetic outsider political actors in the press and in government, and an ability to expand the scope of the conflict beyond the local level to the state and national levels.

Key Terms

Challenge primary A primary election held only if the candidates receives a show of support in their party's nominating convention.

Closed primary A primary election in which only identifiable party supporters may vote. Only Republicans may vote in the Republican primary, and only Democrats may vote in the Democratic primary.

Direct action Refers to such tactics to influence public policy as group protests, civil disobedience, strikes, and sit-ins.

Direct democracy Refers to the initiative, referendum, and recall.

District election See *Ward election*.

Initiative A device that lets voters draft legislative proposals and, if they gather enough petition signatures, put their proposals on a ballot, where they can be decided directly by the people.

Nominating convention A political party's convention for nominating candidates for public office.

Open primary A primary election in which anyone can vote, regardless of party affiliation.

Political machine A tightly knit party organization that controls the party's nominations for public office and controls many patronage jobs.

Primary election An election held to choose nominees to compete for public office in the general election.

Recall A device that allows voters to remove from office an official who has invoked popular displeasure before his or her term ends.

✗ **Referendum** A device for letting the voters decide whether a law just passed by a legislature should be repealed. Also a device for letting voters decide to approve municipal bond issues or to amend the constitution of a state.

Reformed election system A system characterized by nonpartisan, at-large elections.

Tripartite organization The concept of the political party as composed of three components: the party organization, the party in the electorate, and the party in government.

Unreformed election system A system characterized by partisan, ward elections.

Volunteerism A concept used to refer to elected officials who look on themselves as community volunteers doing a civic duty rather than as professional politicians attempting to build a career. Common among suburban local officials.

Ward election An election in which city council members are elected from neighborhood units called wards or districts.

References

1. For further discussion of this point, see John J. Harrigan, *Political Change in the Metropolis,* 3rd ed. (Boston: Little, Brown & Co., 1985), Ch. 4.

2. Gerald Pomper, *Elections in America: Control and Influence in Democratic Politics* (New York: Dodd, Mead, 1968), pp. 254–255.

3. Kenneth Prewitt, "Political Ambitions, Volunteerism, and Electoral Accountability," *American Political Science Review* 64, no. 1 (March 1970): 5–17.

4. Joseph A. Schlesinger, *Ambition and Politics* (Chicago: Rand McNally, 1966), p. 2.

5. M. Kent Jennings and Harmon Zeigler, "The Salience of American State Politics," *American Political Science Review* 64, no. 2 (June 1970): 523–535.

6. Eric M. Uslaner and Ronald E. Weber, "Representing People Who Have Interests" (Paper delivered at the annual conference of the Midwest Political Science Association, Chicago, Ill., April 24–26, 1980), pp. 19–20. Also see Uslaner and Weber, "U.S. State Legislators' Opinions and Perceptions of Constituency Attitudes," *Legislative Studies Quarterly* 4 (November 1979): 563–585.

7. Thomas R. Dye, *Politics, Economics, and the Public: Policy Outcomes in the American States* (Chicago: Rand McNally, 1966), pp. 260–270.

8. Raymond E. Wolfinger and Steven J. Rosenstone, *Who Votes?* (New Haven, Conn.: Yale University Press, 1980), p. 85.

9. Edward C. Olson, "Political Reform in Texas: Big Money Still Talks," in *Practicing Texas Politics,* 5th ed. Eugene W. Jones, Joe E. Ericson, Lyle C. Brown, and Robert S. Trotter, Jr., eds. (Boston: Houghton Mifflin Co., 1983), p. 136; Terry Christensen and Larry N. Gerston, *The California Connection: Politics in the Golden State* (Boston: Little, Brown & Co., 1984), pp. 33–37.

10. Herbert E. Alexander, *Financing Politics: Money, Elections, and Political Reform,* 2nd ed. (Washington, D.C.: Congressional Quarterly Press, 1980), pp. 127–144.

11. Frank J. Sorauf, *Party Politics in America,* 4th ed. (Boston: Little, Brown & Co., 1980), pp. 8–10.

12. Charles W. Wiggins and William L. Turk, "State Party Chairmen: A Profile," *Western Political Quarterly* 23, no. 2 (June 1970): 321–332.

13. Malcolm E. Jewell and David M. Olson, *American State Political Parties and Elections* (Homewood, Ill.: Dorsey Press, 1982), pp. 58–61.

14. Bernard L. Hyink, Seyom Brown, and Ernest W. Thacker, *Politics and Government in California* (New York: Harper & Row, 1985), pp. 52–54.

15. How extensive such party crossover voting is, however, is not really known. One study of presidential primaries in Wisconsin from 1968–1984 estimated such partisan crossover to be no more than 11 percent of the voters. More numerous were Independents who voted in Republican or Democratic primaries (about 34 to 39 percent of the total). The overwhelming majority of primary election voters were people who belonged to the party in whose primary they were voting. See Ronald D. Hedlund and Meredith W. Watts, "The Wisconsin Open Primary: 1968–1984," *American Politics Quarterly* 14, nos. 1 and 2 (January–April 1986): 55–74.

16. *Tashjian v. Republican Party of Connecticut* 107 S.Ct. 544 (1986).

17. On California politics, see Bernard L. Hyink, Seyom Brown, and Ernest W. Thacker, *Politics and Government in California,* 11th ed. (New York: Harper & Row, 1985), pp. 81–83.

18. Jewell and Olson, *American State Political Parties and Elections,* p. 181.

19. James L. Gibson, Cornelius P. Cotter, John F. Bibby, and Robert J. Huckshorn, "Assessing Party Organizational Strength," *American Journal of Political Science* 27, no. 2 (May 1983): 193–222.

20. Timothy Conlan, Ann Martino, and Robert Dilger, "State Parties in the 1980s: Adaptation, Resurgence and Continuing Constraints," *Intergovernmental Perspective* 10, no. 4 (Fall 1984): 6–13.

21. See Alexander P. Lamis, *The Two-Party South* (New York: Oxford University Press, 1984).

22. William Doyle and Josephine F. Milburn, "Citizen Participation in New England Politics: Town Meetings, Political Parties, and Interest Groups," *New England Politics,* Josephine F. Milburn and Victoria Schuck, eds. (Cambridge, Mass.: Schenkman Publishing Co., 1981), pp. 63–64.

23. Paul R. Abramson, "Generational Changes and the Decline of Party Identification in America: 1952–1974," *American Political Science Review* 70, no. 2 (June 1976): 469–478.

24. Charles D. Hadley, "Dual Partisan Identification in the South," *Journal of Politics* 47, no. 1 (February 1985): 255–268.

25. V. O. Key, Jr., *Southern Politics in State and Nation* (New York: Knopf, 1949), Ch. 5.

26. Samuel C. Patterson and Gregory A. Caldeira, "The Etiology of Partisan Competition," *American Political Science Review* 78, no. 3 (September 1984): 691–707.

27. See especially Dye, *Politics, Economics, and the Public,* pp. 293–297; Richard E. Dawson and James A. Robinson, "Inter-Party Competition, Economic Variables, and Welfare Policies in the American States," *Journal of Politics* 25, no. 2 (May 1963): 265–289; Richard I. Hofferbert, "The Relation Between Public Policy and Some Structural and Environmental Variables in the American States," *American Political Science Review* 60, no. 1 (March 1966): 78–82.

28. Virginia Gray studied competition and policy over time and found that when the competition was unstable, two-party competition affected welfare policy outcomes. See Gray, "The Effect of Party Competition on State Policy, A Reformulation: Organizational Survival," *Polity* 7, no. 2 (Winter 1974): 248–263. Gerald C. Wright used a multiple regression of the logarithms of two-party competition and welfare expenditures and found a curvilinear rather than a linear relationship. That is, increasing the degree of competition did not affect policy outcomes until it became very competitive. Once competition approached the maximum possible level, it began to have significant effect on outcomes. See Wright, "Interparty Competition and State Welfare Policy: When a Difference Makes a Difference," *Journal of Politics* 37, no. 3 (August 1975): 796–803. Finally, Richard I. Hofferbert found that two-party competition combined with high voter turnouts produced higher expenditures for education and welfare. See Hofferbert, *The Study of Public Policy* (Indianapolis: Bobbs-Merrill, 1974), pp. 218–221.

29. Herbert McClosky, Paul J. Hoffmann, and Rosemary O'Hara, "Issue Conflict and Consensus Among Party Leaders and Followers," *American Political Science Review* 54, no. 2 (June 1960): 406–427. For a similar finding in relation to the 1980 national conventions, see *New York Times,* August 13, 1980, p. B-2.

30. Robert X. Browning and William P. Shaffer, "Leaders and Followers in a Strong Party State," a paper presented at the annual meeting of the Midwest Political Science Association, Chicago, April 10–12, 1986, pp. 10–12.

31. Robert S. Erikson, "The Relationship Between Party Control and Civil Rights Legislation in the American States," *Western Political Quarterly* 24, no. 1 (March 1971): 178–182.

32. Richard Winters, "Party Control and Policy Change," *American Journal of Political Science* 20, no. 4 (November 1976): 597–636.

33. See, for example, David S. Broder, *The Party's Over: The Failure of Politics in America* (New York: Harper & Row, 1972), pp. xxi, xxiii.

34. See especially Joseph Schlesinger's argument that the parties are being reborn in a form quite distinct from the form they held during the first half of the twentieth century. Joseph A. Schlesinger, "The New American Political Party," *American Political Science Review* 79, no. 4 (December 1985): 1152–1169.

35. Jewell and Olson, *American State Political Parties and Elections*, p. 293.

36. Timothy Conlan, Ann Martino, and Robert Dilger, "State Parties in the 1980s: Adaptation, Resurgence and Continuing Constraints," *Intergovernmental Perspective* 10, no. 4 (Fall 1984): 6–13.

37. James L. Gibson, Cornelius P. Cotter, John F. Bibby, and Robert J. Huckshorn, "Whither the Local Parties? A Cross-Sectional and Longitudinal Analysis of the Strength of Party Organizations," *American Journal of Political Science* 29, no. 1 (February 1985): 139–161.

38. Gibson et al., "Assessing Party Organizational Strength," 193–222.

39. Charles M. Price, "The Initiative: A Comparative State Analysis and Reassessment of a Western Phenomenon," *Western Political Quarterly* 28, no. 2 (June 1975): 243–262.

40. William J. Keefe and Morris S. Ogul, *The American Legislative Process: Congress and the States,* 3rd ed. (Englewood Cliffs, N.J.: Prentice-Hall, 1973), p. 258.

41. Howard D. Hamilton, "Direct Legislation: Some Implications of Open Housing Referenda," *American Political Science Review* 64, no. 1 (March 1970): 127, 131.

42. Raymond E. Wolfinger and Fred I. Greenstein, "The Repeal of Fair Housing in California: An Analysis of Referendum Voting," *American Political Science Review* 62, no. 3 (September 1968): 787.

43. Quoted in Hugh A. Bone and Robert C. Benedict, "Perspectives on Direct Legislation: Washington State's Experience: 1914–1973," *Western Political Quarterly* 28, no. 2 (June 1975): 347.

44. Gladwin Hill, "Initiatives: A Score Card," *Working Papers for a New Society* 4, no. 4 (Winter 1977): 33–37.

45. See Michael Lipsky, *Protest in City Politics: Rent Strikes, Housing and the Power of the Poor* (Chicago: Rand McNally, 1970), especially pp. 163–185.

46. Frances Fox Piven and Richard A. Cloward, *Regulating the Poor: The Functions of Public Welfare* (New York: Random House, 1971).

47. On the decline of black civil rights interest groups since 1965, see Hanes Walton, Jr., *Black Politics: A Theoretical and Structural Analysis* (New York: Lippincott, 1972), pp. 140–160.

Chapter 7
The Institutions of Local Government

Chapter Preview

To understand how state and local governments affect our lives, we need to understand how local government is organized, why it is organized the way it is, and the biases inherent in its organization. We will cover these topics in this chapter by examining:

1. The different types of local governments and the functions they perform.
2. How cities and counties are organized.
3. How machine-style politics came to dominate cities in the nineteenth century but has faded since mid-twentieth century.
4. How reform-style politics emerged as a reaction to machine-style politics, and how reform-style politics has biases of its own.
5. How the metropolitan challenge has been confronted.

Let us begin with an overview of the types of local governments in the United States.

Introduction

Chapters 7 and 8 examine community politics. Chapter 7 will observe the institutions of local government, and Chapter 8, the dynamics of community politics. In discussing community political institutions, we need to focus on (1) the different types of local government, (2) county and city organization, (3) the evolution of reform-style local government, and (4) the metropolitan challenge.

Different Types of Local Government

Local government structure is much more complicated than state government structure. Whereas the fifty states all have very similar constitutions, the 80,000 local governments have an array of structures. Some local governments (counties, municipalities, towns, and townships) have a general purpose and perform a variety of governmental functions. Others (school districts and special districts) have a single purpose and perform only one function.

Single-Purpose Local Governments

The two single-purpose local governments are the **school district** and the special district. The sevenfold decline in the number of school districts since 1942 has been a result of the movement to consolidate school districts. School districts have been pressed to provide new educational services, costly laboratories, and expensive athletic equipment. Small rural school districts often cannot afford these services, and several small districts may find themselves pressured to consolidate into one large district. The trend of school district consolidation, however, appears to have ended between 1977 and 1982, as Table 7–1 shows.

The number of nonschool, single-purpose special districts has more than doubled in the past thirty years. A **special district** is a government that provides a single service. In rural areas, for example, farmers may need a project to conserve soil so that the top soil does not blow away. The affected areas, however, may cross county lines, so that no single county or township can take effective action. To remedy this, the state legislature may create a special district, in this case a soil conservation district, to provide the service. It is a true government, since it has its own taxing powers, its own governing officials, and its own area of jurisdiction. In urban areas, often one special district is used to provide public transit services, another to construct suburban hospitals, another to install sewer systems, another to provide water supply, and still another to handle housing and renewal activities. Another situation that often leads to the creation of special districts occurs in rapidly growing suburban areas, where sewage disposal districts are established to provide that service.

Because the need for their services is so apparent, and their mode of operation so apparently businesslike, the number of special districts has proliferated, and, as Table 7–1 shows, they are still proliferating in the 1980s. They do, however, create two serious problems—coordination and lack of accountability. Especially in metropolitan areas, where governmental coordination is important, the special districts threaten effective governance. Also, since their governing officials are more often appointed rather than elected, they are not very visible. Even when special-district officials are elected, the election turn-

Table 7–1. Number of Governments in the United States

	1942	1952	1962	1972	1977	1982
Counties	3,050	3,049	3,043	3,044	3,042	3,041
Municipalities	16,220	16,778	18,000	18,517	18,862	19,083
Townships and towns	18,919	17,202	17,142	16,991	16,822	16,748
School districts	108,579	67,346	34,678	15,781	15,174	15,032
Special districts	8,299	12,319	18,323	23,885	25,962	28,733
Total local governments	155,067	116,694	91,186	78,218	79,862	82,637
States	48	48	50	50	50	50
Federal	1	1	1	1	1	1
Total all governments	155,116	116,743	91,237	78,269	79,913	82,688

Source: Bureau of the Census, *Statistical Abstract of the United States: 1982-83* (Washington, D.C.: U.S. Government Printing Office, 1982), p. 273.

Note: The growth in local governments since 1972 is accounted for by the continuing proliferation of special districts combined with a dramatic slowdown in the rate of school district consolidations.

outs are pitifully low. In some instances, the elections have not been held because nobody knew when they were scheduled or because nobody ran.[1] For all of these reasons, special districts, in principle, present serious problems of accountability. Political reformers favor the consolidation of school districts, but they oppose the continuing growth in special districts.[2]

General-Purpose Local Governments

The general-purpose local governments are counties, municipalities, towns, townships, and villages. Although they are labeled as general-purpose governments, they are not general purpose in the same sense that the state is a general-purpose government. They are much more limited in what they can do, and their grants of authority are much more specific.

The **county** is the basic administrative subdivision of the state, and its existence is often specified in the state constitution. It is responsible in most states for the local administration of some state services, including law enforcement, justice, welfare, roads, agricultural extension services, and, in some states, education. As a form of government, the county is strongest in the South and Southwest, where the rural character, low population density, and the more elitist nature of local politics facilitated a form of government that covered large geographic areas and required less concentration of authority. Authority was dispersed through a large number of administrative agencies that had little to do with one another. There was little coordination among the county highway department, the county welfare department, and the county courts. Patronage was widespread, and the legislative board of commissioners made little attempt to control the departments.

Although this form of government has worked well in rural settings, it does not work well in metropolitan areas. Of the 3,041 counties, over 700 are now in metropolitan areas.[3] In these areas the county governments not only serve as an arm of the states, as mentioned above, but they also find themselves providing many urban services in the unincorporated suburban areas. These suburban areas contain many professional people who have been socialized into the reform mentality and who work in highly structured business corporations or other organizations. To the extent that such suburban professionals desire public services, they want them run efficiently in accord with the management principles they see in practice in their own work environments. And they often find these principles at odds with the horse-and-buggy nature of rural county government.

In New England, the **town** rather than the county has been the predominant form of local government. Towns perform many of the same functions as counties, but they govern a much smaller geographic area, usually twenty to forty square miles,[4] which encompasses both urban and rural territory. The most distinctive feature of town government is the famous town meeting. This takes place once a year when the voters meet, establish the town budget

Highlight
County Government: The Best That's Ever Been

The tension created between a rural-oriented county commissioner and a reform-oriented professional person is graphically illustrated in the following excerpts from a Texas university professor's interview with a prominent Harris County (Houston) commissioner, E. J. "Squatty" Lyons. Lyons expresses his scorn for modern techniques of public administration, from merit systems of personnel management to unity of command to home rule.

Interviewer: One of the basic principles of organizational theory is that of unity of command, that organizations should be based on a single hierarchy with one official at the top to direct and coordinate the organization's activities. Does county government need a strong executive?

Lyons: You're talking about a dictatorship.

Interviewer: Or the type of arrangement we have with the president and executive branch at the national level, or the strong mayor system that Houston has.

Lyons: It's the strong mayor system that makes Houston city government so . . . bad. You got thousands of employees and every one of them is the mayor's employee—you got dictatorship in Houston.

Interviewer: Is the county administration too politicized? Would the adoption of a civil service system lead to more professional administration?

Lyons: How can you point to a civil service as such a great thing? You've got a perfect example in the city of Houston. I mean, officials for the following year, enact ordinances, and set the town policies. The town meeting has been proclaimed as America's unique contribution to direct democracy.[5] Between town meetings, day-to-day operations are carried out by elected, part-time officials.

The **township** as a form of government exists primarily in the Midwest. Townships are primarily rural units of government. They perform at the local level many of the functions that the county performs at the countywide level. Thus a township constable performs local police functions that supplement those of the county sheriff. Local roads may be maintained by the township, whereas county roads are maintained by the county. Townships are governed by a town meeting and township officers similar to those used in the New England towns. As township territory gets invaded by growing metropolitan populations, the territory is quite often annexed to suburbs or central cities, which are better able to provide the public services that the urban populations require.

The **municipality** is the form of government in cities. Most Americans live in municipalities. Unlike the counties, which are basic subdivisions of the state, municipalities (or city governments) only come into existence when they are incorporated by a charter. The charter prescribes the basic structure of city government and outlines its powers. The city charter has been a target of the political reform movement.

---

just have one hell of a time keeping loyalty or anything else among employees.

They sit back and say kiss my foot . . . and that's the biggest fun in the world, to tell the people who are signing your paycheck to kiss my foot.

Interviewer: . . . [W]ould you favor a home-rule amendment to the constitution giving counties the authority to design their own governing structures?

Lyons: Now, people like that word *home rule* but it's a misnomer. . . . What it amounts to is boss rule. You put some big jackass up there [as county manager] who's been appointed by five or seven or nine people to run the show and the only way the taxpayer can get to that S.O.B. is to have enough influence with the majority of those who appointed him. . . . He can just ignore the individual citizen.

Interviewer: What concluding statement would you like to make on behalf of county government?

Lyons: I like county government because you can vote for or against the man responsible for the specific service. . . . You can take your blackboard government. . . . You can draw up a plan where every S.O.B. who follows it is going to be a millionaire in twenty years. But you just don't get things done drawing on blackboards. People with their blackboard governments just don't know what they're talking about. It just doesn't work that way in practice.

Source: David Fairbanks, "County Government— The Best That's Ever Been: An Interview with E. J. 'Squatty' Lyons," Eugene W. Jones, et al.: *Practicing Texas Politics*, Sixth Edition. Copyright © 1986 by Houghton Mifflin Company. Used by permission.

Local Charters

The legal authority for local governments differs fundamentally from the legal authority for states. The state governments are truly governments with general powers. The United States Constitution reserves to the states all the governmental powers not given by the Constitution exclusively to the national government or reserved exclusively to the people. Local governments, on the other hand, are creatures of the state and have only those powers that are specifically given to them by the state constitution, the state legislature, or the state charter. If a city wants to do something not specified in the charter or constitution or legislation, then the courts usually prohibit the city from action by applying **Dillon's Rule.** Dillon's Rule is named after Judge John Dillon, who established the principle of law that city governments' powers are very restricted. Cities may exercise only the powers specifically mentioned in their charter. Dillon wrote, "Any fair, reasonable, substantial doubt concerning the existence of power is resolved by the courts against the [city government], and the power is denied."[6]

The city charter spells out the precise powers that the local government possesses and determines how the government is to be organized. The charters fall into five categories—special charters, general charters, classified charters, optional charters, and home rule charters. *Special charters* arose shortly after independence when the legislatures enacted different charters for each city. As a result, the patterns of city governance had very little uniformity, and the legislatures were more deeply involved in city governance than many people desired.

In reaction, states began enacting a *general charter* for cities that provided uniform patterns of governance but also imposed a straitjacket on city governing structures. A city of a few thousand people need not be governed in the same way as a city of a million. Consequently, the *classified charter* was established to separate cities by population size. Cities of the largest class have the greatest grants of authority.

A number of states provide an *optional charter,* which allows cities within the same population classification to choose among a number of optional kinds of government.

Most reformers prefer the *home rule charter,* which allows the residents of a city to choose whatever form of government they want. Such a charter is drafted by a local charter commission and submitted for voter approval through referendum.

Division of Local Government Responsibilities

As Table 7–2 shows, there is some overlap in the functions served by the different local governments. But there also is some specialization. Counties

Table 7-2. Division of Local Government Responsibilities

General category of local service	Expenditures for all services in the category by type of local government: 1981-82 (in billions), excluding public education					
	County	Municipality	Township	Special district	School district	Total
Human and social services (welfare, hospitals, public health, corrections)	$24.0 (60.0%)	$10.5 (26.3%)	$0.2 (0.4%)	$5.3 (13.3%)	0 (0%)	$40.0 (100%)
Physical maintenance (highways and streets, sewerage, water supply, parks and recreation, libraries, natural resources)	$9.6 (27.4%)	$18.4 (52.4%)	$2.6 (7.4%)	$4.5 (12.8%)	0 (0%)	$35.1 (100%)
Other traditional city government services (police protection, fire protection, sanitation)	$5.0 (19.0%)	$19.1 (72.6%)	$1.6 (6.1%)	$0.6 (2.3%)	0 (0.%)	$26.3 (100%)
Redevelopment activities (transit, housing and urban renewal, airports)	$1.4 (10.9%)	$7.3 (56.6%)	$0.1 (0.8%)	$4.1 (31.7%)	0 (0%)	$12.9 (100%)
Education	$9.6 (8.4%)	$10.1 (8.9%)	$2.7 (2.4%)	$0.1 (0%)	$91.4 (80.3%)	$113.9 (100%)

Source: United States Bureau of the Census, *Census of Governments, 1982,* Vol. 4, *Government Finances,* No. 5, *Compendium of Government Finances* (Washington, D.C.: U.S. Government Printing Office, 1984), p. 2.

(outside of New England) bear the biggest burden for human and social services, yet they handle very little in the way of redevelopment activities. Cities have the biggest burden for public safety in urban areas and for the physical maintenance of the urban infrastructure (streets, sewers, water supply, and park space.) School districts have the biggest burden for public education. And other special districts share with cities the main burden for redevelopment activity and physical maintenance.

The Organization of Counties and Cities

Counties

Counties have one of two forms of legislative body, the **county board of supervisors** or the **county board of commissioners.** Under the commissioner form, the county is usually divided into districts, with each district electing its own commissioner. Under the county supervisor form, the various towns and townships are usually represented directly on the county board.[7] Under either form, the county board is typically very weak and fragmented. Some southern and southwestern states refer to the chairperson of the county board as the County Judge and give that office some judicial as well as legislative responsibilities.[8]

Although some of the most important public services—such as welfare, public health, sheriff's patrol, county jail—are delivered by county governments, these governments are generally the most fragmented of all major local governments. The executive power is typically divided among several agencies, which report individually to the county board rather than to a chief executive. This gives the agencies considerable independence, especially the larger departments, such as welfare and highway maintenance. Many of the smaller agencies, such as tax assessors and bureaus of vital statistics, are dominated by local political factions and are hotbeds of patronage employment. These factions effectively resist and oppose centralized administrative control. Some department heads, such as sheriffs, are often elected directly, giving them an independent electoral base and making them even more insulated from the county board. In Texas, for example, independently elected county officials include the sheriff, county attorney, county clerk, tax assessor, treasurer, auditor, and county surveyor.[9]

In order to reform these executive weaknesses of traditional county government, reformers have posed three alternatives—the county administrator, the county manager, and the elected county executive. The county administrator is the most popular form and has been adopted by about 29 percent of all counties.[10] The administrator, hired directly by the county board, helps the board set the budget and tries to coordinate operations of the various departments.

The county manager form of government is somewhat more powerful than the county administrator. Like the administrators, the county managers are hired by their county boards and help set the budgets. Additionally, they have broad budgetary and supervisory control over the county agencies. Only about 6 percent of all counties have a county manager. The most prominent is Dade County (Miami), Florida.

Finally, the elected county executive is similar to the strong-mayor form of city government, which will be discussed. As an elected official, the county executive has more political influence to deal with administrative agencies and with the county board. Only about 6 percent of all counties have adopted the elected county executive. The largest is Milwaukee, Wisconsin.

Municipalities

City councils can be described as reformed or unreformed. The reformed city council is characterized by several features of the early twentieth-century progressive reform movement, especially nonpartisan and at-large elections and lack of direct control over the city administrative departments. The unreformed councils, in contrast, are characterized by partisanship, ward elections, and considerable intervention of council members in the internal affairs of the departments. Council members put pressure on the departments to hire their relatives or political supporters, and they interfere with departments by demanding special services and favors for the neighborhoods in their own districts.

Whether a city council is reformed or unreformed seems to have some policy impact. Probably because of their partisan and neighborhood basis, unreformed councils respond more effectively to political divisions within the city than do reformed councils. The unreformed councils also tend to tax more and spend more money on city services than do reformed councils.[11]

Table 7-3 shows the most popular forms of city executive. About 55 percent of all cities use the mayor form and about 35 percent use the manager form. Only 3 percent use the commission form.

The Commission

The commission form of government was created in Galveston, Texas, after a tidal wave in 1900 killed 5,000 people. This disaster required emergency action that the weak-mayor form of government was unable to provide, so a commission of prestigious businessmen was appointed to run the city during the emergency. This commission carried out its task so effectively, the

Table 7–3. Frequency of Local Government Forms

Population group	All cities	Form of government (number and percent)			
		Mayor-Council	Council-Manager	Commission	Town meeting[a]
Over 1,000,000	6	6 (100%)	—	—	—
500,000 to 1,000,000	17	12 (71)	5 (29%)	—	—
250,000 to 499,999	34	17 (50)	15 (44)	2 (6%)	—
25,000 to 249,999	1,009	371 (37)	569 (57)	44 (4)	25 (2%)
10,000 to 24,999	1,545	705 (46)	666 (43)	54 (3)	120 (8)
2,500 to 9,999	4,028	2,594 (64)	1,053 (26)	75 (2)	306 (8)
Total (all cities over 2,500)	6,639	3,705 (56)	2,308 (35)	175 (3)	451 (6)

Source: Calculated from International City Management Association, *The Municipal Yearbook 1986* (Washington, D.C.: International City Management Association, 1986), Table 3, p. xv.

[a]Includes representative town meeting.

Note: The mayor-council form of government is most popular in very large and very small cities. The council-manager form is most popular in medium-sized cities. The commission form continues to lose popularity.

leading citizens got a charter change that permanently installed the commission form of government.

Commission government unites executive and legislative functions in the same people. Each commissioner is the head of a city department, as shown in Figure 7–1. While this form of government apportioned out responsibility clearly enough to take decisive action during the Galveston tidal wave disaster, it had some inherent defects when installed on a permanent basis. As department heads, the commissioners tended to defend the interests of their particular departments during the city council meetings. Budget sessions turned into logrolling contests in which alliances were established and the department heads left out of the alliance were given budgetary leftovers. Since neither a chief executive nor a legislative body was independent of the existing departments, the commissioners tended to be unreceptive to new spending needs outside of their limited responsibilities. Under this system, executive leadership was thwarted. Although the commission form of government spread rapidly in the early 1900s, the defects of the system began to appear and it swiftly lost favor. By 1987 only two cities of over 250,000 still maintained the system (Tulsa and Portland).

City Manager

The second and more lasting reform-style government is the **city manager,** or, as it is sometimes called, the *council-manager.* Where the commis-

Figure 7–1. Manager and Commission Forms of Government

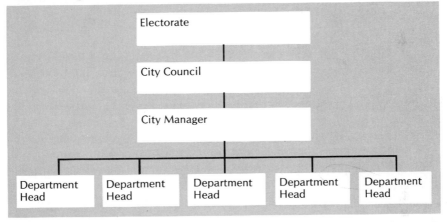

Commission Government

Electorate

Board of Commissioners

| Department of Public Safety | Department of Public Works | Department of Finance | Department of Libraries and Public Buildings | Department of Parks and Recreation |

Council-Manager Government

Electorate

City Council

City Manager

| Department Head | Department Head | Department Head | Department Head | Department Head |

In the commission form of city government, each city council member (commissioner) is also a department head. In the council-manager form, executive and legislative functions are separated.

The council theoretically sets policy, whereas the manager theoretically confines himself or herself to administering the city. In practice, as the text discusses, the manager is indeed political.

---

sion unites the legislative and administrative functions, the city manager form separates them. It also tries to separate politics from administration. Reformers viewed the city council as the legislative and political body. It is engaged in the politics of campaigning, lobbying with the state legislature, establishing political support for the city government, and adopting overall city policies. The manager is hired by and serves at the pleasure of the city council. The manager's job is to administer the policies established by the council and to take charge of all personnel matters, budget preparation, and other administrative details.

In practice, does the manager form of government really remove politics from administration? The answer depends on what is meant by the term *politics*. If politics is defined narrowly as partisanship and campaigning for office, the answer appears to be yes, the city manager is nonpolitical.[12] The city manager does protect the city administration fairly well from partisan politics, campaign pressures, and patronage. However, if politics is defined more broadly to include the process of public policymaking, city managers are definitely political.[13] They make most of the policy proposals that city councils adopt.[14] Council members and city residents perceive the managers as political, and successful managers align themselves with members of the dominant coalition of the council. When the council majority changes, the manager either realigns his or her loyalties or faces dismissal by the council.

The nonpartisan intent of the city manager role works best in medium-sized cities, especially suburbs, where the populations are less heterogeneous and less divided politically than they are in large cities. As Table 7–3 shows, a majority of all cities in the 25,000 to 250,000 range have the manager form of government. Only five of the twenty-three cities over 500,000 population have a city manager. In these large cities, the political divisions often become too acrimonious to be handled smoothly by a manager appointed by a council that is likely to reflect the political divisions of the city. This could be seen in San Diego, where a city manager form presided smoothly over a city growth period during the 1950s and 1960s. By 1970, San Diego had grown to nearly 700,000 people. Severe opposition arose to the ethos of unrestricted growth, and the city manager proved unable to negotiate effectively between the city's pro-growth and no-growth political factions. This led to the emergence of Mayor Pete Wilson in the 1970s, who gradually strengthened the mayor's office, weakened the city manager, built a strong electoral coalition, and successfully balanced the city's competing pro-growth and no-growth factions.[15]

Mayors

Table 7–3 points out that the mayor form of executive is most popular in large cities and small towns. The major difference between the city manager and the mayor is that the mayor is elected and the manager is appointed by the council. This gives the mayors an independent base of political support and strengthens their hand in dealing with the council.

Two types of mayor—the weak mayor and the strong—are illustrated in Figure 7–2. The **weak mayor** resulted from the traditional American distrust

Figure 7–2. Strong- and Weak-Mayor Forms of Government

Weak Mayor Government

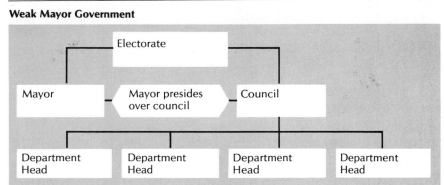

Strong Mayor Government

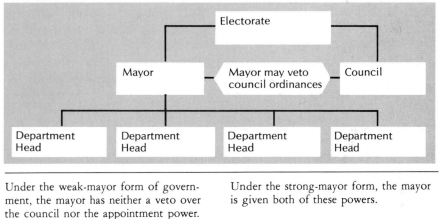

Under the weak-mayor form of government, the mayor has neither a veto over the council nor the appointment power.

Under the strong-mayor form, the mayor is given both of these powers.

of strong executives. Because of this distrust, city departments were set up independent of each other and of the mayor. Often the department heads were directly elected by the people and were given political patronage jobs to hand out. The weak mayor has little appointive power, very limited budget-making powers, and often cannot veto measures of the city council. The **strong mayor,** in contrast, has broad appointive powers, presides over council meetings, sets its agenda, has strong budget-making powers, and has a veto. In large cities the mayor often has a chief administrative officer or a deputy mayor who runs the day-to-day operations of the city departments and leaves the mayor free to deal with the larger areas of policy and leadership.

The Evolution of Reform-Style City Politics

The evolution of reform-style local government forms, such as county manager, city manager, and strong mayor-councils, was a direct product of the **progressive political reform movement** of the early twentieth century. This movement sought to replace boss-dominated, machine-style politics with a style of politics that reformers hoped would be less corrupt and less partisan in nature.

Machine-Style Urban Politics

Political machine refers to a state or local political party that has organized itself so strongly it dominates politics in its region. The political machine differs from just any political party, however, in several respects. The machine is led by a single boss or a unified central committee. The organization controls the nominations to public office. The machine leaders are often of working-class or lower-class social origins. They usually do not hold public office. The machine's workers are kept loyal through material rewards (such as patronage jobs) and nonideological psychic rewards (such as fellowship or ethnic recognition). Finally, the machine controls extensive patronage.[16]

Machine politics had an ethnic basis. The rise and decline of machine politics coincided with the massive immigration of Europeans to American cities between 1840 and 1930. During those ninety years, thirty-seven million people migrated to the United States from Europe. By 1900 only two cities east of the Mississippi River had a population over 100,000, of which the majority were native-born white Americans. A majority of the thirty-seven million immigrants came from only five nationality groups—Germans, Irish, Italians, Poles, and Russians. Most of these people settled in the big cities of the Northeast and Midwest, and their impact on the politics and development of the cities was profound.

As the number of immigrants increased, the political parties—notably the Democratic party—began nominating European ethnic minorities to run for office in the hope that these ethnic candidates would attract other immigrant voters. This development has been called the politics of recognition,[17] and through it the Democratic party began to secure the voting loyalties of the European ethnics.

The machines also provided assistance to lower-class immigrants. This assistance was always granted on an individual basis to people who could be expected to support the machine's candidates. Although the assistance was not given universally or institutionalized by law, it had the effect of creating a large body of supporters for the machine. In the nineteenth century, Tammany Hall's district leader George Washington Plunkitt bragged that whenever a family in his district was burned out of its home, he showed up on the scene to provide lodging and assistance.[18] When young people got into trouble with the courts and the police, the machine politicians like Plunkitt often acted as mediators. The machines also found city jobs for their supporters, the so-called patronage jobs. To keep these patronage jobs, city workers were expected to work for the party during election campaigns, to contribute money to the parties, and to promote the party's welfare.

The oldest and most famous machine is New York City's Tammany Hall, founded in 1789 as a social club. It became politicized under the Irish, who used it as a central device for controlling the district bosses. A district boss was a machine leader responsible for getting out the vote for the machine in his district (sometimes called ward) of the city. The leader of Tammany Hall controlled New York's elections, patronage, and treasury. From the end of the Civil War until the early 1900s, New York City was intermittently controlled by a succession of Tammany Hall leaders—William Marcy "Boss" Tweed, Charles F. Murphy, and Richard Croker.

Boss Tweed is probably the most famous of all the bosses. He started his career as a foreman for the fire department and worked up through alderman, congressman, and finally the leader of Tammany Hall. As boss of Tammany Hall, he exerted considerable influence over government contracts, franchises, licensing, and construction activity. He stole millions from the city treasury and finally was arrested. He died in prison.[19]

For the most part, machine politics is largely a relic of the past, existing today in scattered locations and seldom dominating a region's style of politics as Tammany Hall did a century ago. The most important machine today is Chicago's, which was dominated from 1955–1976 by the legendary Mayor Richard J. Daley and which has been wrapped up in a struggle for control ever since.[20] The heart of the Chicago machine is the Cook County Central Committee, which is made up of one committeeman from each of the city's fifty wards, plus the suburban municipalities. As both mayor of the city and chairperson of the county central committee, Daley was able to control the two most powerful tools of the machine—patronage and nominations. With these tools, he swiftly consolidated his control over the ward bosses and ran the city government like his own personal fiefdom for twenty years.

Daley could control the Cook County Democratic Central Committee in part because the voting system on the committee centralized power in the hands of Daley and a small group of inner city committeemen. Each committeeman had as many votes on the central committee as his or her ward had given to the Democratic Party in the previous election. This voting device ensured that the Chicago committeemen would always be able to outvote the suburban committeemen. Under Daley an inner group of the most powerful committeemen would decide whom the party should endorse for elective offices, and the whole central committee usually ratified their choices. Daley himself presided over these deliberations with meticulous concern, and the resulting slate of endorsed candidates was carefully constructed to represent Chicago's polyglot of ethnic and racial neighborhoods. Milton Rakove wrote:

> Every ethnic, racial, religious, and economic group is entitled to have some representation on the ticket. Thus, in Chicago, the mayor's job has been an Irish job since 1933. The city clerk's job belongs to the Poles. The city treasurer can be a Jew, a Bohemian, or a black. On the county ticket, the county assessor, the state's attorney, and the county clerk must usually be Irish, but the county treasurer, the county superintendent of public schools, or the sheriff can be a member of one of the other ethnic or racial groups. A judicial slate is made up of three or four Irishmen, two or three Jews, two or three Poles, several blacks, a Lithuanian, a German, a Scandinavian, several Bohemians, and several Italians.[21]

These ethnically balanced tickets worked well to represent most ethnic groups as long as the European ethnics predominated in the city's population. But by the 1980s, European ethnics had become a distinct minority. Today, blacks alone account for over 40 percent of the city's population, and Hispanics, over 15 percent;[22] and both minority groupings want a greater share of the machine's benefits.

When Daley died in 1976 the machine angered blacks by refusing to replace Daley with the city council's black president pro tempore. Instead, one of the machine's old guard, Michael Bilandic, was selected. When Bilandic was challenged in the 1979 mayoral race by Jane Byrne, black wards voted overwhelmingly for Byrne. Byrne, too, ignored some black community demands—for a black superintendent of schools and a black police chief, and many black observers began to argue that the Chicago machine had become a liability to black advancement rather than a facilitator of it.[23]

When Byrne came up for reelection in 1983, the machine was deeply split between blacks and whites as well as between Byrne's supporters and the machine's old-guard leaders she had overthrown. One faction of the machine supported Byrne, another supported the son of former mayor Daley, and a third supported black Congressman Harold Washington. Washington won the close three-way primary and then went on to win the racially polarized general election, in which large elements of the white machine supported the Republican candidate, Bernard Epton, who openly exploited racial issues in the campaign.

The results of the 1983 election put Washington in the mayor's office but left the city council controlled by Edward Vrdoliak, the leader of the anti-Washington white faction of the machine. At stake were control over the city council's policymaking powers and thousands of patronage jobs in the city bureaucracy. For the next three years, open hostility between the two factions marked Chicago politics. The key turning point came in a special council election in 1986. In a contest marred by gunfire, fire bombing, and open intimidation, Washington's candidates won that election, finally giving Washington control over the city government. Washington solidified his control by gaining reelection in 1987 and placing his supporters in key decision-making positions in the city council and elsewhere in Chicago government.[24]

Who Benefited from Machine Politics?

The biases of the political machines are obvious. First, they were biased against ideological or programmatic politics. The machine politicians had no ideologies; they had no plans to end poverty, provide housing, improve education, or end discrimination. Rather, they dealt in the concrete transactions of trading favors for services.

Second, the machines also were biased in favor of the lower- and working-class immigrants who secured patronage jobs and political positions. In the process of controlling city government, the machines helped integrate the European immigrants into American society, find them employment, get them into the political system, and get them registered to vote. Sociologist Robert Merton referred to these functions as the *latent functions* of the machines. He distinguished them from the machine's *manifest function* of gaining control of the government.[25] As shown by the Chicago example, however, these latent functions did not work very well for later migrants to the cities, such as blacks and Hispanics.

The Progressive Reform Movement

To the upper class and the upper-middle class, it was intolerable to have city government controlled by machine politicians who catered to the lower-class immigrants. Historian Samuel P. Hays has documented very painstakingly that the initiative for progressive reform in the late nineteenth and early twentieth centuries came primarily from the cities' top business leaders and upper-class elite.[26]

These businessmen-reformers sought to make direct financial gains by overthrowing the corrupt machine politicians. But they also had philosophical reasons for displacing the machine politicians. Historian Richard Hofstadter has contrasted the political vision of the typical reformer with the vision of the typical machine politician. The immigrant politician viewed politics in personal terms. Government was "the actions of particular powers. Political relations were not governed by abstract principles; they were profoundly personal."[27] In contrast, the upper-middle-class reformers looked upon politics as "the arena for the realization of moral principles of broad applications—and even, as in the case of temperance and vice crusades—for the correction of private habits."[28]

The Mechanics of Reform

The political reformers devised several mechanisms to make it more difficult for the machines to operate. The most prominent reform mechanisms were the merit system of public employment, the direct primary, at-large elections, nonpartisan elections, the short ballot, and the city manager and commission forms of government. No one single measure destroyed the machines, and some machine organizations showed a tenacious ability to persist despite the reforms. The reformers hoped that the combination of reforms would have a detrimental effect on the machines.

The Merit System

If the machine bosses relied on patronage to keep themselves in power, then the obvious antidote was **civil service** and the **merit system.** From the point of view of reformers, it was inconceivable that partisanship should have anything to do with the delivery of public services. The machine politicians, however, thought that partisanship had a great deal to do with delivery of services. Tammany Hall district leader George Washington Plunkitt once remarked that civil service is the "curse of the nation. . . . Parties can't hold together if their workers don't get the offices when they win."[29]

The Direct Primary

The convention system of nominations favored the political machines. Because the bosses controlled the selection of delegates to the conventions, they easily controlled the nominations for public office. The reformers' cure was a system wherein nominations were made directly by the voters in a **direct primary** election, thus weakening the political bosses' influence.

At-large Elections

Election from wards enabled ward leaders and councilmen to provide enough services and close personal contact with their constituents to control their votes. The reformers' rejoinder was **at-large elections,** in which a candidate runs in the city as a whole rather than from a specific district. They hoped that at-large elections would force the voters to adopt a citywide vision of how the government was supposed to operate. With elections conducted at-large, reformers hoped the ward politicians would find it more difficult to give people favors in exchange for their votes.

Nonpartisan Elections

Partisan elections also benefited the bosses. The likely reform was **nonpartisan elections.** With the party designation removed from the ballot, the machine's choices for office would be much less obvious and other endorsing organizations, such as good government leagues, newspapers, and interest groups, would presumably gain influence.

The Short Ballot

The bosses promoted weak mayors who had no control over city agencies and bureaucracies, many of which were headed by elected officials. Because the department heads and elected officials competed with each other and depended on the machine to keep them in office, it was easy for the boss to control them and, in turn, the city government. The obvious antidotes were the **short ballot** and either the city manager or the commission form of government. The short ballot has the voters elect only those few offices that set overall policy—preferably just the mayor and the city council. It is distinguished from the long ballot, in which a large number of purely administrative and nonpolicymaking positions are elective. The more names on the ballot, the more individual voters have to rely on recommendations of endorsing organizations. As the best-organized endorsing organization, the political machine has the most influence under the long ballot. By substituting a short ballot, the voter is better able to focus attention on the candidates.

Reformed City Government

Finally, the city manager and commission forms of government provided professional administration for city functions, thereby weakening machine influence. These reforms do not always cause machines to die, but where all the reform mechanisms went into effect, machines found it difficult to survive.

The Bias of Progressive Reform

If political machines were biased in favor of white, working- and lower-class ethnics, reform politics also had their biases. They made it easier for upper- and upper-middle-class people to gain influence in city politics. Correspondingly, low-status voters lost influence. Nonpartisan elections, for example, produce council members of higher socioeconomic status than do partisan elections.[30] And reform-style politics generally make it harder for city government to be responsive to majority demands in the city. One study found that local officials in cities with partisan elections were much more likely to agree with a majority of city residents about the city's problems than were officials in cities with nonpartisan elections.[31] These findings suggest that reform-style politics make it harder for the leaders of the city to be responsive to peoples' concerns and interests.

A major reason for this lies in the types of people recruited to city council positions in reformed cities. Very few of them look on the city council as a stepping stone to building a political career. Rather, they are characterized by an attitude that Kenneth Prewitt calls **volunteerism.** Prewitt interviewed over 300 city council members in the Oakland–San Francisco Bay area and found that they perceived themselves as volunteers serving on city councils as a civic duty. For the most part they were not interested in higher office and not greatly concerned about reelection. For this reason they felt free to make their own decisions on matters that came before the city councils rather than paying great attention to citizens' opinions.[32]

Recent Reforms

Political reform, of course, did not end with the progressive era. Numerous devices have been employed in recent years in the hope of making city governments more effective and more accountable to the citizenry. As a result of the Community Development Block Grant program (see Chapter 3), for example, many cities have set up neighborhood councils and city advisory committees to give residents a voice in the spending of the community development block grant funds. New York, Boston, and some other cities experimented with little city halls, which were neighborhood offices that served as an outreach arm for the mayor. But many of these were disbanded in the budget-retrenchment years of the early 1980s. In 1973, Detroit established an **ombudsman** office, which is an independent office responsible for handling citizen complaints about city government services. By 1981 the office was handling over 13,000 complaints a year. Its ability to improve services varied, not surprisingly, with the intractability of the problems involved. It proved easier, for example, for the ombudsman to get trees trimmed and storm sewers unclogged than to resolve problems associated with abandoned buildings in poor neighborhoods.[33] Finally, as cable television becomes widespread, another device aimed at improving ties between citizen and local government may be the televised city council meeting. Not enough is yet known to determine whether this development will have a positive or negative impact. A study of such televised meetings in Kansas found that, despite a tendency for members to play to the cameras, televising the meetings increased the feed-

back council members got from city residents, and the viewers were disproportionately people of lower socioeconomic status.[34]

The Metropolitan Challenge

A **metropolitan statistical area (MSA)** consists of any county containing a city or contiguous cities of 50,000 people plus the surrounding
counties that are economically integrated into the central county. Areas
lacking a central city of 50,000 can also qualify if their built-up, urbanized
area contains 100,000 people. There are 337 MSAs today, and they house
three-fourths of Americans. The typical metropolitan area is a patchwork of
community identities and governing institutions. In no metropolitan area is
there a central political authority that can speak for the metropolis as a whole.
The mayor is the most visible spokesperson for the city, and the governor the
most visible spokesperson for the state. But the intermediate metropolitan
level has no highly visible spokesperson. Lack of such a visible spokesperson
makes it almost impossible to create a sizable metropolitan constituency with
any interest in metropolitan problems. The lack of such a constituency makes
it hard for government to tackle metropolitanwide problems.

A typical MSA is built up around a central city, sprawls over into two or
more counties, and embraces dozens of municipalities, school districts, and
special districts. Some of the most serious problems (air pollution, crime control, housing, education, transportation, racial discrimination) lap over into all
of these governmental jurisdictions. Because of this fact, the past thirty years
have seen many attempts to create governmental structures that could deal
with metropolitanwide problems with the same authority that mayors and city
councils deal with individual city problems.

The Hopes for Metropolitan Government

Following World War II (1941–1945), many metropolitan areas appeared
headed for trouble, because of the lack of metropolitanwide institutions to
cope with metropolitanwide problems. In the older Northeast and Midwest
regions of the country, three quarters of the metropolises of a million or more
saw their central city populations peak in 1950 and decline steadily afterward.
These cities became surrounded by incorporated suburbs. In the South and
Southwest sunbelt regions, many central cities were still growing (and indeed
still do not appear to have reached their population peaks), but suburbanization continued apace there as well. By the mid-1980s, all of the twenty largest

metropolitan areas in the nation had more people living outside their central cities than in them.

The rapid suburbanization of this period led to numerous problems, especially local governments' inability to provide the normally expected urban services in the suburban fringes. Central city water and sewer lines, for example, were usually not extended into the new suburban subdivisions, and homeowners often had to rely on private wells and backyard septic tanks. As populations grew, this combination led to inevitable pollution of wells. Although it was often possible for cities or water supply districts to drill deep wells, it was much harder for a small community to set up a central sewage treatment plant.

Compounding the task of resolving these service problems was the fact that by 1945 no metropolis in the nation possessed a governmental mechanism for coping on a coordinated, areawide basis with such problems as air pollution, sewage disposal, water supply, solid waste disposal, mass transit, and public health, which were beyond the abilities of any individual community to solve. Instead, the responsibility was divided among literally hundreds of governments. The New York City region had 1,400 different local governments; Chicago had 1,100. Little thought was given to coordinating the policies of these many units, which led to overlapping of responsibilities, intergovernmental conflicts, and important gaps in service.

From the viewpoint of political reformers, the great hope for coping with problems of this sort was to scrap the existing system of governance and create a single general-purpose authority at the metropolitan level. Two strategies eventually evolved for doing this.

City-County Consolidation

The ideal strategy was to develop one acting government, normally achieved by **city-county consolidation** of the central city with the surrounding county. A single countywide council would replace the previous city council and county board of commissioners, and the city and county service departments would be merged. This synthesis would prevent the formation of new municipalities in the suburbs and reduce the need for more special districts. Prominent successes in city-county consolidation occurred in Nashville-Davidson County, Tennessee (1962), Jacksonville-Duval County, Florida (1967), and Indianapolis-Marion County, Indiana (1969).[35]

The Two-Tier Government Strategy

A second strategy for metropolitan reform was the development of **two-tier government.**[36] Local units would perform the governmental functions best suited for localities, and a regional authority would handle the broader functions, such as sanitation, transportation, and regional planning. The inspiration for this strategy came from Canada, where federative forms of metropolitan government were established in Toronto, Ontario, and Winnipeg, Manitoba.[37] A variation of this approach was achieved in Miami-Dade County, Florida, in 1957. The county government was reorganized that year and given expanded regional service responsibilities for transportation, sewage, water supply, and land-use planning. The existing twenty-six municipalities continued to provide such local services as police patrolling and zoning.

The Great Hopes Dashed

Despite these great hopes for major surgery on the metropolitan governmental body, proposals for metropolitan government failed about 75 percent of the time that they were submitted to the electorate for a vote.[38] And with the few exceptions noted above, most of the successes occurred in relatively small metropolitan areas, where the problems were least serious.

Several reasons have been given for the failure of metropolitan reform. First, many reform proposals encountered severe resistance from suburban voters, who viewed the reform as an attempt by central city politicians to grab their tax base, schools, amenities, and above all their autonomy.[39] Second, resistance also tended to come from many local political elites, who foresaw a loss in their own influence if the reforms were approved.[40] Since the establishment of a centralized regional government intentially reduces the influence of leaders in suburban municipalities, special districts, and isolated county offices, their opposition was probably unavoidable.

A final reason for the failure of metropolitan reform has been the satisfaction of central-city and suburban voters with their existing governmental arrangements. The proponents of reform often phrased their definitions of the problems in such abstract terms as "inefficiency" and "overlapping functions," which had little meaning to the average voter. They often failed to demonstrate convincingly that reorganization would mean better services or lower taxes. By contrast, when voters did have a high level of dissatisfaction with public services (as in Jacksonville, Miami, and Nashville), and the reformers campaigned on the basis of those dissatisfactions, people often voted for the reforms.

An Incremental Approach to Metropolitan Reform

Despite the defeat of metropolitan reform proposals, the problems of the metropolis did not go away. In many ways they worsened. In response, metropolitan areas around the nation began experimenting with incremental approaches to coping with metropolitan problems. Typical of these incremental approaches was the spread of metropolitan planning agencies and councils of governments. A **metropolitan planning** agency seeks to develop long-range plans for regional land use and also to develop plans for the rational extension of major public services (such as roads, public transit, sewers) into the growing suburban fringes. A **council of governments (COG)** is a metropolitanwide organization composed of representatives from the counties and larger municipalities. It seeks to promote cooperative solutions to areawide problems that touch all the governments in the region. COGs expanded rapidly during the 1960s as a consequence of federal grants for metropolitan planning and federal requirements during the 1960s and 1970s that local-government grant applications for federal aid be reviewed by a COG-like metropolitan agency. For the most part, COGs have been a major disappointment, having failed to solve any major problems[41] and having been hurt by the cutbacks of federal aid in the 1980s.

The most distinctive example of effective incremental approaches to metropolitan reform are probably those in Minneapolis–Saint Paul, Minnesota, and Portland, Oregon. In Minneapolis–Saint Paul, the metropolitan reform has been closely guided by the state legislature. A Metropolitan Council was created to handle metropolitan planning and policy formulation, and it was ordered to find a solution to the area's sewer problems. The fast-growing suburbs were not able to tie into the central cities' sewage system. As a result, hundreds of thousands of suburbanites were drinking contaminated water, and the Federal Housing Administration threatened that it would not insure any more new home mortgages if these homes lacked access to a sewer system. The Metropolitan Council handled this sewage crisis successfully, and the state legislature increased the council's powers in each of the legislative sessions for the next ten years. By the 1980s the Metropolitan Council had become a true metropolitan government in everything but name. It did not operate public services directly, but it set areawide policies for issues of metropolitan significance, and it had considerable power to overrule municipalities, counties, special districts, and metropolitan agencies that acted contrary to the council's policies.[42]

Conclusion

In this chapter, we have examined the major governing institutions at the community level. It is important to stress that none of these institutional forms are politically neutral. The reformed structures of city government (commission, city manager, at-large elections, nonpartisan elections) were promoted by upper-class elites who wanted to get control over city government out of the hands of machine politicians and the lower-status European ethnics to whom the machines were responsive. The more recent attempts at metropolitan reform have often been defeated because many citizens and entrenched local elites see them as curbing the power of existing political elites and strengthening the power and authority of elites who might not be very accessible.

It is important to stress that most cities and metropolitan areas today present serious problems in governability. Many, if not most, urban leaders lack the authority and effective power to cope comprehensively with urban problems. The governability problem is especially acute at the metropolitan level, where metropolitan problems have persisted despite the lack of progress in metropolitan reorganization. In the absence of effective metropolitanwide institutions, power and authority over some problems (such as pollution control and transportation) have drifted to the federal- and state-level agencies, while power and authority over other problems (such as land use and racial integration) have proved elusive.

Summary

1. There are over 80,000 local governments (counties, municipalities, school districts, special districts, towns, and townships) in the United States. The number continues to grow as special districts proliferate.

2. The most important distinction to make about local governments is that some are reformed and some are unreformed. Reformed counties have a county manager or an elected county executive. Unreformed counties have no chief executive power, and numerous county agencies report independently to a board of supervisors or commissioners. Reformed city governments are characterized by city manager or strong-mayor forms of executive, the at-large city council, and nonpartisan elections.

3. The sprawling metropolis presents serious governmental challenges. Through the 1970s, political reformers had great hopes for metropolitan reform, such as city-county consolidation or two-tier metropolitan government. Such proposals were rejected by the voters about 75 percent of the time, however, and reformers have been forced to be content with less extensive incremental reforms, such as metropolitan planning and councils of government. Two of the more successful examples of incremental reform are found in Minneapolis–Saint Paul, Minnesota, and Portland, Oregon.

Key Terms

At-large election A city council election in which a candidate runs in the city as a whole rather than from a specific district.

City-county consolidation A metropolitan reform strategy in which the city and its surrounding county are merged into a single government.

City manager A city chief executive who is a professional administrator picked by the city council and serves at the pleasure of the council.

Civil service A form of recruitment for government jobs in which people are hired on the basis of merit, as measured by their performance on competitive examinations.

Commission government A form of city government in which the council members (commissioners) also serve as the city's executives.

Council of government (COG) A metropolitanwide agency composed of representatives from counties and larger municipalities.

County The general-purpose local government that is the basic geographic subdivision of the state. Used throughout the country except for New England.

County board of commissioners See *County board of supervisors*.

County board of supervisors The legislative body for the county in states where towns and governmental units have representatives on the board. Called *board of commissioners* in counties where the representatives come from districts or are elected at-large instead of coming from existing governmental units.

Dillon's Rule The principle that city government powers must be interpreted very narrowly.

Direct primary A means of nominating a party's candidates for office. The nominees are chosen directly by the voters at the ballot box.

Merit system (employment) A recruitment method for government jobs that hires and promotes people on the basis of their training and competence to perform specific jobs. See *Civil service*.

Metropolitan planning The attempt to develop long-range plans for land use and the extension of urban services throughout the metropolis.

Metropolitan statistical area (MSA) The official United States government definition of a metropolitan area. Prior to 1983, the term used was *standard metropolitan statistical area (SMSA)*.

Municipality A city government.

Nonpartisan election An election in which the party affiliation of the candidates is not printed on the ballot.

Ombudsman An office established to follow up on citizen complaints about government services and seek to get the complaints resolved.

Progressive political reform movement An early-twentieth-century political movement that sought to replace boss-dominated machine-style politics with a less corrupt and less partisan form of politics.

School district A government that runs a school system.

Short ballot An election in which only a few offices are contested.

Special district A government that performs only a single function, such as a waste control commission.

Strong mayor A mayor who has power to appoint the city department heads and the authority to play a strong role relative to the city council.

Town A general-purpose form of local government especially prominent in New England.

Township A form of local government in rural areas, prominent in the Midwest.

Two-tier government A metropolitan reform strategy that divides public services into those to be performed by a metropolitanwide central government and those others to be performed by local governments.

Volunteerism An ethic common among city council members that they are serving as volunteers doing a civic duty rather than as professional politicians building a career.

Weak mayor A mayor who cannot appoint the city department heads or play a strong role relative to the city council.

References

1. See Stanley Scott and John Corzine, *Special Districts in the San Francisco Bay Area: Some Problems and Issues* (Berkeley, Calif.: Institute of Governmental Studies, 1964).

2. See Advisory Commission on Intergovernmental Relations, *The Problems of Special Districts in America,* Report A–22 (Washington, D.C.: U.S. Government Printing Office, 1964); and Advisory Commission on Intergovernmental Relations, *Regional Decision Making: New Strategies for Substate Districts* (Washington, D.C.: Advisory Commission on Intergovernmental Relations, 1973), Ch. 2.

3. United States Department of Commerce, National Bureau of Standards, *Standard Metropolitan Statistical Areas.* FIPS Publication no. 8–4, Change No. 9, August 1, 1981.

4. Russell W. Maddox and Robert F. Fuquay, *State and Local Government,* 4th ed. (New York: Van Nostrand, 1981), p. 333.

5. Two students of New England local government argue that, even today, residents in places where town meetings exist are more knowledgable about local government affairs than are residents in places without the town meeting. See William Doyle and Josephine F. Milburn, "Citizen Participation in New England Politics: Town Meetings, Political Parties, and Interest Groups," *New England Politics,* Josephine F. Milburn and Victoria Schuck, eds. (Cambridge, Mass.: Schenkman Publishing Co., 1981), pp. 36–37.

6. John F. Dillon, *Commentaries on the Law of Municipal Corporations,* 5th ed. (Boston: Little, Brown & Co., 1911), Vol. I, sec. 237.

7. Advisory Commission on Intergovernmental Relations, *Profile of County Governments: An Information Report,* Report M–72 (Washington, D.C.: U.S. Government Printing Office, 1972), p. 13; Advisory Commission on Intergovernmental Relations, *For a More Perfect Union: County Reform,* Report M–71 (Washington, D.C.: U.S. Government Printing Office, 1971).

8. On Texas, see Eugene W. Jones, Joe E. Ericson, Lyle C. Brown, and Robert S. Trotter, Jr., *Practicing Texas Politics,* 5th ed. (Boston: Houghton Mifflin Company, 1983), pp. 221–222. On Missouri, see Stephen C. S. Chen, *Missouri in the Federal System* (New York: University Press of America, 1983), pp. 204–205.

9. Jones et al., *Practicing Texas Politics,* p. 233.

10. These data are derived from Advisory Commission on Intergovernmental Relations, *Profile of County Governments,* Report M–72, and *For a More Perfect Union,* Report M–61.

11. Robert L. Lineberry and Edmund P. Fowler, "Reformism and Public Policies in American Cities," *American Political Science Review* 61, no. 3 (September 1967): 701–716; Terry N. Clark, "Community Structure, Decision Making, Budget Expenditures, and Urban Renewal in 51 American Communities," *American Sociological Review* 33, no. 4 (August 1968): 576–593.

12. See H. G. Pope, "Is the Manager a Political Leader? No," *Public Management* 34 (February 1962).

13. See Gladys Kammerer, "Is the Manager a Political Leader? Yes," *Public Management* 34 (February 1962): 26–59.

14. One survey of over 1,700 cities found that 94 percent of city managers sought to set the policy agenda for their city councils. Robert J. Huntley and Robert J. McDonald, "Urban Managers: Managerial Styles and Social Roles," *Municipal Yearbook, 1975* (Washington, D.C.: International City Management Association, 1975), pp. 149–159.

15. Glen Sparrow, "The Emerging Chief Executive: The San Diego Experience," *National Civic Review* 74, no. 11 (December 1985): 538–547.

16. The first four points are taken from Fred I. Greenstein, "The Changing Pattern of Urban Party Politics," *Annals of the American Academy of Political and Social Science* 353 (May 1964): 3.

17. Raymond E. Wolfinger, *The Politics of Progress* (Englewood Cliffs, N.J.: Prentice-Hall, 1974), p. 69.

18. *Plunkitt of Tammany Hall,* recorded by William L. Riordan (New York: Dutton, 1963), pp. 46, 53.

19. For background on Tammany Hall, see Gustavus Myers, *The History of Tammany Hall* (New York: Boni and Liveright, 1917). On Boss Tweed, see Seymour Mandelbaum, *Boss Tweed's New York* (New York: Wiley, 1955); Harold Zink, *City Bosses in the United States* (Durham, N.C.: Duke University Press, 1930).

20. There are several background works on Daley. For a polemical treatment, see Mike Royko, *Boss: Richard J. Daley of Chicago* (New York: Dutton, 1971). A critical but much less polemical account that gives considerable insight to Chicago politics is given by Milton Rakove, *Don't Make No Waves—Don't Back No Losers: An Insider's Analysis of the Daley Machine* (Bloomington: Indiana University Press, 1975).

21. Rakove, *Don't Make No Waves—Don't Back No Losers: An Insider's Analysis of the Daley Machine,* p. 96.

22. The 1980 census calculated the black population at 39.8 percent and the Hispanic population at 14.0 percent of Chicago's total population. Both figures have undoubtedly grown since then. *Statistical Abstract of the United States, 1986* (Washington, D.C.: U.S. Government Printing Office, 1985), p. 16.

23. See especially Michael B. Preston, "Black Politics and Public Policy in Chicago: Self-Interest Versus Constituent Representation," in *The New Black Politics: The Search for Political Power,* Michael B. Preston, Lenneal J. Henderson, Jr., and Paul Puryear, eds. (New York: Longman, 1982), pp. 159–186; and Twiley W. Barker, "Political Mobilization of Black Chicago: Drafting a Candidate," *PS* 16, no. 3 (Summer 1983): 482–485.

24. See *New York Times,* May 4, 1987, p. 1.

25. Robert K. Merton, *Social Theory and Social Structures* (Glencoe, Ill.: Free Press, 1957), pp. 78–82.

26. Samuel P. Hays, "The Politics of Reform in Municipal Government in the Progressive Era," *Pacific Northwest Quarterly* 55 (October 1964): 157–166.

27. Richard Hofstadter, *The Age of Reform: From Bryan to F.D.R.* (New York: Knopf, 1935), p. 181.

28. Ibid.

29. Riordan, *Plunkitt of Tammany Hall,* pp. 11, 13.

30. Carol A. Cassel, "Social Background Characteristics of Nonpartisan City Council Members: A Research Note," *Western Political Quarterly* 38, no. 3 (September 1985): 493–501.

31. Susan Blackall Hansen, "Participation, Political Structure, and Concurrence," *American Political Science Review* 69, no. 4 (December 1975): 1181–1199.

32. Kenneth Prewitt, "Political Ambitions, Volunteerism, and Electoral Accountability," *American Political Science Review* 67, no. 4 (December 1973): 1288–1307.

33. Lynn W. Bachelor, "The Impact of the Detroit Ombudsman on Neighborhood Service Delivery" (Paper delivered at the annual conference of the Midwest Political Science Association meeting, Chicago, Ill., April 20–23, 1983).

34. Elaine B. Sharp and Allen Cigler, "The Impact of Televising City Council Meetings" (Paper presented at the annual conference of the Midwest Political Science Association meeting, Chicago, Ill., April 20–23, 1983).

35. See Daniel R. Grant, "Urban and Suburban Nashville: A Case Study in Metropolitanism," *Journal of Politics* 17, no. 1 (February 1955): 82–99; Brett W. Hawkins, *Nashville Metro: The Politics of City-County Consolidation* (Nashville, Tenn.: Vanderbilt University Press, 1966).

36. See Committee for Economic Development, *Reshaping Governments in Metropolitan Areas* (New York: Committee for Economic Development, 1970).

37. See Advisory Commission on Intergovernmental Relations, *A Look to the North: Canadian Regional Experience,* Vol. 5 of *Substate Regionalism and the Federal System* (Washington, D.C.: U.S. Government Printing Office, 1973), Chs. 3, 6.

38. Vincent L. Marando, "City-County Consolidation: Reform, Regionalism, Referenda, and Requiem," *Western Political Quarterly* 32, no. 4 (December 1979): 409–422.

39. Sharon P. Krefetz and Alan B. Sharof, "City-County Merger Attempts: The Role of Political Factors," *National Civic Review* (April 1977): 178.

40. Thomas A. Henderson and Walter A. Rosenbaum, "Prospects for Consolidation of Local Governments: The Role of Local Elites in Electoral Outcomes," *American Journal of Political Science* 17, no. 4 (November 1973): 695–720.

41. Joseph F. Zimmerman, "Can Governmental Functions Be Rationally Reassigned?" *National Civic Review* 73, no. 3 (March 1983): 130.

42. John J. Harrigan and William C. Johnson, *Governing the Twin Cities Region: The Metropolitan Council in Comparative Perspective* (Minneapolis: University of Minnesota Press, 1978).

Chapter 8
The Dynamics of
Community Politics

Chapter Preview

Having examined the institutions of local government in the previous chapter, in this chapter we go on to explore the dynamics of community politics today. Discussed in turn are:

1. Two competing theories for explaining who runs community politics.
2. The emergence of functionally organized power and the problem it poses for strong community leadership.
3. The federal government's influence on community politics and the consequences of that influence.
4. Urban mayors and the quest for community leadership.
5. The challenge of the urban political economy.

Let us begin with an examination of a classic passage in the literature of community power studies—the X family.

Introduction

What can citizens do to influence public policy and affect the way public services are delivered to them? Some pessimists think that most people can do very little, and that power is concentrated in a very small, closely knit group of elites who dominate the lives of the rest of the people in their communities. This viewpoint was articulated fifty years ago by a Middletown resident complaining about the extent to which his life was dominated by Middletown's most prominent family, the X family.

If I'm out of work I go to the X plant; if I need money I go to the X bank, and if they don't like me I don't get it; my children go to the X college; when I get sick I go to the X hospital; I buy a building lot or house in an X subdivision; my wife goes downtown to buy clothes at the X department store; if my dog strays away he is put in the X pound; I buy X milk; I drink X beer, vote for X political parties, and get help from X charities; my boy goes to the X Y.M.C.A. and my girl to their Y.W.C.A.; I listen to the word of God in X-subsidized churches; if I'm a Mason I go to the X Masonic Temple; I read the news from the X morning newspaper; and, if I am rich enough, I travel via the X airport.[1]

Is this pessimistic view of elite dominance of community life accurate? Was it ever accurate? And whether or not it is accurate, what roles do interest groups, citizens, and political parties play in American communities? Are individual citizens gaining or losing influence over the public services that affect their lives? What are the dynamics of community politics?

To answer these questions, we must approach them from two different perspectives. First, we must examine two opposing theories about the way power is distributed in American communities. Second, we must trace the historical development of political power through four distinct but overlapping historical stages—the age of political machines, the age of political reform, the age of functional fiefdoms, and the age of Washington dominance over community politics.

Theories of Community Power

"Who really runs American communities?" is one of the most long-standing and intensely debated questions in American politics. Some people think that community power resides in a core of wealthy persons who secretly control all key decisions. Others think that power is widely dispersed among a variety of interested groupings that participate democratically in running the community. These two schools of thought are the *elitist* and the *pluralist* theories of community power. In either theory, power can be defined as the ability of groups or individuals to influence what a government does.[2]

The Elitist Theory of Community Power

The elitist theory was developed by a small group of early twentieth-century European sociologists who viewed society as ruled by a relatively small group of leaders referred to as elites.[3] This view influenced American sociologists and anthropologists who began conducting community studies during the 1920s and 1930s[4] and who often found that their communities were dominated by a small business elite. One of the most famous of these studies focused on Middletown (Muncie, Indiana) and its dominance by the X family, described earlier.

Perhaps the most influential of the early elitist studies was Floyd Hunter's book *Community Power Structure.*[5] Hunter concluded that community politics in Regional City (Atlanta, Georgia) in the early 1950s was controlled by a small, closely knit group of elites. These elites were predominantly the people who ran the major business and economic institutions. They manipulated government officials to give the top elite what it wanted. Further, power was viewed as cumulative in that the individual elite person who got power in the economic sphere also began to accumulate power in the social and political spheres. Political decisions flowed from the elite down to ordinary citizens. Because he viewed Atlanta's power structure as a stratified pyramid, Hunter's theory is called **elitist theory** or **stratificationist theory.**

Hunter came to these conclusions using a research method called the **reputational approach.** He began by asking, "Who runs Regional City?" To identify the leadership, he compiled lists of prominent leaders in civic affairs, business, and society. He then selected a panel of knowledgeable people to examine the lists and identify the most influential individuals and organizations. From these selections Hunter identified forty individuals who, he said, constituted the top power structure in Regional City. Most of these forty served on the boards of directors of the same corporations and belonged to the same social clubs. Beneath these top forty leaders were dozens of other important but less prominent persons whom Hunter called *under-structure personnel.* They carried out the will and the instructions of the top power structure.

Hunter contended that this elite power structure initiated most of the development that occurred in Regional City and that it successfully vetoed projects it disliked. Enterprising newspaper or journal writers lost their jobs when they disagreed with the power structure. Social welfare professionals carefully avoided raising issues that might violate the interests of the power structure. Hunter pictured the governor, the United States senators, the key state legislators, the party leaders, and most other officials as subordinated to the top power structure.

This elitist theory rapidly came under criticism,[6] particularly from political scientists who objected to Hunter's conclusion that the political structures were subservient to the economic institutions. Hunter's critics also objected to his assumptions about power and his methods of researching power. By asking knowledgeable observers to identify the most influential leaders, said Hunter's critics, he had not really measured the exercise of power. He had merely measured the reputation for power.[7] To make a valid measurement of power, they argued, one would have to analyze the actual decisions through which power was in fact exercised.

The Pluralist Theory of Community Power

The first major attempt to measure power through a **decision-making approach** was Robert Dahl's study of New Haven, Connecticut, and was reported in his book *Who Governs?*[8] This and several other decision-making studies that followed spelled out the principles of **pluralist theory.**[9] Rather than believing that power is stratified, pluralists believe that a plurality of power centers exists in a city—labor unions, political parties, banks, manufacturing plants, churches, school systems, and government agencies. These power centers compete with each other democratically, and public policy emerges out of their competition. Each of these power centers is powerful only within particular functional areas. Pluralists also reject the stratificationist implication that some permanent, vague powerholder controls situations from behind the scenes. Rather, power exists only when it is exercised through specific decisions by specific individuals. Finally, pluralists reject the stratificationists' belief that power is cumulative.

Dahl deliberately set out to test the hypothesis that New Haven was governed by the kind of economic and social elite that Hunter had discovered in Atlanta. He isolated thirty-four important decisions in the three functional areas of urban renewal, education, and the selection of party nominees for mayor over a period of time that extended from 1941–1959. Contrary to Hunter's findings, Dahl discovered that in New Haven *no significant overlap* occurred between the economic and social elites, that these elites had little influence on the decisions he studied, and that power in New Haven was *noncumulative*—that is, power in one functional area did not lead to power in other functional areas.

In the three issues areas that concerned him, Dahl conducted extended interviews with forty-six top decision makers. He found very few instances in which an individual person was involved in more than one major decision, let alone more than one issue area. The exception to this was the mayor of New Haven, Richard C. Lee. Lee was a supreme political tactician at bargaining with leaders of all the functional power centers in New Haven plus some others in federal and state agencies that ran programs in the city. Through his bargaining skill, he successfully started and carried out the kinds of programs he thought the city needed to grow and prosper. Dahl perceived Mayor Lee as occupying the critical position in what Dahl referred to as an "executive-centered coalition" of a plurality of interest groups in New Haven. Because this view sees power as noncumulative and dispersed among several power centers, Dahl's theories about community power are called *pluralist* theories.

The pluralists have been pointedly criticized also. Especially criticized was Dahl's reliance on decisions as the test of power. Peter Bachrach and Morton S. Baratz charged that concentrating on actual decisions ignored "the fact that power may be, and often is, exercised by confining the scope of decision making to relatively 'safe' issues."[10] If one person can keep a question from being placed on a city council or state legislative committee agenda for action, then that person has exercised power even though no formal public decision has been made. Such an exercise of power is called a **nondecision.**

The key area where nondecisions predominate is in preserving the dominant values, myths, and established political programs of a community. Only certain kinds of questions are put on the agendas of the decision-making agencies. Since other kinds of questions never appear on those agendas, they never reach the point where decisions about them can be made. A researcher who focuses only on actual decisions may fail to notice emerging groups or issues in the political process. In his study of New Haven, for example, Robert Dahl paid little attention to the black community because it did not figure in the decisions he analyzed. Even the urban renewal decisions that deeply touched the lives of New Haven blacks were made without much input from the local black community. When a riot broke out in New Haven in 1967, some persons began to ask why decisions had not been made on questions that the blacks themselves apparently considered important.[11] The answer seems to be that the blacks did not constitute a strong enough interest group to have their demands placed on the decision-making agenda. The needs and demands of people who do not have the backing of strong interest groups and powerful civic leaders are likely to remain in the realm of nondecisions.

Generalizations About Community Power:
Key Differences Between Elitist and Pluralist Theories

Since these tenets were first articulated by Hunter's and Dahl's studies, the research on community power has become voluminous, the research methods very sophisticated, and the results often contradictory (see Table 8–1). A later study of Atlanta, for example, found it to be less elitist than Hunter had claimed,[12] and a later reanalysis of New Haven claimed it to be less pluralist than Dahl had found.[13] Despite the contradictions, a number of findings keep recurring, regardless of whether the researchers were pluralists or elitists and regardless of their methods. Several generalizations can be made.

First, political scientists were much less likely to come to stratificationist conclusions than were sociologists.[14] Second, the role played by business in

Table 8–1. Key Tenets of the Pluralist and Stratificationist Theories

Issue	Pluralist tenet	Stratificationist tenet
Locus of political power	In individual action and individual competence	In positions of economic and institutional leadership
Structure of power	Divided among competing power centers	Stratified in pyramid form
Nature of power	Not cumulative. Power in one area does not necessarily lead to power in a different area	Cumulative. Power in one area tends to lead to power in different areas as well
Most common approach to identifying powerholders	Decision-making analysis	Reputational analysis
Exercise of power	Through decisions only	Through decisions and nondecisions
Role of business community	The business community is only one of many competing power centers. The great diversity of business interests makes it impossible to speak of *the* business-community interest	Business is the dominant interest in the community. Despite its diversity, there is considerable unity on issues important to top business leaders

community and state politics is rarely as dominant as Hunter saw it to be in Regional City. In fact, a later study of Atlanta found that business interests were only one of three groups of community influentials.[15] The business community in any sizable city is divided among several factions, and each faction's influence is usually limited to the one or two areas that affect it. Thus urban renewal agencies routinely seek the advice and collaboration of real estate brokers and the financial community. Other kinds of businesses—such as retail merchants, automobile dealers, and shopping center owners—are often quite uninterested. Utilities seek to promote a city's population, income, and employment, whereas railroads frequently display little interest in city politics.[16]

Third, power is structured differently in different communities, and the structure of power also changes over time. Atlanta of the 1980s, led by a black mayor and a black representative in Congress, is not at all like the Atlanta that Hunter studied in the early 1950s, in which the black community was practically excluded from the top power structure. One of the most sophisticated community power studies was Robert Agger, Daniel Goldrich, and Bert Swanson's comparative study of four American communities over a fifteen-year period.[17] They distinguished between two dimensions of power (see Table 8–2). The *convergent-divergent* dimension measures the unity of the

Table 8–2. Types of Community Power Structures

| | | Distribution of power among citizens | |
		Broad	Narrow
Political leadership ⎰	Convergent	Consensual mass	Consensual elite
⎱	Divergent	Competitive mass	Competitive elite

Source: From *The Rulers and the Ruled*, Rev. Ed., by Robert Agger, Daniel Goldrich, and Bert Swanson. Copyright © 1972 Wadsworth Publishing Company, Inc. Reprinted by permission of Brooks/Cole Publishing Company, Monterey, California 93940.

political leadership of a community. Where the leadership is convergent, or unified, the political leaders generally agree on how expansive government should be and who should benefit from government activity. Where the leadership is divergent, the political leaders do not agree. The other dimension measures how broadly power is distributed among citizens.

The most highly stratified power structure exists in communities where power is very narrowly distributed and the leadership is unified. This is referred to by Agger, Goldrich, and Swanson as a *consensual-elite* form of power structure. In contrast, the most democratic form of power structure is the *competitive mass*, occurring in communities where the elites are split and power is broadly distributed among the residents.

In this terminology, Hunter's description of Atlanta, for example, fits into the consensual-elite category. After Hunter's study of the early 1950s, however, Atlanta's power structure changed. The black community became larger and more influential. The city itself grew dramatically, increasing in the number of interest groups involved in community politics. By the 1980s Atlanta's power structure had altered to the point where it would fit more appropriately into the competitive-elite category.[18]

Fourth, single-elite-dominated power structures are most likely to be found in isolated communities dominated by a single industry and in small homogeneous communities. Pluralist power structures are most likely to be found in metropolitan areas, communities with a heterogeneous population, and communities with a diversity of economic foundations and social cleavages.[19]

Fifth, the number of key community decision makers is very small. Hunter said there were no more than forty in Atlanta. Even Dahl estimated the total number of key decision makers in New Haven to be less than one-half of 1 percent of the city's population.[20]

Sixth, politically important people get their political influence from holding positions of institutional leadership. The participants are business leaders, labor leaders, party leaders, government leaders, or leaders of some other institutions that have interests at stake in the governmental process of their cities.

Last, community politics takes place within a system of politics in which the dominant values, roles, and processes are fairly well structured. Even though a decision might get made through a pluralistic process, some elitists argue, the elites who run the community's institutions control the system.[21]

The Emergence of Functionally Organized Power

However one measures community power, one has to take account of the growing importance of functionally organized political power bases in the state and local government bureaucracies. It would be a mistake to view these bureaucracies as simply the unwitting puppets of the private-sector business elites. These bureaucracies often have policy agendas to which many other political actors respond.[22] They also have strong ties to interest groups in the private sector, which give them political support in dealing with city councils, mayors, and state legislatures.

The Trend Toward Functionally Organized Power Bases

The growth of government bureaucracies as important political actors in community politics stems from the Great Depression of the 1930s, which had devastating impacts on the old city governments and the political machines that dominated many of the cities then. The decline in economic activity and the sudden increase in unemployment meant that many people could not pay their property taxes, causing city government revenue to drop. As revenues shrank, city workers had to be laid off. The political machines no longer had enough money to run their patronage apparatus at full steam, nor did they have funds for the services they had offered their supporters in the past. The machines could no longer provide charity and jobs, at a time when the economic catastrophe of the depression made these services more necessary than ever. To meet the emergency, the federal government stepped in.

The federal government began to create new services. It created a welfare system and unemployment compensation. Starting in the 1930s it provided funds to build airports, construct public housing, and redevelop downtown areas. Few of these new services were turned over to the traditional city governments dominated by the political machines. Instead, the services added from the 1930s to the 1950s were handled by newly formed airport commissions, housing authorities, or urban renewal agencies that were independent of the city councils and mayors. The net effect was to foster a power base organized along functional lines.

In the machine model of politics discussed in the previous chapter, the keynote is the concentration of power in the hands of the boss. In the functional model, the keynote is the fragmentation of power into so many governmental entities and agencies that the mayors and the city councils lost comprehensive control over the governance of the city.

New York City's financial crisis of the 1970s (see Chapter 4) is sometimes attributed to the mayor's inability in those years to control the functionally organized city bureaucracies and the public employee labor unions connected to those bureaucracies. To get elected mayor, conditions necessitated that candidates seek support from the police union, fire fighters' union, sanitation workers' union, and other public employee associations. When it came time to negotiate collective bargaining contracts with those unions, the union leaders found themselves in a stronger bargaining position than the mayor.[23] One New York public employees' union leader quipped, "We have an advantage no private sector union has. We elect our employer."[24] Not only did the public employees have an edge in dealing with the mayor in the 1960s and 1970s, but many city bureaucracies themselves were well insulated from mayoral control. This was particularly true of highway and urban renewal departments, which received a major share of their funding from the federal government and were much more attuned to federal regulations than to mayoral or city council demands. They were bolstered in their independence by supportive interests in the private sector, such as the construction unions, banks, and development firms that stood to profit from highway and urban renewal projects. For all of these reasons, New York's urban renewal czar, Robert Moses, was effectively beyond the control of the city's mayor,[25] as was the Port Authority of New York and New Jersey with its billions of dollars invested in roads, bridges, railways, bus terminals, airports, and office buildings.

Political scientist Theodore Lowi coined the term "functional feudality" to describe the ties between the professional bureaucracies and their related interest groups.[26] The feudal analogy is quite appropriate. Just as the elite nobility in the Middle Ages enjoyed relative autonomy in the conduct of affairs within their fiefdoms, so for the past fifty years the elite bureaucratic officials have traditionally enjoyed considerable autonomy from effective outside interference by citizens and political parties (but not from members of Congress) in the conduct of their specialized operations. Just as the feudal nobility was not elected to its position of dominance but was maintained in it through a complex system of secular and ecclesiastical laws, the bureaucratic elite of contemporary urban America is not elected to office but enjoys tenure through an equally complex system of laws and administrative rules. The major inapplicability of the feudal analogy is that the fiefdoms of the Middle Ages were geographic in scope, whereas the fiefdoms of the contemporary bureaucracies are primarily functional in scope. In sum, contemporary urban America has seen the emergence of the **functional fiefdom** as a basic unit for organizing political influence. The fiefdom consists of a government bureaucracy and its related private-sector interest groups, which operate in that bureaucracy's functional area of public service.

A good example of a functional fiefdom is urban renewal administration. Urban renewal was started under the Federal Housing Act of 1949 and its amendments in later years, especially 1954. Under this legislation, the federal government makes urban renewal funds available to a local public agency. The local public agency's independence from the city government varies from place to place. In machine cities with strong leaders, such as Mayor Daley in Chicago or Mayor Richard C. Lee in New Haven, the local public agencies were controlled by the city government, but in most cities, the council and mayor had little influence over these agencies.[27] This changed in 1974 when federal legislation permitted mayors and city councils to gain more direct control over housing and urban redevelopment authorities.

The Unintended Consequences of Functional Fiefdoms

New York was not unique in the emergence of its functional fiefdoms. What was happening there was also happening to a lesser degree in most metropolitan areas. There were two consequences: First, the governmental apparatus was becoming insulated from citizen opinion. Administrative-agency heads do not owe their jobs to the voters, and often they must be much more attentive to the demands of administrators at the state or federal level then to the needs of voters. Urban renewal agencies and urban freeway planners received most of their money from Washington. No ordinary citizen was able to convince the urban renewal officials or the administrators of the Port Authority of New York and New Jersey that what they were doing had negative consequences for the city. For the functional fiefdoms, citizen opinion is not very important.

The second consequence of the functional model of governance is that the fiefdoms are not subject to effective control or policy guidance by the people elected to run our governments—the mayor and city council. The mayor and city council may *influence* these other functional governments, but they certainly do not control them, nor do they coordinate them very well; and urban governance often runs off in a dozen different directions at once. Strong state legislatures have more policy guidance. But they do not control the day-today implementation of policy. And, as discussed in Chapter 11, the ability of the functional fiefdoms to set administration rules about the implementation of laws can be just as significant for policy formation as passing the laws in the first place.

Federal Influence in Community Politics

Concurrent with the growth of functional fiefdoms in American metropolises has been growing influence of the federal government in community affairs. The metropolitan areas became more and more dependent on the federal government to finance renewal, freeways, housing, hospital construction, and airport construction. Federal domestic programs spread rapidly during the 1960s and 1970s, until over 400 federal programs were operating in urban areas. As we saw in Chapter 4, nearly a quarter of the money spent by state and local governments came from federal grants. Washington had become a major force in urban government. How this occurred is an important story. The critical period of this story took place in the Kennedy and Johnson administrations of the 1960s.

The Kennedy and Johnson Urban Policies (1961–1969)

Until 1960, federal involvement in urban affairs was fairly narrow in scope. Federal aid supported a number of welfare programs (such as Aid for Families with Dependent Children) that operated disproportionately in urban areas, and there were substantial federal subsidies for capital construction projects such as hospitals, airports, urban renewal, public housing, and interstate highways. But the total number of grants-in-aid involved was only about 100, and they involved only about $10 billion.

After 1960 the federal domestic role grew rapidly, until there were nearly 500 programs in the late 1970s that spent $100 billion. By the end of the Johnson administration, social-service spending outweighed spending for big construction projects. So many new needs came to public attention during the 1960s that the Kennedy and Johnson administrations responded with proposals for more and more programs. This was especially the case under Johnson, who called his administration the **Great Society** to underscore his concern for improving opportunities and living standards for millions of Americans living in poverty. Under the Great Society, there was no overall urban policy, only a proliferation of programs.[28] The first attempts at coordination occurred in the Economic Opportunity Act; but under its first director, Sargent Shriver, the Office of Economic Opportunity did not view itself as a coordinating agency, so little took place. The model cities program initiated in 1966 had as its main thrust the coordination of programs within concentrated areas of about 150 big cities.[29]

A key thrust of some important programs in the Johnson administration was the move toward citizen participation, the attempt to make federal programs (such as urban renewal and public housing) more responsive to the demands of the ordinary citizens who were affected by the programs. The precedent here was the Economic Opportunity Act of 1964. This act started the community action programs, which were the heart of Johnson's War on Poverty. This act called for the **maximum feasible participation** of the poor in designing and carrying out antipoverty projects. Over a thousand community action agencies were set up in locales around the nation, and each one was to provide for the direct election of citizens to its board of directors. The community action agencies thus would bring isolated citizens in poverty neighborhoods into a partnership with city hall.

The trend toward citizen participation peaked in 1974 with the Housing and Community Development Act of that year. Before submitting an application for community development grants, a city had to provide for citizen input to its application. Many cities did this by creating citywide citizens' advisory committees to suggest priorities for the community development funds. Other cities divided themselves into districts and had elected neighborhood planning councils recommend how community development funds should be spent in their neighborhoods. By the 1980s, however, the movement toward direct citizen participation in local government was on the decline.[30] Neighborhood district councils still exist, but rarely do they have any real authority.

The Nixon and Ford Urban Policies (1969–1977)

Under Nixon and Ford, national urban policy was characterized by two features. First was a direct assault on many domestic programs of Johnson's Great Society and the Democratic Congress. The Office of Economic Opportunity was dismantled, and model cities, urban renewal, and eight other urban programs were consolidated into the community development block grant program of the Housing and Community Development Act of 1974. Nixon impounded over $11 billion that Congress had appropriated for sewer construction in metropolitan areas. Some highly controversial programs such as the legal services program were depoliticized.

A second feature of the Nixon and Ford urban policy was the attempt to increase the political influence of state government, small town, and rural political forces. These were more favorable to the Nixon administration than were the big cities and their allies in some of the federal bureaucracies. Nixon proposed several initiatives to accomplish this. Effective power over urban policy was concentrated in the Domestic Council and the Office of Management and Budget. Revenue sharing channeled substantial federal funds through state governments. Nixon also proposed to consolidate several categorical grants into large block grants dealing with employment, criminal justice, and community development. These consolidations were designed to increase the influence of state governments and to restrict the influence of big city agencies that operated the categorical grants programs in these areas. Further, the **Community Development Block Grants** were allocated by formulas that over time shifted some federal funds away from big northern cities to the suburbs and the sunbelt region.

The Carter Urban Policy (1977–1981)

More than any other president, Carter sought to articulate a true urban policy that would subordinate all federal urban programs to overall policy guidance. Under this scheme, the federal government would become a facilitator and coordinator seeking to target federal funds to high-priority areas, to reverse the historic anti-urban bias of most federal programs, and to stem the disinvestment from the large, old northern cities (see Chapters 3 and 4). These goals drew enthusiastic endorsement from major state and local public agency groups, such as the National League of Cities, the United States Conference of Mayors, the National Governors Association, and the National Conference of State Legislatures.[31]

In fact, however, this approach to urban policy accomplished very little of lasting importance. The heart of his proposal, an Urban Development Bank, was never created. And much of what was created, such as the urban impact analysis, was simply abandoned by Carter's successor, Ronald Reagan. The most permanent and perhaps most successful innovation under Carter was the **Urban Development Action Grant (UDAG)**, a grant program that enabled the federal government to target funds to selected projects in selected cities. Several cities used UDAG grants in combination with the Community Development Block Grant allocations as seed money to entice private investors into downtown redevelopment projects, which greatly expanded jobs and office space in the central business districts.

The Reagan Approach to Urban Policy (1981–1989)

President Ronald Reagan's approach to urban policy was essentially embodied in the New Federalism discussed in Chapter 3. Unlike Carter, Reagan did not articulate a specific urban policy.[32] Consistent with his traditional political philosophy of conservatism, Reagan strongly believed that the best antidote to urban problems lay in a healthy national economy and that urban development projects were best left to market forces and the private sector rather than direction by such government-sponsored programs as UDAG, which had been so popular under the Carter administration. In Reagan's view, such programs do not encourage the expansion of business; they merely encourage it to shift from one location to another.[33] Rather than relocate the jobs to depressed urban areas where huge numbers of unemployed people live, Reagan preferred to let the people relocate to the places where jobs exist. In the words of Reagan's first budget director, David Stockman, UDAG led to overall inefficiencies in the national economy because it "compensates the private sector for shifting investments to high-cost or less economically efficient areas. This reduces the net economic (although not necessarily the social) gains from any given amount of investment."[34] Given these philosophical viewpoints, it is not surprising that the Reagan administration eventually sought to eliminate the UDAG program.

In a sense, Reagan's approach to urban policy presented a paradox. On the one hand, he favored policies that stimulated economic growth. But on the other hand he disapproved of and cut the budget of UDAG, which was a major federal instrument for guiding economic growth in urban and depressed areas. The Reagan administration's way out of this paradox was to encourage **urban enterprise zones.** As originally conceived, the Department of Housing and Urban Development would be allowed to designate up to twenty-five urban neighborhoods a year to qualify as enterprise zones. Any business company that moved into the qualifying zone would be eligible for special tax concessions from the local, state, and federal governments. Reagan also proposed reducing the minimum wage for the enterprise zones and relaxing federal regulations on the environment and occupational health and safety.[35] With these concessions, businesses could be expected to move into the affected neighborhoods and create jobs for the residents. Although the necessary legislation for the enterprise zones had not yet passed Congress as of this writing, several states went ahead with their own enterprise-zone initiatives.

In sum, Reagan's approach to urban policy was very similar to the laissez-faire philosophy that characterized his approach to the New Federalism (see Chapter 3). The best antidote to urban problems was economic growth. For cities in the Northeast and Midwest that were based on old, heavy industrial manufacturing, Reagan favored letting the armies of unemployed people relocate to the more economically dynamic regions of the South and West rather than pumping large amounts of federal funds into redeveloping those cities. To the extent that he did support a government role in fostering urban economic growth, it came in the form of such initiatives as enterprise zones, designed in the belief that tax and regulatory concessions granted to business corporations would eventually trickle down to low-income residents of poor neighborhoods.

Urban Mayors and the Quest for Leadership

Given the existence of important power centers outside the city government (banks, labor unions, and other interest groups), strong functional fiefdoms, and the emergence of the federal government as a significant actor in community affairs, the power structure of most metropolitan areas has become extremely fragmented. Making the various power centers work together for common goals is an arduous task. And the political office usually considered to exercise such leadership is that of the central-city mayor.

The Changing Urban Setting for Mayoral Leadership

Being mayor of a sizable city is one of the most difficult positions in American politics. As the most visible city official, the mayor is held responsible for solving urban problems, but he or she rarely has enough authority to do that. In large part as a result of the Progressive Reform movement, the devices for accumulating political power have been weakened. The mayor's formal powers are sharply restricted by the state constitution, the legislature, and the city charter. Many of the most important governing functions in cities are carried out, not by the city government, but by other governments. Public health and welfare are usually administered by the counties; public transit, sewers, and airports are under the control of metropolitan agencies; and schools are usually run by independent school districts.

If mayors are to become dynamic executives, at least two things must happen. First, they must be given the legal and political resources to do their jobs. Jeffrey Pressman has identified seven factors that he calls the preconditions for strong mayoral leadership.

Sufficient financial resources with which a mayor can launch innovative social programs.

City jurisdiction in the vital program areas of education, housing, redevelopment, and job training.

Mayoral jurisdiction within the city government in those policy areas.

A salary sufficiently high that the mayor can work full time at his office.

Sufficient staff support for the mayor, such as policy planning, speech writing, intergovernmental relations, political work.

Ready vehicles for publicity, such as friendly newspapers and television stations.

Politically oriented groups, including a political party, which the mayor can mobilize to help him achieve particular goals.[36]

Second, an effective mayor must have a subjective vision of what needs to be done in the city and how it can be done. A mayor who has no vision of how the mayoralty can be used to improve the lives of the city's residents will not become a great mayor, regardless of his or her objective resources. On the other hand, a very dynamic personality with a sharp understanding of what can be accomplished may be able to have a lasting impact on the city even if he or she lacks several of the resources identified by Pressman.

John P. Kotter and Paul R. Lawrence attempted to analyze the subjective-vision factor in terms of the mayor's ability to impose his or her own style on the city.[37] They analyzed the leadership styles of mayors in twenty different cities during the 1960s and isolated several variables that contribute to mayoral strength. Of critical importance were five variables: setting a decision-making agenda, controlling the mayors' time, expanding their political alliances to attract new supporters, building a large staff to whom they could delegate appropriate responsibilities, and gaining political control over the city government. If we juxtapose the objective preconditions with the subjective-vision dimension, we derive four mayor types of leadership: the ceremonial mayor, the caretaker mayor, the crusader mayor, and the program entrepreneur. These are shown in Figure 8-1.

Figure 8-1. Styles of Mayoral Leadership

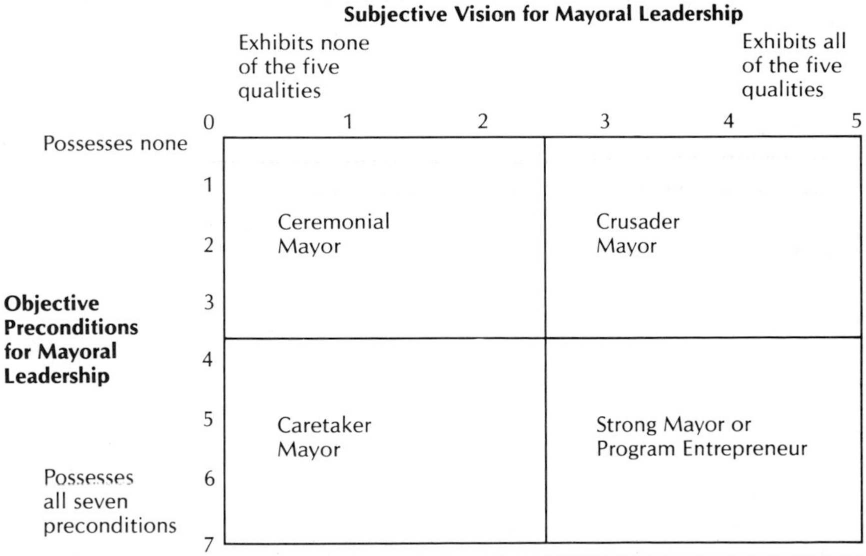

By juxtaposing the objective preconditions with the subjective vision for mayoral leadership, we can identify four major styles of mayoral leadership.

Sources: This figure was composed by juxtaposing criteria developed in Jeffrey L. Pressman, "The Preconditions for Mayoral Leadership," *American Political Science Review* 66, no. 2 (June 1972): 511–24; John P. Kotter and Paul R. Lawrence, *Mayors in Action: Five Approaches to Urban Governance* (New York: Wiley, 1974), Ch. 7; and Douglas Yates, *The Ungovernable City* (Cambridge, Mass.: M.I.T. Press, 1977), p. 165.

Types of Mayoral Leadership

The Ceremonial Mayor

The person with little subjective vision occupying an office that has few preconditions is very likely to follow the style that Kotter and Lawrence call the **ceremonial mayor.** These mayors make little effort to set a decision-making agenda for dealing with city problems. They have no broad goals to be accomplished; rather, they deal with problems individually. They have a modest staff and do not try to build new political alliances to contend with city problems; they rely instead on past friendships and personal appeals. In coping with mayoral tasks, the ceremonial mayor attempts to tackle all the tasks individually rather than delegate authority to others. As an example of a ceremonial mayor, Kotter and Lawrence point to Walton H. Bachrach of Cincinnati (1963–1967). They write of Bachrach:

> Walt was a very personable guy and just about everybody loved him. He'd walk down a crowded street and say hello to nearly everyone—by their first name.
>
> As mayor he spent nearly all of his time in ceremonial activities. He gave speeches at banquets, he welcomed conventions, he cut ribbons at all types of openings, he gave out keys to the city, and so on. He really looked the part and he played it with grace and dignity.[38]

The Caretaker Mayor

The mayor with limited subjective vision who occupies an office that has several of the preconditions is likely to be a **caretaker mayor.** Like the ceremonial mayors, the caretaker mayors also do not set an agenda of goals to be accomplished. They, too, deal with problems individually. They do make more of an effort than the ceremonial mayors to build political alliances, to surround themselves with a loyal staff, and to delegate authority to others, especially to the established bureaucracies.

The prototype of a caretaker mayor was Ralph Locher of Cleveland (1962–1967). Locher dealt with city problems with an unsystematic approach. He let his own daily agenda be dictated by other people who placed demands on him and by regular office routines such as opening the mail and dictating letters. There is no evidence that Locher attempted to establish goals for some of Cleveland's broader social problems. He was simply a caretaker for the city. Locher himself said:

> You know, I suppose it could be said that Burke [another mayor] and I were custodial mayors. We tried to keep the city clean and swept and policed. Some say that wasn't enough. Let me just say this about that

complaint. You can't nurture flowers and good thoughts and ideals when you're living in a rat-infested squalor and your city services aren't being done.[39]

The Crusader Mayor

The **crusader mayor** has the subjective vision for strong leadership to a high degree but occupies an office that lacks several preconditions for strong leadership.[40] The crusader style emerges when the mayor's office is occupied by a very active, imaginative, and ambitious personality who has a very weak political power base. Douglas Yates points to former New York City Mayor John Lindsay as a crusader. Lacking the political strength to control the city bureaucracies and dominate the government, Lindsay adopted a crusading, symbolic style of leadership. During the riots of the 1960s, he went into the streets in the riot-torn sections and urged people to return to their homes. He traveled often to Washington to testify before congressional committees and to serve as a spokesperson for the nation's urban problems. He engaged in political battles with New York State Governor Nelson Rockefeller. Despite the battles, the conflicts, and the publicity, however, it is hard to identify Lindsay with very many significant accomplishments.

The Program Entrepreneur

The **program entrepreneurs** are the most ambitious of all the mayoralty types, and the offices they hold necessarily possess several of the objective preconditions. Their agenda is much more detailed. They not only have broad goals but even a list of objectives or priorities to be covered. Only a small portion of their daily work schedule is spent reacting to events. The rest is spent on activities tied to short- and long-range objectives. The program entrepreneurs skillfully build political alliances and surround themselves with a substantial staff.

The prime example of the program entrepreneur is Richard Lee of New Haven. Lee built a solid alliance around the large interest groups in the city— the city bureaucracy, federal renewal agencies, the city council, the business community, organized labor, the Democratic party, and Yale University.

Much of the basis for Lee's success was his strong political support in New Haven's Democratic party. With this backing, he was assured of renomination and reelection, thus giving him a long tenure as mayor. The long-term mayor has advantages in dealing with the bureaucracy that the short-term mayor does not have.[41] It is easier for bureaucratic officials to oppose or ignore the wishes of the short-term mayor because he or she might not be around very long. One of Lee's first goals on becoming mayor was to establish control over city departments and bureaucracies.[42] He was able to maintain control over New Haven's urban renewal projects, a feat not performed by mayors in other cities, such as Newark and New York.[43] At the center of what Robert Dahl called an executive-centered coalition, Lee was able to line up business leaders, university leaders, union leaders, and other civic leaders behind his redevelopment goals.[44]

The Minority Mayor

Although not a distinct style of leadership, the minority mayor is a very visible and increasingly common type of mayor. Some of the nation's largest cities are now led by mayors who are not upper-middle-class white males. Minority mayors include blacks—for instance, Harold Washington (Chicago), Wilson Goode (Philadelphia), Tom Bradley (Los Angeles), Coleman Young (Detroit), and Andrew Young (Atlanta); Hispanics—for example, Henry Cisneros (San Antonio), Federico Pena (Denver), and Xavier Suarez (Miami); and women, such as Dianne Feinstein (San Francisco), Kathy Whitmire (Houston), Maureen O'Connor (San Diego), and Annette Strauss (Dallas).

Minority mayors may confront problems and opportunities that white male mayors do not face. Writing particularly about black mayors, political scientist Peter Eisinger argues that they are faced with a problem of divided loyalties.[45] In their initial election campaigns, they usually win a small minority of the white vote,[46] which means they rely on overwhelming support from black communities. But to initiate the economic development activities that are needed to increase employment for the cities' minority populations, the black mayors have to make alliances with upper- and upper-middle-class whites who have the economic power to put economic development programs into action. The more that minority mayors cater to their minority election constituencies, the more problems they create with their economic development coalition, and vice versa.

If minority mayors have special problems, they also have special opportunities to increase employment and business prospects for the minority populations. Eisinger's studies of black mayors show that they indeed are able to increase the number of blacks employed by city government at all levels.[47] Grace Hall Saltzstein conducted a similar study among women mayors and found that they are able to increase the number of women holding city jobs.[48]

The Prospects for Mayoral Leadership

There are both positive and negative factors influencing the prospects for cities' getting strong mayoral leadership for the late 1980s and early 1990s.

The negative factors have mostly to do with money and the availability of resources. Due to the sharp cutbacks in federal grants-in-aid to state and local governments and important transformations in the American economy, many cities no longer have the economic and financial resources to support the visions of the program-entrepreneur mayors. In the retrenchment environment of the 1980s, many such mayors have had to function as brokers balancing off the various political pressure groups in the city,[49] or as caretakers aiming at efficient management of the city's scarce resources. In fact, one study of mayoral goals in forty-six cities found that the achievement of efficiency was the highest-ranking goal among the mayors.[50]

On the positive side there is more recognition today than there was twenty years ago of the need for strong mayoral leadership, and some progress appears to have been made toward the seven objective preconditions for strong mayors that were outlined earlier. One study found that mayoral staffs in some cities more than doubled during the 1960s and 1970s.[51] By the mid-1970s, the New York City mayor had a staff of over 1,000 people and a budget of more than $20 million.[52] And a study of mayoral influence in ninety-three cities found that mayors with a strong political base of support tended to enjoy considerable success in getting their program proposals adopted.[53]

Finally, the example of Pete Wilson of San Diego (see Chapter 7, pp. 166–167) shows that a dynamic individual under the proper circumstances can indeed exercise dynamic leadership even in weak-mayor cities. Wilson not only provided dynamic leadership, but he also expanded the formal powers of the mayor's office in San Diego.

Mayoral Leadership and the Urban Political Economy

The name of the game for urban mayors in the 1980s has been economic development. The typical mayor's success has largely been measured by the amount of economic development that has been attracted during his or her administration. A number of development tools exist. Although these will be examined in detail in Chapter 17, we will briefly discuss them here. They can be categorized as either direct subsidies or indirect tax subsidies.

Direct Subsidies

The direct subsidies for economic development have been encouraged in great measure by federal programs, beginning with the urban renewal programs of the 1950s, which for the first time provided federal funds for cities to clear blighted neighborhoods and provide for new commercial and residential development projects in their place. A critical change occurred with the Housing and Community Development Act of 1974, which established a block grant (CDBG) for urban redevelopment and for the first time permitted the mayor's office to take direct charge of redevelopment activities. More than any other single piece of legislation, this act concentrated mayors' attentions on economic development. They used the CDBG grants as seed money to entice private developers into the central cities. As a consequence of this, most cities have undergone a boom in the construction of downtown office buildings and retail shopping facilities. Most cities have also used their CDBG funds to redevelop local historic sites and to "gentrify" some of their historic neighborhoods. In addition to CDBG funds, two other federal programs have provided substantial money for direct subsidy of economic development. These are the Economic Development Administration's economic development grants and the Urban Development Action Grants (UDAGs) started in the Carter administration. All three of these programs were targeted for termination by the Reagan administration. To date they have survived but have suffered significant budget cuts. It is doubtful they will be significant sources of direct subsidies much longer.

Indirect Tax Subsidies

As federal funds for economic development dwindled under the Reagan administration, urban redevelopers were more than able to make up the shortfall by relying on tax subsidies that were made available by the states and by the federal government. The most obvious tax subsidy is for a city simply to give a firm a property tax abatement (that is, forgive the tax) if the firm locates or expands within the city. Most popular was probably the IDRB, or Industrial Development Revenue Bond (see Chapter 4), under which a city helped a company raise investment capital at lower interest rates by using the city's tax-exempt municipal bonding authority. Linked with the use of IDRBs were tax increment financing plans, under which the increased property taxes from a development project would be used to pay off the city's investment rather than going into the city treasury. Finally, because the Reagan administration in 1981 dramatically reduced the number of years over which investors could depreciate their investments in real estate, tax-sheltered investments in central-city office buildings, condominiums, and renovation projects became the rage during the first half of the 1980s.

Looking to the Future

Imaginative and aggressive mayors were able to centralize much of the planning for these economic development activities in their own offices. This helped the mayor of the last dozen years acquire a stature that the office did not have in the 1950s and 1960s. Whether the mayor's new stature will continue, however, is unknown. By the 1990s, economic development as the driving force of urban politics may have abated somewhat. The prospects for continued direct federal subsidies (through CDBGs and UDAGs) do not look very bright, and revisions of the federal income tax code have reduced the attractiveness of IDRBs and real estate tax shelters. Furthermore, there has arisen a glut of central-city office buildings in much of the country by the late 1980s, which is likely to require a period of slow growth or no growth so that demand for office space can catch up with the supply. Finally, criticism of the government-sponsored redevelopment activity of the 1980s maintains that it has not really addressed the severe social and economic problems of the older central cities and the poor residents of the central cities.[54] We will examine these criticisms in Chapter 17.

Summary

1. The question "Who runs American communities?" has evoked a variety of responses from political scientists and political sociologists. Stratificationist theories, first articulated by sociologists, held that a small business elite dominated local politics and that local government leaders were subordinated to this business elite. Pluralist theories, first articulated by political scientists, held that power is divided among a number of competing power centers. Recent research has attempted to compare power structures in different communities. These comparative studies have tended to find degrees of stratification and democracy.

2. Regardless of one's interpretation of community power, a major fact of life in contemporary community politics has been the emergence of functional fiefdoms. As the political machines weakened and as new urban programs, such as public housing, urban renewal, airport construction, and metropolitan freeway construction, emerged, the functionally organized bureaucracies became powerful. Popularly elected city councils, mayors, and school boards were weakened in their ability to control urban bureaucracies.

3. Since 1965, the federal government has performed an increasingly important role in urban affairs. One significant result of the federal government's emergence as an urban actor has been the creation of metropolitan-level planning and policymaking agencies.

4. The major office for providing executive leadership to cope with diverse power centers, the functional fiefdoms, and the federal government is that

of the central-city mayor. Getting mayors who are strong requires giving mayors the objective legal and political resources needed to do their jobs and getting mayors who have a subjective vision of what needs to be done in the city and how to do it.

5. Strong mayors in the 1980s have built their records principally on guiding economic development activities in the cities. Whether this process can continue at its recent pace is doubtful.

Key Terms

Caretaker mayor A mayor with more initiative than the ceremonial mayor, but one who fails to set an agenda of goals to be accomplished.

Ceremonial mayor A mayor who tackles problems individually and devotes much time and effort to ceremonial and symbolic acts.

Community Development Block Grant Formula grant created in 1974 by consolidating several urban-related categorical grants.

Crusader mayor An active and aggressive mayor who lacks many of the preconditions for strong mayoral leadership.

Decision-making approach The approach to analyzing community power that relies on identifying the people who actually make decisions that exert power.

Elitist theory The theory of community power that sees communities as being dominated by a top elite composed principally of major business leaders.

Functional fiefdom The organization of political power along functional lines between a government bureaucracy and allied interest groups in the private sector.

Great Society The name given to the administration of President Lyndon B. Johnson (1963–1969).

Maximum feasible participation The principal that as many of the poor as possible should be involved in designing and carrying out community action programs.

Nondecision The exercise of power by keeping an item off the decision-making agenda of a governmental body.

Pluralist theory The theory of community power that sees communities as being run through the competition of a variety of power centers.

Program entrepreneur A dynamic governor or mayor who sets an agenda of goals to be accomplished and builds alliances with the interests needed to reach the goals.

Reputational approach The approach to analyzing community power that relies on asking a panel of judges to indicate the most powerful people and institutions.

Stratificationist theory See *Elitist theory*.

Urban Development Action Grant (UDAG) A grant program begun by President Jimmy Carter that aimed to target federal development project funds to needy urban areas.

Urban enterprise zone A plan that would give tax incentives and regulatory relief to companies that would locate facilities in designated poor neighborhoods and hire the residents of those neighborhoods.

References

1. Robert S. Lynd and Helen M. Lynd, *Middletown in Transition* (New York: Harcourt, Brace, 1937), p. 74.

2. See Robert A. Dahl, *Modern Political Analysis,* 2nd ed. (Englewood Cliffs, N.J.: Prentice-Hall, 1970), pp. 19–25, 32–34.

3. See especially Gaetano Mosca, *The Ruling Class,* trans. Hannah Kahn (New York: McGraw-Hill, 1939); Roberto Michels, *Political Parties: A Sociological Study of the Oligarchical Tendencies of Modern Democracy,* trans. Eden Paul and Cedar Paul (New York: Free Press, 1962).

4. For a survey of these early studies, see Nelson Polsby, *Community Power and Political Theory* (New Haven, Conn.: Yale University Press, 1963).

5. Floyd Hunter, *Community Power Structure* (Chapel Hill: University of North Carolina Press, 1953).

6. See Polsby, *Community Power and Political Theory;* Herbert Kaufman and Victor Jones, "The Mystery of Power," *Administrative Science Quarterly* 14 (Summer 1954): 2–5; Raymond Wolfinger, "Reputation and Reality in the Study of Community Power," *American Sociological Review* 25 (October 1960): 636–644; Robert A. Dahl, "A Critique of the Ruling Elite Model," *American Political Science Review* 52 (June 1958): 463–469.

7. See Polsby, *Community Power and Political Theory,* pp. 45–56.

8. Robert Dahl, *Who Governs? Democracy and Power in an American City* (New Haven, Conn.: Yale University Press, 1966).

9. See Wallace S. Sayre and Herbert Kaufman, *Governing New York City* (New York: Russell Sage Foundation, 1960); Robert V. Presthus, *Men At the Top: A Study in Community Power* (Ithaca, N.Y.: Cornell University Press, 1964); Aaron Wildavsky, *Leadership in a Small Town* (Totowa, N.J.: Bedminster Press, 1964); Frank J. Munger, *Decisions in Syracuse* (Bloomington: Indiana University Press, 1961); Linton C. Freeman et al., *Metropolitan Decision-Making* (Syracuse, N.Y.: Syracuse University Press, 1962).

10. Peter Bachrach and Morton S. Baratz, "The Two Faces of Power," *American Political Science Review* 56, no. 4 (December 1962): 948.

11. See Bernard Asbell, "Dick Lee Discovers How Much Is Not Enough," *New York Times Magazine,* September 3, 1967, p. 6.

12. Kent Jennings, *Community Influentials: The Elites of Atlanta* (New York: Free Press, 1964).

13. G. William Domhoff, *Who Really Rules? New Haven and Community Power Reexamined* (New Brunswick, Conn.: Transaction Books, 1978).

14. John Walton, "Discipline, Method, and Community Power: A Note on the Sociology of Knowledge," *American Sociological Review* 31, no. 5 (October 1966): 684–689.

15. Jennings, *Community Influentials: The Elites of Atlanta.*

16. See Edward C. Banfield and James Q. Wilson, *City Politics* (New York: Random House, 1965), pp. 261–276.

17. Robert Agger, Daniel Goldrich, and Bert Swanson, *The Rulers and the Ruled*, rev. ed. (Belmont, Calif.: Wadsworth, 1972).

18. Hunter, however, would disagree with this assertion. In a revision of his earlier study he maintained that the rise to influence of blacks did not signal the demise of Atlanta's top community power structure. See his *Community Power Succession: Atlanta's Policy-Makers Revisited* (Chapel Hill: University of North Carolina Press, 1980).

19. Delbert Miller, "Industry and Community Power Structures," *American Sociological Review* 23 (February 1958): 9–15.

20. This was noted by Floyd Hunter in his review of *Who Governs?* in *Administrative Science Quarterly* 6 (1961): 517–518.

21. Clarence Stone, "Systemic Power in Community Decision-Making: A Restatement of Stratification Theory," *American Political Science Review* 74, no. 4 (December 1980): 984.

22. Michael N. Danielson and Jameson W. Doig, *New York: The York: The Politics of Urban Regional Development* (Berkeley: University of California Press, 1982), pp. 15–16.

23. Theodore J. Lowi, "Machine Politics—Old and New," *Public Interest* 9 (Fall 1967): 86.

24. See Roger Starr, "Power and Powerlessness in a Regional City," *The Public Interest* 16 (Summer 1969): 10.

25. See Robert Caro, *The Power Broker: Robert Moses and the Fall of New York* (New York: Vintage, 1974).

26. Theodore J. Lowi, *At the Pleasure of the Mayor* (New York: Free Press, 1964), especially Ch. 7.

27. On New Haven, see Dahl, *Who Governs?* On Chicago, see Martin Meyerson and Edward C. Banfield, *Politics, Planning, and the Public Interest* (Glencoe, Ill.: Free Press, 1955). On other cities, see Jeanne Lowe, *Cities in a Race with Time: Progress and Poverty in America's Renewing Cities* (New York: Random House, 1968), pp. 68–72; Harold Kaplan, *Urban Renewal Politics* (New York: Columbia University Press, 1963).

28. Daniel Patrick Moynihan, "Toward a National Urban Policy," *Public Interest* 17 (Fall 1969): 3–20.

29. James L. Sundquist, *Making Federalism Work: A Study of Program Coordination at the Community Level* (Washington, D.C.: Brookings Institution, 1969).

30. See Edward Hayes, "Presidential Participation/Decentralization from Lyndon Johnson to Ronald Reagan," *Urbanism Past and Present* 8, no. 1 (Winter/Spring 1983): 1–11.

31. Jane F. Roberts, "National Urban Policy: Initial Intergovernmental Readings," *Intergovernmental Perspective* 4, no. 2 (Spring 1978): 7–14.

32. Myron A. Levine, "The Reagan Urban Policy: Efficient National Economic Growth and Public Sector Minimization," *Journal of Urban Affairs* 5, no. 1 (Winter 1983): 17–28.

33. Rochelle L. Stanfield, "Economic Development Aid—Shell Game or Key to Urban Rejuvenation?" *National Journal* (March 21, 1981): 497.

34. Ibid., pp. 494–495.

35. These proposals were enunciated by Reagan in various speeches. For the core of his message on enterprise zones, see *New York Times*, March 24, 1982, p. 14.

36. Jeffrey L. Pressman, "The Preconditions for Mayoral Leadership," *American Political Science Review* 66, no. 2 (June 1972): 512–513, 522.

37. In addition to the three styles mentioned in the text here, they also identified two other styles: the personality individualist and the executive. For a discussion of these, see John P. Kotter and Paul R. Lawrence, *Mayors in Action: Five Approaches to Urban Governance* (New York: Wiley, 1974), Ch. 7.

38. Ibid., p. 107.

39. Ibid., p. 111.

40. Douglas Yates, *The Ungovernable City* (Cambridge, Mass.: M.I.T. Press, 1977), p. 165.

41. Norton Long, "The City as Reservation," *Public Interest* 25 (Fall 1971): 35.

42. Allan R. Talbot, *The Mayor's Game: Richard Lee of New Haven and the Politics of Change* (New York: Harper & Row, 1967), p. 29.

43. Jewell Bellush and Murray Hausknecht, "Entrepreneurs and Urban Renewal: The New Men of Power," *Journal of the American Institute of Planners* 32, no. 5 (September 1966): 289–297.

44. Robert Dahl, *Who Governs?* pp. 200–214.

45. Peter K. Eisinger, "Black Mayors and the Politics of Racial Advancement," in William C. McReady, ed., *Culture, Ethnicity, and Identity* (New York: Academic Press, 1983), p. 106.

46. In Ernest N. Morial's first election as mayor of New Orleans in 1977, he received only 19 percent of the white vote but 95 percent of the black vote. In Richard Arrington's first election as mayor of Birmingham in 1979, he won less than 15 percent of the white vote. Philadelphia's Wilson Goode won about 20 percent of the white vote in his 1983 victory. Chicago's Harold Washington won few white votes but an estimated 95 percent of the black vote in his 1983 election. In his 1987 reelection, Washington expanded his vote in white neighborhoods but still received only a small minority of white votes. The major exception to this trend is Los Angeles's Tom Bradley, who won a majority of white votes in his initial election in 1973. See John J. Harrigan, *Political Change in the Metropolis,* 3rd ed. (Boston: Little, Brown and Company, 1985), p. 134.

47. Eisinger, "Black Mayors and the Politics of Racial Advancement," pp. 95–109.

48. Grace Hall Saltzstein, "Female Mayors and Women in Municipal Jobs," *American Journal of Political Science* 30, no. 1 (February 1986): 128–139.

49. Yates, *The Ungovernable City,* p. 153.

50. John F. Sacco and William M. Parle, "Policy Preferences Among Urban Mayors: A Comparative Analysis," *Urban Affairs Quarterly* 13, no. 1 (September 1977): 49–72.

51. Arnold M. Howitt, "The Expanding Role of Mayoral Staff," *Policy Studies Journal* 3, no. 4 (June 1975): 363–369.

52. Peter Trapp, "Governors' and Mayors' Offices: The Role of the Staff," *National Civic Review* 63, no. 5 (May 1974): 242–249.

53. Wen H. Kuo, "Mayoral Influence on Urban Policy Making," *American Journal of Sociology* 79, no. 3 (November 1973): 637.

54. See Susan S. Fainstein et al., *Restructuring the City: The Political Economy of Urban Redevelopment* (New York: Longman, 1983), Ch. 7.

Chapter 9
State Legislatures
and Public Policy

Chapter Preview

This chapter examines the role of state legislatures in establishing and overseeing public policy. We shall discuss in turn:

1. The three main functions performed by state legislatures.
2. The structure of state legislatures, with an eye to the impact of organizational patterns on policymaking.
3. Legislative processes, including the bill-passing sequence.
4. The impact of legislative reform movements on state legislatures over the past two decades.

Let us begin by looking at legislative functions.

Introduction

The state legislatures are crucial bodies for setting public policies. Each session of each legislature finds it enacting many policies that deeply affect our lives. Legislatures raise or do not raise our taxes. They appropriate money for various purposes, such as higher education, highway maintenance, and public health. They pass laws in attempts to deal with various social issues, such as drunk driving, wildlife preservation, and minority rights. As they go about the task of trying to carry out these difficult responsibilities, they get resoundingly criticized. The great English observer of American politics James Bryce once commented that "the state legislatures are not high-toned bodies."[1]

Many people today would agree with this understated criticism and perhaps express it even more vehemently. Whether the state legislatures still deserve their disrepute is a topic we will examine in this chapter. We will do that by asking four broad questions. First, what do legislatures do? (That is, what are their functions?) Second, how are legislatures organized to carry out their functions? (How are they structured?) Third, what roles do individual legislators play in legislative policymaking? (What are the legislative processes?) Fourth, can legislative performance be improved? (Have the reforms of recent years been effective?) Finally, when we ask these four questions of state legislatures, we must also ask what effects structure, process, and reform have on the kinds of public policies enacted.

Legislative Functions

Legislatures authorize the building of roads, set taxes and budgets, help constituents, and oversee state agencies, among many other things. In trying to categorize what legislatures do, three functions stand out—policymaking, legislative oversight, and representation.

Public Policymaking

One of the most important tasks of legislatures is to establish public policies. They do this in a variety of ways. When the state legislature appropriates money for the state budget, determines which taxes will be used to raise money, or passes special educational programs that are mandatory for local school districts, it obviously establishes a statewide policy that affects many people in numerous ways.

State legislatures, of course, are not the only institutions that set public policies. Governors set policies, as do courts, executive agencies, and mayors. Legislatures are distinct from these other institutions, however, in that the legislatures are the critical arenas for debating the proposed policies and determining whether they should have the force of law. The governor may propose, for example, a policy to increase the state income tax and decrease local property taxes. However, that policy is not enacted until the legislature makes the necessary tax changes and approves a budget with the needed appropriations.

Legislative Oversight

When the legislature establishes a policy or program, it necessarily provides a broad, general plan of action and delegates to the executive agency involved the responsibility for fleshing out the details. To ensure that the executive branch is carrying out the legislative intent of the law, the legislature exercises

legislative oversight. Historically, state legislatures paid haphazard attention to their oversight responsibilities,[2] but recent years have seen them devote increasing attention to the topic.

Traditional means of conducting oversight have been committee review of administrative agencies, **casework** (whereby individual legislators follow up on constituent complaints about their contacts with administrative agencies), and legislative audit (or postaudit) procedures. Under postaudit, a legislative auditing body is established to make studies of selected agencies to see how programs are working and whether the agencies are complying with legislative intent. Today, about two-thirds of the states have postaudit provisions.[3]

The two newest means of conducting oversight are sunset laws and the legislative veto. A **sunset law** (discussed more fully in Chapter 11) attacks the belief that some programs and agencies outlive their usefulness. To combat this, legislatures establish a specific life span for an agency (usually six or seven years). At the end of that time period the agency is slated to expire unless it can convince the legislature that it is still needed. Thirty-five states have adopted sunset review since it was first adopted in Colorado in 1976. The assessments of sunset laws as an oversight mechanism have been mixed. The most comprehensive study of sunset laws found that over 1,500 agencies in all sunset states had been reviewed over a five-year period (1976–1981), resulting in the termination of 300 agencies and modifications in the procedures of 300 others. The remainder were recreated without change.[4] Satisfaction with sunset laws varies from state to state. It gained a very positive response in Tennessee,[5] for instance. But many legislators complain that the sunset review process is too time-consuming. Disillusionment with the process led North Carolina to repeal its sunset law.[6]

If sunset review seeks to attack the problem of programs outliving their usefulness, the **legislative veto** seeks to attack the problem of administrative agencies writing rules and regulations contrary to the intent of the legislature. For example, to ensure the safety and well-being of children in day-care homes and day-care centers, many states have passed laws providing for the licensing of such establishments. Inevitably, such laws delegate to state welfare departments the responsibility for drawing up the specific rules concerning the number of children per center, the number of staff workers per child, the amount of space per child, and similar requirements. If the rules so promulgated are too rigid, day-care providers will complain to their legislators, and the legislators will seek to review the rules to see whether they are consistent with the legislature's intent in passing the legislation in the first place. By 1982, forty-one states had established formal procedures for reviewing such rules, and twenty-nine states had provided for a legislative veto,[7] which enables one or both houses of the legislature to veto the rule within a specified time period (usually thirty to ninety days) and prevent it from taking effect.

Of all these forms of legislative oversight, the legislative veto is currently the most controversial. A Congressional veto was struck down by the United States Supreme Court in 1983 as a violation of the separation of powers principle of the federal constitution. At the state level, the legislative veto has also been struck down in Alaska, Connecticut, New Hampshire, New Jersey, Wyoming, and Montana.[8] But even when it is struck down, legislatures find imaginative ways to accomplish their oversight goals. After Connecticut's legislative veto was struck down, for example, the legislature sought and secured a constitutional amendment permitting it, and California created an Office of Administrative Law with power to reject proposed rules.[9]

Representation

The third major function of the legislature is to represent the people in the government. Three aspects of representation have been of greatest importance in recent decades: how the geographic divisions of a state are represented,

If upheld by the courts, the legislative veto is a powerful weapon for the legislature in its perennial battle with the executive branch.

Source: By Mike Keefe. Copyright © 1983, Field Enterprises, Inc. Printed by permission of North America Syndicate, Inc.

which social sectors get represented, and whom the legislators perceive themselves as representing.

Apportionment, or Geographic Representation

The legislatures are divided into geographic districts. At the beginning of this century the rural dominance of the legislatures reflected the distribution of the population. But the representative districts did not change as the population shifted to urban areas. By the 1960s, metropolitan areas were grossly underrepresented in every state except Wisconsin and Massachusetts.[10]

Although the United States Supreme Court refused to act on the question of **apportionment** in 1946,[11] sixteen years later, in 1962, it heard the landmark case of *Baker* v. *Carr*.[12] The Supreme Court ruled that reapportionment of the Tennessee House of Representatives was a judicial issue. This decision eventually forced all the states to reapportion their lower houses on the basis of one person, one vote. Two years later, in *Reynolds* v. *Simms* (1964),[13] the Supreme Court applied the one-person, one-vote principle to state senates as well as to state lower houses. Chief Justice Earl Warren wrote in the Court's opinion that "legislators represent people, not trees or acres. They are elected by voters, not farms or cities or economic interests." Rural political leaders then sought to amend the United States Constitution to exempt state senates from the one-person, one-vote principle.[14] These attempts did not succeed, and all state legislatures were reapportioned to comply with population shifts found in the 1970 and 1980 censuses. Following *Reynolds* v. *Simms*, the one-person, one-vote principle was also applied to congressional districts and local general-purpose governments.[15]

The Impact of Reapportionment

Did reapportionment have any significant effects on the public policies that state legislatures approved? The earliest studies tended to answer this question negatively and found little significant policy impact from reapportioning the legislatures.[16] Later studies, however, began to find that reapportionment did seem to affect public policy outcomes. Because it takes time for new electoral majorities to create policy changes, reapportionment could be expected to have a delayed reaction on policy outcomes. This appears to have happened.[17] After reapportionment, legislatures became much more attentive to the problems of urban and metropolitan areas,[18] and the states assumed more active roles in dealing with problems such as air pollution, metropolitan planning, housing and urban renewal, and sewerage treatment and disposal.[19] Reapportionment also contributed to increasing black representation in the state legislatures. Reapportionment additionally led to allocation of more state financial aid to local governments. A study of central-city and suburban counties in selected metropolitan areas found that their share of state aid increased after reapportionment.[20] Reapportionment also increased suburban representation more than central-city representation. In a partisan sense, it is hard to make a conclusive statement about the benefits of reapportionment. Democrats seemed to benefit most in the North, and Republicans made gains in the South.[21] The most long-standing impact of reapportionment may well have been that the influx of suburban, minority, younger, and more heterogeneous legislators led to important reforms of the legislatures themselves and made them more capable of confronting today's problems.

Gerrymandering.   Legislative seats can be perfectly apportioned on a one-person, one-vote basis and still discriminate. This can be accomplished through the *gerrymander,* the practice of mapping legislative boundaries into odd shapes so that one party's voters are overconcentrated in a few districts, thus allowing the other party to win a majority of the legislative seats. A Republican-dominated 1981 Indiana reapportionment, for example, concentrated Democratic districts in Indianapolis while splitting the Democratic vote in Fort Wayne. As a consequence, the Democrats won only 43 percent of Indiana's House seats in the following election, despite the fact that they won 51.9 percent of the vote in House races throughout the state. In California, at the same time, Democrats redrew that state's legislative boundaries to the disadvantage of Republicans. Traditionally the federal courts have tended to reject gerrymandering cases on the grounds that they are "political issues," not "judicial issues." But in 1986, the United States Supreme Court reversed this tradition and ruled in the Indiana case that henceforward gerrymandering cases will be considered justiciable.[22] This ruling has not yet forced either California or Indiana to redraw their House boundaries, but the implications for reapportionment after the 1990 census are enormous. Legislative redistricting plans then could be under considerable pressure from federal courts not only to balance off urban and rural regions fairly but also to take partisan interests into consideration and to create districts that are compact and continuous.

Social Sector Representation

Social sector representation refers to the extent to which the various categories of people in society at large are represented in the legislature. In order to gain some insight into the patterns of representation, take the quiz on social representation on p. 216. If your responses show patterns to representation, your answers were realistic. There are patterns to the social sectors represented in legislatures. In some respects legislators are very similar to the people they represent, but in other respects they are not similar at all.

Legislators most resemble their constituents in the *birthright characteristics* of race, religion, and ethnicity.[23] Otherwise, the typical legislator is not very representative of his or her constituents. Although the number of women legislators is growing,[24] about 85 percent of the state legislators are men. Compared to their constituents, legislators tend to have lived in their districts longer, to be more involved in community organizations, and to have a slightly higher social status. They are more educated than the general population and are much more likely to have professional or managerial occupations. A 1979 study found that three-fourths of all state legislators were businesspeople, professionals (such as doctors or dentists), or lawyers.[25] Legislator-lawyers are most likely to be either rural lawyers[26] or *solo practitioners* (small-firm lawyers in business for themselves). For solo lawyers, political work provides a way to make valuable contacts and get favorable publicity.[27]

This all suggests that state legislatures represent the upper-middle sectors of the population much more than the lower sectors. Several social sectors are very underrepresented—women, youth, old people, racial minorities, and low-income people.

Perceptual Representation

In addition to representation by geographic district and by social sectors, representation can also refer to the *perceptions* legislators have about their representational role. The classic presentation of perceptual representation was

You Decide

Who Is Most Likely to Be a State Legislator?

		Yes	No
a.	White person in a black district?	☐	☐
b.	Black person in a black district?	☐	☐
a.	Person of the same religious background as most constituents?	☐	☐
b.	Person of a different religious background as most constituents?	☐	☐
a.	Person with many contacts in local organizations?	☐	☐
b.	Person totally unfamiliar with local organizations?	☐	☐
a.	Person who has lived in district many years?	☐	☐
b.	Person who just moved into the district?	☐	☐
a.	Person high on the socioeconomic ladder?	☐	☐
b.	Unemployed person?	☐	☐
a.	Lawyer, teacher, or businessperson?	☐	☐
b.	Unskilled laborer?	☐	☐

made by the great British theorist Edmund Burke, who distinguished between the trustee role and the delegate role. Burke advocated the **trustee** role, in which the legislators vote according to their own best judgment and not according to the wishes of their constituents. In the **delegate** role, by contrast, the legislators vote according to their constituents' wishes. Legislators sometimes balance the two roles, voting as a trustee on issues that generate little public interest or emotion but voting as a delegate on issues that enflame their constituents. Such legislators are said to play the **politico** role. A study of state legislators in Ohio, New Jersey, Tennessee, and California found that almost two-thirds indicated a trustee orientation, about 14 percent a delegate orientation, and about 23 percent a politico orientation.[28]

This overwhelming preference of legislators to function as trustees rather than as delegates seems to fit a broader set of values held by the public. Researchers in Iowa asked the legislators, a sample of the general public, and a sample of other political influentials who the legislators *should* be most attentive to as they decide how to vote in the legislature. Six possible sources for attentiveness were given—the legislator's conscience, the state, the legislator's district, the political party, the governor, and special interest groups. The results, shown in Table 9–1, show very little difference between the three samples. The general public, the community influentials, and the legislators themselves all wanted the legislators to be most loyal to their own conscience, the state, and their home districts. They wanted legislators to be least attentive to demands coming from the political parties, the governor, and political interest groups.

Table 9–1. Expectations About Perceptive Representation

"Which should a legislator be most attentive to in deciding how to vote?"

Iowa legislators	Sample of Iowa political influentials	Representative sample of Iowa voters
1. Conscience	1. Conscience	1. Conscience
2. State	2. State	2. District
3. District	3. District	3. State
4. Party	4. Party	4. Party
5. Governor	5. Governor	5. Governor
6. Group	6. Group	6. Group

Source: Ronald D. Hedlund, "Perceptions of Decisional Referents in Legislative Decision Making," *American Journal of Political Science* 19, no. 3 (August 1975): 538. Reprinted by permission.

Note: There was great similarity between the expectations of voters, legislators, and the political influentials about whose opinions a legislator should represent. Conscience, state, and district scored high; political parties, interest groups, and governors scored low.

Legislative Structure:
How Organization Affects Policymaking

The fifty states are very similar in their legislative organization. All but Nebraska are bicameral, that is, have two houses. All but Nebraska and the one-party states of the South organize themselves around political party caucuses. And all fifty states rely heavily on committees to do most of their work. Of these three structural features, bicameralism has the least effect on policy formulation.

Bicameralism

Bicameralism developed during the colonial period, when the house members were looked on as the elected representatives of the people and the senators as the appointed representatives of the governor. After the Revolution in 1776, the state senates served mainly to represent wealthy people with property, who feared that the popularly dominated lower houses would redistribute the wealth. By the early nineteenth century, all the states were bicameral. Only Nebraska reverted to the unicameral form, doing so in 1934.[29]

Unicameralism has worked well in Nebraska, and legislative reformers have urged it upon other states. Reformers argue that elimination of one of the two houses would make the legislature operate more efficiently and effectively. It would eliminate the need for conference committees and increase the prestige of the body.[30] In contrast, the supporters of bicameralism say that the two-house legislature helps preserve the traditional principle of checks and balances and impedes the hasty passage of poorly conceived bills by slowing down the legislative process. Whatever its merits, unicameralism is not popular with either legislators or the voters. When put on the ballot, unicameral proposals have been invariably voted down.

The Responsible-Party Model of Centralizing Influence

The **responsible-party model** has been very popular with many reform-minded political scientists, who feel it is the best way to make the legislature accountable to the voters.[31] They allude to the British Parliament as the ideal responsible-party system. Voters in England elect either the Conservative, the Liberal, or the Labor party to office. The winning party controls both the executive and legislative branches of government and enacts its own policies. When the voters become dissatisfied with the government's performance, they can vote the governing party out of office. No American state has a responsible-party system comparable to that in Great Britain, but the states vary widely on the degree of party strength and the ability of the parties to provide leadership in the legislature.

Party Leadership

The key feature of party organization of the legislature is the attempt to provide for leadership through the *centralization of influence* in a few party leaders. The dominant party leader in the lower house is the **speaker of the house,** who is the presiding officer and is chosen from the majority party (or the majority coalition in one-party states). The speaker's powers vary from state to state, but speakers typically have the authority to assign bills to committee, to recognize house members who desire to speak on the floor, to influence committee assignments of the members, to determine the house calendars, and to control the ebb and flow of legislative business on the floor.

Immediately subordinate to the speaker are the **majority leader** (or floor leader) and assistant majority leaders (or whips), whose task is to line up floor votes for party-supported bills. The same job is performed for the minority party by the **minority leader** and the assistant minority leaders. In some strong-party states, such as Rhode Island and Pennsylvania, a regular promotion pattern exists from whip to floor leader to speaker.[32] In strong-party states, speakers tend to hold their position for several years, whereas in the weak-party states a rotation system keeps circulating new people into the leadership positions.[33]

In the state senates, the presiding office is usually called the president. In twenty-eight states, the lieutenant governor serves as president of the senate; in the remaining states the president is elected by the senators. In most states, the president's position is an honorific one with few powers. But in Texas the president is the dominant leader of the senate. Other important party leaders in the senate are the majority and minority leaders. As in the house, they are helped by assistant majority or minority leaders.

From time to time, all the legislators of a party gather in a meeting called the party **caucus,** where they set goals and plan legislative strategies. In almost all states, party caucus meetings are closed to outsiders. At these meetings the party determines who will hold the leadership positions, what bills will demand party discipline, and who will prevail in the recurring battles between opposing factions within the party. If a legislative party is strong, it is able to make a majority of its members vote the party position on most important bills. In New Jersey, which is a strong-party state, the party caucus meets every legislative day and is very successful at maintaining discipline behind the caucus leaders.[34] In the weak-party states and the one-party states, the party caucuses seldom meet. This compounds their problems of building party discipline.

Sometimes party discipline gives way to coalitions built on ideological bases or personal ties. For instance, a conservative coalition of Republicans and Democrats has controlled the New Mexico House of Representatives for most of the 1980s,[35] and deadlocked party competition also led to cross-party coalition government in the Washington House of Representatives in 1979 and the California Assembly in 1981.[36]

Do Strong Competitive Parties Make Any Difference?

Party strength varies from state to state. Figure 9–1 shows the states dominated by Democrats or Republicans or by competition between these parties. In American political theory, two-party competition is expected to result in

Figure 9–1. Interparty Competition in the United States: 1974–1980

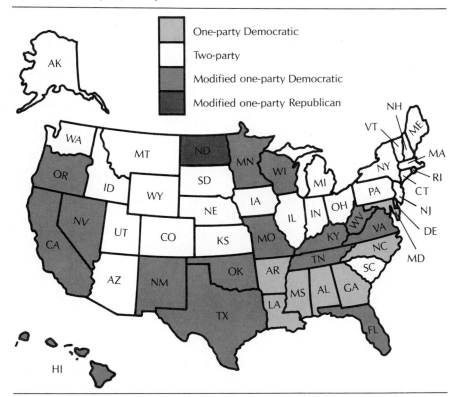

Source: John F. Bibby et al., "Parties in State Politics," Copyright © 1983 by John F. Bibby, Cornelius P. Cotter, James L. Gibson, and Robert J. Huckshorn, in Virginia Gray, Herbert Jacob, and Kenneth N. Vines, eds., *Politics in the American States: A Comparative Analaysis,* 4th ed. Reprinted by permission of Little, Brown and Company.

responsible parties that present alternative policy programs to the voters. As the two parties compete for votes, the competition forces the parties to be more responsive to the voters' wishes. In contrast, the absence of party competition is believed to lead to political factionalism built around personalities and temporary issues. The factions are not permanent, and they fail to translate voter preferences into public policy.[37]

Do strong, competitive parties lead to more liberal policies? Although the results of voluminous studies are not conclusive, four generalizations have emerged.

Highlight
Strong Leaders in Texas and Massachusetts

Two very different patterns of partisan leadership can be seen in Texas and Massachusetts. Texas is a predominantly Democratic legislature in which the major legislative divisions occur between different factions of the Democratic party rather than between Democrats and Republicans. The dominant person in the Texas Senate currently is Democrat William Hobby, who has presided over that body since he was first elected lieutenant governor in 1972. As president of the Senate, Hobby has authority to assign bills to committee, to appoint committee membership, to name committee chairs, to appoint senators to conference committees, and to control the floor agenda of the Senate. He also interprets the Senate's rules when they are disputed and recognizes members who wish to speak on the floor. He participates in debate himself and casts a vote in case it is needed to break a tie. Hobby has used these powers to secure himself as one of the main leaders of the moderate conservative faction in the Texas Democratic party.

Massachusetts is another Democrat-dominated state with a tradition of strong legislative party leadership, at least until

1985, when a revolt unseated the autocratic speaker of the House, Thomas W. McGee. McGee possessed most of the powers cited above for Texas's lieutenant governor. Additionally, he controlled the hiring of all legislative staff personnel and the distribution of office space among legislators. To keep representatives in the dark about legislation, McGee would prevent copies of bills from being printed before debate. Legislators who challenged him were sometimes arbitrarily removed from their committee positions and turned out of their office space. After McGee was voted out of the speaker's position in 1985, the new speaker, George Keverian, introduced a new rules package that maintained most of the speaker's powers but limited future speakers to eight years in office and provided for greater input and participation from rank-and-file legislators.

Sources: Clifton McCleskey, Allan K. Butcher, Daniel E. Farlow, and J. Pat Stephens, *The Government and Politics of Texas* (Boston: Little, Brown and Company, 1982), pp. 69, 108, 200, 344; *New York Times,* December 10, 1983, p. 8; George Goodwin, Jr., "1985 Leadership and Rules Changes in the Massachusetts General Court," *Comparative State Politics Newsletter* 6, no. 5 (October 1985): 16–19.

First, two-party competition does not necessarily lead to more liberal social welfare policies. Thomas R. Dye correlated two-party competition with fifty-four different policy outcomes, such as per-capita expenditures in the areas of education, welfare, and highways. He found several positive relationships between two-party competitiveness and liberalization of state expenditures in these areas. However, he also found that the most competitive states were also the most affluent and economically developed. After eliminating the effects of economic development, Dye found that only two of these fifty-four measures showed a statistically significant relationship between party competition and public policies. Dye concluded, "party competition itself appears to have little independent effect on policy outcomes."[38] The competitive states did not spend more money because they were competitive; they spent more money because they were wealthier.

Second, although two-party competition does not necessarily produce more liberal social welfare policies, there are a number of conditions under which it does. Increasing the level of party competition in a state will lead to more liberal social welfare policies in states where the competition is already fairly close and where the majority party has only a small margin over the minority party.[39] The same thing happens in states where the competition is highly volatile and the majority party has a realistic chance of being defeated.[40]

Third, on nonexpenditure measures, competition seems to make legislatures more responsive to demands. Wayne Francis found that the competitive states were more likely to take action on issues before the legislature than were the noncompetitive states.[41]

Fourth, outside of the South, when Democrats control the legislature, they often enact different kinds of policies than the Republicans would when they have control. Civil rights laws, for example, were much more likely to be passed under Democratic control than under Republican control.[42]

In sum, strong competitive parties can make a difference in the kind of policies a state adopts. This is most likely to happen when the competition is very close and very volatile. Outside of the South, Democrats appear to be more liberal than Republicans. The parties have a much stronger impact on nonbudgetary policy areas than they do in budget areas, however. For budgetary policy, two-party competition is probably less significant than the level of affluence of a state. The affluent states spend more because they have more money to spend.

Committee Organization as a Decentralizing Force

In contrast to party organization, which centralizes political influence in the hands of party leaders, committee organization *decentralizes political influence* to the chairpersons of the various committees that study legislative proposals called bills. The typical legislature will consider two or three thousand measures each biennium. (Massachusetts considered over 18,000 in 1981–1982). And several hundred of them will be enacted into law. New York's legislature was the most active in 1981–1982, enacting nearly 5,200 laws and resolutions.[43] To provide a division of labor capable of processing this massive amount of work, committees are created. Committees receive bills, conduct hearings, change the substance of bills, and vote to approve or disapprove them. There is usually a **standing committee** for each major area of legislation, such as taxes, agriculture, education, or transportation.

In addition to standing committees, **select committees** are created on a temporary basis to study important issues that do not fit readily into the workload of the standing committees. Another type of committee is the **interim committee,** which operates between legislative sessions to study subjects that did not get action at one session but are so important that they will be introduced in the next year's session. Interim committees, however, are not as important as they once were because of the trend toward full-time legislatures and the trend toward having the standing committees meet periodically during the interim.[44] A fourth type of committee is the **joint committee,** which is composed of members of both houses. Connecticut, Maine, and Massachusetts rely heavily on joint standing committees.[45] The advantage of such an arrangement is that it precludes the necessity of a bill's being examined separately by senate and house committees. Finally, a special type of joint committee is the **conference committee,** which is created to resolve the differences between house- and senate-passed versions of a bill.

Legislative Process: How Legislators Make Policy

Before an idea, no matter how brilliant, can be turned into public law, it must work its way through the legislative maze. Some of the procedures for doing this are very formal; others are very informal. Legislators play a variety of roles in this process, and they follow several unofficial and unwritten rules that govern legislative behavior.

Passing a Law

A simplified model of a bill's passage is shown in Figure 9–2. The bill may originally be conceived by a legislator, a lobbyist, a state agency, the governor's staff, a citizen group, or an interested citizen. But it can only be formally introduced by a house or senate member, who is known as the bill's author.

Figure 9–2. Steps in the Passage of a Bill

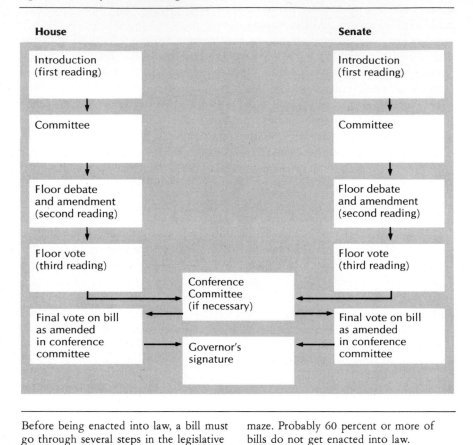

Before being enacted into law, a bill must go through several steps in the legislative maze. Probably 60 percent or more of bills do not get enacted into law.

The bill's first reading* occurs when the clerk announces the bill's number and title to the full house or senate.

After introduction, the bill is referred to a committee. It is very important to the author that the bill be sent to a friendly committee. If it is referred to a hostile committee in a state with strong committees, it may be given an unfavorable recommendation or simply **pigeonholed.** An important bill will be sent to a subcommittee that will conduct public hearings, invite all interested parties to testify, and amend the bill. In states with effective **sunshine**

*It is called a *reading* because the clerks originally read the bills aloud to the full chamber. Although this requirement is still demanded by some state constitutions, bills are never read aloud anymore.

laws, all official committee action is taken publicly in open meetings, records are kept of votes on amendments, and tape recordings of the debate are made available to reporters and the public.

After a bill is reported out of committee, it is put on a **calendar** to await its second reading and floor debate. Debate quite often occurs in a committee of the whole, which is simply the whole house meeting under the less formal committee rules. These allow a smaller **quorum** and make it easier to amend bills. Since the committee of the whole is where the full chamber makes its most serious amendments, the votes in committee of the whole indicate a legislator's intent much more than do the votes on final passage of bills.

Finally, after floor debate and amendment, the bill comes back for final passage as amended. This is the third reading. Most states require roll call votes on the passage of the bill, and forty states use electronic voting devices that flash a green light for an *aye* vote and a red light for a *nay* vote, and automatically record the votes.[46] When roll call votes are not used, or to determine unanimous consent, voice vote may be used.

When the house-passed version of a bill differs from the senate-passed version, a joint conference committee is appointed by the speaker of the house and the president of the senate to resolve the differences. The conference committee has an equal number of senators and representatives. The house and senate must approve or reject the conference committee report without amendment.

Once the chambers pass a single version of a bill, it is printed in final form (called *enrollment*) and sent to the governor for signature. At this stage, the governor has three choices. If the governor signs the bill, it becomes law. If the governor neither signs nor vetoes it, it becomes law without his signature. If the governor vetoes the bill, it does not become law unless the veto is overridden by the legislature. This seldom happens, in part because some states require a two-thirds majority vote in each house to override a veto and in part because many vetoes are made at the close of the legislative session, when the legislators are no longer present to conduct an override vote. To cope with this, more and more states are providing for special override sessions to give the house and senate a chance to override vetoes made after the regular session ends. Finally, some states provide for a pocket veto. If a bill comes to a governor at the close of a session and it is not signed or vetoed within a specified number of days (usually five to fifteen), it does not become law, and the governor is said to have exercised a **pocket veto.**

How Legislators Fit into the Legislative Process

In the bill-passing procedure, legislators play a variety of roles. These roles, which are determined largely by what purpose the legislators see themselves serving, have been described in one study as the **purposive roles** of ritualist, tribune, inventor, and broker.[47]

Ritualists become absorbed with legislative details, such as the rules of parliamentary procedure, that occupy so much of the legislator's time. **Tribunes** view the legislature as a forum for promoting popular issues that create considerable publicity for themselves and for the people whose interests they advocate. The **inventor** continually introduces new ideas into the legislative mill and attempts to get them translated into public policy. The **broker** guides the ideas of the inventors through the legislative maze and works out the compromises necessary for policies to be enacted. Whereas the inventor is oriented toward issues, the ritualist toward legislative details, and the tribune toward popular causes, the broker is oriented primarily toward power.

Some mixture of all these roles is necessary for the legislature to function well. The ritualist helps smooth over the conflicts that are inherent in the legislative process. The tribune helps link the legislature to citizen groups that may not be well represented by the established interest groups. The inventor helps introduce new ideas. And the broker works out the compromises necessary for policy to be made.

How Informal Rules Govern Legislative Behavior

When legislators carry out their various roles in setting public policy, they find themselves constrained by a series of unwritten, informal rules[48] designed to promote group cohesion, to keep personality conflicts from disrupting the legislative process, and to help the legislature resolve bitter conflicts between powerful interests or between individual members. Legislators may oppose one another on one measure but need each other's support on another measure. To survive in such an environment, they follow informal rules that enable them to satisfy the demands placed on them and at the same time cooperate on bills in which they share a common interest. If legislators allowed every bill they authored to become a life-or-death matter, they would soon have so many legislative enemies that none of their bills would pass.

Table 9–2 shows the most commonly accepted rules among 260 senators from eleven states. These informal rules are applied imperfectly, of course, and most of the sanctions used to enforce them are informal. For example, not all legislators are able to refrain from dealing in personalities, a norm subscribed to by 90 percent of the legislators polled in Table 9–2. However, legislators who consistently violate most of these rules encounter unpleasant consequences, such as having their bills obstructed, being ostracized from the dinners, parties, or other socializing events of the legislators, or being reprimanded by senior members. Once they lose the confidence of other mem-

Table 9–2. Informal Rules of the Legislature

Norm	Percent of legislators agreeing with the norm
Do not conceal the real purpose of a bill or purposely overlook some portion of it in order to assure passage.	94.5%
Do not deal in personalities in debate or in other remarks made on the floor of the chamber.	90.5
Do not give first priority to your reelection in all your actions as a legislator.	87.4
Do not introduce as many bills and amendments as possible during any legislative session.	84.6
Do not be a thorn to the majority by refusing unanimous consent.	77.8
Do not become generally known as a spokesperson for some special interest group.	74.4
Do not speak about subjects coming before the legislature on which you are not completely informed.	71.4
Do not become known as a loner who does not have much to do with other senators outside the chamber.	70.2
Do not seek as much publicity as possible from the press in order to look good for the people back home.	66.6
Do not avoid taking any kind of stand on legislation before the final vote or roll call.	63.5
Do not talk to the press or anyone else about decisions that were reached in private.	62.8

Source: E. Lee Bernick and Charles W. Wiggins, "Legislative Norms in Eleven States," *Legislative Studies Quarterly* 8, no. 2 (May 1983): 194–195. Copyright © 1983, Comparative Legislative Research Center. Reprinted by Permission.

bers, they may be subjected to embarrassing cross-examination or ridicule. They might lose political privileges such as patronage or good committee assignments.

How Legislators Are Influenced to Vote

Perhaps the most important aspect of the informal legislative process concerns how legislators are influenced to vote on specific public policies. In our earlier discussion of representation, we asked whether the legislator *should* be a trustee or a delegate. In reality, as illustrated in Figure 9–3, the pressures on legislators are much more complex than this. They consult and are influenced by a wide variety of sources, ranging from fellow legislators to individual constituents. Figure 9–3 suggests that the intralegislative influences are much more important than the extralegislative influences. When asked whom they consulted before making decisions, legislators were much more inclined to name persons in the legislature than to name the governor, constituents, or interest groups. Interest groups, however, may have more influence than Figure 9–3 suggests. A study of lobbyists registered in Iowa found that interest

Figure 9–3. Sources That Legislators Consult

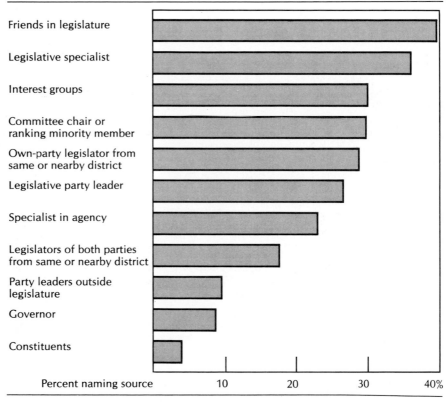

Senators and representatives are much more attentive to such intralegislative sources of influence as friends, specialists, and committee chairs than they are to such extralegislative sources of influence as constituents, governors, or party leaders. The extralegislative source of influence that rates highly is the interest group.

Source: From Eric Uslaner and Ronald Weber, *Patterns of Decision Making in State Legislatures* (New York: Praeger Publishers, 1977).

group lobbyists were more active than other actors. They took positions on 61 percent of the bills before the legislature, compared to 35 percent for the governor, and 26 percent for the house majority caucus. Further, on 84 percent of the bills, there was no conflict between lobbyists. When they came into conflict with the governor or the house majority caucus, however, the interest groups were more likely than the others to lose.[49] Finally, legislators are also affected by their own ideological leanings. A study of voting in the Connecticut and North Carolina legislatures from 1971 through 1974 found that a liberal or conservative orientation of legislators had a greater impact on their vote than did their partisanship or the economic characteristics of the districts they represented.[50]

Legislative Reform: Improving Legislative Performance

As legislatures have gone about their tasks of making public policy, they have been heavily criticized for the way they perform the public's business. Their deficiencies over the years led a number of organizations—such as the Citizens Conference on State Legislatures,[51] the Advisory Commission on Intergovernmental Relations, the Council of State Governments, the Eagleton Institute, and the Committee for Economic Development—to call for extensive legislative reform that would professionalize the state legislatures and streamline their operations. During the past fifteen years, considerable progress has been made toward meeting the criticisms levied by these organizations. A distinguished student of legislative reform, Alan Rosenthal, wrote in 1981: "Years ago state legislatures merited much of the criticism that is aimed at them today . . . [but recently] . . . they have proved to be more deserving; now they merit commendation rather than blame."[52] The general thrust of the proposals for legislative reform and the progress made toward achieving reform are summarized in the following six statements.

1. *Legislatures should be smaller in size.* Just how large a legislature should be cannot be determined. Minnesota—with 67 members—has the largest state senate, and New Hampshire—with 400 members—has the largest house. The Committee for Economic Development recommended that state legislatures be no larger than 100 members. Reformers feel that a smaller legislature would enhance its prestige, make it possible to offer higher salaries, and enable more highly qualified people to run for office. Reducing the size would necessarily force the legislatures to restructure the committees, and pinpointing responsibility would be easier.

   While these arguments seem plausible, there is no evidence that these objectives would necessarily be achieved in smaller legislatures. Smaller legislatures would, however, reduce the representation of racial minorities, women, and the poor. Since racial minority legislators come mostly from small, homogeneous districts, increasing the population and heterogeneity of their districts would decrease minority representation. Because reducing the size would also increase the geographic distance covered by the legislative districts, the legislators in many rural, sparsely populated states would lose intimate contact with many of their smaller communities.

There were a few reductions in legislative size during the 1970s and 1980s. Illinois and Massachusetts, for example, reduced the size of their lower houses by a third. But few states have followed their example.

2. *Legislative sessions should be more flexible.* Historically, legislative sessions were timed to coincide with the work schedules of farmers. This resulted in legislatures that met every other winter for sixty or ninety days. These rigid sessions meant that the legislature had no way to deal with crises during the rest of the two-year period, short of calling special sessions. Because of the pressure to get much legislation passed during the short sessions, legislatures were criticized for passing most of the bills during what was called the "end-of-the-session logjam." This led to abuses. The end-of-the-session logjam provided a convenient excuse for burying bills not favored by the leadership. It enabled the leadership to push through other bills or amendments hastily, without giving the members a chance to deliberate on them. A logjam problem indeed exists. In the 1981–1982 sessions, 38 percent of all bills were passed in last 10 percent of the sessions. But the logjam problem varied widely from state to state. A study of the problem in thirty-seven states found that North Carolina passed *all* its bills in the final 10 percent of the sessions. At the other extreme, Arizona passed only 1 percent of its bills in the final 10 percent of the sessions.[53] Unhappily for reformers, however, states with annual sessions and long sessions did not have any less of a logjam problem than did the other states.

In response to the criticisms about rigidity, the states have greatly extended their meeting times. Forty-three states now meet annually, and nine states are in session so often that for all practical purposes they have become full-time.[54]

3. *Legislatures should become professional, full-time bodies with an adequate salary for the members.* Most legislatures are nonprofessional institutions that do not pay their members enough money to devote full time to the job. Legislative turnover is very high (about 22 percent each term and reaching over 40 percent in some state bodies),[55] making it difficult to provide a body of experienced members who can cope effectively with experienced lobbyists and state agency executives. Reformers usually desire full-time, well-paid, professional legislators with lower turnover rates.

Although compensation has steadily increased in most states, the average annual salary in 1986 was only about $17,000. Additional per diem payments and travel reimbursements would make total compensation somewhat higher, but such a low salary obviously makes it impossible to have a full-time legislature. In response to these criticisms, most states over the past decade have increased pay and lengthened their sessions. But in some states complaints are now being raised that this has led to the worst of both worlds. Except for the few states with full-time legislatures, legislative pay is seldom high enough to enable most legislators to make it their full-time job. However, the time demands have become so burdensome that legislators also find it difficult to hold down a full-time job outside the legislature. Some states have begun reducing session length,[56] and debate has renewed on the value of the part-time amateur versus the full-time professional legislator.[57]

4. *Legislatures need better staff and research capability.* Legislatures without adequate research capabilities are unduly dependent on the research and information provided by interest groups, state agencies, and other interested parties. Trained staff members can do many things to assist legislators and legislative committees—draft bills, analyze bills that the legislators do not have time to read thoroughly, analyze the governor's budget proposals, and evaluate programs being administered by state agencies. In fact, the legislatures increased their staffs substantially during the 1970s. Today the fifty state legislatures collectively employ 16,000 workers year round and take on another 9,000 during the sessions.

5. *Constitutional restrictions on legislatures should be removed.* In addition to the expected constitutional matters dealing with the structure and powers of legislative bodies, most state constitutions provide detailed restrictions on legislative activity. As mentioned previously, some state constitutions prescribe how much pay legislators will receive and the maximum number of days the legislature can meet. Yet the most restrictive constitutional provisions are the ones imposed on state budget-making powers. *Earmarked funds* in the state constitutions restrict legislative flexibility to set the state budget.

6. *Legislative processes need to be cleaned up.* The nature of raising campaign funds indebts some legislators to vested interests. Many legislators have hidden conflicts of interest. They receive benefits from organizations that in turn benefit from policies supported by these very legislators. Accordingly, and as a result of demands created in the immediate post-Watergate era, most legislatures are adopting rules for stricter disclosure of legislators' financial interests, stricter enforcement of fair campaign practices laws, more extensive disclosure of campaign contributions, tighter regulation of lobbyists, creation of ethics commissions to oversee the implemen-

tation of these laws, and sunshine laws that open the legislative process to public scrutiny.

Legislative Reform and Public Policy

To summarize, the ideal reformed legislature is distinguished from the unreformed legislature by several key features. It tends to meet annually in flexible sessions instead of in short, rigid sessions held once every two years. It is moving toward making the office of legislator a full-time, professional position with a high salary rather than a part-time job with a low salary. It is relatively small in size. Its constitutional provisions outline the overall structure and give the legislature broad grants of authority rather than prescribe technical legislative rules. It has adequate staff and research assistance and sufficient office space. Its committees are well organized. Finally, it has provided itself with effective measures to control graft, conflicts of interest, and political corruption.

The Policy Consequences of Legislative Reform

Considerable time, energy, and money were invested during the 1970s and 1980s in drawing up this agenda for reform and getting the reforms adopted by the states. Has this reform activity made any difference? When a state legislature begins adopting these reforms, what are the consequences? Does it really matter in a state's politics and public policies whether its legislature is reformed or not? One study of Illinois came up with some sobering conclusions and suggests that one must be cautious in expecting too much from legislative reform. (See the Highlight on p. 233.)

Several social scientists have attempted to determine the relative influence of the socioeconomic and legislative reform variables. Most have concluded that legislative reform in itself does not lead to more liberal welfare and educational expenditures. Lance T. LeLoup conducted a sophisticated multiple regression statistical analysis that enabled him to test the relationship between one index of legislative reform and policy outcomes after eliminating the effect of economic development. He found that legislative reform was directly related only to two outcomes—the scope of governments and average welfare payments. Some legislative reforms had more impact on policy results than did others. LeLoup concluded that the reforms most likely to have a policy impact were those that brought a more diverse variety of people into the legislature and those that made the legislators more representative of their constituents.[58] In this respect, the legislative reapportionment starting in 1962 probably had more impact on modernizing state legislatures than did other reforms.[59]

These limited results of legislative reform should not be exaggerated, however, to mean that reform has no impact on policy. Legislative reform never takes place in a vacuum. And when it occurs, it can enhance the impact that other variables have on public policy. Viewing the issue this way, Edward Carmines concludes that a professionalized legislature enhances the impact that interparty competition has on public policy. That is, two-party competition is more likely to produce generous welfare policies in states with professionalized legislatures than in states with unprofessional legislatures.[60] Phillip W. Roeder found that legislative reform combined with executive reform has a significant impact on increasing expenditures for police services.[61] In conclusion, legislative reform has made a distinct improvement in state political processes, but the evidence is still inconclusive on how much impact legislative reform has on liberalizing state public policies.

Highlight
Results of Reform in Illinois

Illinois is a state that moved from having one of the least-respected legislatures in the early 1960s to the number-three legislature according to a comparative study in 1971. An influx of suburban legislators in 1965 created pressure for legislative reforms, and a Commission on the Organization of the General Assembly was formed. This commission recommended several reforms to the 1967 session of the legislature, and a number of these recommendations were adopted over the next few sessions—improvements in legislative staffing, better legislative pay, reimbursement of legislative expenses, establishing deadlines for the introduction of new bills in order to ease the end-of-the-session logjam. These improvements were reinforced in 1971 when the new Illinois Constitution eliminated some of the constitutional restrictions on the legislature. Additionally, the legislative process was smoothed by provisions for unanimous consent and recessed sessions. It has been moving increasingly in

the direction of becoming a full-time body. Conflict-of-interest legislation has curbed some of the abuses that occurred during the early 1960s. In short, from the mid-1960s to the early 1970s, Illinois moved from having one of the worst to having one of the most reformed state legislatures. Reforms continued in the 1980s as the size of the house was reduced.

What have been the results of all this? All these changes have improved the quality of legislative procedures in Illinois, but a study of the impact of reorganization on public policy in Illinois was unable to find any identifiable impact of the legislative reorganization on the kinds of public policies that were enacted in that state.

Source: Summarized from Samuel K. Gove, "Policy Implications of Legislative Reorganization in Illinois," in *State Legislative Innovation,* James A. Robinson, ed. (New York: Praeger, 1973), pp. 101–135.

Summary

1. The legislative functions discussed in this chapter are public policymaking, legislative oversight, and representation.

2. A major legislative representation conflict during the early 1960s was over reapportionment. This was settled by the Supreme Court cases that demanded apportionment according to the one-person, one-vote principle. However, instituting that principle did not eliminate partisan gerrymandering, did not make the legislature more socially representative of the population, and did not affect the legislators' tendencies to think of themselves as trustees rather than as delegates.

3. Several patterns were observed in the organization of state legislatures. All but one are bicameral. The two organizing devices are the political parties, which tend to centralize influence, and the committee systems, which tend to decentralize influence. Although state legislative committee systems have typically been much weaker than the congressional committee system, very little development of strong and responsible parties has occurred to strengthen ties between the legislature and the voters.

4. The legislative process seems to put a premium on delay, caution, and checks so that powerful political minorities are able to block bills that threaten them. Throughout the 1950s and 1960s this phenomenon gave the state legislatures a noninnovative image in the face of pressing social changes.

5. Partially in order to restore the autonomy of state legislatures, the legislative reform movement accelerated in the late 1960s and the 1970s. Although the reforms improved the internal procedures of the legislatures, scholars have been able to find few consistent patterns in policies that resulted from legislative reform. This lack of distinct policy change may reflect the tendency of reformers to focus on technical and procedural reforms that did not affect the balance of power in the legislatures.

Key Terms

Apportionment The division of legislative seats among the population. *Malapportionment* refers to a very unequal division of legislative seats. *Reapportionment* refers to the act of apportioning the seats once again to make their division more equal.

Broker The legislative role of guiding the ideas of inventors (see *Inventor*) through the legislative maze and working out the compromises needed for policies to be enacted.

Calendar Generally refers to a list of bills that have been acted on by committee and are waiting for debate or final vote. There are specific types of calendars with a wide variety of names for the specific stages of floor consideration of bills.

Casework The practice of helping constituents handle their problems with government agencies. So called because each constituent's problem becomes a "case" to be solved.

Caucus A group of legislative members who meet jointly to push a legislative program. Usually refers to a party caucus such as the House Republican caucus or the Senate Democratic caucus.

Conference committee A temporary joint legislative committee created to work out a compromise when the house-passed version of a bill differs from the senate-passed version.

Delegate The representation role in which legislators vote as their constituents wish rather than voting their own consciences.

Interim committee A legislative committee that meets during the interim between legislative sessions to provide groundwork for the coming legislative session.

Inventor The legislative role of continually introducing new ideas into the legislative mill.

Joint committee A committee composed of members of the House and Senate.

Legislative oversight The legislature's responsibility to see that the executive branch implements laws as the legislature intended them to be implemented.

Legislative veto A device whereby the legislature can reverse an action of the governor or executive agencies by passing a resolution (the legislative veto) opposing the action within a short period of time after its announcement (usually thirty to ninety days).

Majority leader The majority-party leader responsible for managing legislation on the floor of the legislature.

Minority leader The minority-party leader responsible for managing legislation on the floor of the legislature.

Pigeonholing The act of filing a bill for the record but never taking it up for consideration.

Pocket veto The governor's act of killing a bill he or she has received after the close of a legislative session simply by not signing it within the required number of days (usually five to fifteen).

Politico The representation role in which legislators sometimes vote their consciences and other times vote as their constituents wish.

Purposive role A legislative role by which the legislator acts out what he or she sees as the purpose of being in the legislature. *Inventor, Broker, Tribune,* and *Ritualist.*

Quorum The number of members needed to be present for the legislature to conduct its business. Usually a quorum requires a majority of members to be present.

Responsible-party model A model of parliamentary control similar to that in Britain in which voters elect a party to power and the individual legislators are accountable to the party, which in turn is accountable to the voters. When voters become displeased with the party's performance, they can vote it out of power.

Ritualist The legislative role of being absorbed with minor legislative details and the perquisites of being a legislator, to the detriment of using parliamentary procedure to further legislation.

Select committee A temporary legislative committee that is responsible for legislation that has surfaced in a particular legislative session but that is not expected to recur permanently.

Speaker of the house The key party leader, who presides over the lower house of the state legislatures.

Standing committee A permanent legislative committee that is responsible for legislation in each subject area that recurs in every legislative session, such as education or transportation.

Sunset law A law requiring programs to terminate in a given number of years unless they are reauthorized by the legislature. This forces the legislature to reevaluate the purposes and operations of the sunset agencies and programs.

Sunshine law Legislation requiring that all government business, including legislative business, be open to the public.

Tribune The legislative role of acting as spokesperson for causes.

Trustee The representation role in which the legislators vote their consciences rather than as their constituents wish.

References

1. James Bryce, *The American Commonwealth,* vol. 1 (New York: Macmillan, 1906).

2. Alan Rosenthal, *Legislative Life: People, Process, and Performance in the States* (New York: Harper & Row, 1981), p. 314.

3. Alan Rosenthal, "Legislative Oversight and the Balance of Power in State Government," *State Government* 56, no. 3 (1983): 90–98.

4. Common Cause, *The Status of Sunset in the States: A Common Cause Report* (Washington, D.C.: Common Cause, 1982).

5. William Lyons and Patricia K. Freeman, "Sunset Legislation and the Legislative Process in Tennessee," *Legislative Studies Quarterly* 9, no. 1 (February 1984): 151–160.

6. *State Legislatures* 9, no. 2 (February 1983): 3.

7. Thad L. Beyle, "Governors and Legislatures," *The Book of the States 1984-85* (Lexington, Ky.: Council of State Governments, 1984), pp. 42–43.

8. Rosenthal, "Legislative Oversight and the Balance of Power in State Government," pp. 90–98.

9. Lanny Proffer, "Legislative Veto Alternatives," *State Legislatures* 10, no. 1 (January 1984): 23–25.

10. Gordon E. Baker, *The Reapportionment Revolution: Representation, Political Power and the Supreme Court* (New York: Random House, 1966).

11. *Colegrove* v. *Green,* 328 U.S. 549 (1946).

12. *Baker* v. *Carr,* 369 U.S. 186 (1962).

13. *Reynolds* v. *Sims,* 377 U.S. 533 (1964).

14. It was not only the politicians who objected to the *Reynolds* v. *Sims* decision. Some scholars also objected to it. Political scientist Alfred De Grazia argued that the Tenth Amendment ought to be strengthened to preclude the Supreme Court from handling apportionment cases. See De Grazia, "Righting the Wrongs of Representation," *State Government* 38 (Spring 1965): 113–117. Also see A. Spencer Hill, "The Reapportionment Decision: A Return to Dogma?" *Journal of Politics* 31 (February 1969): 186–213. For a contrary view, see Robert B. McKay, "Don't Amend the Constitution," *State Government* 38 (Spring 1965): 121–125. For a summary of apportionment cases after *Baker* v. *Carr* and the 1970 census, see Ross E. Robson and Parris N. Glendenning, "Apportionment: Judicial Intervention," in *Controversies in State and Local Political Systems,* Mavis Reeves and Parris N. Glendenning, eds. (Boston: Allyn and Bacon, 1973), pp. 132–136.

15. *Wesberry* v. *Sanders,* 376 U.S. 1 (1964) was the congressional case.

16. See Herbert Jacob, "The Consequences of Malapportionment: A Note of Caution," *Social Forces* 63 (1964): 261; Thomas R. Dye, *Politics, Economics, and the Public: Outcomes in the American States* (Chicago: Rand McNally, 1966), p. 273; David Derge, "Metropolitan and Outstate Alignments in the Illinois and Missouri Legislative Delegations," *American Political Science Review* 53 (1958): 1051–1065; Thomas A. Flinn, "The Outline of Ohio Politics," *Western Political Quarterly* 13 (September 1960): 712–721.

17. Cho and Frederickson found, "In a nationwide sense, then, it can be argued that the effects of reapportionment were delayed, but that generally speaking, as a state gets further from the year or session of the initial reapportionment, the effects of that act become more apparent." For example, those that reapportioned early spent more money for general welfare and for urban-related functions such as "public welfare, public health and hospitals, and less for highways, state aid to local governments in general and to local schools in particular. . . . Our findings seem to indicate that reapportionment has had a selective impact which is, like the process of budgeting, incremental, becoming more apparent with the passing of time." Yong Hyo Cho and H. George Frederickson, "The Effects of Reapportionment: Subtle, Selected, Limited," *National Civic Review* 63, no. 7 (July 1974): 357–362. Quote on p. 362.

18. Michael C. Le May, "The States and Urban Areas: A Comparative Assessment," *National Civic Review* 61, no. 11 (December 1972): 542–548.

19. Paul N. Ylvisaker, "The Growing Role of State Governments in Local Affairs," *State Government* 51 (Summer 1968): 150–156.

20. Cited in Cho and Frederickson, "The Effects of Reapportionment," pp. 357–362.

21. See Timothy O'Rourke, *The Impact of Reapportionment* (New Brunswick, N.J.: Transaction Books, 1980).

22. *Davis* v. *Bandemer* 106 S.Ct. 2797 (1986). For background, see: Charles H. Backstrom, Leonard S. Robins, and Scott D. Eller, "Partisan Gerrymandering in the Post-*Bandemer* Era," a paper presented at the American Political Science Association Convention, August 28, 1986, Washington, D.C.; Bill Warren, "The Gerrymander Puzzle," *State Legislatures* 12, no. 9 (October 1986): 21–25; and Debra J. Collins, "Indiana Reapportionment Case Promises Precedent-Setting Ruling," *National Civic Review* (March–April 1986): 99–101.

23. Thomas R. Dye, "State Legislative Politics," in *Politics in the American States: A Comparative Analysis,* Herbert Jacob and Kenneth N. Vines, eds. (Boston: Little, Brown & Co., 1965), p. 166.

24. On women in state legislatures, see Emmy E. Werner, "Women in the State Legislatures," *Western Political Quarterly* 21, no. 1 (March 1968): 40–50. The most extensive study of female legislators is that of Jeanne Kirkpatrick, *Political Women* (New York: Basic Books, 1974).

25. Insurance Information Institute, *Occupational Profile of State Legislators* (New York: Insurance Information Institute, 1979).

26. Michael Cohen, "Community Size and Participation by Lawyers in Community Politics," *Journal of Politics* 31, no. 4 (November 1969): 1107–1110. This study of upstate New York lawyers found that almost two-thirds of the rural county lawyers had held elective public office, whereas less than 20 percent of the urban county lawyers had held such offices.

27. Herbert Jacob, *Justice in America: Courts, Lawyers, and the Judicial Process,* 2nd ed. (Boston: Little, Brown & Co., 1972), pp. 70–72.

28. Heinz Eulau et al., "The Role of the Representative," *American Political Science Review* 53, no. 3 (September 1959): 742–756.

29. For a review of the early history of unicameralism, see George S. Blair, *American Legislatures: Structure and Purpose* (New York: Harper & Row, 1964), pp. 141–145.

30. See Jesse Unruh (former Speaker of the California Assembly), "For a One-House Legislature," *National Civic Review* (May 1971): 253–258.

31. "Toward a More Responsible Two-Party System," *American Political Science Review* 44 (September 1950): supplement.

32. Douglas Camp Chaffey and Malcolm E. Jewell, "The Institutionalization of State Legislatures: A Comparative Study," *Western Political Quarterly* 23, no. 1 (March 1970): 1283.

33. Samuel C. Patterson, "Legislators and Legislatures in the American States," *Politics in the American States: A Comparative Perspective,* 4th ed., Virginia Gray, Herbert Jacob, and Kenneth N. Vines, eds. (Boston: Little, Brown and Company, 1983), p. 162.

34. Donald Morrison, "The Legislatures in Three States: A Farewell to Ignominy," *New York Times,* April 11, 1976, p. E-6.

35. Phil Hain, "Coalition Control of the 1985 New Mexico Legislature," *Comparative State Politics Newsletter* 6, no. 5 (October 1985): 22–23.

36. See "Is the Party Over? Political Parties in State Legislatures," *State Legislatures* 7, no. 10 (November/December 1981): 27.

37. See V. O. Key, *Southern Politics* (New York: Vintage Books, 1949), Ch. 14.

38. Dye, *Politics, Economics and the Public,* p. 258. In analyzing similar data somewhat differently, political scientist John H. Fenton came to the opposite conclusion. See John H. Fenton, "Two-Party Competition: Does It Make a Difference?" in *People and Parties in Politics,* John H. Fenton, ed. (Glenview, Ill.: Scott, Foresman, 1966). Also see John H. Fenton and Donald W. Chamberlayne, "The Literature Dealing with the Relationships Between Political Process, Socio-Economic Conditions and Public Policies in the American States, A Bibliographic Essay," *Polity* 1, no. 3 (Spring 1969): 388–404. Finally, Virginia Gray analyzed competitiveness over time rather than at a single point in time as Dye had done. She discovered that party competition had a significant impact on changes in policy outcomes over time. Virginia Gray, "Models of Comparative State Politics: A Comparison of Cross-Sectional and Time Series Analyses," *American Journal of Political Science* 20, no. 2 (May 1976): 235–256.

39. Gerald C. Wright, Jr., "Interparty Competition and State Social Welfare Policy: When a Difference Makes a Difference," *Journal of Politics* 37, no. 3 (August 1975): 796–803.

40. Gray, "Models of Comparative State Politics."

41. See Wayne L. Francis, *Legislative Issues in the Fifty States: A Comparative Analysis* (Chicago: Rand McNally, 1967).

42. Robert S. Erikson,"Relationship Between Party Control and Civil Rights Legislation in the American States," *Western Political Quarterly* 24, no. 1 (March 1971): 178–182.

43. *The Book of the States: 1982-1983* (Lexington, Ky.: Council of State Governments, 1982), p. 207.

44. William Pound, "The State Legislatures," *The Book of the States: 1982-1983*, p. 183.

45. George Goodwin, Jr., "State Legislatures of New England," *New England Politics*, Josephine F. Milburn and Victoria Shuck, eds. (Cambridge, Mass.: Schenkman Publishing Co., 1981), pp. 117–118.

46. *State Legislatures* (May 1985): 12. Twenty states use electronic voting in both houses. Another twenty use it only in the lower house.

47. John C. Wahlke et al., *The Legislative System: Explorations in Legislative Behavior* (New York: Wiley, 1962), p. 259.

48. Ibid., pp. 146–161.

49. Charles W. Wiggins and William P. Browne, "Interest Groups and Public Policy Within a State Legislative Setting," *Polity* 14, no. 3 (Spring 1982): 548–558.

50. Robert M. Entman, "The Impact of Ideology on Legislative Behavior and Public Policy in the States," *Journal of Politics* 45, no. 1 (February 1983): 163–182.

51. The Citizens Conference on State Legislatures, *The Sometimes Governments: A Critical Study of the 50 American Legislatures* (New York: Bantam Books, 1971).

52. Alan Rosenthal, *Legislative Life* (New York: Harper & Row, 1981), p. 3.

53. Harvey J. Tucker, "Legislative Logjams: A Comparative State Analysis," *Western Political Quarterly* 38, no. 3 (September 1985): 432–446.

54. William T. Pound, "The State Legislatures," *The Book of the States: 1986-87* (Lexington, Ky.: Council of State Governments, 1986), p. 77.

55. *The Book of the States: 1986-87*, p. 88.

56. Pound, "The State Legislatures," p. 77.

57. See Andrea Paterson, "Is the Citizen Legislator Becoming Extinct?" *State Legislatures* 12, no. 6 (July 1986): 22–23; Charles B. Howe, "The Case for . . . the Professional Legislator," *State Government* 47, no. 3 (Summer 1974): 130–136; Michael L. Strang, "The Case for . . . the Citizen Legislator," *State Government* 47, no. 3 (Summer 1974): 130–136. Howe and Strang were members of the Colorado House of Representatives at the time they wrote these articles.

58. Lance T. LeLoup, "The Policy Consequences of State Legislative Reform" (paper delivered at the Midwest Political Science Association meeting, Chicago, Ill., April 29–30, 1976). Other attempts to correlate legislative reform with specific policy outcomes have reached even more pessimistic conclusions than LeLoup's. See especially Leonard Ritt, "State Legislative Reform: Does It Matter?" *American Politics Quarterly* 1 (October 1973): 499–510; Albert K. Karnig, State Legislative Reform and Public Policy: Another Look," *Western Political Quarterly* 29, no. 3 (September 1975): 548–552.

59. LeLoup, "The Policy Consequences of State Legislative Reform."

60. Edward G. Carmines, "The Mediating Influence of State Legislatures on the Linkage Between Interparty Competition and Welfare Policies," *American Political Science Review* 68, no. 3 (September 1974): 1118–1174.

61. Phillip W. Roeder, "State Legislative Reform: Determinants and Policy Consequences," *American Politics Quarterly* 7, no. 1 (January 1979): 51–70.

Chapter 10
Governors and the Challenge of Executive Leadership

Chapter Preview

This chapter examines the role of state governors in providing public policy leadership. We shall discuss in turn:

1. The demand for strong executive leadership.
2. The reformers' goal of increasing the formal powers of governors.
3. Governors' leadership styles.
4. Governors' careers.
5. Other state executives.
6. The impact of strong governors on public policy.
7. Governors and the political economy of states.

Let us begin with a glimpse at some fascinating governors.

Introduction

In most states, the governor is the most visible politician, and over the years governors have been some of the most interesting people in American politics. Woodrow Wilson, Franklin Roosevelt, Jimmy Carter, and Ronald Reagan used the governor's office as a springboard to the presidency.

Many others sought to do so but failed. Huey Long, calling himself the "Kingfish," established a virtual dictatorship in Louisiana (1928–1931), went on to the United States Senate, then was gunned down by an assassin as he plotted a challenge to the incumbent president, Franklin Roosevelt. Jerry Brown of California (1975–1983) chose to live in a small apartment rather than in California's governor's mansion, which he derided as a Taj Mahal, drove a simple Plymouth rather than being chauferred in a state limousine, and urged the people of California to follow his example of a simpler lifestyle. He then went on an African safari with pop singer Linda Ronstadt.

241

Scorned by some as "Governor Moonbeam" but idealized by others, Brown at the age of 38 won upset victories in five out of six presidential primaries in 1976 and was reelected governor in 1978 by 1.3 million votes. Seemingly with no place to go but up, Brown made one disastrous mistake in 1981 and was brought down to earth. When an infestation of the Mediterranean fruit fly threatened to destroy California's agricultural industry in 1981, Brown vacillated on allowing aerial spraying of the crops. California's agribusiness recovered, but Brown did not; the next year he was resoundingly defeated in a bid for the United States Senate.[1]

Other, less-colorful governors have also been bitten by the presidential bug. For New York governors it has almost been an occupational hazard. Republicans Thomas E. Dewey and Nelson Rockefeller, as well as Democrat Averell Harriman, harbored presidential ambitions.

A springboard to national fame may be the most dazzling thing about the governorship today, but there is much more to the office than that. Governors have the opportunity to provide policy leadership in their states, and they are often expected to make sure that the state bureaucracy does its job responsibly, to cope with crises as they arise, and to preside over a strong state economy.

This chapter examines executive power at the state level of government. It looks first at the effects of the political reform movement on the changing expectations about executive leadership. Second, it discusses leadership exercised by governors and other state executives. Third, it examines the importance of career patterns on gubernatorial leadership. Fourth, it asks whether strong executive leadership has any significant consequences for the public policies adopted and for the way in which public benefits are distributed. Finally, it explores the importance of the political economy to governors today.

The Demand for Strong Executives

Executive Representation

Our expectations of the state and local executives have evolved through three historical stages. First, from the 1830s until about 1900 there was a demand for what Herbert Kaufman has called **executive representation.**[2] This demand was based on the belief that the executive branch should represent people just as the legislature does. Its origins were in **Jacksonian democracy,** the concept of the **spoils system,** and the direct election of large numbers of administrative officials through the **long ballot,** so called because of its long list of elective executive offices. Voters choose not only governors and mayors but other statewide administrators, clerks, and many local officials not engaged in broad policymaking. The long ballot persists into the present day. As recently as 1960, for example, Los Angeles voters had to choose from among seventy different candidates and issues.[3]

Philosophically, the demand for executive representation was supported by two arguments. First, it was thought that the long ballot would make the bureaucracy conform to the wishes of the people. To a limited degree, the long ballot, when tied to the nineteenth-century urban political machines, may have helped accomplish this. As the immigrants began to dominate the urban population, they voted their fellow immigrants into office. These officeholders, in turn, hired their immigrant supporters to work in the public bureaucracies, including fire and police departments.

The second argument for executive representation was based on the separation of powers. Early American political philosophers—especially James Madison—taught that the concentration of power is dangerous.[4] They advocated dividing power among many hands. At the state and local levels, the number of elective executive offices was expanded. This change limited the power of governors and mayors to act as chief executives responsible for the overall direction of the executive branch.

The system of executive representation and the machine politics that was closely associated with it, however, soon led to widespread abuses—graft, corruption of law enforcement agencies, undemocratic politics, and inefficient government. These things soon came under attack by the progressive political reformers of the late nineteenth and early twentieth centuries.

Neutral Competence

Reformers demanded that public services be removed from dominance by the political machines. They wanted services to be performed competently and in a politically neutral fashion. The demand for **neutral competence** is reflected most obviously in the merit systems of employment. In 1883 the United States Civil Service System was established. In the same year New York passed a civil service act, and Massachusetts passed one the following year. Today all the states use some variation of a merit system for hiring, promoting, and firing state employees. (For greater elaboration on these points, see Chapter 11.)

The administration of the delivery of public services was another area in which reformers sought neutral competence. As the concept of neutral competence became popular, service delivery agencies were increasingly insulated from political interference by the governor or the legislators. This was particularly the case in public education. Requirements for teacher certification, systems of tenure for teachers, and state education boards composed of citizen members were instituted to protect the education delivery system from political interference. The governor's influence was increasingly restricted to the overall level of funding that the states would provide to local schools.

As demands for more government services grew during the twentieth century, the new services were increasingly provided by government institutions politically independent of governors, legislatures, mayors, and city councils. This trend led to a proliferation of independent agencies, special districts, governing boards, licensing boards, and regulatory agencies, each of which had its own constituency and few of which were under the policy control of the governor and the legislature. As the concept of neutral competence was put into practice, it led to a governmental structure characterized by weak governors, executive authority fragmented among a number of independent agencies, duplication of services, overlapping responsibilities, a lack of coordination, unconcern for overall state policy, and unaccountability to the voters.

Executive Leadership

These deficiencies of neutral competence stimulated a demand for **executive leadership.** Twentieth-century critics wanted the chief executive's office to be strengthened so that it could exercise policy control over the delivery of services. These critics believed that meeting the service needs of the growing populations and establishing modern public policies to deal with these problems required strong governors and strong mayors who could control their bureaucracies. They wanted to counter the excessive fragmentation of authority that occurred as a result of both the executive representation and neutral competence philosophies. Control of administrative functions would be integrated and concentrated in the hands of a governor or mayor who would be chief executive in fact as well as in name.

As the movement for executive leadership has picked up momentum, it has led to a general increase in stature in the office of governor and in the quality of the people who aspire to that office. At mid-twentieth century, the typical governor was more likely to be a "good-time Charlie" than a dynamic manager of government. The last two decades, in contrast, have seen the emergence of a "new breed" of governors who, in Larry Sabato's words, were "better educated than ever, and more thoroughly trained for the specific responsibilities of the governorship."[5]

Executive Leadership at the State Level: Making Governors Stronger

From the preceding discussion, we see that the general trend in state government has been to strengthen the governor in order to provide effective leadership. In a sense, all of the chief executive roles outlined below are aspects of the main role of exerting leadership. As chief legislator, chief administrator, leader of public opinion, and so on, the governor primarily provides leadership in the formulation, adoption, and execution of public policies in the state.

The Governor's Role in Policymaking

The strong governor is the central person in establishing state public policies. More than anyone else, the governor sets the agenda for public policy decision making, coordinates the formulating of policy, and oversees its implementation.

Setting the agenda for policymaking is critical. The legislators can only pass bills that are put on their agenda. Ideas that are never drafted into bills or that fail to gain enough support to merit serious discussion in key committees do not get put on the decision-making agenda. One of the most important things that governors do is to shape the political environment so that their proposals will receive high priority on the legislature's agenda.

The strong governor also coordinates the formulating of state policies. His support is sought for the legislative proposals that are made by state agencies, relevant interest groups, the governor's party, and the governor's staff. Since governors have several bargaining tools, such as the threat of a veto, their legislative requests are seriously considered by the legislators. This is especially true of budget requests. Because of their crucial position in the law-making process, strong governors can propose a legislative program and a budget and be fairly certain of getting much of what they want enacted into law. After the policies are established by the legislature and enacted into law, the strong governor is expected to oversee how well the state administrative agencies are carrying them out. If an agency falls under heavy public criticism for the way it implements the law, the governor is expected to bring that agency into line.

In providing policy leadership, the governor performs a number of roles ranging, as shown in Table 10-1, from chief of state to ultimate judge to chief crisis manager. Many problems do not reach the governor until they attain crisis proportions, and resolving big crises can often put the governor's reputation and future career on the line. Careful agenda building and policy planning by the governor cannot always avoid disasters, such as the nuclear power plant accident at Three Mile Island, Pennsylvania, in 1979 or the infestation of the Mediterranean fruit fly in California in 1981. Pennsylvania Governor Dick Thornburgh enhanced his reputation by his handling of the Three Mile Island crisis, but California Governor Jerry Brown injured his reputation by vacillating on the state's response to the Med fly.[6]

Some Governors Are Stronger than Others

Despite the expectations that the governor will exercise strong leadership in policymaking and policy implementation, many governors lack the legal

Table 10–1.   Governors' Roles

Chief of State
Performs ceremonial functions. Represents the state in Washington, D.C., and in intergovernmental organizations such as the National Governors' Association.

Chief Legislator
Sends legislative proposals and budget proposals to the legislature. Gives an annual state-of-the-state message. Lobbies and bargains with legislators for passage of legislative proposals. Has veto power (except in North Carolina).

Chief Administrator
Appoints officials to many state agencies, regulatory commissions, and advisory boards. Requires state administrators to report on their activities. Prepares the state budget.

Military Chief
Is commander-in-chief of the state national guard. The national guard is often called out to keep peace and order during national disasters and civil disturbances.

Chief of Party
In two-party states, the governor is usually the most prominent party leader, especially if the governor's party also controls the legislature. In one-party states, the governor usually leads only one of the major factions within the party. As chief of party, the governor can seldom control local nominations for the legislature or control statewide nominations. However, by judicious use of patronage and campaign assistance, the governor can often use his assets to build support for the party and in turn get legislators to support his legislative program.

Leader of Public Opinion
Makes public appearances, holds interviews and press conferences, and corresponds with residents. Tries to build support for himself and his program. Takes part in activities, such as planting trees on Arbor Day, that give symbolic support for causes he favors.

Ultimate Judge
Has power to grant pardons. May commute sentences. May grant paroles. May grant a reprieve that postpones the execution of a sentence. Has power of rendition which enables him to return a fugitive from justice to a state asking for the fugitive's return.

Crisis Manager
When a natural disaster occurs or some other crisis erupts, the governor is often expected to organize a state response and resolve the problem.

---

authority to provide that leadership. Thad Beyle constructed an index of formal powers of governors, shown in Table 10–2.[7] The index has five measures of gubernatorial strength: tenure potential (whether the governor can succeed himself or herself and the length of his or her term), appointive powers (how many policymaking state officials are appointed by the governor), budget powers (how much influence the governor has over the state budget), veto powers (the conditions under which he or she can veto laws), and organization powers (the extent to which state administrative agencies are subordinated to the governor). Each measure has a maximum of five points, and the total number of points on all five measures is twenty-five. As Table 10–2 shows, New York and seven other states are judged to have the most powerful governors, while six states are ranked among the weakest. The

Table 10-2. Index of Gubernatorial Strength

Very strong	*Moderate*
New York (24)	Missouri (19)
New Jersey (23)	Nebraska (19)
Pennsylvania (23)	Ohio (19)
Utah (23)	Virginia (19)
Hawaii (23)	Wisconsin (19)
Maryland (23)	Florida (18)
Massachusetts (23)	Georgia (18)
Minnesota (23)	Kansas (18)
	Kentucky (18)
Strong	Louisiana (18)
California (22)	North Dakota (18)
Connecticut (22)	West Virginia (18)
Illinois (22)	Alabama (17)
Michigan (22)	Arkansas (17)
South Dakota (22)	New Mexico (17)
Wyoming (22)	Oklahoma (17)
Arizona (21)	Washington (17)
Colorado (21)	Indiana (16)
Delaware (21)	Oregon (16)
Idaho (21)	Rhode Island (16)
Iowa (21)	Vermont (16)
Alaska (20)	*Weak (10–15 points)*
Maine (20)	Nevada (15)
Montana (20)	New Hampshire (14)
Tennessee (20)	North Carolina (14)
	Mississippi (12)
	Texas (11)
	South Carolina (10)

Source: Thad L. Beyle, "Governors," Copyright © 1983 by Thad L. Beyle, in Virginia Gray, Herbert Jacob, and Kenneth N. Vines, eds., *Politics in the American States: A Comparative Analysis,* 4th ed. Reprinted by permission of Little, Brown & Company.

strongest governors tend to be found in states that are urban, affluent, and have intensive competition between the two political parties.

Challenges to Gubernatorial Leadership

Leading the Legislature

The success of contemporary governors is measured most visibly by how much of their legislative programs pass. Their legislative strength is based primarily on the authority to present messages to the legislature, to recommend laws for passage, to present an executive budget, to veto bills, and to call special sessions of the legislature. With their budget message and their state-of-the-state address, the governors set the agenda for legislative action. But their most dramatic legislative tool is probably the **veto.** All states except North Carolina give the governor the right to veto. Forty-three states additionally give the governor an **item veto** over appropriations bills; that is, they can veto specific appropriations without vetoing the total package. Montana and Illinois grant their governor an **amendatory veto;** the governor can add money to appropriations made by the legislature.

Governors veto only a very small number of bills passed by the legislature. In the 1983 through 1985 sessions, governors in all fifty states vetoed about 3,266 out of 69,139 bills, about 5 percent. Forty percent of these vetoes occurred in only three states (California, Illinois, and New York).[8]

Although the veto is normally a negative tool used to block legislation, it is most effective when used positively to shape legislation. It is especially effective when used as a threat or in combination with the executive amendment provisions. Under executive amendment the governor may return a bill to the legislature and suggest that it be changed. The legislature can either accept the amendments or reject them, but it cannot make any other changes in the bill at that point.[9] If the legislature rejects the amendments, the governor may decide to veto the whole bill. If it accepts the amendments, then the governor has shaped the legislation as intended without resorting to the veto.

Overriding a veto usually takes at least a three-fifths vote in each house. Although overrides are becoming more frequent than they were two decades ago, they are still rare,[10] happening only about 5 percent of the time.[11] Because of this rarity, the veto and the threat of a veto are very potent tools for the governor.

The legislature dominates in some states, such as South Carolina and Texas, whereas some other states, such as New York and New Jersey, have a tradition of dominance by the governor. In most states, in the perennial battle between governor and the legislature, there is reason to believe that the governor is losing ground.[12] Governors' formal powers and the legislative structure have both been greatly improved by the governmental reform movement of the 1960s and 1970s, but one of those reforms' impacts has been to give the legislatures increased staff to assist in negotiating with governors on a more even footing. Added to that has been the tendency of some legislatures to empower themselves to hold veto-override sessions, in which they can cast override votes on vetoes that in previous years they would not have voted on. New York, for example, has a long history of strong governors (Roosevelt, Dewey, Rocke-feller) whose programs sailed through the legislature. In the 1970s, governor–legislature relations became so bad that New York's Democratic governor Hugh Carey called the legislature "a zoo,"[13] and in 1976 the legislature overrode a governor's veto for the first time since 1870. Once that barrier was broken, overrides became "relatively common in the Carey years."[14] Governor Mario Cuomo appears to have had much better relations with his legislature; but Alan Rosenthal asserts that the governorship is not as strong as it once was.[15]

Depiste losing ground to the legislature, the governor remains a formidable force for legislative leadership, especially if the governor's party also controls the legislature and the governor dominates the party. This combination is not easy to bring about, however. Massachusetts Governor Michael Dukakis's strongest opposition often came from his fellow Democrats in the legislature rather than from the Republicans. Said Dukakis, "When you've got majorities of four to one in the legislature—I'm sure you recognize that it is by no means an unmitigated blessing—you've got conservative Democrats, you've got liberal Democrats, you've got moderate Democrats, you've got suburban Democrats, you've got rural Democrats, and you don't have any Republicans."[16]

Running the Bureaucracy

As chief executive, the governor is expected to run the state's administrative agencies. Much of the governor's mail comes from citizens complaining about a specific bureaucratic failure—perhaps a parent of a mentally retarded child who is encountering difficulties in getting the child placed in a desirable training facility. In practice the governors have very little to say about such detailed administration of services, and they tend to pass such complaints directly on to the agency involved. Unless the complaint requires major policy changes, the matter is likely to be handled by one of the governor's staff aides, who at most will contact the appropriate agency, perhaps inquire about procedures, find out if anything can be done, and draft a letter for the governor's signature.[17]

The governor does not have enough time to follow up personally on detailed administrative matters such as the one cited. Except for crises, the governor's interest in administering state bureaucracies usually centers on getting favorable persons appointed to key positions, setting budget limits, and coordinating general policy questions. Such appointive and policymaking matters occupy an increasing amount of the governor's time.[18] But when a natural disaster occurs or when an emergency erupts, the governor's full attention is drawn to specific administrative details. For example, the Attica Prison revolt in New York in 1971 commanded the detailed attention of Governor Nelson Rockefeller, who personally authorized state troopers to invade the prison and free the prisoners' hostages.[19] Prior to the revolt and after the immediate crisis had passed, there is little evidence to suggest that Rockefeller personally concerned himself in administrative questions about the state corrections facilities. Nor is Rockefeller's lack of involvement in corrections unique. Few governors have the time to get deeply interested in more than a few issues. And since any significant issue divides powerful political interests in the state, governors can risk their popularity or be accused of political interference if they get too deeply enmeshed in administrative matters. The governors typically appoint a state corrections commissioner or a governor's crime commission to handle administrative details or to recommend policy changes regarding matters such as state prisons.

Obstacles to Strong Administrative Leadership

Governors face several obstacles in their quest to control the executive branch. First, they are confronted by several other state officers, such as the lieutenant governor, the attorney general, the treasurer, and the auditor, who in most states have been elected to office in their own right. Table 10–3 shows that the average state has from six to seven directly elected state

Table 10–3. Statewide Elected Executives

Office	Number of states in which elective
Governor	50
Lieutenant Governor	42
Attorney General	43
Secretary of State	36
Treasurer	38
Auditor	18
Education Department Head	16
Controller	12
Agricultural Department Head	12
State Board of Education	11
Public Utilities Commission	11
Insurance Commission Head	8
University Board of Regents	5

Number of offices	Number of states with that many elective offices
10 or more	4
8–9	13
6–7	21
4–5	5
3 or less	7
	50

Source: The Book of the States: 1986–87 (Lexington, Ky.: Council of State Governments, 1986), pp. 51–57.

offices. These separately elected officials are seldom elected as a party slate. Some may be Democrats and others Republicans. In 1986, five states had governors of one party and lieutenant governors of another party.[20] In the entire history of Minnesota, only once have all elected state officers been from the same party (1975–1979).

A second obstacle to strong administrative leadership is the autonomy of most individual departments. Some of the most important state departments are administered by a separately elected head or by an independent board or commission. Education is perhaps the most pertinent example. Table 10–3 shows that heads of education departments are separately elected in sixteen states. Moreover, in forty-nine states the state department of education is under a state board of education that often appoints the state superintendent of education and establishes statewide education policies. With the interposition of such a board between the governor and the department itself, educational administration is well protected from gubernatorial interference. To be sure, the governor has considerable influence in determining the amount of state financial aid that is channeled to public education, and the governor can also be a leading force for innovative educational programs, as exemplified in the 1980s by Tennessee governor Lamar Alexander[21] (see Chapter 14). But by and large, the governor has little to say about administrative matters such as personnel, curriculum, and the organization of public instruction.

The third obstacle to strong administrative leadership is the relationship that exists between state agencies and private enterprise. All states have licensing boards that control admission to the professions, administrative agencies that run programs, and regulatory agencies that oversee such functions as pollution control, health care facilities, and utility rates. It is often charged that the regulatory agencies serve the interests of the industries they are supposed to regulate rather than serving the interests of the public.[22] And the licensing boards tend to be peopled by representatives from the sectors they are supposed to oversee.[23] This close relationship between state agencies and specific private sector interests creates an obstacle for gubernatorial leadership, because the private groups often come to the support of agencies when governors try to control them or lead them in new policy directions.

To strengthen the governor's administrative powers, reformers have sought to remove the three administrative obstacles just discussed, by:

1. Eliminating separately elected state executives,
2. Allowing the governor to appoint a cabinet of department heads,
3. Reducing the number of independent state agencies,
4. Centralizing the budgetmaking process in the governor's office,
5. Removing boards and commissions from direct administrative roles.

All of these reforms have been implemented in many states, some in all states. But the effect has *not* been to give the governor undisputed control over the executive. Political scientists over the past twenty years have periodically surveyed state agency heads to find out whether governors or legislators had more control over their agencies. In 1967 Deil S. Wright discovered that a majority of agency heads felt their state legislatures exerted more control over them than did their governors.[24] Since 1967 there has been a considerable strengthening of the governors' administrative powers. But sixteen years later, in 1983, Glenn Abney and Thomas P. Lauth reported that a similar survey of state agency heads still found that a majority of them (53 percent) felt the legislature exerted more influence over them than did the governor.[25] For most governors, successful administrative leadership probably lies less in controlling administrative details than it does in carving out a limited number of policy initiatives, selecting competent agency heads who agree with those policy initiatives, securing a budget that reflects the policy priorities, and avoiding embarrassments in the few staff agencies directly under the governor's authority (usually Planning and Finance).

Strengthening the Governor, in Practice

In practice, the governor has a number of sources of strength in his or her attempts to exert policy leadership. Some of these (such as budgeting) result from increasing his formal powers, and some (such as public relations and political party) result from personal characteristics and political factors.

Budgeting as a Source of Strength

Budgeting helps the governor control the state administration, and the budgeting process will be discussed in detail in the next chapter. The normal budgeting practice is for executive agencies to submit their budget requests to a budget office or a finance commissioner who works closely with the governor. The governor determines overall spending guidelines and tries to establish priorities on how funds are divided among the various programs and agencies. He or she then submits the budget to the legislature, where the governor is expected to fight for its passage.

By establishing overall spending limits and by setting priorities, the governor can exert significant influence on policies and on agencies' procedures for implementing them. Most governors enjoy strong budget powers, and few express any need to seek major extensions of them.[26]

The Governor's Staff as a Source of Strength

Choosing an effective staff is the governor's first cardinal task.[27] Poorly chosen staff members can give the governor a bad image, make poor suggestions on administrative appointments, alienate key legislators, and fail to accomplish important tasks. Governors' staffs have expanded dramatically in recent years, from an average of 4.6 persons in 1957 to 7.3 persons in 1967[28] to 34 in 1979.[29]

Staff members are needed to serve as press secretary, administrative aide, personal secretary, legislative liaison, budget analyst, and policy analysts. In addition to their personal staff, the governors can also make extensive use of state planning agencies and budget offices, which have increasingly been put under direct control of the governor. Finally, federal legislation since the 1960s has required state planning and advisory commissions in a wide number of policy areas ranging from criminal justice to manpower. Since those advisory commissions are normally created directly under the governor, the governor needs full-time policy analysts to work with them.[30]

Public Relations as a Source of Strength

Because the image of leadership can influence actual leadership, most truly successful governors are very attentive to public relations. For one thing, a poor public image decreases the governor's prospects for reelection.[31] Governors use public relations efforts to create popular support for their legislative programs, thus increasing chances of getting those programs passed by the legislature. Malcolm Jewell wrote: "The most renowned governors of this century have been men who were able to lead public opinion. This has been a trademark of New York governors—Smith, Roosevelt, and Rockefeller, for example—and men like Earl Warren in California, Adlai Stevenson in Illinois, and Woodrow Wilson in New Jersey."[32] So important are public relations activities that most governors rely heavily on them, and they seldom miss an opportunity to appear before television cameras.

The Federal System as a Source of Strength

In some respects, the proliferation of federal grants-in-aid programs since the 1960s has given the governor a new role as federal systems officer for the states.[33] In this role the governor lobbies for his or her state and attempts to coordinate the operations of federal programs in the state. This role in turn has increased the governor's planning powers, since many federal programs demand a comprehensive approach to program planning and since state planning agencies have been increasingly placed under the governor's office.[34]

To cope with the growing federal influence, the governors have set up separate offices in Washington, D.C., and joined together to lobby as a group for favorable treatment at the federal level. By 1983 thirty states had offices to lobby for them in Washington. Perhaps the major channel through which governors collectively lobby with the federal government is the National Governors' Association. At its annual meeting, the Governors' Association passes resolutions calling for federal action on specific state problems.[35] It then lobbies Congress for legislation in those areas.

Political Party as a Source of Strength

Finally, the political party is a potential source of strength for governors, although in many states it is a very limited asset. A survey of fifteen governors who left office in the middle 1970s found that they made little use of the political party. They did not turn to the party as a source of either ideas for public policy or appointments to public office. The main uses of party were three. First, because the legislature is divided by party, it helps a governor to have his or her party in control of the legislature. Second, governors are likely to feel that they can deal better with the federal government and the intergovernmental system if their party controls the White House. Third, they need party support to get renominated and reelected.[36]

Exercising Leadership: Governors' Styles

In addition to formal powers, such as the veto power and the power of appointment, the successful governor also needs the less tangible qualities of leadership. Unless a governor has effective leadership qualities, all of the formal powers may still not produce a strong governor. The importance of leadership qualities was seen in an ambitious study by Larry Sabato, who compared 312 governors between 1950 and 1975 according to their hard work, competence, dedication, and ability to meet the needs of their states. He judged 117 (about a third) of them to be outstanding.[37] When those outstanding governors were compared to the nonoutstanding governors by several criteria (including their education and experience, the formal powers that their states gave to the office, and the degree of interparty competition in their states), there was only a slight tendency for states with substantial formal governor's powers (see Table 10–2) to produce outstanding governors."[38] The strongest relationship found was that the outstanding governors were usually younger than the nonoutstanding governors. But youth as a factor may be "largely a proxy measure for personal dynamism and ambition."[39]

In short, the leadership style of governors is just as important in determining their success as is the formal power of their office. Little has been written about the style of governors' leadership. But at least four styles can be identified: the demagogue, the program entrepreneur, the frustrated warrior, and the caretaker.

The Demagogue

The preeminent **demagogue** was undoubtedly Huey Long of Louisiana (1928–1931).[40] Long called himself "the Kingfish," established a virtual dictatorship in Louisiana, manipulated the state judges so they would interpret the constitution to fit his political ambitions, siphoned untold amounts of the state's money into his own political organization, and trampled unmercifully on opponents who dared to challenge him. His term did not lack substantive accomplishments, however. He provided free textbooks for the public schools for the first time in the state's history, broadened public higher education, established the state's basic highway structure, and engaged in well-publicized fights with the state utilities to lower their rates.

Huey Long's greatest success was in manipulating public relations in order to give symbolic gratification to his lower-class supporters. He proudly called for a nationwide "Share Our Wealth" plan that would prohibit anyone from earning more than $1 million a year. He appeared prominently before news cameras at the sidelines of Louisiana State University football games. He showed his disdain for the upper class by greeting a foreign dignitary while dressed in his pajamas. And he proudly showed his affinity with poor farmers by pulling off his shoe in the middle of a speech and displaying that, like them, he still had holes in his socks. As a reward for these antics, the people of Louisiana repeatedly returned him and his political machine's candidates to power. Long ended up in the United States Senate after a bitter struggle in which he had the state courts rule that he could not be succeeded by the lieutenant governor even though that succession was clearly specified in the constitution. Long was by this time enjoying considerable national popularity. He had his eye on the 1936 presidential campaign when his career was ended by an assassin.

The Program Entrepreneur

The **program entrepreneur** was the most popular style of governor during the 1960s and early 1970s, when governments were broadly expanding their public service programs. Nelson Rockefeller of New York (1959–1973) is one of the best examples.[41] Rockefeller proposed programs for housing, highways, higher education, elementary and secondary education, and a host of other services. The program entrepreneur's style of leadership during periods of economic expansion is to propose more and more programs to deal with the state's problems. During periods of recession and economic contraction, the program entrepreneur's style is one of calling for efficient and businesslike management of scarce resources. It is a style particularly suited to contemporary society, in which the educated elites have been socialized into thinking in terms of problem solving. Problems are identified, alternative solutions proposed, and the most rational alternatives chosen. The program entrepreneur fits nicely with this mode of thinking.

The Frustrated Warrior

A frustrated warrior is in essence a governor who sought to be a program entrepreneur but was unsuccessful. For many reasons the frustrated warrior is unable to get his or her programs adopted, and he or she ends the governorship in frustration. New York's Averell Harriman (1955–1959) and Hugh Carey (1975–1979) were frustrated warriors. They, like Nelson Rockefeller, faced a Republican-dominated legislature. Furthermore, personality differences made it difficult for them to deal effectively with the Republican legislative leaders.[42]

The Caretaker

A fourth style of governor is the **caretaker.** Caretakers may be either Democrats or Republicans, but they are usually conservative. They are not demagogues, nor do they push for programs. They see the job largely as one of maintaining the state in operation but not using the state's power to achieve any social goals. Caretakers often have been lieutenant governors who succeeded to the governorship but were unable to win election in their own right. Elected governors who become caretakers usually do so during times of governmental retrenchment, such as the 1980s.

Governors' Careers

There are two significant criteria for becoming governor. First, one must have the appropriate background. Second, one must choose the most appropriate strategy for a campaign. The most likely candidates meet the constitutional requirements for the position, are over forty years of age but not over the middle fifties,[43] and share their constituents' race, ethnicity, and religion. Male aspirants have a distinct advantage over females, but women have enjoyed increasing success (see Highlight on p. 257).

Governors have a higher income, a better education, and a more prestigious job than the average state resident. Most governors are lawyers.[44] And as the Highlight on women governors suggests, the successful aspirant must also be accomplished in politics, business, civic affairs, or professional life to provide visibility.

Once the potential candidates meet these background criteria, they then must decide which route to take to the state house. There are four major routes. The most commonly traveled one is the *political promotion route.* Joseph Schlesinger's study of the career patterns of 995 governors from 1870 to 1950 found that 90 percent had held prior public office.[45] This pattern has strengthened in recent years. Only 4 percent of governors elected since 1970 had no prior experience in public office.[46] The precise promotional pattern varies from state to state. In Iowa there appears to be a hierarchical promotion process within the Republican party. In Mississippi most governors come directly from the legislature. In Texas and several other states a law enforcement pattern of succession has been identified. Attorneys general and prosecuting attorneys gain favorable publicity that has often served as an asset to them when running for the governorship.[47]

A good example of a governor who followed the political promotion route is Jimmy Carter. After serving in the Georgia legislature, he ran unsuccessfully for governor. Capitalizing on the name recognition and publicity he got in that race, Carter returned in the following election to win the governorship.

In contrast to governors who move up through the political promotion route, others are able to use the *preeminent citizen route*. Ronald Reagan, governor of California from 1967 to 1975, provides a good example. Well-known as a movie star, president of the Screen Actors Guild, and host of a General Electric–sponsored television series, Reagan gained political visibility through his work for Barry Goldwater's ill-fated conservative bid for the

Highlight
Women Governors of the 1970s and 1980s

Kentucky: Martha Layne Collins (1983–   )
Party affiliation: Democrat
Age at election: 46
Background: High school teacher
Political experience: Kentucky Lieutenant Governor (1979–83)

Vermont: Madeleine Kunin (1985–   )
Party affiliation: Democrat
Age at election: 51
Background: Immigrant refugee from Fascist Italy in the 1930s; newspaper and TV reporter
Political experience: State legislator (1973–79); Vermont Lieutenant Governor (1979–83); unsuccessful Vermont gubernatorial candidate (1983)

Nebraska: Kay Orr (1987–   )
Party affiliation: Republican
Age at election: 47
Political experience: Nebraska State Treasurer (1981–87); governor's chief of staff (1979–81)

Connecticut: Ella Grasso (1975–80)
Party affiliation: Democrat
Political experience: Connecticut legislator (1953–58); Connecticut Secretary of State (1958–70); U.S. House of Representatives (1971–75)

Washington: Dixie Lee Ray (1977–81)
Party affiliation: Democrat
Background: Marine biologist, college professor
Political experience: Chair, U.S. Atomic Energy Commission (1972–73); Assistant U.S. Secretary of State (1975–76)

presidency in 1964. Capitalizing on this visibility, Reagan sought and won the California governorship in 1966.

An even more advantageous way is the *combination route,* which combines the political promotion route with the preeminent citizen route. Jerry Brown of California typifies this. As the son of one of California's most famous governors, he capitalized on his well-known name and his family contacts with influential politicians and ran successfully for secretary of state. Serving a term in that office helped him establish popular acceptance and recognition in his own right. This left him well poised to run for governor in the following election. Thus he used his preeminent name to get elected to a position that would serve as a promotional stepping stone.

The fourth road to the state house is the *populist route.* This is the most likely one for those who are neither preeminent citizens nor tied to the politi-

---

Highlight
Conditions of the Governor's Office

Legal Qualifications

The governor must be a citizen, and in some states must have been a citizen for a minimum number of years. Most states require the governor to have been a state resident for a minimum number of years. Most states also require a minimum age of thirty, although some states have a minimum age of only twenty-one or twenty-five.

Terms of Office

All states but four have a four-year term of office. Those four (Arkansas, New Hampshire, Rhode Island, Vermont) have a two-year term of office but put no limit on the number of terms a governor may serve. Twenty-six states limit the number of terms a governor may serve. Eleven of these place the limit at two terms, and the remainder place it at one term. Twenty-two states allow an unlimited number of four-year terms.

Compensation

The range of governors' salaries is from $35,000 in Maine to $100,000 in New York. The median is about $65,000. Forty-four states also provide the governor with a mansion, and most states provide an expense allowance.

Succession

Forty-two states provide for a lieutenant governor to succeed to the office when it becomes vacant. Other states provide for a different state official to succeed, usually the president of the senate.

Removal

All states but Oregon have an impeachment process, but only four governors have been removed through impeachment since 1900. Thirteen states provide for a recall, but only one governor, Lynn J. Frazier of North Dakota, has been removed by recall (in 1921). Few states have a workable provision for removing governors in cases of physical or mental disability.

cal promotion route. Lester Maddox typifies this. Maddox was not heavily engaged in Georgia politics until he was forced to desegregate his restaurant after the Civil Rights Act of 1964. He first tried driving the black patrons off his premises with an ax handle and finally closed the restaurant rather than desegregate it. With his ax handle as a campaign symbol, Maddox won the next governor's election.

Governors' future career prospects are also important to their political influence. Governors with prospects for reelection are strengthened. Their influence is enhanced even more if they have bright prospects for going on to the United States Senate, a future cabinet position, or the White House. "The lure of following a national leader to Washington can bring action out of legislators and administrators."[48] This activity is more likely to occur if the governor's party controls both the White House and the state legislature. Most governors, however, do not go on to the Senate or to cabinet positions. Most return to private business or to their private careers.

Other State Executives

Along with the governor, several other state executives are typically elected directly by the people. The most important of these are the lieutenant governor, the attorney general, the secretary of state, the auditor, and the treasurer.

Lieutenant Governor

The office of **lieutenant governor** exists in forty-two states, but in only twenty-two are the governor and lieutenant governor elected jointly as a team. The lieutenant governor succeeds the governor if the office becomes vacant, casts tie-breaking votes in twenty-six states, and in thirty-one states serves as acting governor while the governor is temporarily out of the state. Like that of vice president of the United States, the office of lieutenant governor can be a frustrating position with little authority. Lieutenant governors are often appointed to lead various advisory boards, but they seldom get a very visible role. Hence, many lieutenant governors do little more than wait for the governor's office to become vacant. Because of this fact, many critics have argued that the position is useless and ought to be abolished. In the states where the office does not exist, a line of succession has been established in which either the president of the senate or some other elected state official succeeds the governor. The main exception to this principle of weak lieutenant governors is Texas where Lieutenant Governor William Hobby is one of the most influential leaders in the state.

Attorney General

In most states the **attorney general** is the second most important state-wide office. The attorney general is the official legal adviser to the state and the state's chief prosecutor. After legislation is passed, administrators may ask the attorney general for a legal opinion on the meaning of the law on points where the intent of the law is unclear. Although the attorney general's opinion is not legally binding and could be overturned by the courts, public officials normally will be reluctant to oppose the attorney general's ruling.

Besides giving legal opinions, the attorney general—as state prosecutor—has considerable influence on policy. For example, many states have established consumer protection divisions within their attorney general's office. An attorney general who hires competent investigative attorneys in this division and gives them sufficient staff support will make a significant impact on the delivery of services. Fly-by-night operators will find themselves subjected to investigation and may leave the state voluntarily rather than face prosecution. Investigations and prosecutions will uncover loopholes in consumer protection legislation, and the attorney general will be able to push strongly for new or supplementary legislation to strengthen that state's consumer protection apparatus.[49] The same may be true of nursing home facilities, health insurance provision, corrections systems, and drug and other criminal prosecutions.

By using their prosecution powers aggressively, attorneys general are well positioned to create a popular image that can serve as a springboard to higher office. The two most historic examples of this are Governors Robert M. La Follette of Wisconsin and Thomas E. Dewey of New York. Both prosecuted vice and organized crime to gain the prominence that eventually enabled them to get elected governor.[50]

Although the public prosecutor has considerable potential to use the office for political purposes, it would be misleading to suggest that most attorneys general or other prosecuting attorneys are primarily concerned with doing that. A study of county-level prosecuting attorneys in Kentucky found that only a minority had definite future political ambitions, and the politically ambitious attorneys were just as sensitive to defendants' rights as were the politically unambitious prosecuting attorneys.[51]

Secretary of State

The third major statewide office is the **secretary of state.** This office is found in all states except Hawaii, and it is elective in thirty-six states. Typically, the secretary of state keeps the state archives, supervises elections, compiles election statistics, publishes a *Blue Book* on state government organization, and often serves on state commissions and advisory boards. In some states, the secretary of state issues automobile and drivers' licenses and issues certificates of incorporation. Since these functions are mostly clerical, many scholars of public administration have advocated that the office be made appointive rather than elective.

Auditor

Two tasks of auditing need to be accomplished in state government—a preaudit and a postaudit. The preaudit authorizes payment of state funds, ensures that funds have been appropriated by the legislature, and makes certain that there is a sufficient balance in the appropriate state account. The preaudit is conducted by a person, technically called a controller, who certifies before the state treasurer writes a check that the funds are available.

The postaudit occurs after the expenditure of funds and is made to ensure that the funds were spent in accord with the intent of state law. Because the postaudit provides considerable potential to investigate the honesty and effectiveness of officials at both the state and local levels, public administration specialists normally look on the postaudit as a legislative function that should be performed by an **auditor** accountable to the legislature rather than to the governor or the executive branch. In practice, the preaudit and postaudit functions are usually combined in the same office located in the executive branch. Twenty-five states have elected auditors; thirteen have elected controllers.

Treasurer

Treasurers are custodians of the state's funds. They determine which banks will be the depositories for the state monies, and they authorize the checks that pay for state obligations. Although their duties are largely clerical, they can have a policy impact by, for example, refusing to deposit state money in banks that redline or that fail to take part in central-city redevelopment. Thirty-eight states have elected treasurers, but modern public administration theory suggests that appointed treasurers are preferable to elected ones.

Do Strong Governors Make Any Difference?

Has strong governorship produced any public policy consequences? When we compare the policy achievements of strong-governor states with those of weak-governor states, do we find any difference? Such a study was conducted by Thomas R. Dye, who compared whether the states with the strongest governors (as measured by the index of formal powers in Table 10–2) also spent the most money per capita on education, health care, highways, and welfare. Dye concluded that the level of state expenditures was less dependent on the power of the governor than on the affluence of the state. Strengthening the governors did not necessarily lead to more investments in these public services.[52]

Sarah Morehouse, on the other hand, asserts that even after economic development factors are taken into consideration, the weak-governor states tended to rely excessively on regressive tax structures to finance their public services. Particularly in the case of social welfare policies, the governor's leadership had a significant effect on policy outcomes. She writes, "It takes organization to put forward and pass a sustained program in behalf of the needy. Disorganization can obstruct such a program. A fragmented executive may be a holding operation, a bastion of the status quo."[53] Morehouse's arguments were strongly supported by an elaborate statistical study of governors as a mediating influence on public policy. This study found that, in affluent states with liberal public opinion and competitive parties, strong governors were more likely to produce redistributive policies than were weak governors.[54]

To conclude this survey of research on the impact of governors' powers, three generalizations are warranted. First, the formal powers of the governor do make a difference. It is easier for a person to be a dynamic governor if that position has been given substantial amounts of the formal powers shown in Table 10–2. Second, formal powers alone will not make a dynamic and forceful governor; the governor must also have the personal drive and skill to lead successfully. Third, formal powers alone will not lead to liberal state policies. But, if we accept the arguments of Sarah Morehouse, liberal governors are unlikely to overcome the forces of the status quo unless those governors do have substantial formal powers.

Governors and State Political Economies

What happens in a state's economy is vitally important to the incumbent governor. If a significant part of the state's economy suffers from a prolonged recession, several repercussions are possible, none of them pleasant from the incumbent governor's viewpoint. Increasing unemployment caused by recession can reduce state tax collections, forcing the governor to call for budget cuts and tax increases. Since there is some evidence that raising taxes usually does not help one's reelection prospects,[55] governors are usually eager to avoid recessions during their terms of office. If a tax raise is avoided, increasing numbers of unemployed people filing for unemployment compensation and welfare benefits can overload the state's capacity to provide those benefits, which will reflect poorly on the governor's leadership. And even if these things do not happen, many people demonstrate their economic frustrations by voting against the incumbents, regardless of whether the incumbents have any real power to combat the economic conditions. For all of these reasons, governors feel pressured to do something about their states' economies.

Even aside from recessions and fluctuations in the economic cycle, the American economy has been undergoing a revolution in recent decades. Older, manufacturing sectors of the economy (especially those based in the Northeast and Midwest) have not kept pace with the nation's economic growth and have been badly damaged by foreign competition. The newer service sectors of the economy have led the nation's economic growth. This has been a boon to the South and Southwest. But energy-producing states of the West, after experiencing explosive growth in the 1970s, were decimated by the oil glut and falling energy prices in the mid-1980s.

Few, if any, states are untouched by these changes today. Economic life of the 1980s has been characterized by intense competition between states to attract new economic development and to keep businesses they already have. At the center of this competition are the governors. They are the most visible political leaders in their states, and people expect their governors to do something about the state's economic conditions.

Given these considerations, it is not surprising that a National Governors' Association survey found that the number-one concern of governors for 1983 was the economy and jobs, followed—as a distant second—by fiscal matters.[56] How governors react to these concerns and how they promote economic development will be examined in detail in Chapter 17.

Summary

1. Although the substance of voters' demands on governors changes over time, the one persistent demand that stays constant is that governors be strong leaders.

2. The demand for strong executive leadership has evolved through three historical stages revolving around the progressive reform movement.

3. The governors' main sources of leadership strength are legislative powers, administrative powers, budget powers, public relations powers, the capabilities and resources of their personal staffs, and influence that they derive from their new roles as federal systems officers.

4. The governor's ability to lead in part depends on the gubernatorial style he or she adopts. Four styles were outlined: the demagogue, the program entrepreneur, the frustrated warrior, and the caretaker.

5. Four different paths lead to the governor's mansion—the political promotion route, the preeminent citizen route, the combination route, and the populist route. How governors get to the state house can affect their influence. Getting an uncontested nomination in a party that controls the legislature gives a governor greater leverage over the legislators than would winning nomination after a bitter primary or convention fight. Once in the state house, the more potential a governor has to get reelected or go on to high federal office, the more leverage he or she can exert over legislators and state administrators.

6. In addition to the governor, several other state officials are elected—principally the lieutenant governor, attorney general, secretary of state, treasurer, and auditor.

7. Empirical evidence suggests that strong governors and strong mayors are needed in order to continue promoting programs to meet public needs.

Key Terms

Amendatory veto Power of the governor in some states to add sums to appropriations bills.

Attorney general The chief law enforcement officer of a state.

Auditor The state officer responsible for ascertaining that funds are spent properly and legally.

Caretaker A gubernatorial style in which the governor maintains the operations of the office but rarely pushes for new legislation, new programs, or new authority.

Demagogue A political leader who builds his or her political support by enflaming people's passions over emotional political issues. A gubernatorial style practiced by Governor Huey Long of Louisiana (1928–1931).

Executive leadership The demand that the chief executives in governmental jurisdictions (principally governors and mayors) should exercise considerable authority over other executives.

Executive representation The demand that people should be represented in the executive branch by elected executives just as they are represented in the legislative branch by elected legislators.

Item veto Power of the governor in some states to veto specific provisions of appropriations bills without vetoing the entire bill.

Jacksonian democracy A governing concept attributed to the period of President Andrew Jackson (1829–1837) that government should rule for the benefit of the common people.

Lieutenant governor A statewide officer who succeeds the governor if the governor leaves the governorship.

Long ballot An election ballot containing many offices to be filled by election.

Neutral competence The demand that public services should be provided competently and in a politically neutral fashion.

Program entrepreneur A dynamic governor or mayor who sets an agenda of goals to be accomplished and builds alliances with the interests needed to reach the goals.

Secretary of state A statewide office responsible for administering the state election system, publishing a legislative manual, and conducting various clerical duties.

Spoils system A patronage theory of public hiring that the winning candidates in elections should be able to find jobs for their supporters in the public bureaucracies. "To the victors go the spoils" was the slogan of this theory.

Treasurer The state officer responsible for custody of state funds and for writing the checks that pay state obligations.

Veto Power of a governor to negate a bill passed by the legislature and prevent it from becoming law.

References

1. On Huey Long, see T. Harry Williams, *Huey Long* (New York: Bantam Books, 1970); Alan Sindler, *Huey Long's Louisiana: State Politics 1920-1952* (Baltimore: Johns Hopkins Press, 1956). On Jerry Brown, see Terry Christensen and Larry N. Gerston, *The California Connection: Politics in the Golden State* (Boston: Little, Brown and Co., 1984), pp. 103-106, 114-115.

2. These three stages were articulated by Herbert Kaufman in "Emerging Conflicts in the Doctrines of Public Administration," *American Political Science Review* 50 (1956): 1057.

3. Duane Lockard, *The Politics of State and Local Government* (New York: Macmillan, 1969), p. 322.

4. See especially *Federalist Papers* no. 10 and no. 51.

5. Larry Sabato, *Goodbye to Good-time Charlie: The American Governor Transformed*, 2d ed. (Washington, D.C.: Congressional Quarterly Press, 1983), p. 52.

6. On Brown, see Wallace Turner, "More than Fruit Flies Are Clouding Brown's Future," *New York Times*, July 19, 1981, p. 6-E. On Thornburgh, see Neal R. Peirce, "Good Management Sells for Governor," *Minneapolis Tribune*, March 23, 1980, p. 17a.

7. Just how to make the best measurement of the formal power of governors has been a subject of intense debate among political scientists. The index used here has the advantage of being recent and including the governor's organizational powers. For some other approaches, see Keith J. Mueller, "Explaining Variation and Change in Gubernatorial Powers, 1960-1982," *Western Political Quarterly* 38, no. 3 (September 1985): 424-431; and Nelson C. Dometrius, "Measuring Gubernatorial Power," *Journal of Politics* 41, no. 2 (May 1979): 589-610.

8. *The Book of the States: 1986-87* (Lexington, Ky.: Council of State Governments, 1986), pp. 114-116.

9. On the executive amendment provision, see Coleman Ransone, Jr., *The Office of*

Governor in the United States (Tuscaloosa, Ala.: University of Alabama Press, 1956), pp. 182–184.

10. On the increasing frequency of overrides, see Charles W. Wiggins, "Executive Vetoes and Legislative Overrides in the American States," *Journal of Politics* 42, no. 4 (November 1980): 1110–1112. The California legislature failed to override even a single governor's veto from 1946 to 1974; New York's, from 1877 to 1976; Texas', from 1941 to 1979. See Noel J. Stowe, *California Government: The Challenge of Change* (Beverly Hills, Calif.: Glencoe Press, 1975), p. 138; Eugene J. Gleason and Joseph Zimmerman, "The Strong Governorship: Status and Problems, New York" *Public Administration Review* 36, no. 1 (January–February 1976): 92–95; Clifton McCleskey et al., *The Government and Politics of Texas,* 7th ed. (Boston: Little, Brown and Co., 1982), p. 176.

11. In the 1983 through 1985 legislative sessions there were 146 overrides of 3,276 vetoes. *The Book of the States: 1986-87* (Lexington, Ky.: Council of State Governments, 1986), pp. 114–120.

12. Alan Rosenthal, "Legislative Oversight and the Balance of Power in State Government," *State Government* 56, no. 3 (1983): 90–98.

13. Gerald Benjamin, "The Governorship in an Era of Limits and Changes," *New York State Today: Politics, Government, Public Policy,* Peter W. Colby, ed. (Albany: State University of New York Press, 1985), pp. 134–135.

14. Ibid., pp. 134–135.

15. Rosenthal, "Legislative Oversight and the Balance of Power in State Government."

16. National Governors' Association, *Reflections on Being Governor* (Washington, D.C.: National Governors' Association, 1981), p. 65.

17. See David J. Olson, "Citizen Grievance Letters as a Gubernatorial Control Device in Wisconsin," *Journal of Politics* 31 (August 1969): 711–755.

18. See Ronald O. Michaelson, "An Analysis of the Chief Executive: The Governor Uses His Time," *State Government* 45, no. 3 (Summer 1974): 153–160. This study concluded that Governor Richard Olgilvie of Illinois spent an estimated 20 percent of his time dealing with administrative management.

19. In Tom Wicker's treatment of Attica in *A Time to Die* (New York: Quadrange/ New York Times, 1975), pp. 301–322, Rockefeller is portrayed as personally in overall command of dealing with the Attica rebellion. The police charge, however, was not conducted by him, although he ordered it. Although the postriot reforms can be attributed to Rockefeller's policy guidance, the development and implementation of specific reforms were the result of a special state committee that had been appointed by Rockefeller. Even in a situation that personally involves the governor as much as a prison riot, then, the governor gets involved primarily at the moment of crisis. Once the crisis is past, the governor may try to establish policies, but the administration and implementation of those policies are left to others.

20. For the 1985–1987 period, the five states were Delaware, Missouri, North Carolina, Rhode Island, and Vermont. See Steven Williams series of articles on Lamar Alexander in *The Comparative State Politics News Letter.*

21. Steven Williams, "Alexander's Master Teacher Program Fails in Tennessee," *Comparative State Politics Newsletter* 4, no. 3 (May 1983): 11–12; "Master Teacher Program Update," 4, no. 6 (December 1983): 21; and "The First Year of Merit Pay for Tennessee Teachers," 6, no. 5 (October 1985): 33.

22. See Louis M. Kohlmeier, Jr., *The Regulators: Watchdog Agencies and the Public Interest* (New York: Harper & Row, 1969).

23. In Minnesota, for example, of eleven licensing boards listed in the field of health care, ten were prescribed by law to have a majority of the members from the field being licensed. *The Legislative Manual: 1981-1982* (St. Paul: State of Minnesota, 1981), pp. 313–316.

24. Deil S. Wright, "Executive Leadership in State Administration," *Midwest Journal of Political Science* 11, no. 1 (February 1967): 1–26.

25. Glenn Abney and Thomas P. Lauth, "The Governor as Chief Administrator," *Public Administration Review* 43, no. 1 (January–February 1983): 40–49.

26. Thad L. Beyle, "The Governor's Formal Powers: A View from the Governor's Chair," *Public Administration Review* 28, no. 6 (November–December 1968): 540–544.

27. Norton Long, "After the Voting Is Over," *Midwest Journal of Political Science* 6, no. 2 (May 1963): 183–200.

28. See Donald P. Sprengel, *Gubernatorial Staffs: Functional and Political Profiles* (Iowa City: Institute of Public Affairs, University of Iowa, 1969). pp. 34–52.

29. Beyle, "The Governor's Formal Powers," p. 205.

30. On the federal government's impact on governors' staffs, see Peter Trapp, "Governors' and Mayors' Offices: The Role of the Staff," *National Civic Review* 63, no. 5 (May 1974): 242–249.

31. Patrick J. Kenney and Tom W. Rice, "Popularity and the Vote: The Gubernatorial Case," *American Politics Quarterly* 11, no. 2 (April 1983): 237–242. Kenney and Rice examined nineteen gubernatorial elections in four states where polling organizations periodically track governors' popularity (California, Iowa, Minnesota, and New Jersey). In fifteen of the nineteen elections, the governors lost their reelection bid if their final pre-election popularity ratings dropped below 48 percent.

32. Malcolm Jewell, "State Decision Making: The Governor Revisited," *American Governmental Institutions,* eds. Aaron Wildavsky and Nelson Polsby (Chicago: Rand McNally, 1968), pp. 556–557.

33. See Deil S. Wright, "Governors, Grants, and the Intergovernmental System," in *The American Governor in Behavioral Perspective,* eds. Thad Beyle and J. Oliver Williams (New York: Harper & Row, 1972), pp. 187–193.

34. See Thad L. Beyle and Deil S. Wright, "The Governor, Planning, and Governmental Activity," in Beyle and Williams, pp. 193–205.

35. An analysis of Governors' Conference resolutions from 1946 to 1969 can be found in Wright, "Governors, Grants, and the Intergovernmental System," pp. 192–193.

36. Lynn Muchmore and Thad L. Beyle, "The Governor as Party Leader," *State Government* 53, no. 3 (Summer 1980): 121–124.

37. Larry Sabato, *Goodbye to Good-time Charlie: The American Governor Transformed, 1950-1975,* 1st ed. (Lexington, Mass.: Lexington Books, 1978), pp. 50–56.

38. Lee Sigelman and Roland Smith, "Personal, Office, and State Characteristics as Predictors of Gubernatorial Performance," *Journal of Politics* 43, no. 1 (February 1981): 169–180.

39. Ibid., p. 180.

40. On Huey Long, see T. Harry Williams, *Huey Long* (New York: Bantam Books,

1970); Alan Sindler, *Huey Long's Louisiana: State Politics 1920-1952* (Baltimore: Johns Hopkins Press, 1956). Also see Huey Lòng's autobiography, *Every Man a King: The Autobiography of Huey Long* (New Orleans: National Book Co., 1933), and the political novel based on the life of Huey Long by Robert Penn Warren, *All the King's Men* (New York: Bantam Books, 1968).

41. See Alan G. Hevesi, *Legislative Politics in New York State: A Comparative Analysis* (New York: Praeger, 1975).

42. Ibid.

43. Samuel R. Solomen, "Governors: 1960-1970," *National Civic Review* 60, no. 3 (March 1971): 310.

44. Sarah McCally Morehouse, "The Governor as Political Leader," in *Politics in the American States: A Comparative Analysis,* 3d ed., eds. Herbert Jacob and Kenneth N. Vines (Boston: Little, Brown and Co., 1977), p. 204. Of the 156 governors during the 1960s, 92 were attorneys and 32 were businesspersons.

45. See Joseph A. Schlesinger, *How They Became Governors* (East Lansing: Michigan State University, Governmental Research Bureau, 1957), p. 11.

46. Beyle, "The Governor's Formal Powers," p. 185.

47. Schlesinger, *How They Became Governors,* pp. 10–11.

48. Morehouse, "The Governor as Political Leader," pp. 201–202.

49. All attorney general offices have authority to act on consumer protection. See *The Book of The States: 1982-83,* p. 160.

50. For a political biography of La Follette, see Robert S. Maxwell, *La Follette and the Rise of the Progressives in Wisconsin* (Madison: State Historical Society of Wisconsin, 1956). On Dewey's use of the prosecution power to become governor, see Warren Moscow, *Politics in the Empire State* (New York: Knopf, 1948), pp. 29–32. Dewey was not the attorney general, however; he was a special prosecutor appointed to prosecute organized crime figures.

51. Richard L. Engstrom, "Political Ambition and the Prosecutorial Office," *Journal of Politics* 33, no. 1 (February 1971): 190–194.

52. Thomas R. Dye, "Executive Power and Public Policy in the United States," *Western Political Quarterly* 22, no. 4 (December 1969): 926–929.

53. Morehouse, "The Governor as Political Leader," p. 225.

54. David R. Morgan and Jeffrey L. Brudney, "The Mediating Effect of Gubernatorial Power on State Policies," a paper presented to the 1984 meeting of the Midwestern Political Science Association, April 12–14, 1984, Chicago, Illinois.

55. Theodore J. Eismeier, "Votes and Taxes: The Political Economy of the American Governorship," *Polity* 15, no. 3 (Spring 1983): 368–379. In a study of governors seeking reelection over the thirty-year period from 1950 to 1980, Eismeier compared those who raised or proposed to raise taxes with those who did not. He found that 35.6 percent of the tax raisers lost their bids for reelection, compared to only 20.9 percent of those who did not raise taxes.

56. *Governors Priorities 1983* (Washington, D.C.: National Governors' Association, 1983), p. 3.

Chapter 11
Administrators and the Implementation of Policy

Chapter Preview

This chapter examines the role of state and local administrators in carrying out the policies and implementing the programs established by political leaders. The main topics we will explore are:

1. Perennial tensions between administrators and executives.
2. Public approaches to personnel practices.
3. Administrative reorganization as an approach to state government reform.
4. Budgeting and the attempts to reform budgeting as a device for improving executive management.
5. Reform alternatives for improving executive management.
6. The political economy and government productivity.

Let us begin our examination of state and local administration with a look at a typical attitude that many people have toward their public servants.

Introduction

The great whipping boy of the 1980s is the public bureaucracy. The cartoon on p. 270 sums up many people's feelings about government bureaucracies on all levels. In the popular image, the typical bureaucrat's response to a legislative or gubernatorial order for full speed ahead is to fudge, shuffle, hedge, obfuscate, and so on.

When Jerry Brown became governor of California in 1975, he declared war on that state's bureaucracy. One of his first acts was symbolic, a ban on issuing briefcases to state employees. The paperwork generated by bureau-

269

Source: MacNelly, *Chicago Tribune,* February 6, 1977. Reprinted by permission: Tribune Media Services.

crats simply multiplied to fill the briefcases, said the governor, and the paperwork itself is written in a jargon that is incomprehensible to the outsider.[1] Brown eliminated one regulatory agency, reduced the size of three others, and cut the volume of the state's records by 51,500 cubic feet. But he lost the war. Although he wiped out one regulatory agency, he created three others. Although he eliminated 109 staff positions, he created 443. Midway through his first term, Brown admitted that he was losing.[2] And midway through his second term, the state had 18 percent more employees than it had when Brown was first elected governor.[3]

This chapter looks at the major facets of public administration that cause concern to elected officials such as Governor Brown. It examines first a basic tension between executives and administrators that causes executives such as Governor Brown to attack the administrators in the first place and to concede defeat in the second place. The chapter then focuses on three mechanisms that have been or are being created to enable the elected executives and legislative policymakers to control the administrators. These are personnel practices, reorganization, and budgeting. Finally, the chapter will discuss a number of new management devices that have been experimented with since the mid-1960s.

Tension Between Administrators and Executives

In theory, the legislators write the laws and the governors execute them. In practice, the legislators and governors combine to write the laws, and the laws are implemented by numerous state and local government administrative agencies. The job of the governor or the mayor then is to ensure that the administrative agencies implement the law in the way the executives and legislators intended. Governors and legislators, faced with electoral pressures, may demand changes in agency procedures. Administrators defend their routines by actively trying to influence the formulation of policies. The net result is considerable tension and conflict between the governor and mayor executives and the public agency administrators.

This tension between executives and administrators is kept alive by several other factors. First, the administrators are permanent employees, whereas the executives are temporary. The average term of executives is only 5.6 years for big-city mayors and barely 4 years for governors. But top civil service employees remain until they retire or resign, which gives them a longer-range perspective on the services provided by their agencies. If a governor's policy proposals challenge strongly held agency privileges, the civil servants can often stall the demanded changes until the governor is replaced.

A second source of tension is that administrators are professionals in government, whereas the executives are not. The executives, who typically look on themselves as citizen-officials responsible for overseeing the activities of the professionals, are skeptical of the supposedly professional expertise of the administrators.[4]* Technical expertise is necessary in the case of highway engineering, for example. But decisions on the location of roads and freeway interchanges, the awarding of construction contracts, and the choice of urban neighborhoods to be torn up by freeways are primarily political decisions. In making such decisions, executives have to weigh the demands of professional standards against the vocal demands of angry citizens.

A third source of tension is that the professional administrators have much more detailed knowledge about government programs than do the citizen-executives. Administrators are deeply embedded in a significant communications network involving other professionals at the federal, state, and local levels of government. In fact, the professional administrators often either initiate or review new policy ideas that the executives put forward to the public.

---

*One consequence of the tension between professional administrators and citizen-executives is that the citizen-executives tend to have much less respect and empathy for the organizations they head than do business executives for their corporations in the private business world.

Managing Personnel for Better Policy Implementation

A major management problem lies in directing the daily activities of the thirteen and one-half million people who work for state and local governments. Most of these employees, as shown in Table 11–1, work in education, health, and police protection. Nearly three-fourths of them work at the local level. How are these thirteen and one-half million people to be hired, promoted, or fired? Should it be on the basis of favoritism or merit? Should special preferences be given for protected categories of people, such as veterans, racial minorities, and females? Should salaries be determined by executive decision or by collective bargaining? What kind of pension systems should these employees have? And how should those pensions be funded? These questions involve billions of dollars in taxes and go to the heart of the struggle over who should control state and local government.

The Patronage System of Employment

The **patronage** system, or the spoils system, is a recruitment method that gives government jobs to political supporters of the winning candidates. It is useful to distinguish between traditional patronage and contemporary patronage. Traditional patronage affected the rank-and-file government employees, and it was often dominated by the political machines. It was the main public employment system until late in the nineteenth century. It flourishes best today in cities such as Chicago and New York, which have a tradition of machine politics,[5] and it also continues at the county level in many places.[6] But most elected executives find traditional patronage difficult to administer.[7]

Table 11–1. State and Local Government Employment: 1984

Function	Number (in thousands)	Percent
Education	7,022	52
Health and hospitals	1,392	10
Police protection	684	5
Highways	540	5
Public welfare	407	3
Financial administration	314	2
Fire protection	316	2
All other functions	2,819	21
Total	13,494	100

Source: Bureau of the Census, *Statistical Abstract of the United States: 1987* (Washington, D.C.: U.S. Government Printing Office, 1986), p. 282.

A new administration that fired large numbers of workers to make way for political appointees would in most places suffer a severe public relations setback.

The critical blows to traditional patronage started in 1939 when the Hatch Act made it illegal for federal employees to engage in partisan political activity. This prohibition was later extended to cover state and local employees who administered federally funded programs.[8] In 1970 the Intergovernmental Personnel Act provided grants to train administrators, to improve state civil service systems, and to prohibit partisanship in hiring practices if federal funds were involved. The most dramatic restriction of traditional patronage came in 1976 when the United States Supreme Court ruled that politically motivated dismissals could only be made among policymaking officials and could not touch rank-and-file employees.[9] Although these developments have crippled traditional patronage in most of the country, a few places, such as Chicago, still award thousands of jobs on the basis of partisanship.

More important than traditional patronage has been the emergence of what Raymond Wolfinger calls contemporary patronage.[10] One form of contemporary patronage resulted from the broad expansion of government contracts to perform evaluation studies, run programs, or conduct pilot projects. Such contracts have often been awarded to private consultants who have developed intimate connections with program administrators at the federal, state, and local levels. Another form of the new patronage are the advisory boards and commissions that have been broadly expanded at all levels of government. Although appointment to these commissions rarely brings much direct financial reward, the appointments are a matter of prestige and can help aggressive people make contacts that are valuable for either political or career advancement.

The new patronage identified by Wolfinger differs from traditional patronage in two key respects. The old patronage jobs were, first, given to low-income and poorly educated people and, second, were controlled by the political parties and political machines. By contrast, most of the contemporary patronage jobs described above are awarded to highly educated, middle-class people who get the positions through their connections with program administrators and political executives rather than through connections with political machines.

The Merit System of Employment

The **merit system,** or the **civil service system,** is a recruitment method that hires and promotes employees on the basis of their training and competence to perform specific jobs. Once employees are given civil service status, they are protected from arbitrary removal.

One gets civil service status by passing a test. A job description is drawn up for each civil service position. The position is classified at a specific level and assigned a pay range. Promotion to higher positions is achieved by competition, with the promotion ideally going to the candidate whose experience, qualifications, training, and test scores best fit the responsibilities of the job.

The first state civil service system was established in New York in 1883. Since then it has spread to all states[11] and to most large cities.[12] Most of these state and local civil service systems were established after 1939, in response to federal laws and court decisions that prohibited patronage systems in federally funded programs.[13]

Merit systems are administered in one of two ways—either by a civil service commission or by a state personnel agency. In states where the motivation behind the merit system has been primarily to eliminate patronage, a civil service commission is the administering agency because it can be made independent of the governor and the legislature. Where the primary motive is not to eliminate patronage but to provide modern personnel services, then a state personnel department usually administers the system.

Issues in Personnel Management

Just as the traditional patronage system was sharply criticized in the late nineteenth century for not meeting the demands of neutral competence, contemporary merit systems have been bitterly criticized in the late twentieth century. The primary issues have been systematic bias in the hiring and promotional patterns, comparable worth, collective bargaining, the viability of public employee pension funds, and civil service reform.

Bias and the Concept of Representative Bureaucracy

Civil service systems have been increasingly accused of bias in hiring and promoting. Racial minorities complain that civil service procedures are biased against them. Feminists complain that the procedures systematically exclude women from the highest civil service positions. Both charges are confirmed by employment data. Starting in the 1960s, the federal government attempted to cope with this bias by promoting **equal employment opportunities.** Federal grants and loans for programs administered by state and local governments could be denied unless the recipient government hired its employees without regard to race, sex, religion, or country of origin. This equal employment opportunity principle was written into the 1970 Intergovernmental Personnel Act. However, equal opportunity did not substantially increase the number of women and minorities in top policymaking positions.

Because of the failures of equal opportunity principles to overcome traditional biases in hiring practices, minorities and women began promoting the concept of **affirmative action.** Each state and local agency receiving federal funds must develop an affirmative action plan for increasing the number of women and minorities in top positions. Perhaps because of these efforts and because minorities have more success finding public-sector jobs than private-sector jobs, blacks tend to have a high proportional share of state and local government jobs.[14] Thus blacks are overrepresented in government jobs. Women, by contrast, tend to be slightly underrepresented.[15] For both blacks and women, opportunities are greatest at the lower-level jobs. A 1974 study found that only 2 percent of state agency heads were minority, and only 4 percent were women. But by 1986, 18 percent of all state cabinet-level posts were held by women.[16]

Closely associated with contemporary concerns over bias in personnel practices is the concept of the representative bureaucracy. This is the concept that the bureaucracy can represent the population as well as the legislature can. As discussed in Chapter 10, this notion surfaced as the demand for executive representation during the period of Jacksonian Democracy (1829–1837) and reached its zenith in the heyday of machine politics (1870–1930), when the European immigrants demanded that they have representatives in the public bureaucracies as well as in the state legislatures and city councils. As executive representation under the political machines degenerated into political favoritism and patronage, civil service practices and merit systems of employment were promoted to create a fairer system of hiring and dismissing public employees. But if machine politics led to a personnel system biased in favor of European ethnics, civil service systems led to a personnel system, as said above, biased against minorities and women. The apparent motives of minorities and women in seeking affirmative action are in some ways reminiscent of the motives of the European immigrants a century ago. In both instances they wanted jobs and hoped that getting some of their own people into the bureaucracies would assure them better treatment by the bureaucracies.

Comparable Worth

A personnel issue of the 1980s of particular concern to women is that of **comparable worth,** the demand that jobs of equal skill requirements receive comparable pay. This demand is different from the more familiar demand of equal pay for equal work. The equal pay for equal work principle would guarantee that a female licensed practical nurse (LPN) would earn the same salary as a male LPN with the same seniority and experience. But it would not guarantee that LPNs (a field dominated by women) earn as much income as persons in male-dominated fields with comparable or lower-skill requirements. For example, state-employed LPNs in Minnesota (95 percent of them women) in 1979 earned $1,382 per month, whereas state-employed general repair workers (99 percent of them men) earned $1,564 monthly. A state study evaluating the jobs on the basis of knowledge, skill, problem solving, accountability, and working conditions gave the LPN job 183 job-evaluation points and the general repair worker job only 134 points.[17] Despite having jobs that were more demanding, the female LPNs received about 12 percent less pay than the male general repair workers.

There are two general ways to reduce this inequity. Opponents of the comparable worth point out that the pay differences for different jobs reflect the differing economic values of the jobs as determined by the marketplace. Accordingly, they argue, women who wish to earn more money should seek jobs that pay more. Proponents of comparable worth argue that the value of all jobs in a state or local government should be assessed on objective, gender-free criteria and the pay scales for those jobs set accordingly.

This issue came to national prominence in 1983 when a federal district court ruled that the State of Washington had discriminated against many female employees by paying them much less than it paid male employees in jobs with similar or lower value. This ruling called on the State of Washington to readjust its pay schedule to reflect the content of each job. As a result, the state was ordered to pay about half a billion dollars in back pay to 15,000 female workers for the previous four years. In many other states, chapters of the American Federation of State, County, and Municipal Employees took a cue from the Washington case and began pressing for comparable worth studies in their states. To date, comparable worth legislation has been defeated in four states (Florida, Missouri, Nebraska, and Pennsylvania) and is being implemented in four other states (Iowa, Minnesota, New Mexico, and Washington); and twenty states have begun the process of gathering data related to pay-equity studies.[18]

Collective Bargaining

Collective bargaining among public employees made very little progress until the 1960s.[19] During that decade, strikes of teachers, police officers, and other public employees led to state laws that permit employees to bargain collectively and in many states to strike under certain circumstances. By the mid-1970s most states permitted some form of collective bargaining for public employees, and some states even gave them the right to strike.[20]

The foremost public employees union is the **American Federation of State, County, and Municipal Employees (AFSCME)**, which by 1983 had 959,000 members.[21] By 1982, 40 percent of all state and local government employees were unionized, with the greatest unionization occurring among firefighters, sanitation workers, and teachers.[22]

In a collective bargaining situation, the group of employees (called the

You Decide
Seniority Versus Affirmative Action

The principle of job seniority came into a classic confrontation with the principle of affirmative action in Boston in the early 1980s. Because of a severe fiscal crisis, the city of Boston laid off large numbers of white firefighters and police officers with high seniority. At the same time a federal district court order prevented the city from laying off newly hired blacks and Hispanics with less seniority. In taking these actions, the city and the federal district court set aside a Massachusetts civil service law that protected seniority rights.

The laid-off firefighters and police officers sued to be reinstated, and it did not take long for their suit to reach the United States Supreme Court. However, in the meantime, a state law was passed that rehired them and guaranteed that the seniority principle would have to be followed in any subsequent layoffs of public employees for fiscal reasons. Having been reinstated in their jobs, the employees now asked for back pay for the time they had been laid off, contending that the layoffs had been illegal.

Since the employees had been rehired, the issue of reinstatement was moot. But the Court's decision would transmit a clear pro- or anti-affirmative action position to public officials in similar situations around the country. There were essentially three issues before the Court. First, the public employees' union (supported by the Reagan administration) wanted the affirmative action order by the district court to be struck down because the union considered it an unconstitutional and illegal instance of reverse discrimination. Second, the employees wanted back pay for the time that they were illegally (in their view) laid off. However, this issue was not formally included in their original appeal to the Supreme Court. Third, the NAACP (supported by other civil rights groups) wanted the Supreme Court to uphold the validity of the original layoffs, thereby strengthening the affirmative action position in potential similar cases around the country.

Assume that you were a member of the Supreme Court dealing with this case. You essentially have four options. You can vote for or against any of the above three issues. Or, as a fourth option, you could vote to dismiss the case. How would you decide on these issues? And what would be your rationale?

	Yes or *No?*	*Rationale*
1. Strike down the original layoffs.	_____	_____
2. Award back pay.	_____	_____
3. Uphold the original layoffs.	_____	_____
4. Dismiss the case.	_____	_____

To learn the Supreme Court's response to these issues, see the Highlight on p. 279.

bargaining unit) typically negotiates a master contract that stipulates conditions of employment, grievance procedures, salary schedules, and seniority provisions. Although existing evidence does not show that collective bargaining is necessarily incompatible with the merit principle,[23] the seniority provisions of most collective bargaining contracts do indeed place a higher premium on seniority than they do on rewarding job performance or affirmative action. If low tax revenues force public agencies to lay off people, the seniority clause of the contract causes the layoffs to be made on the basis of seniority, with no regard for job competence or for affirmative action. These conflicts have appeared repeatedly in the 1980s. A typical conflict is presented for you to resolve in the accompanying "You Decide" on p. 277.

In sum, collective bargaining today is a potent political force in state and local government. Although it has led to notable and badly needed improvement in public employees' pay levels, it has also been counterproductive to the merit principle and to affirmative action.

Public Employee Pensions

A major problem facing taxpayers in the 1990s will be paying for public employee pensions. As the public work force has grown, millions of employees have been added to the public pension plans. Eventually, all these workers will retire, and the public will have to pay retirement benefits to them. If the public pension plans were fully funded from workers' contributions so that each worker's benefits were paid out of the investment earnings on his or her contributions, there would be no problem. In fact, however, many very large state and local pension plans have not been funded adequately, and as the employees retire, the taxpayers will have to shoulder a very heavy burden. The benefit levels for retirees vary widely from state to state. The average for all states in 1984 was only $453 per month, but average payments ranged from a low of $159 per month in Nebraska to a high of $888 per month in Alaska.[24]

A second pension problem has been *double dipping*, which occurs when someone retires early from one government job, begins receiving a pension, and then takes another government job that will eventually pay another pension. Double dipping is most common among military personnel, who can begin collecting retirement benefits in their late thirties and then take jobs as public school teachers or as other state or local employees.

Additional public pension problems have been cited. Several states have had very lax disability pension procedures. Others have not maintained strong legislative watch over the public employee pensions. And with the advent of collective bargaining, many government officials have not responsibly monitored the actual costs of the benefits they were granting.

Civil Service Reform

The public employee personnel problems mentioned have raised serious questions over whether anybody really is able to control public personnel practices. One consequence has been a resurgent movement in the late 1970s to reform state civil service systems. The most prominent reform was probably in Wisconsin, highlighted by a two-week strike in the summer of 1977 and the passage of a civil service reform law later that year.[25] The main feature of the Wisconsin reform was an increase in the number of top-level, policymaking officials that the governor can appoint. A second feature was the placement of a new personnel management department directly in the governor's cabinet. Wisconsin also limited the veterans' preference provisions in state hiring. Other states are likely to reform their civil service procedures along similar lines during the 1980s. The general aim of this reform is to enhance the governor's influence over state agencies, to increase the number of high-level political appointees, to eliminate some of the roadblocks to affirmative action, and to make it easier to dismiss poorly performing employees.

Highlight
Seniority Versus Affirmative Action

In May 1983, the Supreme Court responded to the Boston case discussed in the "You Decide" on p. 277 by dismissing it. In this way the Court made an affirmative action decision in this particular case, but it set no precedent for future cases and gave no clues to what the Court might do in future cases. The employees' request for back pay was hindered by the fact that such a request was not included in their original petition to the Supreme Court. And their request for striking down the original layoffs was hindered by the fact that they had already been rehired. This meant they were presenting a moot case to the Court. But the Court will only hear actual cases and controversies in which a litigant is suffering or has suffered actual losses. Having decided not to give a decision supportive of the workers, there was no need for the Court to do anything more than dismiss the case.

Although this case did not set a legal precedent for future courts to follow, the Supreme Court has in fact tended to uphold the legality of affirmative action plans in cases where prior racial discrimination existed. In 1986, for example, the Court upheld an affirmative action plan in Cleveland that gave black and Hispanic firefighters promotion preference over whites.

Source: Boston Firefighters Union v. *Boston Chapter, NAACP* 103 S.Ct. 2076 (1983).

Reorganizing for Better Policy Implementation

There is a strong feeling that political executives at both the state and local levels could do a better job of managing the public bureaucracies and implementing public policies if the bureaucracies were organized in a rational and hierarchical way. Traditional administration has its authority fragmented into so many different bureaus and agencies that neither the governor nor the legislature exerts comprehensive control over its state bureaucracy.

The Administrative Reorganization Movement

A reform movement to end this fragmentation of authority began at the national level when President William Howard Taft established a Commission on Economy and Efficiency (1910–1912) to recommend improvements in the federal government. At the state level, reorganization took place in three separate periods. The first major reorganization occurred in 1917 in Illinois under Governor Frank D. Lowden. Over 100 independent agencies, boards, and commissions were consolidated into nine departments, and their heads were made appointive by the governor. Following Illinois' lead, in the next ten years over a dozen states made some effort at reorganization.

A second stimulus to state reorganization was the publication in 1949 of the report of the National Commission on the Organization of the Executive Branch of the Government, known as the Hoover Commission, after its chairman, Herbert Hoover. In the five years following the report, thirty-five states formed so-called **Little Hoover Commissions** to study reorganization. These commissions generally argued for a hierarchical form of state government structure to be built on the following six principles.[26]

1. Concentrate authority and responsibility in the governor.
2. Consolidate the many separate agencies into a small number of departments so that all agencies working in similar service areas will be grouped together under the same functional department.
3. Eliminate boards for purely administrative work.
4. Coordinate staff and other administrative services.
5. Provide an independent audit.
6. Provide a governor's cabinet.

Despite their massive documentation of the need for state reorganization, the commissions' reports had little immediate impact. By 1953 only two of twenty-four states where Little Hoover Commissions reported had the legislatures responded positively to the proposals. In nine of the twenty-four states, the legislative response was negative. In the remaining thirteen states, the response was mixed with between 30 and 50 percent of the commission proposals being adopted.[27]

A third wave of reorganization efforts occurred in the late 1960s and the 1970s. In those two decades over twenty states underwent major administrative reorganizations that incorporated one or more of the six principles cited above.[28] Reorganization has been more successful since 1965 because of the growing popularity of two effective reform strategies.

The first reform strategy is a constitutional amendment requiring the consolidation of all state agencies into a limited number of departments by a specific date. This strategy forces the governor and the legislature to accept the broad structure of reform but leaves up to them the details of the consolidation. This strategy was successful in Missouri[29] and North Carolina.[30] Missouri, for example, passed a constitutional amendment in 1972 that required the consolidation of all state agencies into no more than fourteen departments. Some agencies were assimilated totally into the new departments, and others, especially the regulatory agencies with quasi-judicial powers, were allowed to retain their policy independence.

The second reform strategy is to pass a law that gives the governor authority to reorganize the executive branch. If the legislature or the constitutionally elected state officers affected do not veto the reorganization within a specified period of time, it takes effect. This approach was successfully used by Governor Jimmy Carter in Georgia, where the major portion of a reorganization plan proposed by an appointed special committee went into effect in 1972.[31]

Assessing Reorganization: Some Caveats

No conclusive studies have assessed the impact of the reorganization of state government on the kinds of policies adopted and on the delivery of services. The reformists assume that more public services can be delivered at a lower per-capita cost if (1) state administrative activities are coordinated, and (2) the governor has authority to control all state programs. Political scientist York Willbern questions both of these assumptions. He asks whether coordination is really necessary. The large state programs of highways and education, for example, have little or no relationship to each other, and there is no inherent reason why both those commissioners should sit in a governor's cabinet. Overlapping responsibilities could be coordinated through negotiated agreements.

Willbern also questions the belief that focusing responsibility on the governor leads to better government. He suggests that some state governmental activities have broader public importance than others and thus may need more executive control. Other agencies may need less control by the governor.[32]

For example, would state services to the blind, the physically disabled, the mentally retarded, and the emotionally disturbed be better administered by grouping them all under one bureau for the disabled and then appending that bureau to a large department of health or welfare represented in a governor's cabinet? Or would state services to these people best be improved by allowing each service to have its own autonomous agency? The first option provides a more comprehensive approach to the disabled. And it may provide better services to people whose disabilities are multiple or to people who have a disability for which a specialized agency does not exist. On the other hand, interest groups for the disabled generally fear that, under consolidation, services for disabled people would be subordinated to the main mission of the larger department.

In recent years a number of researchers have found that reorganized states do not necessarily provide equal services for fewer dollars than unreorganized states.[33] One such study used twelve criteria to compare the performance of state departments headed by a single executive (favored by reformers) with the performance of departments headed by boards or commissions (a practice disapproved of by reformers). Not only did the study fail to find that single-head departments consistently outperformed multi-head departments, but the multi-head departments had some advantages lacking in the single-head departments. Multi-head commissions improve representation in the bureaucratic process, and they absorb public criticisms when things go poorly in the department.[34]

By the mid-1980s, interest in comprehensive executive reorganization had waned.[35] Administrative reform today is much more likely to be targeted at specific administrative problems. New Jersey, for example, streamlined its administrative bureaucracy by eliminating hundreds of middle-management positions.[36] Targeted administrative reform might well avoid the objections to all-encompassing consolidation discussed above. A study of hazardous-waste management, for example, found that consolidation of hazardous-waste bureaucracies did in fact lead to an improvement in a state's hazardous-waste management policies.[37]

Budgeting as a Device for Improving Executive Management

Budgeting is the most important weapon that governors and legislatures have for imposing policy control over their administrators. To the extent that they control the budget, governors can influence the overall level of expenditures, and they can decide which agencies will get the largest share of the budgetary pie. This decision-making power is an important lever for executives in getting the cooperation of administrators. The executive's ability to wield this leverage, however, depends on the extent to which a state has moved from traditional budgeting practices to newer approaches such as program budgeting and zero-based budgeting.

Traditional Budgeting

Incrementalism

Traditional budgetmaking is an incremental process.[38] An *increment* is simply a small step, and an *incremental process* is one that moves in one direction in small steps. Budgeting is an incremental process because most agencies get a budget increase each year that makes the budget slightly larger than the previous year's. Only under extraordinary circumstances, such as the creation of a new agency or the introduction of a new federal program, does a department or agency get a substantial increase that greatly exceeds the overall budget increase. **Incrementalism** produces stability in the budgeting system. Since each agency knows it will get a slight increase each year, it also knows that it will not get cut back sharply or cut out entirely.

The Budget Timeline

The incremental process fits well into the traditional budget timeline. Although the Montana timeline highlighted on p. 284 was selected because it has fewer complications than most states', the basic process is similar in all the states. State agency heads make initial budget requests that far exceed their expectations. This allows the governor and the budget director to cut the requests without harming any of the agency's programs. The governor leaves the total requests high enough so that the legislature can make more cuts without damaging the governor's priorities. Finally, the legislature makes cuts that leave the agency an amount slightly larger than the previous year's budget.[39] In this way, both the governor and the legislature can tell tax-conscious citizens how much money they saved. And the program administrators can count on getting just about as much money as they really had expected.

It is not clear how closely other states fit the incremental process described here,[40] but it is clear that most agencies' budget levels go up or down in only small increments each year. Even the rapid increase in urban and social programs in the late 1960s did not alter the patterns of incrementalism. A study of twelve state budgets conducted at that time found that the states that got the largest increases in federal grants for urban and social programs in health, education, and welfare were the same states that had the largest staffs and the biggest programs to begin with.[41]

Why do budgets change in incremental steps rather than in response to changing policy priorities? One reason is the reluctance of governors and legislators to make a comprehensive review of the whole budget document each year. Such a comprehensive annual review would make it impossible for program administrators or clients to count on a program's permanence.[42] Nor would public employees be able to count on keeping their jobs permanently. To terminate whole sectors of state employees and public services each year as priorities change would make state government chaotic.

Other Features of Traditional Budgeting

In addition to incrementalism, two other features of traditional budgeting that limit executive control are earmarking and line-item budgeting. *Earmarking* limits executive control, as pointed out in Chapter 4, because it places significant parts of the budget beyond the influence of the elected executives.

Line-item budgeting refers to the way that budget authorizations are listed. For example, the budget for a bureau of vocational rehabilitation might authorize expenditures for the line items of salaries, postage, mailing expenses, supplies, telephone expenses, travel, in-service training for employees, and contracted services. Although these line items enable the bureau chief to keep track of the bureau's expenditures, they do not enable him or her to compare how the bureau's money is being divided among its various programs. Nor do they allow the bureau chief's supervisor, the department head, to compare how money is apportioned on a program basis. At no point do

---

Highlight
A Budget Timeline: Montana Biennium 1989–1991

September 1, 1988
    State departments and agencies must submit their budget requests to the Director of the Office of Budget and Program Planning in the governor's office.

September 1, 1988, to January 1989
    The governor and the Director of Budget and Program Planning review agency budget requests and change the budgeted amounts in order to meet the governor's priorities.

First Monday in January 1989
    The governor submits the budget to the legislature.

January to the end of the session in spring 1989
    The legislature has unlimited power to make any changes in the budget. After the legislature makes its appropriations, the governor has item veto power.

July 1, 1989
    The fiscal year starts and the state budget takes effect. The budget is for the biennium (two years) and is in effect until June 30, 1991.

Source: The Book of the States: 1986–87 (Lexington, Ky.: Council of State Governments, 1986), pp. 220–221.

the budget director, the governor, or the legislative appropriations committees tie the line-item budget requests to actual programs in any comprehensive way. Since many services are delivered by more than one agency, the budget review process is to a considerable extent divorced from the actual operation of programs.

Budgeting Innovations

Until the late 1970s, the incremental increases in state and local agency budgets were possible because of the yearly increase in funds available to the public sector and the steadily growing federal grants-in-aid. Since about 1978, however, state and local revenues declined, in real dollars, as did federal aid (see Chapter 4). By the 1980s, state and local budget officers had to contend with allocating budget reductions and program cuts rather than allocating growing resources. The traditional incremental budget process was not a very useful tool for confronting these new financial problems. This new task put a premium on a number of innovations in budgeting that sought to give governors and mayors greater control over the allocation of state and local resources.

Program Budgeting

In the early 1960s the United States Department of Defense introduced a new concept, planning program budgeting. The concept quickly spread to other departments and then to the states[43] before it was abandoned in the early 1970s. Although abandoned, it was an important experiment because it spun off such innovations as program budgeting, cost–benefit analysis, the definition of program objectives, and zero-base budgeting, some of which are still used today.

Planning program budgeting (PPB) was an extremely complicated budgeting device that attempted to eliminate the separation between program planning and budget planning that was inherent to the line-item budget. Instead of organizing the budget by traditional line items, PPB organized a budget by programs. In addition, PPB also demanded that each program's objectives be defined. Rather than simply asking for more funds to continue activities that had been carried on in previous years, agencies were obliged by PPB to define each activity's objectives and to indicate how the budget amounts related to the objectives, how to accomplish the objectives in alternative ways, and whether the objectives were being accomplished. This procedure involved a **cost–benefit analysis** of programs. If five different programs operated by three different agencies deal with the education of retarded children, PPB in theory enables the policymakers to compare the results of these programs in terms of the costs involved and the benefits received.

Tying all these elements of PPB together turned out to be such an enormously complicated task that the federal government eventually abandoned it, but some effective variations of program budgeting were established in Hawaii, Pennsylvania, Wisconsin, Alaska, and some other states. However, in most states the elaborate PPB process never got off the ground.[44]

Zero-Base Budgeting

As PPB began to wither, budget reformers turned their attention to **zero-base budgeting** (ZBB). Under ZBB, each agency is forced to justify its own budget from a base of zero dollars as though it were just starting to operate for the first time. The most concerted attempt to implement ZBB was probably that of New Mexico (see the Highlight on p. 287). Ideal conditions existed in that state because only 35 percent of the budget was earmarked and the legislature had authority over the rest. Even under these favorable conditions, however, the results were fairly modest.

Since New Mexico had made such great strides in the direction of ZBB and performance-level budgeting, why was the 75 percent performance level abandoned in 1974? The main reason seemed to be that the state had a large budget surplus that year, that would give most agencies a budget increase of 10 to 20 percent. A moot exercise of setting priorities for a budget at the 75 percent level had little support, therefore.

Some other governments besides New Mexico's have abandoned ZBB after brief experimentation. Pima County (Phoenix), Arizona, abandoned the practice when county officials became discouraged because ZBB failed to meet their needs.[45] And at the state level, Montana abandoned the practice after a four-year experiment. The deputy director of budgeting in that state complained that "the benefits derived from ZBB were marginal compared with the problems encountered in implementing the system. ZBB . . . was fundamentally incompatible with actual conditions experienced in state government budgets."[46] Among the problems encountered in trying to implement were a fourfold increase in paperwork to complete the budget process, and a lack of legislative commitment. The Montana legislature itself ignored the ZBB format in favor of the line-item format whenever it was possible.

In contrast to these negative experiences with ZBB, New Jersey Governor Brendan Byrne successfully used ZBB to cope with a financial crisis in 1974. Each department was required to rank its programs in order of priority and to set performance levels for each program. This enabled the governor to apply the zero-base concept as he cut low-priority programs and reallocated the state's limited revenue among the surviving programs.[47]

The state of Delaware also had a successful experience with ZBB.[48] Initiated in 1977 with only 3 percent of the state budget covered, by 1979 it had gradually expanded to cover the entire budget. ZBB brought several benefits to Delaware budgeting. It helped the governor to control state costs and to reallocate state funds from low-priority programs to high-priority programs. Also, it helped bring program managers into the budgeting process and facilitated communication between the executive and legislative branches. Analyzing the Delaware experience, one team of researchers offered four guidelines for increasing the chances for successful implementation of ZBB.[49] First, there must be commitment of the executive and legislative leadership to the process. Second, ZBB should be phased in gradually, starting with a limited number of programs and expanding slowly to cover the entire budget. Third,

Highlight
Zero-Base Budgeting in New Mexico

In 1971 New Mexico's legislative Finance Committee instructed ten agencies (which together spent about 1 percent of the state's appropriations) to justify their programs as though they were starting from zero. As a result of the justifications presented, the committee recommended abolishing three agencies, substantially reducing programs in two, and giving a business-as-usual budgeting treatment in the remaining five. This, of course, was in keeping with the zero-base concept. The three agencies that could not provide a sufficient justification of their programs had, under the zero-base concept, to be eliminated. The legislature as a whole was unconvinced by this argument, however, and only one agency was actually abolished.

In the following year, 1972, the legislative Finance Commitee introduced the "level-of-effort" concept. Sixteen agencies (which together spent about 4 percent of the state budget) were examined and asked to submit performance criteria for their budget. Under performance criteria, the committee instructed each agency to specify which programs would be cut if the agency's budget were established at 75, 95, or 100 percent of its current spending level.

This introduction of performance criteria and levels of effort did force the agencies to establish priorities on their programs. However, it constituted an abandonment of the zero-base concept, since the agencies did not have to justify any program from a base of zero. The procedure worked smoothly, nevertheless, and in the following year, 1973, the legislative Finance Committee expanded the concept to thirty-five agencies, which comprised about 40 percent of all state expenditures. Included in the thirty-five agencies were all major agencies except higher education and public schools. Finally, in 1974 the legislature modified the concept of performance level so that the minimum performance level for which the agencies were required to budget was no longer 75 percent of the current budget but 100 percent. The 1974 approach clearly abandoned the zero-base concept. No longer did the agencies have to justify programs and rank priorities among them. They simply had to establish priorities on which ones were to get increases.

Source: John D. La Faver, "Zero-Base Budgeting in New Mexico," *State Government* 47 (Spring 1974): 112.

judicious use must be made of budgeting experts. Fourth, it is necessary to follow up on the implementation process and monitor feedback from the program managers to improve the process as it goes on.

The New Jersey and Delaware experiences show that the newer budgeting concepts have become useful. Although PPB failed, it did serve the important function of introducing the states and cities to new budgeting concepts—program budgeting, cost–benefit analysis, definition of program objectives, zero-base budgeting, and the establishment of performance levels for agencies. None of these reforms has totally replaced the traditional, line-item, incremental budget,[50] so they are not cure-alls for state and local budgeting problems. Nevertheless, judicious application of them can be an important and useful governing tool.

Alternatives for Improving Executive Management

In addition to budget innovations, recent years have seen several other creative approaches to improving executive management at the state and local levels. These include program evaluation, management by objectives, sunset legislation, and legislative review of administrative rules. (For this last approach see Chapter 9.)

Program Evaluation

Legislatures often pass programs without criteria for evaluating their success. Executives cannot make reasonable decisions about allocation of resources unless they can evaluate whether programs attain their objectives. Without evaluation, they cannot know which programs are successful, which administrative practices work, and even which groups of employees are competent.[51]

There are three types of **program evaluation.** First is the *social science or behavioral approach.* A social science evaluation might, for example, conduct surveys of residents in a redevelopment neighborhood to determine the impact of the program on their lives. Experimentation has also been used. Different neighborhoods might be identified as control and experimental sites to test rent subsidy or social service programs. The social science approach has definite uses, but it also has limits. Administrators can affect the conclusions of the evaluation, and programs administered in separate cities may differ so much that they cannot be compared as part of controlled experiments.[52]

One of the most prominent social science evaluation projects in recent years was a national survey of the population, called *Bureaucratic Encounters,* seeking to measure how much contact people had with public bureaucracies and how they evaluated those bureaucracies. Based on a national sample, the study found that well over a majority of the population (58 percent) had used government services provided at the federal, state, and local levels. These services included employment services, welfare services, and health services. Some of the study's most important findings on how clients evaluated the services were paradoxical. People tended to give higher evaluations to the agency they encountered than to government agencies in general. For example, 71 percent of the people said that the agency they contacted had solved their personal problem satisfactorily, and 79 percent felt they had been treated fairly. When the same people were asked to evaluate government offices generally, however, only 30 percent thought that the agencies could take care of problems, and only 42 percent thought that government offices treated people fairly.[53] These findings suggest that although government bureaucracies perform satisfactorily for their specific clients, they have serious image problems among the general population.

A second approach is based on *cost-effective* models, which assume that costs and benefits for specific programs can be measured. When forced to choose between alternatives, administrators can choose the approach that has the lowest cost–benefit ratio—that is, the approach that produces the most benefits for the least cost. While attractive in theory, the cost–benefit approach has been difficult to implement. Many programs have multiple goals that are difficult to rank and that can evolve over time. Administrators tend to state goals in vague, general terms to give themselves as much flexibility as possible. All this makes evaluation of goals difficult, and it also makes it difficult to measure whether the goals are attained.

A third type of evaluation is eclectic.[54] *Eclectic* means selecting unsystematically from various approaches. For example, when asking for a large budget increase in a given program, administrators might make an eclectic evaluation of the program by listing a series of rationales and data to show that the program is effective. Such data will be unsystematically gathered and perhaps totally unrelated to the prestated objectives of the program. But if the data are presented well, the administrator may be able to use this kind of evaluation effectively.

Management by Objectives

Under **management by objectives (MBO)**, each agency director stipulates his or her objectives for the upcoming year.[55] A director of a state vocational education agency, for example, might make it an agency objective to reduce the number of dropouts from the state vocational schools. Once the agency head's objectives are defined, the bureau chiefs under the director propose their objectives, which will be consistent with the director's. The subordinates of the bureau chiefs then define their objectives for the year in relation to those of the bureau chief. Theoretically, all of the employees of a given department work to attain a common set of objectives for the department as a whole. Throughout the year, supervisors evaluate their subordinates' progress toward the objectives. In systems that provide merit pay, MBO can be tied to pay increases for employees; employees who exceed their objectives get extraordinary raises. In this way, MBO and merit pay can be tied together in a comprehensive system of incentives.

In practice, of course, MBO rarely works this neatly. Public employee unions generally resist MBO if it involves the concept of merit pay. Nevertheless, the concept of MBO has become popular with high-level administrators, who feel it has greatly increased their capacities to control the services they administer.

Sunset Legislation

In 1976 Colorado passed the nation's first **Sunset law.** This law set a termination date for a third of the state's regulatory boards and commissions. The termination was to take effect after seven years, and the only way that the boards could continue to exist after that date was by convincing the legislature to renew them for another seven years.

The Colorado law was passed in large part because of the lobbying effort of the Colorado branch of Common Cause. The legislature selected licensing boards for the first sunset review, for they were the most marginal agencies. Considerable duplication appeared among the licensing boards, and some of these boards had been caught in questionable if not outright corrupt practices.[56]

As a result of its first round of sunset reviews, the Colorado legislature eliminated four small agencies and made a number of minor changes in its regulatory legislation, indicating that the sunset process has had some success. In the second round of sunset reviews, in 1979, no agencies were permanently eliminated, although several changes were made in regulatory practices.[57] But it would be unreasonable to expect too much from sunset legislation. No state is likely to eliminate its department of education. Nor is any major educational program likely to be abolished. Even the marginal programs have client groups that will make their elimination very difficult, regardless of the evaluation made of them.[58]

If the goal of sunset is actually to terminate agencies, it has not been a very effective reform. If, however, the goal is to use sunset as a form of legislative oversight to improve government performance, the experience of Colorado and other states indicates that sunset is a very useful tool.[59] By 1982, thirty-five states had adopted sunset laws. Supporters of sunset hope that it will at the very least require legislators to conduct meaningful evaluations of agencies and programs and force agency administrators to justify what they are doing.

Political Economy and Government Productivity

As public resources have become scarcer in the 1980s, there has been a growing demand for increasing the productivity of public employees. This demand is reflected in most of the reform measures examined in this chapter—improving personnel practices, reorganization of government, budget improvements, and management by objectives. All of these measures reflect an assumption that it is possible to get more work out of government employees than currently. This can be done, it is thought, either by performing existing services with fewer dollars or by getting better performance out of the dollars already being spent. In the 1980s, two approaches in particular have focused on improving government service at lower cost: privatization and waste control.

Privatization of Public Services

One of the hottest concepts in state and local administration in the 1980s has been **privatization,** the use of private organizations to produce certain public services. Governments responsible for a given service are increasingly contracting out to private companies to produce the service for the government. The government then becomes an overseer of the service rather than a producer of it.

Privatization received a substantial boost in the 1970s when a body of research began comparing the cost of public service delivery with private delivery of similar services. It was found, for example, that it cost New York City garbage collectors $39.71 to collect a ton of garbage, whereas private garbage companies in adjacent suburbs could collect the same amount of refuse for only $17.28.[60] In Chicago, the city spent $1.23 to read a single water meter, but a private firm in Indianapolis was able to do the same job for 27½¢.[61] To the extent that public services generally could be produced more cheaply by private companies, governments had a tremendous incentive to contract out as many services as feasible.

Scottsdale, Arizona, gained nationwide publicity when it contracted out all its fire protection services to a private company.[62] Other jurisdictions followed suit, contracting out a variety of services, from residential treatment centers for delinquent children to jails. At the local level, the services most often contracted out are refuse collection, streetlight operation, vehicle towing, hospital management, solid-waste disposal, street repair, and traffic signal mainte-nance. Twenty-five percent of all cities contract out those services.[63]

Privatization of services is not problem-free, however. There is tremendous potential for contracting out to become a form of patronage (see p. 273) associated with bid rigging, political favoritism, and financial kickbacks through campaign contributions. The savings by going private may disappear if the contractor makes a "low-ball" bid the first year and then recovers the losses by boosting prices once the contract has been won. If contractors default or fail to perform adequately, the city may be left holding the bag. St. Paul, Minnesota, contracted out the operation of a facility to run a machine to turn diseased elm trees into wood chips that could be marketed as cheap fuel. The private contractor never learned how to run the machine and failed to market the chips successfully. The city was saved from a financial loss on the operation only when the chips accidentally caught fire and were de-stroyed.[64] Finally, privatization inevitably draws bitter opposition from the American Federation of State, County, and Municipal Employees, which has launched a campaign to inform the public of the many ventures in which privatization increased rather than decreased costs.

Waste Control

A second popular approach to improving public employee productivity in the 1980s has been controlling the amount of government waste. Following the example of the federal government's Grace Commission, which identified many ways to eliminate waste in the federal government, at least four states (Illinois, New Jersey, North Carolina, and Texas) have established Little Grace Commissions. The New Jersey commission recommended a number of cost-cutting measures, including a better accounting system and eliminating the duplication of services.[65]

Assessment

In the tighter budgetary environments of the 1980s, it has become impera-tive for state and local governments to improve their productivity. There is more at stake than simply reducing the cost of public services, however. The effective delivery of urban services makes a significant difference in the qual-ity of our lives and the ability of private-sector institutions to function. If the potholes in our streets are not filled, our lives are less comfortable. If the police do not respond to our calls, our lives are less secure. It is reported that when residents of the South Bronx need emergency help fast, they often pull the fire alarm rather than call the police.[66] They know that the fire department

Source: Bob Englehart, *Dayton Journal Herald.* Reprinted by permission.

always responds quickly, but they do not know how fast—or even whether—the police will arrive. This, of course, is a very expensive way of getting help. And for public managers in the 1980s, it illustrates some of the main problems discussed in this chapter. How do they ensure that the most appropriate agencies deliver the right services most effectively to the target people on time? And how do they meet the demands of cost-conscious groups that all these services be delivered at the lowest possible cost per unit of service?

Summary

1. A basic tension exists between career administrators and policy-level executives, such as governors and their appointed department heads.

2. With over thirteen million state and local employees, personnel management has become an awesome governmental task. Traditional patronage systems of recruitment have given way to more modern civil service personnel management practices. Some of the most serious problems confronting personnel management are racial and sexual bias in hiring and promotional patterns, collective bargaining, public employees' pensions, and the inability to create a system of incentives that rewards top performance and makes it possible to discharge incompetent employees.

3. State and local governments have traditionally been organized in a fragmented and ineffective manner. In order to modernize their governments, nineteen states reorganized their executive branches between 1965 and 1975. The goals of these reorganizations are to concentrate more authority in the governor, to create a hierarchical form of organization, and to consolidate hundreds of scattered agencies into a limited number of departments that would be directly accountable to the governor. Two reform strategies have been most successful. The first is to pass a constitutional amendment that limits the executive branch to a specified number of departments, which forces the legislature to enact the necessary enabling legislation. The second strategy is to grant the governor the authority to reorganize the executive branch, subject to legislative veto.

4. A major device for improving the governor's or mayor's ability to manage administrative departments is the budget. Budgeting at the state level has become the task of a budget director, who is usually tied closely to the governor. At the local level, budgeting is less centralized. It is most centralized in city-manager and strong-mayor systems and least centralized in weak-mayor, commission, and traditional county governments.

A second step to improve the budget as a management tool has been to get away from traditional practices that were characterized by incrementalism and the line-item budget. Attempts in the late 1960s to impose planning program budgeting in the states and cities failed, but as a result of the attempts at PPB, many state and local governments have adopted some form of program budgeting. And over twenty states have adopted some form of zero-base budgeting.

5. A number of alternatives have been experimented with to improve executive management at the state and local levels. The most far-reaching of these have been program evaluation, management by objectives, sunset legislation, and legislative review of administrative rules.

6. In the 1980s, attention has focused on increasing the productivity of public employees and bureaucracies, sometimes through privatization.

Key Terms

Affirmative action   The principle that special preference should be given to minorities and women in hiring for public jobs. The objective of affirmative action is to make up for past discriminations against women and minorities.

American Federation of State, County, and Municipal Employees (AFSCME)   The largest state and local government employees union.

Civil service system   A form of recruitment for government jobs in which people are hired on the basis of their performance on competitive examinations or merit.

Collective bargaining The process of workers banding together and bargaining as a unit with their employer over wages and job conditions.

Comparable worth The principle that jobs of equal skill requirements should receive equal pay.

Cost–benefit analysis A budgeting procedure that weighs the costs of different programs against the benefits to be derived from them so that officials can select the programs that achieve agency goals at the lowest cost–benefit ratio.

Equal employment opportunity The practice of giving equal opportunity to all job applicants, regardless of race or religion.

Incrementalism A budgeting process in which budgets increase annually at about the rate of inflation.

Line-item budgeting A form of budgeting in which budgets are organized by specific expenditures unrelated to specific programs.

Little Hoover Commission A type of commission appointed in the 1950s to study the organization of state government and make recommendations for improvement. About thirty-five states formed such commissions.

Management by objectives (MBO) A procedure in which managers and supervisors set annual objectives that are consistent with agency goals. Their performance is then measured by their ability to attain their objectives.

Merit system (employment) A recruitment method for government that hires and promotes people on the basis of their training and competence to perform specific jobs. See *Civil service system.*

Patronage A recuitment method for government jobs in which people are hired as a reward for their political support of the winning candidates.

Planning program budgeting A form of budgeting organized around programs rather than line items and planned out two or three years into the future.

Privatization The practice of governmental contracting with private firms to provide public systems.

Program evaluation A procedure for determining if programs meet their objectives. There are three different approaches to program evaluation.

Sunset law A law requiring programs to terminate in a given number of years unless they are recreated by the legislature. This forces the legislature to reevaluate the purposes and operations of the sunset agencies and programs.

Zero-base budgeting A budgeting procedure in which agencies must set various performance levels and indicate which services will be reduced as budget levels are reduced. This enables officials to set priorities on different services and programs.

References

1. *New York Times,* July 12, 1977, p. 12.

2. Ibid.

3. Calculated from *The Book of the States: 1982–83* (Lexington, Ky.: Council of State Governments, 1982), p. 341, and *The Book of the States: 1976–77,* p. 155.

4. Ira Sharkansky, "State Administrators in the Policy Process," in *Politics in the American States: A Comparative Analysis,* 2d ed., eds. Herbert Jacob and Kenneth N. Vines (Boston: Little, Brown and Co., 1971), p. 238.

5. Martin Tolchin and Susan Tolchin, *To the Victor: Political Patronage from the Clubhouse to the White House* (New York: Vintage Books, 1972), Chs. 2 and 4.

6. W. Robert Gump, "The Functions of Patronage in American Party Politics: An Empirical Reappraisal," *Midwest Journal of Political Science* 15, no. 1 (February 1971): 87–107.

7. Frank J. Sorauf, "Patronage and Party," *Midwest Journal of Political Science* 3, no. 2 (May 1959): 115–126.

8. See *Oklahoma* v. *U.S. Civil Service Commission,* 330 U.S. 127 (1947).

9. *Elrod* v. *Burns,* 427 U.S. 347 (1976).

10. Raymond Wolfinger, "Why Political Machines Have not Withered Away and Other Revisionist Thoughts," *Journal of Politics* 34, no. 2 (May 1972): 365–398.

11. *The Book of the States: 1982-83* (Lexington, Ky.: Council of State Governments, 1982), pp. 312–313.

12. An official of the Bureau of Intergovernmental Personnel Program of the United States Civil Service Commission cites a survey that indicates that 95 percent of all local employees are covered by some form of merit system. Whether all of these systems are free of political influence, however, seems debatable. See Andrew W. Boesel, "Local Personnel Management: Organizational Problems and Operating Practices," *Municipal Yearbook: 1974* (Washington, D.C.: International City Management Association, 1974), pp. 92–93.

13. York Willbern, "Administrative Organization," in *The 50 States and Their Local Governments,* ed. James W Fesler (New York: Knopf, 1967), pp. 341–342.

14. Richard C. Elling, "State Bureaucracies," *Politics in the American States: A Comparative Analysis,* 4th ed., eds. Virginia Gray, Herbert Jacob, and Kenneth N. Vines (Boston: Little, Brown and Co., 1983), p. 257.

15. Ibid.

16. Deil Wright, Mary Wagner, and Richard McAnaw, "State Administrators: Their Changing Characteristics," *State Government* 50, no. 3 (Summer 1977): 152–159; *New York Times,* October 24, 1986, p. 13.

17. Marion Reber, "Comparable Worth: Closing a Wage Gap," *State Legislatures* 10, no. 4 (April 1984): 26–31.

18. Keon S. Chi, "Developments in State Personnel Systems," *Book of the States: 1983-84* (Lexington, Ky.: Council of State Governments, 1984), pp. 289–291; Debra A. Stewart, "States and Local Initiatives in the Federal System: The Politics and Policy of Comparable Worth in 1984," *Publius* 15, no. 3 (Summer 1985): 81–96.

19. See Boesel, "Local Personnel Management," pp. 87–90.

20. Ibid., pp. 87, 90.

21. Bureau of the Census, *Statistical Abstract of the United States: 1986* (Washington, D.C.: U.S. Government Printing Office, 1985), p. 423.

22. Ibid., p. 425.

23. Elling, "State Bureaucracies," p. 263.

24. *The Book of the States: 1986-87,* pp. 314–315.

25. See Neal R. Peirce in *Minneapolis Tribune,* December 11, 1977, p. 19-A. Also see Dennis L. Dresang, "The Politics of Civil Service Reform: Lessons from Wisconsin" (Paper delivered at the annual conference of the Midwest Political Science Association, Chicago, Illinois, April 1978).

26. The original outlining of these six principles is usually attributed to A. E. Buck, *The Reorganization of State Governments in the United States* (New York: Columbia University Press, 1938), pp. 14–28. Also see York Willbern, "Administrative Organization," in *The 50 States and Their Local Governments,* ed. James W. Fesler (New York: Knopf, 1967), p. 343. These provisions were also reiterated in an influential document of the Committee for Economic Development, *Modernizing State Government* (New York: Committee for Economic Development, 1967), pp. 49–60.

27. Karl A. Bosworth, "The Politics of Management Improvement in the States," *American Political Science Review* 47, no. 1 (March 1953): 84–99.

28. Elling, "State Bureaucracies," p. 251.

29. R. P. Knuth, "Reorganization Bill Enacted in Missouri," *National Civic Review* 63, no. 4 (April 1974): 195–196.

30. Alva W. Stewart, "New State Plan in North Carolina," *National Civic Review* 61, no. 2 (February 1972): 76–78.

31. Albert B. Saye, "Georgia Revamps State Agencies," *National Civic Review* 61, no. 3 (March 1972): 136–137.

32. York Willbern, "Administrative Organization," pp. 341–342.

33. See Kenneth J. Meier, "Executive Reorganization of Government: Impact on Employment and Expenditures," *American Journal of Political Science* 24, no. 3 (August 1980): 396–412.

34. Charles T. Goodsell, "Collegial State Administration: Design for Today?" *Western Political Quarterly* 34, no. 3 (September 1981): 447–466.

35. Thad L. Beyle, "The Executive Branch: Elected Officials and Organizations," *The Book of the States: 1984-85,* pp. 44–45.

36. James Conant, "State Reorganization: A New Model?" *State Government* 58, no. 4 (1986): 130–138.

37. James P. Lester, James L. Franke, Ann O'M. Bowman, and Kenneth W. Kramer, "Hazardous Wastes, Politics, and Public Policy: A Comparative State Analysis," *Western Political Quarterly* 36, no. 2 (June 1983): 257–283.

38. There are two different versions of incrementalism. The *rational incremental* version argues that the largest increments go to the agencies that run programs consistent with the short-term political interests of the legislators who approve the budget. See Charles E. Lindblom, "Decision Making in Taxation Expenditures," in National Bureau of Economic Research, *Public Finances: Needs, Sources and Utilization* (Princeton, N.J.: Princeton University Press, 1961), pp. 295–329. In contrast, the *role-constrained* model of incrementalism argues that the budget increments get determined by individual actors playing out predetermined roles. It is essentially this model that is described in the text. See Thomas J. Anton, "Roles and Symbols in the Determination of State Expenditures," *Midwest Journal of Political Science* 11, no. 1 (February 1967): 27–43.

39. Anton, "Roles and Symbols," pp. 27–40. Anton's model was derived from a study of the budgeting process in Illinois.

40. Ira Sharkansky studied budgets in twelve states and concluded that the role-constrained model did not apply in those states. See his "Agency Requests, Gubernatorial Support and Budget Success in State Legislatures," *American Political Science Review* 62, no. 4 (December 1968): 1220–1231. An attempt to test Anton's role-constrained theory in all fifty states did not find enough consistency in growth in specific budget areas to

support the model for all states. See Gerald E. Sullivan, "Incremental Budget-Making in the American States: A Test of the Anton Model," *Journal of Politics* 34 (May 1972): 639–647.

41. Sharkansky, "Agency Requests, Gubernatorial Support and Budget Success in State Legislatures," pp. 1220–1231.

42. Sharkansky, "State Administrators in the Policy Process," p. 259.

43. See Allen Schick, "PPB: The View from the States," *State Government* 45, no. 1 (Winter 1972): 13.

44. Aaron Wildavsky says of PPB, "I have not been able to find a single example of successful implementation of PPB," and he makes specific reference to attempts at zero-base budgeting in the U.S. Department of Agriculture. See Wildavsky, *The Politics of the Budgetary Process*, 2d ed. (Boston: Little, Brown and Co., 1974), pp. 195, 200. Also see John A. Worthley, "PPB: Dead or Alive?" *Public Administration Review* 34, no. 4 (July–August 1974): 393.

45. Keith J. Mueller, "Can Hungry Bureaucrats Be Forced to Diet? Zero-Base Budgets in Local Government," (Paper delivered at the annual meeting of the Midwest Political Science Association, Chicago, Illinois, April 24–26, 1980).

46. John S. Fitzpatrick, "Montana's Experiment With Zero-Base Budgeting," *State Government* 53, no. 1 (Winter 1980): 11–16.

47. Michael J. Scheiring, "Zero-Base Budgeting in New Jersey," *State Government* 49, no. 3 (Summer 1976): 174–179.

48. J. Robert Krebill and Ronald F. Mosher, "Delaware Budgets for Productivity," *State Government* 53, no. 1 (Winter 1980): 17–21.

49. Ibid.

50. Elling, "State Bureaucracies," p. 273.

51. For an assessment of program evaluation generally, see Carol H. Weiss, *Evaluation Research: Methods of Assessing Program Effectiveness* (Englewood Cliffs, N.J.: Prentice-Hall, 1972).

52. Orville F. Poland, "Program Evaluation and Administrative Theory," *Public Administration Review* 34, no. 4 (July–August 1974): 334.

53. Daniel Katz et al., *Bureaucratic Encounters: A Pilot Study in the Evaluation of Government Services* (Ann Arbor, Mich.: Institute for Social Research, 1975), pp. 120, 182.

54. Poland, "Program Evaluation and Administrative Theory," pp. 333–338.

55. On MBO, see Jong Jun, "Introduction: Management by Objectives in the Public Sector," *Public Administration Review* 36, no. 1 (January–February 1976): 1–4; Frank Sherwood and William Page, "MBO and Public Management," *Public Administration Review* 36, no. 1 (January–February 1976): 5–11. For general overviews, see Robert D. Miewald, *Public Administration: A Critical Perspective* (New York: McGraw-Hill, 1978), pp. 153–155.

56. See Robert D. Behn, "The False Dawn of the Sunset Laws," *Public Interest*, no. 49 (Fall 1977): 103–118.

57. Ronald E. Gregson, "Sunset in Colorado: The Second Round," *State Government* 53, no. 2 (Spring 1980): 458–462.

58. Behn, "The False Dawn of the Sunset Laws."

59. See *The Status of Sunset in the States: A Common Cause Report* (Washington, D.C.: Common Cause, 1982). Also see Patricia Freeman and William Lyons, "The Impact of

Sunset Legislation in Tennessee" (Paper delivered at the Midwest Political Science Association annual meeting, Milwaukee, Wis., April 29–May 1, 1982).

60. E. S. Savas, "Municipal Monopolies Versus Competition," in *Improving the Quality of Urban Management,* Vol. 8, *Urban Affairs Annual Reviews,* eds. Willis D. Hawley and David Rogers (Beverly Hills, Calif.: SAGE Publications, 1974), p. 483.

61. Robert L. Lineberry, *Equality and Urban Policy: The Distribution of Urban Services,* Vol. 39, SAGE Library of Social Research (Beverly Hills, Calif.: SAGE Publications, 1977), p. 167.

62. On Scottsdale, see Edward C. Hayes, "In Pursuit of Productivity: Management Innovation in Scottsdale," *National Civic Review* 73, no. 6 (June 1984): 273–277.

63. Data from a 1985 survey by the International City Management Assoc. Reported in the *New York Times,* May 28, 1985, p. 9.

64. Peter Hames, "When Public Services Go Private: There's More Than One Option," *National Civic Review* 73, no. 6 (June 1984): 282.

65. Keon S. Chi, "Private-Public Alliances Grow," *State Government News* 29, no. 1 (January 1986): 10–13.

66. See Dennis Smith, *Report From Engine Co. 82* (New York: McCall Books, 1972), p. 27.

Chapter 12
Courts, Crime, and Corrections in American States

Chapter Preview

One of the most important concerns of state and local government is the courts and their handling of crime. In this chapter we will survey this topic by examining, in turn:

1. How the courts play important roles establishing and implementing public policy.
2. The decentralized nature of court organization and the demands of judicial reformers for more centralization and more accountability of judges.
3. How politics is inherently embedded in the judicial process in American states.
4. The problem crime poses for American society and how state courts process criminal charges.
5. The importance of political values in setting and carrying out criminal justice policies.

Let us begin by looking at how one particular state supreme court handled a very difficult case of public policy.

Introduction

On September 3, 1976, workers in New Jersey for the first time had a 2 percent state income tax charge deducted from their paychecks. Many New Jerseyites did not like this new tax. One crowd of demonstrators dumped a crate of tea on the doorstep of the governor's mansion to remind him of the

Boston Tea Party of two centuries earlier. Governor Brendan Byrne had become one of the state's strongest advocates of the income tax even though he had campaigned for the governorship in 1973 by telling voters, "I have said loud and clear that I do not think we need an income tax in the forseeable future."[1] Another crowd of 5,000 demonstrators took out their wrath on the legislators by staging a rally at the state capitol.

But the demonstrators were really directing their protest at the wrong targets. Left to themselves, the legislators had repeatedly failed to pass the governor's proposals for an income tax.

The body most responsible for New Jersey's income tax was the state supreme court. In 1973 its decision in *Robinson* v. *Cahill*[2] struck down the state's traditional method of financing public education from local property taxes and ordered that a new, statewide tax plan be devised by December 31, 1974. In response to this court order, Governor Byrne in 1974 proposed a state income tax. But the legislature refused to pass it. The court's deadline of December 31, 1974, passed with no new tax plan enacted. The court responded by extending the deadline another year and ordering that $300 million in state aid be taken from well-to-do suburban school districts and redistributed to central-city school districts. Even then the legislature was unable to pass a new tax plan. By the middle of 1976 the supreme court's patience was exhausted. Three years had passed, and still the state's schools were operating on a finance plan that had been declared unconstitutional. Seeing no alternative course of action, the supreme court in May 1976 ordered all of the state's public schools closed after July 1 of that year.

This was the seventh supreme court ruling on the case in three years. Opponents asked the federal courts to overrule the state supreme court order, but the federal courts refused to do so. On July 1, all New Jersey schools closed. No summer school or special educational programs for the handicapped or retarded were permitted to continue. Faced with the inevitable pressures that came from parents and teachers to get the schools opened, the legislature, on July 9, 1976, finally passed a 2 percent income tax plan, and the schools reopened.[3]

The New Jersey school finance case illustrates well the impact that state and local courts have on our lives. Not only do the courts resolve personal legal problems we may have, but they are a tremendously important political force. They also play critical roles in setting and implementing public policy on crime. In this chapter, we examine five major facets of the state and local court systems: (1) public policy and the courts, (2) the organization of court systems, (3) the role of politics in American courts, (4) crime and the legal system in America, and (5) political values as they affect criminal justice policies.

Public Policy and the Courts

State and local courts play three major roles in the creation and implementation of public policy. First, the courts resolve legal disputes. Second, they help set many public policies. And third, they get intimately involved in the administration of some of these policies.

① Resolving Legal Disputes and Administering Justice

The primary role of the courts is to resolve legal disputes. These may be disputes of **civil law** or **criminal law.** In civil cases, one individual or group sues another, and the court's job is to settle the dispute and determine whether damages will be awarded. Typical civil cases involve divorce, settlement of estates, and malpractice suits. In criminal cases, the government prosecutes an individual for violating a law. The court is called on to determine whether the accused person is guilty and, if guilty, to apply a jail sentence, fine, or other punishment prescribed by state law. A serious crime such as murder, arson, or theft of large amounts of money is called a **felony.** A lesser crime is called a **misdemeanor.** Generally, misdemeanors cannot bring a jail sentence of more than a few months or a fine of more than $1,000, but the precise limits vary from one state to another. Although criminal cases usually get more media attention, the overwhelming majority of cases handled in court are civil cases.

② Setting Public Policy

As they go about their primary business of resolving disputes, state courts often establish public policies. They do this mainly by interpreting the law and by determining whether a law is constitutional (**judicial review**). When a state supreme court declares a law unconstitutional, nobody can be convicted of violating that law. This not only makes the law unenforceable, it establishes new policies. In the case of *Robinson* v. *Cahill,* discussed earlier, the New Jersey Supreme Court in effect changed the state's public policies for financing educational services.

The judicial review role of the state courts is carried out almost exclusively by the state supreme courts. The lower courts are limited to applying the law. Most cases are simply applications of previous decisions, referred to as *precedents.* Only a minimum of lower-court decisions are appealed to the state supreme courts, and few of those appeals are heard by the higher courts. Lower state courts can nevertheless make an impact on public policy by issuing declaratory judgments, injunctions, and cease-and-desist orders. A **declaratory judgment** is a legally binding court order, and anyone who disobeys it is liable for a fine or a jail sentence. The **injunction** and the **cease-and-desist order** are court orders to stop some particular action. Such court orders can be used to set public policy. For example, courts that consistently use these powers to stop strikes or to permit nonunion workers to take the jobs of striking workers are clearly setting a legal policy that is pro-management and anti-union.

Finally, in eleven states the supreme court can affect public policy by giving **advisory opinions.** Such opinions warn people in advance how the judges feel about the constitutionality of proposed actions or bills. The remaining thirty-nine states follow the example of the United States Supreme Court and do not allow their courts to issue advisory opinions, leaving that task to their attorneys general.

Law Makers or Law Interpreters?

A major controversy about the courts' policymaking role is whether they should confine themselves to law interpretation or use their judicial review powers to engage in law making. One reason why the New Jersey Supreme Court was able to force an income tax on the state was because New Jersey has a long tradition of judicial law making. Another state with such a tradition is California. In this respect, California and New Jersey behave similarly to the United States Supreme Court, which plays an extensive law-making role. But California and New Jersey are the exceptions rather than the rule among state courts. Most state supreme courts are much less activist than the California, New Jersey, or federal courts. When the less innovative supreme courts do engage in law-making types of decisions for their states, they tend to justify those decisions in part by citing precedents from cases decided by the more prestigious state supreme courts, especially California, New York,* and Massachusetts.[4]

When judges engage in law making, they are sometimes said to exercise **judicial activism;** and when they limit themselves to interpreting the law, they are said to exercise **judicial restraint.** Whether judges should be law makers or law interpreters is a highly controversial issue that is seldom separated from the purposes for which judicial activism is used. Conservatives object to judicial activism used for liberal purposes, as in *Robinson* v. *Cahill.* Liberals object when it is used for conservative purposes.

Distributive or Redistributive Policies?

The most frequent conflict between liberal values and conservative values in court occurs when judges must choose between a **distributive policy** and

---

*In New York State, the court of last resort is called the Court of Appeals, and the term *Supreme Court* refers to the trial courts. See p. 305.

a **redistributive policy.**[5] Throughout most of American history, state and local court policies have been distributive; that is, they have followed a conservative pattern of reinforcing the existing distribution of wealth and influence. But in the New Jersey school finance case, the court's action was clearly redistributive, because it had the effect of taking money away from people in well-to-do areas of the state and redistributing it to poor school districts.

Another redistributive court practice is the **class-action suit** in consumer protection cases. By permitting isolated individuals with the same grievance to join together and file a single suit as a group, class-action suits encourage a redistribution of wealth and power from large corporations and institutions to isolated but organizable individuals.

Administration of Public Services

In addition to resolving legal disputes and setting public policies, some courts also administer certain services. The most notable examples are the family courts that resolve divorce cases. If a couple cannot agree on a division of property, the court will make that division for them. The court may also provide counseling services for couples seeking divorce. In cases where both the mother and father want custody of the children, the court may conduct custody studies to determine which party is better able to care for the children. Juvenile courts provide counseling and other services for juvenile offenders, and they monitor juvenile probation officers. Probate courts assign lawyers to administer the estates of people who die without leaving a will.

Court Organization and Reform

A dual court system exists in the United States—the federal court system and the state court systems. But there is a fair amount of overlap in their jurisdictions, for crimes such as kidnapping, sale of illegal narcotics, and robbery of federally insured banks violate both state and federal laws. For such crimes, a person could be prosecuted in either the state or the federal courts, depending on a number of factors, although most such prosecutions occur in state courts. The judgment of the state courts is final and cannot be appealed to the United States Supreme Court unless the case involves a *federal question*—a violation of either federal law or the United States Constitution.

A Decentralized Court System

In Figure 12–1 the organization of a typical state court system looks hierarchically structured. At the top is the court of last resort, usually called a

Figure 12-1. Structure of a Typical Court System

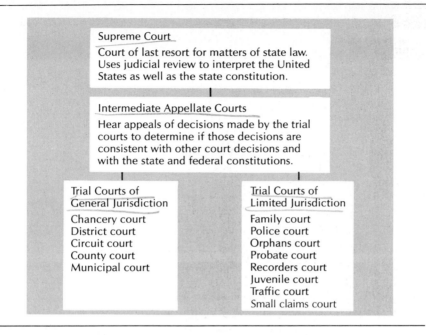

supreme court.* It hears appeals from the trial courts. Thirty-three states have created intermediate appellate courts under the supreme court to reduce the work loads of the supreme courts. Like the United States Supreme Court, these courts primarily hear appeals only to determine if proper judicial procedures were followed in the trial court or to make an interpretation of the law or the constitution. With the task for making such decisions removed from the supreme courts, the supreme courts can concentrate more fully on the most important constitutional and legal problems. In states with intermediate appellate courts, the supreme courts are felt to do a more thorough job than the supreme courts in states without the intermediate courts.[6]

At the bottom of the organization chart are the trial courts, where the parties present their testimony, facts are investigated, and a court decision is made. For trial courts of general jurisdiction, the state is divided into districts, and thus these courts are usually called district courts, county courts, municipal courts, or sometimes circuit courts or chancery courts. All major criminal and civil cases are tried in these courts.

---

*Two states—Maryland and New York—simply call the court of last resort the court of appeals. Confusing matters somewhat, New York uses the words *supreme court* to refer to its trial courts of general jurisdiction. Texas and Oklahoma have two supreme courts, one for civil cases and the other for criminal cases.

For minor criminal cases such as misdemeanors, for civil cases involving relatively small sums of money, or for specialized problems such as traffic tickets and divorces, courts of limited jurisdiction are used. Small claims courts, for example, deal with civil cases where the amount of damages is small and the parties can present their testimony in person without the expense of hiring a lawyer.[7]

Although this court organizational structure seems hierarchical and integrated, most state court systems actually are not well integrated. There are over 17,000 state and local courts, and they have a variety of organizational patterns. New York, for example, has eleven different kinds of trial courts, each specializing in its own type of lawsuit.[8]

Reforming Court Organization

In an attempt to impose a better-functioning structure on this decentralized judicial apparatus, reformers propose a unified court system. The unified court structure would consolidate all the courts of a state into a single judiciary with general jurisdiction over the entire state. A statewide trial court would have jurisdiction over all types of criminal and civil cases. The large states would have an intermediate appellate court between the trial courts and the supreme court. Having ultimate administrative authority over this unified state court system would be the chief justice of the state supreme court. He or she would assume major responsibility for assignment of cases and the hiring of court personnel. To handle these tasks, the chief justice would be given an administrative staff. In many states, full-time administrative officers have been hired to oversee the staff and assist the chief justice. Unified court systems have been adopted in Colorado, Illinois, and Minnesota, but most states continue to have decentralized courts.

Although modern administrative techniques have been widely adopted in most other major institutions, many judges have opposed their introduction to the courts. Critics charge that the traditional judge is reluctant to use a team approach to handling cases in court, to arrange the court calendar according to team priorities, to deal formally rather than informally with lawyers and other court participants, and to give up complete control over the disposition of cases as they proceed through the courts.[9] These traditionally organized courts have difficulty in keeping up with the rapid increase in lawsuits. Consequently, most courts have large backlogs of unheard cases.

A second demand of court reformers is to make judges accountable to professional standards. There is little to restrain a judge from vindictive or unprofessional behavior while on the bench, and every state has its own examples of this. Four Chicago judges and a court clerk were convicted of bribery and corruption for fixing cases.[10] The Rhode Island chief justice resigned in 1986 under threat of impeachment for his ties with organized crime.[11] And a Wisconsin judge was recalled in 1977 for statements offensive to women in his handling of a sexual abuse case (see Highlight, below).

But recall, impeachment, and criminal prosecution are not systematic ways of holding judges accountable. To provide systematic restraints, several states have created judicial-performance commissions to investigate charges of judicial impropriety. New York's Commission on Judicial Conduct investigated 317 complaints against judges in one recent year, resulting in formal disciplinary action against twenty-four judges.[12] The most famous judicial-performance commission is probably the California Commission on Judicial Performance, which is responsible for recommending the retirement, removal, or censure of judges found unfit for the **bench** (another term for the court). The Commission usually investigates only lower-court judges, who often retire quietly once an investigation begins rather than suffer public embarrassment and possible dismissal. But in 1977 the Commission brought about the forced retirement of an eighty-two-year-old Supreme Court justice who was senile and engaging in what the Commission called bizarre behavior on the bench.[13]

Perhaps the most controversial work of the Commission came in 1979 when it investigated the Supreme Court itself. The Commission held open hearings on charges that some Supreme Court justices had delayed making unpopular decisions until after the 1978 election, when four of them were up

Highlight
How Should Judges Be Removed?

Unless they severely violate deeply felt community values, judges can normally serve for as long as they want or until they reach their state's mandatory retirement age. Judge Archie Simonson blatantly affronted community values in Madison, Wisconsin. In 1977 two black youths, aged fourteen and fifteen, were charged with sexually assaulting a sixteen-year-old white girl in a Madison high school. A third teenage boy became a state's witness and was not charged. Judge Simonson sent the fourteen-year-old boy to a group home in Milwaukee but released the fifteen-year-old to the custody of his parents. The prosecuting attorney argued that the fifteen-year-old should also be placed in a group home. Judge Simonson replied that Madison was a sexually permissive community and suggested that the youth had been reacting normally in committing the sexual assault. When asked to apologize for these remarks, Simonson refused. Feminist groups in Madison collected enough petition signatures to set up a special recall election. The election was held in September 1977, and Judge Simonson was replaced by Moira Krueger, a specialist in juvenile law. This was the first time in thirty-five years that a judge anywhere in the United States had been recalled.

Source: New York Times, September 8, 9, 11, 1977.

for reelection. The hearings had barely begun when a court ruled that the open hearings must cease. The Commission continued its investigation behind closed doors and eventually came out with a report that made no charges or explanations of what it had discovered.[14] For all practical purposes, this report had the effect of condoning the delay of the decisions by the justices. The whole affair, however, somewhat reduced the stature of the California Supreme Court, which has generally been considered one of the most prestigious in the nation. Holding the investigation in secret seems to have violated the spirit of openness in government. And the revelations of pettiness and acrimony among the justices did not help their image.

Politics in American Courts

Politics can enter the judicial process in four ways. First, the selection of judges is itself a political act. Second, judges dispense patronage and make other political decisions. Third, judicial decisions are influenced by the political and socioeconomic backgrounds of the judges. Last, the courts become the focus of interest group activity.

Selecting Judges

Five selection methods exist, as Table 12–1 shows, and all five are political. Political party interests benefit most from partisan elections of judges or from direct appointments by the governor or the legislature. Under these methods, party supporters and contributors with many years' service to the party, legislators, or the governor can be rewarded with nominations or appointments to the bench. In states with strong political machines, such as New York and Pennsylvania, the judges can be called on to contribute a portion of their salaries to political campaigns. If politically sensitive issues come before these courts, the party in power can hope that the judges will look out for the party's vital interests. Not surprisingly, judges with political party connections in those states benefiting from party selection resist proposals for a merit plan of selection.[15]

Judicial reformers strive for nonpartisan elections or, better yet from their viewpoint, **merit plans** of selection. Since the first merit plan was put into practice in Missouri in 1930, such plans are known as **Missouri Plans.** Under this plan a nominating commission suggests a list of three nominees to the governor, who must select the judge from among those three. The nominating commission usually includes a governor-appointed citizen member, a judge, and representatives of the bar association. The bar association is a for-

Table 12–1. Methods of Selecting Judges for Appellate and Major Trial Courts

Much party influence and little bar influence		Little party influence and much bar influence	
Partisan election	Appointment	Nonpartisan election	Merit plan
Alabama	*By governor*	Georgia	Alaska
Arkansas	California[g]	Idaho	Arizona[a]
Illinois	Delaware	Kentucky	California[a]
Mississippi	Hawaii	Louisiana	Colorado
New Mexico	Maine	Michigan	Florida[a]
New York[e]	Massachusetts	Minnesota	Indiana[a]
North Carolina	New Hampshire	Montana	Iowa
Pennsylvania[f]	New Jersey	Nevada	Kansas
Tennessee[d]	Vermont	North Dakota	Maryland[h]
Texas		Ohio	Missouri[b]
West Virginia	*By legislature*	Oregon	Nebraska
	Connecticut	Washington	Oklahoma[a]
	Rhode Island[c]	Wisconsin	South Dakota[a]
	South Carolina		Utah
	Virginia		Wyoming

Source: Calculated from *The Book of the States: 1986–87* (Lexington, Ky.: Council of State Governments, 1986), pp. 162–163.

    a. Appellate courts on merit plan; some trial courts nonpartisan elections.
    b. Appellate courts on merit plan; some trial courts partisan election.
    c. Appellate courts appointed by legislature; trial courts appointed by governor.
    d. Intermediate appellate courts on merit plan.
    e. Governor appoints appellate judges; trial courts partisan elections.
    f. Partisan ballot for initial election; nonpartisan for reelection.
    g. Governor appoints appellate judges; some trial courts nonpartisan elections.
    h. Appellate courts on merit plan; some trial courts appointed by governor.

mal organization of lawyers that sets standards for admitting lawyers to practice and ethical codes that govern the lawyers' conduct. Under the merit plan, bar associations usually dominate the selection of nominees sent to the governor. After appointment by the governor, the judge stays in office for a year and then must stand unopposed in a retention election on the merits of his or her record in office. Needless to say, very few judges lose their elections for retention. (See Table 12–2 for various length of terms of state judges.)

Does Merit Selection Make Any Difference?

Notwithstanding its merits, the merit plan does not remove politics from the judicial selection process. Missouri, the birthplace of the merit plan, was

Table 12-2. Length of Terms of State Judges

Length of term	Number of states with terms of this length for:		
	State supreme courts	Intermediate appellate courts	Major trial courts
Life (or to age 70)	3	1	3
14-15 years	1	0	2
10-12	17	8	3
6-8	29	25	36
4-5	0	2	9
Less than 4	0	0	0
Total	50	36	53[a]

Source: Calculated from *The Book of the States: 1986-87* (Lexington, Ky.: Council of State Governments, 1986), pp. 155-158.

[a]The total is greater than fifty because some states have several major trial courts with different lengths of terms for each.

rocked by a scandal in 1985 that involved overt partisan manipulation of its merit plan of selection. One Supreme Court appointment went to an allegedly poorly qualified governor's aid, and two other Supreme Court appointments were apparently engineered by the Republican State Party chairperson.[16]

The most controversial example of the inherent political nature of judicial selection involves California Chief Justice Rose Bird. Appointed by Governor Jerry Brown in 1977, she narrowly won her first retention election in 1978; and in her 1986 reelection bid she faced a $7-million conservative Republican campaign to unseat her because of her opposition to the death penalty. Two other Supreme Court justices went down to defeat with Bird in November 1986, thus enabling conservative Governor George Deukmejian, an outspoken Bird foe, to appoint a new, conservative majority to the Court.[17]

In addition to depoliticizing the process, the merit plan of reformers also had the objective of getting judges who have training from the more prestigious law schools and relevant legal experience. However, studies of judicial selection in California, Iowa, and Missouri suggest that the merit plan has not led to these results. In Missouri, researchers found that the governors still "used their appointments to reward friends or past political supporters" and have implemented the plan very largely from a "personal and political viewpoint."[18]

It was also assumed that highly qualified judges would make better decisions than would poorly qualified judges. Since appointed judges do not have to gain popular support, it could reasonably be argued that appointed judges, more than popularly elected judges, would support upper-class economic interests and be tougher on criminal defendants. Burton Atkins and Henry R.

Glick studied the highest appellate courts in the fifty states to see if decisions would indeed follow this pattern. They found that the method of selecting judges had no significant impact on the kinds of decisions made. Elected judges were as likely as appointed judges to espouse upper-class economic interests or to favor the prosecution rather than the criminal defendant.[19]

Judicial Patronage and Political Consequences

A second way that politics can enter the courts is through patronage, the hiring of public employees as a reward for political support. Few states follow the example of Colorado and provide a civil service system of employment for court administrative jobs. In most states judges hire people to work in a variety of administrative positions; these include clerks, court reporters, bailiffs, and secretaries. In communities with a tradition of machine politics, judges often exercise extensive and lucrative patronage powers. In Pittsburgh and Philadelphia, judges appoint the board of education and the park commissioners.[20] In New York they appoint executors for the estates of people who die without leaving a will. Since an executor's fee is a percentage of the estate, this is a lucrative patronage appointment. Lawyers who want such appointments must stay in favor with the judges. Politically motivated judges can use such appointment powers to secure campaign contributions and other cooperation from the lawyers.

In addition to the political effects of patronage, judges make decisions that can have political consequences. For instance, they resolve disputed elections and decide conflicts between governmental agencies.

The Influence of Judges' Backgrounds

Studies of judicial decisions have consistently found a relationship between the backgrounds of judges and the kinds of decisions they make. In workers' compensation cases, for example, Catholic or Democratic judges are much more likely than are Protestant or Republican judges to hand down decisions that favor workers over employers. In criminal cases, Catholic or Democratic judges are much more likely than Protestant or Republican judges to rule in favor of defendants rather than plaintiffs.[21]

Although the patterns vary from state to state,[22] significant partisan differences were found on fifteen different kinds of cases, ranging from unemployment compensation to the governmental regulation of business. You are much better off in front of a Democratic or Catholic judge if you are a tenant being sued by a landlord, a consumer seeking damages for shoddy merchandise bought under misleading sales tactics, a person injured in an automobile accident, or a government tax lawyer seeking to collect more taxes from a taxpayer. Conversely, you are much better off in front of a Republican or Protestant judge if you are the landlord, the merchant being sued for unfair sales tactics, the insurance company being sued in the automobile case, or the taxpayer being sued for more taxes by the government.

Pressure Group Influence

Pressure group activities are more subtle in the judicial arena than in the legislature or administrative agencies. Although lobbyists can contribute to judges' reelection campaigns, they cannot use business luncheons, cocktail parties, or other entertainments to influence judicial opinions. They also have to be more restrained and formal in presenting information they hope will sway judges' opinions. They are restricted largely to two major tactics: initiating litigation and presenting **amicus curiae** (or "friend of the court") briefs in cases filed by other contestants.

Political interests in New Jersey used both of these tactics to try to influence the courts in the *Robinson* v. *Cahill* case cited at the beginning of this chapter. As an eleven-year-old child from a middle-class family, Kenneth Robinson had neither the financial resources nor the legal knowledge to wage what would be a six-year legal battle to reform New Jersey's system of school finance. He was carefully recruited to file the suit by the mayor of Jersey City and his legal adviser. Once the suit was filed, several interest groups—including local chapters of the National Association for the Advancement of Colored People (NAACP) and the American Civil Liberties Union (ACLU)—filed amicus curiae briefs in which they provided the court with strong arguments and much data to support the striking down of New Jersey's reliance on local property taxes to finance public education.[23]

Crime and the Legal System

One of the most important roles of the courts, obviously, is to deal with crime. To understand this role, we need to examine (1) the different kinds of crime and trends in crime, (2) how the courts process criminal cases, and (3) how different political values influence law enforcement and correctional policies.

Crime

Because different kinds of crime have different degrees of impact on society, it is useful to detail the important distinctions among them.

Index Crime

Index crime refers to the crimes listed annually in the Uniform Crime Reports of the Federal Bureau of Investigation (FBI). These are all the crimes reported each year by police departments. They are divided into two major categories—crimes against property (larceny of $50 or more, burglary, auto theft) and crimes against persons (assault, forcible rape, robbery, murder). *Assault, auto theft, rape,* and *murder* are self-explanatory. *Robbery* is stealing someone's property through the threat or use of force. *Burglary* is the act of entering a building unlawfully to commit a felony or a theft. In robbery the thief directly threatens the victim or forces him or her to hand over a purse, wallet, or some other valuable. In burglary, usually no direct confrontation occurs between thief and victim. Over twelve million index crimes are reported by the police each year.

Because index crime refers only to reported crimes, the Uniform Crime Reports index has been subjected to considerable criticism.[24] Since most crimes go unreported,[25] the Uniform Crime Reports index greatly understates the amount of actual crime, especially rapes and assaults. Police departments are widely known to distort their reports for political purposes—to get a bigger budget, to respond to newspaper criticisms, or to cover up administrative problems.[26] For all these reasons, the FBI has been studying ways to improve the Uniform Crime Reports.[27] **White-collar crimes** (embezzlement, fraud, and commercial theft, for example) are not included in the FBI index. The President's Commission on Law Enforcement and the Administration of Justice argued that white-collar crime was just as costly to society, if not more so, than index crime.[28]

Organized Crime

The FBI crime index also does not provide a sufficient accounting of *organized crime*. The index does not indicate how much crime is attributable to organized criminal elements and how much of it is done by isolated individuals or gangs.

United States government reports during the 1960s argued that in the United States a national confederation exists of twenty-four criminal organizations or families called La Cosa Nostra or the Mafia.[29] These families are located in the big cities of the Northeast, the Great Lakes states, the South, and the Southwest. They control prostitution, narcotics, and gambling activities—especially gambling on major league sports such as football and horse racing. The twenty-four families comprise about 5,000 men who, these reports say, are all Italian. This "Italian organization in fact controls all but an insignificant proportion of the organized-crime activities in the United States" and may involve as many as 100,000 people.[30]

This official version of organized crime has been criticized as too romantic, too mystical,[31] too inclined to assume a business organization structure of crime,[32] and too inclined to associate organized crime with Italian communities.[33] Actually, many ethnic groups have contributed heavily to organized crime, and a path of ethnic succession has been traced.[34] Until the 1920s it was dominated by Irish, Jews, and Germans.[35] Italian dominance came later and appears to have peaked in the 1950s. Much of the lower-class narcotics and numbers-racket activities has been taken over by blacks, Latinos, and Asians in minority neighborhoods.[36] Italian spokespersons have vigorously objected to linking their nationality to the Mafia.

The existence and profitability of organized crime, however, are evident. Organized gambling on professional sports is illegal in most states, yet such gambling exists. And the extensive supplies of illegal narcotics would not be possible without organized crime.

Organized crime is probably growing fastest in the Sunbelt. Today the South and West have higher crime rates than the rest of the nation.[37] In Arizona, organized criminal elements invested heavily in land schemes that fleeced individuals by convincing them they were paying for a retirement home. When a Phoenix, Arizona, newspaper reporter began a 1976 series exposing the links between the land deals, Arizona politicians, and organized crime, he was murdered.[38] At the eastern end of the Sunbelt, Miami, Florida, has become a center for the importation of illegal drugs; and drug trafficking is believed to be one major reason why crime rates have soared in Florida.

The Crime Explosion

As shown in Figure 12–2, the growth rate of crime was explosive in the 1960s and 1970s but has declined in the 1980s. Some of the growth in the 1960s and 1970s probably reflects an improvement in crime reporting and crime statistics.[39] To get reimbursed by their insurance companies, robbery or burglary victims usually must make a police report. However, the fact that the number of reported crimes increased so much faster than the population (about four times faster) makes it unlikely that the increase is solely a matter of better reporting. It seems much more likely that a true crime explosion took place.

From a demographic perspective the most interesting fact about crime is that a majority of all persons arrested today are under age 24; which has been the case for many years.[40] This leads some authors to conclude that the crime explosion of the 1960s and 1970s was caused by the increase in the numbers of *youths* in racial minority ghettos during those years.[41] Not only were there more youths in the cities, but youth unemployment rates were higher after 1960 than they had been previously. If this demographic intrepretation of the

Figure 12-2. The Crime Explosion

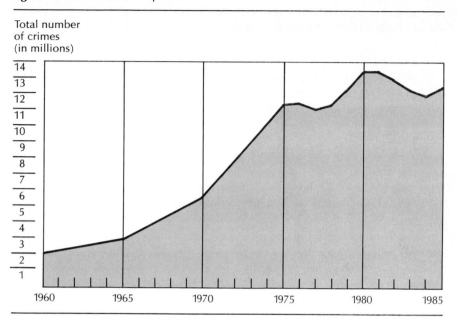

Total number
of crimes
(in millions)

Source: Bureau of the Census, *Statistical Abstract of the United States: 1987* (Washington, D.C.: U.S. Government Printing Office, 1986), p. 155.

crime explosion is accurate, then part of the decline in the 1980s can be attributed to a decline in the youth population.

This demographic explanation for the crime explosion of the 1960s and 1970s is disputed, however, by James Q. Wilson, who attributes it to the interaction of the demographic factor and a rising self-expressive ethic that scorns such Victorian virtues as thrift, hard work, and concern for the community. The self-expressive ethic emerged in the 1920s but was halted during the 1930s and 1940s by the Great Depression and World War II. It was the reflowering of this ethic combined with the booming youth population of the 1960s and 1970s that gave rise to the crime explosion of those years, according to Wilson.[42]

Crime and the Courts

The courts, of course, play a major role in the governmental response to crime because it is the courts that determine guilt or innocence and set punishments for specific offenses. In their attempts to mete out justice, the courts have come under considerable criticism. Of interest here are four targets of criticism—the jury system, the role of money in justice, plea bargaining, and the attempts of some courts to establish minimum standards of justice.

The Jury System

There are two types of juries—the grand jury and the trial jury. The **grand jury** is an official panel of citizens who investigate a crime and determine whether there is enough evidence to warrant filing charges. If a grand jury finds sufficient evidence, it reports a *true bill,* or indictment. Few states require indictment by grand jury. A majority of states gives the prosecutor some discretion in calling a grand jury. Prosecutors file most of the criminal charges. They rely on the grand jury only for cases that are extremely sensitive, such as those involving public officials or organized crime.

Trial **juries** can be used in either civil cases or criminal cases. In civil cases the trial jury decides which party deserves to be awarded damages and sometimes sets the amounts. In criminal cases, the trial jury's role is to determine whether a defendant is guilty. Traditionally, conviction requires a unanimous verdict of twelve jurors persuaded "beyond a reasonable doubt" that the defendant is guilty. It often is very difficult to obtain such unanimity among twelve jurors. In reaction, some states have relaxed this requirement. Louisiana has permitted convictions on a vote of only nine of the twelve jurors;[43] Florida now permits six-member juries instead of the traditional twelve.[44] Experience with the smaller juries suggests that they put defendants at a disadvantage. As jury size gets smaller, the chances of a hung jury decrease. Relying on this experience and a number of empiricial studies showing that large juries performed better, the Supreme Court in 1978 refused to approve five-person juries.[45]

These changes in trial juries reflect a growing skepticism about the ability of juries to apply the law fairly and consistently. The law has become so complex that it is difficult for average jurors to follow the legal arguments of lawyers and to suspend their personal biases when making their decisions. Because of these problems, juries are seldom used in Europe and are declining in use in civil cases in the United States.

Money and Criminal Justice

A second area of concern in criminal justice involves the role of money. A trial inevitably involves court fees, lawyers' fees, fees for investigators, and court recorders, and, if the case is complicated enough, costs for getting witnesses to testify and for specialists such as accountants, psychiatrists, and other scientists. The two greatest costs may be lawyers' fees and bail. If a possible prison sentence is involved, states are obliged to provide lawyers for people who cannot afford to hire one.[46] But the quality of these state-appointed lawyers varies from state to state.[47] In civil cases the federal government has established the Legal Services Corporation to provide lawyers for poor people.

Bail is a sum of money an accused person deposits with the court to ensure that he or she will show up for trial. People without money must borrow from a bail bondsman at a very high interest rate or stay in jail until their case comes to trial. For persons acquitted of the charges against them, the time spent in jail awaiting for trial is a true travesty of justice. The Vera Institute in New York has experimented successfully with a program to get judges to release suspects without bail—on their own recognizance—if the suspect is a reputable person and has a job and a stable residential history. Kentucky's experience with this and other bail reforms was so successful that it abolished all commercial bail bondsmen.[48]

Plea Bargaining

A third target of criticism is the practice of **plea bargaining**. The prosecutor may have several possible charges on which to prosecute the defendant, but the evidence on the most serious charge may not be strong enough to win a conviction. So the prosecutor may offer to drop the most serious charge if the defendant will plead guilty to a lesser charge. From the defendant's point of view, it may be preferable to accept the certainty of a short sentence for the lesser charge than to risk the uncertainty of a conviction and a possibly long sentence on the serious charge. The defendant and the prosecutor thus bargain with each other until they reach an agreement about the plea that the defendant will make. Hence the term *plea bargaining*. Plea bargaining is so popular that probably no more than 20 percent of all persons charged with a felony go to trial.[49] The overwhelming majority plead guilty to a lesser charge.

Plea bargaining has both its opponents and its defenders. As suggested in the cartoon on page 318, opponents of plea bargaining view the compromises made as inherently contrary to the ideal of impartial justice. The bargaining inevitably leads to different punishment levels for the same crime. Defenders of plea bargaining point out that criminal courts would be intolerably overloaded with cases if plea bargaining were eliminated. In this view, the overloaded courts and the long delays in getting to trial would provoke much more injustice than does plea bargaining. These arguments appear to be persuasive to state legislators who have chosen not to abolish plea bargaining and to the American Bar Association, which would prefer to see the practice refined and improved.[50]

Minimum Standards of Justice

Attaining a high quality of justice also depends upon the substantive decisions that judges make and the tactics that police use to get evidence. The

Plea Bargaining Approved by Supreme Court

idea of justice would be a sham, for example, if court standards were so lax that police were permitted to torture their suspects in order to gain confessions or if court standards were so rigid that nobody ever got convicted.

Between these extremes has been a wide variety of minimum standards of justice in the fifty states. Although some disparities may be acceptable, the United States Supreme Court has ruled that most of the provisions of the Fourth, Fifth, Sixth, and Fourteenth Amendments to the United States Constitution should be applied with consistency in all the states. The application of these federal constitutional provisions to the states is called *incorporating* them.

Although the Supreme Court never stated that the establishment of minimum standards of justice was its goal, its decisions have effectively accomplished this. Table 12–3 outlines the major Supreme Court cases addressing the question of minimum standards of justice. Probably the most controversial cases have been those involving the exclusionary rule, the Miranda rule, and the death penalty.

The **exclusionary rule** states that illegally seized evidence may not be used against a defendant in a trial. The rule was first applied to the states in *Mapp* v. *Ohio*.[51] Cleveland police officers had asked to search the home of Dollree Mapp for a suspect in a bombing. When she refused to let them enter, they forcibly broke in and searched the house. They did not find the suspect they claimed to be seeking, but they did find pornographic materials

Table 12–3. Setting Minimum Standards of Justice:
Incorporating the Bill of Rights into State Criminal Law

Expanding the minimum standards	*Relaxing the minimum standards*
1957 If a suspect is not taken before a judge as soon as possible after arrest, any unnecessary delay will make it impossible to admit into court any confession made prior to being brought before the judge. *Mallory* v. *United States.*	1971 If a suspect during a legal interrogation contradicts any voluntary statements made prior to seeing a lawyer, those prior statements may be used as a basis for further questioning. *Harris* v. *New York.*
1961 If a person's constitutional rights have been violated by a police officer, that person may sue the police officer in federal court. *Monroe* v. *Pape.*	1972 A unanimous jury verdict is not necessarily required for a verdict of guilty in felony cases. Nine of twelve jurors is sufficient if permitted by state law. *Johnson* v. *Louisiana.*
1961 Evidence collected in an "unreasonable" search and seizure may not be used against a person in court. Established guidelines for obtaining evidence and conducting searches. *Mapp* v. *Ohio.*	1976 The death penalty may be imposed if the legislation establishing it and the judicial sentencing procedures provide safeguards against arbitrariness and capriciousness. *Gregg* v. *Georgia.*
1963 Free legal counsel must be provided in felony cases for defendants who cannot afford to hire a lawyer. *Gideon* v. *Wainwright.*	1976 States may not impose a mandatory death penalty. *Woodson* v. *North Carolina.*
1964 A person is not required to testify against himself or herself. *Mallory* v. *Hogan.*	1980 Exclusionary rule relaxed in a case where a prisoner may have been tricked into providing incriminating evidence without benefit of a lawyer. Being transported in a patrol car past a school for handicapped children, Thomas Innis overheard a police officer express hope that the murder weapon not be found by one of the children. Innis led the officer to the spot where he had left the weapon, and it was used as evidence against him. *Rhode Island* v. *Innis.*
1964 If police obtain a confession from a suspect before letting him or her see an attorney, that confession cannot be used in court. *Escobedo* v. *Illinois.*	
1966 A suspect must be warned of the right to be represented by a lawyer and to remain silent. If such warning is not given, no information provided by the suspect may be used against the suspect in court. *Miranda* v. *Arizona.*	
1967 The right to free counsel is guaranteed to juveniles being tried in juvenile court. *Re Gault.*	1984 Good-faith exception to the exclusionary rule permitted. *United States* v. *Leon;* and *Massachusetts* v. *Sheppard.*
1972 In any case for which a jail sentence might be imposed, free legal counsel must be provided for defendants who cannot afford to hire a lawyer. *Argersinger* v. *Hamlin.*	1987 Death penalty expanded so it could apply to accomplices in murder cases even though they did not kill or plan to kill. *Tison* v. *Arizona.*
1972 The death penalty was struck down as unconstitutional because it was applied capriciously and arbitrarily. *Furman* v. *Georgia.*	1987 Death penalty expanded by rejection of the contention that the death penalty is racially discriminatory because of the statistical fact that blacks who murder whites get the death sentence more often than blacks who murder blacks. *McCleskey* v. *Kemp.*

that were illegal under an Ohio statute. The police confiscated the materials and prosecuted Ms. Mapp for violating the pornography ordinance. In court the police could not produce a search warrant entitling them to search the Mapp home, thus making the search illegal. Mapp was convicted on the basis of the evidence, but the Supreme Court overturned the conviction on the grounds that the illegally seized evidence should have been excluded from the trial.

The **Miranda rule** was established in *Miranda* v. *Arizona*.[52] In that case, the Supreme Court ruled that the police must advise a suspect of the right to speak to a lawyer before interrogation. At issue was Miranda's conviction for rape. Miranda had confessed while being interrogated by the police; however, Miranda had not asked to see an attorney. The Supreme Court overturned his conviction and issued very specific rules prescribing that police must inform suspects of their constitutional rights to remain silent and to see an attorney. As a result of this case, police officers began carrying so-called Miranda cards. These cards spelled out the suspect's constitutional rights to remain silent and to see a lawyer. On arresting a suspect, the police officer would read the card out loud to the suspect.

In recent years the exclusionary rule and the Miranda rule have been relaxed somewhat. The Supreme Court upheld the conviction of a man who had given police incriminating evidence before he had a chance to see his attorney. Thomas Innis had been picked up by police on suspicion of murder and was being transported by police officers in a police car. When the car passed a home for retarded children near the scene of the crime, one of the officers began speculating aloud that one of the retarded children might find the gun used in the murder and get injured or injure someone else. Innis then led the officers to the gun, and it was used as evidence in his trial. Although his lawyers later asked to have the gun excluded as evidence because it violated both the Miranda rule and the exclusionary rule, the evidence was not excluded, Innis was convicted, and the Supreme Court upheld his conviction.[53]

The exclusionary rule has been heavily attacked in the 1980s. President Ronald Reagan denounced the exclusionary rule as absurd, and Attorney General Edwin Meese sought to abolish it.[54] The Supreme Court began whittling away at the rule by making it easier to obtain search warrants[55] and by permitting a "good-faith exception" that would allow illegally seized evidence to be used in court if the police officer involved believed in good faith that the seizure was legal.[56]

A third area where the setting of minimum standards has generated controversial court decisions involves the death penalty. In 1972 the Supreme Court struck down the death penalty as arbitrary and capricious.[57] In reaction to that decision, several states rewrote their death penalty laws in order to make them less arbitrary, and most of these have been upheld. Thirty-seven states now have death penalty laws, and there are over 1,500 inmates on death row. To date, each execution has been accompanied by considerable publicity, and the topic has become highly volatile. About three-fourths of the American public support the death penalty.[58] And, as we saw above, California Chief Justice Rose Bird lost her retention election in 1986 in large part because of her opposition to capital punishment.

Political Values and Conflicts over Criminal Justice Policy

How we deal with social problems depends in great measure on how we think about them, what we think causes them, and how we think they might best be solved (if, indeed, we think they can be solved). This is as true of crime as of all social problems.

Governments have a choice in how they cope with crime. The way political officials deal with crime reflects certain assumptions about its causes. These assumptions are based in part on ideological orientations that the officials have or that the officials think their constituents may have about crime. The political candidate who campaigns against crime on a platform of giving the police more weapons, giving them more discretion to use those weapons, increasing the penalties for crimes, and making prisons more punitive is acting on certain assumptions about how to control crime and what solutions are acceptable to the voters. Another candidate who argues that police should be increased in number but stripped of lethal weapons and that prisons should be phased out in favor of community-based correctional facilities that try to rehabilitate offenders uses an entirely different set of assumptions about what works and what is acceptable to the voters.

The candidates and voters need not be ideologues to be influenced by ideologies. Most, in fact, are not ideologies.[59] However, they do make assumptions about what works and what is acceptable. These assumptions can be traced to different ideological positions. Which ideological positions prevail among the electorate and the political leaders greatly influence the approaches and programs that are actually carried out.

Approaches to Coping with Crime

As we noted in Chapter 1, these political ideologies can be visualized along a liberal–conservative, left–right continuum. Although the percentage of people at either extreme is very small, it is useful to describe the ideologies in their extreme versions, for this gives us criteria for evaluating what political

Table 12–4. Overview of Theories of Crime and Punishment

	Liberal	Conservative
Major cause of crime	Social injustice	Individual defects
View of the criminal offender	Can be rehabilitated	Probably cannot be rehabilitated
View of punishment	No useful function	Deters others from committing crime
View of prisons	Reduce to the minimum needed to incarcerate dangerous criminals; prefer community corrections.	Prisons preferred over community corrections
View of police	Skeptical	Positive
Preferred policy solutions	Make educational, employment, and social reforms to reduce the stimuli to crime.	Make punishment more severe, and increase the likelihood of getting caught and being punished.

leaders tell us. It also enables us to examine our own attitudes about crime in connection with ideological positions. To what extent do our beliefs on crime and punishment reflect leftist philosophies? Rightist philosophies? Are our beliefs consistent with our underlying set of values about society? Once we draw these connections between our beliefs and values and ideological positions, we are in a good position to evaluate campaign promises of candidates and anticrime bills put before the legislatures. The liberal and conservative ideological positions on crime and punishment are summarized in Table 12–4.

The View from the Right—The Criminal Is Depraved

The traditional extreme conservative views crime as a moral or psychic defect in the individual person. Crime is an irrational deviation from social norms that exhort us not to kill, steal, rape, and so on. The criminal is diseased, and there is not much hope for a cure. This conservative has a strong concern for social order and emphasizes the government's role in preserving social order and preventing violence. In reaction to the Supreme Court decisions protecting the rights of criminal suspects, such as *Miranda* v. *Arizona* (see p. 318), a typical conservative might point out that society also has the right to be protected from violent crimes.

The traditional conservative policy for crime logically follows. If crime is a moral defect, the criminal must be punished for the transgression. Most criminals cannot be rehabilitated; thus, the punishment must be both harsh and certain to deter others from committing the same crimes. Consistent with their concern for social order, conservatives view the police favorably as the keepers of order. They favor increasing the size of police forces; giving the police sophisticated hardware such as helicopters, computers, Mace, and lethal weapons; and experimenting with crime-prevention tactics. They see a need for prisons to house habitual criminals who are too dangerous to be returned to society, where they can prey on innocent victims.[60]

The View from the Left — Crime Is Rooted in Social Injustice

In contrast to conservatives who think crime is caused by defects in the individual person, liberals trace the causes of crime to social injustice. Most index crimes are committed by poor people against other poor people living in poor neighborhoods. The liberal views this as evidence that poverty, economic deprivation, and lower-class social conditions are the main causes of crime. These conditions alienate criminally disposed persons from society and make them unreceptive to middle-class social values. At the extreme left, the radical carries this argument one step further: Crimes for money are rational— the insecurity and competitiveness of capitalist societies naturally lead people at all class levels to commit crimes in order to acquire the material goods they want.[61]

Just as the conservative policy responses of force and punishment are consistent with conservative beliefs on the causes of crime, so are leftist policy responses consistent with leftist beliefs. At the extreme left, the radical believes that crime will wither away in the just society. The radical argues that "we cannot realistically expect to 'solve' the problem of crime in the United States without first effecting a fundamental redistribution of power in our society."[62] At the moderate left, the liberal aims at two things—rehabilitating the criminal offender and improving the social conditions that breed crime.

The left views the police much more negatively than does the right. Radicals view the police as instruments of class oppression, the means by which the upper classes maintain the lower classes in their place. The moderate liberal notes that police officers have frequently been hostile toward racial minorities and lower-class white communities. Rather than giving the police more lethal weapons to deal with criminals, moderate liberals seek to sensitize the police to these communities' needs and to increase the number of minority police officers.

The moderate liberal also supports reform efforts to overhaul the criminal justice system. This includes professionalizing police departments and implementing court reforms such as bail reform and the uniform court system. Reform also emphasizes rehabilitation programs that train offenders in marketable job skills and reorient their value systems so that they can function better in society.[63]

Critique of the Rational Economist: Crime Pays

Until the late 1960s, most social science research on crime and punishment was conducted by sociologists, social psychologists, and criminologists. Because they found criminal behavior directly related to social class, their findings have generally supported the leftist rather than the rightist philosophy of crime. Further, the main thrust of psychological counseling and behavior modification experiments supported the notion that rehabilitation is possible.

Conservative criminologists got some significant research support from economists, who began to take an interest in crime in the 1960s. In 1968 a seminal article by Gary Becker outlined the basis of the rational economic conservative theory.[64] Like the traditional conservative, the rational economist attributes crime to individual free choice. Rather than assuming that the individual criminal is ill or morally depraved, the rational economist asks whether the criminal act is a rational thing to do. That is, does crime pay? Does the criminal earn more money at crime than would be possible at a legitimate occupation?

These researchers first note that the risk of arrest for any specific crime is small. In Pennsylvania the chances of going to prison for a specific act of burglary were less than twenty-nine to one in the early 1970s. Even of those convicted of burglary, only 58 percent went to prison.[65] In Chicago in the same period the chance of imprisonment for any specific offense was less than three out of a thousand, and for a juvenile it was less than two out of a thousand.[66]

Although the risk of imprisonment is negligible for any specific offense, the person who habitually commits crime will end up in prison. However, the stays in prison will probably be short.

The economists then note that a good burglar can earn more money at burglary than at most legitimate occupations for which he or she might qualify. The average burglar lacks the skills to make much money at legitimate jobs. A study of all imprisoned burglars from Norfolk, Virginia, found that they averaged $1.55 per hour in wages at legitimate jobs in 1966 and only worked for thirty weeks. When researchers divided the total amount of jailed burglars' income from their burglaries and subtracted the amount of income lost during the average thirteen months they spent in prison for their crimes, they found that the burglar got almost three times as much income from their burglaries as they could have earned legitimately.[67]

A similar study of burglaries in Chicago in 1969 calculated an average net return of $36.70 per burglary. If a juvenile worked at burglary at the rate of one burglary a day for five days a week, and if the time spent in jail for those crimes is considered as unemployment, the juvenile still made two-and-one-half times as much income from working as a burglar than could have been earned working forty hours a week legitimately.[68] An early-1970s study of Pennsylvania burglars led to conflicting interpretations. One economist, using one set of assumptions, found that each burglary brought its perpetrator a net loss of $197 over what could have been earned legitimately. But another economist, using different assumptions, discovered a profit of $15 per burglary.[69]

The message of the rational economists is clear. If you are a low-wage, unskilled laborer who suffers periodic bouts of unemployment, and if you do not mind the risk of spending twenty to thirty months in prison now and then, you would be much better off to go into burglary than into virtually any legitimate occupation for which you could qualify. Burglary pays. To the rational economist, the only sensible policy response to combat burglary is to make punishment so certain, so extreme, and so unpleasant that crime will no longer pay. In this view, punishment deters crime.[70]

Corrections as an Approach to Crime

Nowhere is the impact of these diverse viewpoints more dramatically seen than in recent trends in corrections philosophy. Until the 1930s, the dominant views of corrections were primarily punishment and deterrence. Most felt that criminals could not be rehabilitated. From the 1930s to the 1970s the concept of rehabilitation came into greater favor. With the tools of modern psychology, counseling, and the teaching of marketable skills in prison, it was hoped that prisoners could be rehabilitated to rejoin society in a productive capacity.

As time went on, however, it became apparent that the correctional institutions did not rehabilitate many criminals. Many released inmates ended up back in prison once again. This is called recidivism. About two-thirds of all persons arrested for felonies had previously served time in prison. To some observers, these high rates of recidivism suggested that the prisons were training young offenders to become better criminals instead of rehabilitating them.

In most instances, rehabilitation was not taken seriously. Only a fifth of all corrections personnel work in rehabilitation or in treatment.[71] Many vocational programs teach skills that are unmarketable. For example, many vocational programs teach barbering; yet in most communities, felons may not become barbers.[72]

Nobody really knows which rehabilitation programs might cut down recidivism. Robert Martinson surveyed 231 experimental studies of juvenile and adult offenders of both sexes. The experiments included vocational training for inmates, individual counseling, transforming the atmosphere of the prison to be less custodial and more rehabilitative, the use of drugs and surgery, manipulating the length of the sentence, and moving the inmates to community-based facilities. In each study the experimental group in the rehabilitation program was compared to a control group in a regular prison population. After this intensely thorough review of all these experiments, Martinson came to the conclusion that "with few and isolated exceptions, the rehabilitative efforts that have been reported so far have no appreciable effect on recidivism."[73] Some isolated programs seem to hold some promise, but Martinson's overall conclusion was pessimistic.

Martinson's findings sparked intense controversy among criminologists. Some later research discovered that some offenders were indeed amenable to

You Decide
Public Policy for Crime

Assume that you have just been hired as the chief criminal justice adviser to the mayor of your city. The mayor wants to make a serious attempt to reduce crime and has called on you to outline policy alternatives. To do this, you must use your general knowledge about crime and corrections and create practical policy proposals. As you go through this exercise for the mayor, several things become apparent.

First, you must determine whether the mayor seriously wants to reduce crime or whether the real goal is to make symbolic gestures that will gain newspaper publicity and voter support. If the goal is symbolic gestures, then the mayor will respond favorably to proposals for crackdowns on vice or juggling police crime reports to show crime reductions on paper. A crackdown on prostitutes for a few months combined with arresting an occasional male customer may get the mayor publicity, but it will have little effect on actual crime.

Second, as you try to assess the practical consequences of the liberal and conservative philosophical positions, you will note that both positions help us understand crime, but neither has a monopoly on the truth. At

least two generalizations seem warranted by empirical social science research. First, research by the rational economists and by Robert Martinson provides impressive (although inconclusive) evidence that liberals have emphasized rehabilitation too much and have not paid enough attention to the fact that some crime does pay. At the same time, other research findings that most of the index crimes are committed by people low on the socioeconomic ladder impressively suggest that the conservative position does not pay enough attention to the impact social injustices have on crime rates.

Unfortunately for the mayor, he or she does not exert much influence over either of these things. Questions of punishment rates and determinate versus indeterminate sentencing are in the hands of legislators, not mayors. Sentences, convictions, paroles, and rehabilitation programs are the domain of the courts and corrections departments, neither of which are under the mayor. Finally, issues of social justice and providing a livable income for all the city's residents are not controlled by the mayor either.

What the mayor can do, however, is to use the visibility of the mayor's office to rehabilitation while others were not, and this suggests that different approaches should be taken to the two different types of offenders. Also, studies in Utah and Illinois showed that strict supervision of youthful offenders decreased the frequency with which they were subsequently rearrested.[74]

Despite these qualifications to Martinson's findings, it was Martinson's pessimism about rehabilitation approaches that had the greatest impact on criminal justice policymakers in the 1970s.[75] Many policymakers returned to a punishment philosophy of corrections,[76] as the trend toward *determinate* rather than *indeterminate* sentencing indicates. Under rehabilitation theory a judge issues an indeterminate sentence of perhaps five to twenty years. Felons who take part in rehabilitation programs and convince their parole boards that they are good risks can often get released after only a few years in prison.

---

lobby for appropriate legislation and to drum up public opinion on behalf of his or her criminal justice goals.

Third, you can recommend utilizing the mayor's ability to propose law enforcement strategies to the city's police department. Even if the mayor does not immediately oversee the police, the police will respond to political pressures created by the mayor. A local criminal justice crime reduction commission can survey law enforcement strategies that have been successful in other cities and investigate their appropriateness for your city. Crime attack strategies, community service strategies, or police deployment strategies may be appropriate in your city. Once these are identified, the mayor is in an influential position to get the police department to adopt some of them.

Fourth, the mayor can urge reforms in the state and county corrections agencies. It may take courageous intervention by the mayor to get certain neighborhoods to accept community-based facilities. The mayor's support for reforms in sentencing, parole boards, juvenile justice, and the administration of state prisons may be instrumental in getting such reforms adopted by the legislature.

Fifth, the mayor must take a strong role in raising money for these experiments and reforms. The mayor's staff clearly needs a grants person who can get federal funds for projects. An active mayor testifying before the legislative appropriations' committees will get more funds for the projects than a passive mayor who neglects to testify.

In taking this swift look at what a mayoral aide might suggest that the mayor do about crime and corrections, three broad generalizations are evident. First, the strategies the mayor adopts will reflect the mayor's personal philosophical perspectives on crime and his or her assessment of the prevailing attitudes among the city's voters. Second, since responsibilities for dealing with crime are spread out among all levels and agencies of government, any comprehensive attack on crime is obviously an intergovernmental enterprise. Third, because crime is disproportionately concentrated in central cities, the central city mayor has a unique opportunity to exercise leadership and influence to solve problems.

Under **determinate sentencing** the judge must give a sentence for a fixed number of years, regardless of the inmate's participation in rehabilitation programs. According to deterrence theory, mandatory punishment and determinate sentencing increase the likelihood that criminals will cease commiting felonies.[77] Although few states have adopted this full-blown version of determinate sentencing, there has been a general trend toward increasing the length of prison sentences, making parole more difficult to get, and setting minimum sentences for certain crimes, such as those involving drugs.[78]

Unhappily for the rational economists, the get-tough policies they advocated and that were widely adopted in the late 1970s had unintended consequences of their own. There is no evidence that recidivism rates went down. A Department of Justice study in the early 1980s found that one-third of all inmates were still back in prison three years after their release.[79] Additionally, the lengthening of sentences increased the already-crowded conditions in prisons. By 1986, thirty-nine of the fifty states had overcrowded prisons and faced the prospect of significantly increased costs to build more prison space. At an estimated construction cost of $125,000 per cell and an annual operating cost of $20,000 per inmate, the politics of getting tough was getting expensive.[80]

Overcrowding exacerbated already-unpleasant prison conditions in many states. Prison conditions in Alabama were so bad in 1981 that a federal judge ordered the state to release nearly 300 inmates.[81] And in 1982 another federal judge ordered extensive reforms in Tennessee prisons, which he characterized as "unfit for human habitation."[82] Tennessee had been one of the leading states in toughening up prison sentences in the 1970s, but by 1982 it found itself unable to add any new prisoners. In 1985 Tennessee reduced prison terms for new offenders, granted early release to some existing prisoners, and sought alternative forms of sentencing in order to make room for new inmates without incurring the costs of constructing new space.[83]

Privatization and Prisons

If determinate sentencing was the corrections fad of the 1970s, the fad of the 1980s is privatization. Because of get-tough laws passed in the 1970s, prison populations shot up to all-time highs by the mid-1980s.[84] This put most states in a dilemma, because the tight budgetary situations of the 1980s did not give the states much leeway to construct new prison space to accommodate the burgeoning populations. Some states reacted to this situation by exploring the contracting out of prison operations to private companies.

Private companies had run many community-based programs for years, but only in the 1980s have they taken over the operations of county jails and state prisons. The largest such company is the Corrections Corporation of America, which runs detention facilities in Texas, Tennessee, and North Carolina.[85] The trend toward privatization of prisons is not without controversy, however. On the positive side, it is argued, most state prisons are so inhumane and incapable of rehabilitating inmates that private industry ought to be given an opportunity to see if it can do better. On the negative side, many in the legal profession argue, privatization of prisons would necessarily create a strong interest group lobbying for more frequent and longer prison sentences (because more money could be made that way). The balance of the 1980s will determine how these issues are resolved.

Summary

1. Courts in America resolve legal disputes, help set many public policies, and become intimately involved in the administration of some policies.

2. A dual court system exists in the United States: a single federal court system and fifty separate state systems. The state and local court systems are typically decentralized and not integrated. Reformers seek unified court systems along the models of Illinois and Colorado. Reformers also seek procedures for keeping judges accountable.

3. Politics enter the judicial process in several ways: through the selection of judges, the dispensing of patronage, the political nature of some judicial decisions, the socioeconomic backgrounds of judges, and the activities of interest groups.

4. Crime presents an important legal and social problem in the American states. Crime rates mushroomed between 1960 and 1980, but experts have no consensus on how crime can best be combated. The conservative orientation attributes crime to defects in the individual and looks to prison as a means of punishment and deterrence. The liberal orientation attributes crime to social injustices and looks to prisons as a place where criminals can be rehabilitated.

5. Empirical social research does not provide unequivocal support for either of these two orientations. Research by the rational economists supports the conservative view by finding that much crime is more profitable than legitimate work and by suggesting a punitive approach to corrections. Punitive approaches adopted in the 1980s led to problems of their own, principally serious prison overcrowding.

6. Courts play a major role in dealing with crime. Considerable criticism has been aimed in recent years at the jury system, the role of money in justice,

plea bargaining, and the attempts of some courts to establish minimum standards of justice.

Key Terms

Advisory opinion An opinion advising someone of the intent of the law on a particular point. Does not have the force of law, but if it is issued by an attorney general or a supreme court it can legitimize a particular course of action.

Amicus curiae Friend of the court. Refers to a third party permitted to file a brief arguing on behalf of one of the two parties involved in a suit.

Bench A court.

Cease-and-desist order A court order to a person to stop carrying out a particular act.

Civil law That portion of law that deals with conflicts between individuals and groups rather than with official legislation.

Class-action suit A suit that permits isolated individuals with the same grievance to join together and file a single suit as a group.

Criminal law Law that deals with the violation of legislative statutes.

Declaratory judgment A legally binding court order.

Determinate sentencing The practice of sentencing inmates to very specific prison terms rather than giving a sentence with a wide range of possible time in prison, adjusted to the inmate's behavior in prison.

Distributive policy A policy that allocates benefits to citizens but does not upset the prevailing distributions of wealth and influence. Also called *distributive services*.

Exclusionary rule The rule that prohibits illegal evidence from being used in a trial.

Felony A major crime.

Grand jury A group of citizens empaneled to examine a particular situation and determine whether enough evidence exists to indict somebody for a crime.

Index crime The seven types of crime listed annually in the FBI's Uniform Crime Reports.

Injunction A court order prohibiting a person from carrying out a particular act.

Judicial activism Judges' practice of using judicial review to impose their own beliefs on the law and to overrule policies set by legislators and executives.

Judicial restraint Judges' practice of making limited use of judicial review and generally refraining from overruling the policies set by legislators and executives.

Judicial review The power of courts to determine the constitutionality of acts of other government actors.

Jury (trial) A group of citizens selected to determine the innocence or guilt of a person being tried.

Merit plan A plan for judicial selection on the basis of qualification for office. See *Missouri Plan*.

Miranda rule The rule that police officers must warn suspects of their constitutional rights to remain silent and to be represented by an attorney before they question the suspect.

Misdemeanor A lesser crime, which usually brings a limited fine or short jail sentence.

Missouri Plan A merit plan for judicial selection under which a nominating commission suggests a list of three nominees to the governor, who makes the appointment from one of the three.

Plea bargaining Offering a defendant the chance to plead guilty on a lesser charge in exchange for not being prosecuted on the more serious charge.

Recidivism The act of returning to prison after once having been released.

Redistributive policy A policy that takes wealth or income from one class of citizens and gives it to another class.

White-collar crime Crimes such as embezzlement, fraud, and commercial theft.

References

1. Richard Lehne, *The Quest for Justice: The Politics of School Finance Reform* (New York: Longman, 1978), p. 103.

2. *Robinson* v. *Cahill*, 355 A.2d 129, 69 N.J. 1449 (1976).

3. This account of *Robinson* v. *Cahill* is taken from Lehne, *The Quest for Justice.*

4. Gregory A. Caldeira, "The Transmission of Legal Precedent: A Study of State Supreme Courts," *American Political Science Review* 79, no. 1. (March 1985): 178–194.

5. On this point, see Kenneth N. Vines and Herbert Jacob, "State Courts and Public Policy," in *Politics in the American States: A Comparative Analysis,* 3d ed., eds. Herbert Jacob and Kenneth N. Vines (Boston: Little, Brown and Co., 1976), pp. 243–246.

6. Herbert Jacob, "Courts," *Politics in the American States,* 4th ed., eds. Virginia Gray, Herbert Jacob, and Kenneth N. Vines (Boston: Little, Brown and Co., 1983), p. 226.

7. See Alfred Steinberg, "The Small Claims Court: A Consumer's Forgotten Forum," *National Civic Review* 63 (June 1974): 289; John H. Weiss, "Justice Without Lawyers: Transforming Small Claims Courts," *Working Papers for a New Society* 2, no. 3 (Fall 1974): 45–54.

8. Joseph F. Zimmerman, "The Organization of New York Courts," *Comparative State Politics Newsletter* 4, no. 6 (December 1983): 23.

9. See Beverly Blair Cook, "Role Lag in Urban Trial Courts," *Western Political Quarterly* 25, no. 2 (June 1972): 234–248.

10. See *New York Times,* December 19, 1984, p. 10; May 31, 1984, p. 11; March 16, 1984, p. 8; December 15, 1983, p. 1.

11. See *New York Times,* May 29, 1986, p. 7.

12. Joseph F. Zimmerman, "Judicial Conduct in New York," *Comparative State Politics Newsletter* 4, no. 4 (August 1983): 10.

13. Michael J. Ross, *California: Its Government and Politics* (North Scituate, Mass.: Duxbury Press, 1979), p. 125.

14. *New York Times,* November 10, 1979, p. 22.

15. On New York, see *New York Times,* October 23, 1985, p. 22; on Pennsylvania, see *New York Times,* January 4, 1984, p. 8.

16. Jerry Brekke, "Politics and the Missouri Court Plan," *Comparative State Politics Newsletter* 7, no. 1 (February 1986): 2.

17. See *New York Times*, March 20, 1985, p. 10 and January 17, 1986, p. 23; *Washington Post National Weekly Edition*, November 11, 1985, p. 12; *Minneapolis Star and Tribune*, November 6, 1986, p. 15a.

18. Richard A. Watson and Rondal G. Downing, *The Politics of Bench and Bar: Judicial Selection Under the Missouri Non-Partisan Court Plan* (New York: Wiley, 1969), pp. 338–339. For the research on California and Iowa, see Larry L. Berg et al., "The Consequences of Judicial Reform," *Western Political Quarterly* 28, no. 2 (June 1975): 263–280.

19. Burton M. Atkins and Henry R. Glick, "Formal Judicial Recruitment and State Supreme Court Decisions," *American Politics Quarterly* 2, no. 4 (October 1974): 427–429.

20. Vines and Jacob, "State Courts and Public Policy," p. 250.

21. See Stuart Nagel, "Political Party Affiliation and Judges' Decisions," *American Political Science Review* 55 (December 1961): 851–943; Nagel, "Ethnic Affiliation and Judicial Propensities," *Journal of Politics* 24 (1962): 92–110; Sidney Ulmer, "The Political Variable in the Michigan Supreme Court," *Journal of Political Law* 11 (1963): 552–562.

22. In the Wisconsin Supreme Court, political party background did not have an independent effect on justices' voting records. David W. Adamany, "The Party Variable in Judges' Voting: Conceptual Notes and a Case Study," *American Political Science Review* 63, no. 1 (March 1969): 57–73. But a study of Michigan justices found that when party background is consistent with other background factors, such as religious denomination and social status, there is a cumulative effect on justices' voting behavior. Malcolm M. Feeley, "Another Look at the Party Variable in Judicial Decision Making: An Analysis of the Michigan Supreme Court," *Polity* 4, no. 1 (Autumn 1971): 91–104.

23. Lehne, *The Quest for Justice*, pp. 28, 34.

24. See Wesley G. Skogan, "The Validity of Official Crime Statistics: An Empirical Investigation," *Social Science Quarterly* 55 (June 1974): 25–38. Skogan compared reported crime in ten cities with crime discovered through survey research. While reported crime apparently understated the actual level of crime, Skogan found a high correlation between the two methods of measuring crime rates. He concluded that reported crime rates do have valid uses.

25. A Department of Justice study in the mid-1980s concluded that two-thirds of crimes go unreported. *Minneapolis Star and Tribune*, December 2, 1985, p. 13-A.

26. Arthur Niederhoffer, *Behind the Shield: The Police in Urban Society* (Garden City, N.Y.: Anchor Books, 1967), pp. 14–16.

27. *New York Times*, November 19, 1984, p. 13.

28. President's Commission on Law Enforcement and the Administration of Justice, *The Challenge of Crime in a Free Society: A Report* (Washington, D.C.: U.S. Government Printing Office, 1967), pp. 155–159.

29. The governmental viewpoint is fairly well summarized in two documents by the President's Commission on Law Enforcement and the Administration of Justice, *The Challenge of Crime in a Free Society*, Ch. 7; the Commission's Task Force on Organized Crime, *Task Force Report: Organized Crime* (Washington, D.C.: U.S. Government Printing Office, 1967). The testimony of former FBI Director J. Edgar Hoover has been widely used in promoting the notion of the dominance of the Mafia over all organized crime in this country. See Hoover's testimony in U.S. Congress, Senate, Permanent Subcommittee

on Investigation of the Senate Committee on Governmental Operations, *Organized Crime and Illicit Traffic in Narcotics,* 89th Cong., 1st sess., 1965, S. Rep. 72. See also U.S. Congress, House, Appropriations Subcommittee of the House Committee on Appropriations, testimony of J. Edgar Hoover, *Hearings Before the Subcommittee of Departments of State, Justice, and Commerce, the Judiciary and Related Agencies,* 89th Cong., 2nd sess., 1966, H. Rep. 273.

30. Ralph Salerno and John S. M. Tompkins, *The Civic Confederation: Cosa Nostra and Allied Operations in Organized Crime* (Garden City, N.Y.: Doubleday, 1969), p. 89.

31. Gordon Hawkins, "God and the Mafia," *Public Interest* 14 (Winter 1969): 24–51.

32. See Ramsey Clark, *Crime in America* (New York: Simon & Schuster, 1970), p. 73; Andrew F. Rolle, *The Immigrant Upraised* (Norman: University of Oklahoma Press, 1968), p. 106.

33. Francis A. J. Ianni, "The Mafia and the Web of Kinship," *Public Interest,* no. 22 (Winter 1971): 78–100; Francis A. J. Ianni and Elizabeth Reuss-Ianni, *A Family Business: Kinship and Social Control in Organized Crime* (New York: Mentor, 1973).

34. See Ianni, "The Mafia and the Web of Kinship," p. 97; Daniel Bell, *The End of Ideology: On the Exhaustion of Political Ideas in the Fifties* (Glencoe, Ill.: Free Press, 1960), pp. 128–136.

35. For some interesting accounts of Irish, Jewish, and German organized crime before the 1920s, see Herbert Asbury, *The Gangs of New York: An Informal History of the Underworld* (New York: Capricorn Books, 1970, originally published 1927).

36. See Ianni, "The Mafia and the Web of Kinship," p. 97; Salerno and Tompkins, *The Civic Confederation,* p. 376; Francis A. J. Ianni, "New Mafia: Black, Hispanic and Italian Styles," *Society* 11, no. 3 (March–April 1974): 26–39.

37. Bureau of the Census, *Statistical Abstract, 1986* (Washington, D.C.: U.S. Government Printing Office, 1985), p. 167.

38. See *New York Times,* June 14, 1976; November 26, 1976; May 9, 1977, p. 32; November 7, 1977, p. 1; October 18, 1980, p. 6.

39. See James Q. Wilson, *Thinking About Crime* (New York: Basic Books, 1975), p. xix.

40. *Statistical Abstract, 1987,* p. 163.

41. See Jackson Toby, "A Prospect for Less Crime in the 1980s," *New York Times,* October 26, 1977, p. 35.

42. James Q. Wilson, "Crime and American Culture," *Public Interest* no. 70 (Winter 1983): 22–48.

43. This was upheld by the United States Supreme Court in *Johnson* v. *Louisiana,* 406 U.S. 356 (1972).

44. Upheld by the United States Supreme Court in *Williams* v. *Florida,* 399 U.S. 78 (1970).

45. *Ballew* v. *Georgia,* 435 U.S. 223 (1978).

46. *Argersinger* v. *Hamlin,* 407 U.S. 25 (1972).

47. An analysis of the advantages of different methods of providing legal assistance in criminal and civil cases was made by Stuart Nagel in his "Reaching a Decision on How to Provide Legal Counsel for the Poor," *Policy Studies Journal* 2, no. 3 (Spring 1974): 199–205.

48. See Julian M. Carroll, "Pretrial Release: The Kentucky Program," *State Government* 49, no. 3 (Summer 1976): 187–189.

49. H. Ted Rubin, *The Courts: Fulcrum of the Justice System* (Pacific Palisades, Calif.: Goodyear, 1976), pp. 26, 37.

50. See Herbert Jacob, *Justice in America: Courts, Lawyers, and the Judicial Process,* 2d ed. (Boston: Little, Brown and Co., 1972), pp. 171–172. On the American Bar Association, see Rubin, *The Courts,* p. 26. On legislators' attitudes, see Mike Kennensohn and Winifred Lyday, "Legislators and Criminal Justice Reform," *State Government* 48, no. 2 (Spring 1975): 122–127.

51. *Mapp* v. *Ohio,* 367 U.S. 643 (1961).

52. *Miranda* v. *Arizona,* 384 U.S. 436 (1966).

53. *Rhode Island* v. *Innis,* 446 U.S. 291 (1980).

54. See *New York Times,* May 13, 1985, p. 10-A.

55. *Illinois* v. *Gates,* 103 S.Ct. 2317 (1983).

56. *United States* v. *Leon,* 104 S.Ct. 3405 (1984), permitted searches with an invalid search warrant. *Massachusetts* v. *Sheppard,* 104 S.Ct. 3424 (1984), permitted the use of a warrant that did not specify the materials to be seized.

57. *Furman* v. *Georgia,* 408 U.S. 238 (1972).

58. A Gallup Poll in 1985 found 72 percent favoring the death penalty. See *Gallup Report* nos. 232 and 233 (January/February 1985): 4.

59. The Survey Research Center, which regularly samples the American electorate, reports that few people have a coherent and consistent ideological orientation to politics, especially to elections. For a review of this and other research on that question, see William H. Flanigan and Nancy H. Zingale, *Political Behavior of the American Electorate,* 4th ed. (Boston: Allyn and Bacon, 1979), pp. 117–126.

60. See David M. Gordon, ed., *Problems in Political Economy: An Urban Perspective,* 2d ed. (Lexington, Mass.: D.C. Heath, 1977), p. 356.

61. Ibid., p. 359.

62. Ibid.

63. Ibid.

64. Gary Becker, "Crime and Punishment: An Economic Approach," *Journal of Political Economy* 76, no. 2 (March–April 1968): 169–217.

65. Michael Sesnowitz, "The Returns to Burglary," *Western Economic Journal* 10, no. 4 (December 1972): 477–481.

66. Gregory Krohm, "The Pecuniary Incentives of Property Crime," in *The Economics of Crime and Punishment,* ed. Simon Rottenberg (Washington, D.C.: American Enterprise Institute for Public Policy Research, 1973), p. 33.

67. William E. Cobb, "Theft and the Two Hypotheses," in Rottenberg, *The Economics of Crime and Punishment,* pp. 19–30.

68. Krohm, "The Pecuniary Incentives of Property Crime," pp. 31–34. Adult burglars, however, only fared better if their *in-kind* earnings in jail (that is, free food, clothing, and lodging) were added to the benefits they derived from burglary.

69. For the net loss argument, see Sesnowitz, "The Returns to Burglary." For the net profit argument, see Gregory C. Krohm, "An Alternative View of the Returns to Burglary," *Western Economic Journal* 11 (September 1973): 364–367.

70. Gordon Tullock, "Does Punishment Deter Crime?" *Public Interest* 36 (Summer 1974): 103–111.

71. Alan E. Bent and Ralph A. Rossum, *Police, Criminal Justice, and the Community* (New York: Harper & Row, 1976), p. 156.

72. Ibid.

73. Robert Martinson, "What Works? Questions and Answers about Prison Reform," *Public Interest* 35 (Spring 1974): 25.

74. James Q. Wilson, "'What Works?' Revisited: New Findings in Criminal Rehabilitation," *Public Interest*, no. 61 (Fall 1980): 3–18.

75. Ibid.

76. See Tullock, "Does Punishment Deter Crime?"

77. On determinate and indeterminate sentencing, see Suzanne de Lesseps, "Reappraisal of Prison Policy," *Editorial Research Reports*, March 12, 1976, p. 189.

78. See *New York Times*, December 13, 1985, p. 1.

79. *Minneapolis Star and Tribune*, December 3, 1984, p. 3A.

80. James Austin, "Too Many Prisoners," *State Legislatures* 12, no. 5 (May/June 1986): 12–19.

81. *New York Times*, July 16, 1981, p. 11; December 16, 1981, p. 14.

82. *New York Times*, August 13, 1982, p. 7.

83. Steven D. Williams, "The Tennessee Legislature's Special Session on State Prisons," *Comparative State Politics Newsletter* 6, no. 6 (December 1985): 11–12.

84. Total prison population reached 490,041 by 1985, up from 464,858 in 1984 and 438,248 in 1983. *New York Times*, September 16, 1985, p. 12.

85. *New York Times*, February 19, 1985, p. 9.

Chapter 13
Poverty and Social Welfare Policies

Chapter Preview

Few phenomena are more of a challenge to the widely held American value of upward social mobility than the continued existence of widespread poverty. And few public policy areas evoke as much emotion as trying to determine what to do about poverty in America. This chapter explores these issues by examining:

1. Poverty as a social problem.
2. The importance of conservative, liberal, and radical values to understanding poverty policy.
3. The roles of federal, state, and local governments in carrying out social welfare policy.
4. The major social welfare programs.
5. Health care policies.
6. The attempts to reform social welfare policy since the 1960s.
7. The reciprocal relationship between social welfare policy and the political economy of states.

Let us begin by looking at three individual poor people and how they became poor.

Introduction

America, we are taught, is the land of opportunity. Immigrants arrived, worked hard, saved their money, and saw their children move up a rung on the social ladder. **Horatio Alger** grew rich writing stories about boys who climbed to the top of the social ladder in a single lifetime. This message was so popular that his books sold more than twenty million copies.[1] And there were plenty of real-life examples to sustain this Horatio Alger myth. The ingenious Thomas Edison rose from telegraph boy to become the nation's foremost inventor. Andrew Carnegie, an impoverished immigrant, became the nation's foremost steel magnate. Even in our own day, the dynamic American economy has provided unmatched opportunities to reach the top. Between 1970 and 1980 the number of people earning $1 million or more in income quadrupled.[2]

Upward **social mobility** may be common in America, but many people, for whatever reasons, fail to partake of it. Ed Criado was eighty-seven when Studs Terkel interviewed him for his book *Division Street: America*. He had worked at a skilled trade as a tool and die maker only to end, if not in poverty, certainly in a very precarious financial situation.

> Now when I retired, I had in the neighborhood of eight thousand dollars in the bank. Well, I thought, that's gonna keep me, I'm seventy-seven. I probably won't live another five, six years. Well, you know that's dwindled down to six hundred dollars in ten years. Between the sickness that I had, and her [his wife's] illness. It's absolutely out of order.[3]

If Ed Criado was retired poor, Lucy Jefferson, fifty-two, was working poor. She was a physical therapy aide in a Chicago hospital but did not make enough money to rent a decent apartment in the private housing market. She lived with her two children in a subsidized public housing project in a black section of the city. Too proud to accept public assistance, she managed to squeak by on the margins of poverty—seeing a movie every two or three months, buying meats only on sales at the supermarkets, pinching pennies from paycheck to paycheck, and terribly worried about her son, who was doing poorly in one of the city's poorest schools. Lucy was not destitute, but she also was not upwardly mobile.[4]

Tally Jackson and his friends experienced a type of poverty entirely different from that of Ed Criado or Lucy Jefferson. Tally was a cement finisher in his thirties who hung out on a street corner in Washington, D.C., with about twenty other male unskilled laborers. They worked fairly steadily, but they never earned enough to provide their families with the luxury goods they saw advertised on television. They were broken men. They drifted in and out of marriages, lost all confidence in their ability to lead the middle-class life-style to which they aspired, stole from their employers to make up for their low wages, had numerous brushes with the law, and lost all hope that their future would be any better than their present.[5]

According to U.S. Census Bureau data, over thirty-three million Americans lived in poverty in 1984. This was down from the thirty-five million of the previous year but still exceeded the number in poverty two decades earlier (see Figure 13–1). Their poverty challenges the relevance of the Horatio Alger

Figure 13–1. Number and Percent of People Below the Poverty Line

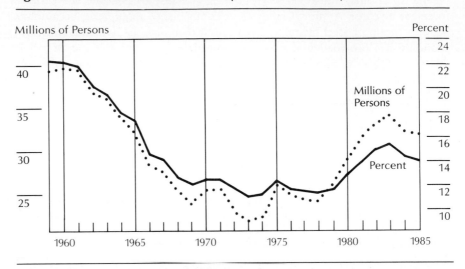

Sources: Bureau of the Census, *Current Population Reports: Poverty in the United States, 1959 to 1968*, Series P-60, no. 68 (Washington, D.C.: U.S. Government Printing Office, 1969), pp. 21, 24; Bureau of the Census, *Current Population Reports: Characteristics of the Population Below the Poverty Level, 1981*, Series P-60, no. 138 (Washington, D.C.: U.S. Government Printing Office, 1983), p. 7; Bureau of the Census, *Statistical Abstract of the United States: 1987* (Washington, D.C.: U.S. Government Printing Office, 1986), p. 442.

myth for contemporary America and raises several questions. What is poverty? Why does it exist? Who is poor? Do different kinds of poverty require different kinds of public policies? Do state and local governments have a significant role to play in setting the public policies that deal with poverty? Or, as some persons charge, is poverty essentially a national problem that must be dealt with by national welfare policies?

These questions will occupy this chapter. We will first examine poverty as a social problem. Second, we will look at conflicting views on the causes of poverty and the ways to deal with it. Third, we will differentiate between the roles played by the federal, state, and local levels of government in setting and implementing social welfare policies. Fourth, we will outline the major welfare programs that operate at the state and local levels. Fifth, because health care programs are the single most expensive area of social welfare expenditures, we will examine them in greater detail than the other programs. Sixth, we will discuss the attempts to reform social welfare programs from the 1960s to the 1980s. Finally, we will look at the relationship between social welfare policy and political economy.

Poverty as a Social Problem

What Is Poverty?

Poverty can be defined in two ways. The first definition is **absolute deprivation,** and the second is **relative deprivation.** Both of these definitions are somewhat arbitrary and judgmental, and as will become apparent, one's definition of poverty affects the policies one favors. Calling poverty absolute deprivation leads to one policy approach; calling it relative deprivation often leads to other policy approaches.

Poverty as Absolute Deprivation

In absolute terms, poverty can be defined as the minimum subsistence income needed to survive without deprivation. Anybody below that income level is judged to live in poverty. Based on the assumption that poor families spend one-third of their income on food, the U.S. Social Security Administration sets an official **poverty line** at three times the amount of income needed to eat according to a modest food plan.*

The official poverty level is adjusted each year to compensate for inflation. Table 13–1 lists the official poverty-level income, by family size and by year. Because the poverty line is one of the criteria used to determine eligibility for federal programs, it is important that this line be set at a realistic level. However, some critics argue that the level is too low. Other critics argue that the assumptions behind the poverty line are no longer valid. One economist argues that the poverty line ought to be set at four times the economy food plan instead of three times.[6] At whatever level the poverty line is set, compensating for special circumstances of different families is impossible. Obviously, $11,000 will cause less deprivation for a family that owns its house than for a family still making rent or mortgage payments. It will cause less deprivation for a family in subsidized housing than for a family in nonsubsidized housing. If all government assistance programs, such as public housing, food stamps, and medical assistance, were counted in determining poverty status, the number of people considered to be living in poverty would be sharply reduced.[7] This fact obviously complicates the task of defining poverty, and its implications for government policy have stimulated considerable debate among social welfare policy specialists.

---

*This modest food plan is actually the economy food plan prepared by the United States Department of Agriculture. The Department of Agriculture annually estimates the cost of buying food on an economy plan, a low-cost plan, a moderate plan, and a liberal plan. See Michael Harrington, "The Betrayal of the Poor," *Atlantic* (January 1970): 71–72. Also see Martin Rein, "Problems in the Definition and Measurement of Poverty," *Poverty in America,* rev. ed., eds. Louis Ferman et al. (Ann Arbor: University of Michigan Press, 1968), pp. 123–125.

Table 13–1. The Poverty Level: 1986 and Previous Years

The 1986 poverty level for different-size nonfarm families		The poverty level in selected years for a four-person, nonfarm family	
Size of family	Average poverty line	Year	Average poverty line
1 Person	$ 5,360	1986	$11,000
2 Persons	7,240	1985	10,989
3 Persons	9,120	1984	10,609
4 Persons	11,000	1983	10,178
5 Persons	12,880	1982	9,862
6 Persons	14,760	1981	9,287
7 Persons	16,640	1980	8,414

Sources: Bureau of the Census, *Current Population Reports: Characteristics of the Population Below the Poverty Level: 1980.* Series P-60, no. 133 (Washington, D.C.: U.S. Government Printing Office, July 1982), pp. 186–187. *Social Security Bulletin* 49, no. 4 (April 1986): 13.

Note: The poverty line rises with the rate of inflation and varies with family size.

Poverty as Relative Deprivation

Partly because of the difficulty in making an absolute deprivation definition of poverty, some critics prefer to define poverty relative to society's overall standard of living. According to this view, as the standard of living goes up, the poverty level should also rise. A majority of poor people today have conveniences that only a generation ago would have been considered luxuries—a television set, a refrigerator or freezer, an oven, hot water, access to a telephone, a private bath, and a flush toilet.[8]

Some writers have suggested that a realistic definition of poverty would draw the relative poverty line at 50 percent of the median income.[9] The median income is the point at which half the people earn more and half earn less. Since the median family income in 1984 was $26,433, poverty income by this measure would be $13,216. About 21 percent of the families lived on incomes below this amount.[10]

Despite the theoretical advantages of defining poverty in relative terms, the United States government continues to use its official definition based on a principle of absolute deprivation. That definition is important for determining eligibility for several federal social programs and for allotting several federal grants-in-aid to states and communities. Because of these reasons, this chapter also will rely on the official poverty definition in discussing trends in poverty.

Who Is Poor?

Some people have an above-average chance of being poor (see Table 13–2). The people with the highest likelihood of being poor are racial minor-

Table 13–2. People Likely to Be Poor

Characteristics	Percent below the poverty line, 1985
All persons	14.0%
Whites	11.4
Blacks	31.3
Spanish origin	29.0
Children under age 15	21.5
In households headed by a white female	45.2
In households headed by a black female	66.9
In households headed by a female of Spanish origin	72.4
All persons in female-headed households	34.0
In households headed by a white female	27.4
In households headed by a black female	50.5
In households headed by a female of Spanish origin	53.1
Persons in families with:	
A family head with less than eight years of schooling	26.2
A family head under age 25	30.2
No wage earner	36.7
Five or more children	49.6

Source: Bureau of the Census, *Money Income and Poverty Status of Families and Persons in the United States: 1985.* Series P-60, no. 154 (Washington, D.C.: U.S. Government Printing Office, 1986), pp. 3, 21, 29.

ities and families headed by a woman. Poverty is also endemic for persons in large families and persons in families headed by a high school dropout, or an unemployed person. More poor people live in the South than in other parts of the country.

The most disturbing change in the composition of the poverty population has been a dramatic increase in poverty among children, especially children in black, female-headed households. A Congressional study in 1985 found that over two-thirds of children in such families lived in poverty and the number of female-headed households (white and minority) was rising dramatically.[11] Unlike previous patterns of poverty in America, poverty in the 1980s is increasingly concentrated among women and children.[12]

Kinds of Poverty

Permanently vs. Marginally Poor

In trying to decide what, if anything, should be done about poverty, it is important to distinguish between the *permanently poor* and the *temporarily* or *marginally poor.* One family may fall into poverty for a two- or three-year period immediately following a divorce, for example, but subsequently re-cover. During that two- or three-year period, the single parent may need job training, placement counseling, and direct financial assistance. Poverty, in this case, is a temporary status.

The Survey Research Center traced the economic fortunes of over 5,000 families for a nine-year period and found that only a fifth of those under the poverty line had lived in poverty all nine years.[13] This suggests that of the thirty-five million poor people calculated by the Census Bureau, only about seven million live below the poverty line most of the time.

However, the Survey Research Center study also found that poverty is much more widespread than suggested by the Census Bureau. Nearly a third of all American families fell into poverty in at least one of the nine years in which they were interviewed. This means that as many as seventy million people live in a fairly precarious situation. Normally they earn enough money to live comfortably, but they fall into poverty during various stages of their lives—when they are laid off work because of a recession, when they get divorced and have to divide their incomes between two homes, when they get fired or widowed or face a medical or financial disaster, when their pension fund goes broke, or, like Ed Criado, when they retire on a fixed-income pension that cannot keep pace with inflation.

These marginally poor do not get a proportionate share of the national income. They do not accumulate much savings. They have few assets other than their houses, and many do not own their homes. The overwhelming majority work as regularly as possible, but they are extremely vulnerable to technological change, social developments, and other events over which they have no control.

The Working Poor and the Nonworking Poor

Another important distinction is between the *working poor* and the *non-working poor*. Nearly half of all poverty families are headed by somebody with a job.[14] However, their jobs do not pay enough to keep them above the poverty level.

Tally and his friends worked. They were busboys, dishwashers, parking lot car jockeys, and unskilled construction laborers. However, those jobs did not protect them from poverty.

> The busboy or dishwasher who works hard becomes, simply, a hard-working busboy or dishwasher. Neither hard work nor perseverance can conceivably carry the janitor to a sitdown job in the office building he cleans up. And it is the apprentice who becomes the journeyman electrician, plumber, steam fitter, or bricklayer, not the common unskilled Negro laborer.

Figure 13-2. Trends in Income Inequality, 1929-1983: Percentage of the National Income Earned by Each of Three Income Groups

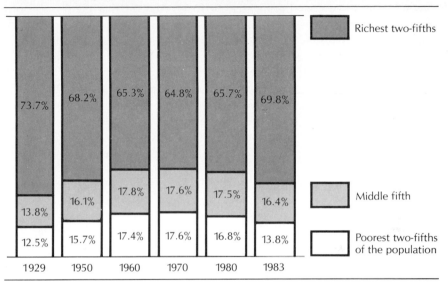

						Richest two-fifths
73.7%	68.2%	65.3%	64.8%	65.7%	69.8%	
13.8%	16.1%	17.8%	17.6%	17.5%	16.4%	Middle fifth
12.5%	15.7%	17.4%	17.6%	16.8%	13.8%	Poorest two-fifths of the population
1929	1950	1960	1970	1980	1983	

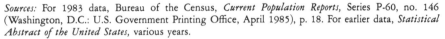

Sources: For 1983 data, Bureau of the Census, *Current Population Reports,* Series P-60, no. 146 (Washington, D.C.: U.S. Government Printing Office, April 1985), p. 18. For earlier data, *Statistical Abstract of the United States,* various years.

Thus the job is not a stepping stone to something. It is a dead end. It promises to deliver no more tomorrow, next month, or next year than it does today.[15]

As Figure 13-2 shows, the plight of the working poor and the marginally poor is getting worse today. The poorest two-fifths of Americans saw their share of the national income steadily grow from 12.5 percent in 1929 to 17.6 percent in 1970 and then decline slightly to 16.8 percent in 1980. Since then it has fallen dramatically to 13.8 percent, almost back to where it was fifty-five years earlier. During the same period of time, the richest two-fifths of Americans saw their share of the national income decline until about 1970, and then rise until today, when it is higher than it has been since mid-century. Figure 13-2 clearly illustrates that income inequality in America is growing, with income shifting away from the 60 percent majority of Americans to the 40 percent who are the richest. If this trend continues, the plight of the marginally poor and the working poor will get worse, and many of today's college students will join those ranks.

Why is this happening? There are many reasons, but analysts point to two overriding reasons. First, the transformation of the American economy from one based on manufacturing to one based on services eliminated 11.5 million well-paying manufacturing jobs from 1979 to 1984. Only 60 percent of those workers found new jobs during that period.[16] At least that many new jobs were created in the same period, but these were primarily lower-paying service jobs in such enterprises as restaurants, hotels, and hospitals. More family members must work more hours for their families to make less money in the 1980s than was true a dozen years earlier.[17]

A second reason for the growing inequality in incomes can be traced to the changes in national tax and welfare policies during the Reagan administration. As will be discussed later in this chapter, these policies had the effect of reducing the incomes of low-income families by about $390 per year while increasing the take-home pay of rich families by $8,390 per year (see Figure 13–4, p. 366).

Political Values and Poverty

A variety of perceptions exist about the causes of poverty and how it can best be dealt with. These perceptions can be placed along the leftist–rightist continuum.

On the right end of the ideological spectrum, conservatives argue that the dynamic, capitalistic American economy provides millions of opportunities for self-advancement. The individual is master of his or her fate; and if the individual is too lazy, too dumb, too unstable, or too sick to work, then that is the individual's own fault. "If the poor would only work, there would be no poverty."[18] In Tally's case, he simply failed to take advantage of abundant opportunities to become literate, learn a job skill, and acquire the middle-class work ethic.

Conservatives tend to view poverty not only as an individual matter but also as inevitable. Life circumstances will always put some people into poverty, but the people with initiative will overcome their poverty. For this reason, the conservative is likely to attribute great significance to the difference between temporary and permanent poverty. Many people may be temporarily thrown into poverty by external circumstances such as a divorce, but those people usually climb out of poverty.

More disturbing to the conservative, however, is the long-term poverty of the lower classes. Some social critics argue that a **culture of poverty** exists among lower-class people. These people become cynical about the social system. They fail not only to develop marketable job skills but to develop positive attitudes that would enable them to work eight hours daily and cause no trouble to their supervisors. Edward C. Banfield writes, "Lower-class poverty . . . is 'inwardly' caused [by psychological inability to provide for the future, and all that this inability implies . . .]. Extreme present-orientedness, not lack of income or wealth, is the principal cause of poverty in the sense of 'the culture of poverty.' Most of those caught up in this culture are unable or unwilling to plan for the future, to sacrifice immediate gratifications in favor of future ones, or to accept the disciplines that are required in order to get and spend."[19]

In its most extreme form during the early twentieth century, the classic conservative explanation for poverty was **Social Darwinism.** Charles Darwin argued that natural evolution occurred through the survival of the fittest. Social Darwinists, such as Herbert Spencer,[20] applied that argument to the evolution of society. Poverty is a mechanism for the survival of the fittest in the social sphere. It weeds out the weakest members of the species, and the overall result is a healthier society.

The extreme conservative would carry this argument to its logical conclusion and deny that the government has any responsibility to combat poverty. Indeed, Charles Murray argues that government welfare programs have only made problems worse by sapping poor people of their initiative and making them dependent on the welfare system.[21] The classic conservative believes that the best antipoverty policy is one of **laissez-faire,** a policy of the government leaving the marketplace alone and not intervening. More moderate conservatives do favor some intervention in the marketplace and some programs to help people who have fallen into poverty. If the government must intervene, however, the conservative would usually prefer that the government give financial incentives to private industry to carry out government objectives. Conservatives, for example, do not usually look favorably on massive public employment programs in which the government creates jobs to reduce unemployment rates. Rather, conservatives prefer that the government provide financial incentives to private industries to hire more workers.

Some conservatives emphasize the distinction between absolute poverty and relative deprivation. Edward C. Banfield, for example, argues that most poverty today is little more than a gap between poor people's limited capabilities and their inflated aspirations for an upper-middle-class life-style.[22]

In contrast to the conservative emphasis on individualism, leftist theories stress that much poverty is structural and would still exist if everybody had a future-oriented value system.[23] This view prevails among liberal social scientists, journalists, and political leaders, who dominate liberal thought. Tracing their views back to the Great Depression of the 1930s and President Franklin Roosevelt's New Deal response to it, liberals point out that private enterprise cannot by itself produce enough jobs for everybody. Even during the late 1960's high tide of the greatest economic boom in history, the unemployment rate remained above 4 percent. The liberal policy approach for dealing with poverty reflects this belief in the structural causes of poverty. Government spending should stimulate economic growth so that full employment can be maintained, and specific government programs such as unemployment compensation should strive to protect people from recessions that occur in the business cycle. The conservative is pessimistic about individuals, but the liberal is optimistic. The liberal supports education programs, retraining programs, and job placement programs that give individuals an opportunity to take advantage of structural changes in the economy.

At the extreme left, radical thought argues that poverty is caused by major economic institutions and the small class of very wealthy people who control those institutions. Radicals believe those people share a consensus opinion that the prevailing class structure of the society must be maintained. This class structure requires a relatively small impoverished class, a fairly substantial class of marginal workers who can be moved into and out of employment as conditions dictate, and a fairly sizable group of upper-middle-class people who can serve as doctors, lawyers, professionals, supervisors, and other managers to run the major institutions of the society.

Neither liberals nor radicals deny the importance of individual traits for social mobility. Some gifted and ambitious people can work their way from the bottom to the top of the social ladder. Leftists stress, however, that unless the basic structure of society is changed, the pool of permanently and marginally poor people will continue to exist. Moreover, the class structure perpetuates itself over generations. Most poor people have parents who are poor. Most rich people have parents who are rich. And twenty-five years from now most poor people will be the sons and daughters of today's poor people.

To cope with poverty, leftists basically have a two-pronged approach, which reflects the differences between the more moderate liberals and the radicals. Recognizing that upward mobility can occur on an individual basis, liberals seek to upgrade individual skills and make structural changes to equalize advancement opportunities. Radicals seek solutions that would change the basic private enterprise nature of the economy. Leftist theory also favors redistributing income from the upper classes to the lower classes.

State, Local, and Federal Roles in Social Welfare Policy

These theories of poverty have had a profound influence on the social welfare system that evolved in the United States. Prior to the depression of the 1930s, classic laissez-faire conservatism was the dominant theory of social welfare, and the government intervened minimally in the economy. The depression was such a monumental catastrophe, however, that laissez-faire was no longer a viable policy. The economy's total output of goods and services (the **gross national product, or GNP**) dropped 45 percent between 1929 and 1933 and did not get back to its 1929 level until 1941. By 1932 a quarter of the work force was unemployed. Traditional systems of welfare, or relief, as they were called in those days, were overloaded with requests for help. These traditional relief systems were run and financed by local governments that were unable to cope with the depression.

In response to the disaster of the Great Depression, a social welfare system emerged that intricately involved all three levels of government. The federal role initially attempted to provide financial support for local governments to give traditional relief.

Federal Roles

In time, a completely new intergovernmental welfare system evolved. The federal government's role in this system now embraces four elements. First, through the grant-in-aid system, the federal government provides financial incentives to the states to run a variety of social welfare programs. These programs, which range from AFDC to unemployment compensation, will be described shortly.

Second, the federal government established minimum payment levels for the programs run by the states. Third, because the federal government provides financial incentives, it effectively plays the key role of deciding which poverty problems will be tackled and what programs will exist to tackle them. Fourth, in addition to setting up and financing programs for the states to run, the federal government directly operates a number of programs itself. Medicare, for example, is handled exclusively by the federal government.

State Roles

Whereas the federal government determines the overall structure of social welfare programs and minimum payment levels, the states implement most programs and set the policies that govern eligibility for program benefits and the ultimate benefit levels. Taking the **Aid for Families with Dependent Children (AFDC)** program as an example, Congress wrote the program into the **Social Security Act of 1935.** The initial objective was to provide financial relief to children in single-parent families that lacked an independent source of income. The federal government provides a minimal AFDC payment level. The state legislatures supplement this amount. Because some states provide more generous supplements than do others, AFDC benefit levels vary widely from one state to another: in 1983 the average monthly

AFDC payments per family ranged from a low of $92 in Mississippi to a high of $566 in Alaska. Finally, after the legislature sets policy for the benefit levels, implementation of the AFDC program is turned over to the state and local welfare departments. The state welfare department draws up the rules and regulations to implement the policy set by the legislature, and it oversees how well these rules and regulations are carried out by the local welfare departments.

Local Roles

Local welfare departments, which are usually found at the county level of government, are most often the agencies that run the AFDC programs. Persons apply for AFDC at the local level. Local officials determine whether the applicant is eligible and what level of benefits the applicant will receive. If the applicant's minor children are older than six years, the local officials register

You Decide
A Dilemma in Welfare Eligibility

Deciding who should receive welfare under what conditions is very difficult and often arbitrary. Getting a fair judgment in some cases would tax the wisdom of Solomon. Such was the case of Wendy Sabot of Suffolk County, New York.

In July 1974, Ms. Sabot applied for AFDC. Although at that time she was receiving $350 per month in child support payments from her former husband, her rent alone was $300 monthly, leaving little for other necessities.

One AFDC eligibility rule requires that recipients have no other liquid assets. Ms. Sabot had no other liquid assets, but her children had accumulated $1,221 in savings. Ms. Sabot told reporters, "Some of it they had earned themselves—baby-sitting, washing cars, working a newspaper-delivery route—and the rest was gift money from birthdays and Christmas. I made the children deposit all of their gift money and half of

what they earned in their accounts."

The Suffolk County Social Services Department told Ms. Sabot that she would not be eligible for welfare payments until she had either spent the children's savings or turned them over to the department. She asked the Legal Aid Society to help her appeal this decision but was turned down because very few poor people would benefit from her case. So she went to a law library and prepared a lawsuit. When the trial court ordered the Social Services Department to make her eligible for welfare, the department appealed the case to New York State's highest appellate court. Finally, three years later, in October 1977, the appellate court upheld Ms. Sabot. "The broad humanitarian purpose of the social services law," read the court's opinion, "does not contemplate that a person must be stripped bare, emotionally and economically."

The Sabot case presents some difficult

the applicant for the WIN (Work Incentive) program. WIN tries to find jobs for the applicants or to provide job training for those who lack work skills. If the applicant is female, the local welfare officials try to find the father of the children and through the courts force him to make higher or more regular child support payments. After going through all these steps to ensure the applicant's eligibility and to boost her outside sources of income, the local welfare department begins to send monthly AFDC checks. Sometimes welfare department officials find it difficult to set eligibility rules that are fair and equitable, as the "You Decide" exercise below shows.

Why Welfare Policies Differ Among States

States differ greatly in the generosity of their welfare benefit levels (see Figure 13–3). Alaska, with its average monthly AFDC payment of $566 in 1983, was more than six times as generous as Mississippi, with its average

---

dilemmas for welfare officials trying to determine eligibility rules. On the one hand many observers would agree with Ms. Sabot that it was "unreasonable" for the Social Services Department to take away the children's money before the family could get help. "It wasn't my money. It never was. . . . Taking away their money would have taken away their incentive. I don't want them to perpetuate the welfare system. I want them to be independent. I didn't want them to grow up to become welfare recipients and have children who were welfare recipients."

On the other hand, the same observers could probably sympathize with the Social Services Department commissioner that "it is questionable whether the public should be required to support this family at a subsistence level while it has $1,200 in the bank." The Sabot case opens the possibility that other AFDC applicants might transfer their own savings to their children's accounts in

order to keep their cash reserves and still receive welfare payments.

The Sabot case gave the Suffolk County welfare officials the difficult task of writing a new set of regulations that would be more humanitarian and at the same time not susceptible to fraud.

If *you* were a public official responsible for this task, how would *you* approach this problem? How much in assets should a family be permitted and still be eligible for AFDC benefits? How would you guard against parents transferring their savings to their children in order to gain AFDC eligibility? And if children were to lose AFDC benefits when they saved money, how would you teach them the value of saving to acquire assets?

Figure 13–3. Affluence and AFDC Benefit Levels by State, 1985

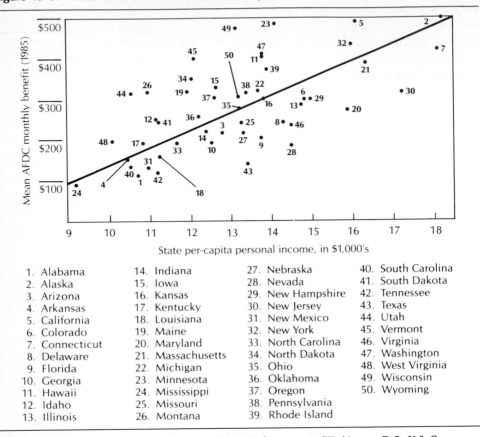

1. Alabama	14. Indiana	27. Nebraska	40. South Carolina
2. Alaska	15. Iowa	28. Nevada	41. South Dakota
3. Arizona	16. Kansas	29. New Hampshire	42. Tennessee
4. Arkansas	17. Kentucky	30. New Jersey	43. Texas
5. California	18. Louisiana	31. New Mexico	44. Utah
6. Colorado	19. Maine	32. New York	45. Vermont
7. Connecticut	20. Maryland	33. North Carolina	46. Virginia
8. Delaware	21. Massachusetts	34. North Dakota	47. Washington
9. Florida	22. Michigan	35. Ohio	48. West Virginia
10. Georgia	23. Minnesota	36. Oklahoma	49. Wisconsin
11. Hawaii	24. Mississippi	37. Oregon	50. Wyoming
12. Idaho	25. Missouri	38. Pennsylvania	
13. Illinois	26. Montana	39. Rhode Island	

Source: Bureau of the Census, *Statistical Abstract of the United States: 1987* (Washington, D.C.: U.S. Government Printing Office, 1986), pp. xxiv, 365.

payment of only $92. Why do states differ so much in their level of welfare benefits?

Affluence as an Explanation

The main explanation for the disparities seems to be the level of affluence of the state. Alaska can be more generous than Mississippi in large part because Alaska has a higher per-capita income than Mississippi, and the cost of living is higher there. Figure 13–3 presents a scattergram that arranges the states according to their average monthly AFDC benefit levels and their per-capita incomes. This scattergram shows that the states with the highest benefit levels tend to be the richest states, and the states with the lowest benefit levels tend to be the poorest states.

Although affluence partially explains the difference in benefit levels, it is not a completely satisfying explanation. Alaska is six times as generous as Mississippi, but it is not six times as rich. Other factors must be involved. One possibility is that political forces in some states lead them to choose higher benefit levels.

Politics as an Explanation

One popular **hypothesis** among political scientists has been that welfare benefits will be highest in the states where Democrats compete vigorously with Republicans for voter support and where voter turnout is high. The assumption behind this hypothesis is that the voters will choose the party that gives them the most benefits, causing the two parties to outbid each other. The higher the turnout and the greater the competitiveness, the more incentive the parties have to bid against each other for voter support. In states with little competition and low voter turnout, the dominant party has little fear of losing office and thus has no incentive to give the voters high benefit levels. This hypothesis is not supported by empirical data, however. Although highly competitive states and high voter-turnout states do give higher welfare benefits than one-party and low-turnout states, the competitive, high-turnout states are also the most affluent states. Although the influence of partisanship cannot be ignored, most statistical analyses have concluded that the level of affluence is much more significant for determining welfare benefits than is the degree of two-party competition or whether the state is controlled by Democrats rather than Republicans.[24]

More important than two-party competition and high voter turnout is the extent to which the working classes and lower classes have politically influential interest groups. The strength and militancy of labor unions does appear to have a significant impact on social welfare benefits. Frances Fox Piven and Richard Cloward argue that AFDC costs rose so fast in the 1960s primarily because of the increasing militancy of welfare recipients, the formation of the National Welfare Rights Organization, the deliberate attempts of community organizers to register people for welfare and to get higher welfare benefits, and the urban riots of the 1960s.[25] Other observers, however, discount this explanation.

The political culture of states also helps explain the differences in welfare benefits. Governmental intervention in the economy, it will be recalled from Chapter 2, is favored much more in moralistic political cultures than it is in traditionalistic or individualistic cultures. Ranking states by the AFDC benefit levels they pay, all but four of the top twenty states have a moralistic strain in their political culture, whereas only three of the bottom twenty states have such a strain. Conversely, only two of the top twenty states have a traditionalistic strain, but sixteen of the bottom twenty states have a traditionalistic strain.

In sum, state and local governments play a vital role not only in administering federal welfare programs but also in determining the generosity of the benefit levels. The most significant variables for determining the generosity of state welfare policies appear to be the level of affluence, the degree of militancy, and the type of political culture in the state. Economic and political factors interact in rather complex ways to influence welfare policies.[26] But, in general, benefits are most generous in states that are affluent, that have strong labor unions and poor people's interest groups, and that have a moralistic strain in their political culture. Benefit levels are the lowest in states that are poor, that lack strong labor unions or poor people's interest groups, and that have a traditionalistic strain in their political culture. The generous states are found disproportionately in the Northeast, Midwest, and Pacific regions, and the least generous states tend to be in the South and Southwest Sunbelt region.

The Major Social Welfare Programs

There is no agreement on what programs are included under the term *welfare*. Some people apply the term only to programs (such as AFDC) in which the recipient receives money even though he or she did not pay into the program. Other people apply the term to a wide variety of programs, ranging from AFDC to Medicare. We will use the larger definition of welfare in order to see how programs such as AFDC fit into the broader complex of dozens of social programs. We will categorize these programs according to the type of assistance and the major beneficiaries of the assistance.[27] As Table 13–3 shows, social welfare programs provide three types of assistance: (1) social insurance transfer payments, (2) cash transfer payments that are not social insurance, and (3) in-kind assistance.*

Social Insurance Transfer Payments

A **transfer payment** is a direct payment of money by the government to individuals. It is not a payment for purchasing goods or services, as are federal expenditures. Nor is it a payment to run a program, as are the services listed in

---

*The table is meant only for illustrative purposes. In order to keep it as simple as possible, a number of social welfare programs, such as veterans' benefits, were not included.

Part 3 of Table 13–3. It is called a transfer payment because its net effect is simply to transfer money from the people who pay taxes to the people who receive the cash. Some transfer payments, such as OASDHI, are **social insurance.** That is, individuals make payments into a social insurance trust fund much as they would make payments into a private insurance policy. Later on they receive benefit payments when they become eligible. The three major social insurance programs—OASDHI, Medicare, and Unemployment Compensation—were established by the Social Security Act of 1935 and its later amendments.

Old Age, Survivors, Disability, and Health Insurance (OASDHI)

OASDHI is widely viewed as a social insurance program, not a welfare program. While working you make regular payroll contributions to the social security trust funds. When you retire, become disabled, or die, you or your beneficiaries receive a monthly payment just as would happen under a pension program or a life insurance plan. Since most people's social security benefits vastly exceed the amount of money they contribute to the trust fund, it is much more of a welfare program than is generally believed.[28]

Social security benefit levels were drastically expanded in the 1970s; and today, through **indexation,** they rise to keep pace with the rate of inflation. By 1983 the social security retirement fund had run out of money, and Congress was forced to pass extensive reforms involving benefit reductions and tax increases to keep the program solvent through the rest of the 1980s.

Medicare

Persons over age sixty-five are eligible for Medicare. They pay a small monthly premium that entitles them to medical services. Doctors send their bills directly to the federal government for payment.

Unemployment Compensation

Unemployment compensation is a social insurance program. While you work, your employer makes regular contributions to an unemployment compensation trust fund; if you become unemployed, you can draw benefit checks for up to twenty-six weeks. Unemployment compensation was initiated by the Social Security Act of 1935. It is financed jointly by employers, the states, and the federal government, but it is administered by the individual states. During the recession of 1981–1982, unemployment rates in some states got so high that several state unemployment trust funds began running out of money and had to borrow from the federal government in order to meet their obligations.[29]

Table 13–3. Approaches to Social Welfare Policy

Approach and program	Major recipients of the assistance	Level of government that writes the checks or administers the delivery of the service	Federal dollars spent 1982 (in billions)	Spent 1986	Budgeted 1988
1. Social insurance transfer payments					
a. Old Age Survivors Disability and Health Insurance (OASDHI)	Retired people and/or the survivors of workers who died; mostly non-workers; all income categories	Federal	154.1	199.8	219.4
b. Medicare	The aged; all income categories; both the working and the non-working poor	Federal	46.6	70.2	73.0
c. Unemployment compensation	Mostly the bottom 40 percent of the income recipients; workers who are temporarily unemployed	State	23.8	17.8	17.7
			$224.5	$287.8	$310.1
2. Nonsocial insurance cash transfer payments					
a. Aid for Families with Dependent Children (AFDC)	The nonworking poor; the bottom 20 percent of the income recipients; mostly single, divorced, or widowed mothers and their children	State and county	8.0	9.9	9.8
b. Food stamps	The bottom 40 percent of the income recipients; both the working and the nonworking poor	Federal and county	11.0	12.5	12.8
c. Supplemental Security Income (SSI)	The aged, the blind, and the disabled; the nonworking poor; the bottom 20 percent of the income recipients	Federal	7.7	10.3	12.3

Program	Beneficiaries	State and county	No federal funds		
d. General public assistance (excluding AFDC and SSI)	The nonworking poor; the bottom 20 percent of the income earners; mostly destitute and homeless people who do not qualify for AFDC, SSI, or unemployment compensation	State and county	$ 26.7	$ 32.7	$ 34.9
3. *In-kind assistance*					
a. Housing programs	Mostly the bottom 40 percent of the income recipients; both the working and the nonworking poor	Municipal or county housing authorities	8.0	12.4	13.4
b. Medicaid	The bottom 40 percent of the income recipients; both the working and the nonworking poor	State and county welfare departments	17.4	25.0	26.9
c. Other health programs	All income categories; mostly concentrating on the bottom 40 percent; people with special health problems; health care professionals	Federal, state, and county	9.1	9.8	11.1
d. Legal Services Program (LSP)	The bottom 40 percent of the income recipients; both the working and the nonworking poor	Federal	0.26	0.3	0
e. Employment programs	Middle 40 percent of the income recipients; the working poor who are unemployed	Federal, state, county, and municipal	6.0	5.6	6.5
f. Other social services (e.g., child day care, foster care, family planning, services for the mentally retarded)	The bottom 40 percent of the income recipients; both the working and the nonworking poor; people with special needs and special problems	State, county, and municipal	5.9	7.1	8.5
			$ 46.66	$ 60.2	$ 66.4

Sources: Actual dollars spent for FY 1982 from *The Budget of the United States Government: Fiscal Year 1984* (Washington, D.C.: U.S. Government Printing Office, 1983), Part V, pp. 86–87, 102–103, 114–115, 138. Actual dollars for FY 1986 and proposed dollars for FY 1988 are from the outlays listed in *The Budget of the United States Government: Fiscal Year 1988. Supplement* (Washington, D.C.: U.S. Government Printing Office, 1987), Part V, pp. 89, 109, 115, 123, 136, 147.

355

Transfer Payments That Are Not Social Insurance

In contrast to the above social insurance programs, some other transfer payment programs, such as AFDC, are not social insurance. People can receive assistance from those programs when they meet the eligibility requirements and if they can pass a **means test;** that is, if their income or assets fall below a certain level. The main cash transfer payments of this type are AFDC, food stamps, SSI, and General Public Assistance.

Aid for Families with Dependent Children (AFDC)

AFDC is the most controversial transfer payment. It provides a direct monthly payment to single parents with dependent children. In 1985 AFDC payments averaged $348 per family.[30] The number of recipients rose fivefold in less than thirty years—from 2.2 million in 1950 to over 11.4 million in 1975; since 1975, however, the number has declined slightly. The large increase was caused by several factors—the rising divorce rate, the rising rate of children born out of wedlock, the extensive post–World War II in-migration of racial minorities and poor whites from rural areas to the big cities, the extensive immigration of destitute Chicanos and Puerto Ricans, the rise of militancy and political activism among poor people in the 1960s, a broad expansion of federal funding for social programs during the Lyndon Johnson presidency (1963–1969), and the recurrence of economic recession.

The AFDC program is controversial not only because of the vast sums of money involved but also because of a very negative stereotype attributed to AFDC recipients. According to this stereotype, the typical recipient misspends AFDC checks on alcohol, gambling, and frivolities. Nevertheless, rigorous research has shown that AFDC recipients spend more of their income on food and housing and less on frivolities than do non-AFDC recipients.[31] Another stereotype is that the recipient is able-bodied enough to work but is simply ripping off the system by drawing AFDC checks. Federal investigations find that only a small minority of AFDC recipients are ineligible.[32] The overwhelming majority of people on the AFDC rolls are young children, and most of the rest are single or divorced women. Another stereotype is that the typical AFDC mother becomes permanently dependent on welfare. The fact is that 60 percent of AFDC recipients receive this benefit for less than three years. Only about 8 percent have received benefits for more than ten years.[33]

Food Stamps

Another controversial measure has been the **food stamp program,** which was started in 1961 as a pilot project and then established on a permanent basis in 1964. It is totally funded by the federal government but is administered by the federal Department of Agriculture jointly with the state and county departments of welfare.

Food stamps serve both the working and the nonworking poor. To qualify, the family income must be below a certain cutoff level. Eligible households receive a monthly allotment that is tied to the amount of money needed for the Agriculture Department's "thrifty food plan."[34] Food stamps were attacked strenuously by President Reagan, whose administration tightened eligibility requirements and sought to reduce the number of recipients. This tactic worked, since the number of recipients has declined to less than 20 million[35] after reaching a peak of 22.4 million in the recession of 1981.[36]

Supplemental Security Income (SSI)

Supplemental Security Income (SSI) is a federal program that provides aid to the aged, the blind, and the permanently or totally disabled. Prior to 1972 these programs were handled by the states. The Social Security Administration sends a monthly SSI check to each recipient, and each state is permitted to supplement the federal payment. SSI is clearly a relief program, not a social insurance program. It is aimed exclusively at the nonworking poor.

General Public Assistance

The final transfer payment program is general public assistance (GPA), or general relief. This is administered and financed exclusively by state and local governments. Homeless and destitute persons who do not qualify for other public assistance programs can get general relief from their state and county welfare departments.

In-Kind Assistance Programs

In addition to transfer payments, the federal, state, and local governments have a wide range of specific services for the poorer part of the population. These are sometimes called **in-kind assistance** because they provide assistance that has a cash value, even though it is not received in cash. Five of the most prominent social services are outlined in Table 13–3—public housing, health programs, Medicaid, legal services, and employment services. Housing and health will be discussed elsewhere in this chapter, so only the last two will be dealt with here.

Employment Programs

All states provide employment services through which they help people find jobs. In addition, a number of federal and state programs have existed over the years to provide training, job location services, and public jobs. The most prominent of these in recent years was probably CETA, the Comprehensive Employment Training Act, passed in 1973. Under CETA, the United States Department of Labor funded state and local agencies to provide job training and to hire people for public service jobs. A school district, for example, could seek CETA funds to hire and train a recreation supervisor. At its peak in the late 1970s, CETA provided 750,000 opportunities for training and work experience.

When CETA came up for review in 1981, Ronald Reagan was in office. President Reagan was philosophically opposed to the program, especially its public-works jobs aspect, and all funds for public-works jobs were deleted from the 1982 budget. Federal employment programs were then restructured by the Training for Jobs Act of 1982, which dropped the CETA label from federal jobs programs, eliminated the concept of federally subsidized public jobs, and reoriented federal efforts toward training and youth employment. These training programs and youth jobs programs were to be run by the state governments rather than by the cities and counties, as had been the case under CETA, and the legislation gave the states considerable discretion on how they spent the federal funds.[37]

Legal Services

One of the most controversial social services has been the **legal services program (LSP)**. It was created in 1965 as part of the **War on Poverty**. Under this program, federally paid lawyers handle legal problems, such as divorce filings, disputes with landlords, and consumer complaints of individuals against government bureaucracies. In 1974 Congress forbade poverty lawyers from engaging in political activities or giving legal advice on controversial political issues such as abortion, the draft, military desertion, school desegregation, and homosexual rights. With the political impact of the program neutralized, it picked up considerable support for its strictly legal services. By 1978 it had a budget of $205 million and 3,200 lawyers in 700 offices around the country.[38] The Reagan administration sought to eliminate the program, but to date Congress has not yet complied.

Other Social Services

In addition to the above programs, state and local governments also provide a wide variety of other social services, such as child day care, adoption, homemaker services for the elderly, and child-protection services. Federal involvement in these programs is traced to the 1975 Title XX amendment to the Social Security Act, which established a social services block grant. State discretion under the block grant was further expanded by the Omnibus Budget Reconciliation Act of 1981, which reduced federal funds for the twelve main social services by 20 percent. States now no longer have to match the federal funds in order to receive federal aid for the Title XX Social Services.[39]

Health Care Policies: The Intergovernmental System in Practice

State and local governments have traditionally maintained public health departments to curb communicable diseases and to promote the general public health. Additionally, counties in metropolitan areas have maintained large public hospitals where needy persons could go for emergency care.

A Growing State and Local Government Role

In recent years, the state and local government role in health care has expanded far beyond traditional roles. In most instances the state and local expansion occurred as a response to new federal programs. One of the first was the Hill-Burton Act of 1946, which provided funds for hospital construction. Later amendments to this act provided federal funds for rehabilitation facilities and nursing homes. Federal funds went to both public and private facilities.

As public and private health care facilities expanded, the states saw themselves forced into a much stronger regulatory role. A major consequence of the Hill-Burton Act, for example, was the overbuilding of hospital capacity and bed space, thus contributing to the inflation of health care costs. As the cartoon on p. 360 implies, the public pays for the extra bed space whether the beds are used or not. In order to gain better control over hospital construction costs, most states have passed certificate-of-need laws. These require any organization to get state certification that the new construction is actually needed before it can add to its hospital, nursing home, or clinic, or before it can buy expensive diagnostic equipment. Allowing states this much regulatory control is commonplace in the 1980s, but it was unheard of a few decades ago.

State and local governments are also heavily involved in the direct provision of health care services to the poor. This role expanded dramatically after the passage of the Medicaid Act in 1965. Medicaid must not be confused with its partner, Medicare; the two are very different. **Medicare** is a health insurance program for elderly people of all income levels. **Medicaid** provides medical services for people who cannot afford health care on their own. All public assistance recipients (AFDC, SSI, GPA) are eligible for Medicaid, as are the aged who cannot afford the Medicare premiums. Under Medicaid,

Source: Jerry Fearing, *Saint Paul Dispatch*, September 21, 1977.

states are required to provide eight basic health services, and they may add up to seventeen other services if they choose. A cost-sharing formula is scaled to the state's per-capita income. Thus the thirteen richest states split Medicaid costs equally with the federal government, whereas the poorest state, Mississippi, pays only 23 percent.[40]

Issues for the 1990s

As more and more government funds have gone to health care, a number of issues have surfaced that will plague governments at all levels throughout the balance of the 1990s. First is the skyrocketing inflation of health care costs. In 1985 health care expenditures totaled $425 billion and consumed 10.7 percent of the GNP, up from only 5.3 percent of the GNP in 1960.[41] So expensive has health care become that some health care specialists have begun discussing the idea of rationing health care in order to curb costs.[42] In the face of these rising costs, state governments have come under pressure to regulate the rates that health care producers (doctors, hospitals, nursing homes, and so forth) charge insurance companies and that the insurance companies pass on to their policyholders in the form of higher premiums.

A second issue is **catastrophic health insurance.** Some illnesses can run up medical bills of twenty or thirty thousand dollars that normal health insurance will not cover. Destitute people have Medicaid to cover such costs, but working and middle-income people would have to lose their entire life savings and become destitute before they could qualify for Medicaid. To cope with this problem, some states now require insurance companies to make catastrophic health insurance available to all their policyholders. For persons not covered by private plans, some states have state-run funds.

A third issue is malpractice insurance. As juries began awarding damages of several hundred thousand dollars to people who sued physicians for malpractice, insurance companies raised their malpractice insurance rates. California doctors retaliated by withholding medical services rather than paying the higher rates. This forced California and most other states to adopt some form of malpractice insurance reform. The most far-reaching was Indiana's, which set up arbitration panels to process claims and limited damage awards to $500,000.

A fourth major issue has arisen over the rapid growth of prepaid health plans called **Health Maintenance Organizations (HMOs).** In return for a prepaid monthly fee, an HMO acts as an insurance company to cover subscribers' bills and provides clinic use without additional charges. Since all expenses are prepaid, the HMO has a strong financial incentive to emphasize preventive medical care. By 1970, thirty states had passed laws that effectively prohibited the formation of HMOs. But federal legislation in 1973 required employers in all states to offer HMO coverage as an optional health plan if an HMO existed in the region. This law sparked a rapid growth in HMOs so that by 1984 there were 310 serving about 6 percent of the population.[43]

Finally, if the AIDs disease spreads as extensively as current projections suggest it will, large portions of state health budgets will be consumed just caring for indigent AIDs patients. In addition to these major issues, in the 1990s state governments will try to reform their health care licensing procedures; to seek more effective programs for alcoholism, drug abuse, mental retardation, emotional disturbances, and occupational safety and health; and to allow advertising of health care services. The primary battlegrounds for most of these conflicts will be the state legislatures, the state health boards, and the substate health systems agencies.

Reforming Social Welfare

The American public exhibits a schizophrenic view of social welfare programs. National surveys find broad support for government aid to helpless people, but the *word* "welfare" is greeted with overwhelming hostility. A good example of this schizophrenic view was seen in a 1977 *New York Times*/CBS poll that found that 58 percent of the people did not approve of government welfare programs.[44] Yet when asked if they would support a program to help poor people buy food at reduced prices, an implicit reference to the food stamp program, 81 percent of the people said yes. When asked if they would support financial aid for children in low-income, one-parent homes, an implicit reference to the AFDC program, 81 percent again said yes. And when asked if they would support paying health costs for poor people, an implicit reference to the Medicaid program, 82 percent said yes.

One possible reason for the general public mistrust of welfare is the widespread publicity given to many abuses committed in various programs. *Some* welfare recipients—about 5.5 percent of AFDC recipients, according to federal calculations[45]—have fraudulently taken benefits to which they were not legally entitled. These well-publicized frauds tarnish the reputations of the 95 percent of welfare recipients who do have a legal claim to their benefits. Perhaps another 5 percent are overpaid, and overpayments of all sorts add up to about $1 billion per year.[46]

Not only are abuses in social welfare programs widely publicized, but the programs are an administrative nightmare. A large number of agencies is needed just to administer the many different programs. At the federal level, social welfare policymaking is handled by twelve different Congressional subcommittees and at least four executive departments or agencies (HHS, HUD, USDA, VA).[47] At the state and local levels, welfare administration is decentralized to several different subcommittees in each of the 99 separate houses of the state legislatures, 3,000 counties, and at least that many bureaucratic agencies at the state, local, and regional levels.

Because of the unpopular image of welfare, the well-publicized abuses, the administrative complexities in implementing welfare policies, and the widely divergent benefit levels from one state to another, welfare reform has been promoted for years. The three most significant attempts to deal with welfare took place in the 1960s, the 1970s, and the early 1980s, respectively.

The 1960s: War on Poverty

The Lyndon Johnson administration (1963–1969) did not really have a welfare reform plan; instead, Johnson proposed a war on poverty itself. Once poverty was eliminated, the need for welfare programs could decrease. The war on poverty had two complementary thrusts. First, social service programs were massively expanded. Second, the poor were encouraged to organize to gain political influence and to fight their own poverty.

The Great Society years saw dramatic increases in funding for the transfer payment and social service programs discussed earlier. Some programs, such as Medicare, Medicaid, and legal services, were creations of the 1960s. The keystone of the war on poverty was the **Economic Opportunity Act of 1965,** which created the Office of Economic Opportunity to conduct experiments in social services and to coordinate all the poverty-related efforts of the agencies of the federal government. In 1966 the model cities program was created to concentrate and coordinate federal programs in specific neighborhoods of 150 selected major cities. However, neither the model cities nor the economic opportunity programs were successful in coordinating the poverty efforts at either the federal or the local level.[48]

Perhaps the most significant impact was their requirement that the people affected by the programs participate in drawing up the program plans. In each locality receiving War-on-Poverty funds, a community action agency (CAA) was created to draft a community action plan for those communities. The net effect was to stimulate community organizing efforts in poor neighborhoods. In particular, the CAAs developed community leadership in black neighborhoods, provided jobs for poor and middle-class blacks, and organized residents of those neighborhoods to battle for better services from the city government, to vote, to combat absentee landlords, and to become politically active.

Although these social programs did not eliminate poverty, it would be a mistake to assume that the War on Poverty failed.[49] The social programs of the 1960s produced very significant consequences. They put more economic resources into the hands of more poor people, and they were a major factor in cutting in half the percentage of people living in poverty.[50]

The 1970s: Aborted Attempts at Income Maintenance

President Richard M. Nixon proposed a plan to maintain everybody's income above a subsistence level. He labeled this **income maintenance** proposal the **Family Assistance Plan (FAP).** A four-person family with no income would receive $1,600. For each dollar the family earned, the government's payment would decrease by fifty cents. When the family's earnings reached $3,920, the government benefits would be phased out completely.

Although this was a truly revolutionary approach to welfare reform, it never became law. Liberals, who had previously pushed for income maintenance as the ideal tool for income redistribution, feared that FAP would phase out other major programs, such as food stamps.[51] They complained that Nixon's proposed benefit levels were too low and would reduce overall welfare benefit levels in most states.[52] Conservatives objected that FAP would reward poor families for not working. Social work professionals had no incentive to support FAP, since it would reduce the need for AFDC caseworkers. Finally, there was no broad public support for the concept of income maintenance. A *New York Times*/CBS poll in 1977 found that 50 percent of the people opposed a guaranteed minimum income and only 44 percent supported it.[53] Unable to build the political support needed for his plan, Nixon himself grew cool to it. A version of it twice passed the House of Representatives, but it died in the Senate.

When Jimmy Carter became president in 1977, he resurrected the income maintenance concept and proposed a work benefit and income support program to replace the existing AFDC, SSI, and food stamp programs.[54] Carter's plan provided a mandatory work requirement for adults classified as able to work. To ensure an adequate supply of employment opportunities, he proposed an extensive expansion of public service jobs at the minimum wage. And to help out the working poor, he proposed a cash payment to supplement the earned incomes of workers whose wages were so low as to keep them below the poverty level. For a family of four, a basic work benefit of $2,300 would be paid if the family's total outside income was less than $3,800. For each dollar earned above $3,800, the work benefit payment would be reduced by fifty cents until it was completely phased out at $8,400. The same $8,400 maximum in income support would also be available for families of four that lacked an adult classified as able to work.

Although Carter's proposal had considerable appeal to the advocates of welfare reform, the plan immediately ran into the same kind of opposition that had killed Nixon's family assistance plan earlier in the decade. The benefit levels were attacked as too high by the chairmen of the House and Senate tax committees[55] and too low by both the AFL-CIO and the congressional black caucus.[56] The mandatory work provisions were criticized. Carter's public service jobs, it was said, would have people earning the minimum wage working side by side with people who earned six or seven dollars per hour. Labor leaders also feared that the program might give local governments an incentive to fire their regular employees and hire them back at the minimum wage with federal funds. Faced with this opposition, Congress again aborted the income maintenance approach and instead expanded the food stamp program.[57]

The 1980s: Curbing the Welfare Rolls

When Ronald Reagan became president in 1981, he took an approach to welfare that differed dramatically from the War on Poverty and income maintenance approaches of earlier years. Reagan charged that welfare programs sapped people of their will to become self-supporting,[58] and he believed that plenty of work was available for those who truly wanted to work. In contrast to Nixon and Carter, who had sought to provide incentives for the working poor, Reagan's welfare reforms hit the working poor the hardest.[59] Reagan's plan had the following elements:

1. Sharp cuts in most social services and in-kind assistance programs, in the hope of pushing those recipients into the job market.
2. Workfare, or the requirement that a person be dropped from government assistance programs if he or she refused to seek and accept work.
3. Protection of most benefit levels in the social security pension plan, which was the largest safety net in Reagan's program.
4. Provision of sharp income-tax cuts for middle- and upper-income groups, to spur the investment and spending that would produce an economic recovery. This recovery would provide jobs for the people being displaced from the government assistance programs.

Most of these measures were reflected in the 1981 Budget Omnibus Reconciliation Act and the 1981 Economic Recovery Tax Act, which have been discussed previously in reference to the programs listed in Table 13–3. There were sharp cuts in most of those programs. Benefit levels were reduced, and eligibility requirements were stiffened. Figure 13–4 shows that these measures, combined with the 1982–1984 income tax cuts, had a sharp negative impact on low-income households.

One of the most debated parts of Reagan's approach to welfare was the workfare requirement that welfare recipients work off their benefits. In fact, a work requirement (called Work Incentive Program, or WIN) had been in place since 1967. Under the WIN program all AFDC recipients with children over the age of six must register with their state employment agencies, seek jobs from provided leads, and accept any jobs that are offered. In fact, however, WIN was a failure. A 1975 study found that only one-sixth of all those registered in the WIN program that year received training or found permanent employment.[60]

What makes the workfare of the 1980s different from the WIN program is the recognition at the state level that welfare mothers can only be successful in the job market if certain conditions are met: There must be jobs available for them, they must have the skills and attitudes to win the jobs, and they must have day-care help (which currently costs $50 to $70 per week per child). The pioneers in seeking to meet these conditions are California's GAIN plan (Greater Avenues to Independence) and Massachusetts' ET plan (Employment and Training). GAIN was passed in California through a fascinating political compromise between liberal Democrats (who agreed to the conservative demand for a mandatory work requirement) and conservative Republicans (who agreed to the liberal demand for putting up money for training and child-care expenses). The result has been an elaborate program

Figure 13–4. The Impact of Tax and Budget Cuts on Household Income

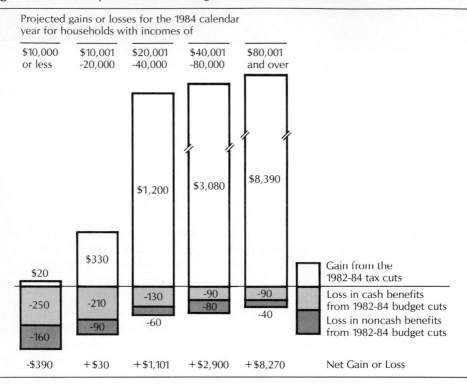

Projected gains or losses for the 1984 calendar year for households with incomes of

$10,000 or less	$10,001 -20,000	$20,001 -40,000	$40,001 -80,000	$80,001 and over	
		$1,200	$3,080	$8,390	
	$330				
$20					Gain from the 1982-84 tax cuts
-250	-210	-130	-90 / -80	-90	Loss in cash benefits from 1982-84 budget cuts
-160	-90	-60		-40	Loss in noncash benefits from 1982-84 budget cuts
-$390	+$30	+$1,101	+$2,900	+$8,270	Net Gain or Loss

Source: Congressional Budget Office, *The Combined Effects of Major Changes in Federal Taxes and Spending Programs Since 1981* (Washington, D.C.: Congressional Budget Office, April 1984).

begun in 1985 that screens participants into appropriate training programs, creates "job clubs" to teach them how to find jobs, and gives them money for child care while they are in training and for their first year on the job.[61] Workfare programs on the GAIN or ET model are not cheap. The Massachusetts ET budget is four times as costly as its previous AFDC costs.[62] But the state expects these costs to be more than made up by moving welfare recipients into permanent jobs so they will no longer depend on public assistance and will instead be paying income taxes to the state.

Whether these fond hopes will materialize is too early to know. Most state workfare schemes, unlike those of California and Massachusetts, seem aimed more at making welfare recipients work off their benefits in menial public service jobs than at providing the costly supportive services to help the recipients become truly independent.[63] And in the last analysis, even if the supportive training and child-care services are provided, the number of welfare recipients who can be moved into permanent, full-time jobs depends on the strength of the national economy and the number of jobs that are created. In the meantime, California's GAIN plan and Massachusetts' ET will be closely watched in the hope that a carefully crafted work/welfare program can lead large numbers of people to independence.

Social Welfare and the Political Economy

In the past decade, profound changes in the American economy have affected state and local social welfare policies in important ways. As noted in previous chapters, the major changes are three. First is the shift from an economy based on heavy, so-called smokestack industries (such as automobiles, steel, and rubber) to one based on services, communications, and high-technology industry. Second, and reinforcing this first change, is the growing challenge of foreign competition to American basic industry. This challenge has been most dramatic in recent years in the automobile industry, where foreign competition rose from a minimal share of the American automobile market to capturing nearly a third of it by the early 1980s. These two developments provoked high unemployment rates in the Northeast and Midwest states, where much of America's heavy industry was located. The third economic trend has been the rise of the Sunbelt economies and the strains put on the Frostbelt economies of the Northeast and Midwest.

These economic developments are related to poverty and social welfare policies in some important ways. Because of the economic dislocations mentioned above and the recessionary environment that prevailed in the first three years of the decade, the 1980s have seen sharp increases in the percentage of people in poverty and sharp increases in the demands placed on unemployment compensation and other social assistance programs. But just as the needs grew for those programs, the federal government, under the direction of the Reagan administration, began cutting back on the federal role in financing social welfare. As we saw in Chapter 3, this administration also sought, with some success, to increase state responsibility for social welfare.

As these developments progressed in the early 1980s, many states found themselves strapped to meet the welfare demands placed upon them. The situation was perhaps worst in the old industrial states of the Northeast and Midwest, where the economic dislocations of the early 1980s appeared to be creating conditions of permanent impoverishment for hundreds of thousands of workers whose jobs failed to return, even when the recessions ended. To the extent that those displaced workers remained in the Frostbelt, they put a drain on the social service and welfare budgets of those states. Many, however, chose to migrate to other regions, especially the Sunbelt, in search of employment. But the large numbers of marginally employable people arriving in the South and Southwest overloaded the job markets in those regions as well, and soon this began increasing the pressure on the welfare and social services budgets of those states. Even the energy-rich states, such as Texas, Oklahoma, and Alaska, were not immune to the economic dislocations of the times. As oil revenues declined in the 1980s, those states, too, found it more difficult to meet all the commitments that had been made when revenues were rolling in.

No one, of course, can predict with any certainty whether the trends of the past will carry into the future. A strong and sustained economic recovery would alleviate many of these problems for the political economies of the states. But the fundamental economic changes taking place seem likely to continue to threaten the economic status of blue-collar workers and the lower-middle-income groups. As we saw earlier, these groups are receiving a smaller share of the national income than they did a decade earlier. For these reasons, unless and until the American economy regains a competitive edge in the international economy, individual state and local governments in this country are very likely to find their social welfare budgets squeezed very tightly for some years to come.

Summary

1. The official United States poverty income line is based on the amount of money needed to purchase food on a modest food plan. The percentage of people below the poverty line declined from nearly 25 percent in 1960 to about 12 percent in the early 1970s. In the 1980s it began to rise again.

2. Leftist and rightist theorists present conflicting views on the causes of poverty and the ways that government should deal with poverty.

3. The implementation of welfare policies is done on an intergovernmental basis, with complicated interactions among federal, state, and local governments. This decentralized process of implementation has led to differing benefit levels from one state to another and has made administering welfare policies rationally and efficiently very difficult.

4. Welfare benefit levels vary from state to state in part because of differences in affluence and levels of political competition, the militancy of the working and lower classes, and differences in political cultures.

5. The major social welfare programs can be grouped under three general headings: (1) social insurance transfer payments, (2) cash transfer payments that are not social insurance, and (3) in-kind assistance programs.

6. The most costly welfare policies are probably the health care policies. A number of volatile health care issues will confront the state governments in the 1990s, and the federal government will continue to be confronted with the question of creating a national health insurance system.

7. Despite the administrative deficiencies of existing welfare programs and despite popular dissatisfaction with the general concept of welfare, attempts to reform the welfare system by consolidating the categorical programs under an income maintenance plan and by nationalizing more of the program failed consistently during the 1970s. In the 1980s, the Reagan administration succeeded in sharply reducing spending for most social welfare programs, increasing eligibility requirements, and decreasing benefit levels.

Key Terms

Absolute deprivation A measurement of poverty that says that one is deprived of the necessities of life if one falls below a specific income line.

Aid for Families with Dependent Children (AFDC) A program that provides cash assistance for single parents without income but with dependent children.

Catastrophic health insurance An insurance program that provides protection against financial loss due to extremely expensive and long-duration illnesses, such as some forms of cancer.

Culture of poverty A term used to describe a combination of psychological traits among many people who are permanently poor. These traits include cynicism toward the social system, lack of hope for escape from their plight, inability to defer gratification, and inability to plan for the future.

Economic Opportunity Act of 1965 The fundamental legislation of President Johnson's War on Poverty. It created the Office of Economic Opportunity to conduct experiments in social services and to coordinate all the poverty-related efforts of the agencies of the federal government.

Family Assistance Plan (FAP) An income maintenance proposal of the Nixon administration that did not pass Congress.

Food stamp program A program that provides vouchers to low-income people to help them buy food.

Gross national product (GNP) A nation's total output of goods and services.

Health maintenance organization (HMO) An organization that provides medical clinics and prepaid health care, with an emphasis on preventive medicine.

Horatio Alger An author who grew rich writing stories about boys who climbed to the top of the social ladder. The term "Horatio Alger myth" is synonymous with upward social mobility.

Hypothesis A scientific term that refers to an educated guess about the factors that explain some phenomenon.

Income maintenance An approach to social welfare that seeks to provide cash assistance that will maintain people's income above the poverty line.

Indexation The practice of adjusting income tax brackets to rise with the cost of living. Also refers to the practice of making benefit levels in certain programs adjustable for changes in the inflation rate.

In-kind assistance Social programs, such as medical aid, that provide help that has a cash value, even though the help is not received in the form of cash.

Laissez-faire The concept that government should leave the economy to the forces of the marketplace and should not seek to regulate the economy.

Legal services program (LSP) A program that provides legal aid to poor people in civil cases, but not in criminal cases.

Means test A test that makes eligibility for benefits dependent on a person's ability to show need, usually by falling under a specified income level.

Medicaid A program that provides medical assistance for people who cannot afford health care on their own.

Medicare A government-run health insurance program for elderly people of all income levels.

OASDHI Old Age, Survivors, Disability, and Health Insurance. The fundamental social insurance programs for retirement, disability, and Medicare set up under the Social Security Act.

Poverty line The federal government's official definition of poverty, based on the assumption that three times the income needed to buy food on the modest food plan constitutes poverty.

Relative deprivation A measurement of poverty that says that a person can only be considered poor in relation to the rest of the people in a society.

Social Darwinism An application to the social sphere of Darwin's theory of natural selection and survival of the fittest. Accordingly, Social Darwinists oppose social welfare policies.

Social insurance A societal program in which one pays money into a government-sponsored trust fund and draws benefits from that fund later, when the person becomes eligible.

Social mobility Movement upward or downward in society's class structure.

Social Security Act of 1935 The original legislative authority for much of the social welfare programs existing today.

Transfer payment A direct payment of government money to individuals.

War on Poverty President Lyndon Johnson's Great Society approach to poverty. Johnson vastly expanded social service programs in the hopes of eliminating poverty.

References

1. Robert E. Spiller et al., eds., *Literary History of the United States: Bibliography* (New York: Macmillan, 1974), p. 226.

2. Bureau of the Census, *Statistical Abstract of the United States: 1982-83* (Washington, D.C.: U.S. Government Printing Office, 1982), p. 256.

3. Studs Terkel, *Division Street: America* (New York: Avon Books, 1967), pp. 271–272.

4. Ibid., pp. 39–46.

5. Commentary on Tally Jackson are extracted from Elliot Liebow, *Tally's Corner* (Boston: Little, Brown and Co., 1967).

6. For critiques of the methods of drawing a poverty line, see Lee Rainwater, "Economic Inequality and the Credit Income Tax," *Working Papers for a New Society* 1, no. 1 (Spring 1973): 50–61; Michael Harrington, "The Betrayal of the Poor," *Atlantic* (January 1970): pp. 71–72; Martin Rein, "Problems in the Definition and Measurement of Poverty," *Poverty in America*, rev. ed., eds. Louis Ferman et al. (Ann Arbor: University of Michigan Press, 1968), pp. 123–125; Daniel M. Gordon, "Trends in Poverty," *Problems in Political Economy: An Urban Perspective*, 2d ed. (Lexington, Mass.: D.C. Heath, 1977), pp. 297–298. Also see Alan Haber, "Poverty Budgets: How Much Is Enough?" *Poverty and Human Resources Abstracts* 1, no. 3 (1966): 6.

7. Timothy M. Smeeding, *Alternative Methods for Valuing Selected In-Kind Transfer Benefits and Measuring Their Effect on Poverty* (Washington, D.C.: U.S. Bureau of the Census, 1982).

8. Thomas R. Dye, *Politics in States and Communities*, 3d ed. (Englewood Cliffs, N.J.: Prentice-Hall, 1977), p. 439.

9. For a review of this suggestion, see Gordon, "Trends in Poverty," pp. 299–300. Also see Victor R. Fuchs, "Redefining Poverty and Redistributing Income," *Public Interest* 8 (Summer 1967): 91.

10. Calculated from data on family incomes in Bureau of the Census, *Current Population Reports: Money Income of Households, Families and Persons in the United States: 1984*, Series P-60, no. 134 (Washington, D.C.: U.S. Government Printing Office, 1986), p. 29.

11. This study was conducted by the House Ways and Means Committee. See *New York Times*, October 20, 1985, p. 1.

12. These were two conclusions of a 1986 study by Congress's Joint Economic Committee. See *New York Times*, December 22, 1986, p. 1.

13. James N. Morgan et al., *Five Thousand American Families: Patterns of Economic Progress* (Ann Arbor: University of Michigan, Institute for Social Research, 1974).

14. Bureau of the Census, *Current Population Reports: Characteristics of the Population Below the Poverty Level: 1977*, Series P-60, no. 119 (Washington, D.C.: U.S. Government Printing Office, 1979), p. 4.

15. Liebow, *Tally's Corner*, p. 63.

16. From a study by the Congressional Office of Technology Assessment. See *New York Times*, February 7, 1986, p. 1.

17. See *New York Times*, May 20, 1984, p. 35.

18. Howard M. Wachtel, "Looking at Poverty from a Radical Perspective," *Review of Radical Political Economics* 3, no. 3 (Summer 1971): 7.

19. Edward C. Banfield, *The Heavenly City* (Boston: Little, Brown and Company, 1970), pp. 125–126.

20. See Herbert Spencer, *Social Statics* (London: John Chapman, 1851).

21. Charles Murray, *Losing Ground* (New York: Basic Books, 1984), p. 9.

22. Banfield, *The Unheavenly City*, p. 118.

23. A summary of ideological orientations to poverty is presented by David M. Gordon in his *Problems in Political Economy: An Urban Perspective*, 2d ed. (Lexington, Mass.: D.C. Heath, 1977), pp. 272–281.

24. See especially Thomas R. Dye, *Politics, Economics and the Public* (Chicago: Rand McNally, 1966); Richard E. Dawson and James A. Robinson, "Interpreting Competition, Economic Variables and Welfare Policies in the American States," *Journal of Politics* 25, no. 2 (May 1963): 265–289; and Gary L. Tompkins, "A Causal Model of State Welfare Expenditures," *Journal of Politics* 37, no. 2 (May 1975): 392–416. These and more recent studies, however, are subject to important methodological criticism for often lacking coordination between the time periods in which they gather their data on policy results, party competition, and levels of affluence. See Harvey J. Tucker, "Interparty Competition in the American States: One More Time," *American Politics Quarterly* 10, no. 1 (January 1982): 93–116; and Harvey J. Tucker, "It's About Time: The Uses of Time in Cross-sectional State Policy Research," *American Journal of Political Science* 26, no. 1 (February 1982): 176–196.

25. See Frances Fox Piven and Richard Cloward, *Regulating the Poor: The Functions of Public Welfare* (New York: Pantheon, 1971), especially pp. 285–338.

26. An excellent review of the relative influence of economic and political variables on public policy is Jack Treadway, *Public Policy-Making in the American States* (New York: Praeger, 1985), pp. 131–176.

27. For an excellent summary of the major social welfare programs, see "Social Security Programs in the United States," *Social Security Bulletin* 49, no. 1 (January 1986): 5–61.

28. On the definitions of welfare, see Gilbert Steiner, *The State of Welfare* (Washington, D.C.: The Brookings Institution, 1971), pp. 1–4.

29. *New York Times,* July 19, 1982, p. 1.

30. Bureau of the Census, *Statistical Abstract of the United States, 1987* (Washington, D.C.: U.S. Government Printing Office, 1986), p. 363.

31. Teh-Wei Hu and Norman Knaub, "Effects of Cash and In-Kind Welfare Payments on Family Expenditures," *Policy Analysis* 2, no. 1 (Winter 1976): 81–82.

32. Office of Management and Budget, *Budget of the Government of the United States for FY 1978* (Washington, D.C.: U.S. Government Printing Office, 1977), p. 172.

33. *Statistical Abstract of the United States, 1986,* p. 382.

34. *Congressional Quarterly Almanac, 1977,* pp. 458–462.

35. *New York Times,* May 24, 1986, p. 6.

36. *Statistical Abstract of the United States, 1986,* p. 123.

37. *Congressional Quarterly Almanac, 1981.*

38. *New York Times,* July 31, 1976, p. E-4.

39. *The Book of the States: 1982-83,* p. 504.

40. Ibid., p. 513.

41. Jeffrey L. Lake and James T. Dimas, "State Health Agency Programs," *The Book of the States 1984-1985* (Lexington, Ky.: Council of State Governments, 1984), pp. 403–406.

42. On costs, see *Statistical Abstract of the United States, 1987,* p. 84. On rationing, see *Wall Street Journal,* January 9, 1987, p. 6.

43. *Statistical Abstract of the United States, 1986*, p. 102.

44. *New York Times*, August 3, 1977, p. 1.

45. Office of Management and Budget, *FY 1978 Budget*, p. 172.

46. *Minneapolis Tribune*, March 13, 1980, p. B-8.

47. Steiner, *The State of Welfare*, p. 14.

48. See James E. Anderson, "Coordinating the War on Poverty," *Policy Studies Journal* 2, no. 3 (Spring 1974): 174–178; and James L. Sundquist, *Making Federalism Work: A Study of Program Coordination at the Community Level* (Washington, D.C.: Brookings Institution, 1969).

49. This argument is made by Sar A. Levitan and Robert Taggart, "Great Society Did Succeed," *Political Science Quarterly* 91 (Winter 1976–77): 601–618.

50. See John E. Schwarz, *America's Hidden Success: A Reassessment of Twenty Years of Public Policy* (New York: W. W. Norton & Co., 1983), especially pp. 57–59.

51. Ellen Kelman, "Welfare Reform," *Dissent* 24 (Spring 1977): 126–128.

52. Lester C. Thurow, "The Political Economy of Income Redistribution Policies," *Annals of the American Academy of Political and Social Science* 409 (September 1973): 146–155.

53. *New York Times*, August 3, 1977, p. 1.

54. See President Jimmy Carter's welfare reform message in *New York Times*, August 7, 1977, pp. 1, 40.

55. Senate Finance Committee Chairman Russell Long and House Ways and Means Committee Chairman Al Ullman, *New York Times*, September 16, 1977, pp. 4–13; December 11, 1977, p. 43.

56. *New York Times*, September 16, 1977, p. 13.

57. *Congressional Quarterly Almanac 1977*, pp. 458–462.

58. In his weekly radio address of February 15, 1986, Reagan blamed welfare programs for teenage pregnancies, family breakups, worsening poverty, and the creation of a permanent state of dependency among the poor. See *New York Times*, February 16, 1986, p. 27a.

59. Bob Kuttner and Phylis Freeman, "Women to the Workhouse," *Working Papers* (November/December 1982): 23. Based on the example of a woman supporting herself and three children on work earnings of $544 per month, Kuttner and Freeman show how Reagan's cuts in AFDC and food stamp work incentives would reduce this woman's spendable income. Prior to the Reagan program she would have $742 per month to spend; under the Reagan program that would be reduced to $558. This was only $27 more than she could have received if she quit work and relied exclusively on the $531 she could get with AFDC and food stamps.

60. Irene Lurie, "Work Requirements in Income-Conditioned Transfer Programs," *Social Service Review* 52 (December 1978): 551–565.

61. David L. Kirk, "The California Work/Welfare Scheme," *The Public Interest* 83 (Spring 1986): 34–48.

62. Joe Davidson, "Welfare Revised: More States Now Ask Recipients of Aid to Train and Take Jobs," *Wall Street Journal*, July 23, 1986, p. 1.

63. See Bradley R. Schiller, "Workfare Not Such a Sweeping Success," *Wall Street Journal*, May 14, 1986, p. 24.

Chapter 14
Education

Chapter Preview

One of the most important services provided by state and local governments is public education. That service spends more tax dollars and employs more people than any other state or local policy area. In the 1980s, the public school systems came under widespread criticism, and as we move to the 1990s much of education politics focuses on improving the quality of education. We will examine this phenomenon in this chapter by studying:

1. How state, local, and federal governments work together in providing public education.
2. How political values affect the role people think education should play in society.
3. How state and local governments cope with major educational problems today.
4. How state and local governments have responded in the 1980s to the demands for educational reform.
5. How education is linked to the political economies of states and communities.

Let us begin with a look at two people who made their way through the educational system, Edward Donohue and Herman the Pushout.

Introduction

Public education in the United States has traditionally been viewed as the means by which people can learn skills and attitudes that will make them employable, enrich their lives, or help them move up socially. But it did not work out that way for Edward Donohue and Herman the Pushout.

374

Edward Donohue, white, sued the Copiague, New York, school district in 1977 for graduating him the previous year even though he was functionally illiterate. Edward's reading ability was so poor that he failed his driver's test; he could not read the instructions for the written examination. When he bought clothes, he had to have clerks in the store read him the labels on the clothes. When he applied for jobs, he had to bring the application blanks home so his mother could fill them out for him.

Edward's teachers admitted to reporters that the high school followed an unwritten policy of pushing through potential problem children and trouble-makers rather than making them repeat courses in which they did unsatisfactory work. Teachers who failed too many students got informal reprimands from the principal. Problem students and those with special learning disabilities went unhelped. So Edward passed enough courses to graduate, although he apparently had only a faint idea of what the courses covered. He could not even write the traditional few words and an autograph in the other graduates' yearbooks.[1]

Herman the Pushout, black, was transferred to a desegregated school at the age of ten in 1966. Pursuant to federal court orders, the black school he attended in North Carolina was merged with a nearby white school. The black principal and administrators lost their jobs, since the new, desegregated school would be staffed by white administrators and teachers. Herman did not mingle well with the white children and had trouble at the new school. His new white teacher told him in front of the class that she hoped he would be executed someday. The white boys went unpunished for calling him "nigger," but he was often punished for fighting with them. While still in grade school he got into deep trouble for allegedly writing a note of affection to a white girl. Local segregationists wanted him jailed for that, and school district psychologists told him his behavior was not normal.

Herman did not do well in class. He finally quit high school and never graduated. Some would say that Herman dropped out. Others would argue that he was pushed out by a hostile and alien school system that was unable to cope humanely with the throes of desegregation. By the late 1970s Herman, in his early twenties, worked as an unskilled laborer when he could find a job. Mostly he drifted about and spent time with other male friends who were also unskilled laborers and high school dropouts.[2]

Edward Donohue and Herman the Pushout illustrate the human dimension of two of the most serious problems facing public education today—quality of education and desegregation. Implicit in these problems is a third—finding and distributing the financial resources for public education. These and a complex of problems involving discipline, safety, violence, and drugs have been identified by Gallup polls as the education problems that have caused the most concern to American people during the 1980s.[3]

The blackboard reads, repeatedly in cursive, diminishing line by line:

I will do my best to improve my methods and upgrade the system.
I will do my best to improve my methods and upgrade the system.
I will do my best to improve my methods and upgrade the system.
I will do my best to improve my methods and upgrade the system.
I will do my best to improve my methods and upgrade the system.
I will do my best to improve my methods and up—
I will do my best to improve my methods.
I will do my best to improve my
I will do my best to

LORCHER 1983 CHICAGO TRIBUNE

Source: Lorcher. Reprinted by permission. Tribune Media Services.

These concerns came dramatically to public prominence in the mid-1980s. The **National Commission on Excellence in Education** in 1983 issued *A Nation at Risk,* a devastating report charging that now, for the first time in American history, the average school graduate is less well educated than the average graduate a generation earlier, and that American students performed poorly in comparison to the students of other industrialized nations. "If an unfriendly foreign power had attempted to impose on America the mediocre educational performance that exists today," reported the commission, "we might well have viewed it as an act of war. As it stands, we have allowed this to happen to ourselves. . . . We have, in effect, been committing an act of unthinking, unilateral educational disarmament."[4] As a consequence of this report, education suddenly became an issue, both at the national level and in the states.

In this chapter we will examine these educational concerns. We will first look at the tradition of local control over education and the conflicts growing out of the increasing state and federal responsibilities. Second, education will be viewed from the left and right philosophical perspectives. Third, the way governments cope with the main problems of education will be examined in detail. Fourth, we will explore developments in educational reform since the 1983 publication of *A Nation at Risk*. Last, we will discuss the role of education in the political economy.

State, Local, and Federal Roles in Education

Local Roles

The dominant role of local government in public education is shown in Table 14–1. Most public schools are organized into local school districts that are independent of other units of local government—cities, towns, or counties. These **independent school districts** are governed by local **boards of education,** which are popularly elected in about 85 percent of cases. Only three public school systems are organized at the state level without any local districts. The local school boards establish local school district policies, set the budget, and decide the tax levy.

In practice, the initiative in these matters usually is taken by the local **superintendent of schools,** not the school boards. The superintendent proposes policies and budgets to the board, sets the school board meeting agendas, and presents the board with a limited number of options. The board members, who are rarely professional educators, usually lack the educational expertise to dominate their superintendents. An analysis of relations between superintendents and school boards in four states found that barely a third of the boards actively and successfully challenged their superintendents.[5]

Table 14–1. Organization of Public Education

Type of public school system	Number of systems	Public school enrollment (in thousands)
Independent school districts	14,851	35,614
Other school systems		
State (Hawaii, Alaska, Maine)[a]	24	176
County	578	3,420
Municipal	286	3,429
Township (and "town")	650	912
Subtotal for other school systems	1,538	7,938
Total for all states	16,389	43,551[b]

Source: Bureau of the Census, *1982 Census of Governments: Governmental Organization*, Vol. 1, *Governmental Organization* (Washington, D.C.: U.S. Government Printing Office, 1983), p. xv.

[a]Alaska administers twenty-two state-dependent school systems.

[b]Enrollment totals do not add up correctly because of rounding errors.

The Trend Toward Greater State Centralization

While local levels have traditionally been dominant in public education, centralization at the state level has increased. This is reflected in the decreasing number of local school districts—from over 127,000 in 1932 to 16,389 in 1982. Small districts with only a few dozen or a few hundred students lacked resources to finance modern laboratories, elaborate extracurricular activities, and the other expensive features of today's schools. Consequently, legislatures forced many small districts to consolidate. State centralization can also be seen in the increasing levels of state financial aid to local schools and in the increasing state-level concern with educational policies. As Table 14–2 shows, the percent of public education funded by the state has increased in recent years. The federal share increased steadily during the 1960s and 1970s, then dropped sharply during the Reagan years.

The keystone of state educational policymaking is the **state education agency (SEA)**. The SEA is composed of a state board of education, a chief state school officer the state calls a **commissioner** or **superintendent of education,** and a department of education. The state board of education adopts the overall educational policies for the state. It sets minimum high school graduation requirements. It legitimizes decisions made by the state department of education. It insulates the department from the governor, and it appoints the chief state school officer in half the states. Sixty percent of the state boards of education are appointed directly by the governor.

Although historically the SEAs have exercised little influence on local school districts, their influence has grown in recent years. The local school districts, the governor, and the legislature look to the SEA to provide educational leadership—to initiate new ideas, to ask for money, to see that local

Table 14–2. Centralization of Public School Finance

Level of government	Percent of public school expenditures financed				
	1960	1970	1975	1980	1985
Federal	4.4%	8.0%	9.0%	9.8%	6.2%
State	39.1	39.9	42.2	46.8	49.0
Local	56.5	52.1	48.8	43.4	44.8

Sources: Calculated from the Bureau of the Census, *Statistical Abstract of the United States: 1982–83* (Washington, D.C.: U.S. Government Printing Office, 1982), p. 154; *Statistical Abstract of the United States: 1986* (Washington, D.C.: U.S. Government Printing Office, 1985), p. 142.

districts carry out national and state policies, and to maintain a positive public image for public education. The SEA distributes the state foundation aids, sums awarded according to a formula set by the legislature (see pp. 389–390). It approves requests for categorical grants. It provides basic research and information to legislative committees that must deal with school problems. The more these other actors look to the SEAs for leadership and services, the more important the SEAs become.[6]

Federal Roles

The federal government has historically played a small role in public education. It now provides less than 10 percent of all public school funding, and it was not until 1965 that the federal government passed a broad program of aid to all public school districts (see Table 14–3).

The federal government's biggest impact on elementary and secondary education has come in two areas: desegregation and special programs for the disadvantaged.[7] Since desegregation will be discussed in detail later in this chapter, this section will focus on programs to help the disadvantaged.

The 1965 **Elementary and Secondary Education Act** Title I provided for **compensatory education** for disadvantaged children. In addition to Title I, the federal government during the 1960s initiated a number of other special programs. Head Start was designed to give culturally deprived children some preschool preparation for the first grade. Jobs Corps was begun with the Economic Opportunity Act of 1964 to give education, vocational training, and work experience to unemployed youths between ages sixteen and twenty-one. In 1976, Congress passed the Education for All Handicapped Children Act, which amounted to an educational bill of rights for the nation's eight million children with handicaps ranging from mental retardation to physical disability. According to a 1980 study, federal programs have been effective in improving the education of poor children.[8] In 1981, several of these categorical grants were consolidated under the **Education Consolidation and Improvement Act,** which reduced the amount of federal funds involved but increased the authority of states over how the funds would be spent.[9]

In an attempt to provide better coordination of federal educational programs and demonstrate a commitment to public education, Congress in 1979 created the cabinet-level Education Department. President Reagan sought to eliminate the department by converting it into a government foundation that would fund education projects but would lose the power to regulate schools and colleges.[10] This plan ran into opposition in Congress, however, and the department was not abolished.

Table 14–3. Federal Aid to Education

Before 1945

1785   Northwest Ordinance. Reserved one section of each township in the Northwest Territory for the endowment of schools.

1862   The Morrill Act. Provided grants of federal land to set up land-grant colleges for agriculture and mechanical arts.

1917   The Smith-Hughes Act. Provided federal grants for vocational education at the precollegiate level.

1944   The Servicemen's Readjustment Act (GI Bill of Rights). Provided educational benefits to World War II veterans. Later expanded to include Korean, Cold War, and Vietnam veterans.

Elementary and secondary education since 1945

1946   National school lunch and milk programs. Provided for lunches and milk to be served in public and private schools.

1950   Impacted-areas legislation. Provided special federal aid for school districts that were "impacted" with federal activities, for federal property, and for Indian reservations.

1958   National Defense Education Act (NDEA). Provided grants for equipment.

1965   Elementary and Secondary Education Act (ESEA). This act, plus its later amendments, set the framework for contemporary aid to education. Title I provided funds for compensatory education for children in poverty areas. Title II provided grants for library resources, books, and printed instructional material. Title III provided grants to stimulate innovative programs. Other titles funded educational research centers, attempted to strengthen state departments of education, encouraged programs for the mentally retarded and the physically handicapped.

1972   Emergency School Aid Act (ESAA). Authorized $2 billion to eliminate minority group segregation and discrimination at the elementary and secondary levels. The funds were intended principally for local school districts that had to incur added expenses in order to implement their desegregation plans.

1981   Education Consolidation and Improvement Act. Consolidated several categorical grants, including ESEA Title I, and gave states considerable discretion in deciding how these funds would be spent.

Higher education since 1945

1950   National Science Foundation (NSF) established. The NSF encouraged scientific research and the education of scientists. In the late 1960s, NSF's budget was greatly expanded, and it became an important source of assistance to graduate students and established scholars.

1958   National Defense Education Act (NDEA). Provided low-interest loans for college students and fellowships for graduate students.

1964   Work-study program established. Provided grants to colleges to pay 90 percent of the wages of students working part time at the college.

1965 National Endowments for the Arts and Humanities established (NEA and NEH). Established to stimulate the arts and humanities similar to the stimulus that NSF provided for science.

1965 Higher Education Act. This act, plus its later amendments, set the basic framework for federal aid to higher education. Title I provided matching grants for community service programs. Title II provided grants for library materials. Title III provided special aids for small colleges, especially black colleges. Title IV made provision for student financial assistance such as Upward Bound, scholarships, loans, work-study, and cooperative education. Title VI provided matching grants for equipment purchases. Title VII provided grants for college building construction. Other titles aided intercollege cooperation, graduate programs, community colleges, and clinical experience for law students.

1972 Basic Educational Opportunity Grant (later called Pell Grant) program started. Initiated federal assistance programs for college students.

1978 Middle Income Student Assistance Act. Extended guaranteed student loans to all students regardless of income.

1981 Omnibus Budget Reconciliation Act. Sharply reduced amount of federal aid available for student grants and loans, established a means test, and reduced the number of eligible students.

Postsecondary Public Education

At the postsecondary level, the most significant institutions are the state universities, the state college systems, the community college systems, the postsecondary vocational schools, and the private colleges. The central campuses of the state universities get the biggest share of the state higher education budget. They have the most affluent undergraduates. They generally pay their faculty higher salaries than are paid by other higher education facilities. They tend to be research-oriented institutions. And they get most of the grants awarded to higher education in the state for research, experimentation, and program implementation.

Less prestigious than the major campus of the state university is the state college or the state university system. These colleges often started as teachers' colleges early in the century but were expanded into extensive university systems to accommodate the boom of students during the 1950s and 1960s.

The state community college system is composed of two-year schools, which have traditionally been treated as the poorer cousins of higher education. On the average, they get the least money, have the poorest libraries, and give their instructors the heaviest teaching loads. A Brookings Institution study in 1981 charged that the community colleges have diluted academic rigor in their attempts to increase their budgets and enrollments. Only 10 percent of community college students graduated from the two-year programs, and fewer yet transferred to four-year programs at colleges and universities.[11]

Vocational and technical schools expanded during the 1970s as the educational focus switched increasingly to job training and career education. This was one of the earliest areas in which the federal government became involved in education. The Smith-Hughes Act of 1917 provided grants-in-aid for teacher training in trades, home economics, and agriculture. By the mid-1970s, federal aid was helping state and local governments to provide career training for post–high school as well as high school students in a variety of fields that ranged from home economics to computer programming.

In the 1980s, higher education has come under attack. The most noted critic is United States Secretary of Education William J. Bennett, who in a 1986 speech at Harvard University assailed the quality of higher education in the country. Bennett faulted the nation's colleges for not providing a moral grounding to their studies, for being too concerned over money, for being too liberal politically, and for not seeing to it systematically that their students achieved quality education. Bennett's criticisms were echoed by a report of the Carnegie Foundation issued about the same time. The Carnegie Foundation called for more coherent undergraduate curricula, the scaling back of athletic programs, increased general education requirements, and a requirement that all undergraduates write and defend a senior thesis before graduating.[12]

These criticisms came at a particularly difficult time for colleges and universities, because of great financial pressures due to reductions in federal aid and the decline in the number of traditional college-age people. As federal aid and federal initiatives decline, the states—especially their governors—are looked to for leadership.[13] In the tight budgetary environment of the 1980s, difficult choices have to be made. Will the elite, research-oriented universities be favored? Or will the less elite, teaching institutions be favored? What public assistance can be given to private institutions? Will public funding continue to be enrollment driven? And if so, what effects will this have in the late 1980s and the 1990s, when enrollments are expected to decline by about 6 percent?[14] Given the growing attention to high-technology occupations in today's changing economy, will resources be shifted away from the humanities and into technology? If college costs continue to rise and if federal student aid fails to keep pace, how will the millions of low- and middle-income people finance their educations?

Because of overlap in the target populations as well as in the programs of the different kinds of institutions of higher education, there is a great need for coordination. By 1980 all but two states had created higher-education coordinating boards responsible for coordinating budgets, plans, and programs of the various institutions of higher education.

Political Values and Public Education

The View from the Right

Conservatives view public education as a force for promoting upward social mobility and developing the human capital (skills, knowledge, attitudes) that will improve overall economic productivity. For Edward Donohue, Herman the Pushout, and the hundreds of thousands of other high school dropouts and functional illiterates, public education has failed.

Conservatives view these failures partly as a failure of the individuals and partly as a failure of the schools. Insofar as Edward Donohue and Herman the Pushout are individual failures, Edward Banfield wrote, "There will be *some* number of students who are simply not capable of doing high school work."[15] That these individuals tend to be concentrated in the lower classes and the racial minorities is attributed by some writers to a culture of poverty, which inhibits the desire for achievement, self-improvement, and deferred gratification.[16] The "lower-class person cannot as a rule be given much training," wrote Banfield, "because he will not accept it."[17] Other writers have tried to relate poor educational achievement to genetic factors.[18]

Conservatives blame the degree to which Edward Donohue and Herman the Pushout represent a failure of the schools on liberal educational philosophies traced back to John Dewey. Educational permissiveness has let the schools drift away from the basics of education, which focus on reading, writing, and mathematical skills, and stress rote drilling. Conservatives also emphasize rigid discipline; in some instances they favor giving schools the right to suspend or expel students identified as troublemakers. Many of these ideas found expression in the Report of the National Commission on Educational Excellence mentioned earlier. Conservatives are very concerned about the ability of the educational system to provide a competent work force for American business.

The View from the Left

On the moderate left, the liberal shares with the conservative the assumption that the functions of education are to provide economic opportunity, assure upward social mobility, and produce skilled workers for the economy.[19] The liberal, having an optimistic view of human nature, also views education as a force for human development, the expansion of minds. Unlike the conservative, the liberal views Edward Donohue and Herman the Pushout as failures of the school system, not the individual. To the liberal the basic problems lie in segregated schools and in poor people's lack of control over their educational environment. The liberal also believes that, with the exception of the severely mentally retarded, everyone has the potential to acquire knowledge and develop employable skills. What prevents this development is that the school systems have never reformed themselves enough to cope with a broad range of students' cultural backgrounds. Many reform efforts of the Great Society were cut short before they were really given a chance.

The liberal advocates more reforms and more experimentation and often rejects the conservative emphasis on basic skills, rigid discipline, and rote learning. Much liberal support goes to such school reforms as open schools, programs that allow great permissiveness in the classroom, and programs to keep disruptive youngsters in the classroom rather than expelling them. The liberal seeks more desegregation and supports involuntary busing. The liberal also tends to support programs for greater decentralization, community control, and citizen participation in the educational process. Most of these causes are out of favor in the 1980s.

On the extreme left, the radical argues that public education fails to provide upward social mobility because it was never meant to do this for a great number of students. The radical argues that the public education system "screens potential workers through a sieve, sorting them according to their capacities to work persistently, to respond to incentives like wages, to conform to work requirements, and to defer gratification."[20] This sifting function can be seen most clearly in the system of formal credentials issued by the colleges and universities. People with professional degrees get sorted into upper-middle-class occupations like medicine and law. More typical middle-class occupations, such as public school teacher, social worker, accountant, computer programmer, and registered nurse, come disproportionately from the state college systems and from the less prestigious private colleges.

The radical contends that this sifting process also works below the college level. Graduates of high schools, technical schools, and trade union apprentice programs get sifted into occupations such as laboratory technician, hairdresser, dental assistant, and police officer. At the bottom of the occupational ladder are the high school dropouts, who become dishwashers, unskilled laborers, and public relief recipients.

Coping with Educational Problems

Desegregation

De Jure Segregation

In 1954 the Supreme Court struck down school segregation as a violation of the equal protection clause of the United States Constitution. To clearly understand the current struggle over desegregation, it is necessary to examine the development of constitutional law on the subject of segregated schools.

The equal-protection clause of the Fourteenth Amendment to the United States Constitution asserts that no state may deny any citizen the equal protection of the law. In a famous case in 1896, the Supreme Court set down the legal justification for segregation. The Court approved separate public facilities for blacks and whites as long as the separate facilities were equal.[21] This was the famous **separate-but-equal doctrine.** Several states used this ruling to justify the establishment of separate school systems for whites and nonwhites, and in 1927 the Supreme Court specifically approved this practice.[22] By mid-twentieth century, seventeen states plus the District of Columbia legally required segregated schools, and another four states permitted segregation at the local level.

Segregation consisted of a dual school system—one for white children and an entirely separate system for nonwhite children. Because this system was established by law, it is referred to as **de jure segregation.** The nonwhite system was never given as many resources as the white system, thus making a mockery of the provision that the separate systems be equal.

Black civil rights leaders, working through the National Association for the Advancement of Colored People (NAACP), spent the first half of the twentieth century attempting to get these dual systems declared unconstitutional. Their first victory came in 1938 in Missouri. The University of Missouri Law School refused to admit blacks even though the state had no separate law school for blacks. It attempted to meet the separate-but-equal requirement by offering scholarships to send blacks out of state to law school. The United States Supreme Court struck this down as unconstitutional.[23]

Ten years later the University of Oklahoma was obliged to admit blacks to its law school.[24] The university did not treat its newly admitted black students equally with the white students, however. They were not allowed to use the cafeteria at the same time as the white students or to use the regular desks in the reading room of the library, and they were required to sit for classes in an anteroom adjoining the classroom, where they could not see the professor. This practice, too, the Supreme Court struck down as unconstitutional.[25] Texas attempted to meet the separate-but-equal requirement by building a separate law school for blacks, but the United States Supreme Court ruled that no such segregated school could possibly be equal to the University of Texas at Austin with its excellent library, its top-notch faculty, and the prestige that its law degree enjoyed among the state's attorneys.[26]

All of these developments came to a climax in the famous 1954 *Brown* v. *Board of Education* decision, in which the Supreme Court unanimously struck down the dual school systems as violating the **equal-protection clause** of the United States Constitution.[27] The schools were ordered to desegregate with all deliberate speed. However, the desegregation that followed was much more deliberate than speedy, making slow progress in its first ten years.[28] In the next ten years, however, the pace of integration speeded up, and by the 1980s considerable progress had been made in desegregating the once legally segregated school systems of the South.

De Facto Segregation

By the 1970s, the major segregation problem was no longer de jure dual school systems; it was the much more difficult problem of **de facto segregation,** that is, segregation that exists in fact even though there are no laws or rules requiring it. The schools are segregated in fact because minorities live in one part of the city and whites live in another.

Coping with de facto segregation is much harder than coping with de jure segregation. Although a variety of techniques have been attempted in de facto segregated cities to get black and white children into the same classrooms (magnet schools, voluntary transfers, open enrollment plans, paired schools), the most direct tactic was the involuntary busing of both black and white children to integrated schools. In *Swann* v. *Charlotte-Mecklenberg Board of Education* (1971),[29] the United States Supreme Court ruled that federal district courts may impose forced busing to desegregate if there is evidence that the segregation results from legal measures to alter school boundaries or to impose residential segregation.

The Federal Role in Desegregation

The federal government has five main tools for imposing desegregation: unfavorable publicity for the school system involved; use of federal armed forces; withholding federal funds; initiating law suits; and court-ordered involuntary busing.

Unfavorable publicity works only when the desegregating officials really care what outsiders think about them. Use of armed forces is extremely rare and is only done as a last resort. It was done to desegregate the high school in Little Rock, Arkansas, in 1957. Threatening to cut off federal funds is also a limited weapon because it is a two-edged sword. When federal education officials threatened to cut off funds from Georgia school districts that were practicing segregation, the schools simply operated without the funds rather than desegregate. Because most of the money involved was Title I compensatory education funds targeted for black schools, cutting them off had the paradoxical effect of hurting the very children that the federal officials were trying to help. And federal funds coming from noneducational federal agencies (such as the Department of Agriculture's school lunch program) continued even after the federal education officials imposed their cutoff. Georgia's recalcitrant school districts did not really desegregate until the Department of Justice (DOJ) sued the state to impose desegregation on the offending local systems.[30]

Table 14–4. Public Opinion on Busing as a Way to Achieve a Better Racial Balance in Public Schools

	Favor	Oppose	Don't know
Whites	17%	78%	5%
Blacks	59	31	10

Source: The Gallup Report, no. 185 (February, 1981), p. 29.

The example of Georgia suggests that it has been primarily the willingness of the DOJ to sue local school districts and the Supreme Court's willingness to uphold court-ordered busing plans that have brought about most desegregation. The 1964 Civil Rights Act gives the DOJ the authority to sue states or local school districts that fail to desegregate. And it gives the Department of Education authority to withhold federal funds from those districts. These federal tactics are most likely to be successful when the president encourages the DOJ to enforce the Civil Rights Act's provisions on desegregation and when the president and Congress give full support to the Court's decisions. During the Kennedy and Johnson administrations (1961–1969), the White House strongly supported civil rights legislation and the use of federal administrative powers to enforce that legislation. Later administrations have been less enthusiastic about enforcing desegregation, with the Reagan administration adamantly backing off from desegregation measures, especially forced busing.

Is Busing Effective?

The most polarizing means to desegregate schools has been court-ordered busing. It is resoundingly opposed by whites, as Table 14–4 shows, but it gathers majority support from blacks. The problem, as Frederick Wirt has pointed out, is that "no one has yet figured out how to desegregate very much without busing."[31]

Forced busing placed the burden of desegregation disproportionately on the shoulders of working and lower-middle-income central-city residents; the suburbs normally were exempted from forced busing. A court ruling in 1974[32] refused to extend busing to the suburbs unless the suburban school districts had drawn their boundaries deliberately to exclude minorities.* This meant

---

*In Delaware the court ruled that this had been done. Delaware passed a consolidation plan in 1968 that changed all school district boundaries except for Wilmington's. The court ruled that these boundary changes had the effect of legally concentrating Delaware black students in the Wilmington School District and this constituted de jure segregation. In this instance the court ordered busing between suburbs and the central city.

that persons affluent enough to move to the suburbs or to send their children to private schools could flee the whole problem of desegregation.

This phenomenon is called **white flight.** In cities where forced busing was met with organized opposition and violence, busing did seem to precipitate white flight. In Atlanta, busing went into effect in 1972. Between then and 1975 the black share of school enrollment increased from 56 percent to 87 percent. In Memphis, busing started in 1973, and by 1976 the black share of enrollment had increased from 50 percent to 70 percent.[33] In the North's most celebrated desegregation case, the Boston schools lost over a third of their white pupils while their minority population increased in the two years following the start of busing in 1973.[34] In 1973, non-Hispanic whites comprised 65 percent of the schools' population. By 1985 that had dropped to 28 percent.[35]

While these percentages are important, they cannot be attributed solely to busing. Even where busing did not occur, white enrollment declined. Christine Rossell studied the enrollment records of eighty-six central-city school systems between 1963 and 1973. Only four of these cities had a statistically significant decline in white enrollment after busing began.[36] The biggest enrollment declines appeared to occur immediately before and after the busing decision. In subsequent years, enrollment trends returned to their prebusing patterns. Even where busing was met with violence, a similar pattern emerged. During the three years after Boston started busing in 1973, the reaction was so violent that police had to be stationed all year in some of the schools. Descriptions of the South Boston High School made it sound more like a battlefield than a school. But by the fall of 1977 most of the antibusing fervor had dissipated, and the children were bused to school without incident.

On balance, forced desegregation has positive effects on the actual children involved, especially those who underwent desegregation in the early grades. This was the conclusion reached by Willis Hawley after an elaborate study of ten court cases, desegregation activities in seventeen cities, and a review of over 1,200 other studies of desegregation.[37] Hawley found that achievement scores of white children did not go down. He maintains that the desegregation also reduced the racial isolation of minorities. And as desegregation proceeded, it also seemed to encourage families to move into their children's new attendance areas, thus helping to break down housing segregation. In Charlotte, North Carolina, for example, residential integration has increased to the point where *less* busing is needed to provide racial balance today than was needed a decade earlier.[38]

Despite Hawley's optimistic conclusions about the advantages of busing, there is little support for busing today among elected political leaders. The Reagan administration in particular has been very vocal about its distaste for busing. Under Reagan, federal funds to finance desegregation activities were reduced, and the Secretary of Education announced his intention not to file any busing suits.[39] Additionally, many big central-city school systems have so few white students left that there are only limited desegregation gains to be made by busing exclusively within central-city boundaries. Most suburbs, however, object to being drawn into desegregation plans. As long as the Supreme Court adheres to the principle set in *Millikin* v. *Bradley* (1974), it will not force the suburbs to participate in busing plans unless they were involved in some official actions that sought to promote de jure segregation. In 1983 an interesting agreement was reached between the St. Louis, Missouri, school district and twenty-two surrounding suburbs to engage in a voluntary busing plan that would increase the white population of St. Louis schools and increase the minority populations in suburban schools.[40] If this plan works successfully, it could signal a breakthrough in the attempt to establish metropolitanwide desegregation. In 1986, however, the Supreme Court gave an opposite signal when it allowed Norfolk, Virginia, to end its court-ordered busing plan, even though that meant an increase in the number of children attending all-black schools. This decision set many school officials asking whether busing had run its course and was on the way out.[41]

How Schools Are Financed

Table 14–5 shows that about 45 percent of the money for public schools comes from local governments, almost exclusively from the property tax, the traditional means for financing public education. In order to supplement local property taxes, the states have historically provided two forms of school aid. First is the **foundation aid program.** The states give each school district a certain number of dollars for each pupil in the schools. In addition, many states also build an equalization formula into the foundation aid so that more money goes to districts with many poor students and a small property-tax base. The second type of state aid is *categorical aid,* aid directed at a specific need. For example, many states reimburse local districts for most of the cost of hiring special education teachers to teach mentally retarded children.

Fiscal Disparities in School Finance

In places where a majority of school money comes from local property taxes, a small school district with an electric power plant, a large shopping center, or an industrial park will have abundant tax resources for public schools, whereas a neighboring district without these developments will be short on tax resources. The term for this uneven distribution of property tax resources is **fiscal disparities.** In some states, the disparities from one district to another are extreme. The Greenwich school district in Connecticut, for example, had $156,564 in taxable property for each pupil in 1976, while

Table 14–5. Financing the Schools

I. Percent of public school revenue derived from:		
Federal sources: 6.6%	State sources: 48.3%	Local sources: 45.1%

II. Percent of public school revenue (1980–1981)
derived from local sources (selected states):

States least dependent on local sources		States with litigation on the method of financing schools		States most dependent on local sources	
Hawaii	0.5%	California	26.1%	Massachusetts	51.9%
New Mexico	11.5	Arizona	37.1	Connecticut	55.1
Alaska	15.6	Texas	46.6	Vermont	60.1
Kentucky	21.2	New York	52.9	Michigan	61.9
California	26.1	Connecticut	55.1	South Dakota	62.5
		New Jersey	56.6	Nebraska	66.4
		Michigan	61.9	Wyoming	67.6
		Wyoming	67.6	New Hampshire	88.9

Source: Calculated from Bureau of the Census, *Statistical Abstract of the United States: 1986* (Washington, D.C.: U.S. Government Printing Office, 1985), p. 142.

the Sterling school district in the same state had only $17,441. In order for Sterling to provide the same services as Greenwich, Sterling homeowners would have had to pay nine times as much in property taxes as Greenwich homeowners.[42]

The problem of fiscal disparities came to a head in 1971 in the California court case of *Serrano* v. *Priest.*[43] Serrano had a very bright child and was told by the child's teacher that Serrano should move to a different district with programs to help achieve the child's full potential. These programs did not exist in Serrano's school district because of the lack of property tax resources. Serrano was not affluent, and the houses in the nearby richer districts were more expensive than he could afford. Consequently, rather than move, Serrano sued the state of California for not providing equal educational opportunity for all children and all school districts in the state. The California Supreme Court agreed that the fiscal disparities inherent in the property tax financing of public education violated the California Constitution and ordered California to find an alternative financing method.

No sooner had the California Supreme Court made this decision than parents in other states sought to get the principle applied nationwide under the equal-protection clause of the United States Constitution. A San Antonio, Texas, case came to the Supreme Court for decision in 1973. San Antonio was divided into different school districts for different neighborhoods, and the district for the Chicano community had very few property tax resources to support its schools. However, in *Rodriguez* v. *San Antonio School District*, the United States Supreme Court refused to apply the Serrano principle under federal law. The Court agreed that the states had relied too heavily and too long on the property tax. However, unless the state's constitution had a provision covering the allocation of school resources, the Supreme Court would not hear the case. The "ultimate solution must come from the lawmakers and from the democratic pressures of those who elect them."[44]

Despite the Supreme Court's refusal to apply the Serrano principle to the United States Constitution, the basic conflict has continued to surface in state after state. As discussed in Chapter 12, the most volatile conflict took place in New Jersey, where the state supreme court virtually forced the state legislature to adopt a state income tax for funding schools.

Approaches to Equalizing School Finance

It has been much easier for the courts to order equalization of school tax resources than it has for legislators to find a solution to the problem with enough political support to pass. Three general approaches have been made in the states.[45]

State Assumption of School Financing.   In Hawaii no local school taxes are levied; the state assumes all costs of school financing. No other states have followed Hawaii's lead, however. Considerable resistance exists to statewide funding of education. State funding would probably mean substantial increases in the state income and sales taxes. Fiscal conservatives feel that holding down school costs is easier under local control than it would be under state financing. If the state paid all the school costs, conservatives fear that local school boards would have no incentive to economize or to negotiate rigorously with their local teachers and other employee unions. Thus, many conservatives fear that statewide funding will cause salaries to skyrocket.

Resource Equalization.   A second option is to take some of the money raised in property-tax-rich districts and redistribute it to the districts that lack a sufficient property tax base. Variations of resource equalization have been partly worked into the school financing plans of several states.* In effect, the revenue-raising power of the school property tax is equalized throughout the state, and total school expenditures do not necessarily rise.

Although very confusing and mathematically complicated, this proposal appeals to people who do not want to increase state sales or income taxes.

---

*Colorado, Kansas, Maine, and Michigan. See *The Book of the States: 1976-77* (Lexington, Ky.: Council of State Governments, 1976), p. 315.

However, since it means that the tax-rich districts directly subsidize the tax-poor districts, resource equalization tends to be bitterly opposed by residents and officials of the districts blessed with considerable property-tax base.

Basic Education Plus a Local Enrichment Levy.   The third and most popular option is for the state to pay for much of the cost of education through foundation aid and categorical grants and allow local school districts to levy only a small amount of property taxes for enrichment purposes. Any taxes over this small amount would have to be approved by the voters in a referendum. This was how the California legislature initially responded to the challenge of *Serrano* v. *Priest*.[46] This also is essentially the way that Texas responded to *Rodriguez* v. *San Antonio*. A 1977 Texas law required that state foundation aids be used to equalize educational services in the state. However, local districts are allowed to levy additional taxes on top of their foundation aids, and—in the words of one team of observers—the state's "efforts to reduce educational inequalities among the districts of the state have met with only limited success."[47]

Problems with School Finance Equalization

By the mid-1980s, the drive for school finance equalization had lost much of its steam. In part it fell victim to the more conservative period of the 1980s; conservatives do not favor equalization. And in part it ran up against some hard realities. Rich districts were understandably opposed to equalization if it meant that they would be brought down to the level of the poor districts. Few people were willing to pay the huge costs of bringing the poor districts up to the level of the rich districts. Nevertheless, progress was made as some of the worst disparities between districts were reduced. And today, the states pay a greater share of the school bill than they did in the early 1970s. But equalization of finances seems as elusive now as it did then.

Other Education Issues

In addition to integration and finance, a host of other problems affect public schools. Rather than catalogue all of them, this discussion will focus on just three interrelated issues that have troubled school administrators in recent years: safety, religion, and quality of education.

Discipline/Safety

One major problem with some public schools can be traced to a very undisciplined and at times unsafe environment that impedes the learning process. In many big cities teenage gangs have literally taken over some schools. They decide where children will sit in the cafeteria and openly recruit gang members without interference from teachers and administrators.[48] A survey by the National Education Association estimated that over 100,000 teachers were assaulted during the 1978–1979 school year. The situation in New York City became so dangerous that the United Federation of Teachers published a booklet on personal security in the schools. The booklet warned that even the practice of teachers locking their classroom doors did not protect them from assault and violence.[49] The booklet also advised teachers not to sit alone in the faculty lounge and not to arrive at school more than thirty minutes before classes start. The decline of security also is reflected in increased vandalism; by the mid-1970s, vandalism cost the public schools more than half a billion dollars yearly.[50]

To cope with these discipline, safety, and vandalism problems, schools are taking a number of steps. It is not rare in metropolitan school districts for police officers to be assigned to high school buildings. Some districts provide, free of rent, mobile homes parked permanently on school grounds to persons who agree to report any disturbances. Schools are forced to buy increasingly elaborate security paraphernalia, such as floodlights, closed-circuit television, alarm systems, and ultrasonic alerters.

Religion

Religion has presented several problems over the years for public education. The Supreme Court ruled that the practice of public school classes saying prayers violates the First Amendment's **establishment clause**.[51] This clause forbids the "establishment of religion." School prayers, reasoned the court, would establish such a prohibited religious practice.

These decisions, however, turned out to be very unpopular. Prayers continued in many remote schools despite the Supreme Court ruling.[52] During the early 1980s, substantial opposition began to build against the Supreme Court decision. Bills were introduced in Congress that would curb the Supreme Court's authority to hear school prayer cases, and President Reagan openly supported a right to hold prayer sessions in public schools. To date, however, none of these bills has passed Congress. An imaginative approach to the question was taken in some states, which passed laws requiring a moment of silence each school day during which each student could pray or meditate. The Supreme Court struck down Alabama's "Moment of Silence" law, which had specifically directed that the quiet time could be used for voluntary prayer;[53] but this decision left open the possibility that the Court might approve other states' laws if they were worded slightly differently.

A second religious issue involves the curriculum. What should be taught? Certain fundamentalist Christian groups object to the teaching of evolutionary theories in biology classes. Under their influence, the Arkansas and Louisiana Legislatures passed laws requiring that equal time in biology classes be given to teaching creationist theories of the origins of human life. However, federal courts struck down this law as a violation of the Constitutional separation of church and state.[54] By the mid-1980s fundamentalist Christians were making a broad assault on a variety of textbooks and other teaching materials that they claimed promoted "secular humanism," a vague concept that could be applied to many things. Some fundamentalists, for example, sought to have a story on Leonardo da Vinci removed from the schools because of its secular humanism.[55] A group of fundamentalist parents in Tennessee successfully got federal courts to exempt their children from public school reading classes that featured readings the parents opposed on religious grounds. In particular, the parents had objected to *The Diary of Anne Frank,* because in that book Anne Frank asserted that all religions were equal. And in 1987 a federal judge banned over forty books from Alabama schools on the grounds that they promote the religion of secular humanism.[56] Whether the United States Supreme Court will allow these decisions to stand and how fundamentalist Christians handle their conflicts with mainstream American cultures will be important issues for the balance of the 1980s.

A third religious issue involves the extent to which governments can provide financial aid to church-related schools or their pupils. To date the Supreme Court has allowed governmental aid, such as funds for textbooks or transportation, that assists the students rather than the schools and that does not promote a particular church belief.[57] However, aids that go directly to church-related schools, such as tuition tax credits, were fairly consistently struck down by the Supreme Court until 1983. In that year the Supreme Court upheld a Minnesota law that provided state income tax deductions for a portion of tuition expenses.[58]

The Supreme Court's decision in the Minnesota case is likely to encourage those groups that have been pressing for some form of aid that would give parents an alternative to sending their children to the public schools. The prominent educational sociologist James S. Coleman, whose early studies were so influential in helping promote school desegregation (and whose later works helped inhibit it), completed a new study in 1981. This study asserts that private schools, on balance, are more orderly, more disciplined, and more effective at educating children than are most central-city public schools.[59] Coleman also has supported a voucher plan under which governments would give parents a voucher they could use to send their children to the school of their choice.[60] Public school administrators and teachers' associations fear that such a **voucher plan** would be devastating to the public school system, and they resoundingly oppose it.

Quality of Education

The quality of education has received considerable publicity in recent years. If, as in the case of Edward Donohue, one can graduate from high school and still not be able to read well enough to fill out a job application, what is a high school diploma really worth? Even admitting that students such

Figure 14–1. Trends in Average Annual SAT Scores

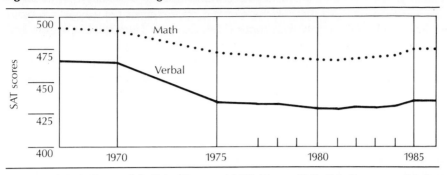

Sources: *Statistical Abstract of the United States: 1986* (Washington, D.C.: U.S. Government Printing Office, 1985), p. 147; The Educational Testing Service, Princeton, N.J.

as Edward constitute a small minority of the population, more standard indicators, such as the average SAT test scores shown in Figure 14–1, also point to a declining quality of public education. These trends gave rise to movements in the 1980s to reform and improve American public education.

Reforming Public Education

As these indicators of educational quality became widely known in the 1970s, a rising citizen interest developed, especially among conservatives, to impose more rigorous academic standards. Sometimes called **back-to-the-basics,** this movement urges less free time in schools, more homework, and more rigid graduation requirements. With responsibilities for desegregation, socialization, and instruction in various social causes, as well as being buffeted by changing educational philosophies over the years, the schools had been asked to do too many things. It was time to get back to the fundamental pursuit of cognitive, academic, and intellectual rigor.[61] The educational reform movement received a very prestigious boost in 1983 when the National Commission on Excellence in Education proposed several measures to improve the schools—raising teachers' salaries, creating a cadre of master teachers, lengthening the school year, and raising requirements for graduation. Within a year, a half-dozen other prestigious commissions presented similar proposals.[62] The get-tough philosophy had struck the public schools.

School Reform and Its Implementation

Some of the proposed reforms proved easier to implement than others. Within two years of the 1983 publication of *A Nation at Risk,* forty states had raised graduation requirements, and thirty-six states had provided more student testing for minimum academic competencies.[63] A majority of the states had adopted at least five of the specific reform measures suggested by *A Nation at Risk,* and only four states (Nevada, New Hampshire, Oregon, and Rhode Island) failed to adopt any.[64]

More difficult to implement were the proposals for dramatic increases in teachers salaries and for merit pay for teachers. Tennessee presents an excellent case in point. Governor Lamar Alexander proposed a Master Teacher Program in 1983. Despite approval by a large majority of Tennesseans, the $200-million price tag was opposed by fiscal conservatives, the merit pay features were adamantly opposed by the Tennessee Education Association (TEA), and the program was defeated in the legislature. Alexander then took the initiative with an imaginative fight for his program. He appeared on national television and gave interviews to national magazines to promote it. He managed to enlist the American Federation of Teachers to criticize the TEA for its opposition. He ran television ads plugging the program and changed its title from "Master Teachers" to the "Better Schools Program."

Finally, in 1985, the Tennessee legislature raised the state sales tax to provide the money for one of the country's most extensive educational reform packages. The centerpiece of the proposal is a career-ladder provision under which teachers move up to the higher-paying ladder positions on the basis of their classroom competence rather than the number of graduate course credits they have accumulated.[65]

In addition to Tennessee's comprehensive reform, North Carolina Governor James B. Hunt promoted the North Carolina School of Science and Mathematics as a public school where gifted eleventh and twelfth graders could be taught by highly qualified teachers. Minnesota Governor Rudy Perpich proposed an open-enrollment system that would essentially allow any child to attend any public school in the state on a space-available basis. This was resoundingly opposed by the Minnesota Education Association and the public school administrators. Confronted with a stiff reelection contest in 1986, Perpich withdrew his open-enrollment plan in order to avoid organized electoral opposition from the Minnesota Education Association. Former Texas governor Mark White ran into similar opposition when he pushed for competency testing of teachers and for forcing high school football players to have passing grades if they wanted to stay on their teams. White persisted, however, and in 1984 the Texas legislature passed a comprehensive educational reform package that included these measures as well as raising teacher salaries and reducing the fiscal disparities between school districts.[66]

From a political perspective, these examples illustrate the importance of aggressive and unrelenting leadership by the governor. Tennessee got its reforms in large part because the dynamic leadership of Governor Lamar Alexander was able to overcome the educational bureaucracy and the teachers' associations. Minnesota lost its chance to become the first state to have an open-enrollment policy in no small part because election needs made it impossible for Governor Rudy Perpich to persist in his vision.

Finally, from an educational perspective, it is an open question whether these reforms are sufficient to produce the well-educated and trained citizenry that educational reformers are seeking. Given the working conditions of many American public school systems and the psychological assault on the integrity of public employees that seems to be endemic in the 1980s (see Chapter 11), it is not at all clear that higher teacher salaries by themselves are going to attract brighter and more enthusiastic college students into teaching. Nor is it clear that merit pay provisions will necessarily improve student achievement.[67] An impressive body of comparative research at both the state level and the school-district level suggests that graduation rates and SAT scores are less influenced by increasing expenditures for public schools than they are by socioeconomic factors.[68] If this is the case, then instead of dramatically increasing school expenditures, a better approach to raising a state's average SAT scores might be to decrease the number of school children living in poverty or in female-headed households.

Education and the Political Economy

Historically, education has occupied a critical place in the American political economy. Through the public and private school systems, people were educated to play a variety of roles in an industrial and highly sophisticated society. Children received the educational basics they needed to become skilled workers, technicians, engineers, accountants, and professionals. Furthermore, education was assumed to play a great equalizer role in American democracy. So many millions of people enjoyed upward social mobility partially as a result of skills, knowledge, and credentials acquired at school that it became easy to believe that education was the answer to many social problems. Much of the battle over desegregation, for example, focused on desegregating schools because of the assumption that they were the key to equality for the racial minorities. Another assumption was that society itself could be made more humane by broadening the school curriculum to include more social studies and humanities courses.

Today, many of these assumptions are being questioned. The National Commission on Educational Excellence performed a great service for educational reformers by complaining that the school systems are not preparing children well for the high-technology type of society those children will inherit. If the Commission's criticisms are accurate, important changes will have to be made in order for schools to carry out their traditional role of educating a workforce to meet the nation's needs.

This cartoon by Mike Peters reflects the fear of many people that high technology will not provide much economic opportunity for the average citizen, regardless of how good their education may be.

Source: Mike Peters, 1983. Reprinted by permission of United Feature Syndicate, Inc.

Given these considerations, it is not surprising that much of the support for public school reform has come from the business community. Most of today's students will work for business corporations tomorrow, which gives those corporations an important interest in seeing that its recruits are literate and have the attitudes necessary to work eight-hour shifts. Business needs exist at least at two levels. First, keeping America competitive with the rest of the world requires highly skilled engineers, scientists, researchers, and technicians who can function comfortably in today's high-tech world. Hence the concern among businessmen over literacy, the ability to write, the quality of scientific learning, and declining SAT scores. In all probability, however, the number of highly lucrative high-tech jobs is quite limited.

Second, since most of the jobs created since 1980 have been very low-tech jobs—in restaurants, hotels, and other service establishments—what is needed arc large numbers of people willing to work at repetitive tasks for long hours, day in and day out. This need is expected to become especially acute in the 1990s, when the number of young people entering the job market will be smaller than in recent years. Hence, many corporations are working closely with local school districts to acculturate teenagers into this kind of job environment. A "Boston Compact" in 1982 required every public school student to hold a part-time job between the summer of tenth grade and graduation.[69]

Perhaps the most obvious link between public education and the political economy occurs with higher education. The link is especially strong between business corporations and the large research-oriented universities. Corporations benefit from the technical research done at those universities. And universities benefit from equipment donations, consulting contracts, and friendly ties with the corporations. From the point of view of state government, a well-functioning university system is a definite asset in attracting more industry.

Summary

1. Local school districts have historically been the dominant unit of school governance. However, educational problems such as desegregation and financing could not be solved by small districts; thus, in recent years, policymaking and financing have been increasingly centralized at the state level, and the federal government has become more and more involved in public education. The federal government's greatest impact has been in the desegregation of public schools.

2. Theorists of the right view declining achievement and growing discipline problems as both failures of individual students and failures of the public school systems. They attribute the failures of the school systems to liberal educational philosophies that have led to permissiveness in the classroom, open schools, and poor discipline. Liberals attribute the failures of the school systems to inadequate implementation of and insufficient dedication to progressive educational programs. On the far left, radicals doubt that the public schools were ever meant to be major agents of upward social mobility for most students.

3. According to findings of the Gallup poll, the educational problems that cause the most concern to American citizens are desegregation, quality of education, financing schools, and a complex of discipline problems involving safety, violence, and drugs.

4. The impetus for desegregation has come mostly from the federal courts. The Supreme Court first struck down de jure segregation as unconstitutional. The courts have had less success in ending de facto segregation. The most volatile desegregation controversy of the 1970s was over the use of forced busing to desegregate schools.

5. The main school finance problems stem from fiscal disparities in the distribution of property-tax resources. State governments supplement local school resources with foundation aids and categorical grants. Several state

courts, most notably those in California and New Jersey, have struck down excessive reliance on local property taxes to finance public education. Three general approaches to school finance equalization have been used: (1) state assumption of school financing, (2) resource equalization, and (3) basic education plus a local enrichment levy. Support for school finance equalization comes from liberal sources much more than it does from conservative sources.

6. Public concern over declining scores on achievement tests has led to an educational reform movement called *back to the basics*. The states have enacted numerous educational reform measures in recent years.

Key Terms

Back-to-the-basics movement An educational movement seeking to impose more rigorous standards on public schools and to limit the number of subjects taught.

Board of education The governing board of a local school district.

Commissioner of education See *Superintendent of Schools*.

Compensatory education The tenet that disadvantaged children suffer from poor preparation for school and must be given special educational help to compensate for their backgrounds. See *Elementary and Secondary Education Act of 1965*.

De facto segregation Segregation that arises because of residential practices rather than because of laws requiring segregation. See *De jure segregation*.

De jure segregation Segregation that is imposed by law rather than by informal residential practices. See *De facto segregation*.

Education Consolidation and Improvement Act of 1981 A law that consolidated several educational categorical grant programs into a block grant, reduced the total funding for the programs involved, and increased state discretion in dispensing the funds.

Elementary and Secondary Education Act of 1965 The first extensive form of federal aid to public schools. Famous for its Title I compensatory-education provisions. See also *Compensatory education*.

Equal-protection clause The provision of the Fourteenth Amendment that forbids any state to deny persons in its jurisdiction the equal protection of the laws.

Establishment clause The Constitution's First Amendment provision that "Congress shall make no law respecting an establishment of religion."

Fiscal disparities The situation in which neighboring governmental jurisdictions vary widely in their ability to raise revenue. One jurisdiction may have a substantial tax base, while a neighboring one has a meager tax base.

Foundation aid program A program of state aid for public schools under which the state provides a given number of dollars to each school district for the number of full-time pupils enrolled in that district.

Independent school district The basic governing unit for public schools.

National Commission on Excellence in Education A commission that reported in 1983 that the nation's school systems are failing to provide children with the quality of education they need in the contemporary world.

Separate-but-equal doctrine The principle established in *Plessy* v. *Ferguson* (1896) that segregated facilities do not violate the equal protection clause as long as the separate facilities are equal.

State education agency (SEA) State educational policymaker, composed of the state board of education, the chief state school officer, and the department of education.

Superintendent of schools The chief executive officer for public schools. May be either a local or state superintendent. The state superintendent is sometimes called the *commissioner of education*.

Voucher plan (school) A proposal that would give parents vouchers to pay the cost of sending their children to the school of their choice.

White flight The theory that middle-class whites have in large numbers withdrawn their children from the central-city public schools in order to avoid school desegregation.

References

1. *New York Times,* February 20, 1977, p. 1.

2. J. J. Jackson and C. C. Harris, "You May Be Normal When You Come Here, But You Won't Be Normal When You Leave: Or Herman the Pushout." *Black Schollar* 8 (April 1977): 2–11.

3. *The Gallup Report,* No. 252 (September, 1986): 12.

4. National Commission on Excellence in Education, *A Nation at Risk: The Imperative for Educational Reform* (Washington, D.C.: U.S. Government Printing Office, 1983).

5. Michael O. Boss and Harmon Zeigler, "Experts and Representatives: Comparative Basis of Influence in Education Policy-Making," *Western Political Quarterly* 30, no. 2 (June 1977): 255–262.

6. See Burton Dean Friedman, *State Government and Education Management in the State Education Agency* (Chicago: Public Administration Service, 1971).

7. See Robert W. Tyler, "The Federal Role in Education," *Public Interest,* no. 34 (Winter 1974): 164–187.

8. M. W. Kirst and R. Jung, "The Utility of a Longitudinal Approach in Assessing Implementation: A Thirteen-Year View of Title I, ESEA," *Educational Evaluation and Policy Analysis* 2 (1980): 17–34.

9. *The Book of the States: 1982-83* (Lexington, Ky.: Council of State Governments, 1982), p. 432.

10. *New York Times,* January 28, 1982, p. 10.

11. Cited in *St. Paul Pioneer Press,* December 6, 1981, p. 16.

12. For Bennett's speech, see *New York Times,* October 11, 1986, p. 8. For the Carnegie report, see *New York Times,* October 10, 1986, p. 15.

13. Clark Kerr, "The State and Higher Education: Changes Ahead," *State Government* 58, no. 2 (Summer 1985): 45–50.

14. Total 1983 enrollment in higher education institutions was 12,465,000. By 1993 this is expected to drop to 11,676,000. See *Statistical Abstract of the United States: 1986* (Washington, D.C.: U.S. Government Printing Office, 1985), p. 151.

15. Edward C. Banfield, *The Unheavenly City* (Boston: Little, Brown & Co., 1970), p. 134.

16. This was especially the theme of Oscar Lewis. See his *La Vida* (New York: Random House, 1965). Also see Barbara E. Coward, Joe R. Feagin, and J. Allen Williams, Jr., "The Culture of Poverty Debate: Some Additional Data," *Social Problems* 21, no. 5 (June 1974): 621–633.

17. Banfield, *The Unheavenly City*, p. 139.

18. The proponents of this view are Arthur Jensen and William Shockley. See H. J. Eysenck, *The I.Q. Argument* (New York: Library Press, 1971).

19. See David M. Gordon, *Problems in Political Economy: An Urban Perspective*, 2d ed. (Lexington, Mass.: D.C. Heath, 1977), pp. 108–112.

20. Ibid., p. 213.

21. *Plessy* v. *Ferguson*, 163 U.S. 537 (1896).

22. *Gong Lum* v. *Rice*, 275 U.S. 78 (1927).

23. *Missouri ex rel. Gaines* v. *Canada*, 305 U.S. 337 (1938).

24. *Sipuel* v. *Oklahoma*, 332 U.S. 631 (1948).

25. *McLaurin* v. *Oklahoma State Regents*, 339 U.S. 637 (1950).

26. *Sweatt* v. *Painter*, 339 U.S. 629 (1950).

27. *Brown* v. *Board of Educ.*, 347 U.S. 483 (1954).

28. Charles S. Bullock III and Harrell R. Rodgers, Jr., "Coercion to Compliance: Southern School Districts and School Desegregation Guidelines," *Journal of Politics* 38, no. 4 (November 1976): 987–1013.

29. *Swann* v. *Charlotte-Mecklenberg B. of Educ.*, 402 U.S. 1 (1971).

30. Bullock and Rodgers, "Coercion to Compliance," pp. 987–1013.

31. Frederick M. Wirt, "Institutionalization: Prison and School Policies," *Politics in the American States: A Comparative Analysis*, 4th ed., eds. Virginia Gray, Herbert Jacob, and Kenneth N. Vines (Boston: Little, Brown & Co., 1983), p. 310.

32. *Millikin* v. *Bradley*, 418 U.S. 717 (1974).

33. Mary Costello, "Busing Reappraisal," *Editorial Research Reports*, December 26, 1975, pp. 948–949.

34. Diane Ravitch, "The 'White Flight' Controversy," *Public Interest* no. 51 (Spring 1978): 142.

35. *New York Times*, August 22, 1985, p. 1.

36. Christine H. Rossell, "School Desegregation and White Flight," *Political Science Quarterly* 90, no. 4 (Winter 1975–76): 692. This is a very controversial article. It has been criticized for its methods and its policy suggestions; see Ravitch, "The 'White Flight' Controversy," pp. 135–150. Also see the exchange of views by Christine H. Rossell, Diane Ravitch, and David J. Armor, "Busing and 'White Flight,'" *Public Interest*, no. 53 (Fall 1978): 109–115.

37. Willis D. Hawley, ed., *Effective School Desegregation* (Beverly Hills, Calif: SAGE Publications, 1981).

38. See Wirt, "Institutionalization," pp. 310–311.

39. *New York Times,* March 16, 1981, p. 11.

40. *New York Times,* February 23, 1983, p. 1; March 10, 1983, p. 10.

41. For background, see *New York Times,* November 4, 1986, p. 1; *Newsweek,* November 17, 1986, p. 60.

42. *New York Times,* April 24, 1977, p. E-5.

43. *Serrano* v. *Priest,* 5 Cal. 3d 584 (1971).

44. *Rodriguez* v. *San Antonio School District,* 411 U.S. 59 (1973).

45. Jerome Zukosky, "School Finance Reform: Challenge for the States," *National Civic Review* 62, no. 4 (April 1973): 176–183.

46. John Pincus, "Spending for Education," *Center Magazine* 10, no. 2 (March–April 1977): 60–70.

47. Clifton McCleskey, Allan K. Butcher, Daniel E. Farlow, and J. Pat Stephens, *The Government and Politics of Texas,* 7th ed. (Boston: Little, Brown and Co., 1982), p. 306.

48. See Suzanne de Lesseps, "Violence in the Schools," *Editorial Research Reports,* August 13, 1976, pp. 583–600.

49. Ibid., p. 595, reports the New York booklet. For the 100,000 assaults, see *St. Paul Dispatch,* July 5, 1979, p. 23.

50. de Lesseps, "Violence in the Schools," p. 583.

51. *School Dist. of Abington Township* v. *Schemp,* 374 U.S. 203 (1963).

52. Bullock and Rodgers, "Coercion to Compliance," pp. 987–1013.

53. *Wallace* v. *Jaffree,* 105 S.Ct. 2479 (1985).

54. *New York Times,* January 6, 1982, p. 1; June 20, 1987.

55. *New York Times,* July 15, 1986, p. 8.

56. On the Tennessee case, see *New York Times,* February 28, 1986, p. 11; October 25, 1986, p. 1. On the Alabama case, see *New York Times,* March 5, 1987, p. 1; March 7, 1987, p. 7; March 10, 1987, p. 14.

57. *Everson* v. *Board of Educ.,* 330 U.S. 1 (1947); and *Board of Educ.* v. *Allen,* 392 U.S. 236 (1968).

58. *Committee for Pub. Educ. & Religious Liberty* v. *Nyquist,* 413 U.S. 756 (1973); *Mueller* v. *Allen,* 463 U.S. 388 (1983).

59. James S. Coleman, "Public Schools, Private Schools," *Public Interest,* no. 64 (Summer 1981): 19–30.

60. See Coleman's letter to the editor, *New York Times,* April 19, 1981, p. 16.

61. See Diane Ravitch, *The Troubled Crusade: American Education 1945-1980* (New York: Basic Books, 1983). Also see Deborah Meier's excellent critique in "Getting Tough in the Schools," *Dissent* (Winter 1984): 61–70.

62. Task Force on Education for Economic Growth, *Action for Excellence: A Comprehensive Plan to Improve Our Nation's Schools,* Education Commission of the States, June 1983; The National Science Board, *Educating Americans for the 21st Century,* 1983; The Twentieth Century Fund Task Force on Federal Elementary and Secondary Education Policy, *Making the Grade,* 1983; John I. Goodlad, *A Place Called School: Prospects for the Future* (New York: McGraw-Hill, 1983); Ernest L. Boyer, *High School: A Report on Secondary Education in America* (New York: Harper & Row, 1983); Theodore R. Sizer, *Horace's Compromise—The Dilemma of the American High School* (Boston: Houghton Mifflin, 1984).

63. Peggy M. Siegel, "School Reform Momentum Continues," *State Legislatures* 11, no. 3 (March 1985): 11–15.

64. Don Shinn and Jack Van Der Slik, "A Model for Analyzing School Reform Legislation," *Comparative State Politics Newsletter* 7, no. 1 (February 1986): 5–6.

65. The history of Alexander's proposals have been traced by Steve Williams in a series of articles in the *Comparative State Politics Newsletter*. See "Alexander's Master Teacher Program Fails in Tennessee," 4, no. 3 (May 1983): 11–12; "Master Teacher Program Update," 4, no. 6 (December 1983): 21; and "The First Year of Merit Pay for Tennessee Teachers," 6, no. 5 (October 1985): 33.

66. Peter LeMann, "Texas: A Choice Without a Difference," *The Atlantic* 255, no. 5 (November 1985): 28.

67. Harvey J. Tucker and David B. Hill present data suggesting that higher salaries will indeed attract higher-quality people into teaching. See their "Teacher Quality and Expenditures for Public Education," *State Government* 58, no. 3 (Fall 1985): 105–107. On the other hand, Harry P. Hatry and John M. Greiner argue that merit pay will not necessarily improve student achievement or attract higher-quality teachers. See their *Issues in Teacher Incentive Plans* (Washington, D.C.: The Urban Institute, 1984).

68. See David R. Morgan and Sheila S. Watson, "Comparing Education Performance Among the American States," *State and Local Government Review* 19, no. 1 (Winter 1987): 15–20.

69. Joel Spring, "From Study Hall to Hiring Hall," *The Progressive* 48, no. 4 (April 1984): 31.

Chapter 15
Infrastructure Policies: Transportation, Housing, and Community Development

Chapter Preview

One of the most important roles of state and local governments is building and maintaining the physical infrastructure of modern society. In this chapter we will examine three areas of infrastructure policy and analyze them from the perspective of political values and their social consequences. We will discuss in turn:

1. Transportation policy.
2. Housing policy.
3. Community development policy.
4. Political values and the social consequences of infrastructure policy.

Let us begin this examination with a short introduction to what is meant by infrastructure policy and why political values are significant to it.

Introduction

One of the most important roles played by state and local governments is building, maintaining, and overseeing the physical infrastructure without which our modern society would not be possible. This chapter examines that part of the physical **infrastructure** that includes roads, transportation systems, housing, and community development projects. Some of these infrastructures, such as roads, are built by governments. Others, such as housing, are mostly built by private entrepreneurs but are extensively regulated and subsidized by governments. Others, such as metropolitan bus systems, were originally privately owned but in most metropolises have been taken over by public transit commissions.

The politics of these infrastructure services vitally affect the allocation of the costs and benefits of government. The construction of urban freeways, for example, required the uprooting of inner-city neighborhoods; and in the early 1970s city after city saw bitter conflicts as neighborhood groups fought against the destruction of their communities to make way for the superhighways. One of the most famous battles took place in Boston, where residents of working- and middle-class neighborhoods teamed up with urban planners from the Massachusetts Institute of Technology and stopped plans for a freeway there.[1] Similar conflicts began to arise over urban redevelopment projects. The federal government's urban renewal programs of the 1950s became so renowned for tearing up black communities that black leaders dubbed the program "Negro removal."

These conflicts raise important questions about the values underlying infrastructure policies as well as the consequences and biases of those policies. If neighborhoods have to be torn up for government projects, can the burden be borne equally by all ethnic groups and social classes? Or do only certain ones pay the cost? Who benefits from infrastructure policies? Most infrastructure projects, without doubt, provide a public good. Everybody, for example, benefits from well-maintained streets, but do some groups of people benefit more than others? Finally, what impacts do infrastructure policies have on the social problems we examined in the two previous chapters? Is de facto racial segregation in most metropolises truly just a by-product of the choices people make privately about where they want to live? Or did transportation, housing, and community development policies play a role in establishing the segregated metropolis?

We cannot answer all these questions in this chapter, but we will touch on many of them and try to provide a factual base for you to make your own judgments. We will examine transportation policy first, since the building of roads and transportation networks greatly influences where people are able to live and which communities will prosper. Second, we will examine housing and community development policies. Third, we will examine the role of political values in these areas. And last, we will speculate on the prospects for these policy areas in the 1990s.

Transportation

Since the mid-twentieth century, the American transportation system has been dominated by automobiles, trucks, and highways. Typically, most Americans get around by car. The widespread use and popularity of automobiles has given most Americans more mobility than any other people in history.

This phenomenon has produced a number of positive results. The extent of our reliance on automobiles, however, has also led to an imbalance in the transportation system as other forms of transit have deteriorated. This imbalance has produced a number of negative consequences. Perhaps a third of the population is too old, young, disabled, or poor to own and drive an automobile. Probably a fifth of all households do not own an automobile. This 20 to 33 percent of the population is unable to take advantage of the extensive mobility offered by automobiles, roads, and freeways. And the lack of balance between automobiles and other modes of transit has helped pollute the air and congest existing roadways.

These transportation conditions pose several important questions for state and local governments. First, how did automobiles, trucks, and highways become dominant in the transportation system? Why were railroads and mass-transit commuter systems allowed to deteriorate? Second, what prospects exist for public transit today? Third, what respective roles can states, communities, and the federal government play in bettering our transportation planning?

The Rise to Dominance of the Highway System

In large part the dominance of the highway system can be attributed to technological change. Table 15–1 shows that the American transportation network has evolved through a series of stages, each stage depending on the technology of its time.

The earliest forms of transit—the turnpikes, canals, and riverboats—depended heavily on human or animal power for locomotion. They were labor-intensive in that they required numerous workers to construct and operate the facilities. Yet, except for the canals, large amounts of capital were not required to build these networks. The rivers already existed, and many of them were navigable for great distances. All that was required was to construct riverboats. At crucial points it became necessary to connect some of the waterways with canals. The most famous of these was the Erie Canal, which opened in 1824 to link the Hudson River with the Great Lakes. At key points along the canals and rivers, bustling new cities grew up as transfer and service points for this river-canal-lake transit system.

All of this changed in the second quarter of the nineteenth century with the introduction of the railroads. The bustling centers of the river-and-canal era now shrank as the railroad centers grew to prominence. The railroads required much more capital and energy than the river-canal-turnpike system. Large sums of money were needed to build the tracks, to maintain them, and to update the equipment. The considerable energy required was supplied first by coal and later by diesel fuel.

Table 15–1. Technology and Changes in Transportation

Mode of transport	Time period of most importance	Source of locomotion	Intensiveness			Representative city
			Capital	Labor	Energy	
Turnpike — Most important cargo: people, supplies for personal needs	1800–1840	Animal and foot	Low	Very high	Very low	Cumberland, Md.
Canal — Most important cargo: grain from West to East	1820–1850	Barge: first animal, then steam	Medium	High	Very low	Rome, N.Y.
River — Most important cargo: grain, agricultural products generally, people	1840–1875	Steam, then diesel	Low	High	Very low	Galena, Ill.
Railroad — Most important cargo: agricultural products, coal, manufactured goods, people	1850–1920	Steam, then diesel	High	High	Medium	Vandalia, Ill.
Air/auto/motor — Most important cargo: people, manufactured products	1920–?	Gasoline engine, diesel and jet engines	Very high	Medium	Very high	Las Vegas, Nev.
Electronic communications — Most important cargo: information	1965–?	Telecommunications, computers, facsimile, cable television	Very high	Low	Very high	Suburb or satellite city of a metropolis

Source: From John J. Harrigan, *Political Change in the Metropolis*, p. 30. Copyright © 1976 by Little, Brown and Company (Inc.). Reprinted by permission.

A third, and for our day crucial, change in technology occurred in the twentieth century when the automobile was mass produced. Just as the river and canal towns declined with the advent of the railroad, early railroad towns began to decline with the mass production of the automobile. To accommodate the automobile, thousands of miles of roads had to be built, and states began to create state highway departments.

The state highway departments were responsible for building and maintaining the state's **primary road system**—the system of roads connecting the state's urban centers. A **secondary road system** was created to get farmers' products to market, and a **tertiary road system** was constructed within the urban areas. This tertiary system consists of city streets and other roads in metropolitan areas.

As the road system grew in the twentieth century, the shortcomings of railroad passenger service became increasingly apparent. The railroads either would not or could not improve passenger service to the level of most European nations. As a result, they carried only a fraction of the people carried by European railroads.[2] American trains were virtually useless for local transportation. An analysis of railroad schedules during the 1910s found that a round trip from New Washington, Ohio, to the county seat of Bucyrus only fourteen miles away took nine hours and required a train change on both trips.[3]

Given this poor railroad service, it is not surprising that people preferred to travel by automobile once cars became reasonably priced. Especially in rural areas, cars met an economic need not fulfilled by any other system of transport. Americans are often accused of having a love affair with their cars[4] and being unwilling to use public transportation, but it must be recognized that the widespread use of the automobile was due just as much to economic necessity as to love.

The Federal Role in Highway Development

The federal government played an important role in the creation of the road system. In 1916 Congress created the Bureau of Public Roads, which was authorized to provide federal highway funds to the states on a fifty-fifty matching grant basis. To get federal funds, the states had to create state highway departments that would draw up highway construction plans and submit them to the Bureau of Public Roads for approval. To ensure that the state-built roads would tie together into a national system, the Bureau of Public Roads was empowered to establish construction standards and to see that the routes joined at state boundary lines. In 1921 federal aid to each state was restricted to the primary state highway system that connected the major urban centers and ran mainly through rural areas.

In 1944 Congress passed a law calling for an extensive system of national highways, although money for it was not provided until the **Federal Aid**

Highway Act of 1956. This act earmarked the revenues from a new four-cents-per-gallon gasoline tax (increased in 1983 to nine cents) for the highway trust fund that was used to construct the **interstate highway system.** With a generous ninety–ten matching formula, each state received $100 million in federal funds for each $10 million it put up.

The interstate system of 42,500 miles was designed to be completed by 1972 at a total cost of $37.5 billion. Today all but 1,700 miles, mostly in metropolitan areas, has been constructed. The new target date for completion is 1990, and the total cost by that time will be nearly $100 billion. This massive expenditure of funds helped generate the so-called **highway lobby,** which has been one of the most potent political forces at both the state and national levels. As the cartoon on p. 411 illustrates, the highway lobby has effectively sought funds for highway construction while showing little sensitivity to related transportation needs.

The State Role in Highway Development

Historically, states provided aid to counties and municipalities that in turn built and maintained the roads. Under the federal stimulus of the Bureau of Public Roads, however, the state governments began taking over direct responsibility for building the system of state highways, and by 1924 every state had a department of highways.

Highlight
Traveling by Rail

The immense difficulty of using the railroad for local travel was documented by a vaudeville entertainer, Fred Allen, who wrote of his troubles in getting to various small towns and cities of the Midwest:

There never seemed to be a direct way the actor could go from one date to another without changing trains once or twice during the night and spending endless hours at abandoned junctions waiting for connecting trains. One trip always annoyed me. Terre Haute and Evansville, both in Indiana, were a split week. The acts playing the Hippodrome Theater in Terre Haute for the first three days went to the ﹍ant Theater in Evansville for the last three. ﹍d been possible to go directly from one ﹍ the other, the trip could have been

in three hours. It took the actors eight hours. Finishing at Terre Haute, they would leave there on the midnight train. After riding for an hour, they had to get off at some small town and wait four hours for a train to pick them up to ride the remaining two hours to Evansville. Most of the railroad stations were deserted at night. . . . Through the years, I have spent a hundred nights curled up in the dark, freezing railroad stations in the Kokomos, the Kenoshas, and the Kankakees, waiting for the Big Four, the Wabash, or C&A trains to pick me up and whisk me to the Danvilles, the Davenports, and the Decaturs.

Source: Fred Allen, *Much Ado About Me* (Boston: Little, Brown & Co., 1956), pp. 186–187.

Until the 1930s, highway construction and maintenance were financed primarily from general revenues. Gasoline tax revenues were not sufficient to pay for the immense costs of building and maintaining highways. As automobile ownership grew rapidly during the 1920s and 1930s, gasoline tax revenues soon exceeded the amount of money needed to build roads. To prevent the diversion of those gas tax revenues into the general treasury, the highway lobbies urged that gas tax revenues be earmarked for specific purposes.[5]

By 1970 forty-two states had **antidiversion legislation,** and twenty-eight states had written these antidiversion provisions into their constitutions.[6] The most common purposes for which gas taxes were earmarked were highways, airports, state police, water transport, and boating. Few states designated gas tax revenue for public transit purposes.

The Consequences of Imbalanced Transportation

These developments in the highway system have had several important consequences for the lives of most Americans. First, because of the unprecedented mobility it gave people, the highway system helped disperse the metropolitan life-style throughout the countryside. The highways and the electronic communications systems of telephone, television, radio, and com-

On a clear day you can see forever.

Source: Reprinted by permission from *Herblock's State of the Union* (New York: Simon & Schuster, 1972).

puter terminals now link the small town intimately to the metropolis. Possessing these communications links, many corporations increasingly construct new facilities in small towns beyond the fringes of the metropolis rather than in the heart of it.

The small town of the 1980s does not face the isolation that the same town might have faced a century earlier. The early-1900s characters of the novel *Main Street* were terribly isolated from the nearest metropolis, even though they were only a hundred miles away. Today, small-town residents can be just as urban by most criteria as the residents of the big city. They may have middle-class, managerial occupations in a state university, a branch office of a national corporation, or a local franchise outlet for a national retailing firm. The small-city residents may even have the best of both worlds. The residents of Tyler, Texas, can enjoy the advantages of Houston and Dallas and yet live a considerable distance away. They can drive to Houston in the morning in their air-conditioned automobiles, shop at Neiman-Marcus or some other prominent department store, attend an afternoon ball game in the Astrodome, have dinner at any number of excellent restaurants, and be back home in Tyler in time to watch the 10:30 movie on television. Never before has this kind of mobility been possible.

This unprecedented mobility has permitted, paradoxically, both a *decentralization* and a *recentralization* of social activities. For Tyler, Texas, the automobile has spread the metropolitan life-style into the countryside. Until the 1920s, cities developed along streetcar lines,[7] but the combination of excellent roads and mass-produced automobiles permitted real estate developers to build subdivisions in suburban areas not served by streetcars or buses. Retail merchants began to abandon the congested central business districts for attractive, new suburban shopping centers that had plenty of parking space. In this way, the road network decentralized the metropolis.

The road system has also reconcentrated social activities in the suburbs and far-flung, freestanding cities such as Tyler, Texas. Social institutions, especially public schools, became bigger in size and fewer in number. The road system made it possible to transport children to large schools; in this way small neighborhood schools gave way to large centralized ones.

A second consequence of the automobile age became apparent during the Arab oil embargo of 1973–1974. The United States was importing about one-third of the petroleum used to drive automobiles and heat buildings. This made the new diffuse life-style extremely vulnerable to interruption of foreign supplies.

A third consequence of the automobile age was the decline of the central cities of the Northeast and Midwest.[8] The freeways enabled retailers to abandon the central business district for the shopping centers in the suburbs, making it unnecessary for most people to venture into the old business districts except for an occasional excursion. The freeways built in the central cities tore up large numbers of homes and split up neighborhoods. In some cities, such as Los Angeles, Chicago, and Denver, they produced smog serious enough to require people with respiratory diseases to remain indoors during smog alerts. The third of the population that was too old, young, disabled, or poor to drive automobiles was increasingly compressed into central cities, where they had access to bus lines. The automobile did not by itself cause all of this, but increasing reliance on the highways after 1945 was one of the important factors in the decline of the central cities.

A fourth problem that has become serious in the 1980s is that the cost of maintaining the road system came to exceed available revenues. The highway trust fund paid only for constructing the interstate system; maintenance costs were left to the states. Congress in 1976 passed a four-R program (resurfacing, rehabilitation, restoration, and reconstruction). But the road systems have continued to deteriorate. A Federal Highway Administration report in 1981 estimated that over the next 15 years, 83 percent of all interstate highways would need repaving.[9]

Part of the deterioration of the interstate highways can be traced to big trucks. Heavy trucks present a problem because trucks weighing up to 80,000 pounds are now allowed on the interstate system, but those roads were not designed to accommodate loads that heavy.[10] The Congressional Budget Office estimated that taxes on trucks in this size range paid for only half of the wear and tear they added to the roadways.[11] To help alleviate these problems, Congress in 1982 and 1983 increased the road taxes that truckers would pay and also increased the federal gasoline tax by five cents per gallon. Four of those five cents were earmarked for interstate highway maintenance and one cent for mass transit. Several states also raised their gasoline taxes. These measures are beginning to slow down the deterioration of the nation's roads, but simply maintaining the roads at their current level until the end of the century will cost $18 billion per year.[12]

The Uncertain World of Public Transit

While automobile usage continues to climb, ridership on public transit (see Table 15–2) declined steadily from the 1940s until 1972. It then rose for the next ten years, peaking in 1982. Whether public transit usage will return to the short-term renaissance it enjoyed in the 1970s depends on several factors.

Disenchantment with Freeways

Part of the public transit renaissance in the 1970s was due to a growing disenchantment with urban freeway systems. Whereas the state highway departments successfully overrode neighborhood objections to the metropolitan

Table 15–2. Changing Ridership on Public Transit (in millions of passengers)

Year	Railway Streetcar	Railway Subway and elevated	Railway Total[a]	Trolley coach	Motor bus	Grand total
1935	7,276	2,236	9,512	96	2,618	12,226
1940	5,943	2,382	8,325	534	4,239	13,098
1945	9,426	2,698	12,124	1,244	9,886	23,254
1950	3,904	2,264	6,168	1,658	9,420	17,246
1955	1,207	1,870	3,077	1,202	7,250	11,529
1960	463	1,850	2,313	657	6,425	9,395
1965	276	1,858	2,134	305	5,814	8,253
1970	235	1,881	2,116	182	5,034	7,332
1971	222	1,778	2,000	148	4,699	6,817
1972	211	1,731	1,942	130	4,495	6,567
1973	207	1,714	1,921	97	4,642	6,660
1974	150	1,726	1,876	83	4,976	6,935
1975	124	1,673	1,810	78	5,084	6,972
1976[b]	112	1,632	1,759	75	5,247	7,081
1977[b]	103	1,610	1,728	70	5,408	7,286
1978	104	1,706	1,825	70	5,721	7,616
1979[b]	107	1,777	1,899	75	6,156	8,130
1980[b]	133	2,108	2,256	142	5,837	8,235
1981	123	2,094	2,232	138	5,594	7,964
1982	136	2,115	2,266	151	5,324	7,741
1983	137	2,167	2,307	160	5,422	7,889

Source: Transit Fact Book: 1970–71 (Washington, D.C.: American Public Transit Association), p. 6; *Transit Fact Book:* 1981, p. 54; *Transit Fact Book,* 1985, p. 32.

[a]Total includes some other rail forms of transit.

[b]The large changes in specific transit modes between 1976 and 1977 are mostly due to changes in the definition of passenger trips. The large changes in specific modes between 1979 and 1980 are mostly due to changes in the method of data collection.

freeways during the 1950s and 1960s,[13] by the 1970s several freeway projects were bogged down in legal and political infighting. In 1967, Memphis, Tennessee, residents successfully blocked the construction of a freeway through city parks.[14] In Washington, D.C., a decade-long battle persisted over proposals to construct a freeway through the city's affluent northwest section and a new bridge over the Potomac River. In Boston, neighborhood residents teamed up with urban planners from the Massachusetts Institute of Technology and political activists to block a stretch of freeway through their neighborhoods to downtown Boston.[15] And a protest of New Yorkers in 1985 brought an end to that city's so-called Westway project, a four-mile-long highway redevelopment project slated to cost $15,782 *per inch*.[16]

Federal Incentives for Public Transit

Equally important for the renaissance of public transit in the 1970s was a series of financial incentives that had started a decade earlier. The **Federal Aid Highway Act of 1963,** prohibited the use of federal highway funds in metropolitan cities unless those cities had a multimodal plan covering public transit as well as highways. This requirement that cities engage in transit planning was given further support the following year by the **Urban Mass Transportation Act of 1964,** which made the first federal grants for public transit planning. And nine years later, in 1973, the Interstate Transfer Program allowed any state to cancel nonessential portions of the interstate highway system and transfer the allotted money to local roads, rapid rail systems, or other mass transit. But relatively little money was actually diverted this way.[17]

None of these acts directly appropriated federal funds for urban transit construction or operations. This did not occur until 1970, when $3.1 billion was authorized for a five-year period. It was followed by the **Urban Mass Transit Act of 1974,** which authorized another $11.2 billion through 1979, roughly $2.2 billion per year. When this program expired, another $22 billion was authorized in 1980. In sum, $38.5 billion was authorized between 1970 and 1980; most of that money was actually appropriated and spent.*

The key legislation in this series of developments, the Urban Mass Transit Act of 1974, provided federal funds for operating expenses of transit systems. All previous federal funding had been limited to planning, construction, and other capital expenditures. These limits, however, had some counterproductive results. They encouraged a number of areas to plan for rapid rail systems even though they lacked the density of population to support such systems. They also caused buses to be replaced prematurely. One study of Cleveland and Chicago claimed that such purchases actually wasted 23 percent of the federal subsidy.[18]

Although limiting federal subsidies to capital expenditures has drawbacks, opening up federal subsidies for operating expenses also raised grave dangers. They would make the local transit systems more vulnerable to wage demands of unionized transit employees, and they would reduce the local agencies' incentives to run their operations efficiently.[19]

When Ronald Reagan became president in 1981, he proposed the elimination of operating subsidies and drastic reductions in all federal mass transit subsidies. After a long deadlock with him over these issues, Congress finally passed the **Surface Transit Assistance Act of 1982.** This act earmarked,

---

*When Congress *authorizes* expenditures, it provides the legal authority for spending, but the money cannot actually be spent until Congress in another vote *appropriates* the money. Because of this difference, funds spent seldom exactly match the amounts authorized.

through 1988, one cent of the federal gasoline tax to public mass transit. Although Reagan failed to get his proposed elimination of operating subsidies, the $17.7 billion authorized for public transit (from 1983 through 1986) amounted to about a 20-percent reduction from the amount being spent when Reagan took office.[20] When these funds approached expiration, Congress in 1987 authorized another $18 billion for mass transit through 1991.

At the heart of these conflicts over funding public transit is the realization that most public transit systems cannot be run at a profit. Only about 44 percent of public transit revenues come from fares and advertising. The rest comes from state (47 percent) or federal (9 percent) subsidies.[21] Even at the peak of public transit ridership in the early twentieth century, transit operations lost money. In Boston early transit operators built their streetcar systems primarily to transport people to real estate property they were developing on the fringes of the city. They not only lost money on their transit operations, they used their real estate profits to subsidize transit operations. Once the real estate was sold, they had no more incentives to subsidize the transit; and at that point they appealed to the city for financial aid. This occurred several times in Boston's history,[22] and the pattern was repeated throughout the United States. Schaeffer and Sclar write:

> The device was simple. A trolley line, charging low fares, was built beyond the city to marginal land, owned by the speculators. This land was then subdivided into building lots. The result was a manifold increase in the value of these real-estate holdings, which more than made up for operating trolley lines that were at best barely profitable. This connection between real estate profits and transit availability was thoroughly understood by the U.S. land speculators from coast to coast.[23]

An Increasing State Role

As federal aid for transit began to decline from the peak years of the 1970s, state and local governments took on an increased role. Transit fares went up, and state governments were forced to considering increasing their own transit subsidies. Some states and communities, of course, were more able to meet these challenges than were others. On one extreme, transit systems in Chicago and Boston were so plagued with financial difficulties that they cut service, raised fares, and saw their riderships decline. At the other extreme, San Diego relied exclusively on state and local funds to build its famous light rail system, and Dallas voters increased the sales tax to build a rapid rail system in their area.

Transit Options for the Nineties

In planning for effective public transit, each community must select the combination of transit vehicles that is most appropriate for its particular transit problem. Five major vehicle systems are available—expanded bus service, light rail systems, personal rapid transit (PRTs, or people movers), rapid rail systems, and commuter railroads.

Expanded Bus Service

Buses will remain the core of most transit systems. The greatest advantage of the bus is its flexibility. It can be driven any place where streets are paved. Buses can also be used in a variety of ways. Many metropolitan areas have experimented successfully with buses on special lanes in the freeways. Cars are prohibited from the reserved lanes, so that the buses can move faster than the traffic. *Para transit* refers to small vans that cruise fixed routes and pick up and drop off passengers at any point. *Minibuses* or *shop-and-ride* buses have been used for shuttle purposes between central business shopping areas and outlying parking lots. *Dial-a-ride* is a system of small buses: when residents telephone, a minivan cruising in the neighborhood is dispatched to the resident's home to transport the resident to some point within the area serviced by the dial-a-ride.

In addition to flexibility, bus service has the lowest capital costs of any existing public transit system. *Capital costs* refer to the cost of building or purchasing a facility, and they are distinguished from *operating or maintenance costs,* which are the costs of running the facility once it is built.

The major disadvantage of buses is that they are labor-intensive. Each bus, van, minibus, or other vehicle must have a driver. Drivers unionize. They bargain for higher wages, which increases the costs of operation. Bus operating expenses are also high for the large number of bus routes that do not attract enough passengers to pay for themselves.

Light Rail Systems

The light rail system is an updated version of the old streetcar. Streetcars are large, electrically powered vehicles that ride on tracks in the street. Most streetcar systems disappeared in the 1940s, when the transit companies changed to buses and paved over the streetcar rails. Between 1935 and 1970 the number of streetcar track miles declined from 25,000 to 762. In Los Angeles, which had an extensive streetcar system, the public transit company was purchased by a consortium owned by General Motors, Firestone, and Standard Oil, which tore up the tracks and replaced the streetcars with buses.[24]

In the late 1970s streetcars, or **light rail vehicles (LRVs),** as they were renamed, gained new popularity. Unlike buses, they do not pollute the air and they are not vulnerable to petroleum shortages. They can carry many more passengers (up to 500 in three cars linked together) and they have a longer expected life than do buses (thirty years compared to thirteen). San Diego opened a sixteen-mile system in 1981. By 1985 LRV systems were operating in a dozen cities.

PRTs, or People Movers

Personal rapid transit (PRT) is a proposal to have small cars running on a fixed rail system. Whereas subway cars and streetcars may carry up to 175 people, each PRT car would carry only six to ten people. Ideally, PRT lines could be constructed in a grid pattern with the lines no more than a mile apart, putting every resident of the city within walking distance of a PRT station. Because PRT cars are small, the fixed guideways needed for a PRT system would be much less costly than the fixed guideways needed for the subway or other rapid rail systems.

PRT promoters argue that it is the first major innovation in transit since the construction of electric subways in Boston in 1898. It exceeds the flexibility of the bus and is unaffected by motor fuel shortages. Because the cars can be computer-directed and need no driver, PRT's labor problems would be minimal.

Small-scale systems have been constructed and run successfully at some airports. The only attempts to establish a PRT or people mover system as a major element of city transit occurred in Morgantown, West Virginia (see p. 420), and Detroit, Michigan. Both systems were plagued by expensive cost overruns and ridership that fell short of original projections.[25]

Rapid Transit

The fourth option for urban transportation is the traditional **rapid transit**—electrically driven trains that run in subways, on ground, or on elevated guideways. Such systems currently exist in New York, Philadelphia, Boston, Cleveland, Chicago, San Francisco Bay Area, Atlanta, Miami, Baltimore, and Washington, D.C. The major advantage of rapid transit is that it can move more passengers than any other mode of transit. A comparison of the modes of travel in urban America can be seen in Table 15–3.

Table 15–3. How People Travel in Urban America

Mode of Travel	Millions of passenger miles logged, 1970	Percent of Total
Automobile	736,689	93.9%
Bus transit	20,864	2.7
Rail transit	16,928	2.2
Commuter rail	4,600	0.6
Taxicab	5,126	0.6
Total	784,207	100.0

Source: United States Department of Transportation, *1972 National Transportation Report* (Washington, D.C.: U.S. Government Printing Office, 1972), Table 6–1, p. 189.

Rapid rail transit is not appropriate in all places. Because it costs so much to build, it is most appropriate in areas with large populations, high densities, and large numbers of people moving into the central business district each day.[26] Even in such places rapid rail has had many problems. San Francisco's BART (Bay Area Rapid Transit), which opened in 1972, was the first rapid rail system to be built since the early 1900s. It has been heavily criticized for its initial cost overruns, its inability to run at a profit, and its failure to reduce traffic congestion in the San Francisco Bay–Oakland Area.[27] Atlanta's rapid rail system has been plagued by muggings, assaults, and other crime.[28] And Miami's Metrorail has suffered from disappointing ridership—only one-fifth of original projections.[29]

All of the new rapid rail systems, except for BART, were 80 percent built with federal grants, and their operating losses are partly made up for by federal operating subsidies. As the Reagan administration cut back on mass transit funding and sought to eliminate federal operating subsidies, new rapid rail systems were badly hit. Without the federal aid, Detroit and Miami, for example, cannot buy or build the feeder lines they had counted on to raise ridership on their people mover and Metrorail, respectively.

Given all these considerations, at the moment it appears as though the smartest cities were the ones that resisted the temptation to use federal grants to build rapid rail or people mover systems. But it is conceivable that history may judge otherwise. Of all the new systems, only BART has been operating for over a decade. And this may well be too short a time in which to evaluate such an expensive undertaking as a people mover or a rapid rail system. Conceivably, both New York and Chicago could have shown disappointing results only a few years after their subways first opened. Yet today those subway systems are invaluable, and in forty years San Francisco Bay Area residents, Atlantans, and Miamians may well be grateful for the wisdom of today's leaders in constructing their rail systems.

Commuter Railroads

The fifth major transit option is the commuter railroad. This mode of transit has suffered the sharpest decline in ridership. Except in extremely dense locations, such as New York and Chicago, commuter railroads cannot compete with automobiles. They are much more expensive to run than subway systems, and the fares are higher.

The Dubious Future of Public Transit

It is not clear whether mass transit can reverse its current decline and pick up with the renaissance it enjoyed in the 1970s. That renaissance had in great measure been financed by $54 billion in federal grants between 1970 and

Highlight
PRT in Morgantown

Morgantown, home of West Virginia University, was the scene of a daily traffic jam between the university's three campuses and the city's central business district. To relieve this congestion, the university requested a $13.5-million grant from the federal Department of Transportation (DOT) to construct a 3.6-mile, $18-million PRT system with six stops that would connect the university's parking lots, its three campuses, and downtown Morgantown. The forty-five vehicles would be 6 feet wide by 15 feet long, would seat eight and take another twelve standing commuters. The chauffeurless cars were to be electrically driven at 30 miles per hour by a computer. The system runs on an elevated concrete guideway that on completion was to extend 5.4 miles. The riders signal for a car by placing their fare cards in a slot and pressing a designation button. This signals the computer to dispatch a car to the riders' station to take them to their destinations.

Early in the planning, Morgantown's PRT got caught in national politics. DOT decided it wanted to dedicate the Morgantown PRT guideway before the 1972 presidential election, but it did not yet know how heavy the cars would be. To accommodate the heaviest possible car, it built a much heavier and thus much costlier structure than the one originally anticipated. Planning and construction were rushed, the project manager was changed, designs were altered, inflation hit double digits, and the cost of the project quickly overran the original estimates.

When the first phase was completed, costs had reached $59.8 million. Rather than a 5.4-mile system reaching all three university campuses, it was only 2.2 miles long and reached only two campuses. Rather than six stations, the system had only three. At one point, when the development of vehicles was delayed, the university ran golf carts along the guideway.

The university complained that this abbreviated system did not meet its needs and threatened to tear it down at a cost to DOT of $7 million if DOT did not move into phase II, which would complete the original plans. Phase II was projected at the time to cost another $53.8 million. This would bring the total cost for the system to $113.6 million, nearly $100 million more than the original estimate of $18 million. DOT agreed to finish phase II, which would add two more stations and complete the 5.4 miles of guideways.

By 1975 phase I was in operation and at peak rush hours could ferry 2,500 to 3,000 riders per hour. This could be doubled by reducing the headway between cars from the then-prevailing 15 seconds to 7.5 seconds. Whether the PRT system has reduced automobile congestion in Morgantown is not yet certain. DOT and the original promoters at the university consider the project a success. Some other observers are not quite so sure.

Source: "Trouble in Mass Transit," *Consumer Reports* 40, no. 3 (March 1975): 190–195.

1988. Under the Reagan administration, federal funding for urban mass transit declined sharply from its peaks of the late 1970s. The one-cent gasoline tax, which currently raises about $400 million per year for mass transit–operating subsidies, is scheduled to expire in 1988. And the massive federal deficits of the 1980s do not leave much room for expanding federal aid after 1988.

On the positive side, states and metropolitan areas have a transit planning apparatus in existence (which did not exist prior to the 1960s) to identify and propose solutions for transit problems. The action of Dallas voters in approving a sales tax to finance a rapid rail system for their area suggests that it may be possible for some areas to find local sources for transit expansion. And the absence of federal aid will force communities to consider their options more carefully in the light of local needs rather than on the availability of federal dollars. Eighty-percent funding for rapid rail or people mover construction is very hard to turn down. Left to their own devices and their own sources of funds, Detroit and Morgantown probably would not have made the mistakes they made with their people movers.

Finally, the 1980s' trend towards privatization is affecting public transit as well as other public services. There are some things that private companies can do that large public transit commissions cannot. This probably includes much para transit and jitneys. But there is also a danger of divesting to private companies the most profitable bus routes, leaving the large public transit commission to provide costly services on the less lucrative routes.

Housing and Community Development

A second area of infrastructure policy involves the framework for housing people and activities. In discussing these policy areas we need to examine: (1) the basic problems associated with housing and central-city deterioration; (2) the roles that states, communities, and the federal government play in housing and redevelopment policies; and (3) alternatives to present-day housing and community development programs.

The Basic Problems of Housing

Housing for Low-Income People

The first basic housing problem is that most low-income people cannot obtain decent housing at a reasonable cost. There is no agreement on what decent housing is, but certainly it would be superior to what the Census Bureau calls substandard. Substandard housing is physically dilapidated or lacks at least one of the three basic plumbing facilities (hot and cold piped water, a flush toilet, and a shower or bathtub). In 1980, 2.4 million families lived in substandard housing, down from 7.9 million in 1960 and 4.4 million in 1970.[30] A second measure of decent housing focuses on overcrowding. The accepted definition of overcrowding is more than one person per room. In 1980, 2.3 million families lived in overcrowded units, down from 6.0 million in 1960 and 5.1 million in 1970.[31] If we use these minimal definitions of overcrowded and substandard units to define decent housing, then between 2.3 and 4.4 million housing units in 1980 could be called indecent.

Although considerable progress has been made over the last twenty years in reducing the percentage of poor people living in substandard or overcrowded housing units, the poor have lost ground on getting that housing at a reasonable cost. The usual criterion for reasonable cost is that rent or mortgage payments should not exceed 25 percent of a household's income. In 1980, a solid majority of all central-city renters (55 percent) paid more than this amount, compared to only 44 percent who exceeded that amount in 1973.[32]

The most commonly given explanation for the poor quality and high cost of low-income housing is an insufficient supply of housing. The Federal Housing Act of 1968 stated that the national housing goal of a decent home for every American family would require the construction or rehabilitation of twenty-six million housing units over ten years, six million of these for low- and moderate-income families. In fact, the nation's builders came very close to meeting this goal. About twenty-one million new housing units were added to the nation's housing supply during the 1970s.[33] Nevertheless, housing supply was tight because of the growing trend toward one-person households, the rise in divorce rates, and the entrance into the housing market of the children of the 1950s baby boom. This demand for housing should begin to abate in the late 1990s as these trends are absorbed and as fewer people come into the age range in which they will buy houses.

Housing for the Moderate Income

For moderate-income families, whose goal most often is to own their home rather than rent it, the major problem today is the cost of buying a home. On the face of it, it would seem these people are clearly not priced out of today's housing market. By the mid-1980s, almost two-thirds of American families owned their own homes, up from 44 percent in 1940.[34] However, many middle-class families are able to afford a home only if both spouses work. For these families, the single biggest factor in determining what housing unit, if any, to buy, is the monthly mortgage payment they will have to make.

The monthly mortgage payment is a function of three factors: the purchase price of the house itself, the property taxes on the dwelling, and the interest

Figure 15–1. The Cost of Buying a Home (Median Sales Prices of Homes Sold)

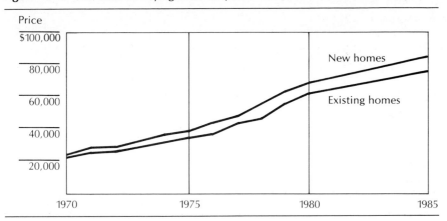

Sources: U.S. Bureau of the Census, *Statistical Abstract of the United States, 1982–83* (Washington, D.C.: U.S. Government Printing Office, 1982), p. 749; *Statistical Abstract of the United States, 1987* (Washington, D.C.: U.S. Government Printing Office, 1986), p. 707.

rate on the mortgage. The median purchase price of housing, as Figure 15–1 shows, has more than tripled since 1970. In some markets, such as California and the Northeast coast, costs have inflated even more. Like the inflation of purchase price, property taxes have also escalated steadily in most states. And mortgage interest rates have fluctuated widely. They have ranged from a low of 7.5 percent in the early 1970s to a high of over 13 percent in the early 1980s, dropping back to the 9 percent to 11 percent range in 1987. On a thirty-year fixed-rate mortgage, a rise of only 2 percentage points in the interest rate on a $75,000 mortgage drives up the monthly mortgage payments by $110.

The cartoon on p. 424 illustrates well the trade-off faced by most families: Should they buy a not-so-nice house with comfortable mortgage payments or a very nice house with uncomfortable mortgage payments? When inflation was rampant in the 1970s it made sense to go deeply into debt, because rising paychecks and rising home values would eventually build up a person's net assets and bring housing costs in line with his or her income. In the dis-inflationary environment of the 1980s, however, the reverse held true. Many people who went deeply into debt in 1979 or 1980 at the highest mortgage interest rates in American history did not receive large enough pay increases to bring their incomes in line with their expenses, and their home values did not escalate enough for them to sell out at a profit. The result? The percentage of home mortgages foreclosed increased each year during the first half of the 1980s.[35]

Source: Jerry Fearing, *St. Paul Pioneer Press*, 1979.

Racial Separation in Housing

Racial and cultural minorities find more obstacles in their search for decent housing than do whites of similar income levels. Only in 1948 did the Supreme Court hold that deed covenants that prohibited the sale of property to a noncaucasian were unenforceable in the courts. Federal Housing Administration (FHA) loans to nonwhites were prohibited as late as 1962. It was not until the Housing Act of 1968 that discrimination in the sale and rental of housing was made illegal.

This legislation expanded housing opportunities for many middle-income racial and cultural minorities. And racial separation is measurably less today than it was twenty years ago.[36] Nevertheless, separation and discrimination continue to exist. As late as 1976 the Department of Housing and Urban Development (HUD) was financing public housing in Chicago that was practicing the most blatant discrimination.[37] Suburbs continue to be mostly white, and only a small percentage of racial minorities live in suburbs. White populations continue to decline in most cities with large minority populations.

In the face of strong national legislation against racial discrimination in housing and in the face of apparent lessening of racial tensions in recent years, how can it be that racial separation in housing is still the predominant pattern throughout the nation? Part of the racial separation can be attributed no doubt to whites freely choosing not to live among blacks and blacks freely choosing not to live among whites. But much of it also is due to exclusionary zoning practices in the suburbs. **Exclusionary zoning** exists when a suburb requires each house to have expensive amenities, such as a large lot, a garage, a paved driveway, and other costly building-code demands, plus prohibiting low-rent apartment buildings. The more such requirements, the more expensive it is to build housing in a community. An elite suburb, as shown by the Highlight below, can easily keep out low-income people this way. Since racial minorities disproportionately earn low incomes, minorities necessarily bear the biggest burden of exclusionary zoning. The motivation behind exclusionary zoning is class-based rather than race-based, but the practice clearly has racial consequences. By keeping out low-income people, a community can effectively keep out most blacks and other minorities.

In 1975 New Jersey initiated a practice called **inclusionary zoning.** In that year the New Jersey Supreme Court refused to allow Mount Laurel township to zone out low-income housing. Instead, it required every town to "include" low-income housing in their development plans. Hence the term *inclusionary zoning*. Implementation of inclusionary zoning has been plagued with difficulties, and in 1983 the court reaffirmed its decision that all communities must include low-income housing. In 1985 the New Jersey state legislature created a Council on Affordable Housing to determine how the principle would apply in each town and each development project.[38]

Highlight
Keeping Minorities Out of Birmingham

Birmingham, Michigan, is an upper-income Detroit suburb with few blacks or other racial minorities among its 26,000 residents.

In fall 1977 Michigan's Housing Development Authority agreed to finance a 150-unit apartment complex for the elderly if Birmingham would in turn rehabilitate fifty existing houses for rental to low- and moderate-income families. Assuming that the low- and moderate-income families would be poor blacks, 4,600 Birmingham voters signed a petition urging the Birmingham Commission (the city council) to turn down this bargain.

When the city commission voted to approve the bargain, opponents began a petition drive to recall the six city commissioners who had voted for the plan. In April 1978 three of those city commissioners stood for reelection and were defeated by candidates who opposed the housing plan. Also on the ballot was a referendum on the housing plan itself. It was resoundingly defeated.

Source: New York Times, April 12, 1978.

Deterioration of Central-City Neighborhoods

A fourth housing problem is neighborhood deterioration, particularly acute in the big, old central cities of the Northeast and Midwest. In the early twentieth century the Jews, Poles, and Italians inherited housing formerly owned by the Irish and Germans. Now this housing is being turned over to the racial minorities. In the 1950s the Rogers Park section of Chicago, for example, was a prosperous, middle- and working-class, predominantly Jewish neighborhood. Today it is turning into a slum inhabited chiefly by Chicanos, Puerto Ricans, blacks, and Appalachian whites. The housing is a quarter century older now, and landlords are often reluctant to provide good maintenance for their buildings.

Neighborhoods such as Rogers Park are also hit hard by the practice called **red-lining.**[39] Banks and insurance companies supposedly draw a red line around deteriorating neighborhoods where it is a risky investment to make a mortgage loan or to insure a building. This makes mortgage loans and insurance hard to get in red-lined neighborhoods. In Brooklyn it was estimated in 1977 that 89 percent of the assets of mutual savings banks located in that city were invested in mortgages outside of Brooklyn.[40] When apartment owners are unable to get loans to improve their buildings, their more affluent tenants move out and are replaced by the less affluent. Homeowners who are lucky enough to get financing to sell their homes move to better neighborhoods. The red-lining practice accelerates the flight of the middle class to the suburbs. The incoming low-income people have more problems, and the inevitable result is that urban neighborhoods such as Rogers Park that are denied mortgage funds rapidly deteriorate.

Once the process of neighborhood deterioration starts, it is very difficult to stop. The South Bronx in New York City was plagued during the late 1970s by the abandonment of buildings by slum landlords, their vandalization by youths, and their destruction by arson. In some neighborhoods of the South Bronx, whole blocks were leveled, giving the appearance of a city struck by wartime bombing. In the late 1970s and early 1980s many cities began to see a small influx of middle-income and professional people back into certain inner-city neighborhoods. This has been called the **gentrification** process, and many city leaders hope that it signals an end to the cycle of neighborhood deterioration described here.

Displacement

Gentrification has been characterized by upper-middle-income and professional people moving into certain inner-city neighborhoods, refurbishing the homes there, and turning old apartment buildings into condominiums. In most cities the gentrifying neighborhoods are usually near the downtown area, are blessed with houses that have distinctive aesthetic qualities, and are often large enough to be converted into two- or three-unit condominiums. On the positive side, gentrification has led to neighborhood restoration, added to the urban tax base, and attracted an upper-middle-income population. This in turn provides an economic base for restaurants and chic shopping facilities. However, gentrification, like most developments, has not been an unmitigated blessing. On the negative side, it has led to the **displacement** of lower-income people, usually racial minorities, who are driven out of the houses and apartments that are in the process of being gentrified.[41] This phenomenon occurs because the gentrification process drives up property values to the point where landlords can no longer charge cheap rents. As low-income people are displaced from their former homes, they are forced to rent newer ones in adjacent neighborhoods, usually at higher prices.

The Intergovernmental Connection in Coping with Housing Problems

Governmental initiatives to deal with these housing and community development problems began in the late nineteenth century at the local level.* First, social reformers attacked the spread of urban slum housing[42] by enacting **building codes** that established minimum requirements for space, electricity, plumbing, and health matters such as garbage disposal. The first building codes were adopted in New York City in the 1860s after a cholera epidemic had spread through slum neighborhoods. By the early twentieth century most cities and states had adopted some form of housing regulations.[43] These codes had the paradoxical effect of driving up the cost of new housing for the poor; builders could not erect new housing that met rigorous housing codes and still keep the cost down.

The second early housing initiative was the enactment of zoning regulations, which divide a community into zones restricted to specific uses. The **zoning codes** were largely designed to protect residential, middle-class, single-family-home neighborhoods from low-income apartments, industrial establishments, and other developments that were considered undesirable. This second initiative has been enforced more effectively than have building codes.[44]

A third stage of governmental involvement in housing problems occurred in the 1930s in response to the Great Depression. The federal government set

---

*It could be argued that the federal Homestead Act of the 1860s was the first housing program. This act gave free land to people who would move into the western territories and live on the land for five years. But this was primarily an attempt to stimulate the westward movement and has little significance for contemporary housing problems.

up programs that the state and local governments were charged with implementing. This intergovernmental approach still characterizes housing and community development policymaking.

Helping Out the Middle Class — Mortgage Protection

The Federal Role. The Great Depression of the 1930s effectively destroyed the existing system of financing home purchases. The most common method to finance a home then was the so-called **balloon mortgage.** This required a down payment of 35 to 40 percent, and the life of the loan extended for ten to fifteen years. During those years the home buyer made only interest payments and was required to pay off the entire principal with a single, so-called balloon payment at the end of the period. If the home buyer had not accumulated enough savings to make the final payment, the lending institution foreclosed the mortgage, sold the house, and used the proceeds of the sale to pay the balance of the loan and other bank charges. Whether the home buyer got back any of the down payment depended entirely on whether home values had risen.

The Great Depression set off a vicious cycle of events that destroyed this system. By 1932 nearly 25 percent of the work force was unemployed. Those unemployed workers were unable to make their mortgage interest payments, thus depriving the banks, savings and loan associations, and credit unions of needed income. Lacking a national system of insured savings accounts, this declining income made it impossible for savings institutions to pay their depositors. In order to generate income, the lending institutions regularly foreclosed on mortgages that fell behind in interest payments. The supply of foreclosed homes vastly exceeded the demand for them, and home values dropped sharply. Unable to sell their foreclosed houses at a profit, unable to attract new depositors, and unable to pay existing depositors, many banks simply closed their doors. In 1930, 150,000 homes were foreclosed, and in 1933, over 4,000 banks failed. These record levels have never been exceeded.

The federal government responded by creating programs to aid the mortgage lenders. The Federal Housing Administration's (FHA) mortgage insurance, started in 1934, and the Veterans Administration (VA), started after World War II, insured mortgage loans and paid them off if the bank was forced to foreclose on a mortgage. These programs provided lower interest rates, lower down payments, longer mortgage periods, and a buildup of equity. In 1938 the Federal National Mortgage Association (FNMA) was created to purchase original mortgages, which enabled the issuing banks to use the new money to make more loans, pay off depositors, and meet other obligations.

Deposit insurance also strengthened the home mortgage market. By insuring savings accounts for up to $100,000, the federal government protected not only the depositors but also the lending institutions from a repeat of the disaster they had faced in the early 1930s.

These complicated mechanisms of mortgage protection were phenomenally successful. They helped increase the profitability of the mortgage lenders;[45] the number of bank failures declined from over 4,000 in 1933 to barely 300 during the balance of the 1930s. The new system also strengthened the control of large mortgage-lending institutions over the production, buying, and selling of homes.[46] And these new mortgage practices revolutionized the patterns of home ownership. Because of the rigid mortgage practices before the 1930s, home ownership was limited to barely 40 percent of all families. By the mid-1970s this proportion had risen to two-thirds, where it has stayed.[47]

State and Local Roles.   These programs giving mortgage help for middle-class housing have been primarily a transaction between federal government agencies and private lending institutions. State and local governments play a regulatory role. They charter and regulate the lending institutions. They establish the building codes and zoning regulations to which the newly built FHA and VA homes must conform. Many states also have usury laws that limit the amount of interest that can be charged on loans. Finally, many states have active programs of their own to generate housing opportunities for middle- and moderate-income people.

Housing Programs for the Poor — Public Housing

The Federal Role.   The Housing Act of 1937 provided for the Public Housing Administration (since 1965 a division of HUD) to contract with a local housing authority (LHA) to build apartment units that would be rented to low-income tenants at a subsidized rate. By 1974, when housing programs were overhauled, over 1.3 million housing units were rented by over five million families.[48] Most cities had long waiting lists of people applying to public housing projects.

Public housing was originally designed to provide housing assistance for middle- and working-class people who had been temporarily driven out of decent housing by the depression. Because very little housing was constructed from 1929 until the end of World War II, by 1945 an enormous housing shortage existed. During the next thirty years a housing construction boom took place largely in the suburbs and in the fast-growing cities of the South and Southwest. By the early 1960s the supply of middle-class housing had caught up with the demand. Upwardly mobile tenants abandoned the public housing projects in the 1950s and 1960s. They were replaced by the poor, primarily by black migrants from the South and by Latinos.

State and Local Roles.   Although initiated and overseen by the federal government, public housing was actually implemented by a local government agency, the local housing authority (LHA). The local city council establishes the LHA and approves its contract with the Public Housing Administration to build low-income apartments. Most LHAs were formed in the large central cities.[49] Once created, the LHA sold tax-exempt municipal bonds to raise the funds needed to buy land and build the projects. The LHA administers the project and retires the debt through the rent it collects from tenants. Since these rents are never high enough to let the project break even, the Public Housing Administration subsidizes the LHA for each low-income family in the project.

If success is measured by the demand for a product, then public housing has been very successful. Long waiting lists exist for most projects. Nevertheless, public housing has its problems and has been bitterly criticized. It increasingly concentrated low-income blacks in big-city ghettoes. In some places, public housing was used deliberately to relocate blacks from scattered locations throughout the cities to a few large ghettoes.[50] Some public housing projects concentrated large numbers of people with extensive social problems into the same residential area, leading to unsatisfactory living conditions for the majority of the residents of those projects. One of the worst of these was the Pruitt-Igoe project in St. Louis, which finally had to be closed.

Pruitt-Igoe was not typical of all public housing projects. Other cities followed different site patterns. In Dade County, Florida, public housing was located on 100 sites scattered throughout the county. In New York, Chicago, and St. Louis, it was commonly located in high-rise apartments. An analysis of crime statistics in housing projects in New York City found that the high-rise projects were much more prone to violent crime than were the low-rise buildings.[51]

Many of the public housing defects were attributed to the program's tendency to concentrate racial minorities, broken families, families subsisting on welfare, and recent migrants into the big cities. Concentrating people with several social problems together into large, high-rise buildings without supportive social services probably made social disorganization in the public housing projects inevitable. These problems are compounded by the poor upkeep maintenance that characterizes most projects. The LHAs function like slum landlords.

Housing for Low- and Moderate-Income People

Public housing operated mainly for people at or near the poverty line. The FHA and VA mortgage protection programs operated mainly for the middle classes. But a large number of people fell between those categories. Their incomes were too high to qualify for public housing but too low to qualify for traditional VA, FHA, or conventional mortgages.

During the 1950s and 1960s, a number of federal programs were passed to assist low- and moderate-income people. These programs used a variety of techniques, including subsidizing the interest rate of loans to builders and to tenants and subsidizing part of tenants' rents. Some of the programs sought to stimulate construction of low-income housing and others to encourage demand for this housing. None of the programs worked satisfactorily.[52] In 1974 a reorganization of low- and moderate-income housing programs brought forth the Section 8 program. This was a program for leased public housing, which will be discussed later in the chapter.

Urban Renewal

Distinct from federally sponsored housing programs was the **urban renewal** program, which was created by a 1949 amendment to the Housing Act of 1937 and which allowed part of the housing money to be used for commercial development. The resulting program was called *urban renewal.*

The primary objective of urban renewal was to clear blighted areas and redevelop them with a mixture of commercial and residential establishments

Highlight
The Death of Pruitt-Igoe

The most criticized of all public housing was probably the Pruitt-Igoe project in St. Louis, although it had received wide praise from architectural critics when it was built in the 1950s. It originally was built to house both blacks and whites, with the whites in the Igoe part and the blacks in the Pruitt part. After federal courts prohibited segregation in public housing, the two sections were integrated. The whites slowly moved out, and eventually the project became overwhelmingly black. The residents were continually harassed by teenage gangs that mugged and raped women. Broken windows went unrepaired, and glass scattered on the ground below went uncleared. Residents complained that the elevators were unsafe and were continually used for toilets. The laundry facilities were unsafe. One resident

commented that although her apartment itself was much nicer than homes she had previously lived in, the surrounding environment was dirty, dangerous, and unsanitary.

So dangerous and unpleasant was the Pruitt-Igoe project, in fact, that people refused to live in it. Its 2,700 apartments never maintained high occupancy rates. And in 1972 the failure of this project was publicly admitted when the buildings were vacated and some of them torn down.

Sources: Lee Rainwater, "The Lessons of Pruitt-Igoe," *Public Interest* (Summer 1967): 116–126; Eugene J. Meehan, *Public Housing Policy* (New Brunswick, N.J.: Rutgers University Press, 1975); and Nicholas J. Demarath, "St. Louis Public Housing Study Sets Off Community Development to Meet Social Needs," *Journal of Housing* 19 (October 15, 1962): 472–478.

that would truly renew the old neighborhoods. Urban renewal was thus distinguished from public housing in that it focused on commercial redevelopment. Also in contrast to public housing, urban renewal developments were turned over to private entrepreneurs rather than owned by a government body, the local housing authority.

To qualify for urban renewal funds, a city had to create a local public agency (LPA), which was sometimes the same as the local housing authority. The LPA designated land to be cleared with urban renewal funds and submitted to the federal urban renewal agency a *workable program* for redevelopment.

When the local plan was approved, the federal urban renewal agency provided funds for the LPA to acquire the land, clear it, and reinstall the public facilities such as sewer and water. After this was completed, the LPA offered the land to redevelopers, who bought it at a much reduced price and erected their establishment on it. The federal government typically paid two-thirds of the LPA's net cost (acquisition, clearance, and upgrading costs less the price paid by the redeveloper), and the rest was made up through local bonds, cash, or other funds.

The residents and former merchants in the redevelopment area had to relocate to new areas. The LPA was obliged to give relocation assistance to the residents, but in fact this aid was seldom adequate[53] and displacement of these residents became one of the biggest complaints against urban renewal. One study of urban renewal found that over 60 percent of 750 displaced former merchants never reopened their businesses after being forced to move.[54]

In sum, the major impact of urban renewal was to redevelop the central business districts (CBDs) and other commercial areas of the major cities. Although urban renewal was instrumental in rebuilding many CBDs, it was resoundingly criticized from a variety of fronts. Community activists and architectural critics objected to it for destroying functioning communities.[55] Black leaders referred to urban renewal as Negro removal. Conservatives criticized it for using governmental authority to take property from one group of private citizens (the private homeowners and merchants) and turning it over to another (the redevelopers).[56] Perhaps the clinching argument against urban renewal was that despite the billions of dollars spent between 1949 and 1974, the central cities were not renovated. Nor did urban renewal stop the decline of central cities. Although Pittsburgh, for example, made one of the most concentrated and renowned renewal efforts, its population dropped from 677,000 in 1950 to 520,000 in 1970.

The benefits of urban renewal have gone primarily to the redevelopers, the builders, the bankers, and the new users of the renovated land. The costs have been borne by the low-income people and merchants who have been forced to relocate and by the taxpayers who provide the revenue.[57]

Restructuring Housing and Renewal Programs:
The 1974 Housing and Community Development Act

By the early 1970s federal housing and urban renewal programs were resoundingly criticized. They also were caught in bitter infighting between the White House and Congress. President Nixon wanted a program that would be cheaper and simpler to administer. In early 1973 he proposed consolidating several categorical grants into a single community development program that would give cities and states complete discretion to spend the funds as they saw fit. Nixon also impounded the money that Congress had appropriated for housing, urban renewal, model cities, and several other programs that were to be replaced by his community development project.

The impoundments enraged most big-city officials and most racial minority leaders. Although these leaders had criticized urban renewal and public housing, they swiftly perceived that Nixon's new approach would decrease the amount of federal money going to big cities, would dilute the funds by spreading them out to many communities, and would decrease the federal government's ability to target its assistance to the poor, the needy, and the racial minorities.

The final result of this infighting was the **Housing and Community Development Act of 1974.** This act made the most drastic changes in housing policy since the urban renewal program was started in 1949. As indicated by the title, the 1974 act focused on two general provisions—community development and housing.

The community development provisions consolidated seven categorical grant programs, including urban renewal, into a community development block grant (CDBG) of $8.4 billion annually from 1975 to 1977. Successive renewals in 1977, 1980, and 1983 have kept it alive. Cities may use their community development funds for urban renewal purposes, more public housing, or other activities ranging from code enforcement to improving certain public services. To get its funds, a community submits a community development plan, which identifies its development needs and outlines a program to meet those needs. Under a complicated formula, each community of over 50,000 is automatically entitled to a specific sum. And in the initial round of CDBG grants, a *hold harmless* provision assured that no community would receive less than the annual average it had received under the consolidated programs over the preceding five years. During the Reagan administration, CDBG funds were reduced sharply, but localities were given much more flexibility on how they could use the funds.[58]

The housing portion of the 1974 Housing and Community Development Act authorized annual expenditures of $1.225 billion under a rent supplement program called **Section 8.** Under Section 8, the LHA provides rent assistance for tenants whose total family income is less than 80 percent of the median income for the area. Tenants pay between 15 and 30 percent of their income (depending on the size and circumstances of the family) to the landlord. The LHA uses federal funds to pay the landlord the difference between that amount and a maximum allowable rent established by HUD.

Compared to earlier housing and urban development programs, the 1974 act vastly decentralized control to the local level in three ways. First, the consolidation of previous categorical grant programs into one block grant gave city councils much greater discretion over the use of these funds. Second, the funds went directly to the city governments rather than to the LPAs and LHAs, as had occurred under the urban renewal and public housing programs. These agencies thus became more closely controlled by the city councils than they had been. Third, the new law demanded citizen participation in planning.

Did the 1974 act achieve all its goals? Assessments suggest that the act is not doing as much as its supporters hoped or its opponents feared. As its supporters desired, the new program clearly strengthened the city councils in dealing with the LPAs and LHAs. One analysis of the community development program concluded that it decentralized power away from Washington while it gave more influence to the locally elected chief executives.[59] How CDBG funds were used seems to vary greatly from city to city. In St. Paul, Minnesota, a strong mayor exerted considerable influence to promote several large redevelopment projects downtown. In four New England cities, by contrast, the mayors exerted very little influence, and CDBG funds were scattered to neighborhood projects throughout the cities.[60] In much of the South, a civil rights group complained, compliance with CDBG requirements for citizen participation mostly ignored activists in poor communities.[61] But in Austin, Texas, poor neighborhoods were well represented.[62]

In contrast to the community development portion of the 1974 act, the Section 8 rent supplement portion seems to be working effectively. By guaranteeing landlords a fair rent in return for upgrading their apartments to local building codes, Section 8 has created a major incentive for rehabilitating existing housing rather than demolishing it. Section 8 rent supplements also made it possible to spread subsidized housing into white, middle-class neighborhoods. Although these neighborhoods had historically been willing to accept subsidized housing for the elderly, they usually balked at providing such units for poor families, and previous attempts at scattered-site public housing had failed. The Section 8 program was more successful than previous public housing at spreading subsidized housing into the suburbs.

Though Section 8 has simplified federal housing programs and has run fairly smoothly during the 1970s, it has not been free of problems.[63] For example, critics argue that the main housing problem in the 1980s will not be the adequacy of standard housing so much as its cost. Housing costs inflated so drastically during the 1970s that most low- and moderate-income people were spending high proportions of their incomes for rent or mortgage payments. Since Section 8 subsidizes the difference between actual rent and 30 percent of a tenant's income, it can be a very expensive program.[64]

Housing Options for the 1990s

Although the 1974 Housing and Community Development Act has corrected some of the worst abuses that existed under previous programs, criticisms of the community development block grant program and the Section 8 housing program suggest that new options may be needed for the 1990s. These options tend to fall under one of two strategies. The **filter-down strategy** seeks to stimulate new housing construction primarily for upper-income people, whose old homes will "filter down" to lower-income people. From this point of view, it makes little sense to construct new housing for the poor. Such housing is invariably quite expensive and consequently is seen as an inefficient way to increase total housing supply. The **direct-production strategy** seeks to do the opposite. It argues that the filter-down approach does not provide enough housing for poor or moderate-income people and necessarily leads them to pay a high percentage of their income for housing. The direct-production strategy thus favors the direct construction of housing for the poor either under the Section 8 program, the old Public Housing program, or a number of other construction programs.[65] Three housing options in particular reflect these two strategies. They are outlined next.

Population Relocation

One possible alternative is a combined federal-state initiative to relocate families to new communities. The federal government attempted to do this twice during the 1960s. The New Communities Act of 1968 proposed construction of sixteen federally subsidized new towns over a twenty-year period. The original idea was to promote new towns as a device for channeling suburban growth into designated areas, as the British had done with their new towns around London.[66] This plan would curb suburban sprawl and would open moderate-income housing opportunities in the suburbs. Within six years, however, the program was in shambles, and it was terminated by the 1974 Housing and Community Development Act.[67] HUD had a huge financial loss because several new town projects were started but never completed.

The second federal initiative was the concept of **new towns in town.** Using federally owned land in several large cities, the Johnson administration in 1967 planned to coordinate several existing federal programs to build new communities to demonstrate that federal programs could serve as a revitalization focus to attract people back to the cities. The program was eventually abandoned without a single new-town-in-town. In the words of one observer, it "was unequivocally a failure."[68]

Despite the failures of the New Communities Act and the new-towns-in-town concept, population relocation goes on all the time. When NASA built its Cape Kennedy space center it literally created a new metropolitan area in Florida's Broward County. However, it did none of the advanced planning that goes into the new-town concept. The two most successful new towns in America—Reston, Virginia, and Columbia, Maryland—stand as evidence that new towns can be a viable option to suburban sprawl. Both of these were planned and built by private developers.

The Reagan Voucher Plan

President Ronald Reagan in 1981 proposed reorganizing federal housing aid through a **housing voucher plan.** Under this plan, which was consistent with his conservative philosophy, eligible people would receive a voucher to pay for rent on any unit in the private housing market. An experimental housing-allowance program that served over 20,000 people in the 1970s[69] was cited as evidence that vouchers would work. Theoretically such a program would reduce the role of public housing authorities in running apartment complexes of their own or in determining what other apartments qualify for the Section 8 program. Whether such a housing voucher program would actually meet people's housing needs, of course, would greatly depend on how poor one had to be to qualify and what the value of the voucher would be. On both of these criteria, the Reagan proposals were quite stringent. They proposed complete replacement of the Section 8 program with vouchers that would go only to people whose income was 50 percent below the median income for their area and paying rents that exceeded 50 percent of their income.[70] Such requirements were far beyond the eligibility requirements for existing housing programs at the time.

For the first two years of the Reagan administration little happened in national housing policy because of a stand-off between the White House's filter-down strategy of vouchers and the production strategy favored by Democrats in the House of Representatives. Finally, in 1983, a compromise housing bill renewed the CDBG program for three more years, allotted $1.3 billion for construction under the old public housing program, authorized $9.9 billion for Section 8, and set aside $242 million for a demonstration housing-voucher program that would serve 15,000 people. Repealed was any new rental housing construction under Section 8.[71]

Innovations in Home Financing

In the early 1980s, people who wanted to buy housing were being served less and less well by the long-term, low-interest, low-down-payment, government-insured mortgages pioneered by the FHA during the Great Depression of the 1930s. This was in great measure a function of skyrocketing inflation rates and soaring interest rates. When inflation rates stay high, mortgage bankers suffer losses (because they are getting paid back in dollars that have lower purchasing power). For this reason, banks and savings and loan associations were reluctant to make long-term loans unless they could charge extremely high interest rates or adjust their interest rates over the years. Housing prices soared during these years, and this made it difficult for low-income people and young people to make the required down payments and monthly payments.

If it had not been for a number of mortgage innovations and **creative financing** ideas that emerged during these years, the housing market might well have collapsed. Creative financing refers to a variety of arrangements in which the seller lends part of the mortgage money to the buyer, often by accepting part of the down payment in the form of a balloon loan that matures in three to five years. To assist young people who cannot afford mortgage payments under conventional plans, mortgage lenders introduced *flexible mortgage rates* and *graduated payment mortgages.* Conventionally, a borrower's monthly payment is the same amount in the first month of the mortgage as it is in the last, a payment schedule that puts a heavy burden on the borrower in the first years of the mortgage but lightens that burden as his or her income rises. The graduated payment plan would start with low monthly payments that barely cover the interest costs. As the borrower's income goes up, however, the monthly payments also go up. This plan thus makes home mortgages available to people who currently cannot initially afford them. Under flexible mortgage rate plans, the lending bank is permitted to raise or lower the mortgage interest rate in future years to conform to national trends in interest rates.

Also designed to help out young people with little down-payment money are the *shared appreciation plans,* in which the lender shares some of the equity in the house and the borrower is obliged to buy out that equity within a specified number of years.

The *reverse mortgage* was approved in 1978 by the Federal Home Loan Bank Board. This plan is designed to provide cash to people who have their home mortgages paid off and want to use that equity to supplement their monthly income. Under this plan, a couple might take out a $48,000 mortgage on their $60,000 house and receive a $450-per-month check for a number of years until the $48,000 is used up. At that point, if inflation continues, the house can be sold for enough money to pay off the new debt. Some nonprofit institutions are willing to provide a variation of the reverse mortgage in which an elderly couple donate their property to the institution when they die. In exchange for this the institution permits the couple to live expense-free in the house. Because the recipient institution will ultimately get the equity in the house, it can afford to pay them a monthly amount until they die. In this way, the couple is able to take advantage of the equity in their house to maintain an expense-free home and a guaranteed monthly income.

Political Values and the Social Consequences of Infrastructure Policy

Infrastructure policies do not take place in a vacuum. They reflect political values of society at large. And they have important social consequences.

Political Values and Infrastructure Policy

The importance of political values to infrastructure policy can be seen clearly in relation to housing policies. The conservative perspective[72] seeks to minimize public-sector involvement in direct subsidy of housing as much as possible. Thus conservatives opposed the original Public Housing Act in 1937, and in 1949 they used their influence to involve the private sector in the Urban Renewal amendments to the Housing Act. They favor income tax deductions to help middle-class people pay for their mortgages.

Conservatives are reluctant to provide housing assistance to the poor for the same reasons that they are reluctant to provide welfare assistance in general to the poor. Poverty is seen as an individual defect rather than a product of the social structure. To the extent that conservatives support housing assistance to the poor, they tend to favor housing allowances or vouchers, as proposed by the Reagan administration. From a philosophical point of view, vouchers have a decided advantage over public housing programs because they maximize freedom of choice. There is some contradiction in conservative thinking on vouchers, however. Philosophically, conservatives are sympathetic to the working poor and unsympathetic to those who will not work to support themselves. In practice, however, conservatives tend to put very stringent eligibility requirements on vouchers so that the working poor are necessarily eliminated from participation.

In contrast to the conservative perspective, liberals prefer housing aid as in-kind assistance through direct-production strategies. Thus they are more favorable to the rental housing construction and rehabilitation components of Section 8 than they are to housing vouchers. Liberals fear that widespread use of housing vouchers will only drive up rents and effectively negate the impact of the aid. Liberals usually face an uphill battle for housing aid (as with other welfare aids) against majority political forces that want to provide only minimal welfare or housing assistance. This puts liberals in the position of having to make compromises that undermine the very programs they are trying to create. R. Allen Hays made this point succinctly when he wrote:

> Liberal politicians usually have to fight hard to get any sort of program put in place, no matter how limited in scope or design. Yet, the limits they must accept make the program vulnerable to valid criticisms from other liberal scholars, journalists, and policy advocates concerning its design, administrative procedures, comprehensiveness, or equity. . . . Such critiques may actually serve to undermine political support for existing programs, rather than generate pressures for expansion.[73]

In relation to transportation policy, liberal-conservative differences are not as marked as they are in housing and social welfare areas. Nonetheless, differences exist. Conservatives are more receptive to highway aid than they are to public transit aid. It is more consistent with their philosophy of freedom of choice. Public transit can take you only where the transit lines run, but automobiles can take you virtually anyplace you want to go. Furthermore, a highway construction in today's environment is likely to follow development rather than seek to channel it into predetermined sectors of the region. Conservatives also favor privatization of public transit systems by having them divest themselves of services that could be run profitably by private companies.

Liberals, since they also drive automobiles, do not reject highway aid. But they are much more sympathetic to public transit aid than are conservatives. Liberal ideology is also much more sympathetic to the notion that metropolitan development should be planned and coordinated. And they favor the use of public transit planning as a means to control and channel metropolitan growth. Liberals are skeptical of the current trend toward privatization of public transit systems. They fear that the most lucrative services will be spun off to private companies, and minimally subsidized public transit commissions will end up fighting uphill battles to get funds to run the unprofitable bus routes. Pointing out that probably a third of the population cannot get around without public transit, liberals would much prefer that all services be centralized in a metropolitan transit commission so that the profitable transit services could subsidize the unprofitable ones.

The Social Consequences of Infrastructure Policy

If infrastructure policy reflects ideological differences, it also has important social consequences for the social services discussed in Chapter 13. First, as seen from our review of transportation and housing policies, these policies over the past half-century played important roles in creating the racial residential patterns of de facto segregation. The great central cities, for example, might have kept expanding and never been ringed by independent suburban municipalities had it not been for a number of government policies and practices: federal highway aid, which helped build the suburbs; lax state municipal incorporation laws, which permitted suburban governments to form; and rigid annexation laws, which prevented central cities from expanding through annexation. Added to these were policies that enabled many suburbs to segregate: restrictive covenant clauses in deeds that prohibited the sale of such houses to noncaucasians and that were not struck down until 1948;[74] FHA regulations that financed much of suburbia but that prohibited mortgage loans to noncaucasians until 1962; local exclusionary zoning ordinances, which drove up the price of homes to the point where few minorities could afford them; deliberate attempts by some housing authorities to keep minorities out of housing projects in white neighborhoods or white suburbs; and deliberate attempts (as in the case of Birmingham, Michigan) to keep public housing out of specific suburbs. Some observers look at these facts and conclude that there is no such thing as de facto segregation (see Chapter 14), that government involvement at all levels was so extensive in building the segregated metropolis that most segregation is in fact de jure.

A second way in which infrastructure policies have social consequences is that they impede upward social mobility for the very poor. The housing displacement that results from urban renewal and highway construction usually forces the affected people into more expensive homes that take a larger share of their income. Redevelopment projects that replace mom-and-pop stores with shiny office buildings reduce entrepreneurial opportunities in poor neighborhoods. Policies promoting suburban sprawl transform the most dynamic economic areas many miles from poor residential neighborhoods. And policies that promoted the decline of public transit made it harder for poor people to get to locations where jobs are growing at the most rapid rate.

Of course, not all physical development policies hindered upward mobility. Public housing programs helped poor people meet their housing costs. In short, most of the infrastructure policies have a middle-class bias. The poor may have benefited from housing and transportation policies to some degree, but not nearly to the degree that the middle class has benefited.

Summary

1. The basic transportation problem in America is lack of balance. Excessive reliance on the highway system has left a substantial minority of the population without mobility, has made our transportation vulnerable to foreign

supplies of fuel, and has created a maintenance problem that may be more costly than the original highway construction.

2. Several factors have led to the rise of the highway system to its dominant position in transportation—technological changes, railroad neglect, the emergence of the highway lobby, and the earmarking of gasoline tax revenues to highways by both state and federal governments.

3. The 1970s saw what appeared to be a renaissance in public transit. Public transit ridership began to increase for the first time in a generation, and substantial federal aids were earmarked for transit purposes for the first time. By the 1980s, however, public transit ridership was no longer rising, and federal transit expenditures were no longer growing. States were forced to assume greater responsibility for financing public transit.

4. Urban transit options are most often discussed in terms of the kind of *vehicle* that should be used. The five major options are expanded bus service, light rail systems, people movers, rapid rail systems, and commuter railroads.

5. Housing problems have led to the evolution of housing and community development programs that are intergovernmental in scope. Federal housing programs are implemented by local public housing authorities. Until 1974 urban renewal programs were administered by local public agencies, which had considerable autonomy from local mayors and city councils.

6. The 1974 Housing and Community Development Act completely restructured housing and renewal programs. It consolidated ten categorical grants into a single community development block grant. It gave the city councils greater control over the LPAs and LHAs. It gave local governments more discretion over the use of housing and community development funds. It required citizen participation in planning the use of community development funds. And it put the emphasis on rent supplements rather than on construction of more public housing projects.

7. Three options likely to attract some attention during the 1990s are population relocation, more variety in home mortgage practices, and President Reagan's housing voucher plan.

Key Terms

Antidiversion legislation State laws that prohibit gasoline taxes and highway-use funds from being used for purposes not related to highways and automobiles or trucks.

Balloon mortgage A mortgage plan in which one makes interest payments over the life of the mortgage but does not make any repayment of principle until the end of the mortgage, when the entire principle is due in a single, so-called balloon payment.

Building code A municipal ordinance that establishes minimum requirements for space, electricity, plumbing, and health matters for residential buildings.

Creative financing A plan of financing home mortgages in which the seller uses a variety of devices to effectively lend money to the buyer. It became popular during the late 1970s and early 1980s, when inflation and interest rates were high.

Direct-production strategy The housing production strategy that focuses on providing housing assistance directly to low-income people.

Displacement The phenomenon whereby low-income people are forced to move out of their homes by urban renewal agencies, by the gentrification process, or by freeway construction.

Exclusionary zoning The practice by a municipality of putting expensive construction requirements in the local zoning plan and building code. This drives up the cost of new housing and thus excludes low-income people.

Federal Aid Highway Act of 1956 The act that established the federal gasoline tax that was earmarked for construction of the interstate highway system.

Federal Aid Highway Act of 1963 The act that prohibited the use of federal highway funds in metropolitan areas unless those areas had a multimodal transportation plan.

Filter-down strategy A housing production strategy that focuses on constructing new housing for upper-middle-income people on the assumption that their old housing will "filter down" to the poor and moderate-income people.

Gentrification The process whereby upper-middle-income whites move into inner-city neighborhoods and rehabilitate the homes there.

Highway lobby An alliance of cement manufacturers, construction firms, trucking firms, and certain labor organizations that for years has successfully lobbied for highway construction projects.

Housing and Community Development Act of 1974 The federal legislation that established the Section 8 housing program and the Community Development Block Grant program.

Housing voucher plan A proposal of the Reagan administration to replace existing housing programs with a voucher plan in which poor people could receive government vouchers that would be redeemable for rent payments much in the same way that food stamps are redeemable for buying groceries.

Inclusionary zoning The practice, as adopted in New Jersey, of requiring municipalities to include in their housing plans provisions for low-income people.

Infrastructure The roads, buildings, sewers, water supply systems, and similar structures essential for an economy to operate.

Interstate highway system The system of over 40,000 miles of divided, limited-access highways that crisscross the United States.

Light rail vehicle (LRV) A modern-day version of the streetcar. A large vehicle powered by overhead electric cables, run on tracks in city streets, and capable of carrying up to 200 passengers.

New-towns-in-town A federal program seeking to use federally owned land in cities to construct elaborate redevelopment projects that would include commercial, residential, and cultural facilities.

Primary road system The major set of roads connecting a state's urban centers.

Rapid transit The traditional big-city subway or elevated train systems that run large, electrically driven trains along fixed guideways that may be at ground level, elevated, or underground.

Red-lining The practice of mortgage lenders and insurance firms not providing mortgages or home insurance in risky areas of cities. So called because the lending associations have supposedly drawn a red line around the affected areas.

Secondary road system A set of roads lining farms and remote urban areas to a state's primary road system.

Section 8 A housing program initiated by the Housing and Community Development Act of 1974. It provides for leased public housing by authorizing a local housing authority to pay a portion of poor people's rent directly to the landlord.

Surface Transit Assistance Act of 1982 A federal law that earmarked, through 1988, one cent of federal gasoline tax revenue for public transit.

Tertiary road system The street system within urban areas.

Urban Mass Transit Act of 1974 The act that authorized the first extensive federal funding of mass transportation, including operating expenses as well as capital expenses.

Urban Mass Transportation Act of 1964 The act that provided the first federal grants for public transit planning.

Urban renewal A federal redevelopment program started in 1949 under which local public agencies used federal funds to clear blighted areas and resell the land to private developers, who would construct apartments or commercial buildings on the sites.

Zoning code A municipal ordinance that divides the city into different zones, with each zone being limited to specific kinds of structures. Some zones permit only single-family residences. Others permit retail commercial buildings. Others permit heavy industry.

References

1. Alan Lupo, Frank Colcord, and Edmund P. Fowler, *Rites of Way: The Politics of Transportation in Boston and the U.S. City* (Boston: Little, Brown and Co., 1971).

2. K. H. Schaeffer and Elliott Sclar write: "Even in their heydays around 1920 the U.S. railroads on a per-capita basis carried only a third of the passengers of the British and German railroads, or a fifth of the passengers of the Swiss system." *Access for All*, Transportation and Urban Growth (Baltimore: Penguin, 1975), p. 41.

3. Ibid., p. 44.

4. See Marshall McLuhan, *The Mechanical Bride: Folklore of Industrial Man* (New York: Vanguard, 1951).

5. Schaeffer and Sclar, *Access for All,* p. 48.

6. Advisory Commission on Intergovernmental Relations, *Toward More Balanced Transportation: New Intergovernmental Proposals,* Report A-49 (Washington, D.C.: U.S. Government Printing Office, 1974), p. 218.

7. See Sam Bass Warner, Jr.'s analysis of Boston's growth in his *Streetcar Suburbs: The Process of Growth in Boston, 1870-1900* (Cambridge, Mass.: Harvard University Press, 1962).

8. On the costs of central-city expressways to the city's residents, see Anthony Downs, *Urban Problems and Prospects* (Chicago: Markham, 1970), Ch. 8.

9. Bob Gatty, "Highways that Changed a Nation," *Nation's Business* 69, no. 5 (May 1981): 24–31.

10. *New York Times,* February 4, 1983, p. 27.

11. See Ralph Craft, "Shifting Gears: Federal Transportation Policy and the States," *State Legislatures* 8, no. 9 (October 1982): 13.

12. Data from a Department of Transportation report. Cited in *New York Times,* May 30, 1985, p. 10.

13. See Alan Altshuler, *The City Planning Process: A Political Analysis* (New York: Cornell University Press, 1965).

14. *Citizens to Preserve Overton Park, Inc.* v. *Volpe,* 401 U.S. 402 (1971).

15. See Lupo, Colcord, and Fowler, *Rites of Way.*

16. *Newsweek,* August 19, 1985, p. 28.

17. *New York Times,* March 1, 1977. By 1977 only $2.1 billion had been diverted. And none of that actually came directly out of the revolving highway trust fund. Rather, the money was taken from the general tax revenues appropriated to the Urban Mass Transit Administration. This was necessary in order to appease the highway lobby and get around its opposition to the breakup of the trust fund.

18. Arthur F. Schreiber, Paul K. Gatons, and Richard B. Clemmer, *Economics of Urban Problems: An Introduction,* 2d ed. (Boston: Houghton Mifflin, 1976), p. 232.

19. Ibid.

20. *Congressional Quarterly Almanac 1982* (Washington, D.C.: Congressional Quarterly, Inc., 1982), p. 320.

21. Robert Benenson, "Mass Transit's Uncertain Future," *Editorial Research Reports* (June 21, 1985): 464.

22. Schaeffer and Sclar, *Access for All,* pp. 30, 39, 61–79, 97.

23. Ibid, p. 30.

24. See Jonathan Kwitny, "The Great Transportation Conspiracy," *Harper's* (February 1981): 14–21. Also see Schaeffer and Sclar, *Access for All,* p. 45; and Arnold W. Reitze, Jr., and Glenn L. Reitze, "Lau: Deus Ex Machina," *Environment* 16 (June 1974): 3–5. On streetcar track mileage, see *Transit Fact Book: 1970-71* (Washington, D.C.: American Public Transit Association, 1971), p. 12.

25. See *New York Times,* November 23, 1984, p. 17; *Minneapolis Star and Tribune,* December 8, 1985, p. 32A.

26. See Advisory Commission on Intergovernmental Relations, *Toward More Balanced Transportation,* pp. 45–48.

27. See Melvin M. Webber, "The BART Experience—What Have We Learned?" *Public Interest* 45 (Fall 1976): 79–108; and "Trouble in Mass Transit," *Consumer Reports* 40, no. 3 (March 1975): 190–195.

28. *New York Times,* May 22, 1986, p. 10.

29. *New York Times,* March 9, 1985, p. 8.

30. Bureau of the Census, *1970 Census of Housing: Plumbing Facilities and Estimates of Dilapidated Housing,* Final Report HC (6), 1973 (Washington, D.C.: U.S. Government Printing Office, 1974); definitions on pp. vii–viii, data in Table 1, pp. 1–5. Bureau of the Census, *Statistical Abstract of the United States: 1982-83* (Washington, D.C.: United States Government Printing Office, 1982), p. 751.

31. For 1970, see Bureau of the Census, *1970 Census of Housing. Subject Reports: Structural Characteristics. The Housing Inventory,* Final Report HC (7)-4 (Washington, D.C.: U.S. Government Printing Office, 1973), Table A–1, p. 1. For 1960, see Bureau of the Census, *U.S. Census of Housing: 1960. Components of Inventory Change, Part 1A: 1950-1959 Components.* Final Report HC (4), Part 1A-1 (Washington, D.C.: U.S. Government Printing Office, 1962), Table 1, p. 30. Bureau of the Census, *Annual Housing Survey: 1980.* Part A, *General Housing Characteristics,* Current Housing Reports, Series H, 150–180 (Washington, D.C.: U.S. Government Printing Office, 1981).

32. Data from Bureau of Census and Department of Housing and Urban Development, *Annual Housing Survey.* Reported in R. Allen Hays, *The Federal Government and Urban Housing: Ideology and Change in Public Policy* (Albany: State University of New York Press, 1985), p. 68.

33. Between 1970 and 1980, 20,713,000 new units were added. *Statistical Abstract of the United States, 1986* (Washington, D.C.: U.S. Government Printing Office, 1985): p. 735.

34. *Statistical Abstract of the United States, 1986* (Washington, D.C.: U.S. Government Printing Office, 1985), p. 731.

35. Data from the Mortgage Bankers Association. Reported in *New York Times,* February 18, 1985, p. 1.

36. Karl Taeuber calculated a segregation index for twenty-eight central cities and found a 9 percent decrease in racial separation between 1970 and 1980. See Karl Taeuber, *Racial Residential Segregation, 28 Cities, 1970-1980,* Working Paper 83-12 (Madison, Wisc.: Center for Demography and Ecology, University of Wisconsin, March 1983). A similar calculation for metropolitan areas rather than central cities found an 8 percent decrease in racial separation between 1960 and 1970. See Thomas L. Van Valey, Wade Clark Roof, and Jerome E. Wilcox, "Trends in Residential Segregation, 1960–1970," *American Journal of Sociology* 82, no. 14 (January 1977): 836.

37. *Hills* v. *Gautreaux,* 425 U.S. 284 (1976).

38. *New York Times,* February 21, 1986, p. 35; February 24, 1986, p. 13.

39. The Rogers Park example is described in *Wall Street Journal,* April 5, 1974, p. 1. For other news stories on red-lining and efforts to combat it, see *New York Times,* May 1, 1977, p. E-7; May 11, 1977, p. 1; and May 20, 1977, p. A-24.

40. See *New York Times,* May 20, 1977, p. A-24.

41. See Chester Hartman, Dennis Keating, and Richard L. Gates, with Steve Turner, *Displacement: How to Fight It* (Berkeley, Calif.: National Housing Project, 1982).

42. An influential example of this early critique was Jacob Riis's *How the Other Half Lives* (New York: Charles Scribner's Sons, 1904).

43. For a summary of these early developments, see Marian Lief Palley and Howard A. Palley, *Urban America and Public Policies* (Lexington, Mass.: D. C. Heath, 1977), pp. 161–164.

44. Anthony Downs, *Urban Problems and Prospects*, 2d ed. (Chicago: Rand McNally, 1976), p. 89.

45. Larry Sawyers and Howard M. Wachtel, "Who Benefits from Federal Housing Policies?" in *Problems in Political Economy: An Urban Perspective*, 2d ed., ed. David M. Gordon (Lexington, Mass.: D. C. Heath, 1977), p. 502.

46. Michael E. Stone, "The Politics of Housing: Mortgage Bankers," *Society* 9, no. 9 (July–August 1972): 31–37.

47. Bureau of the Census, *Statistical Abstract of the United States: 1986* (Washington, D.C.: U.S. Government Printing Office, 1985), p. 731.

48. Bureau of the Census, *Statistical Abstract of the United States: 1976* (Washington, D.C.: U.S. Government Printing Office, 1976), p. 742.

49. Sawyers and Wachtel, "Who Benefits from Federal Housing Policies?" p. 484.

50. Theodore J. Lowi, *The End of Liberalism: Ideology, Policy and the Crisis of Public Authority* (New York: Norton, 1969), pp. 251–266.

51. Oscar Newman, *Defensible Space: Crime Prevention Through Urban Design* (New York: Vintage Books, 1975).

52. Hays, *The Federal Government and Urban Housing*, pp. 79–106.

53. See Chester W. Hartman, "A Rejoinder: Omissions in Evaluating Relocation Effectiveness Cited," *Journal of Housing* 23, no. 2 (February 1966): 88–89. Also see Herbert Gans, "The Failure of Urban Renewal: A Critique and Some Proposals," *Commentary* (April 1965): 29–37.

54. Gordon, *Problems in Political Economy*, p. 504.

55. This in particular is the lament of Jane Jacobs, *The Death and Life of Great American Cities* (New York: Vintage Books, 1961).

56. See Martin Anderson, *The Federal Bulldozer* (Cambridge, Mass.: M.I.T. Press, 1964).

57. Sawyers and Wachtel, "Who Benefits from Federal Housing Policies?" p. 504.

58. Myron A. Levine, "The Reagan Urban Policy: Efficient National Economic Growth and Public Sector Minimization," *Journal of Urban Affairs* 5, no. 1 (Winter 1983): 24.

59. Raymond A. Rosenfeld, "Implementation of the Community Development Block Grant Program: Decentralization of Decision-making and Centralization of Responsibility" (paper presented to the Midwest Political Science Association, Chicago, Ill., April 21–23, 1977).

60. Donald F. Kettl, "Can Cities Be Trusted? The Community Development Experience," *Political Science Quarterly* 94, no. 3 (Fall 1979): 437–452.

61. Raymond Brown with Ann Coil and Carol Rose, *A Time for Accounting: The Housing and Community Development Act in the South* (Atlanta: Southern Regional Council, 1976).

62. Ibid., pp. 86–87.

63. For criticisms of Section 8, see Irving Welfeld, "American Housing Policy: Perverse Programs by Prudent People," *Public Interest*, no. 48 (Summer 1977): 128–144.

64. Edgar O. Olsen, "Housing Programs and the Forgotten Taxpayers," *The Public Interest* no. 66 (Winter 1982): 97–109.

65. Arthur P. Solomon, "Housing and Public Policy Analysis," *Public Policy* 20, no. 3 (Summer 1972): 443.

66. See Lloyd Rodwin, *Nations and Cities: A Comparison of Strategies for Urban Growth* (Boston: Houghton Mifflin, 1970), Ch. 2.

67. Daniel A. Mazmanian and Paul A. Sabatier, *Implementation and Public Policy* (Glenview, Ill.: Scott, Foresman and Company, 1983). See especially Ch. 3, "New Communities, The Promise Unfulfilled." Also see Helene W. Smookler, "Administrative Hara-Kiri: Implementation of the Urban Growth and New Community Development Act," *Annals of the American Academy of Political and Social Science* 422 (November 1975): 133–137.

68. Martha Derthick, *New Towns In Town: Why a Federal Program Failed* (Washington, D.C.: Urban Institute, 1972), p. xiv.

69. This experiment is discussed favorably from several perspectives in Joseph Friedman and Daniel H. Wernberg, eds., *The Great Housing Experiment*, Urban Affairs Annual Reviews, Vol. 24 (Beverly Hills, Calif.: SAGE, 1983). See especially the chapter by Ira S. Lowry, "The Supply Experiment."

70. Rolf Goetze, *Rescuing the American Dream: Public Policies and the Crisis in Housing* (New York: Holmes and Meier Publishers, 1983), p. 90.

71. *Congressional Quarterly Almanac: 1984* (Washington, D.C.: Congressional Quarterly, Inc., 1984), p. 415.

72. An excellent overview of ideology and policy can be found in R. Allen Hays, *The Federal Government and Urban Housing*, Ch. 2, "Ideological Context of Housing Policy."

73. Ibid., p. 33.

74. *Shelley* v. *Kraemer*, 334 U.S. 1 (1948).

Chapter 16
Regulatory Policies: The Environment, Energy, and the Economy

Chapter Preview

In this chapter we will explore the regulatory roles of state and local governments. We will examine in turn:

1. Pollution control and regulation of the environment.
2. The evolution of energy regulatory policies.
3. The regulation of business and professions.
4. The reciprocal relationship between state and local governments and regulation on the one hand and the political economy of states on the other.
5. A cost–benefit approach to assessing regulatory politics.

Let us begin by asking *why* state and local governments exercise their regulatory roles.

Introduction

State and local governments play major regulatory roles in our lives today. Among other things, government regulators force us to have our pets inoculated, send our children to certified schools, purchase automobile insurance if we wish to drive, and, in many states, submit our cars for annual safety inspections. In addition to restricting the behavior of individuals, state and local regulators also impose a host of restrictions on business corporations. Regulators stipulate many provisions of health insurance and life insurance coverage, determine the conditions under which alcoholic beverages can be sold, and decide which corporations will be granted exclusive franchises to market electricity, cable television, and natural gas within sizable geographic areas.

Why do governments intervene in our lives in these ways? Governments intervene when they are called on to correct for failures in the marketplace. In the mixed, public-private, capitalistic type of economy that exists in the

United States, most major goods and services are sold by private companies competing with each other in a market economy. According to traditional capitalistic theory, this competition ensures that goods and services will exist over a wide range of quality and prices. In theory, the public good is served through unrestrained competition in the marketplace. In the real world, however, the market-directed economy often fails to serve the public good, and government is called upon to correct for these market failures.

What kinds of market failures could justify governmental intervention and regulation? Economists have identified three types of market failures. First are those involving **externalities**—that is, costs that are not borne directly by the buyers or sellers of a particular product. Automobiles, for example, produce air pollution. Historically, the sales price of the car did not include any fee for cleaning up that air pollution. For this reason, automobile-produced air pollution could be viewed as a cost that was external to the cost of the car. If society wanted to deal with the externality of air pollution, it needed to give government an environmental regulatory role.

A second type of market failure involves **social goods.** A public recreational area or park, for example, is a social good. Its benefits are indivisible and nonexclusive in that everybody in the community can enjoy them without depriving anyone else of their use. Because private companies are in business to make profits, they have a very limited ability to provide free parks or other social goods for the general public. A community that wants a well-developed park system will necessarily have to purchase the park land publicly and create a public agency to develop and maintain the facilities.

A third type of market failure involves **merit goods.** Merit goods are those that society deems everyone deserves. In America today, merit goods include free public education, medical care by doctors and dentists who meet minimal professional standards, and the right to assume that foods and medicines sold in the marketplace are not contaminated. To ensure that the public receives these merit goods, governments either provide them directly (as in the case of schools) or regulate their provision by private entrepreneurs (as in the cases of medical care and food inspection).

Historically, government's regulatory role was much less extensive than it is today. State and local governments were the primary regulators, and the federal government played a less dominant role than it does today. In the 1960s and 1970s, however, the sheer volume of regulation expanded dramatically. Much of this increase was due to a broad expansion of the federal government's regulatory role. As the federal government increased its regulatory responsibilities, federal legislation and regulations began forcing states to modify their own regulatory policies. These developments were quite controversial because of the intricate intergovernmental conflicts they aroused and because the federal government began playing a dominant regulatory role in areas that had previously been considered state responsibilities: environmental protection, occupational health and safety, consumer protection, civil rights, and equal opportunity principles in employment, education, and housing. As all of these changes took place, the whole topic of regulation itself came into question. By the 1980s proponents and opponents of regulation were debating whether the benefits of all this regulation outweighed the costs.

This chapter will examine three areas of public regulation—the environment, energy, and business. In examining these regulatory areas, we will pay particular attention to the intergovernmental politics involved, the question of cost–benefit analysis, and the implications for state and local political economies.

Environmental Regulation

In the Love Canal neighborhood of Niagara Falls, New York, the air was so foul in 1978 that the mail carrier began wearing a gas mask. Radishes in backyard gardens turned coal black. Basements smelled like dead animals. Apparent congenital defects in the children vastly exceeded normal expectations: one child had an extra row of teeth, another a clubfoot; another was retarded. Miscarriages were exceedingly high in 1978, and during that summer five children were born with congenital defects.[1] Love Canal had been the dumping site for eighty different waste chemical compounds (eleven of which cause cancer) from 1947 to 1952. After the dumping ceased, the toxic wastes were covered with earth. Several years later a real estate subdivision was built along the canal. In 1978, twenty-six years after the dumping ceased, a season of heavy rains brought the buried toxic chemicals to the surface. Getting complaints from neighborhood residents, government officials installed instruments to measure the air quality in local basements. The readings in many homes showed highly dangerous concentrations of eleven toxic chemicals, including two that were carcinogenic (that is, cancer-causing). So dangerous was the environment along Love Canal that New York State provided money to help relocate thirty-seven families with children under the age of two. The local elementary school was closed for health reasons. Further research found other people endangered, and a complicated program of federal and state funding was set up to enable New York State to buy up the contaminated homes. By 1983, lawsuits for damages by the affected citizens against various governments and the company that had done the dumping totalled more than $3 billion.

Love Canal may be one of the extreme horror stories of environmental degradation in American communities, but it is not unique. In Donora, Pennsylvania, in 1948, twenty people died from industrial air pollution in a single week, and nearly half the city's population became ill. In Portland, Oregon, in the 1920s, construction workers refused to work at a dockside because the pollution of the Willamette River had produced an unbearable stench. In Cleveland, Ohio, the Cuyahoga River became so polluted with combustible wastes that it once caught fire in the 1960s, treating the city's residents to the extraordinary spectacle of a river blazing like a bonfire.

State and local governments have the primary responsibility for coping with disasters such as these and managing the effects on the environment. It was not until 1970 that the federal government entered in a big way into environmental management, intervening with its greater resources of money and its ability to set national standards that must be enforced at the state and local levels. The politics of this ecological management have become very intense, especially in the 1980s, when the Reagan administration sought to reduce the federal role and shift environmental responsibilities to the states.

The result of all these developments since 1970 is a wide range of public policy areas that interconnect: air and water pollution, visual and noise pollution, solid and hazardous waste disposal, litter, the exhaustion of natural resources, water supply, nuclear energy, and so on. In order to present a sufficiently detailed discussion, this chapter is limited to three aspects of environmental management—air and water pollution control, hazardous-waste management, and energy regulation. In this examination, several questions arise. What steps have been taken at all levels of government to protect the environment? How does the intergovernmental system work? What policies have been established? How are they implemented? Have the policies and their implementation been effective? And, of course, are things getting better or worse? What are the trends?

A National Environmental Policy:
New Tools for Environmental Management

The evolution of pollution-control policymaking has completely reversed the traditional relationship between the states and the national government. Prior to World War II, primary responsibility for pollution control lay with the states. During the 1950s and 1960s, however, the federal government became increasingly involved, and the intergovernmental mechanism began to resemble cooperative federalism rather than the traditional dual model. A partnership existed between the state and federal governments in which the federal government assisted the states in defining their own policies and priorities. This system did not work effectively, however, and by the 1970s the mechanism had changed to the centrally directed federalism discussed in Chapter 3. A key step in this direction was the **Environmental Protection Act of 1970.**

This act declared "a broad national policy for environmental protection."[2] It created the Environmental Protection Agency (EPA) to coordinate and oversee the federal government's wide-ranging activities in the field of environmental protection. It also established the Council on Environmental Quality (CEQ) within the executive office of the president to monitor progress in environmental quality and make annual recommendations to the president for improving it.

The National Environmental Protection Act also created the **environmental impact statement (EIS)**. Each federal agency is required to file with the CEQ a statement outlining the environmental impacts of any major construction project it plans to undertake. The EIS must outline adverse environmental effects of the project, alternatives to it, and its relation to maintaining and enhancing the long-term productivity of the environment.[3]

The EIS concept originally applied only to federal agencies, but it quickly spread to the states. Most development projects are actually carried out by or licensed by state and local governments. For this reason, state EIS requirements have much more potential for curbing environmental abuse than do the federal EIS requirements. Yet, most state EIS requirements do not fulfill this potential. They do not apply to projects of local governments or private enterprise, and they do not designate a statewide agency with authority to review and approve the statements.

The Council on Environmental Quality found that many of the early EISs were sloppy and incomplete. Even when complete, they are often so technically complex that local officials have difficulty understanding them. One environmental impact statement filed for a project to build 6,000 housing units in New Jersey was so complex that local officials found it difficult to evaluate the statements objectively.[4] Some impact statements ran thousands of pages and took years to prepare. In 1978 the CEQ revised the federal EIS guidelines to make them shorter, simpler, and more useful to decision makers.[5]

Water Pollution Management

At the Federal Level:
Setting National Policy

Until 1965 the federal government's role in managing water pollution was limited to studying water quality and providing federal matching grants for waste treatment plants. In 1965 Congress passed the Water Quality Act, which increased federal funds for sewage treatment plants but left the primary responsibility for action with the states. The states were charged with setting water quality standards and drafting plans to implement the standards. Despite this stronger federal initiative, the states did not respond swiftly. By 1971 fewer than thirty states had passed acceptable plans.[6]

While the states delayed implementation of the federal Water Quality Act, federal administrators began searching for other ways to stop the discharge of effluents* into the nation's waterways. An almost forgotten law, the Federal Refuse Act of 1899, made it illegal to discharge any refuse into a navigable waterway without a permit from the United States Army Corps of Engineers. Government administrators drew up a list of 18,000 companies that would have to clean up their waste discharges in order to get a permit under this act. However, government suits against these companies were eventually dismissed by the federal courts. If a permit system were to be established, new legislation would be required.

The **Water Pollution Control Act of 1972** (also called the **Clean Water Act**) set the overall framework for water pollution management that still exists. It set the goal of making all the nation's waters fishable and swimmable by 1983, and the goal of eliminating all polluting discharges into the nation's waterways by 1985; but both deadlines have been extended, as we will discuss below. Federal enforcement powers were increased. The act also distinguished between point-source and non-point-source pollution.

Point-source pollution refers to pollution that can be traced to a specific point of introduction into the water—hazardous wastes dumped in a river by a chemical company, for example, or untreated human waste discharged into a river by a city's sewers.

The act had two major provisions to deal with point-source pollution. First, it established the National Pollution Discharge Elimination System (NPDES). The NPDES requires any organization that discharges effluent into a waterway to obtain a permit. National standards for discharges were established, and any discharge that exceeds those standards is not permitted. Second, the act also obliged municipal sewer systems to install secondary sewage treatment facilities by 1977. The Environmental Protection Agency (EPA) is responsible for administering the act, but it delegates its authority to the states. If a state or local government fails to set up a permit system or if its water-quality standards do not meet EPA criteria, then the EPA can take over. Most states did act, and only a small minority preferred to have the EPA administer the program in their states. To assist the state and local governments in costly planning and sewer system construction, the 1972 act authorized $18 billion in grants-in-aid on a three-to-one matching fund basis.

Non-point-source pollution in waterways comes from a variety of sources that cannot be traced to a specific point of entry. The most prominent example would be pesticides and fertilizers, which wash into lakes, streams, and underground aquifers when it rains. Northern states that salt their roads to prevent ice in the winter find that the salt flows into the waterways and

---

Effluents are discharges into waterways and water bodies.

pollutes them during the spring thaw. Air pollution ends up in the waterways when the rain cleans the air and washes the pollutants into streams and lakes. Thus, automobile emissions are a non-point source of water pollution. Even solid-waste material buried in sanitary landfills can contaminate the underground water supplies of spring-fed lakes.

Section 208 of the 1972 act provides funds for setting up agencies to develop an environmental management system. By 1977 EPA had set up these so-called Section 208 agencies in 176 different regions of the country.[7] The Section 208 agencies were given a two-year planning period to develop their environmental management systems, but the task of coping with all the varied non-point sources of pollution was so overwhelming that few Section 208 agencies were able to meet this deadline.[8] Even when the plans were drawn up, the problem of non-point-source pollution proved much more intractable than originally thought, and progress on this front has been negligible, according to the Council on Environmental Quality.[9]

Whereas the 1972 Clean Water Act set the basic framework, subsequent legislation and amendments fine-tuned the system of water-quality control. The Safe Drinking Water Act of 1974 and its later amendments directed the EPA to set maximum allowable levels for certain chemical and bacteriological pollutants in the nation's water systems. The 1977 Clean Water Act amendments extended until 1987 some of the deadlines for ending the dumping of pollutants into the nation's waterways and authorized another $24.5 billion for sewage treatment–plant construction.

Today this water quality–control system is at a crossroads. Over $50 billion in federal and state funds have been spent since 1972 in constructing public sewer systems and waste treatment plants. The EPA estimates that constructing new waste treatment plants, or rehabilitating existing ones, plus making needed replacements of defective urban water supply and treatment facilities could cost another $134 billion by the end of the century.[10] The steps taken to date have halted the deterioration of the nation's water quality, but the budgetary squeeze on all levels of government raises questions about public willingness to continue existing high levels of investment in water-quality control. These doubts are amplified by some technical questions about the effectiveness of much of the equipment that has been purchased and installed. In the Minneapolis–St. Paul metropolitan area, for example, millions of dollars of sewage treatment equipment simply did not work.[11] Finally, existing pollution control efforts have focused almost exclusively on surface water (lakes and streams), but half of the nation's drinking supply comes from ground water that in many regions is endangered by toxic and chemical wastes that seep into underground water sources.[12] After several years' stalemate between the Reagan administration (which wanted to weaken the provisions) and Congress (which wanted to strengthen them),[13] the Clean Water Act was finally reauthorized in 1987.

At the State and Local Level:
Cleaning Up the Willamette

Although the 1972 Water Pollution Control Act gave the Environmental Protection Agency primary authority to establish water-quality standards, the states were charged with implementing these standards and monitoring compliance. Consequently, accomplishing the "fishable" and "swimmable" goals of the 1972 act will depend on the desire of all levels of government to cooperate in cleaning up the waterways in their jurisdictions. Perhaps one of the most successful examples of such cooperation has been the cleaning up of the Willamette River in Oregon.

The Willamette is the twelfth longest river in the United States. It runs 150 miles from the western range of the Rocky Mountains to Portland, Oregon, where it joins the Columbia River. Nearly two million people, 70 percent of Oregon's population, live in the Willamette basin. Three sizable cities are located along the river—Eugene, Salem, and Portland.

Until 1950 every city along the river dumped untreated human wastes into it. The river also received the discharges of several highly polluting industries—especially lumber sawmills, paper mills, and vegetable-processing plants. During the summer, when the Willamette River is at low flow, tidal action and backflow of the Columbia River trap all the pollutants in the vicinity of Portland. These factors combined to make the Willamette one of the nation's most polluted rivers. During the 1920s civic groups traced much of the pollution to the discharge of raw sewage into the river. Despite this identification of the problem, it was not until 1937 that the Oregon legislature finally required sewage treatment. However, that bill was vetoed by the governor because of the financial hardships it would have imposed on the municipalities that would have been forced to build their own treatment plants. Not until 1938 was the newly created state sanitary authority charged with developing and enforcing a statewide water-sanitation program.

The sanitary authority ran into a special problem with the paper mills, which objected to installing primary treatment facilities for their effluents. Some companies threatened to move to a friendlier state, but passage of federal water quality legislation in 1965 and 1972 reduced the mills' ability to play states against each other and effectively strengthened Oregon in its own regulatory capacity.

As a result of these actions, the quality of the Willamette improved tremendously. For the first time, Chinook salmon moved upstream to spawn in the fall. Recreational use of the river also increased, and the state approved a greenway plan for developing a system of riverside parks and for preserving the river from real estate and commercial development.

The Council on Environmental Quality attributed Oregon's successful cleanup of the Willamette to four factors. First, the problems were identified early, and steady progress was made between the creation of the sanitary authority in 1939 and the availability of extensive federal support in the 1960s. Second, the cleanup efforts had broad popular support. Citizen organizations sparked the initial research into the river's condition in the 1920s and 1930s. And new, ecology-minded interest groups during the 1960s continued the pressure for improvement and for the greenway plan. Third, strong political leaders supported the cleanup. Finally, the growing federal role after 1965 strengthened Oregon in dealing with the private paper mills. Additionally, federal grants-in-aid eased the financial burden on the municipalities.[14]

Air Pollution Control

At the Federal Level:
Setting National Policies

The first federal air pollution law was enacted in 1955. Like the first water pollution efforts, it limited the federal government to providing support to state and local governments for research. The federal role was increased by the 1963 Clean Air Act, which established a $95 million grant-in-aid program to help states set and enforce air pollution standards. In 1965 Congress authorized emission standards for motor vehicles. The 1967 Air Quality Act divided the nation into 247 air quality–control regions, so that levels of air pollution could be monitored and cities could issue air pollution alerts when the air quality declined to dangerous levels.

Just as the water-quality provisions of the 1960s were largely ignored by the states, the air-quality standards were also ignored, leading to the **Clean Air Act of 1970,** whose six major provisions set the basic framework for coping with air pollution (see Highlight on p. 457).

Some of the 1970 act's provisions proved difficult to implement, particularly the automobile emission standards. Implementing the primary and secondary air-quality standards also was difficult. Implementation required extensive interaction among federal, state, and local levels of government and among the legislative, executive, and judicial branches. The air-quality standards are set by the EPA. The states can set more rigid standards but not looser ones. To do this, the states draft **state implementation plans (SIPs)** to indicate how they will meet the standards in each of their air quality–control districts.

By 1977 it became apparent that most states would not be able to meet that year's deadlines for achieving the air-quality goals. Congress reacted by passing the **Clean Air Act Amendments of 1977,** which extended various deadlines, tightened a number of air-quality standards, and increased the enforcement powers of the EPA. In summary, the 1977 Clean Air Act Amendments did the following:[15]

Extended the deadline for cities to meet the ambient air-quality standards until the end of 1982, and extended the deadline for meeting auto emission standards to include 1981 and 1982 model cars.

Subdivided existing air quality–control regions into over a thousand local air quality–control regions, which were often coterminous with counties.

Established three classes of areas that would be required to have air cleaner than the national standards, and mandated the nondeterioration of air quality in those areas. National wilderness areas, for example, would be required to have such clean air that it would be very difficult for extensive mineral or energy exploration to occur there.

Required states to revise their SIPs; required EPA to review them by 1981; and required EPA review each succeeding five years.

Determined stiffer regulations for nonattainment areas (regions not meeting the EPA air-quality standards). States with nonattainment areas were required to (1) adopt auto vehicle emission and maintenance inspec-

Highlight
Main Provisions of the 1970 Clean Air Act

1. The EPA should set **primary** and **secondary air-quality standards.** Primary standards aim at protecting public health. Secondary standards aim at protecting crops, vegetation, forests, animals, and other materials essential to the public welfare.
2. States should draft their state implementation plans (SIPs) for EPA approval, proposing how they would meet the EPA air-quality standards.
3. Emissions from automobiles should meet rigorous limits beginning with the 1975 model year. For these cars, polluting emissions would have to be reduced by 90 percent from the 1970 level. The automobile manufacturers were given the right to appeal for a year's extension.
4. The EPA should set emission standards for stationary power plants.
5. The EPA was empowered to ban the sale of any fuel or fuel additive that would endanger the public health.
6. Citizen groups were empowered to sue the EPA or polluters for enforcement of the act.

Source: Congressional Quarterly Almanac: 1975 (Washington, D.C.: Congressional Quarterly, Inc., 1975), p. 246. Copyrighted information reprinted with permission, Congressional Quarterly, Inc.

tions, and (2) adopt a permit system for approving or disapproving any
new industrial facilities that might cause air pollution.

Authorized EPA to withhold federal highway funds from noncomplying
states, to withhold federal grants for sewage treatment, and to impose
a ban on issuing permits for industrial expansions that might cause air
pollution.

Created the National Commission on Air Quality to monitor progress in
meeting the act's goals and to make recommendations for further
legislation.

This extremely complicated system of air-quality regulation reflects the
equally complicated problem of controlling pollution in a high-technology
society. In many ways this system also reflects the complexities of the federal
system of government, which requires national, state, and local cooperation to
achieve program goals. How such intergovernmental politics works in practice is shown in Charles O. Jones's excellent study of cleaning up the air in
Pittsburgh.

At the State and Local Level:
Cleaning Up Pittsburgh

Pittsburgh is well known for its dirty air. As early as 1862 Anthony Trollope
called Pittsburgh "without exception, the blackest place I ever saw. The city
itself is buried in a dense cloud."[16] Pittsburgh began passing smoke abatement
ordinances as early as the 1860s, but these were seldom enforced. Either the
corporations simply ignored them (as the railroads illegally continued burning
the heavily polluting bituminous coal in their locomotives) or the courts ruled
the ordinances invalid (as in the attempts to get emission standards for steel
mills in 1895 and 1906). The first effective smoke abatement ordinance was
not passed until 1941; because of the need to increase steel production during
World War II, enforcement was delayed.

The first effective leadership in cleaning up Pittsburgh's air came after
World War II from Richard King Mellon of Pittsburgh's influential Mellon
family. He helped found the Allegheny Conference on Community Development (ACCD), which took the lead in redeveloping the city's central business
district and in seeking industrial compliance to the smoke abatement ordinance. Mellon also used his personal influence to get the railroads to stop
using the highly polluting bituminous coal in their locomotives. In 1947 the
Pennsylvania Railroad opposed legislation that would give the county authority to prohibit bituminous-coal-burning locomotives. Legislative leaders
found it impossible to round up the necessary votes for passage, so they appealed to Mellon.

Mellon was a director of the railroad company and one of its principal stockholders. He let its top management know that if the line failed to comply, or continued to block the new law, the companies he controlled would probably switch their freight haulage to other, competitive lines. Other customers of the railroad company took similar stands.

In a matter of days, the smoke control bill passed through the legislature unamended. Soon the Pennsylvania line started replacing its old engines with diesel equipment.[17]

The key political leader for renewal and clean air was Pittsburgh Mayor David Lawrence. One of Lawrence's first acts as mayor was to set immediate deadlines for compliance with the 1941 smoke abatement ordinance. Lawrence worked hard during his long tenure as mayor (1941–1959) to establish a cooperative business and political alliance in the smoke-control struggle.

Because smoke crossed municipal boundaries, it was necessary to combat it on the county as well as the city level. Allegheny County appointed a Smoke Control Advisory Committee that was dominated by representatives of the major polluting industries and their labor unions. Thus the pollution-control system was, for all practical purposes, a system of self-regulation by the industries.

By the end of the 1950s, this cooperation between government and the polluting industries had achieved mixed results. Considerable progress had been made in clearing the air of dense smoke, but little had been done to eliminate less visible emissions such as particulates and gases.

The limitations of the cooperative approach were seen in the case of the U.S. Steel Corporation. In 1960 U.S. Steel agreed to a ten-year plan to install pollution collectors in order to reduce the emission of pollutants. The company discovered early in the ten-year period that the equipment to reduce pollution emissions was not working, but it did not report these findings to the advisory committee until it was too late for the company to meet its ten-year deadline.[18]

In the late 1960s public concern over the environment rose sharply, and militant environmental groups formed around the nation. Given Pittsburgh's air pollution problems, environmentalists there cleverly named their organization GASP (Group Against Smog and Pollution). GASP had an extraordinary knack for getting favorable publicity and pulling off highly imaginative public relations stunts: awarding "Dirtie Gertie" prizes to polluting companies, selling cans of clean air, lobbying for improvements in regulations, and rounding up support for stronger air pollution regulations.

Militant environmentalists also succeeded in expanding the scope of the conflict beyond the closed doors of Allegheny County's industry-dominated advisory committee. In addition to attracting attention with their imaginative tactics, environmentalists also looked to the federal government for stronger curbs on air pollution. These pressures led both the county and the state to draft stiffer regulations than had originally been anticipated.

The new regulations, adopted in the fall of 1969, replaced the industry-dominated advisory committee with a new Allegheny County Variance Board, whose members had few ties with the steel industry. For the first time the regulatory body had the authority to enforce its rules and regulations. The burden of proof was put on the companies. If a company could not meet the air-quality standards, then it had to either get a permit of noncompliance from the variance board or shut down.

The new regulatory system was tested almost immediately by the U.S. Steel Corporation's Clairton coke-producing plant. Coke is a processed form of coal that burns hotter than coal but produces less smoke. The final step in producing coke is to cool it by quenching it with water. As the water is poured over the coke, it releases several lethal chemicals—phenols, ammonia, cyanide, hydrogen sulfide, and chlorides. Under the regulations of Allegheny County, the state of Pennsylvania, and the federal Clean Air Act of 1970, U.S.

The ticking-time-bomb aspect of abandoned toxic waste–dumping sites is portrayed in this cartoon by Jerry Fearing.

Source: Jerry Fearing, *St. Paul Dispatch,* August 10, 1978.

Steel would have to remove 99 percent of these dangerous chemicals from the steam. Rather than attempt this, the company asked for a variance on the grounds that it did not have the technology to remove 99 percent of the dangerous chemicals. The technology did exist for eliminating 90 percent of the pollutants, but U.S. Steel felt it could not justify expenditures to achieve an emission level that would still be illegal and would leave the company open to lawsuits.

Faced with this uncompromising attitude, the variance board denied the variance and recommended that the issue be transferred to courts that could deal directly with the legal ramifications of the case. The courts attempted to force the board and the corporation to work out a compromise. U.S. Steel was reluctant to accept the compromise devised at the local level because it might be rejected at the federal level. Under the 1970 Clean Air Act, the EPA had authority to veto any implementation plans that did not meet its own emission standards, and it refused to commit itself to any compromise.

In the fall of 1972 the court issued three consent decrees that would achieve a 90 percent reduction in sulfur emissions and would also set standards for other emissions. In exchange for U.S. Steel's agreement to these terms, local officials granted the company a ten-year immunity from being sued and forced them to install new equipment that might become available during the ten-year period.

Hazardous-Waste Management

A third major area of environmental concern lies in the disposal of the sixty million tons of hazardous and toxic waste that are produced each year. These range from low-level radioactive waste from medical testing and treatment facilities to the extremely toxic chemical wastes dumped into Love Canal over the years. The EPA has identified hundreds of dangerous toxic-waste sites around the nation. Cleaning them up and finding suitable locations for other hazardous wastes is a major environmental problem.

The Federal Role

Three major laws established the federal government's response to the hazardous-waste problem. The **Toxic Substances Control Act of 1976** required the EPA to set up regulations for testing new chemical substances before they are marketed, authorized the EPA to ban any chemical it deemed unsafe, and prohibited the sale of the extremely toxic PCBs (polychlorinated biphenyls) not contained in enclosed systems. The **Resource Conservation and Recovery Act of 1976** (RCRA) set up a so-called cradle-to-grave process for controlling and disposing of hazardous wastes. And the Comprehensive Environmental Response Compensation and Liability Act of 1980 set up the $1.6 billion so-called **Superfund** to provide the financing needed to clean up some 300 abandoned dumping sites around the nation that threatened ground-water supplies and surrounding neighborhoods. Seven-eighths of the money for the Superfund was to be raised from a special tax on certain chemicals and oils, and the other one-eighth was to be appropriated annually by Congress. This bill was scheduled for reauthorization in 1983, but it took three more years to work out a compromise between Congress and the Reagan White House. In 1986, the Superfund was reauthorized and its financing increased to $9 billion. But even with this increased funding, only 8 to 10 percent of the nation's 25,000 hazardous-waste sites will be cleaned up.[19]

Despite this legislation, the progress made on managing hazardous waste has been very disappointing to environmentalists. The EPA was very slow in drafting regulations for pretesting of chemicals, and a major scandal broke out in 1983 when it was discovered that some of President Reagan's political appointees to the EPA had failed to apply toxic-waste regulations to major corporations that they favored.[20] In the meantime, the media publicized new incidents of people being contaminated by hazardous wastes. One of the worst occurred in Times Beach, Missouri. There, 2,000 residents fled after a flood contaminated their town with highly toxic dioxin; years before, this chemical had been sprayed on the town's unpaved streets to hold down dust. The EPA and the state of Missouri agreed to buy out the contaminated town for $36.3 million.[21] But clearly, the Superfund does not have the resources to do this for all Americans exposed to toxic substances.

State and Local Roles

Although the federal government has taken the lead in regulating hazardous wastes, the RCRA provides for the states to run their own programs (with approval from the EPA). Under these programs, each company producing hazardous wastes must get a permit for disposal of the wastes.[22] But few states have provided the funding needed to do an effective job of running and overseeing this permit system.[23] Even when the funding can be found, it is very difficult to find suitable sites for storing toxic and hazardous wastes. This is the so-called NIMBY (Not-In-My-Backyard) syndrome. The need for disposal sites is widely recognized, but few people are willing to have such sites located in their own neighborhoods. Overcoming the NIMBY syndrome requires competent and open political leadership.[24]

Severe funding problems also exist with the Superfund toxic waste–cleanup legislation. For cleanup of privately owned toxic waste, the federal Superfund provides 90 percent of the money and the states 10 percent. For cleanup of municipal sites, the federal government pays for only 50 percent, with the states making up the remainder. Most states have been unwilling or unable to put up the funds to accomplish a thorough cleanup of existing hazardous sites. The result has been heavy foot-dragging on getting sites cleaned up. The Southeast had forty-six sites identified on the EPA's priority list of sites to be cleaned up. But three years after the passage of the Super-fund, no action had yet been taken at 48 percent of these sites.[25]

Despite these difficulties with hazardous-waste regulation, however, it should not be concluded that the states are sitting on their hands. In fact, considerable policy has been established in the states to deal with the issue. The most far-reaching policy has been set in states where the problem is most severe and in states that score well on indices of legislative professionalism and bureaucratic consolidation.[26]

Does the Pollution-Control System Work?

Is the pollution-control system actually cleaning up the nation's air and water? And is it likely to meet the environmental goals that have been established? Important steps were taken to reduce water pollution during the 1970s, and those steps helped stop further deterioration of the nation's sur-face-water supply. Much of this progress can be attributed to the construction of sewage treatment plants and the National Pollution Discharge Elimination System effluent discharge–control system.

Similarly, measurable improvements have been made in air quality since the late 1960s.[27] The Council on Environmental Quality (CEQ), which monitors concentrations of five major air pollutants at numerous sites nationwide, re-ports there was a significant decline in these pollutants by the early 1980s.[28]

As progress has been made in these areas, other areas have seen setbacks. Acid rain, which was only dimly perceived as a problem in the early 1970s, has gotten much worse. Underground water supplies (as distinct from surface waters) face greater threats from non-point-source pollution today than they did in the early 1970s. And hazardous-waste regulation, despite some strong initiatives, is proving to be a very difficult problem. The seriousness of these problems is magnified by the fact that the political and budgetary environ-ments are less favorable to environmental protection than they were in the 1970s. This can be attributed to several factors. First, environmental concerns have gone through a cycle that is typical of many regulatory movements. In the early phase the problem was identified, but attracting political support for the solutions proved difficult. In Pittsburgh, for example, the sources of smoke pollution had been identified as early as the 1860s; and in Oregon, the pollution of the Willamette had been pointed out in the late 1920s. In both cases, though, it took decades to develop enough political support to solve the problems.

During the late 1960s and early 1970s, the environmental movement be-came highly politicized. Environmental protection became a fashionable cause, and Congress and state legislatures responded with far-reaching legislation. Eventually, popular support for environmental protection began to dissipate. After the Arab oil boycott of 1973–1974, interest in the environmental crisis was replaced by interest in the energy crisis.

In this changing political atmosphere, national and state legislators abandoned their interest in pursuing further environmental legislation. The scene of environmental politics started to shift from the legislative halls to the administrative agencies and the courtrooms. Whereas environmentalists in the early 1970s had succeeded in broadening the scope of the conflict in the public's view, industry interest groups by the late 1970s were able to capitalize on waning public attention to *narrow* the scope of conflict once again.

A second factor limiting further progress in environmental protection is that many people perceive it as conflicting with other highly valued goals—especially energy production and economic growth. Environmentalists, of course, argue that environmental protection is not at odds with either of these objectives. Simply allowing the environment to deteriorate is a cost in itself. Environmentalists refer to these as damage costs, and the CEQ estimates that the damage costs, if nothing is done about environmental deterioration, might well be greater than the costs incurred in reducing environmental deterioration.[29]

Environment and the New Federalism

Most environmentalists viewed Reagan's New Federalism proposals as a threat. As Table 16–1 shows, there is some justification for their fears. The reauthorization for several key pieces of environmental legislation was delayed for years because of conflicts between the White House and Congress. Reagan sought to reduce federal regulations and turn that responsibility over to the states. This philosophy was articulated by Reagan's first EPA director, Anne Gorsuch Burford, who made the following statement at her confirmation hearings:

> I believe that far better environmental protection can be achieved if we will allow the level of government closest to the point of control enough flexibility to implement the protection program best suited to the area and the people who must live in it.[30]

Under Reagan the EPA took a three-pronged approach to the environment. First, Reagan sought to phase out all EPA grants to states for treatment-plant construction and other environmental purposes. This approach was rejected by Congress. Second, the administration submitted EPA regulations to a cost–benefit analysis that sharply reduced the number of rules written by the EPA each year. Third, the president threw his support behind

Table 16–1. Status of Key Environmental Legislation

Legislation	Goal	Reauthori- zations	Status for reauthorization
National Environ- mental Protection Act of 1970	Created the EPA and the CEQ	NA	NA
Clean Water Act of 1972	Set framework for water pollu- tion control	1977, 1987	Was due 1982; reauthorized 1987
Clean Air Act of 1970	Set framework for air-quality control	1977	Was due 1982; currently deadlocked
Safe Drinking Water Act of 1974	Directed the EPA to set maxi- mum allowable levels of chemicals in drinking water	1977, 1979	Was due 1982; currently deadlocked
Nuclear Waste Policy Act of 1982	Set procedures for choosing two repositories for the na- tion's nuclear wastes	NA	NA
Resources Conser- vation and Recov- ery Act of 1976	Set up a cradle-to-grave pro- cess for controlling toxic wastes	1980, 1984	Due 1988
Toxic Substances Control Act of 1976	Authorized the EPA to test new chemicals for safety and to prohibit the sale of PCBs in nonenclosed systems	1979, 1981	Was due 1983; currently deadlocked
Superfund Act of 1980	Established a fund for toxic- waste cleanup	1986	NA

Note: NA = does not apply.

efforts to rewrite environmental protection laws in ways that would abdicate an effective federal role. How this event occurred can be seen in the debate over attempts to rewrite the Clean Air Act in 1981 and 1982.

Apparently heartened by the New Federalism, many business interests sought to water down the Clean Air Act when it came up for reauthorization in 1981. The chairman of General Motors lobbied openly for such moves, called for easing of auto-emission standards, and claimed that such steps could help GM lower its car prices as much as $300 each.[31] Pressure from industry was joined by pressure from states that were finding the Clean Air Act procedures cumbersome. States especially resented having to establish vehicle emission–inspection programs (only twenty-eight had done so by 1983) and the long delays by EPA in approving state SIPs or modifications in them. Furthermore, nearly 500 counties had failed to meet the EPA's primary air-quality standards by the end of the 1982 deadline and were in danger of suffering EPA sanctions if Congress did not rewrite that portion of the Clean Air Act. EPA director Burford threatened thirty-one states with strict sanctions in the hope that those states would lobby Congress to weaken the Clean Air Act.[32] Finally, certain regions and interests complained that the Clean Air Act helped their competitors. The 1977 amendment that required smokestack scrubbers on all coal-burning power plants, for example, gave high-sulfur coal in the East a price advantage over low-sulfur coal in the West.[33]

When the Reagan administration threw its support behind the move to dilute the Clean Air Act, intense debate broke out among many interest groups. Environmental groups initiated numerous lawsuits against administration officials whom they perceived as failing to carry out environmental legislation. Public opinion polls in 1981 found overwhelming opposition to any relaxing of the standards of the Clean Air Act.[34] Faced with these conflicting interests on revising air-quality rules and perceiving strong public support for the Clean Air Act, Congress found itself stalemated on the issue.

In addition to its efforts to dilute the Clear Air Act, the Reagan administration also opposed a 1986 revision of the Clean Water Act. Reagan vetoed the legislation at the end of the Congressional session in 1986 on the grounds that it authorized too much money ($18 billion) for sewage treatment facilities. In 1987, Congress repassed the bill, setting the stage for another confrontation with the president over the federal government's commitment to water pollution control. After Reagan again vetoed the bill, Congress overrode his veto.

The key test of the New Federalism approach to the environment is whether the states have increased their environmental efforts as the federal government has backed off. And the record here is not very encouraging. James P. Lester studied the impact of New Federalism on environmental policy in thirty-one states and found that two-thirds of those states did not replace reductions in federal environmental protection monies with their own funds. The few states that did, limited their funding increase to one year and just a small number of program areas (air pollution, hazardous-waste management, and safe drinking water).[35] In sum, the decentralization and reduced funding of environmental protection under the New Federalism has hurt overall efforts to protect the environment in the 1980s.

Energy Regulation

The availability of energy in the United States has followed a roller coaster pattern over the last two decades. In the early 1970s American use of energy was already outstripping supply. The Ford Foundation in 1974 projected that, at the then-current rate of consumption, total American energy use would triple by the year 2000.[36] Scientists and energy specialists had serious reservations that such a level of energy use would be environmentally sound. Further, because it would require extensive imports, American energy supplies would be highly vulnerable to foreign political turmoil. The Arab oil embargo of 1973–1974 dramatized these fears for every American. As the embargo wore on, gasoline supplies began to dwindle, and long lines of cars waited at service station entrances. In a few short months, the energy crisis replaced the environmental crisis as the preeminent public policy issue.

In the mid-1980s the situation reversed. Rising oil prices had led to over-production around the globe, and by 1986 the price of oil had dropped more than 60 percent. Given this roller coaster pattern of energy supplies, it has been impossible for any level of government to follow a consistent, long-term energy policy.

The Federal Role

The major responsibility for energy-supply policy belongs to the federal government, which has not followed a single consistent policy. During the 1970s, when energy supplies were scarce, Congress enacted legislation that:

1. Phased out government controls on the price of domestically produced petroleum and natural gas. This helped drive up prices, encourage conservation, and promote exploration.
2. Passed a windfall oil profits tax to recapture some of the huge profits that occurred as domestic oil and gas rose in price.
3. Provided tax incentives to encourage people to conserve energy.
4. Required automobile manufacturers to produce more fuel-efficient cars.
5. Created a Synthetic Fuels Corporation designed to help fund development projects to convert coal into gas or liquid fuel.
6. Established a six-month emergency supply of oil by injecting petroleum into huge caverns in Louisiana.

During the 1980s, when energy supplies were once again bountiful, the Reagan administration cut back the incentives for conservation, speeded up the deregulation of oil and gas prices, and terminated the Synthetic Fuels Corporation. About that time, worldwide recessions and energy conservation produced a glut of petroleum on world markets, and energy prices began dropping.

State and Local Roles

If coping with energy supplies is primarily a national problem, what roles are left to the state and local governments? These governments cannot influence overall supplies or usage nearly as much as the federal government can.

Nevertheless, they play extremely important roles in energy policy in at least seven areas. These areas, and the number of states that had developed plans in those areas by the end of the 1970s, are:

State funding for energy research and development	25
Comprehensive energy resource–development plan	7
State-sponsored energy-demonstration projects	28
Tax incentives for energy conservation by industry	14
Tax incentives for energy conservation by individuals	27
Energy forecasting or modeling plans	23
Interstate cooperation for energy-resources development	20

By the end of the 1970s only three states (Alabama, Delaware, and New Hampshire) had not adopted any of these seven measures, and six states (Arizona, New Mexico, New York, North Carolina, Oregon, and Texas) had adopted six of them.[37]

Enacting legislation in these areas, however, does not necessarily mean that a state's energy policy is well directed to its own particular conditions and needs, which vary widely from state to state. The conditions and needs of Texas, for example, are quite different from those of Maine or New Hampshire. A survey of research on state energy programs concluded that state energy programs have not been very consistent with state energy conditions and needs and that the programs had limited impact on states' energy conditions.[38] One study concluded that state energy programs were little more than "paper programs . . . unrelated to the needs or resources of the states."[39]

By the mid-1980s the worldwide oil glut had taken much of the pressure off of the energy-dependent states, leading states to relax some of their stringent measures for conserving and distributing energy. When the price of oil, gasoline, and heating fuel dropped sharply in 1985 and 1986, there seemed to be little political support for spending precious state revenues on energy programs. How long this situation will last and how long oil, natural gas, and gasoline supplies will stay bountiful, however, is not at all certain.

Economic Regulation

A third area of major regulatory responsibility for state and local governments deals with the economy. The states played important regulatory roles as early as 1776.[40] We need to examine three aspects of state economic regulation—the regulation of business and professions, the impact of regulation on the political economy, and the cost–benefit analysis of regulation.

Regulation of Business and Professions

Most professions are regulated by state governments rather than by the federal government. It is the states rather than the federal government that set requirements for licensing physicians, veterinarians, and other professionals. In most states this job is done by state licensing boards, which are dominated by professionals in the field being regulated. These licensing boards protect the economic well-being of already-licensed professionals by limiting the total number of professionals allowed into the field. If physicians, for example, can limit the number of chiropracters, podiatrists, osteopaths, midwives, and other medical-care providers, they can thereby protect themselves from competition. Thus, although such licensing serves the public by assuring a minimum level of professional competence, it clearly serves the professionals to an even greater degree. Economist Murray Weidenbaum, for example, charged that the net effect of California's prohibiting advertisements for eyeglasses was to make eyeglasses in that state three times as expensive as in Texas, where advertising is permitted.[41]

In addition to regulating professions, states also regulate numerous industries. The most controversial of these are probably public utilities, insurance companies, and banks. Public utilities are usually regulated by public service commissions, which have the power to set rates for electricity and natural gas sales. Rates permitted vary widely from state to state, in that some states, such as California, are very consumer-oriented, while other states, such as Ohio, are more oriented toward protecting utility profits.

Insurance regulation has been politically volatile in that insurance companies tend to locate their offices in states that put the fewest restrictions on them. After Texas limited investments by insurance companies, twenty-nine companies closed offices in Texas and moved to states that were more lenient. This phenomenon makes it difficult for states to regulate insurance with much rigor. Indeed, a federal government survey of seventeen states found that only two conducted their own analyses when approving company requests for rate increases. The other fifteen states relied on analyses provided by the companies and routinely approved the rate increases.[42]

Banks also have found it possible to move certain operations to friendly states. Many states, for example, have high income taxes and usury laws that limit the amount of interest that can be charged on loans. South Dakota has no income tax and a very high usury limit; for this reason it is now becoming a haven for credit card operations by various large banks.

Regulation and The Political Economy

As the examples of the insurance and banking industry suggest, state regulatory practices can influence a state's economic development. During the 1970s and 1980s a number of states with low tax structures, weak labor unions, low welfare benefits, and regulatory agencies friendly to business have actively used those factors to attract new plants and offices from expanding corporations. Particularly at issue here is **workers' compensation.** This is a social insurance program in which employers pay premiums to cover the insurance payments to workers who are injured on the job. The workers' compensation benefits provide income to workers who are fully or partially disabled from such injuries. The three points of conflict over workers' compensation usually are: Are the premium payments too low or too high? Are the benefit payments too low or too high? Should the insurance trust fund be run by the state or by private insurance companies? On the first two issues, business interests usually argue that both premiums and benefits are too high, while unions usually argue that benefits are too low. In general, the stronger the unions in a state, the higher workers' compensation benefits are likely to be.

Figure 16–1. Types of Regulatory Politics

| | **Benefits of Regulation** | |
	Diffuse	Concentrated
Costs of Regulation — Diffuse	Majoritarian Politics (e.g., Social Security)	Client Politics (e.g., utility rate regulation)
Costs of Regulation — Concentrated	Entrepreneurial Politics (e.g., environmental and hazardous waste disposal)	Interest Group Struggle Politics (e.g., workers' compensation)

Source: Adapted from *The Politics of Regulation*, edited by James Q. Wilson. Copyright © 1980 by Basic Books, Inc. Reprinted by permission of the publisher.

In Arkansas, for example, only 17.6 percent of the work force was unionized in 1978, and it paid a maximum weekly benefit of $87 to workers who were totally disabled. In West Virginia, by contrast, 40.4 percent of the work force was unionized, and it paid maximim weekly benefits of $208.[43] Benefits also tend to be higher and a greater percentage of premiums paid in benefits in those states that run their own workers' compensation trust fund than in those states where private insurance companies run the funds.[44]

As the competition for industry and economic development grew more intense in the 1980s, states found themselves under pressure to ease workers' compensation benefits, to relax environmental and occupational safety regulation, and to provide a climate that business would interpret as friendly. And this fact itself becomes an issue in the debate over government's regulatory role. Environmentalists, consumer advocates, and union leaders interpret this fact to support the argument that the federal regulatory role should be strengthened to prevent states from becoming weak regulators as they compete with each other for economic development. Business interests, on the other hand, often find it easier to work with state rather than federal regulators, if the state's political climate and the particular regulatory issue are favorable. Certainly, as long as President Reagan is in office the federal regulatory role is unlikely to expand significantly.

Costs and Benefits of Regulation

Who pays the costs of and who derives the benefits from state regulatory politics? One way to approach this question is to determine whether the costs and benefits are disseminated throughout society or are concentrated on particular groups of people.[45] James Q. Wilson and Bruce A. Williams make this distinction between "diffused" and "concentrated," as shown in Figure 16–1. The types of regulatory policies discussed in this chapter fall into three of the four possible types of regulatory politics shown in this figure. They are entrepreneurial politics, client politics, and interest group politics. The fourth type of regulatory politics—majoritarian politics—is not typically found at the state and local level. It occurs primarily at the national level in programs such as social security, in which both the costs and benefits of paying for the program is diffused across virtually the entire working population.

Hazardous-waste disposal is essentially a case of entrepreneurial politics. The benefits are broadly diffused in that the policies aim to protect everyone from the ravages of toxic and hazardous wastes. The costs of regulating hazardous-waste disposal, however, are narrowly concentrated on those companies that have to contribute fees to the federal Superfund and various state superfunds that have been established for hazardous waste–site cleanups. Although the benefits of hazardous-waste policy and environmental policy in general are widely diffused, the benefits to any particular person are so small and the individuals are so widely dispersed that it is difficult for them to articulate their concerns. They are, in a sense, latent groups, as discussed in Chapter 5. Wilson writes, "Since the incentive to organize is strong for opponents of the policy but weak for the beneficiaries, and since the political system provides many points at which opposition can be registered, it may seem astonishing that regulatory legislation of this sort is ever passed."[46] It is primarily when environmental activists or political entrepreneurs such as Ralph Nader come forward to turn the latent interests into activist groups that public officials are forced to act. For this reason, this pattern of regulatory politics is called *entrepreneurial politics*. The difficulty of entrepreneurial politics, as we saw in the discussion of environmental policy, is that a policy cycle exists in which issues eventually move out of the public limelight, the entrepreneurial groups weaken or dissolve, and the regulation becomes routinized.

If entrepreneurial regulation is difficult to achieve and maintain, client-type regulation is relatively easier to achieve. In fact, entrepreneurial regulation has a tendency to turn into client regulation. Client regulation occurs when the benefits of regulation are concentrated on a small group of people but the costs are widely diffused throughout the society. The regulation of utility rates for electricity, telephones, and natural gas serves as a good example. As discussed on page 469, these rates are usually approved by public service or public utility commissions. Utility companies regularly request rate increases that will concentrate profits in the company and its shareholders. Because the costs will be so broadly spread among the general population, each person's share of the cost will be so small that he or she will hesitate to invest time or energy in opposing the rate increases. In a sense, the public utilities and other regulated industries can be seen as the clients of the regulatory commissions. The regulatory commissions were created to protect consumer interests, but regulated industries themselves spend large sums of money in pressing their cases and lobbying before the commissions. Public utilities commissioners are often appointed by the governor, which means that the companies themselves have ample opportunity to influence the governor's appointment choices. Until the costs of energy began to skyrocket in the 1970s, the public utilities commissions tended to approve rate increases with little opposition and only minor adjustments. As energy costs went up, however, consumer groups, environmental groups, and other groups began to oppose the automatic increases.

A final type of regulation suggested in Figure 16–1 involves regulating the interest group struggle, especially the labor–management struggle. As discussed on page 470, a typical issue in this struggle occurs with workers' compensation. On this issue, both the costs and the benefits are concentrated on small groups—the benefits on workers with job-related injuries and the costs on their employers. Because labor groups and business groups are continuing organizations in state politics, their conflict seems a permanent one, with the state regulatory bodies serving as both the forum for the conflict and the referees for who apportions the benefits.

In sum, it is very difficult to determine just what the costs and benefits of regulatory policy are. Involved is not only the obvious question of whether the costs outweigh the benefits, but also the question of who pays which costs and who gets what benefits. As we have seen, there are three typical patterns in operation in the states—the client-politics pattern, the entrepreneurial pattern, and the interest group–struggle pattern. Business groups are most likely to dominate the client-politics pattern. Consumerists and environmentalists are most likely to dominate the entrepreneurial politics pattern. But they find it difficult achieving permanent, effective regulation, because the entrepreneurial interest groups tend to weaken and dissolve, and the regulatory apparatus that was established tends to degenerate to the client-politics pattern. Unless the entrepreneurial groups can create permanent interest groups to look after their welfare during the politics of interest-group regulation, as organized labor does, they may not achieve many of their goals on a permanent basis.

Summary

1. The Environmental Protection Act of 1970 declared "a broad national policy for environmental protection." It established the Environmental Protection Agency (EPA) and the Council on Environmental Quality (CEQ) and invented the environmental impact statement.

2. Water pollution management requires joint federal, state, and local action. The key federal legislation is the Water Pollution Control Act of 1972 and its later amendments, which set goals of making all the nation's water fishable and swimmable by 1983 and of eliminating all polluting discharges into the nation's waterways by 1985. To deal with point-source pollution, the act established the National Pollution Discharge Elimination System (NPDES). To deal with non-point-source pollution, the act established so-called Section 208 agencies, environmental planning agencies in 176 different regions of the country. The 208 agencies work through an intricate involvement of federal, state, and local interests.

3. One of the remarkable examples of successful water pollution cleanup occurred with the Willamette River in Oregon.

4. The key air pollution legislation at the federal level were the Clean Air Act amendments of 1970 and 1977. These directed the EPA to set primary and secondary air-quality standards. The states draft state implementation plans (SIPs) to indicate how they will meet the EPA standards. The Reagan administration sought to rewrite the Clean Air Act and soften its requirements, but that revision has not yet occurred.

5. A noteworthy example of air pollution cleanup took place in Pittsburgh. As examined in Charles O. Jones's study, Pittsburgh started with a system of voluntary partnership between government and business but ended with a system of mandatory compliance.

6. The federal role in hazardous-waste management stems primarily from three acts: the Toxic Substances Control Act of 1976, which requires EPA to provide for testing of new chemicals and banning of unsafe ones; the Resource Conservation and Recovery Act that established a cradle-to-grave process for hazardous wastes; and the Comprehensive Environmental Response Compensation and Liability Act of 1980, which established the so-called Superfund to finance the cleaning of abandoned dump sites for toxic materials. Most of the responsibility for finding new disposal sites rests with the states.

7. The extent to which these environmental regulation measures work is hard to determine. The least progress has probably been made in managing hazardous wastes, and the most progress has probably been made in reducing air pollution. In water pollution control, substantial progress has occurred in reducing the discharge of pollutants into the lakes and streams. But much doubt remains about whether all cities can comply with requirements for sewage treatment plants. And little has been done to date to protect the quality of ground water.

8. By the 1980s, federal energy-regulation policy had begun to deregulate the price of oil and natural gas and to force conservation measures, such as more fuel-efficient automobiles. The states and localities have been more imaginative in their approaches to energy conservation and energy policy than has the federal government.

9. Economic regulation is deeply intertwined with regulation of the environment and energy. States exert direct regulatory responsibility for the licensing of people in many professions. States also regulate some key industries, such as insurance and banking. As the competition for economic development has grown keen in recent years, states are finding themselves under pressure to relax some of their regulations.

10. Regulatory policies at the state level fall into three categories: entrepreneurial regulation, client-politics regulation, and interest group–struggle regulation.

Key Terms

Clean Air Act Amendments of 1977 Amendments that extended several deadlines for meeting the standards set in the 1970 Clean Air Act, stiffened standards, and gave the EPA increased authority to enforce them.

Clean Air Act of 1970 The act that established the fundamental authority for the federal regulation of air quality.

Environmental impact statement (EIS) An assessment of the environmental impacts of a proposed development project. Required before the project can be approved. Applies to federal agencies and to some states.

Environmental Protection Act of 1970 The keystone of federal authority to regulate the environment. It established the Environmental Protection Agency and the Council on Environmental Quality and declared a broad national policy for environmental protection.

Externalities Costs that are not borne directly by the buyers or sellers of a particular product. For example, the costs of cleaning up air pollution produced by automobiles are not included in the price of cars.

Merit goods Goods that society judges all citizens should have as a matter of right.

Non-point-source pollution Pollution whose specific point of entry into the water cannot be traced. Acid rain, which starts from smokestacks of coal-burning facilities and then disperses over a wide region and falls in the form of rain, is an example.

Point-source pollution Pollution that is introduced into the water supply at a specific, identifiable point of entry, such as a storm sewer opening into a river.

Primary air-quality standards Established by the 1970 Clean Air Act, these aim at protecting public health.

Resource Conservation and Recovery Act of 1976 This act set up a cradle-to-grave process for controlling and disposing of hazardous wastes.

Secondary air-quality standards Set by the 1970 Clean Air Act, these aim at protecting crops, vegetation, forests, animals, and other materials essential to the public welfare.

Social goods Goods whose benefits are nondivisible and nonexclusive. Their enjoyment by one person does not prevent their enjoyment by others.

State implementation plan (SIP) A plan that states are required to draft to show how they will meet the primary and secondary air-quality standards set by the EPA.

Superfund A federal fund set up to finance the cleanup of hazardous-waste sites.

Toxic Substances Control Act of 1976 The act that gave the EPA authority to test new chemicals it considers unsafe and to prohibit sale of PCBs except in enclosed systems.

Water Pollution Control Act of 1972 (Clean Water Act) The keystone of federal environmental policy for water quality. Established the pollution discharge–elimination system and required municipalities to install secondary sewage treatment facilities.

Workers' compensation A government system for providing benefits to workers injured on the job who become partially or totally disabled.

References

1. *St. Paul Pioneer Press,* August 13, 1978, p. 1.

2. See Thaddeus C. Trzyna, *Environmental Impact Requirements in the States: NEPA's Offspring* (Washington, D.C.: U.S. Environmental Protection Agency, Office of Research and Development, 1974), p. 7.

3. Ibid., p. 19.

4. Michael R. Greenberg and Robert M. Hordon, "Environmental Impact Statements: Some Annoying Questions," *American Institute of Planners Journal* 40, no. 3 (May 1974): 164–175.

5. *New York Times,* December 18, 1977, p. 39.

6. Walter A. Rosenbaum, *The Politics of Environmental Concern* (New York: Praeger, 1973), pp. 140–142. Also see Paul A. Sabatier, "State and Local Environmental Policy," *Policy Studies Journal* 1, no. 4 (Summer 1973): 217–225.

7. Ora Huth, "Managing the Bay Area's Environment: An Experiment in Collaborative Planning," *Public Affairs Report* 18, no. 2 (April 1977): 4 (Bulletin of the Institute of Governmental Studies, University of California, Berkeley).

8. Ibid.

9. Council on Environmental Quality, *Environmental Quality: The Eleventh Annual Report of the Council on Environmental Quality* (Washington, D.C.: U.S. Government Printing Office, 1980), p. 133.

10. Jon Grand, "Environmental Management: Emerging Issues," *The Book of the States: 1984-85* (Lexington, Ky.: Council of State Governments, 1984), p. 451.

11. *St. Paul Pioneer Press,* May 15, 1983, p. 1.

12. Congressional Quarterly, *Environment and Health* (Washington, D.C.: Congressional Quarterly, Inc., 1981), p. 43.

13. See Congressional Quarterly Almanac, 1985 (Washington, D.C.: Congressional Quarterly, Inc., 1985), p. 2736, and 1986, pp. 262, 677.

14. This discussion is taken from the U.S. Council on Environmental Quality, *Environmental Quality Annual Report: 1973* (Washington, D.C.: U.S. Government Printing Office, 1973), pp. 43–71.

15. Congressional Quarterly Almanac, 1977 (Washington, D.C.: Congressional Quarterly, Inc., 1977), p. 627.

16. Charles O. Jones, *Clean Air: The Policies and Politics of Pollution Control* (Pittsburgh: University of Pittsburgh Press, 1973), p. 21.

17. Jeanne Lowe, *Cities in a Race with Time: Progress and Poverty in America's Renewing Cities* (New York: Random House, 1968), p. 138.

18. Jones, *Clean Air,* pp. 97–98.

19. Paul Doyle, "The New Superfund: Will It Work This Time?" *State Legislatures* 13, no. 2 (February 1987): 10–14.

20. See Congressional Quarterly Weekly Report, 1983, pp. 839, 1094, 1640.

21. *New York Times,* January 10, 1983, p. 1; *Wall Street Journal,* March 1, 1983, p. 1.

22. For a good background article on the RCRA, see Richard Barke, "Policy Learning and the Evolution of Federal Hazardous Waste Policy," *Policy Studies Journal* 14, no. 1 (September 1985): 123–131.

23. Bruce A. Williams and Albert R. Matheny, "Testing Theories of Social Regula-

tion: Hazardous Waste Regulation in the American States," *Journal of Politics* 46, no. 2 (May 1984): 436–438.

24. Albert R. Matheny and Bruce A. Williams, "Knowledge vs. NIMBY: Assessing Florida's Strategy for Siting Hazardous Waste Disposal Facilities," *Policy Studies Journal* 14, no. 1 (September 1985): 70–80.

25. Ann O'M. Bowman, "Hazardous Waste Cleanup and Superfund Implementation in the Southeast," *Policy Studies Journal* 14, no. 1 (September 1985): 100–109.

26. James P. Lester, James L. Franke, Ann O'M. Bowman, and Kenneth W. Kramer, "Hazardous Wastes, Politics, and Public Policy: A Comparative State Analysis," *Western Political Quarterly* 36, no. 2 (June 1983): 257–283.

27. A slight improvement from 1969 to 1977 is indicated by the *National Wildlife* annual environmental-quality index. See "The 1982 Environmental Quality Index," *National Wildlife* 20, no. 2 (February–March 1982): 32.

28. U.S. Council on Environmental Quality, *Environmental Quality Annual Report: 1983* (Washington, D.C.: U.S. Government Printing Office, 1984), pp. 18–19.

29. U.S. Council on Environmental Quality, *Environmental Quality Annual Report: 1973* (Washington, D.C.: U.S. Government Printing Office, 1973), pp. 78–93.

30. Congressional Quarterly Weekly Reports, November 27, 1982, p. 2917.

31. *New York Times,* October 4, 1981, p. F-2.

32. On sanctions, see Congressional Quarterly Weekly Reports, December 4, 1982, p. 2920.

33. Pater Navarro, "The Politics of Air Pollution," *Public Interest* no. 59 (Spring 1980): 36–44.

34. Walter A. Rosenbaum, *Environmental Politics and Policy* (Washington, D.C.: Congressional Quarterly Press, 1985), pp. 64–68.

35. James P. Lester, "New Federalism and Environmental Policy," *Publius* 16, no. 1 (Winter 1986): 149–165.

36. See the Ford Foundation Energy Policy Project, *Exploring Energy Choices: A Preliminary Report* (New York: Ford Foundation, 1974).

37. James L. Regens, "State Policy Responses to the Energy Issue: An Analysis of Innovation," *Social Science Quarterly* 61, no. 1 (June 1980): 44–55.

38. Stephen W. Sawyer, "State Energy Conditions and Policy Development," *Public Administration Review* 44, no. 3 (May/June 1984): 204–214.

39. Thomas R. Dye and Dorothy K. Davidson, "State Energy Policies: Federal Funds for Paper Programs," *Policy Studies Review* 1, no. 2 (1982): 255–262.

40. Bruce A. Williams, "Bounding Behavior: Economic Regulation in the American States," *Politics in the American States: A Comparative Analysis,* 4th ed., eds. Virginia Gray, Herbert Jacob, and Kenneth N. Vines (Boston: Little, Brown and Co., 1983), p. 336.

41. Murray L. Weidenbaum, *Business, Government and the Public* (Englewood Cliffs, N.J.: Prentice-Hall, 1977), p. 163.

42. Williams, "Bounding Behavior," p. 346.

43. Ibid., p. 360.

44. Ibid., p. 359.

45. Ibid., p. 342, and James Q. Wilson, ed., *The Politics of Regulation* (New York: Basic Books, 1980), pp. 357–394.

46. Wilson, *The Politics of Regulation,* p. 370.

Chapter 17
State and Community Economic Development Policies

Chapter Preview

This chapter examines the politics of promoting economic development at the state and community levels. We will explore in turn:

1. How changes in the national economy and foreign competition have affected states and communities.
2. The economic development strategies that states and communities follow to improve their economic situation.
3. The political strategies that states and communities follow to influence economic development.
4. Important issues that are raised for state and community politics by the quest for economic development.

Introduction

In February 1986, pop singer Bruce Springsteen returned to his hometown of Freehold, New Jersey, and gave an impromptu concert in support of local workers protesting the closing of 3M Corporation's audiotape manufacturing plant there. Able to produce the same tapes more cheaply in a more modern plant elsewhere, the 3M Corporation decided to close the Freehold plant, throwing 700 people out of work and dealing a heavy economic blow to the town as it awaited the shock of losing 700 regular paychecks. Freehold gained fleeting notoriety because of Springsteen's brief appearance. But with less media fanfare, similar plant closings—with their resulting local economic hardship—have been replayed regularly over the last several years, from com-

478

munities as diverse as iron-mining towns in northern Minnesota[1] to former energy-boom towns in Wyoming,[2] and even to the huge, bustling metropolis of Houston, which was hit hard in the mid-1980s by falling energy prices.[3]

When a plant being closed is dominant in the local economy, the state and community involved get doubly hit. First, the loss of a major employer brings economic and social havoc. As the town's income declines, mortgages fall into arrears, savings get depleted, local businesses close, alcohol abuse and family violence mount, the town's physical appearance grows seedier as people become afraid to invest their scarce savings in maintenance and repair. For those seeking to move on to more prosperous areas of the country, houses become impossible to sell except at a fraction of their former worth. A second adverse impact involves the state and community governments. Because of the economic decline, states and communities face a greater demand for welfare and social services to help the people who are displaced. But the state and community governments are less able to provide such services because their own revenue base declines with the local economy.

In contrast to Freehold, Spring Hill, Tennessee, enjoyed an unprecedented transformation in the 1980s from a sleepy hamlet to the growing site of a General Motors manufacturing plant for its new Saturn automobile. Unlike the unfortunate residents of Freehold, the residents of Spring Hill enjoyed the luxury of dollars being pumped into their economy, escalating property values, new stores and services, and an abundance of jobs and economic opportunities.

What, if anything, should governments do to cope with the dramatically changing economic conditions exemplified by Freehold and Spring Hill? To answer these questions and gain a broader insight into the dynamics of state and local political economies, we will examine four broad issues in this chapter. First, how does the changing American economy affect state and community politics? Second, what economic development strategies can states and communities pursue to protect themselves? Third, what political strategies can they follow? And fourth, what issues surface in the quest for economic development?

The Changing Climate for State and Community Economies

To appreciate the causes of Freehold's problems and Spring Hill's good fortune, we must first examine three broad trends taking place in the American economy. First is the transformation from an industrial to a postindustrial economy. Second is the intensification of foreign competition. Third is the changing class structure of American society.

Table 17–1. Changes in the American Economy

Selected aspects	Year	Percentage
International Interdependence		
1. Percent of new automobiles sold that were	1965	94%
manufactured domestically	1985	74
	2015	?
2. Exports as a percent of GNP	1965	5.9%
	1985	9.3
	2015	?
3. Imports as a percent of GNP	1965	4.6%
	1985	11.2
	2015	?
Postindustrialization		
Growth of labor force employed in manufacturing as a percent of growth of total civilian labor force, 1970–1980:		
Manufacturing		4.1%
Total economy		23.7

Source: U.S. Bureau of the Census, *Statistical Abstract of the United States, 1981* (Washington, D.C.: U.S. Government Printing Office, 1981), pp. 390, 421, 624, 733; *Statistical Abstract, 1987*, pp. 417, 585.

From Industrial to Postindustrial Economy

Economists distinguish among three sectors of the economy. The *primary sector* refers to extractive activities such as oil production, mining, timber production, and farming. The *secondary (industrial) sector* refers to manufacturing activities. And the *tertiary sector* refers to a broad range of service activities, from retail trade to banking to hospital management. As Table 17–1 shows, the growth of manufacturing jobs in the secondary (industrial) sector in recent years has lagged far behind the growth of the labor force in general. In contrast to the manufacturing section, which produces fewer jobs and less income (relative to the whole economy) than it did in the past, the service sector of the economy has been growing. The relative decline of industrial manufacturing and the relative growth of the service sector have led some social scientists to note that America has been shifting from an industrial base to a **postindustrial economy.**[4]

Within the manufacturing sector of the economy, dramatic changes are also occurring that have devastating impacts on places like Freehold. The most dynamic growth in the manufacturing sector has involved high-technology products such as computers, lasers, and sophisticated medical equipment. Those industries have been more competitive against foreign industries than have manufacturers of traditional products such as steel, automobiles, and television sets, which have been badly damaged by foreign competition and have lost heavily in their share of the market. At some point, the decline in manufacturing will level off or possibly reverse itself.[5] But until that point is reached, millions of Americans in hundreds of communities will continue to suffer economic dislocation.

Intensification of Foreign Competition

Although America has never been totally independent of the world economy, her economic interdependence today dwarfs the interdependence of the past. Table 17-1 shows that exports have nearly doubled their share of the gross national product (GNP) between 1965 and 1985, and that imports have more than doubled their share. These percentages are likely to continue to grow in the future.

On the positive side, this interdependence enriches the quality of American life by making a greater variety of imported goods and services available. Moreover, aggressive expansion of American exports opens up larger world markets to American companies, thus creating more jobs and income. In theory, the increased need to compete in both the import and export markets leads to better products at more reasonable prices.

On the negative side, many corporations and communities are poorly prepared to compete in international markets. Foreign nations have become increasingly successful in their abilities to manufacture and market high-quality consumer products such as automobiles and television sets. Much American manufacturing is done in outmoded plants (such as the 3M plant in Freehold), using old-fashioned production methods as compared with the highly automated plants in Japan with its extensive use of robots and other innovations. And industrializing third-world countries such as Brazil, Korea, and Taiwan have set up manufacturing plants that are able to hire workers at a fraction of the wages paid in developed countries such as the United States and Japan. Apple Computer Corp., for example, now does most of its manufacturing in plants set up in third-world countries. Further complicating the problem for American communities is the fact that much of the foreign competition comes from countries with authoritarian governments that curb free labor unions, hold down wages for multinational corporations, and do not enforce environmental and safety standards that are prevalent in the United States. Additionally, the host governments often subsidize the export of their products to the United States (what American-based manufacturers call "dumping"). Despite huge transportation distances and costs involved, these and other factors combined in the 1970s and 1980s to give many imported products a distinct price advantage over comparable American goods.

Table 17-2. The Dwindling Middle Class

	Percent of population in:	
Household income	1967	1982
Lower Income Under 75% of median household income (Under $15,100 in 1982)	35.5%	37.7%
Middle Income 75% to 125% of median household income ($15,100 to 25,200 in 1982)	28.2	23.7
Upper Income Over 125% of median household income (Over $25,200 in 1982)	36.3	38.6

Source: Lester C. Thurow, "The Disappearance of the Middle Class," *New York Times,* February 5, 1984, p. F-3. Copyright © 1984 by The New York Times Company. Reprinted by permission.

The Dwindling Middle Class

As the American economy adapts to these technological and foreign challenges, that adaptation is provoking profound consequences on the social and political structures of towns such as Freehold and Spring Hill. Economist Lester Thurow charges flatly that the American middle class is shrinking. As shown in Table 17-2, the percentage of middle-income families has decreased since 1967, while the number of lower- and upper-income families has increased. This suggests that America may be moving toward a bipolar society in which a much smaller middle class than in the past is less able than in the past to reduce tensions between the wealthy and the poor.

Strategies for Economic Development

In the quest to promote jobs and attract industries, states and communities follow a number of strategies. Among the most important of these are public relations, promoting a positive business climate, creating incentives for business growth, and facilitating community development.

Public Relations

The most visible and inexpensive approach to economic development is public relations. Some states spend lavishly to promote their state as a good place for business. States with significant tourist advantages (such as Colorado and Florida) use public relations to attract tourist dollars. And states with extensive retirement communities, such as Arizona, use public relations to enhance their image as an attractive place to resettle. Retirees with their pension checks and tourists with their recreational dollars are just as effective a means of pumping money into a state and creating jobs as is a new manufacturing plant or a high-technology venture.

Promoting a Favorable Business Climate

Of key interest in many states is the **business climate** that will make the state attractive to the business community. What makes a positive business climate is not absolutely clear, however. The Chicago-based Grant-Thornton Company annually rates the states' business climates for manufacturing firms. Their ratings focus heavily on factors that are important to manufacturing firms, such as labor costs. Not surprisingly, states with strong unions and generous workers' compensation and unemployment compensation programs score poorly.[6] In contrast, *Inc. Magazine* rates business climates for small companies, for whom labor costs are less important than is the availability of venture capital to help them get under way and to expand when appropriate. Not surprisingly, *Inc. Magazine*'s ratings differ sharply from those of the Grant-Thornton Company. For example, in 1983 *Inc. Magazine* rated Minnesota fifth in climate favoring small businesses, whereas Grant-Thornton rated it thirty-second in climate for industrial manufacturing.[7]

Taxing and Spending

Of the issues most involved in creating a favorable business climate, taxes and the level of government expenditures on public services are the most politically controversial. Many business organizations argue that the low-tax, low-spending states of the South and Southwest are more attractive to industry than are states with high taxes and high levels of public expenditures. According to this viewpoint, when firms decide to relocate or to expand they often go South or West in order to avoid the punitive tax structures of the Northeast and Midwest. But how true is this assumption?

Roy Bahl surveyed numerous studies of the impact of taxes on decisions to relocate from one state to another and concluded that although taxes do affect relocation within a metropolis, "the consensus of a great deal of such research would seem to be that taxes are not a major factor in interregional location."[8] State taxes represent a relatively small percentage of a firm's income, and most firms can save relatively little on taxes by moving from one state to the next.

The limited impact of taxes on locational decisions was also discovered by Roger W. Schmenner's study of location decisions by 410 of the Fortune 500 companies. Schmenner found that "tax and financial incentives have little influence on almost all plant location decisions." At best they are "tie break-ers" when competing sites are otherwise equally desirable.[9]

Labor Costs

More important to the business climate than taxes are the costs of labor. At issue is whether or not a state's labor force is extensively unionized and whether unemployment compensation and workers' compensation benefits are high. Unemployment compensation is paid to laid-off workers for up to six months while they are between jobs. Workers' compensation awards pay-ments to workers who suffer handicapping injuries on the job (for example, loss of an arm or a leg). Not surprisingly, workers' compensation, unemploy-ment compensation, wages, and benefits tend to be higher in states with strong unions. Most southern and southwestern states have passed so-called **right-to-work laws** that prohibit the union shop (see Chapter 5, p. 109). Most northeastern and midwestern states do permit the union shop.

Offsetting this factor, however, is the fact that many firms also want a labor force that is relatively well educated and has a reputation for reliable, hard work. For this reason a state that reduces taxes by cutting back on public schools and higher education, which help produce quality work forces, may in the long run worsen its business climate rather than improve it. Mississippi, for example, scores high on the business climate criteria of low taxes, low spending, and anti-union legislation. But it also scores among the nation's lowest in educational levels, and for that reason Mississippi is not a very desirable location for corporations that require a well-trained or well-educated work force.

Uncontrollable Factors

Finally, many locational criteria are not very directly under a state's control. Other things being equal, a moderate weather climate would be more attrac-tive than an extreme climate. Access to low-cost energy was a major plus for Texas in attracting industry during the energy-conscious 1970s, for example. A region with a variety of first-class cultural, sports, and entertainment amenities would be more attractive than a state without such amenities. And perhaps most important, a region close to a firm's markets would be more attractive than a region far from a firm's markets.

Does Business Climate Make Any Difference?

In sum, a state's business climate depends on many factors, and each state has its own peculiar combination of strengths and weaknesses. For example, South Dakota has little in the way of metropolitan cultural or entertainment amenities. Yet it has enjoyed a fair amount of success attracting the credit-card billing operations of major banks by relaxing limits on interest rates and by having no personal or corporate income tax.

Seldom discussed, however, is the question of how much difference the business climate actually makes in promoting a state's economy. If business climate were the single most important factor in economic development, then states like South Dakota and Mississippi would be among the highest in economic development, and states like New York and California would be underdeveloped. In fact, the reverse is true. Table 17–3 presents an overall comparison of the relationship between business climate rankings in 1985 and the number of jobs gained or lost in each state in that year.

If there were a perfect relationship between business climate and job growth, then twenty-four states would appear in cell A of Table 17–3, and the other twenty-four would appear in cell D. In fact, the states are fairly evenly distributed among the four cells. This indicates either that no relationship exists between business climate and economic growth or that the relationship is overshadowed by other factors, such as size (because the largest states scored the largest gains) and temporary economic conditions (because net job losses occurred in economically depressed farm states and oil states during that year). Nor do the states with a good business climate score especially well in projected future job growth. The National Planning Association estimates that nearly half the total growth in jobs between 1986 and the year 2000 will occur in just thirty metropolitan areas, only twelve of which are located in

Table 17–3. Business Climate and Economic Growth, 1985

	Number of jobs gained in 1985	
	Number of states in top half (most jobs gained)	Number of states in bottom half (fewest jobs gained)
Number of states ranking in top half (best climates)	A 11	B 13
Number of states ranking in bottom half (worst climates)	C 13	D 11

Business climate (left vertical label)

Sources: Jobs gained in 1985: Bureau of Labor Statistics. Business climate rankings are from Grant Thornton, *Survey of Manufacturing Climates, 1985.* Reprinted by permission of Grant Thornton. Copyright 1986. This study is a summary of subjective assessments by state manufacturing associations on twenty-two criteria, including taxes, welfare expenditures, unemployment benefits, workers' compensation costs, state and local debt per capita, vocational education enrollments, extent of labor unrest, percent of adult population who are high school graduates, energy costs, wages, and extent of unionization.

Note: Only forty-eight states are tallied here because the available business climate rankings did not include Hawaii or Alaska.

states with a good business climate, and seventeen of which are in states with a poor business climate.[10]

None of these data imply that business climate is irrelevant to corporations when they make location decisions. Rather, they reflect the fact that corporations do not have unlimited flexibility in relocating their facilities. Corporations continuously monitor their branch operations (deciding to open some new plants, expand some existing ones, and shut down others), but they do not commonly relocate entire facilities from one state or region to another. One of the most widely respected studies of the impact of corporate in- and out-migrations on jobs was David Birch's study of over two million firms in the early and middle 1970s. He found that such migrations had a negligible impact on the number of jobs a state gains or loses.[11]

Creating Incentives for Business Growth

Whatever the facts may be about the importance of company migrations from state to state, governors, mayors, and legislators in the 1980s find themselves pressured by political forces to provide an extensive array of incentives for business growth. Thus, many states pass legislation allowing local governments or state agencies to offer an array of tax packages, seed monies, and other inducements to attract industry. Most states in recent years have set up venture capital funds to help new businesses start up. Other states have offered tax credits to help corporations spin off new companies and help them get started. Finally, Connecticut, Florida, Kentucky, and some other states pioneered in establishing **urban enterprise zones.** These are zones in blighted neighborhoods in which taxes are reduced and government regulations relaxed for any firm that will set up shop and employ local residents. In Connecticut, for example, up to six enterprise zones were authorized for any city neighborhood in which 25 percent of the population was below the poverty line, on welfare programs, or unemployed. A firm that locates in one of these zones and hires more than 30 percent of its employees from the zone will have its Connecticut corporate income tax cut in half for ten years, will receive a $1,000 state grant for every zone job created, and will have its local property tax reduced by 80 percent for five years.[12]

Facilitating Community Development

Perhaps the most visible thing that states do to promote business growth is to facilitate strategies for economic development in local communities. Communities rely on states for legal authority and financial or tax authority to offer development packages. Working together, states and communities can offer a variety of specific incentives to companies to expand in place rather than move somewhere else.

Tax Abatement

Perhaps the most widespread local inducement to economic development is the **tax abatement**.[13] This is the tactic of forgiving a firm's property taxes for a number of years if it expands in a particular city. One of the most generous tax abatement programs exists in Missouri, which permits local governments to forgive real estate taxes on property improvements for up to twenty-five years.[14]

Federal Seed-Money Programs

Cities can also provide seed money for firms to locate within their boundaries. For example, suppose a firm wishes to expand in Bigtown, USA, but is hampered by lack of developable land. Using its powers of eminent domain, the city of Bigtown can force the owners of a desirable piece of land to sell the land to the local government, usually to a local development agency or a port authority. Purchasing and clearing such land is extremely expensive, but cities have many sources of financial aid for this purpose. From the federal government, there are Community Development Block Grant (CDBG) funds, Urban Development Action Grant (UDAG) funds, or Economic Development Administration funds to purchase and clear the land and lay groundwork for road and sewer installations. These expenditures can be viewed as seed money because they prepare the land and make it attractive for private developers and corporations to build on the new sites.

Industrial Development Revenue Bonds

A city can issue **Industrial Development Revenue Bonds** (IDRB) to raise money for a development project. The city in effect acts as an intermediary to help a company raise development money at a lower cost than if the company had to go directly to the market and sell its own bonds. Because the interest earned by municipal bonds is exempt from federal income tax (and usually state income tax in the issuing state), such bonds carry lower interest rates than corporate bonds. A city will entice a corporation to expand by issuing IDRBs, and the bonds will be paid off with revenues from the company's development project. Thus, for most corporations interest costs are reduced, and at no expense to the city, for the federal and state governments bear the entire cost in the form of lower income-tax revenues. Until 1987, IDRBs were the single most popular method of funding urban economic development. But Congress in 1986 put a cap on the total amount of IDRBs that each state is allowed.[15]

Tax-Increment Financing

Under **tax-increment financing** (TIF), a city declares a tax-increment financing district in the neighborhood it wants to develop. The city issues bonds to clear the land and entice a developer to build a commercial structure on the site. Because the new structure is usually more valuable than the former use of the land, it generates more property taxes. This increment, or increase, in generated property taxes is used to pay off the tax-increment financing bonds. Thus the new development does not bring new property taxes into the city's general revenue until *after* the TIF bonds are paid off. But the development itself will probably create many new jobs for city residents and ultimately improve the city's fiscal picture.

Venture Capital

At least twenty states today have **venture capital** programs to invest start-up capital in new companies that have excellent prospects for growth. The Sky Computer Co. of Lowell, Massachusetts, for example, badly needed capital in 1982 to market plug-in computer boards for scientific and engineering applications. The Massachusetts Technology Development Corporation (MTDC) then invested public funds in the company to help it get off the ground. Within three years the company's work force expanded from fifteen to eighty-five, and annual sales shot up to $10 million. By using its governmentally supplied venture capital for projects like this, MTDC has been able to increase the number of jobs in the state. Between 1979, when it was created, and 1984, the MTDC invested about $5.7 million of venture capital in twenty-seven companies, which has added over 1,000 jobs and $2 million a year in state income-tax collections.[16] In addition to public venture capital corporations like MTDC, three states (New York, New Jersey, and Michigan) allow public employee pension funds to invest in venture capital projects.[17] Although venture capital is extremely risky, the Massachusetts example shows that under the proper circumstances it can produce benefits far exceeding the costs.

Lease-Backs

Finally, an exotic developmental fund raiser, the **lease-back,** was inadvertently created by President Ronald Reagan's tax policy from 1981 to 1987, which allowed investors to depreciate investment buildings over a fifteen-year period instead of the much longer thirty- to forty-year periods previously allowed. A person with a $100,000 income could conceivably eliminate his or her federal income taxes by borrowing a million dollars and using it to buy a million-dollar income-producing building. City-owned income-producing buildings generate no such tax savings, however, since cities do not pay federal income taxes. But a city could build a convention center, for example, sell it to a private investor, lease it back from the investor for fifteen years, and agree to buy it back at the end of the fifteen-year period. In terms of the operation of the center, nothing changes; it is still run by the city. But the private investor gains an enormous federal income-tax break. The city works out a financial package that recaptures part of that tax break in the form of lower building service costs or higher sales price. The city gets a convention center, at no cost to city taxpayers, and the entire expense is borne by the federal treasury in the form of reduced income-tax revenues.[18] Under the Tax Reform Act of 1986, lease-backs will probably not be economically feasible in the future, because real estate investors can no longer shelter as much of their income with paper losses.

Assessing Economic Development Strategies

Cities are under so much economic and fiscal pressure that they have little choice but to take any reasonable action that seems likely to improve the local economy. However, before a city enters a public-private venture such as St. Paul's Galtier Plaza (see Highlight below), a number of questions should be (but apparently seldom are) asked.

Highlight
Urban Economic Development in Action: St. Paul's Galtier Plaza

The flashiest project in a twelve-year period of economic expansion presided over by St. Paul's entrepreneurial-minded mayor George Latimer was a palatial skyscraper called Galtier Plaza. A forty-story building with luxury shops, movie theaters, elegant restaurants, business offices, and upscale condominiums, Galtier Plaza served many key goals in the city's downtown economic development. It would transform a low-rent, low-tax, low-value real estate site into a high-rent, high-tax, high-value site that would provide income, jobs, and economic activity for the central business district. And the expensive condominiums would bring new, affluent residents into the downtown area. Aesthetically, the glass-faced exterior and glossy interior of the building would complement and add life to the small park that abutted it.

It was not possible to get private developers to design and put up the project without special inducements, however. To entice a private firm into the project, the city and the Port Authority promised the developer substantial public subsidies while leaving the corporation itself to reap the lion's share of any profits the project might make. Financing the $127-million building involved most of the economic development tools described in the text. Public funding accounted for over three-fourths of the total initial cost of the project. But construction delays led to the loss of major retail tenants, and before the project was even completed it was faced with possible bankruptcy. At this point the Port Authority sold its interest to Chemical Bank of New York, narrowly avoiding a costly and embarrassing bankruptcy.

First, does the development project result in a *net* increase in jobs? Although development projects always generate new jobs, they also destroy jobs that existed on the site prior to the project. The city should also ask whether the people who lose jobs will find new ones in the city.

Second, does the project bring a *net* fiscal benefit to the area? Wellston, Ohio, for example, suddenly got 980 new jobs when Jeno's, Inc., decided to consolidate its $200-million-per-year pizza-making facilities in that city. To help Jeno's relocate to Wellston, the local county and the state of Ohio lent the firm over $5 million at a very generous 1⅞-percent interest rate. But once the new facility began operations, its waste products clogged the city sewage system with a mass of cheese, meat, and other ingredients the consistency of toothpaste and the color of tomato soup. When the EPA threatened to close down the plant as an environmental danger, Ohio had to give the firm $500,000 to find a way to clean up the wastes.[19] In the long run, Jeno's may be a net fiscal contributor to Wellston, the county, and the state. But in the short run, the location inducements appear to have been fairly costly.

Third, does a public-private redevelopment project actually generate new economic activity? Or does it just relocate activity that would have occurred anyway? Much of the redevelopment of the 1970s and 1980s focused on central-city downtown areas. It is a fair guess that if the city governments had not acted, most of the investments would have been made anyway. They probably would not have been made downtown, but in the suburbs of the same metropolitan areas. Larger suburbs have learned that they, too, must compete for new development; so now they also are engaged in the game of offering a variety of tax or bond inducements to promote development. Many older regions probably had good reasons to redevelop their old, run-down central business districts. But from a broader perspective, one has to ask whether it any longer makes sense to have different communities in the same metropolitan area competing with one another by offering tax incentives for development projects that in all likelihood would occur somewhere in the same metropolitan area even without government inducement.

To find out just how influential state development policies are in promoting development that would *not* occur without state aid, political scientist Susan B. Hansen conducted a sophisticated regression analysis to measure the comparative impact of development policies and a variety of other economic and development forces, such as level of education, tax level, and extent of unionization. Her findings offer very little support for the proposition that economic development policies make a significant difference in job creation:

> Despite a few modest correlations, most state industrial development policies have had a minimal impact on state deviation from regional trends, at least for the short time periods considered here. Consider an

example: Pennsylvania's Ben Franklin Partnership claims to have created over 200 firms since its inception in 1983, resulting in over 3,600 jobs. But compared to the work force in a state the size of Pennsylvania (over five million), the number unemployed (486,000 in late 1985), and the total number of new firms created in the state (17,000 in 1985 alone), the Partnership's effort appears to have had a marginal impact on the state's economy; several neighboring states are doing considerably better.[20]

It was partially concern over the effectiveness of federally subsidized development policies that prompted Congress in 1986 to restrict the amount of IDRBs that a city or state could issue in order to promote its own growth. With the federal government under great criticism for its own huge budget deficits, Congress became less willing to let the federal treasury underwrite a huge volume of development projects that might well have occurred without federal subsidies. The Reagan administration also began pushing for the elimination of development subsidy programs, especially the CDBG, UDAG program, and Economic Development Administration development grants. The language of the 1968 legislation by which Congress first approved tax exemptions for IDRBs for economic development activities suggests that the purposes of the program included: stimulating business investment generally; reallocating capital to small, risky, startup firms desperately in need of capital to survive; and stimulating investment in depressed areas. It is not known how well the IDRB program achieved these goals, but one analysis of their use in Ohio suggests that in fact they were not used to assist economically depressed areas.[21] A persistent criticism of the IDRBs has been of their use to build supermarkets, fast-food restaurants, and other retail establishments that might well have been built anyway and that do not create large numbers of permanent full-time jobs.

Finally, in addition to their economic feasibility, economic development projects must also be weighed for their political feasibility. Generally, public opinion supports state and local economic development efforts—but not always. Substantial tax incentives to lure new industries can sometimes draw the ire of existing businesses, which may feel they are not getting their share of tax breaks. And public opinion as well can sometimes oppose economic development efforts.

The most dramatic example of a situation where public opinion rejected economic development strategies took place in Rhode Island in 1984. A so-called "Greenhouse Plan" to nurture research and development for high-technology firms, to target subsidies at new industries, and to establish training programs for the local work force was put together by an elite commission of representatives of government, big business, and organized labor. The Greenhouse Plan was to be financed by an increase in the state income tax, which would require a constitutional amendment before it could be applied.

Rhode Island desperately needed some sort of initiative to spur its economic growth. In 1985 that state ranked forty-seventh on the Grant-Thornton business-climate index. It had one of the slowest job-growth rates of any state in the nation. And it was not listed among the areas expected to gain the most jobs over the next decade and a half. (See p. 48.) Despite this desperate need and despite an extensive public relations campaign by the state's government, business, and labor leaders to sell the Greenhouse Plan to the public, it was rejected by the voters by a huge four-to-one margin in June 1984. A postreferendum survey of Rhode Islanders found that a majority of people thought that the Greenhouse Plan would make no difference in their own lives, and a third of them thought they would be hurt by it in some way. Over 60 percent thought the main beneficiaries would be bankers and big business, and only 20 percent perceived the plan as beneficial to working people, low-income people, small-business owners, women, or minorities.[22] In sum, Rhode Island's Greenhouse Plan experience suggests that public support is very thin for economic development subsidies that will impose highly visible costs on taxpayers for benefits that will be narrowly distributed.

Political Combat Strategies

The economic development strategies discussed above are essentially positive, forward-looking strategies that seek to use public resources to promote private economic development. Sometimes the strategies do not work, however, and communities are obliged to follow more combative political strategies to protect themselves from the fallout of broken economic dreams.

Plant-Closing Legislation

States usually cannot prevent plants from closing, and most economists would probably maintain that in most instances they should not do so. From a national economic perspective, it makes little sense to force a corporation to keep in existence an inefficient plant that can be replaced by a new, more automated, more efficient one. Protecting such inefficiencies, so the argument goes, will in the long run only make American manufacturers less competitive in the world economy. Instead, we should encourage disinvestment from failing industries so that those resources can be reinvested in more viable economic activities.[23]

Although states cannot prevent plant closings, they can pass legislation that softens the blow to local communities.[24] Four states, in fact, have done so (Connecticut, Maine, Massachusetts, and Wisconsin). The most extensive legislation is in Massachusetts, which encouraged companies to give ninety days' notice of a plant closing so that the workers will have more time to plan and make the necessary adaptations. The legislation also provides for an extra three months of health insurance, unemployment compensation, and job retraining.[25] At a minimum each state would seem to want to require the closing companies to provide severance pay and funds for retraining and job counseling. Many companies do provide severance benefits. But the results are not always as good as the promises. U.S. Steel Corporation (now called USX Corp.) established a job counseling program for laid-off workers when it closed its Clairton mills outside Pittsburgh. Despite the counseling and the motivational sessions, few workers were able to find full-time jobs in the area. Heavily dependent on the now-closed mills, the local economy simply was not strong enough to absorb all the laid-off workers.[26]

A substantial boost to plant-closing legislation occurred in 1987 when the United States Supreme Court upheld the Maine law requiring employers to pay severance pay to workers who lost their jobs because of plant closings. The Fort Halifax Packing Company was sued by 125 laid-off workers who argued that state law required the company to give them severance pay. After losing in the Maine courts, the company appealed the case to the federal courts on the grounds that federal pension and labor laws do not require severance pay plans. Arguing that federal laws have precedence over state laws, the company asked the Supreme Court to strike down the Maine law.[27] But the Supreme Court rejected this argument.

Buy the Plant and Run It

A far more daring strategy is for the local community itself to purchase and operate the failing facility. Twenty-five states have passed **Employee stock ownership plan** (ESOP) laws that provide financial aid and other assistance to help employees purchase plants that are threatening to close. But few communities have been able to do this successfully. Formidable obstacles lie in their way.

The obstacles involved in purchasing a plant were demonstrated in Youngstown, Ohio, in 1977. Religious leaders sought to purchase a factory of the Youngstown Sheet and Tube Company, which announced it would close its Youngstown plant, putting 5,000 people out of work. One month after the announcement, a group of religious leaders led by Catholic Bishop James Malone formed an Ecumenical Coalition to find a way for the community and workers to buy the doomed plant. Barely had these plans been formed than opposition developed. The parent company of the steel plant (Lykes Corporation) opposed the sale for fear of creating a plant that would compete with its remaining steel mills in other parts of the country. Local leaders of the United Steel Workers (USW) did not support the plan, because of their ambivalence about being put into a managerial role if the workers were to become part-owners of the mill. Putting a viable plan together took several months, during which the markets served by the now-closed Youngstown plant had turned to other suppliers, making it doubtful that the Youngstown mill could recapture the lost market share. Finally, banks refused to lend the coalition the $500 million needed to purchase the plant, unless the United States Government would guarantee the loan. But that the United States Government refused to do. In the face of these obstacles, the Ecumenical Coalition was unable to complete its purchase of the plant.[28]

Fighting Back in Court

A special legal and moral problem arises when a company that has received extensive public assistance to open a plant seeks to close it. This was the case in Yonkers, New York. In 1972, Yonkers had put together a $13.9-million package to help Otis Elevators, which employed 1,300 workers, to expand an elevator-manufacturing plant in that city. Four years later, Otis was bought out by United Technologies Corporation, which eventually decided to shut down the Yonkers plant. Unsuccessful in his attempt to negotiate with the firms, Yonkers' Mayor Angelo Martinelli threatened to sue United Technologies to force it to repay some of the aid that had been extended.[29] This threat transformed a moral issue into an important legal issue. Firms that accept aid packages and then leave town may have a *moral* obligation to pay back all or part of the aid, but do they have a *legal* obligation to do so? And if so, under what circumstances would this legal obligation come into play? As more plant closings occur, questions like these are increasingly likely to be brought to the courts for resolution.

Issues in the Search for Economic Development

High Technology and the Quest for Its Holy Grail

In contrast to the decline of heavy industries (such as automobiles and steel) in the Midwest during the 1970s and early 1980s, there was a boom in high-technology industries, such as computer hardware, computer peripheral equipment, computer software applications, medical technology, and biotechnology. California's Silicon Valley and Boston's Route 128 symbolized this new boom as an unprecedented number of high-technology companies were created and expanded in those two areas. Certain other areas, such as Austin, Texas, and Research Triangle, North Carolina, did almost as well. These places became the models that other communities tried to emulate. Why not use economic development packages such as those just discussed to create high-technology industrial parks? The logic of the argument was compelling. The economic development tools existed, and high-technology industry seemed to be much more insulated from foreign competition than were basic industries. The Japanese, Brazilians, and Koreans might be able to manufacture better automobiles more cheaply than could Detroit, but they were years behind the United States in high-technology research. So compelling was the argument for high tech that most states began to try to stimulate as much high tech as they could. Just as the computer age has spawned a new generation of computer wizards seeking to design this season's advanced computer, it has also created a new generation of community leaders seeking to turn their communities into next season's version of Silicon Valley.

But the quest for high technology is no more likely to produce economic salvation today than the quest for the Holy Grail produced salvation during the Middle Ages. There are two reasons for this. First, high technology in fact is no more immune to foreign competition and recession than is basic industry. Silicon Valley, for example, was pushed into a severe recession in the mid-1980s because of foreign competition in microchips and other computer products. The second reason is that few communities have the combination of characteristics that facilitated the concentration of high-technology companies in places such as Silicon Valley, Boston, and Austin, Texas. These places all were located near major research universities. There already existed numerous high-technology industries that could supply the materials needed by the new and expanding high-tech firms. And the areas had a sophisticated work force capable of making high-technology research productive and profitable. In short, some communities are more blessed than others.

If there is no future in basic industrial manufacturing, and if high technology is not in the future for most communities, then what activities can provide the growth that community leaders desire? The answer to this question, according to John Mollenkopf, is government jobs, third-sector institutions (for example, hospitals, universities, foundation headquarters), and advanced corporate services (such as legal work, accounting, computing, advertising, insurance, and investment banking).[30] The expansion of advanced corporate services has been especially important, because cities with many such services become very attractive sites for corporate headquarters.

Mollenkopf argues that three types of cities are emerging in the 1980s. First are the old, industrial cities, like Gary, Indiana, and Youngstown, Ohio. Despite dramatic changes in the national economy that have seen the industrial manufacturing sector decline relative to the service sector, these old cities have clung to their industrial economic bases. Gary and Youngstown are especially good examples, because their basic industry (steel manufacturing) is heavily dependent on the fortunes of the automobile industry. As that industry suffered major setbacks in the 1970s and early 1980s, Gary, Youngstown, and many other old, industrial cities were economically shattered. Furthermore, when the automobile industry rebounded in the mid-1980s, the steel industry benefited very little. This was due in large part to the increased use of cheaper and more flexible plastics to replace steel and also to the increased use of foreign parts, which, of course, were not built with American steel.

In an entirely different situation are the newer service and administrative centers of the Southwest. Cities such as Phoenix and San Diego have attracted administrative and service corporations and high-technology industries that weathered the economic storms of the 1970s better than did the old, basic industries of the Midwest.

Finally, contends Mollenkopf, a third type of city has transformed its economy from old industry to banking and other advanced corporate services. Typical cities in this category are New York, Chicago, Philadelphia, Boston, and San Francisco. Although all have suffered significant population declines, they have maintained themselves as important locales for corporate headquarters and service-sector activities.

Regional Variations and Economic Competition

States and communities, in recent years, have waged intense competition to attract industrial development to their locales. For example, in 1985 the Bloomington, Illinois–Normal, Illinois, area offered $10 million in land donations, $20 million in property tax concessions, and up to $100 million worth of other incentives to entice Chrysler Corporation and Mitsubishi Motors Corporation to construct a $500-million automobile plant.[31] Because the benefits of such a plant are so enormous (an estimated 2,500 jobs in the factory itself, plus another 9,000 jobs in the community), no responsible community leader can afford not to enter the competition.

From the perspective of the national economy, however, there are two problems involved in this competition between regions and states for economic development. First, as indicated earlier in discussing the business climate, it is not clear that tax concessions of this sort actually make a great deal of difference in locational decisions. Although the state of Tennessee offered General Motors much less in the way of concessions than many other states, General Motors decided to build its Saturn Plant in Spring Hill, Tennessee. This suggests that, in their competition for development, states are probably offering generous tax concessions that are not even necessary to attract the development projects they seek.[32] From a national perspective, this is very wasteful.

A second problem with interstate and interregional competition for economic development is that it compounds the task of producing the economic cooperation needed to mitigate the effects of regional recessions. As Table 17-4 shows, different regions of the country participate in the national economic cycle in different ways. The so-called Oil Patch and Farm Belt states,

Table 17–4. Variations in Regional Economies

Region	Economic condition during:		
	1950s	Mid-1970s	Mid-1980s
Oil Patch (Texas, Louisiana, Oklahoma)	Growth	Boom	Depression
Rust Belt (Pennsylvania, Ohio, Indiana, Illinois, Michigan)	Growth	Recession	Stagnation
California	Growth	Recession	Growth
Massachusetts	Decline	Stagnant	Boom
Farm Belt (the Great Plains)	Growth	Boom	Depression

for example, were booming during the energy-crisis days of the 1970s but have been in a deep recession throughout most of the 1980s. Massachusetts suffered severe economic decline in the 1970s but has been enjoying an unprecedented boom in the middle to late 1980s. National economic policy is not very well attuned to these regional variations in the business cycle. Presidents, be they Democrat or Republican, promote taxing, spending, and monetary policies that seek to stimulate growth during recessionary times and to ease inflation during inflationary times. But these crude instruments of national economic policy do not cope very well with the economic condition of the mid-1980s that saw depressed economic conditions in the Farm Belt, the so-called Oil Patch, and much of the so-called Rust Belt heavy-industry states at the same time that unprecedented growth was being registered in the Northeast, California, and a few well-blessed metropolitan areas in between. Coping with regional variations in the business cycle probably requires a more flexible set of national economic management tools than now exists.

Biases in the Fight for Economic Development

Finally, the use of government resources to promote economic development is not a neutral process. It helps some sets of interests and harms others. Three biases in particular should be noted. First, despite the infusion of new money into community redevelopment projects, the economic benefits for the poor and minorities have been disappointing. As indicated earlier, central cities have experienced devastating losses in the number of jobs over the past two decades. Even in the Sunbelt, where cities are still growing, population increases may have outpaced job increases, and most of the growth occurs on the expanding edge of the metropolis, not in the low-income residential neighborhoods. Whatever the reason, the percentage of most cities' residents who are in poverty, unemployed, or on welfare is as high today as it was two decades ago. Furthermore, poor people are not benefiting from the types of central-city jobs being created by economic development. From 1970 to 1984, for example, New York City gained 239,800 jobs for workers with some college education; but it lost 492,000 jobs for workers with less than a high school education.[33]

Second, part of the reason for the lack of improvement in the cities' poverty statistics must be attributed to the biases inherent in the redevelopment process itself. One of the most commonly used redevelopment tools, the industrial development revenue bond (IDRB), for example, does not appear to be utilized to stimulate economically depressed regions, despite the fact that the rationale offered in the legislation establishing it usually names that as a prime objective. To examine how extensively IDRBs were aimed at depressed locations, Thomas A. Pascarella and Richard D. Raymond sought to see if high-unemployment areas in Ohio used IDRBs more than low-unemployment areas. They found no relationship.[34] IDRBs are now used in forty-seven states, and they are so popular they comprise 70 percent of all municipal bond issues, whereas in 1970 they comprised only 33 percent.[35] The most frequent use of IDRBs has been for the installation of pollution-control equipment, for the construction of hospitals, and for the construction of publicly subsidized housing. They also are often used to finance fast-food franchises, discount-store locations, and similar commercial facilities that have little developmental power. In short, the IDRB as often used has done little to generate permanent, well-paying jobs in poverty-stricken neighborhoods. In part because of these disappointments, Congress in 1986 limited the further issuance of IDRBs.

There are limits to what a city can raise money for, Paul Peterson has argued.[36] In Peterson's view, a city that tries to raise too much money for redistributive services for needy residents will drive out its middle-income residents to the less redistributive–oriented suburbs. Cities that focus on raising money for economic development are on a much sounder footing, according to Peterson.

Whether Peterson's view is accurate or not is impossible to prove. But most cities engaged in the redevelopment game today act as though it is accurate. That is, the most praised and successful redevelopment in the 1970s and early 1980s has focused on economic activities in the mainstream of the nation's economy—primarily providing support and office space for service industries and retail commerce. Much has also gone into retaining or attracting manufacturing facilities. This has not reversed the decline of heavy industry in the Frostbelt, but it may have been helpful to industrializing efforts in the South and Southwest over the past decades. Urban redevelopment activities seem to be reinforcing the polarization of cities between the upper-middle class and the low-income classes while driving out the middle-income groups. Much public money has been spent supporting downtown projects and gentrification projects. But no one has yet found the formula that would provide enough economic opportunities to make a permanent dent in the ranks of the urban poor. Small, owner-run retail establishments, which in the past assured the city of a substantial middle-class population, are squeezed out.

People find it very difficult to evaluate much of the urban redevelopment and gentrification activities of the past decade. Remembering the seedy and run-down appearance of many big-city downtown areas two decades ago, comparing them to the elaborate redevelopments in many of these same cities today, and noting the increased number of people, jobs, and activities, it is hard to say that the cities should not have initiated these projects. At the same time, however, many central-city residential neighborhoods have had trouble holding their own as their former middle-class occupants moved to the suburbs, and today they are increasingly occupied by people subsisting on marginal incomes. Many cities are moving toward a bipolar status, as George Sternlieb and James Hughes expressed it,[37] and urban redevelopment activities have not slowed that trend down—they may even have hastened it.

Summary

1. States and communities are today buffeted by dramatic changes in the national economy. Among the most important of these are (a) the transformation from an industrial to a postindustrial economy, (b) the intensification of foreign economic competition, and (c) the declining size of the middle-income groups in comparison to the upper-middle and lower-income groups.

2. To cope with these changes, states and communities have turned increasingly in the past decade to economic development strategies. These strategies include (a) public relations campaigns to attract tourists and industry, (b) promotion of a favorable business climate, (c) creation of business-growth incentives, and (d) the facilitation of community development. The most common community development approaches are tax abatements, the use of federal seed-money programs, industrial development revenue bonds, tax-increment financing, venture capital, and lease-back arrangements.

3. In assessing economic development strategies it is important to consider the negative consequences of these approaches as well as the positive ones.

4. To combat the out-migration of businesses, state and local governments have used plant-closing legislation, strategies to facilitate the purchase of plants by the local communities, and the threat of legal action against firms that move out after receiving local subsidies.

5. Major issues in the search for economic development include questions over the quest for high-technology industries as a salvation to local economic problems, what to do about the competition that arises from variations among regional economies, and biases in the fight for economic development.

Key Terms

Business climate A term used by the business community to refer to the receptivity of a state to the business community. Although different ways of assessing the business climate exist, the business community usually prefers a business climate characterized by low taxes, low public expenditures, and limited state regulation.

Employee stock ownership plan Also called **ESOP**. A plan to aid workers to find financing to take ownership of failing companies. Permits workers, unions, and their pension funds to buy stock in the company.

Industrial Development Revenue Bond A tax-exempt municipal bond that a city sells to enable a local business or development project to obtain financing at below-market interest rates.

Lease-back A local development financing process under which a local government sells a facility to private investors and then rents the facility back from them.

Postindustrial economy The economy of contemporary America, which is increasingly being based on the provision of services rather than on industrial production.

Right-to-work law Legislation that prohibits the union shop.

Tax abatement The forgiving of local property taxes for a firm that dramatically expands a facility.

Tax-increment financing A local development financing process under which the increases in property-tax revenue from a development project are reserved for a number of years to pay off the local government's subsidies or bonds issued for the project.

Urban enterprise zone A blighted urban neighborhood that is designated as an enterprise zone where safety, health, and environmental restrictions would be eased and where companies would be offered generous incentives for locating facilities there.

Venture capital Investment capital targeted for small start-up firms that have trouble raising investment funds through more conventional means.

References

1. Between employment peaks from the late 1970s to 1984, eight northern Minnesota mining towns lost 7,340 jobs, a drop of 49 percent. *Minnesota Tribune,* January 22, 1984, p. 8-A; *Wall Street Journal,* November 19, 1986, p. 6.

2. See *New York Times,* March 12, 1985, p. 16.

3. See Robert H. Bork, Jr., "On the Waterfront: The Port of Houston," *Forbes,* December 17, 1984, pp. 108–116. Also see *New York Times,* October 22, 1985, p. 1.

4. See John Kenneth Galbraith, *The New Industrial State* (Boston: Houghton Mifflin, 1967); and Daniel Bell, *The Coming of Post-industrial Society* (New York: Basic Books, 1973).

5. See Robert J. Samuelson, "Manufacturing Renaissance?" *Newsweek,* November 17, 1986, p. 72.

6. Dan Pilcher, "Assessing State Business Climates," *State Legislatures* 9, no. 8 (August/September 1983): 9–12.

7. *St. Paul Pioneer Press,* October 23, 1983, p. D-1.

8. Roy Bahl, *The Impact of Local Tax Policy on Urban Economic Development* (Washington, D.C.: U.S. Department of Commerce; Economic Development Administration; Urban Consortium Information Bulletin, September 1980), p. 15.

9. Robert W. Schmenner, *Making Business Location Decisions* (Englewood Cliffs, N.J.: Prentice-Hall, 1982), pp. 50–51.

10. Data reported in the *St. Paul Pioneer Press and Dispatch,* June 4, 1986, p. 10-B.

11. David L. Birch, *The Job Generation Process* (Cambridge, Mass.: M.I.T. Program on Neighborhoods and Regional Change, 1979), p. 21.

12. Robert Mier and Scott E. Gelzer, "State Enterprise Zones: The New Frontier?" *Urban Affairs Quarterly* 18, no. 1 (September 1982): 39–52. For specific details on the Connecticut urban enterprise zones, see the *New York Times,* July 7, 1981, p. 1.

13. Bahl, *The Impact of Local Tax Policy,* pp. 8–9.

14. Ibid.

15. Congressional Quarterly Weekly Report, October 4, 1986, p. 2354.

16. Jane Carroll, "Economic Development Through Venture Capital," *State Legislatures* 11, no. 3 (March 1985): 24–25.

17. *New York Times,* June 23, 1986, pp. 1, 9.

18. St. Paul, Minnesota, used a $60-million lease-back package to finance $10 million of maintenance needed on its civic center. When the construction costs of New York City's new convention center began to overrun the original budget, that city began investigating a $600-million lease-back that would save the city $77 million in construction costs. *New York Times,* November 16, 1983.

19. *St. Paul Pioneer Press,* March 13, 1983, p. A-11.

20. Susan B. Hansen, "State Perspectives on Economic Development: Priorities and Outcomes," a paper presented at the Midwest Political Science Association Convention, Chicago, Ill., April 10–12, 1986.

21. Thomas A. Pascarella and Richard D. Raymond, "Buying Bonds for Business: An Evaluation of the Industrial Revenue Bond Program," *Urban Affairs Quarterly* 18, no. 1 (September 1982): 73–89.

22. John Carrol, Mark Hyde, and William Hudson, "Economic Development Policy: Why Rhode Islanders Reject the Greenhouse Concept," *State Government* 58, no. 3 (Fall 1985): 110–112.

23. Lester Thurow, *The Zero Sum Society: Distribution and Possibilities for Economic Change* (New York: Penguin Books, 1980).

24. See especially Barry Bluestone and Bennett Harrison, *The Deindustrialization of America* (New York: Basic Books, 1982), pp. 8, 35, 63–66, 86–92.

25. Thomas J. Leary, "Deindustrialization, Plant Closing Laws, and The States," *State Government* 58, no. 3 (Fall 1985): 113–118. *New York Times,* July 12, 1984, p. 7.

26. David Corn, "Dreams Gone to Rust: The Monongahela Valley Mourns for Steel," *Harper's* 273, no. 1636 (September 1986): 56–64.

27. *Fort Halifax Packing Co.* v. *Coyne* (June 1, 1987).

28. Terry F. Buss and F. Stevens Redburn, "Religious Leaders as Policy Advocates: The Youngstown Steel Mill Closing," *Policy Studies Journal* 11, no. 4 (June 1983): 640–647.

29. *Minneapolis Star and Tribune,* June 5, 1983, p. 6-D.

30. John H. Mollenkopf, *The Contested City* (Princeton, N.J.: Princeton University Press, 1983), pp. 31–36.

31. See *Washington Post,* October 7, 1985, p. A-14.

32. See Larry C. Ledebur and William H. Hamilton, "The Great Tax-Break Sweepstakes," *State Legislatures* (September 1986): 12–15.

33. These data are from a University of North Carolina analysis of Census Bureau data. *New York Times,* October 22, 1986, p. 1.

34. Thomas A. Pascarella and Richard D. Raymond, "Buying Bonds for Business: An Evaluation of the Industrial Revenue Bond Program," *Urban Affairs Quarterly* 18, no. 1 (September 1982): 73–89.

35. John E. Peterson, "The Municipal Bond Market: Recent Changes and Future Prospects," in Norman Walzer and David L. Chicoine, eds., *Financing State and Local Governments in the 1980s: Issues and Trends* (Cambridge, Mass.: Oelgeschlager, Gunn & Hain, Publ., 1981), Ch. 7.

36. Paul E. Peterson, *City Limits* (Chicago: University of Chicago Press, 1981).

37. George Sternlieb and James W. Hughes, "The Uncertain Future of the Central City," *Urban Affairs Quarterly* 18, no. 4 (June 1983): 455–572.

Appendix
Career Prospects in State and Local Government

What kind of career can you build for yourself in state and local government? Virtually any that you are likely to think of, if you wish to work in the public sector. From stock clerk in a government purchasing office to physician in a public hospital, over thirteen million state and local government employees work at nearly as many varied tasks as do employees in the private sector. To give you a better idea of state and local employment possibilities, we have outlined below several career categories in state and local politics. For each category, you are given estimates on employment outlooks through the mid-1990s, the type of work involved, and the educational and other requirements for the position. Following this list is a list of related occupations and career areas that are not normally thought of as public-sector occupations, even though many jobs in these areas are found in the public sector as well as the private sector. Unless otherwise noted, all data on salaries and employment opportunities are taken from the *Occupational Outlook Handbook: 1986-87* (Washington, D.C.: Bureau of Labor Statistics, 1986). You can consult this very useful reference book for more information on most of the following careers and for other sources of information on career planning.

One useful way to test whether you might like a particular job is to take an internship in the area. This will enable you to gain college credit and at the same time explore a career possibility.

Administrator
(Chapters 7, 8, 11–17)

The term *administrator* refers to the highest level of permanent employee below the level of politically appointed executives. Administrators seek to ensure that all parts of their agency work together and carry out the policies set by elected or appointed political leaders. Although some agency administrators are brought in from outside the agency, most work up through the agency ranks. Most administrators have training in a related professional occupation (engineering, for example, in the Transportation Department; or social work in the Welfare Department). Increasingly, administrators bolster

503

their professional experience by acquiring a master's degree in public administration. Salaries and benefits tend to be fairly generous, especially in large agencies. The position of administrator is not entry level, and opportunities for promotion to the administrative level will be limited by the currently slow growth rates of government and the existence of large numbers of managerial personnel competing for administrative jobs.

Budget Officer
(Chapters 7, 8, 10–17)

Most large units of government have a budget specialist who helps prepare budget documents, sometimes controls the release of budgeted funds, and usually is one of the major financial advisers in the particular governmental unit. Because they control agency spending, budget officers find themselves in the thick of many political battles. Qualifications include a college degree, substantial training in, or at least understanding of, accounting practices. A master's degree in public administration, business, or accounting is desirable.

Corrections Officer
(Chapter 12)

Corrections officers work as guards in jails, prisons, and other corrections facilities. The minimal education requirement is a high school diploma, although some college course work in criminology, psychology, and sociology is increasingly required. There were 130,000 corrections officers in 1984, most of them working for the public sector rather than the private sector. If the incarcerated population continues to rise as it has in the 1980s, employment prospects in the corrections field will be expected to grow much faster than the average through the mid-1990s. Starting pay for corrections officers at the city and county levels averaged $15,600 in 1984, but pay varies widely from region to region.

Court Administrator
(Chapter 12)

The increasing complexity of running the nation's courts has given rise to a relatively new position in public administration, that of court administrator. This professional organizes the calendar for courts, hires the personnel, and oversees the day-to-day administrative details of the court's operations. Although legal training is not a prerequisite, many court administrators have been trained as lawyers before moving into administration. If judicial caseloads continue rising as they have in recent decades and if the judicial reform movement keeps pressing for modernizing and professionalizing state and local court systems, then it seems likely that the demand for court administrators will continue to grow.

Economic Developer
(Chapter 17)

So intensive is the demand for people to spearhead and oversee economic development projects that many communities have begun hiring Certified Industrial and Economic Developers (CID/CED). Economic developers need an understanding of their local communities as well as training and experience in development financing tools, zoning processes, accounting, and marketing. Excellent communications skills are a must. Certification for the CID/CED is handled by the American Economic Development Council, which demands five years of work experience in economic development plus appropriate course work.

Through 1986, more than 400 people held a CID/CED certification; about 15 percent of them were women. Employment is found throughout the country in a variety of private and public institutions, such as banks, chambers of commerce, port authorities, and state government agencies. Because of the widespread perceived need for communities to do whatever is feasible and reasonable to attract industry, the demand for economic developers seems likely to continue growing over the near future. For more information, write: American Economic Development Council, Schiller Park, IL 60176.

Fire Fighter

Minimum educational qualification for a fire fighter is usually a high school diploma. Most fire fighting jobs are found at the municipal level. Employment tends to be stable, layoffs infrequent, and fringe benefits generous, especially in unionized states. Beginning annual salaries averaged about $17,300 in 1984, but top salaries are not usually very high. Employment opportunities are expected to grow at about an average rate through the mid-1990s.

Forester and Conservation Scientist
(Chapter 16)

An important area of environmental protection involves forest management and conservation, to protect the nation's forests, soils, and wildlife. Training qualifications usually include at least a bachelor's degree in forestry or range sciences. Employment opportunities are expected to grow more slowly than the average through the mid-1990s. There are about 25,000 such jobs today, about one-fifth of which are in state government, half in the federal government, and the balance in the private sector. The begining federal government salary for foresters, range managers, and soil conservationists in 1985 was $14,400.

Health Services Manager
(Chapter 13)

Health services managers are needed to run hospitals, nursing homes, health maintenance organizations, rehabilitation centers, urgent-care facilities, and the offices of doctors, dentists, and chiropractors. Because of the growing complexity of medical and health care provision, professional managers have been increasingly taking the responsibility for management of health care facilities out of the hands of medical personnel such as physicians and nurses, whose specialty is medical and health care treatment rather than management. Health services personnel range from executive directors in charge of an institution, to internal managers, to specialized staff. There were over 330,000 health care professionals employed in 1984, a great many of them in public or nonprofit facilities.

Responsibilities of health care managers include budgeting, personnel administration, information management, marketing, strategic planning, systems analysis, and labor relations. Managers need a knowledge of management principles and most likely a master's degree in health administration (MHA) or in business administration (MBA) or public administration (MPA) with a health services concentration. Employment opportunities in the 1990s are expected to grow much faster than average. Starting salaries for recent MHA's averaged $27,000 in 1983.

Inspector, Licensor, and Compliance Officer
(Chapters 7, 11–13, 16, 17)

A great many people are employed at all levels of government to carry out a variety of inspection, licensing, regulatory, and compliance functions, including health inspectors, consumer safety inspectors, food inspectors, environmental health inspectors, motor vehicle inspectors, traffic inspectors, occupational safety and health inspectors, wage-hour compliance inspectors, equal opportunity representatives, and building inspectors. About 120,000 inspectors and compliance officers were employed in 1984, about 31 percent of them at the state level, 25 percent at the local level, and the balance at the federal level or in private industry. Training and job requirements vary greatly because of the great diversity of functions. And because of the recent reductions in government regulatory responsibilities, employment growth is expected to be lower than the average through the mid-1990s.

Legislative Aide
(Chapter 9)

Every legislature hires people to do a variety of specialized and professional tasks, ranging from policy research to putting into legal form the ideas for bills that legislators present. Some of these positions require legal training, some computer training, and others training in accounting. For policy analysts, a master's degree in policy analysis, public affairs, or public administration is highly desirable. These analysts may work for committees, for a Democratic or Republican caucus, or even for a specific legislator. Beginning salaries vary greatly from state to state. Due to the increasing complexity of government in the United States, it seems likely that the number of legislative aide positions will continue to grow. One convenient way to test whether you would like to work as a legislative aide is to do an internship with your legislator or some committee of the legislature.

Lobbyist
(Chapters 3, 4, 5, 7–17)

Although no state has a lobbying industry as large as that dealing with the federal government, lobbying at the state and local levels is important and most likely will continue to be so. There will be a continuing need for people who can effectively represent clients before state legislatures, city councils, and regulatory agencies. Lobbyists represent every conceivable sector of society, from welfare recipients to multinational corporations. Some lobbyists work for large organizations; others are self-employed persons who hire themselves out to clients. Effective lobbying requires excellent communications skills, interpersonal skills, intimate knowledge of the government agencies being lobbied, and a willingness to work long hours. Although there are no formal requirements for becoming a lobbyist, lawyers and former legislators have some distinct advantages over other people.

Personnel and Labor Relations
(Chapters 7, 11)

With over thirteen million employees, many of them unionized, state and local governments rely heavily on personnel officers and labor relations specialists. Personnel officers manage the procedures for hiring, promotion, and dismissal. Labor relations specialists help manage relations between government agencies and the collective bargaining agents of their employees. Related jobs include compensation analysts, employee-benefits managers, and training specialists. The goal behind these positions is to provide a competent and productive work force. Because of the diversity of these jobs, training and other requirements vary widely. For entry-level positions, undergraduate course work in personnel or labor relations is helpful, as is a degree or certificate in the field. Little growth is expected in public sector–personnel positions through the mid-1990s, and about average growth is expected in the private sector.

Police Work
(Chapters 7, 11, 12)

Police-related occupations include police officers, state highway patrol, detectives, and investigators. Ability to handle people is a prime prerequisite for these jobs. Qualifications include excellent physical condition and the ability to pass competitive written examinations. Although small communities require only a high school diploma for police officers, some college education and often a college degree is increasingly required in metropolitan areas. Employment opportunities are expected to grow about as fast as the average through the mid-1990s. Salaries vary widely, depending on the state and on the size of the community. The average starting salary for patrol officers was $18,000 in 1984.

Public Education Employment
(Chapter 14)

The major professional occupations in public education are teachers, principals, and central-office administrators (superintendents, data processors, purchasing officers, curriculum development specialists, for example). There are about 125,000 public school principals and assistant principals, 1.8 million teachers, and over 200,000 other professionals. These professionals bear the primary educational responsibility for preparing the next generation of American citizens to live in an increasingly competitive and complex world. To work effectively these professionals need excellent communications and interpersonal skills.

Requirements for teaching positions include teacher certification and undergraduate course work in education. Principals, superintendents, and other high-level administrators also need several years' teaching experience, graduate training in school administration, and certification. Job outlook and salaries vary widely by state and region. Nationwide, the need for elementary teachers and principals is expected to grow through the mid-1990s, but secondary-school employment is expected to decline until 1990, when it will probably begin to rise again.

Public Relations Specialist
(Chapters 5–7, 9–12)

Most large organizations, public or private, use public relations tactics to promote their image and maintain positive relations with the public. In government agencies, public relations is often the responsibility of offices of public information. These offices produce news releases, pamphlets, multimedia shows, and other materials designed to further the goals of their agencies. Major employment qualifications usually consist of a college degree plus public relations experience. A BA or MA in journalism or public relations is helpful. Public relations professionals need highly developed writing and speaking skills as well as the ability to work with people. There were about 95,000 public relations jobs in 1984, a sizable percentage of them in the public sector. Employment opportunities are expected to grow much faster than the average through the mid-1990s.

Social Worker
(Chapter 13)

Demand for social workers has been strong in recent decades because of several societal forces discussed in the text: the aging of the population, the existence of a large, impoverished subpopulation, the change of the population from predominantly rural to predominantly metropolitan, and the need to offer protection services for abused and neglected children, the handicapped, and the disabled. Effective social workers need a variety of important skills: communications skills, knowledge of principles of behavior, ability to work with people, and familiarity with relevant social legislation and administrative rules. The main training qualifications for social work are a bachelor's degree in the social sciences or social work (BSW) or, even more likely, a master's degree in social work (MSW).

Employment opportunities for social workers are expected to grow faster than the average through the mid-1990s. Salaries vary widely from state to state and from the public to the private sector within states. In 1984 the average starting salary for MSWs in hospitals and medical centers was $19,300.

Urban and Regional Planner
(Chapters 7, 8, 11, 15–17)

City planners, urban planners, and regional planners advise local and regional officials on decisions involving the growth and redevelopment of cities, suburbs, regions, metropolitan areas, and rural communities. Because planners are called on to make recommendations concerning land use, environmental issues, health issues, and economic development, planners must combine a broad knowledge of public issues with a technical ability to apply contemporary tools of statistical and policy analysis. Most planning jobs require a master's degree in urban or regional planning. Planners may also be certified by the American Institute of Certified Planners, a branch of the American Planning Association.

Employment opportunities for planners are expected to grow more slowly than the average through the mid-1990s, and demand for them will obviously be greater in the rapidly growing areas of the country, such as the South and Southwest, than in the more stable Northeast and Midwest. About 17,000 people held urban and regional planning jobs in 1984, the majority of them in local government agencies. Median salaries for planners in 1984 ranged from $28,100 in local governments to $35,000 in private consulting firms.

Related Occupations

The following occupations are not distinctly public service careers, since the majority of people working in them are employed in the private sector. Nevertheless, substantial numbers of these people also work in the public sector where their skills are needed.

Accountant and Auditor

These professionals prepare financial reports, analyze financial data, and provide the up-to-date financial data that governments need in order to make responsible decisions. Job requirements may include certification as a Certified Public Accountant. Employment outlook through the mid-1990s is expected to grow much more than the average, and compensation can be very lucrative.

Lawyer

Given the high complexity of life today, the large number of laws enacted by legislatures, and the even larger number of rules issued by regulatory and administrative agencies, lawyers continue to be widely employed by state and local governments in a variety of capacities. Minimum requirements are the LLB degree and in some instances passage of the state bar examination. Eighty percent of lawyers work in the private sector, and the majority of public-sector lawyers work at the local level. Lawyers also seem to have an edge working as lobbyists. And being a solo-practitioner lawyer is often considered a good starting place for a career in elective politics. Future employment demand for lawyers is difficult to gauge. Because of the doubling in the number of law school graduates since 1970, some observers predict that the competition for law-related jobs will become increasingly keen. Other observers, however, predict that the demand for lawyers will continue to grow at above-average rates through the mid-1990s.

Energy-Related Careers

If energy costs begin to rise in the 1990s, as many observers expect, there will be a need for educated people in many energy-related occupations. In the public sector, energy-related employment opportunities are likely to be found in federal agencies such as the Departments of Energy, Interior, Treasury, Commerce, Transportation, State, Agriculture, and Defense. State-level counterparts of some of these departments will also need energy-related workers.

Environment-Related Careers

Although the deregulation trends of the 1980s curbed spending for environmental protection, there is going to be no reduction in the need to protect the air, water, and atmosphere from further degradation. Accordingly, there will continue to be a need for people to serve in a variety of environmentally related occupations. Some of these include forester, range manager, recreationist, soil conservationist, soil scientist, wildlife conservationist, zoo keeper, landscape architect, urban planner, civil engineer, and biologist.

Table A–1. The Twenty Fastest-Growing Metropolitan Areas, 1980–1984

Metropolitan statistical area	Average annual population growth, 1980–1984	Metropolitan statistical area	Average annual population growth, 1980–1984
Fort Myers–Cape Coral, Fla.	4.9%	Houston, Tex.	3.4%
Melbourne, Fla.	4.4	Bakersfield, Calif.	3.2
Austin, Tex.	4.3	Stockton, Calif.	3.2
West Palm Beach, Fla.	4.3	Phoenix, Ariz.	3.0
McAllen, Tex.	4.1	Colorado Springs, Col.	2.8
Fort Worth–Arlington, Tex.	3.8	Salt Lake City, Utah	2.8
Orlando, Fla.	3.8	Dallas, Tex.	2.8
Daytona Beach, Fla.	3.5	Tampa–St. Petersburg, Fla.	2.7
Las Vegas, Nev.	3.5	Tucson, Ariz.	2.7
Riverside–San Bernardino, Calif.	3.5	Atlanta, Ga.	2.5

General Considerations on Public Employment Prospects

Regional Considerations

Because job prospects are heavily influenced by population trends and business conditions, a person should be aware of these in career planning. In general, the Southeast and the Southwest have seen the most dynamic population growth and business growth during the 1980s; but within these huge regions are significant variations from state to state. Governments in Texas, Oklahoma, Louisiana, and Alaska have been under extremely tight budget constrictions in the 1980s because of the petroleum glut. But employment prospects in those states would most likely grow if another energy crisis appeared in the 1990s. The Midwest's so-called Rust Belt lost jobs and population during the first half of the 1980s, and except for isolated locations there appears to be little prospect for dynamic growth over the next ten years.

To give you an idea of where job growth is likely to occur, the twenty fastest-growing metropolitan areas (1980–1984) are listed in Table A–1. You cannot, however, automatically conclude that professional-level jobs will necessarily grow proportionately with the numbers shown. McAllen, Texas, for example, is one of the fast-growing areas, but it is also one of the poorest metropolitan areas. This suggests that McAllen will lack the resources to support extensive growth in professional-level jobs. Some of the other Texas cities listed in the table have seen their employment opportunities shrink dramatically since 1984 as a consequence of the oil glut, and it would not be reasonable to expect a resumption of dynamic growth unless and until Texas oil production booms again.

Index of Names

The letter n after a page number indicates an endnote or a footnote.

Index of Subjects

The letter n after a page number indicates an endnote or a footnote.